The Rhetoric of Remembrance

Siphrut
Literature and Theology of the Hebrew Scriptures

Editorial Board

STEPHEN B. CHAPMAN   *Duke University*
TREMPER LONGMAN III   *Westmont College*
NATHAN MACDONALD   *Universität Göttingen and University of St. Andrews*

1. *A Severe Mercy: Sin and Its Remedy in the Old Testament*, by Mark J. Boda
2. *Chosen and Unchosen: Conceptions of Election in the Pentateuch and Jewish-Christian Interpretation*, by Joel N. Lohr
3. *Genesis and the Moses Story: Israel's Dual Origins in the Hebrew Bible*, by Konrad Schmid
4. *The Land of Canaan and the Destiny of Israel: Theologies of Territory in the Hebrew Bible*, by David Frankel
5. *Jacob and the Divine Trickster: A Theology of Deception and Y*HWH*'s Fidelity to the Ancestral Promise in the Jacob Cycle*, by John E. Anderson
6. *Esther: The Outer Narrative and the Hidden Reading*, by Jonathan Grossman
7. *From Fratricide to Forgiveness: The Language and Ethics of Anger in Genesis*, by Matthew R. Schlimm
8. *The Rhetoric of Remembrance: An Investigation of the "Fathers" in Deuteronomy*, by Jerry Hwang

The Rhetoric of Remembrance

An Investigation of the "Fathers" in Deuteronomy

Jerry Hwang

Winona Lake, Indiana
EISENBRAUNS
2012

© 2012 by Eisenbrauns Inc.
All rights reserved
Printed in the United States of America

www.eisenbrauns.com

Library of Congress Cataloging-in-Publication Data

Hwang, Jerry.
  The rhetoric of remembrance : an investigation of the "Fathers" in
    Deuteronomy / Jerry Hwang.
      p. cm. — (Siphrut : literature and theology of the Hebrew Scriptures ; 8)
    Includes bibliographical references and indexes.
    ISBN 978-1-57506-238-9 (hardback : alk. paper)
    1. Bible. O.T. Deuteronomy—Criticism, interpretation, etc. I. Title.
  BS1275.52.H83 2012
  222′.15066—dc23
                                                              2012012672

The paper used in this publication meets the minimum requirements of the American National Standard for Information Sciences—Permanence of Paper for Printed Library Materials, ANSI Z39.48-1984.

We must examine anew the question whether or not Deuteronomy considered Israel to be under the "law," that is, whether or not it taught Israel to earn its salvation. It is true that even today Deuteronomy is called in almost all scholarly works a "book of the law," or even a "law code." But it is not difficult to show that this designation is not appropriate, and that it misses the essential characteristic of the book completely.
—Gerhard von Rad

The marvel of Deuteronomy is that while it warns against disobedient imagination, it is itself an act of radical obedient imagination. And that radicalness is measured by its own norms of covenant. Any imaginative act in statement consonant with covenant is permitted and even welcomed.
—Walter Brueggemann

Contents

Preface ix
Glossary of Terms x
Abbreviations xi

1. The "Fathers" in Deuteronomy: Introduction 1
   An Overview of Occurrences 3
   A Nexus for Current Methodologies in OT Studies 4
   Conclusion 11

Part 1
The "Fathers" and the Land Promise in Deuteronomy

2. The "Fathers" and the Land Promise in Deuteronomy:
   History of Research and Method 15
   Terminology of Land and Place in Deuteronomy 16
   Deuteronomic Variations in Verbal Actions and
      Recipients of the Land Promise 24
   Past Approaches to the Variations
      in the Land-Promise Formulas 28
   Conclusion 30

3. The "Fathers" and the Land Promise in Deuteronomy:
   Analysis of Texts 31
   Land and the "Fathers" in Deuteronomy 1 32
   Land and the "Fathers" in Deuteronomy 6 50
   Land and the "Father(s)" in Deuteronomy 26 61
   Land and the "Fathers" in Deuteronomy 30 73
   Land and the "Fathers" in Deuteronomy 34 81
   Conclusion 88

Part 2
The "God of the Fathers" and the Divine Promises in Deuteronomy

4. The "God of the Fathers" and the Divine Promises in
   Deuteronomy: History of Research and Method 91
   Terminology for Israel's God in
      Deuteronomy and the Old Testament 93

The Divine Name and the "God of the Father(s)"
   in the Tetrateuch   95
The "God of the Father(s)" in the Deuteronomistic History
   and the Postexilic Historical Books   99
Method for a Study of the Divine Name
   and the "God of the Fathers"   101
Conclusion   108

5. The "God of the Fathers" and the Divine Promises in
   Deuteronomy: Analysis of Texts 109
   The "God of the Fathers" and the
      Promise of Multiplication   110
   The "God of the Fathers" and the Promise of Land   127
   The "God of the Fathers" and Y$_{HWH}$'s Covenant   144
   Conclusion   151

Part 3

The "Fathers" and the Divine-Human Covenant in Deuteronomy

6. The "Fathers" and the Divine-Human Covenant
   in Deuteronomy: History of Research and Method 155
   Past Approaches to Covenant in the Old Testament
      and the Ancient Near East   156
   Speech-Act Theory and Deuteronomic Covenant
      Theology   169
   Conclusion   177

7. The "Fathers" and the Divine-Human Covenant
   in Deuteronomy: Analysis of Texts 178
   An Overview of Deuteronomic Covenant Theology   179
   Divine-Human Covenant and the
      "Fathers" in Deuteronomy 4   183
   Divine-Human Covenant and the
      "Fathers" in Deuteronomy 7–8   207
   Divine-Human Covenant and the "Fathers"
      in Deuteronomy 29   222
   Conclusion   232

8. The "Fathers" in Deuteronomy: Conclusions and
   Avenues for Future Research 233

Bibliography 237

Indexes 273
   Index of Authors   273
   Index of Scripture   278

Preface

This book represents a slightly revised version of my Ph.D. dissertation, which was submitted to Wheaton College in December 2009. I am grateful to Professors Stephen Chapman, Tremper Longman III, and Nathan MacDonald for their editorial suggestions and for accepting my monograph for the series Siphrut: Literature and Theology of the Hebrew Scriptures. The assistance of Jim Eisenbraun, Beverly McCoy, and the team at Eisenbrauns has also been invaluable in bringing this book to print.

I owe a special debt to Dr. Daniel Block, my Ph.D. supervisor, whose blend of scholarly rigor and pastoral care have exemplified what it means to study, do, and teach the word of God (Ezra 7:10). Dr. Richard Schultz, my second reader, was diligent in providing meticulous feedback at every stage of my research, from the original prospectus to the final result contained in these pages. My external examiner, Dr. Duane Christensen, also strengthened this study with his useful feedback.

My research could not have been undertaken without the help of my parents, Mr. and Mrs. Ching-Fa Hwang, who have faithfully provided support in spirit and finances through the years. My wife's parents, Mr. and Mrs. John Wang, have played an integral part in our lives through the years and especially during my doctoral program. I am also thankful to Mr. and Mrs. Eugene Logan for establishing the doctoral fellowship that provided a scholarship and stipend during my studies.

Most of all, this work would have been impossible to complete without the encouragement of my wife, Jackie. Thus I dedicate this book to her and our children, Josie and Jacob, companions together in our journey to bring all nations to the knowledge that "Yhwh, he is God in heaven above and on the earth below; there is no other" (Deut 4:39).

Jerry Hwang
February 2012
Singapore

Glossary of Terms

Bilderverbot. German "prohibition [of] images"; refers to the Decalogue's prohibition against making images of Yʜᴡʜ

Bundesformel. German "covenant formula"; refers to the frequent phrase "I will be your God, and you will be my people" (e.g., Deut 26:16–19; Jer 31:33)

Generationswechsel. German "generation change"; a term used in Deuteronomy scholarship to refer to the book's conflation of generational horizons, especially between the first exodus generation (which died in the wilderness) and the second exodus generation (which entered the land)

Hauptgebot. German "chief commandment"; a term used in pentateuchal criticism to denote the Decalogue's prohibition on serving other gods

Lectio difficilior / Lectio facilior. Latin "the more difficult reading" / "the easier reading"; in textual criticism, refers to the readings found in different manuscripts and their relative probability of being original

Leitmotiv. German "lead motif"; a repeated and prominent theme in a literary work

Leitwort. German "lead word"; in literary theory, refers to a repetition of words and the associated themes that they bring to the foreground

Mise-en-abyme. French "placed in the abyss"; in literary theory, refers to a story embedded within a story: a single narrative episode captures in microcosm the entire book of which it is a part

Numeruswechsel. German "number change"; in Deuteronomy scholarship, refers to the book's tendency to oscillate between second-person singular and plural forms (e.g., Deut 1:20–21)

Parenesis/parenetic. English. In literary theory, refers to a genre that is characterized by urgent exhortation

Promulgationssatz. German "promulgation phrase"; a term coined by Norbert Lohfink to denote an אשר relative clause that identifies a command or promise as coming from God (e.g., "just as Yʜᴡʜ our God commanded us," Deut 1:19)

Textglättung. German "text smoothing"; refers to the tendency of scribes or redactors to smooth over a rough text by introducing easier readings

Urdeuteronomium. German "original Deuteronomy"; a term popularized by Julius Wellhausen to denote the original legal core of Deuteronomy (chaps. 12–26) before the addition of its framing material (chaps. 1–11, 27–34)

Urtext. German "original text"; a term referring to the pristine, original text before it was modified by editors or redactors

Verpflichtung. German "obligation"; the term used by Erhard Kutsch to define Heb. ברית ("covenant") as being devoid of any relational aspects

Abbreviations

General

Akk.	Akkadian
ANE	ancient Near East
chap(s).	chapter(s)
D	Deuteronomistic writer/source
DH	Deuteronomistic Historian
DSS	Dead Sea Scrolls
Dtr^1	preexilic redaction of the Deuteronomistic History
Dtr^2	postexilic redaction of the Deuteronomistic History
E	Elohistic writer/source
f	feminine
Gk.	Greek
Heb.	Hebrew
J	Yahwistic writer/source
LXX	Septuagint
m	masculine
MT	Masoretic Text
NASB	New American Standard Bible
NIV	New International Version
NJPS	New Jewish Publication Society of America Version of the Jewish Bible
NLT	New Living Translation
OT	Old Testament
P	Priestly writer/source
p/pl.	plural
RSV	Revised Standard Version
s/sg.	singular
SP	Samaritan Pentateuch
Sym.	Symmachus
Syr.	Syriac
Tg.	Targum
v(v).	verse(s)
Vulg.	Vulgate

Reference Works

AbOTC	Abingdon Old Testament Commentaries
AB	Anchor Bible
ABD	*Anchor Bible Dictionary.* Edited by D. N. Freedman. 6 vols. New York, 1992
ABRL	Anchor Bible Reference Library
AJT	*Asia Journal of Theology*
AnBib	Analecta biblica
ANES	*Ancient Near Eastern Studies*

AOAT	Alter Orient und Altes Testament
AOTC	Apollos Old Testament Commentary
ASTI	Annual of the Swedish Theological Institute
AsTJ	Asbury Theological Journal
ATANT	Abhandlungen zur Theologie des Alten und Neuen Testaments
AUSS	Andrews University Seminary Studies
BASOR	Bulletin of the American Schools of Oriental Research
BBB	Bonner biblische Beiträge
BBR	Bulletin for Biblical Research
BDB	Brown, F., S. R. Driver, and C. A. Briggs. *A Hebrew and English Lexicon of the Old Testament*. Oxford, 1907
BETL	Bibliotheca ephemeridum theologicarum lovaniensium
BFCT	Beiträge zur Förderung christlicher Theologie
BHS	*Biblia Hebraica Stuttgartensia*. Edited by K. Elliger and W. Rudolph. Stuttgart, 1983
BHQ	*Biblia Hebraica Quinta*. Edited by A. Schenker et al. Stuttgart, 2004–. *Deuteronomy* prepared by C. McCarthy
Bib	Biblica
Bijdr	Bijdragen: Tijdschrift voor filosofie en theologie
BJRL	Bulletin of the John Rylands University Library of Manchester
BN	Biblische Notizen
BSac	Bibliotheca sacra
BWANT	Beiträge zur Wissenschaft vom Alten und Neuen Testament
BZ	Biblische Zeitschrift
BZAW	Beihefte zur Zeitschrift für die alttestamentliche Wissenschaft
CAD	*The Assyrian Dictionary of the Oriental Institute of the University of Chicago*. Chicago, 1956–
CBQ	Catholic Biblical Quarterly
CBR	Currents in Biblical Research
CCT	*Cuneiform Texts from Cappadocian Tablets in the British Museum*
ConBOT	Coniectanea biblica: Old Testament Series
COS	*The Context of Scripture*. Edited by W. W. Hallo. 3 vols. Leiden: Brill, 2003
DDD	*Dictionary of Deities and Demons in the Bible*. Edited by K. van der Toorn, B. Becking, and P. W. van der Horst. Rev. ed. Leiden, 1999
EdF	Erträge der Forschung
EncJud	*Encyclopaedia Judaica*. Edited by F. Skolnick. 22 vols. Detroit, 2007
EstBib	Estudios bíblicos
ETL	Ephemerides theologicae lovanienses
ETR	Etudes théologiques et religieuses
EuroJTh	European Journal of Theology
FAT	Forschungen zum Alten Testament
FB	Forschung zur Bibel
FRLANT	Forschungen zur Religion und Literatur des Alten und Neuen Testaments
FZPhTh	Freiburger Zeitschrift für Philosophie und Theologie
GBS	Guides to Biblical Scholarship
GKC	*Gesenius' Hebrew Grammar*. Edited by E. Kautzsch. Translated by A. E. Cowley. 2nd ed. Oxford, 1910
GTA	Göttinger theologischer Arbeiten

HALOT	Koehler, L., W. Baumgartner, and J. J. Stamm, *The Hebrew and Aramaic Lexicon of the Old Testament*. Translated and edited under the supervision of M. E. J. Richardson. 4 vols. Leiden, 1994–99
HBS	Herders biblische Studien
HBT	*Horizons in Biblical Theology*
HSM	Harvard Semitic Monographs
HTR	*Harvard Theological Review*
HUCA	*Hebrew Union College Annual*
HvTSt	*Hervormde teologiese studies*
IBC	Interpretation: A Bible Commentary for Teaching and Preaching
IBHS	*An Introduction to Biblical Hebrew Syntax*. B. K. Waltke and M. O'Connor. Winona Lake, IN, 1990
ICC	International Critical Commentary
Int	*Interpretation*
ITC	International Theological Commentary
JAOS	*Journal of the American Oriental Society*
JATS	*Journal of the Adventist Theological Society*
JBL	*Journal of Biblical Literature*
JBQ	*Jewish Bible Quarterly*
JBR	*Journal of Bible and Religion*
JETS	*Journal of the Evangelical Theological Society*
JNES	*Journal of Near Eastern Studies*
JNSL	*Journal of Northwest Semitic Languages*
Joüon	Joüon, P. *A Grammar of Biblical Hebrew*. Translated and revised by T. Muraoka. 2 vols. Subsidia biblica 14/1–2. Rome, 1991
JPSTC	Jewish Publication Society Torah Commentary
JSNTSup	Journal for the Study of the New Testament: Supplement Series
JSOT	*Journal for the Study of the Old Testament*
JSOTSup	Journal for the Study of the Old Testament: Supplement Series
JTS	*Journal of Theological Studies*
KAI	*Kanaanäische und aramäische Inschriften*. H. Donner and W. Röllig. 2nd ed. Weisbaden, 1966–69
KTU	*Die keilalphabetischen Texte aus Ugarit*. Edited by M. Dietrich, O. Loretz, and J. Sanmartín. AOAT 24/1. Neukirchen-Vluyn, 1976. 2nd enlarged ed. of *KTU: The Cuneiform Alphabetic Texts from Ugarit, Ras Ibn Hani, and Other Places*. Edited by M. Dietrich, O. Loretz, and J. Sanmartín. Münster, 1995 (= *CTU*)
LHB/OTS	Library of Hebrew Bible / Old Testament Studies (formerly JSOT Supplement Series)
NAC	New American Commentary
NCB	New Century Bible
NEchtB	Neue Echter Bibel
NIBCOT	New International Biblical Commentary on the Old Testament
NICOT	New International Commentary on the Old Testament
NIDOTTE	*New International Dictionary of Old Testament Theology and Exegesis*. Edited by W. A. VanGemeren. 5 vols. Grand Rapids, 1997
NIDNTT	*New International Dictionary of New Testament Theology*. Edited by C. Brown. 4 vols. Grand Rapids, 1975–85
OBO	Orbis biblicus et orientalis
ÖBS	Österreichische biblische Studien

OBT	Overtures to Biblical Theology
OLP	Orientalia lovaniensia periodica
OTE	*Old Testament Essays*
OTL	Old Testament Library
OTS	*Old Testament Studies*
OtSt	Oudtestamentische Studiën
QD	Quaestiones disputatae
RB	*Revue biblique*
ResQ	*Restoration Quarterly*
RHR	*Revue de l'histoire des religions*
SAA	State Archives of Assyria
SB	Sources bibliques
SBAB	Stuttgarter biblische Aufsatzbände
SBLDS	Society of Biblical Literature Dissertation Series
SBLSCS	Society of Biblical Literature Septuagint and Cognate Studies
SBLSem	Society of Biblical Literature Semeia Studies
SBLSymS	Society of Biblical Literature Symposium Series
SBLWAW	Society of Biblical Literature Writings from the Ancient World
SBS	Stuttgarter Bibelstudien
SBTS	Sources for Biblical and Theological Study
SHANE	Studies in the History of the Ancient Near East
SJT	*Scottish Journal of Theology*
SR	*Studies in Religion*
SubBi	*Subsidia biblica*
TD	*Theologie und Philosophie*
TDOT	*Theological Dictionary of the Old Testament.* Edited by G. J. Botterweck and H. Ringgren. Translated by J. T. Willis, G. W. Bromiley, and D. E. Green. 8 vols. Grand Rapids, MI, 1974–
Them	*Themelios*
ThSt	Theologische Studiën
TLNT	*Theological Lexicon of the New Testament.* C. Spicq. Translated and edited by J. D. Ernest. 3 vols. Peabody, MA, 1994
TLOT	*Theological Lexicon of the Old Testament.* Edited by E. Jenni, with assistance from C. Westermann. Translated by M. E. Biddle. 3 vols. Peabody, MA, 1997
TP	*Theologie und Philosophie*
TynBul	*Tyndale Bulletin*
UF	*Ugarit-Forschungen*
VE	*Vox evangelica*
VT	*Vetus Testamentum*
VTSup	Supplements to Vetus Testamentum
WBC	Word Biblical Commentary
WD	*Wort und Dienst*
WMANT	Wissenschaftliche Monographien zum Alten und Neuen Testament
WTJ	*Westminster Theological Journal*
ZABR	*Zeitschrift für altorientalische und biblische Rechtsgeschichte*
ZAW	*Zeitschrift für die alttestamentliche Wissenschaft*
ZTK	*Zeitschrift für Theologie und Kirche*

Chapter 1

The "Fathers" in Deuteronomy: Introduction

The book of Deuteronomy stands at the crucial junction between the Torah and the Former Prophets, not only in narrative and canonical sequence, but also theologically and in the history of interpretation. Even as the older consensus regarding the documentary hypothesis has been challenged in recent decades,[1] Wilhelm De Wette's dating of Deuteronomy or some significant portion thereof to the time of King Josiah's reforms has remained a touchstone of OT scholarship.[2] The question how to distinguish between predeuteronomic and postdeuteronomic material in the Tetrateuch remains a vexing issue today.[3] On the one hand, those who hold to some form of the JEDP documentary hypothesis, such as Joseph

---

1. G. J. Wenham, "Pondering the Pentateuch: The Search for a New Paradigm," in *The Face of Old Testament Studies* (ed. D. W. Baker and B. T. Arnold; Grand Rapids, MI: Baker, 1999) 116–44.
2. W. M. L. De Wette, *Dissertatio critica exegetica qua Deuteronomium a prioribus Pentateuchi libris diversu, alius cujusdam recentioris actoris opus esse monstratur* (Jena, 1805). Scholars who assume De Wette's 7th-century B.C.E. dating of Deuteronomy or some significant portion thereof include J. Wellhausen, S. R. Driver, G. von Rad, B. Halpern, B. Levinson, A. D. H. Mayes, M. Weinfeld, E. W. Nicholson, R. E. Clements, J. R. Lundbom, G. Braulik, and N. Lohfink, among many others.
   However, a minority of scholars hold to an exilic or postexilic date for the earliest material in Deuteronomy. For example, see J. Pakkala, "The Date of the Oldest Edition of Deuteronomy," *ZAW* 121 (2009) 388–401; R. G. Kratz, *The Composition of the Narrative Books of the Old Testament* (trans. J. Bowden; London: T. & T. Clark, 2005) 131–32; P. R. Davies, *Scribes and Schools: The Canonization of the Hebrew Scriptures* (Louisville: Westminster John Knox, 1998) 93–97.
3. Old Testament scholarship has been inconsistent in its use of the descriptors *Deuteronomic* and *Deuteronomistic*. The term *Deuteronomic* usually refers to Deuteronomy itself or the preexilic school that supposedly produced the book. In contrast, *Deuteronomistic* usually refers to the postexilic additions to *Urdeuteronomium*, or the postexilic school that putatively gave Deuteronomy its final form. The hybrid designation *Deuteronom(ist)ic* would then denote the Deuteronomic reforms under Josiah without specific time constraints.
   The terms *Deuteronomic* and *Deuteronomistic* have also been used interchangeably in describing Deuteronomy's influence on other biblical material, as in the identification of the historical books of Joshua–Kings as both the *Deuteronomic History* (e.g., T. E. Fretheim, *Deuteronomic History* [Nashville: Abingdon, 1983]) and the *Deuteronomistic History* (e.g., M. Noth, *The Deuteronomistic History* [JSOTSup 15; trans J. Doull; Sheffield: JSOT Press, 1981]). See the discussion by R. Coggins, "What Does 'Deuteronomistic' Mean?" in *Those Elusive Deuteronomists: The Phenomenon of Pan-Deuteronomism* (ed. L. S. Schearing and S. L. McKenzie; JSOTSup 268; Sheffield: Sheffield Academic Press, 1999) 22–35.

Blenkinsopp, argue that J material antedates Deuteronomy, while P material is exilic and mostly postdates the work of the Deuteronom(ist)ic school.[4] On the other hand, John Van Seters inverts this chronology by arguing that J originated no earlier than the exile and, more importantly, that the theological vision of the Deuteronom(ist)ic school provided the impetus for the entire Torah.[5]

Though research on Deuteronomy continues to play a pivotal role in reconstructing pentateuchal origins, the book's theology has often been caricatured as quid pro quo religion without much analysis of the Deuteronomic description of Israel's past and future.[6] But do Deuteronomy and the school ostensibly associated with the book reflect the "conditional" reworking of older "unconditional" traditions? Or does the Deuteronom(ist)ic movement represent the main starting point for other OT theologies? In order to demonstrate how mired in a false dichotomy between past and future visions of Israel current approaches tend to be, we must reexamine how the narrative world of Deuteronomy presumes prior knowledge of Israel's traditions while concurrently recasting them as homiletic exhortations directed toward future life in the land.

Previous studies on Deuteronomy's relationship to the Tetrateuch have usually focused on diachronic issues in the Decalogues of Exodus 20 and Deuteronomy 5 as well as other discrepancies between the various legal corpora: the Book of the Covenant (Exodus 21–23), the Deuteronomic Torah (Deuteronomy 12–26), and the Holiness Code (Leviticus 17–26).[7] The

---

These ambiguities necessitate clarification. Thus, in this book, I will use *Deuteronomic* to refer to the book of Deuteronomy, *Deuteronomistic* to refer to literary and theological issues related to Joshua–Kings, and *Deuteronom(ist)ic* to refer to the school of tradents that compiled the books of Joshua–Kings. Similarly, the terms *Tetrateuch* and *tetrateuchal* will signify the literary unit of Genesis–Numbers without privileging any particular theory about the Pentateuch's composition (e.g., Martin Noth's Tetrateuch + Deuteronomistic History).

4. J. Blenkinsopp, *The Pentateuch: An Introduction to the First Five Books of the Bible* (ABRL; New York: Doubleday, 1992) 111–26.

5. J. Van Seters, *Prologue to History: The Yahwist as Historian in Genesis* (Philadelphia: Westminster John Knox, 1992) 227–45.

6. E.g., J. Van Seters ("Confessional Reformulation in the Exilic Period," *VT* 22 [1972] 451): "Deuteronomy makes possession of the land conditional upon obedience to the covenant, but this would be contradictory to an unconditional promise made previously to the patriarchs."

7. E.g., B. Lang, "The Number Ten and the Iniquity of the Fathers: A New Interpretation of the Decalogue," *ZAW* 118 (2006) 218–38; B. M. Levinson, *Deuteronomy and the Hermeneutics of Legal Innovation* (New York: Oxford University Press, 1998); F. Crüsemann, *The Torah: Theology and Social History of the Old Testament* (trans. A. W. Mahnke; Minneapolis: Fortress, 1996) 201–75; M. Fishbane, *Biblical Interpretation in Ancient Israel* (Oxford: Clarendon, 1985) 58–60, 174–77, passim. An exception to the usual emphasis on legal corpora is provided by D. E. Skweres (*Die Rückverweise im Buch Deuteronomium* [AnBib 79; Rome: Pontifical Biblical Institute, 1979]), who takes a diachronic approach to the historical flashbacks of Deuteronomy.

characterization of Deuteronomy as a recapitulation of law did not begin with Julius Wellhausen[8] but was encapsulated in the earliest extant interpretation of the book, the LXX translators' problematic rendering of משנה התורה הזאת ("copy of this Torah"; Deut 17:18) as τὸ δευτερονόμιον τοῦτο ("this second law").[9] Accordingly, Deuteronomic covenant theology has been reckoned as a restatement of the "conditional" Israelite covenant rather than the "unconditional" Abrahamic covenant.[10]

An Overview of Occurrences

While many studies have regarded Deuteronomy as a *legal* code, I propose to analyze one particular feature of the book's *narrative* chronology and theology—namely, its nearly fifty references to the אבות, the "fathers" of Israel. Although the repeated appeals to the "fathers" undergird the effectiveness of the Mosaic orations, their precise identity remains an open question: do the "fathers" refer to the patriarchs of Genesis 12–50, the generation(s) of the exodus, or someone else? In five verses, the answer is clear, for the title "fathers" is explicated by the appositive "Abraham, Isaac, and Jacob" (Deut 1:8; 6:10; 9:5; 29:12[13]; 30:20). In other passages, however, the various exodus generations seem to be in view. For example, the literary unit of Deuteronomy 1–11, which contains numerous references to the "fathers," is primarily focused on retracing the journeys of the second exodus generation from Sinai to Moab after the first generation perished in the wilderness. The ambiguities in these references to the "fathers" are reflected in the NASB, which renders אבות variously as "forefathers" (8:1) and "fathers" (8:3).[11]

The importance of the "fathers" in Deuteronomy is also underscored by the occurrence of the title in repeated expressions. The rhetorical force of

---

8. J. Wellhausen (*Prolegomena to the History of Israel* [Cleveland: World Publishing, 1957] 6) famously argued that Deuteronomy is "essentially an independent law-book" and therefore discontinuous from the narratives of the Tetrateuch.

9. D. I. Block, "Deuteronomy, Book of," in *Dictionary for Theological Interpretation of the Bible* (ed. K. J. Vanhoozer; Grand Rapids, MI: Baker, 2005) 166; J. G. McConville, *Deuteronomy* (AOTC 5; Downers Grove, IL: InterVarsity, 2002) 17.

10. The designation *Israelite covenant* is preferable to *Mosaic covenant* or *Sinai covenant*, since the related term *Abrahamic covenant* uses the adjectival modifier (i.e., "Abrahamic") to denote the covenant party rather than the covenant mediator (i.e., "Mosaic") or the place of covenant-making (i.e., "Sinai"). The term *Israelite covenant* is also used by J. Bright, *A History of Israel* (4th ed.; London: SCM, 2000) 152; M. Weinfeld, "ברית," *TDOT* 2:275; W. Eichrodt, *Theology of the Old Testament* (OTL; trans. J. A. Baker; 2 vols.; Philadelphia: Westminster, 1967) 1:43–44.

11. The adjoining context of these two instances of אבות suggests that they should be rendered using the same English term. The NASB translators apparently decided that "forefathers" would refer to the Genesis patriarchs, whereas "fathers" would refer to the exodus generation. If this was the case, the translators were still inconsistent in applying their own principle. In 1:8, where אבות stands in apposition to "Abraham, Isaac, and Jacob," NASB reads "fathers" rather than "forefathers."

4   Chapter 1: The "Fathers" in Deuteronomy

Deuteronomic formulas such as "land that I/Yhwh swore to your fathers,"[12] "God of your fathers,"[13] or "covenant that I/Yhwh made with the/your fathers"[14] hinges on the correct identification of Israel's ancestors. However, the formulaic nature of the references to Israel's ancestors complicates this identification, since only two brief narrative references to the "fathers" exist in Deuteronomy: (1) the group that "went down to Egypt seventy persons in all" (10:22); and (2) the individual who was "a wandering Aramean and went down to Egypt and sojourned there" (26:5). Since these narrative references to the "father(s)" occur without explanation, prior knowledge of oral or written traditions is apparently assumed in both cases. These ambiguous ancestors play a decisive role in the recitation of Yhwh's dealings with Israel.[15]

A Nexus for Current Methodologies in OT Studies

Since the historical referent for the "fathers" ostensibly oscillates between the Abraham-Genesis and Moses-Exodus traditions, the interpreter is faced with two possible reasons for this phenomenon. Either Deuteronomy contains compositional layers that reflect different and competing traditions of the "fathers," or the blurring of the generational horizons functions as an intentional rhetorical device. This tension between redactional and rhetorical approaches suggests that a reassessment of the Deuteronomic "fathers" might also shed light on the proper relationship between diachronic and synchronic methodologies.

Redactional Approaches to the Deuteronomic "Fathers"

Thomas Römer and Norbert Lohfink have most recently applied the redactional approach to the "fathers" in Deuteronomy. In his dissertation, Römer lays the groundwork for subsequent studies by arguing that the "fathers" in Deuteronomy refer primarily to the exodus generation, with the remaining references to "Abraham, Isaac, and Jacob" having been added by a redactor to maintain historical continuity within the Deuteronom(ist)ic agenda.[16] Not surprisingly, Römer's interpretation reflects his view that the

---

12. Deut 1:8, 21, 35; 6:10, 18, 23; 7:13; 8:1; 9:5; 10:11; 11:9, 21; 19:8; 26:3, 15; 28:11; 30:20; 31:7, 23; 34:4.
13. Deut 1:11, 21; 4:1; 6:3; 12:1; 27:3; 29:24[25].
14. Deut 4:31; 7:7–12; 8:18; 29:9–14[10–15]; cf. 5:3.
15. Of the 65 appearances of אב in Deuteronomy, 18 are excluded from this analysis because they do not refer to Israel's ancestors but appear in laws (e.g., "Honor your father and mother"; 5:16) or curses (e.g., "Cursed is he who lies with his sister, the daughter of his father or of his mother"; 27:22).
16. T. C. Römer, *Israels Väter: Untersuchungen zur Väterthematik im Deuteronomium und in der deuteronomistischen Tradition* (OBO 99; Freiburg: Universitätsverlag / Göttingen: Vandenhoeck & Ruprecht, 1990). Römer's detailed redactional proposal was anticipated in outline by Van Seters, "Confessional Reformulation."

Pentateuch is a late Deuteronom(ist)ic document.[17] In a critical reply to Römer, Norbert Lohfink suggests that Deuteronomy's initial identification of the "fathers" as "Abraham, Isaac, and Jacob" (1:8) should function as the default interpretation to analyze subsequent references to the "fathers" in Deuteronomy unless context dictates otherwise.[18]

Römer and Lohfink concur that Deuteronomy draws on known traditions of the "fathers." As I suggested above, however, their positions represent two sides of a potentially false dichotomy whereby one is forced to choose between mutually exclusive traditions. More broadly, their respective approaches reflect two dominant paradigms for the origins of Deuteronomy and the Pentateuch at large. Either one follows Gerhard von Rad's notion of a Hexateuch (i.e., Genesis–Joshua), which holds to the antiquity of the patriarchal traditions (*Das kleine geschichtliche Credo*; 26:5–9);[19] or one follows Martin Noth's notion of a Tetrateuch (i.e., Genesis–Numbers) plus Deuteronomistic History (i.e., Deuteronomy–2 Kings), which regards Israel's exodus from Egypt as the earliest tradition layer.[20] Whether following von Rad or Noth, scholars apply their diachronic presuppositions regarding the Pentateuch's composition and final redaction to prioritize either the patriarchs-Genesis tradition or the Moses-Exodus tradition at the expense of the other. Thus the discussion about the identity of the Deuteronomic "fathers" presents a microcosm of current debates in pentateuchal criticism as well as the interpretive impasses that result even when redaction critics use similar methods.

A Theological Proposal for the Deuteronomic "Fathers"

Though redaction critics typically argue that Deuteronomy's "fathers" represent two competing traditions of Israel's ancestors that were imperfectly joined at a late stage,[21] I will here examine how Deuteronomy blends these traditions rhetorically for the sake of bringing the past to bear on the present. Deuteronomy sometimes uses the "fathers" to refer to the

---

17. Römer, *Israels Väter*, 5.
18. N. Lohfink, *Die Väter Israels im Deuteronomium: Mit einer Stellungnahme von Thomas Römer* (OBO 111; Göttingen: Vandenhoeck & Ruprecht, 1991). Compare with P. Diepold (*Israels Land* [BWANT 15; Stuttgart: Kohlhammer, 1972] 78) and J. H. Tigay (*Deuteronomy* [JPSTC; Philadelphia: Jewish Publication Society, 1996] 61), who are less flexible than Lohfink and argue that the "fathers" invariably denote the patriarchs.
19. G. von Rad, "The Form-Critical Problem of the Hexateuch," in *From Genesis to Chronicles* (ed. K. C. Hanson; trans. E. W. T. Dicken; Minneapolis: Fortress, 2005) 3–5, 41–43.
20. M. Noth, *A History of Pentateuchal Traditions* (trans. B. W. Anderson; Chico, CA: Scholars Press, 1981) 47–62. However, Noth concurs with von Rad that the Sinai theophany represents the latest tradition layer in the Pentateuch.
21. See the recent work by K. Schmid (*Genesis and the Moses Story: Israel's Dual Origins in the Hebrew Bible* [trans. J. D. Nogalski; Siphrut 3; Winona Lake, IN: Eisenbrauns, 2010]), which, however, offers little analysis of the "fathers" in Deuteronomy.

patriarchs, sometimes to the exodus generation, and sometimes to Israel's ancestors in general. But does one need to hold to a strict division among these referents? The book of Deuteronomy evinces a profoundly theological vision of a unified conception of Israel that transcends past, present, and future generations. According to the narrative trajectory of the book, the current generation on the plains of Moab inherits the promises first given to the patriarchs and partially fulfilled through the deliverance from Egypt, in addition to becoming the ancestors of future generations who will reflect back on this seminal moment before Israel entered the land.

The case for such an explicitly theological approach to the "fathers" is reinforced by the incoherence of a strictly historical approach to Israel's generations in the narrative world of Deuteronomy.[22] On the one hand, Moses often identifies his audience as the same individuals who personally experienced the exodus and divine revelation at Horeb. For example, in Deut 5:3, Moses declares that it was "not with our fathers that YHWH made this covenant at Horeb, but with all of us who are alive here today." On the other hand, Moses had previously asserted in Deut 1:35 (cf. 2:14–16) that Israel's disobedience at Kadesh, in refusing to enter the land, resulted in the extermination of that sinful generation in the wilderness and the giving of the land to their children instead.

The first exodus generation should thus be dead, but Moses addresses his hearers as eyewitnesses to the deliverance from Egypt and Horeb theophany. Rather than attributing this anachronism to redactional editing, as diachronic approaches are wont to do, we can see it as Moses' speaking to both living and dead generations as "you" in order to highlight Israel's potential solidarity with both dead and living generations: death for those who disobey and repeat the mistakes of the past and life for those who obey and will enter and remain in the land (30:15–20).[23] Thus every generation of "you" that stands in a filial relationship to the "fathers" must

---

22. Römer also recognizes this incoherence but argues that this provides evidence of the "literarische Fiktion" (*Israels Väter*, 21) of the book rather than a theological perspective on Israel's generations.

23. This is not to say that redactional and theological approaches to Deuteronomy are necessarily at odds. For example, G. von Rad's programmatic essay on the Hexateuch (see n. 19) exemplifies the tension between diachrony and synchrony. On the one hand, von Rad argues for the likelihood of redactional accretions to Deuteronomy ("Problem," 3–7; cf. p. 58). On the other hand, von Rad explores how Deuteronomy's canonical form asserts the corporate solidarity of Israel throughout its generations ("Problem," 20–23). However, my study seeks to go beyond von Rad's in arguing that a theological conception of the generations functions at the *compositional* rather than *redactional* level of the book.

The most recent overview of the tension between diachronic and synchronic methods in Deuteronomy scholarship can be found in J. Taschner, *Die Mosereden im Deuteronomium: Eine kanonorientierte Untersuchung* (FAT 59; Tübingen: Mohr Siebeck, 2008) 26–71. Taschner advocates a synchronic approach similar to the one I am using in this book.

actualize Yhwh's ancient promises "today" through renewing the covenant (Deut 29:9–14[10–15]).[24]

A Rhetorical Proposal for the Deuteronomic "Fathers"

Although scholars have suggested in passing that Deuteronomy's conflation of chronology is a theological move to unify Israel's generations,[25] no rhetorical analysis has yet been devoted to the relationship between the Deuteronomic "fathers" and the so-called *Generationswechsel*.[26] The detailed studies of Römer and Lohfink have downplayed the possibility that the blending of "you" and the "fathers" might function as a rhetorical device in favor of attributing these shifting referents to different redactional layers. However, a rhetorical approach to the "fathers" is especially appropriate in light of three features of Deuteronomy.

First, a rhetorical approach recognizes that the repetitiveness of the Deuteronomic style is a homiletical strategy designed to inculcate the audience with *memory*.[27] The book is shot through with exhortations for Israel to remember the past.[28] Though this repetition has often been attributed to redactional strata, Timothy Lenchak notes that synchronic approaches, especially rhetorical criticism, can provide alternative explanations for the use of repetition in Deuteronomy:

> Historical-critical studies have traditionally viewed repetition and amplification as signs of various layers within a text. Rhetorical criticism,

---

24. R. O'Dowd, *The Wisdom of Torah: Epistemology in Deuteronomy and the Wisdom Literature* (FRLANT 225; Göttingen: Vandenhoeck & Ruprecht, 2009) 31–34; G. von Rad, *Old Testament Theology* (trans. D. M. G. Stalker; 2 vols.; OTL; Louisville: Westminster John Knox, 2001) 2:231; idem, "Problem," 22–23.

25. E.g., von Rad, *OT Theology*, 1:225; B. S. Childs, *Introduction to the Old Testament as Scripture* (Philadelphia: Fortress, 1979) 214–15; Skweres, *Rückverweise*, 102; J. G. Millar, "Living at the Place of Decision: Time and Place in the Framework of Deuteronomy," in *Time and Place in Deuteronomy* (JSOTSup 179; Sheffield: Sheffield Academic Press, 1994) 42–43; J. G. McConville, "Deuteronomy: Torah for the Church of Christ," *EuroJTh* 9 (2000) 38; N. Lohfink, "Reading Deuteronomy 5 as Narrative," in *A God So Near: Essays on Old Testament Theology in Honor of Patrick D. Miller* (ed. B. A. Strawn and N. R. Bowen; Winona Lake, IN: Eisenbrauns, 2003) 266; P. T. Vogt, *Deuteronomic Theology and the Significance of Torah: A Reappraisal* (Winona Lake, IN: Eisenbrauns, 2006) 151–52; O'Dowd, *Wisdom*, 33.

26. For example, Taschner's mostly final-form study on the relationship between the Mosaic speeches in Deuteronomy and their narrative parallels in the Tetrateuch contains only a brief treatment of the "fathers" (*Mosereden*, 107–15).

27. B. A. Strawn, "Keep/Observe/Do — Carefully — Today! The Rhetoric of Repetition in Deuteronomy," in *A God So Near: Essays on Old Testament Theology in Honor of Patrick D. Miller* (ed. B. A. Strawn and N. R. Bowen; Winona Lake, IN: Eisenbrauns, 2003) 215–40.

28. E. P. Blair, "An Appeal to Remembrance: The Memory Motif in Deuteronomy," *Int* 15 (1961) 41–47; G. Braulik, "Deuteronomy and the Commemorative Culture of Israel: Redactio-historical Observations on the Use of *lmd*," in *The Theology of Deuteronomy* (trans. U. Lindbad; N. Richland Hills, TX: BIBAL, 1993) 183–84.

however, sees these devices as attempts to provide presence, stir emotions, give emphasis, and 'fill out' an argument.[29]

Lenchak goes on to demonstrate that Deuteronomy seeks to persuade rather than command Israel,[30] but he restricts his detailed analysis to the third speech of Moses (28:69[29:1]–30:20). A study of the "fathers" in Deuteronomy can expand the scope of Lenchak's rhetorical analysis significantly since the various formulas of the "fathers" occur throughout the book.

Second, a rhetorical approach recognizes that collective memory entails the *transformation* of the past through *actualization* for the present.[31] Rather than providing a disinterested recitation of events "as they actually happened," the preaching of Deuteronomy infuses Israel's history with an urgency that motivates the parenesis found within the book.[32] Such rhetorically charged accounts of history are selective rather than comprehensive in nature, since they are geared toward constituting a community on a shared foundation.[33] When reciting history, the transformative function of memory suggests that historiographical differences between Deuteronomic and tetrateuchal accounts of history might be fruitfully analyzed as a rhetorical strategy rather than as a redactional criterion.

Third, a rhetorical approach to Deuteronomy accords well with the book's self-presentation as "the *words* that Moses *spoke*" (1:1). These words were not only delivered at Moab but were designed to be recited periodically (31:9–13) in order to recreate imaginatively the experiences of Moab for future generations.[34] The book of Deuteronomy assumes a canonical posture by embedding the means of its own oral and written propagation,[35] thereby ensuring that the voice of Moses speaking in the book of Deuter-

---

29. T. A. Lenchak, *Choose Life! A Rhetorical-Critical Investigation of Deuteronomy 28,69–30,20* (AnBib 129; Rome: Pontifical Biblical Institute, 1993) 80.

30. Lenchak, *Choose Life*, 1–37; cf. D. J. McCarthy, *Treaty and Covenant* (AnBib 21a; Rome: Pontifical Biblical Institute, 1981) 53, 187.

31. R. S. Hendel, *Remembering Abraham: Culture, Memory, and History in the Hebrew Bible* (Oxford: Oxford University Press, 2005); J. Blenkinsopp, "Memory, Tradition, and the Construction of the Past in Ancient Israel," in *Treasures Old and New: Essays in the Theology of the Pentateuch* (Grand Rapids, MI: Eerdmans, 2004) 1–17; M. S. Smith, "Remembering God: Collective Memory in Israelite Religion," CBQ 64 (2002) 631–51.

32. B. S. Childs, *Memory and Tradition in Israel* (Naperville, IL: Allenson, 1962) 50–56.

33. D. Patrick and A. Scult, *Rhetoric and Biblical Interpretation* (JSOTSup 82; Sheffield: Sheffield Academic Press, 1990) 45–56.

34. R. J. Pannell, *Those Alive Here Today: The "Day of Horeb" and Deuteronomy's Hermeneutical Locus of Revelation* (Longwood, FL: Xulon, 2004) 41–48; Millar, "Living at the Place of Decision," 41–49; W. Brueggemann, "Imagination as a Mode of Fidelity," in *Understanding the Word: Essays in Honor of Bernhard W. Anderson* (ed. J. T. Butler, E. W. Conrad, and B. C. Ollenburger; JSOTSup 37; Sheffield: JSOT Press, 1985) 21–36.

35. J. Schaper, "The 'Publication' of Legal Texts in Ancient Judah," in *The Pentateuch as Torah: New Models for Understanding Its Promulgation and Acceptance* (ed. G. N. Knoppers and B. M. Levinson; Winona Lake, IN: Eisenbrauns, 2007) 225–36; cf. J.-P. Sonnet, *The Book within the Book: Writing in Deuteronomy* (Leiden: Brill, 1997).

onomy resounds in Israel's ears as a perpetually authoritative speech-act.[36] By acknowledging Deuteronomy's claim to speak to future generations, a rhetorical approach is uniquely equipped to bridge the usual interpretive gap between original and future audiences, between "what it meant" and "what it means."[37] In this regard, speech-act theory will prove an especially helpful tool for contemporizing the Deuteronomic "fathers" as the ancestors of every generation of God's people that, like Moses' audience in Moab, must now renew its commitments to Yhwh.

Rhetorical Criticism in Deuteronomic and Old Testament Scholarship

Before concluding the introduction to this study, I need to make a few methodological remarks on rhetorical criticism because the field has advanced in two divergent directions since James Muilenburg's 1968 SBL plenary address.[38] On the one hand, Muilenburg and his students approached rhetorical criticism as the twofold task of delimiting discrete literary units and demonstrating the relationship between form and content in biblical texts.[39] Rhetorical criticism of this sort often becomes a form of stylistic analysis that is nearly indistinguishable from other synchronic methods that focus strictly on the text, such as "New Literary Criticism."[40]

On the other hand, modern rhetoricians continue the classical approach pioneered by Aristotle and Cicero through elucidating the five components of persuasion: (1) *inventio*, the marshaling of arguments; (2) *collutio* or *dispositio*, the arrangement of arguments; (3) *elocutio*, the stylistics of arguments; (4) *memoria*, the memorization of arguments; and (5) *pronuntiatio*,

---

36. J. G. McConville, "Metaphor, Symbol, and the Interpretation of Deuteronomy," in *After Pentecost: Language and Biblical Interpretation* (ed. C. Bartholomew, C. Green, and K. Möller; Grand Rapids, MI: Zondervan, 2001) 342–46; J. W. Watts, *Reading Law: The Rhetorical Shaping of the Pentateuch* (Biblical Seminar 59; Sheffield: Sheffield Academic Press, 1999) 16–17, 55–57.

37. Patrick and Scult, *Rhetoric*, 23: "[W]e see the religious perspective as essential to genuine rhetorical criticism because . . . the text is designed to persuade its readers to make particular choices which can only be called religious."

38. Published as J. Muilenburg, "Form Criticism and Beyond," *JBL* 88 (1969) 1–18. Cf. D. M. Howard, "Rhetorical Criticism in Old Testament Studies," *BBR* 4 (1994) 87–104; and W. Wuellner, "Where Is Rhetorical Criticism Taking Us?" *CBQ* 49 (1987) 448–63. Howard and Wuellner discuss the two main schools of rhetorical criticism. For a general account of rhetorical criticism in biblical studies, see P. Trible, *Rhetorical Criticism: Context, Method, and the Book of Jonah* (GBS; Minneapolis: Fortress, 1994) 5–84.

39. Muilenburg, "Form Criticism," 8.

40. E.g., J. R. Lundbom (*Jeremiah: A Study in Ancient Hebrew Rhetoric* [SBLDS 18; Missoula, MT: Scholars Press, 1975]) argues that inclusio and chiasm are the primary literary structures in the book of Jeremiah but pays little attention to the orality of the Jeremianic speeches. A similar tendency in Deuteronomy scholarship is found in G. Braulik, *Die Mittel deuteronomischer Rhetorik, erhoben aus Deuteronomium 4,1–40* (AnBib 68; Rome: Pontifical Biblical Institute, 1978).

the delivery of arguments.⁴¹ While these are helpful heuristic categories, their application in OT rhetorical criticism has been rather cumbersome in requiring the interpreter to make multiple "passes" through the biblical text. For example, Lenchak's study results in a significant amount of repetition and compartmentalization in his separate chapters on *inventio*, *dispositio*, and *elocutio* in the third speech of Moses. Lenchak's approach not only neglects to treat the argument of Deuteronomy as a whole; it imposes an Occidental paradigm on an Oriental work.⁴²

The methodology adopted here will attempt to harness the strengths of these two streams of rhetorical criticism while avoiding their weaknesses.⁴³ I will follow Muilenburg's approach by undertaking a close reading of the Deuteronomic "fathers" in their literary context, while also following the "New Rhetoric" in being attuned to oral and persuasive devices in the final form of the text.⁴⁴ After identifying the literary context and flow of a given instance of the "fathers," I will ask several rhetorically oriented questions: How does an appeal to a known tradition of the "fathers" amplify the Mosaic exhortations? What prior awareness of the "fathers" is required on the part of the audience in order for the rhetorical hammer to fall? How do the "fathers" develop as persuasive devices and literary figures in the unfolding argument of the book? Finally, which tradition is more likely cited in a given instance of the "fathers"—the Genesis tradition, the Exodus–Numbers tradition, or perhaps both?⁴⁵ If an inductive procedure of this sort seems less than concrete, it is worth noting that I am in good company for

---

41. G. A. Kennedy, *A New History of Classical Rhetoric* (Princeton: Princeton University Press, 1994). The continuation of classical approaches in modern times, often known as "New Rhetoric," is also discussed by Howard, "Criticism," 91–99.

42. J.-P. Sonnet, "Review of T. C. Lenchak, *Choose Life! A Rhetorical-Critical Investigation of Deuteronomy* 28,69–30,20," *Bib* 76 (1995) 93–98.

43. Cf. T. Renz (*The Rhetorical Function of the Book of Ezekiel* [VTSup 76; Leiden: Brill, 1999]) and R. K. Duke (*The Persuasive Appeal of the Chronicler: A Rhetorical Analysis* [JSOTSup 88; Sheffield: Sheffield Academic Press, 1990]). Renz and Duke retain classical rhetoric's emphases on persuasion and orality without being bound to any particular method.

44. Thus I mainly take a synchronic approach to Deuteronomy. This is not to say that diachronic issues (e.g., the provenance of Deuteronomy) are unimportant but that synchronic readings such as ours can offer new insights on diachronic problems that are currently intractable. R. Polzin similarly asserts the need to perform synchronic analysis before diachronic analysis, without privileging one method over the other:

> [S]cholarly understanding of biblical material results from a *circular* movement that begins with a literary analysis, then turns to historical problems, whose attempted solution then furnishes further refinements and adaptations of one's literary critical conclusions. The priority of synchrony . . . over diachrony is not in rank but only in operation. Thus we are still allowed to call both approaches truly complementary: each must eventually take the other's conclusions into account." (Polzin, *Moses and the Deuteronomist* [New York: Seabury, 1980] 6, italics original)

45. Römer (*Israels Väter*, 543) recognizes the need for a tetrateuchal extension to his work but claims that this mostly lies outside his scope. However, since Genesis and Exodus are the most substantive works in the canon referring to the "fathers," it seems logical that

allowing the shape of the biblical text to dictate the terms of my analysis. Phyllis Trible notes that rhetorical criticism is more of an art deriving from the text than a science driven by method: "Rhetorical analysis unfolds by fits and starts, by hints and guesses."[46]

Conclusion

I am structuring this book in three parts, each of which analyzes a formulaic category of the Deuteronomic "fathers." Part 1 provides a synchronic and theological treatment of the land promise to the "fathers" in dialogue with redaction criticism. Part 2 analyzes the "God of the fathers" in light of the influential views of Albrecht Alt and Julius Wellhausen on patriarchal religion, Mosaic Yahwism, and the putative centralization of Israel's worship. Part 3 examines the covenant of the "fathers" in conversation with form-critical and biblical-theological treatments of covenant in the OT. The analysis of each formulaic category of the Deuteronomic "fathers" varies in methodology because each category has been treated in the past using different methods (e.g., redaction criticism for the land promise to the "fathers" vis-à-vis form criticism for the covenant of the "fathers"). The reexamination of the Deuteronomic "fathers" thus provides a rubric for assessing a wide range of diachronic and synchronic approaches in OT scholarship.

Though the three parts necessarily diverge in their approach, their interpretive strands are woven together to show that Deuteronomy depicts the corporate solidarity of Israel in the land promised to the "fathers" (part 1), under the sovereignty of the same "God of the fathers" across the nation's history (part 2), as governed by a timeless covenant of the "fathers" between Y‍HWH and his people (part 3). In the narrative world of Deuteronomy, the "fathers" begin as the patriarchs, while frequently scrolling forward in time to include every generation that has received Y‍HWH's promises but still awaits their fulfillment.

---

any discussion of the "fathers" should attempt to correlate a Deuteronomic reference with a potentially linked tradition in the Tetrateuch.

46. Trible, *Criticism*, 106.

Part 1

The "Fathers" and the Land Promise in Deuteronomy

Chapter 2

The "Fathers" and the Land Promise in Deuteronomy: History of Research and Method

Gerhard von Rad once observed that the ubiquity of the land promise in the Hexateuch was strangely belied by the dearth of scholarly studies on this topic.[1] Although the force of this observation for the Hexateuch in general has been blunted somewhat in the seven decades since von Rad expressed these sentiments,[2] the situation has only marginally improved for Deuteronomy, the hexateuchal book that speaks most frequently of land. Typically, Deuteronomy's conception of land is examined only as a precursor to using "Deuteronom(ist)ic" land theology as a criterion in source and redaction criticism.[3] In the few instances where synchronic studies have

---

1. G. von Rad, "The Promised Land and Yahweh's Land in the Hexateuch," in *From Genesis to Chronicles* (ed. K. C. Hanson; trans. E. W. T. Dicken; Minneapolis: Fortress, 2005) 59.
2. The most systematic treatments on land in the Pentateuch/Hexateuch from a diachronic perspective have since been provided by M. Weinfeld, *The Promise of the Land: The Inheritance of the Land of Canaan by the Israelites* (Berkeley: University of California Press, 1993); and Diepold, *Israels Land*.
3. For example, S. Boorer (*The Promise of the Land as Oath: A Key to the Formation of the Pentateuch* [BZAW 205; Berlin: de Gruyter, 1993]) proceeds from observations of Deuteronom(ist)ic features in a few scattered texts (e.g., Exod 13:5, 11; 32:13; 33:1; Num 14:23; 32:11) to weave a complex theory of pentateuchal origins. Boorer's analysis of the land promise exists solely for the sake of her redaction-critical proposal. Likewise, D. Nocquet ("Étonnantes variations autour des 'destinataires du pays' dans le Deutéronome: Significations synchroniques et historiques," *ZAW* 119 [2007] 341–54) and L. Perlitt ("Motive und Schichten der Landtheologie im Deuteronomium," in *Deuteronomium-Studien* [FAT 8; Tübingen: Mohr, 1994] 97–108) argue for competing notions of land in Deuteronomy as evidence of multiple strata.
The patriarchal narratives of divine promise, especially Genesis 15, have been the frequent object of redaction-critical study based on "Deuteronomic" conceptions of land. See, for example, E. Noort, "'Land' in the Deuteronomistic Tradition," in *Synchronic or Diachronic? A Debate on Method in Old Testament Exegesis* (ed. J. C. de Moor; Leiden: Brill, 1995) 128–44; B. Gosse, "Le don de la terre dans le livre de la Genèse: En rapport aux rédactions deutéronomiste et sacerdotale du Pentateuque," *EstBib* 52 (1994) 289–301; J. Ha, *Genesis 15: A Theological Compendium of Pentateuchal History* (Berlin: de Gruyter, 1989); N. Lohfink, "Dtn 12,1 und Gen 15,18: Das dem Samen Abrahams geschenkte Land als der Geltungsbereich der deuteronomischen Gesetze," in *Die Väter Israels: Beiträge zur Theologie der Patriarchenüberlieferungen im Alten Testament* (ed. M. Görg; Stuttgart: Katholisches Bibelwerk, 1989) 183–210; H. Mölle, *Genesis 15: Eine Erzählung von den Anfängen Israels* (FB 62;

been conducted on land in Deuteronomy, they have tended to be more theologically oriented.[4]

In this section, I will take a synchronic approach to land in Deuteronomy that analyzes the formulaic references to Yʜᴡʜ's promise of land to the "fathers."[5] These formulaic references occur frequently in אשר relative clauses, generally following the formula "land that Yʜᴡʜ swore to give to the fathers" (e.g., Deut 1:8). Though this investigation must limit itself to these texts for reasons of scope, these references to the land promised to the "fathers" nonetheless furnish a convenient heuristic device for apprehending the broader Deuteronomic theology of land. The recent attention given by scholars to Deuteronomy's account of the land promise to the "fathers" has resulted in further fragmentation of Deuteronomy into redactional layers,[6] thus underscoring the need to reassess the final form of the book.

Terminology of Land and Place in Deuteronomy

Before analyzing the references to Yʜᴡʜ's promise of land to the "fathers," I must overview the rich terminology for land in Deuteronomy. The sophisticated interweaving of the various terms and concepts for land suggests that Deuteronomic land theology cannot be partitioned into discrete redactional strata. In addition to the ubiquitous and flexible terms אֶרֶץ and אֲדָמָה, which I will treat extensively, Deuteronomy uses numerous terms that carry specific geographical or theological nuances. Land can be described in terms of a military objective (אֲחֻזָּה), geographical region (חֶבֶל), divine gift (יְרֻשָּׁה), political boundary (גְּבוּל), feudal grant (נַחֲלָה), or tribal allotment (חֵלֶק). The contrast between fruitfulness and barrenness in the land is frequently reflected in contrasting terms (e.g., שָׂדֶה vs. מִדְבָּר) as well as antithetical phrases (e.g., "land flowing with milk and honey" vs. "great

---

Würzburg: Echter Verlag, 1988); M. Anbar, "Genesis 15: A Conflation of Two Deuteronomic Narratives," *JBL* 101 (1982) 39–55.

4. E.g., W. Brueggemann, *The Land* (OBT; Philadelphia: Fortress, 2002); N. C. Habel, *The Land Is Mine: Six Biblical Land Ideologies* (OBT; Minneapolis: Fortress, 1995) 36–53; P. D. Miller, "The Gift of God: The Deuteronomic Theology of the Land," *Int* 23 (1969) 450–65. Compare with C. J. H. Wright (*God's People in God's Land: Family, Land, and Property in the Old Testament* [Grand Rapids, MI: Eerdmans, 1990] 167–73), who provides detailed analysis of the land promise only in Deut 15:1–2.

5. J. G. Plöger (*Literarkritische, formgeschichtliche und stilkritische Untersuchungen zum Deuteronomium* [BBB 26; Bonn: Hanstein, 1967] 65) provides a convenient chart comparing the similarities and differences in these formulaic references to the land promises to the "fathers" in אשר relative clauses. To the 18 occurrences listed by Plöger (Deut 1:8, 21, 35; 6:10, 18, 23; 7:13; 8:1; 9:5; 10:11; 11:9, 21; 19:8; 26:3, 15; 28:11; 30:20; 31:7, 23), Deut 34:4 ought to be added, because it refers to the patriarchs by name, even though the title "fathers" is missing. A similar chart for the entire Pentateuch is found in G. Giesen, *Die Wurzel* שבע *'schworen': Eine semasiologische Studie zum Eid im Alten Testament* (BBB 56; Bonn: Hanstein, 1981) 231.

6. E.g., Römer, *Israels Väter*; Blenkinsopp, *Pentateuch*, 111–33.

and terrible wilderness"). Deuteronomy's conception of land is also closely related to terminology of place (e.g., דֶּרֶךְ, מָקוֹם).

This book will examine the Deuteronomic terms for land and place in order of increasing frequency. Because rarer terms for land (e.g., נַחֲלָה) typically connote a specific lexical sense, their occurrence frames a discourse context that allows for adjudicating among the various senses of more frequent terms for land (e.g., אֶרֶץ and אֲדָמָה).[7] The collocation of infrequent with frequent terms for land also assists in elucidating the taxonomic relationships between the general terms אֶרֶץ and אֲדָמָה and their less frequent but semantically narrower counterparts.

אָחַז / אֲחֻזָּה

The rarest Deuteronomic term for land is אֲחֻזָּה ("property, possession, plunder"), which appears only in Deut 32:49. At the conclusion of Yhwh's poetic song to Israel (32:1–43), Yhwh commands Moses to ascend Mount Nebo in order to gaze upon the land before dying on the mountain. The land of promise is here described as "the land [אֶרֶץ] of Canaan, which I am giving to the sons of Israel for a possession [אֲחֻזָּה]" (32:49). This appearance of אֲחֻזָּה coincides with the only occurrence in Deuteronomy of the construct phrase "land [אֶרֶץ] of Canaan," a juxtaposition of אֲחֻזָּה with אֶרֶץ that appears elsewhere in texts generally reckoned as Priestly (e.g., Gen 17:8; Lev 14:34; Josh 22:19).[8]

חֶבֶל

The next most frequent Deuteronomic term for land is חֶבֶל ("region"), which appears four times.[9] Deriving originally from a word for "cord" (e.g., 2 Sam 17:13; 1 Kgs 20:31) or "measuring line" (e.g., Mic 2:5; Amos 7:17), it came to denote a measured portion of land, usually the parceling of land into tribal allotments (e.g., Josh 17:5; 19:9).[10] In the narrative sections of Deuteronomy, however, חֶבֶל never refers to Israel's land but is used of Og's

---

7. See P. Cotterell and M. Turner, *Linguistics and Biblical Interpretation* (Downers Grove, IL: InterVarsity, 1989) 155–67, on the progression from lexical to discourse sense.

8. J. S. Kloppenborg ("Joshua 22: The Priestly Editing of an Ancient Tradition," *Bib* 62 [1981] 361) argues for the classification of אֲחֻזָּה as Priestly language in Josh 22:19 and elsewhere. However, a synchronic approach to Deuteronomy 32 may provide an alternative to the Priestly attribution of Deut 32:49. Immediately prior, Deuteronomy's only use of the verb אָחַז ("to seize") occurs as Moses speaks poetically of Yhwh's justice for his people (32:41). Though the poetic and prosaic sections of Deuteronomy 32 are typically dated to different periods (cf. P. Sanders, *The Provenance of Deuteronomy 32* [Leiden: Brill, 1996]), the repetition of אָחַז derivatives across genres suggests a contrast between Yhwh's "seizing" (אָחַז) of justice on Israel's behalf and Moses' failure to lead the nation to its "property" (אֲחֻזָּה). M. Sternberg notes that "generic modulation" in the repetition of verbal roots indicates that poetic and prosaic texts belong together (*The Poetics of Biblical Narrative: Ideological Literature and the Drama of Reading* [Bloomington: Indiana University Press, 1985] 385).

9. Deut 3:4, 13, 14; 32:9.

10. A. R. P. Diamond, "חבל," *NIDOTTE* 2:12–14.

territory in the "region [חֶבֶל] of Argob" (3:4, 13, 14). In the poetic sections of Deuteronomy, חֶבֶל occurs parallel to חֵלֶק ("portion") and in construct with נַחֲלָה ("grant, inheritance, possession"): "Yhwh is the portion [חֵלֶק] of his people / Jacob is the allotment [חֶבֶל] of his grant [נַחֲלָה]" (32:9). The mutuality of Yhwh's relationship with Israel is thus expressed in the way that Yhwh is apportioned to Israel, just as Israel is allotted to Yhwh.

יָרַשׁ/יְרֻשָּׁה

The noun יְרֻשָּׁה ("possession") appears seven times in Deuteronomy[11] and derives from the common verb יָרַשׁ.[12] Like חֶבֶל, יְרֻשָּׁה never refers to Israel's original land of promise but, rather, to territory that Yhwh has given to other nations such as Esau (2:5, 12), Moab (2:9), and Ammon/Lot (2:9, 19). In Deut 3:20, however, the newly conquered land given to the Transjordanian tribes is referred to as their "possession" (יְרֻשָּׁה), to which they may return after helping their countrymen to "possess" (יָרַשׁ) the land west of the Jordan. Not only is the collocation here of יְרֻשָּׁה and יָרַשׁ rare in the OT,[13] the adjacent use of these words from the same verbal root seems to suggest a conceptual relationship or progression between them.[14] On the one hand, the use of יְרֻשָּׁה constitutes a recognition that the Transjordan is foreign land that falls outside Yhwh's promised borders.[15] On the other hand, the repeated use of יָרַשׁ in describing the Transjordan campaign (2:24, 31; 3:12, 18, 20) indicates that this new conquest forms the mirror image to the task of conquering Canaan (e.g., 1:8, 21; 4:1). By describing the conquests of Transjordan and Canaan using identical verbs, Moses makes Israel's success in the Transjordan the prototype for future success in Canaan, in contrast to the failed attempt recorded in Deut 1:26–46. The juxtaposition of יְרֻשָּׁה with יָרַשׁ may provide a lexical bridge for the differences between the original and expanded borders of the land. The notion of flexible borders for Israel receives support in the next word study.

---

11. Deut 2:5, 9 (2×), 12, 19 (2×); 3:20. The word יְרֻשָּׁה should be distinguished from the related noun יְרֵשָׁה, which occurs only in Num 24:18.

12. The verbal form יָרַשׁ appears 71× in Deuteronomy and is distributed evenly across the genres of narrative, direct speech, and law.

13. Cf. Josh 1:15; 2 Chr 20:11.

14. R. Alter (*The Art of Biblical Narrative* [New York: Basic, 1981] 95) notes that repetition of *Leitwörter* from the same verbal root often signals thematic developments in narrative.

15. Weinfeld (*Promise of the Land*, 52–75) attributes the variable descriptions of the land's boundaries (i.e., Num 34:1–12; cf. Deut 1:6–8; 11:22; Josh 1:3–4) to Deuteronomic vis-à-vis Priestly conceptions of the land. However, his redaction-critical approach overlooks the way in which Deuteronomy's various references to גְּבוּל encapsulate a theological vision for the expansion of Israel's borders.

גְּבוּל

The expansion of Israel's borders is also anticipated in גְּבוּל ("boundary"), a word that appears 14 times in Deuteronomy.[16] Like גְּבוּל, יְרֻשָּׁה can refer to other lands such as the land of Esau (2:4), Moab (2:18), Geshur and Maacath (3:14), or Ammon (3:16, 17). Rather paradoxically, the most frequent use of גְּבוּל combines the notions of fixedness and flexibility in Yhwh's promise of land to Israel. On the one hand, Israel's "borders" are the holy גְּבוּל within which no leaven is allowed during Passover (16:4). On the other hand, the exact scope of Israel's גְּבוּל is open-ended and therefore contingent on Israel's obedience, since faithful love for Yhwh will result in conquest from Lebanon and the Mediterranean Sea to the Euphrates River (11:24–25). This expansion of Israel's גְּבוּל will require new sacral regulations far from the "place that Yhwh your God shall choose" (12:20) as well as new cities of refuge (19:3, 8). However, disobedience to Yhwh will eventuate in fruitlessness within Israel's גְּבוּל (28:40).[17] The frequent nexus between theology and geography is exemplified in Deuteronomy 19, where covenant curses are threatened for individuals who unjustly enlarge a גְּבוּל at the expense of a neighbor (19:3, 14 [2×]; cf. 27:17), because Yhwh alone is allowed to augment Israel's גְּבוּלִים as a reward for obedience (19:3, 8).

שָׂדַי/שָׂדֶה

The noun שָׂדֶה ("field") also occurs 14 times in Deuteronomy.[18] It possesses a narrower semantic range in Deuteronomy than in the Tetrateuch and elsewhere. While Deuteronomy also uses שָׂדֶה to mean "open land" (e.g., Deut 5:21; 11:15; cf. Gen 3:18; 34:7; Exod 9:25), as in the idiom "beasts of the field" (Deut 7:22; cf. Gen 2:19; Lev 26:22), it does not use שָׂדֶה to denote a region of a people, tribe, or family (as, e.g., in Gen 36:35; Num 21:20). This semantic function in Deuteronomy seems to be accomplished mainly by using גְּבוּל, יְרֻשָּׁה, חֶבֶל, and נַחֲלָה. Deuteronomy may share with Exodus and Leviticus the tendency to view the שָׂדֶה as the locus of covenant obedience and blessing, for food from the שָׂדֶה is to be left for the poor (Deut 24:19; cf. Lev 19:9) or offered to Yhwh (Deut 14:22; cf. Exod 23:16). However, Deuteronomy tends to express the prosperity of the land by using the word אֶרֶץ or אֲדָמָה rather than שָׂדֶה.[19]

---

16. Deut 2:4, 18; 3:14, 16 (2×), 17; 11:24; 12:20; 16:4; 19:3, 8, 14; 27:17; 28:40.

17. Strikingly, the covenant curses in 28:15–68 describe Canaan in terms identical to the wilderness and Egypt, for Israel's disobedience to Yhwh will turn the promised land into the harshness of Egypt and the wilderness whence the Israelites came. Moses even threatens that apostasy will be punished by a return to Egypt (28:68).

18. Deut 5:21; 7:22; 11:15; 14:22; 20:19; 21:1; 22:25, 27; 24:19 (2×); 28:3, 16, 38; 32:13.

19. The sole Deuteronomic occurrence of the poetic form שָׂדַי (32:13) to refer to Yhwh's provision in the wilderness (32:10–14) is the exception that proves the rule.

מִדְבָּר

The מִדְבָּר ("wilderness") provides the primary geographical and theological foil for land in Deuteronomy, most notably for the word אֲדָמָה.[20] The term מִדְבָּר occurs 19× in the narrative sections of Deuteronomy[21] but is never found in the covenant stipulations of chaps. 12–26. The narrative references to Israel's experience in the מִדְבָּר paint a complex picture. On the one hand, the barren landscape of the מִדְבָּר is vividly underscored in the phrase "great and terrible wilderness [מִדְבָּר]" (1:19; 2:7; 8:15). The מִדְבָּר is also the place of YHWH's wrath against the first exodus generation (9:7, 28; 11:5) and Moses (32:51). On the other hand, the מִדְבָּר is where YHWH imparted life-giving discipline (8:2, 16) and cared for Israel's physical needs (1:31; 2:7; 8:3; 29:4[5]; 32:10). While these differing visions of the מִדְבָּר have been attributed to different strata,[22] a final-form reading of Deuteronomy reveals a theological interconnection between the motifs of obedience and life. Both land and wilderness possess the power to impart life and death,[23] but the critical factor in Israel's destiny remains the nation's decision to obey or disobey YHWH (30:15–20). Whether at home in the land, sojourning in the wilderness, or languishing in exile, Israel's sustenance is guaranteed by divine grace and human obedience rather than by geography.

נַחַל/נַחֲלָה and חָלַק/חֵלֶק

The word pair חֵלֶק ("portion"; 8×)[24] and נַחֲלָה ("grant, inheritance, possession"; 25×)[25] require a joint treatment because חֵלֶק always appears together with נַחֲלָה (Deut 10:9; 12:12; 14:27, 29; 18:1, 8 [2×]; 32:9). The term חֵלֶק refers to an allocation of property (e.g., Gen 33:19; Josh 14:4; 15:3) and derives from חָלַק, a verbal root meaning "to divide, allot" (e.g., Gen 49:27; Josh 13:7; Ps 22:19). In prosaic sections of Deuteronomy, חֵלֶק always refers to the land allotment given to each tribe of Israel, except for Levi (e.g., Deut 10:9; 12:12; 14:27). The juxtaposition of חֵלֶק with חֶבֶל and נַחֲלָה in poetry was noted above.

---

20. L. Rost, "Die Bezeichnungen für Land und Volk im Alten Testament," in *Das kleine Credo und andere Studien zum Alten Testament* (Heidelberg: Quelle & Meyer, 1965) 79–81.

21. Deut 1:1, 19, 31, 40; 2:1, 7, 8, 26; 4:43; 8:2, 15, 16; 9:7, 28; 11:5, 24; 29:4[5]; 32:10, 51.

22. R. Gomes de Araújo (*Theologie der Wüste im Deuteronomium* [ÖBS 17; Frankfurt: Peter Lang, 1999]) argues that the wilderness journey is portrayed in Deuteronomy 1–3 as a negative time of punishment, whereas Deuteronomy 7–11 emphasizes God's miraculous provision and Moses' intercession for the sinful nation. He classifies the negative and positive wilderness traditions as early and late Deuteronomistic, respectively. While Gomes de Araújo rightly recognizes these contrasting conceptions of the מִדְבָּר, his dichotomy between Deuteronomy 1–3 and 7–11 overlooks the positive images in Deuteronomy 1–3— for example, YHWH's tender "carrying" (נָשָׂא) of Israel (1:31).

23. Brueggemann, *Land*, 46.

24. Deut 10:9; 12:12; 14:27; 18:1, 8 (2×); 32:9.

25. Deut 4:20, 21, 38; 9:26, 29; 10:9; 12:9, 12; 14:27, 29; 15:4; 18:1, 2; 19:10, 14; 20:16; 21:23; 24:4; 25:19; 26:1; 29:7[8]; 32:9.

The nominal form נַחֲלָה originally referred to a feudal grant (e.g., Exod 15:17; Ps 79:1; Jer 2:7),[26] with a derived sense of family inheritance (e.g., Gen 31:14; Num 35:2; Deut 3:18; 29:7[8]).[27] In Deuteronomy, the feudal connotations of נַחֲלָה are extended to include the sense of military conquest (e.g., Deut 1:38; 3:28; 4:38; cf. Josh 14:1, 3).[28] The geographical referent of נַחֲלָה in Deuteronomy also expands to encompass the entirety of the land promised by Yhwh to Israel (4:38; 12:9), rather than merely the land of individual clans or tribes such as the Levites (10:9; 14:27).[29]

Both חֵלֶק and נַחֲלָה in Deuteronomy possess a figurative sense beyond their original physical contexts of feudal grant, land gift, and family inheritance. Not only has the entire land become Israel's נַחֲלָה, Israel itself is Yhwh's נַחֲלָה (4:20; 9:26, 29) and חֵלֶק (32:9). For the Levites, who lack a physical נַחֲלָה in the form of land, Yhwh himself is their נַחֲלָה (10:9; 12:12; 14:27, 29; 18:1, 2). These theologically fraught uses of חֵלֶק and נַחֲלָה thus denote a trilateral relationship between Yhwh, Israel, and the land.[30] The certainty of Israel's possession of the land means that the נַחֲלָה will also be known as Israel's מְנוּחָה ("resting place"; 12:9).[31]

מָקוֹם

Though not referring to land per se, Deuteronomy's use of מָקוֹם ("place"; 33x)[32] is intimately related to its dialectic between unsettledness and settledness in Israel's journey towards the land. The phrase הַמָּקוֹם הַזֶּה ("this place") not only signifies Israel's current location in Moab but also denotes contemplative pauses for the purpose of recalling the nation's history since the Egyptian sojourn (1:31; 9:7; 11:5; 29:6[7]). The remembrance demanded

---

26. D. I. Block, *The Foundations of National Identity: A Study in Ancient Northwest Semitic Perceptions* (D.Phil. diss., University of Liverpool, 1981) 422–25; H. O. Forshey, "The Hebrew Root NḤL and Its Semitic Cognates," *HTR* 66 (1973) 505–6; idem, "The Construct Chain naḥᵃlat YHWH/ʾĕlōhîm," *BASOR* 220 (1975) 51–53.
27. Wright (*God's People*, 18–19) is probably incorrect in prioritizing the inheritance dimension of נַחֲלָה at the expense of its originally feudal context. However, the use of נַחֲלָה with both original (i.e., feudal) and derived (i.e., inheritance) connotations in Deuteronomy suggests that Israel is portrayed as both Yhwh's vassal and his son.
28. Habel, *Land Is Mine*, 33–35; J. N. M. Wijngaards, *The Dramatization of Salvific History in the Deuteronomic Schools* (OtSt 16; Leiden: Brill, 1969) 82–84.
29. Von Rad ("Promised Land," 59–69) demonstrates Deuteronomy's innovative use of נַחֲלָה to denote the whole of Canaan, though it is not necessary to follow his view regarding the "declension from grace into law" (p. 68) from unconditional (i.e., JEP) to conditional (i.e., D) notions of land.
30. C. J. H. Wright, "נחל," *NIDOTTE* 3:77; H. M. Orlinsky, "The Biblical Concept of the Land of Israel: Cornerstone of the Covenant between God and Israel," in *The Land of Israel: Jewish Perspectives* (ed. L. A. Hoffman; Notre Dame, IN: University of Notre Dame Press, 1986) 27–64.
31. G. von Rad, "There Remains Still a Rest for the People of God," in *From Genesis to Chronicles* (ed. K. C. Hanson; trans. E. W. T. Dicken; Minneapolis: Fortress, 2005) 82–88.
32. Deut 1:31, 33; 9:7; 11:5, 24; 12:2, 3, 5, 11, 13, 14, 18, 21, 26, 14:23, 24, 25; 15:20; 16:2, 6, 7, 11, 15, 16; 17:8, 10; 18:6; 21:19; 23:17; 26:2, 9; 29:6[7]; 31:1.

at הַמָּקוֹם הַזֶּה will serve to guard Israel against the dangers of idolatry in הַמָּקוֹם הַהוּא ("that place"; 12:3) across the Jordan. Upon arrival in Canaan, Israel must destroy every pagan symbol in כָּל־הַמָּקוֹם ("all the places"; 12:2). In this manner, Israel's geographical and theological journeys towards the land are superimposed on one another through the shift from הַמָּקוֹם הַזֶּה to הַמָּקוֹם הַהוּא. In fact, Israel's ever-increasing proximity to the land is captured by Deuteronomy's penultimate occurrence of the phrase הַמָּקוֹם הַזֶּה, where the geographical referent has shifted forward from Moab to Canaan (26:1–15). Moses here envisions a future of fruitfulness in the land and thereby prescribes a confession of thanksgiving: "Yhwh has brought us to this place [הַמָּקוֹם הַזֶּה] and has given us this land, a land flowing with milk and honey" (26:9). Indeed, the most frequent references to מָקוֹם anticipate Israel's settledness in the land through the formulaic phrase "the place [הַמָּקוֹם] that Yhwh your God shall choose to establish his name" (22×).[33] In Deuteronomy, unsettled Israel has not yet arrived in this settled מָקוֹם but is well on its way.

דָּרַךְ/דֶּרֶךְ

The journey metaphor is also captured through Deuteronomy's creative use of the term דֶּרֶךְ (48×)[34] and its verbal form דָּרַךְ (4×).[35] Like other terms for land and place, דֶּרֶךְ refers to both physical and spiritual aspects of Israel's journey. The physical דֶּרֶךְ (e.g., 1:2, 33; 2:1, 8, 27) through the wilderness must be accompanied by walking in Yhwh's spiritual דֶּרֶךְ (e.g., 8:6; 11:22; 19:9; 26:16; 30:16). Faithful adherence to Yhwh's דֶּרֶךְ will result in the blessing of long life in the land (5:33), thus bringing Deuteronomy's notion of דֶּרֶךְ into close connection with the concept of covenant.[36] The physical and spiritual senses of דֶּרֶךְ can even blur to the point of being indistinguishable, such as when Moses points to Israel's דֶּרֶךְ through the wilderness as a divinely appointed place of humbling and testing (8:2).

אֲדָמָה *and* אֶרֶץ

The most common Deuteronomic terms for land are אֲדָמָה (38×) and אֶרֶץ (197×). The terms are sometimes used synonymously and interchangeably

---

33. Deut 12:5, 11, 14, 18, 21, 26; 14:23, 24, 25; 15:20; 16:2, 6, 7, 11, 15, 16; 17:8, 10; 18:6; 23:17; 26:2; 31:11. G. von Rad ("Deuteronomy's 'Name' Theology and the Priestly Document's 'Kabod' Theology," in *Studies in Deuteronomy* [trans. D. Stalker; London: SCM, 1947] 37–44) argues that Deuteronomy uses Yhwh's "name" as a hypostasis to replace the Priestly theology of his actual presence at the sanctuary. Von Rad's hypothesis of secularization and demythologization in Deuteronomy will be analyzed in the discussion of the "God of the fathers" in chaps. 4–5.

34. Deut 1:2, 19, 22, 31, 33 (2×), 40; 2:1, 8 (2×), 27 (2×); 3:1; 5:33; 6:7; 8:2, 6; 9:2, 16; 10:12; 11:19, 22, 28, 30; 13:6; 14:24; 17:16; 19:3, 6, 9; 22:4, 6; 23:5; 24:9; 25:17, 18; 26:17, 18; 28:7 (2×), 9, 25 (2×), 29, 68; 30:16; 31:29; 32:4.

35. Deut 1:36; 11:24, 25; 33:29.

36. E. H. Merrill, "דרך," *NIDOTTE* 1:989–90.

in formulaic references to the land of Canaan (e.g., 6:10; 30:20).[37] Outside formulaic אֲשֶׁר relative clauses, however, semantic distinctions between אֲדָמָה and אֶרֶץ are still visible, in keeping with their usage elsewhere in the OT. The term אֲדָמָה derives from the Semitic root אדם ("red") and refers to soil or ground, especially in its life-giving and life-sustaining aspects (e.g., Gen 2:7, 19).[38] Accordingly, in Deuteronomy, the אֲדָמָה is the source of the fruit (פְּרִי־הָאֲדָמָה)[39] on which Israel endeavors to live abundantly (חַיִּים עַל־הָאֲדָמָה)[40] or prolong its days (אָרַךְ/רָבָה עַל־הָאֲדָמָה).[41] In contrast, disobedience to YHWH's covenant will cause the אֲדָמָה to cease yielding its "produce" (יְבוּל; 11:17) or even result in removal "from upon" (מֵעַל) the אֲדָמָה (28:21, 63). The immediacy of living on the אֲדָמָה is further emphasized when Moses speaks of "your ground" (אַדְמָתֶךָ; e.g., 12:19; 30:9) as though Israel has already possessed it.

The word אֶרֶץ is the most common Hebrew word for earth and land. As elsewhere in the OT, the term אֶרֶץ is much more common in Deuteronomy than אֲדָמָה and possesses a broader semantic range. Specifically, אֶרֶץ in Deuteronomy entails both political and geographical dimensions. In the political sense, אֶרֶץ occurs frequently as the *nomen regens* of construct chains in referring to the territory of certain peoples or nations,[42] a use never attested for אֲדָמָה. In the geographical sense, אֶרֶץ alone appears as the spatial complement to "heaven" or "water."[43] Most commonly, the term אֶרֶץ is found in formulaic phrases referring to the land of promise. The word אֶרֶץ occurs in expressions emphasizing its attractiveness as the "good land" and "land flowing with milk and honey."[44]

---

37. The meticulous study of Plöger (*Literarkritische, formgeschichtliche und stilkritische Untersuchungen*, 60–129) reveals that, although these terms can be used synonymously (e.g., 11:8–9), אֶרֶץ tends to connote the notion of a "promised" land (e.g., 1:8), whereas אֲדָמָה often connotes the fruitfulness of the land (e.g., 26:2, 15). Compare with similar conclusions by Römer, *Israels Väter*, 12, 175.
38. Block, *Foundations*, 311–17.
39. Deut 7:13; 26:2, 10; 28:4, 11, 18, 33, 42, 51; 30:9. However, the expression פְּרִי הָאָרֶץ is attested once in Deut 1:25.
40. Deut 4:10; 7:13; 12:1; 31:13. The word אֲדָמָה is frequently used with the preposition עַל or לְ. In contrast, אֶרֶץ only occurs with the preposition אֶל.
41. Deut 4:26, 40; 5:16, 33; 6:2; 11:9, 21; 17:20; 22:7; 25:15; 30:18, 20.
42. The most common construct chain involving אֶרֶץ is אֶרֶץ מִצְרַיִם ("land of Egypt"); 1:27; 5:6, 15; 6:12; 8:14; 9:7; 10:19; 11:10; 13:6[5], 11[10]; 15:15; 16:3 [2×]; 20:1; 24:22; 29:1[2], 15[16], 24[25]; 34:11).
43. *Heaven*: Deut 3:24; 4:17, 26, 32, 36, 39; 5:8; 10:14; 11:21; 25:19; 28:24, 26; 30:19; 31:28; 32:1; 33:13, 28. Deut 26:15 is a notable exception, for YHWH's dwelling in heaven is contrasted with man's dwelling on the אֲדָמָה rather than the אֶרֶץ. This verse receives a detailed treatment in the analysis of Deut 26:1–15.
Water: Deut 4:18; 8:7; 10:7; 12:16, 24; 15:23.
44. "Good land": Deut 1:25, 35; 3:25; 4:21, 22; 6:18; 8:7, 10; 9:6; 11:17. "Land flowing . . .": Deut 6:3; 11:9; 26:9, 15; 27:3. In Deut 31:20, the phrase "flowing with milk and honey" is associated with אֲדָמָה, the only instance in Deuteronomy where this expression does not occur with אֶרֶץ. The ANE and geographical background of this expression in denoting lush fertility has been amply demonstrated by P. D. Stern, "The Origin and

Both human and divine individuals perform activities for which אֶרֶץ is the object of the verb. The interplay between human and divine actions is exemplified in the repeated command by YHWH/Moses for Israel to "possess" (יָרַשׁ) the land that YHWH "has given" (נָתַן perfect).[45] The synergism of divine and human agency can also be seen in the juxtaposition of Israel's "entering" (בּוֹא Qal) the land with YHWH's "bringing" (בּוֹא Hiphil) Israel into the land (6:23; 7:1). Moreover, the divine gift requires Israel to obey YHWH's commandments in conquering the land itself (4:40; 11:8) and also to obey after arriving in the land (5:31; 30:16). Indeed, the Deuteronomic legal material exists entirely to govern Israel's conduct in the land (12:1).[46] As Brueggemann notes, the convergence of divine and human actions and agents reveals that Deuteronomy conceives of land as both "gift" and "task."[47]

Deuteronomic Variations in Verbal Actions and Recipients of the Land Promise

In addition to the ongoing interplay between divine actions and the corresponding human imperatives, Deuteronomy also exhibits a remarkable tendency to mix and match the various conceptual elements associated with land into formulaic expressions. Six significant variations occur in Deuteronomy's formulas of YHWH's promise of land: (1) variations in land terminology; (2) variations in verbs of divine action; (3) variations in verbs of human action; (4) variations in verbal aspects; (5) variations in recipients of the land promise; and (6) variations in the identity of the "fathers." The cumulative effect of these manifold variations is that Deuteronomy conceives of the recipients of YHWH's promise of the land as a single corporate entity that transcends chronological and generational distinctions.

Variations in Land Terminology

The usual semantic distinctions between them notwithstanding, both ארץ and אדמה can appear in אשר relative clauses as the objects of YHWH's oath to the "fathers." The only significant difference between the formulas in Deut 6:10 and 30:20 lies in their land terminology:

6:10   הָאָרֶץ אֲשֶׁר נִשְׁבַּע לַאֲבֹתֶיךָ לְאַבְרָהָם לְיִצְחָק וּלְיַעֲקֹב לָתֶת לָךְ
30:20 הָאֲדָמָה אֲשֶׁר נִשְׁבַּע יְהוָה לַאֲבֹתֶיךָ לְאַבְרָהָם לְיִצְחָק וּלְיַעֲקֹב לָתֶת לָהֶם

Significance of 'The Land Flowing with Milk and Honey,'" *VT* 42 (1992) 554–7.554–7; and S. D. Waterhouse, "A Land Flowing with Milk and Honey," *AUSS* 1 (1963) 152–66.152–66. Cf. E. Levine ("The Land of Milk and Honey," *JSOT* 87 [2000] 43–57), who argues unconvincingly that this expression originally denoted uncultivated rather than fertile land.

45. Plöger, *Literarkritische, formgeschichtliche und stilkritische Untersuchungen*, 83. The juxtaposition of YHWH's "gift" (נָתַן) and Israel's "possession" (יָרַשׁ) occurs in Deut 1:8; 3:18, 20; 5:31; 6:18; 8:1; 9:23; 10:11; 12:1; 17:14; 19:2, 3, 14; 21:1; 25:19; 26:1.

46. Miller, "Gift of God," 459.

47. Brueggemann, *Land*, 45–50, 56–62; cf. J. G. McConville, *Law and Theology in Deuteronomy* (Eugene, OR: Wipf & Stock, 1984) 11–13.

Formulaic expressions of the "land" in אשר relative clauses occur more frequently with ארץ (15×)[48] than with אדמה (7×).[49] It is nonetheless striking that ארץ and אדמה can be used nearly synonymously in these constructions, as shown above.

Variations in Verbs of Divine Action

The precise nature of the divine verbal action can vary significantly from formula to formula, especially with regard to the divine "oath" (נשבע) and "gift" (נתן). In the two examples below, the Deuteronomic "fathers" are the recipients of Yhwh's "oath" of the land without any reference to "gift":[50]

6:18   הָאָרֶץ הַטֹּבָה אֲשֶׁר־נִשְׁבַּע יְהוָה לַאֲבֹתֶיךָ
8:1   הָאָרֶץ אֲשֶׁר־נִשְׁבַּע יְהוָה לַאֲבֹתֵיכֶם

In contrast to 6:18 and 8:1, the following two verses demonstrate that the "fathers" can be the recipients of both Yhwh's "oath" and Yhwh's "gift" of the land:

11:21 הָאֲדָמָה אֲשֶׁר נִשְׁבַּע יְהוָה לַאֲבֹתֵיכֶם לָתֵת לָהֶם
30:20 הָאֲדָמָה אֲשֶׁר נִשְׁבַּע יְהוָה לַאֲבֹתֶיךָ לְאַבְרָהָם לְיִצְחָק וּלְיַעֲקֹב לָתֵת לָהֶם

In light of these variations in divine verbal action, redaction critics have often argued for a distinction in Deuteronomy based on whether or not a "gift" (נתן) of the land accompanies the reference to an "oath" (נשבע) to the "fathers."[51]

Variations in Verbs of Human Action

Deuteronomy uses several verbs to denote the requisite human response to Yhwh's "oath" of land to the "fathers." Moses variously commands Israel

---

48. Deut 1:8, 35; 6:10, 18, 23; 8:1; 9:5; 10:11; 19:8; 26:3, 15; 31:7, 21, 23; 34:4.
49. Deut 7:13; 11:9, 21; 26:15; 28:11; 30:20; 31:20.
50. This comparison of Deut 6:18 and 8:1 also reveals the so-called *Numeruswechsel*—namely, variation in grammatical number between singular and plural forms. G. Minnette de Tillesse ("Sections 'Tu' et Sections 'Vous' dans le Deutéronome," *VT* 12 [1982] 53 n. 1) has argued that the plural sections of Deuteronomy use ארץ as a technical term referring to the land or promise, whereas אדמה is used in a general sense. However, Plöger (*Literarkritische, formgeschichtliche und stilkritische Untersuchungen*, 121–24) rebuts this argument by demonstrating that אדמה can also refer to the land of promise in plural sections, as in 11:9 and 12:1. Thus the *Numeruswechsel* is not a meaningful criterion for distinguishing among the references to Yhwh's oath/gift to the "fathers."
51. E.g., Römer, *Israels Väter*, 12–14; Diepold, *Israels Land*, 76–79, 152–54; M. Z. Brettler, "The Promise of the Land of Israel to the Patriarchs in the Pentateuch," *Shnaton* 5–6 (1982) vii–xxiv. Similar arguments for Numbers are offered by N. Lohfink, "Wann hat Gott dem Volk Israel das den Vätern verheissene Land gegeben? Zu einem rätselhaften Befund im Buch Numeri," in *Väter der Kirche—Ekklesiales Denken von den Anfängen bis in die Neuzeit: Festgabe für Hermann Josef Sieben SJ zum 70. Geburtstag* (ed. J. Arnold, R. Berndt, and R. M. W. Stammberger; Paderborn: Schöningh, 2004) 9–30.

to "enter" (בוא), "possess" (ירש), or "cross into" (עבר + ב preposition) the land:

4:5 הָאָרֶץ אֲשֶׁר אַתֶּם בָּאִים שָׁמָּה לְרִשְׁתָּהּ
4:14 בָּאָרֶץ אֲשֶׁר אַתֶּם עֹבְרִים שָׁמָּה לְרִשְׁתָּהּ

In speaking of the conquest of the land, Deuteronomy typically uses a verb of motion (בוא or עבר) accompanied by a purpose clause (ל + infinitive construct of ירש + 3fs suffix).

Variations in Verbal Aspects

In addition to varying the verbs of divine and human action, Deuteronomy exhibits variation between indicative and participial forms. For example, the "gift" of the land can be described in chronological terms of both past (נתן Qal perfect) and present (נתן Qal participle):

12:1 בָּאָרֶץ אֲשֶׁר נָתַן יְהוָה אֱלֹהֵי אֲבֹתֶיךָ לְךָ לְרִשְׁתָּהּ
12:9 הַמְּנוּחָה וְאֶל־הַנַּחֲלָה אֲשֶׁר־יְהוָה אֱלֹהֶיךָ נֹתֵן לָךְ

The blending of indicative with participial forms from the same verbal root (e.g., נתן, ירש, בוא) has many implications for verbal aspect and narrative time. The use of the participle (נֹתֵן) frequently signals that Israel's conquest of the land has commenced,[52] thereby fusing Yhwh's past and present gifts of the land into a single action. In the narrative world of Deuteronomy, the "giving," "entering," and "possessing" of the land of promise have begun even while Israel still stands east of the Jordan. Though this rhetorical blending of chronological horizons is especially evident in Deuteronomy 12, it is more common for Deuteronomy to differentiate the recipients of the land promise according to the particular chronological horizon denoted by the verbal aspect. The "fathers" are typically the recipients of Yhwh's past "gift" (e.g., 6:23; 30:20), whereas the present "gift" is more often offered to the Deuteronomic audience (e.g., 4:21; 19:1). This observation leads to the closely related discussion of variations in recipients of Yhwh's promise of land.

Variations in Recipients of the Land Promise

Though the "fathers" are always the recipients of Yhwh's "oath" (נשבע), the recipients of the land "gift" (נתן) in expressions of this sort may vary between "us," "you," or "them." Strikingly, the land gift to "us" only appears in "creedal" declarations of Yhwh's faithfulness in bringing Israel into the land:

6:23 הָבִיא אֹתָנוּ לָתֶת לָנוּ אֶת־הָאָרֶץ אֲשֶׁר נִשְׁבַּע לַאֲבֹתֵינוּ
26:3 הָאָרֶץ אֲשֶׁר נִשְׁבַּע יְהוָה לַאֲבֹתֵינוּ לָתֶת לָנוּ

---

52. Joüon (§121c) and *IBHS* (§37.6e) observe that the active participle often denotes a continuing, durative, or imminent state of affairs.

History of Research and Method

By prescribing these declarations in first-person plural forms ("us"), Moses requires the speaker to include himself as a confessor of Israel's creeds and beneficiary of Yhwh's past deeds. Deuteronomy also refers to Yhwh's oath of land to the "fathers" as a gift to "you" (both singular and plural, though the so-called *Numeruswechsel* is not found here):

7:13 הָאֲדָמָה אֲשֶׁר־נִשְׁבַּע לַאֲבֹתֶיךָ לָתֶת לָךְ
28:11 הָאֲדָמָה אֲשֶׁר נִשְׁבַּע יְהוָה לַאֲבֹתֶיךָ לָתֶת לָךְ

The literary contexts of 7:13 and 28:11 both emphasize the present reality of the land gift as the basis for covenant obedience. Thus Moses speaks directly to "you" when he desires to motivate his audience with the imminent prospect of conquering the land.

In addition to first- and second-person recipients of the land gift, Moses can also refer to the land given to "them." The referent of "them" can be the "fathers" themselves (11:21; 30:20) or the Deuteronomic audience (31:7), or it may even be left ambiguous with regard to the two aforementioned groups (10:11). Most significantly, two instances of the land-oath formula collapse the generational distinctions between past (i.e., "fathers") and present (i.e., "their seed"):[53]

1:8 הָאָרֶץ אֲשֶׁר נִשְׁבַּע יְהוָה לַאֲבֹתֵיכֶם לְאַבְרָהָם [patriarchs' names] לָהֶם וּלְזַרְעָם אַחֲרֵיהֶם
11:9 הָאֲדָמָה אֲשֶׁר נִשְׁבַּע יְהוָה לַאֲבֹתֵיכֶם לָתֵת לָהֶם וּלְזַרְעָם

In these verses, it is noteworthy that both the "fathers" and "their seed" receive both Yhwh's "oath" and "gift" of the land, thereby hinting that Yhwh's gift of land may be transgenerational in nature.

Variations in Identifying the "Fathers"

The central role of Yhwh's "oath" and "gift" of land to the "fathers" raises the urgent question of their identity, especially in light of the current debate over Israel's origin traditions.[54] The "fathers" can be specified as the patriarchs (e.g., 6:10), or they can stand alone without further identification (e.g., 31:7). The patriarchs even occur in formulaic relative clauses without the appellative term "fathers" (34:4). These three variations in the identification of the "fathers" are seen here:

6:10 הָאָרֶץ אֲשֶׁר נִשְׁבַּע לַאֲבֹתֶיךָ לְאַבְרָהָם לְיִצְחָק וּלְיַעֲקֹב לָתֶת לָךְ
31:7 הָאָרֶץ אֲשֶׁר נִשְׁבַּע יְהוָה לַאֲבֹתָם לָתֵת לָהֶם
34:4 הָאָרֶץ אֲשֶׁר נִשְׁבַּעְתִּי לְאַבְרָהָם לְיִצְחָק וּלְיַעֲקֹב

---

53. Nonformulaic references to "their seed" are found in Deut 4:37; 10:15; 23:3; and 31:21. The use of "fathers" with "their seed" in 4:37 and 10:15 is investigated in chaps. 4–5 below.

54. T. Römer ("Nachwort," in Lohfink, *Väter Israels*, 123) notes that the identity of the Deuteronomic "fathers" lies at the heart of all current problems in pentateuchal scholarship.

Although 6:10 unambiguously identifies the patriarchs as the "fathers," in one instance Deuteronomy speaks of the "fathers" as having already possessed the land:

30:5 הָאָרֶץ אֲשֶׁר־יָרְשׁוּ אֲבֹתֶיךָ וִירִשְׁתָּהּ

Since Deuteronomy speaks predominantly of possession (ירשׁ) of the land as an event in the present (ירשׁ Qal participle) or future (ירשׁ Qal imperfect), this reference to a past possession of the land (ירשׁ Qal perfect) is surprising and requires closer analysis.

Past Approaches to the Variations in the Land-Promise Formulas

The flexible formulations and shifting recipients of Y<small>HWH</small>'s land promise in Deuteronomy have led to numerous redaction-critical attempts to account for this variety in geography, terminology, and theology. Though significant differences can be found in the details of these diachronic proposals, they share the methodological feature of using Israel's dynamic relationship to land as the hermeneutical lens through which individual redactional layers in Deuteronomy can be identified.[55] Typically, the multiplex land theology of Deuteronomy is distilled into two broad phases of Israel's history: (1) settlement in the monarchic era; and (2) the aftermath of the Babylonian Exile. The landed and unlanded periods of Israel's history would roughly correspond to preexilic (Dtr[1]) and postexilic (Dtr[2]) redactions of the Deuteronomistic History, respectively.[56] In this schema, Dtr[1] would portray entry into the land as an unconditional gift of Y<small>HWH</small> that resulted in Israel's spiritual complacency before the exile, whereas Dtr[2] would portray conquest and retention of the land as conditional tasks due to the postexilic need to explain the loss of the land. In contrast to North American scholarship, the so-called "Göttingen school" has been influential among European scholars in arguing for multiple postexilic redactions of the Deuteronomistic History.[57]

---

55. M. Köckert ("Das nahe Wort: Zum entscheidenden Wandel des Gesetzesverständnisses im Alten Testament," *TP* 60 [1985] 496–519) undertakes a similar approach but uses the rubric of law rather than land.

56. In North American circles, the view of a double redaction of the Deuteronomistic History has been advanced by R. D. Nelson, "The Double Redaction of the Deuteronomistic History: The Case Is Still Compelling," *JSOT* 29 (2005) 319–37; idem, *The Double Redaction of the Deuteronomistic History* (JSOTSup 18; Sheffield: JSOT Press, 1981); R. E. Friedman, "From Egypt to Egypt: Dtr[1] and Dtr[2]," in *Traditions in Transformation: Turning Points in Biblical Faith* (ed. B. Halpern and J. D. Levenson; Winona Lake, IN: Eisenbrauns, 1981) 167–92; and F. M. Cross, *Canaanite Myth and Hebrew Epic: Essays in the History of Religion of Israel* (Cambridge: Harvard University Press, 1973) 274–89.

57. R. Smend, "The Law and the Nations: A Contribution to Deuteronomistic Tradition History" (trans. P. T. Daniels), in *Reconsidering Israel and Judah: Recent Studies on the Deuteronomistic History* (ed. G. N. Knoppers and J. G. McConville; SBTS 8; Winona Lake,

The terminological variations in the Deuteronomic formulas of the land promise are treated similarly by redaction critics. Among many others, Diepold and Römer argue for a redaction-critical distinction between land-promise formulas on the basis of the presence or absence of "gift" (נתן) terminology in conjunction with the divine "oath" (נשבע), although they take incompatible approaches. Diepold asserts that the "gift" terminology represents a Deuteronomistic addition to an older, Deuteronomic formulation that only knew of an "oath," with the result that the patriarchs were only receivers of the oath but not the gift of land.[58] Römer reverses Diepold's redactional timeline by arguing that the "gift" to the "fathers" predates the terminology of "oath."[59] Though Diepold and Römer approach the Deuteronomic land promise using similar methods, their conclusions are incommensurable because their disagreements spring from deeper differences in their respective historical-critical accounts of Israel's history (i.e., Wellhausenian vs. Nothian). Regardless of how many historical and redactional periods are proposed for the land theology of Deuteronomy, it is striking that diachronic approaches to Deuteronomic land theology share the conviction that the book's multifaceted conception of land must be explained as a secondary development rather than as a compositional strategy.[60]

IN: Eisenbrauns, 2000) 95–110; T. Veijola, *Das Königtum in der Beurteilung der deuteronomistischen Historiographie: Eine redaktionsgeschichtliche Untersuchung* (Helsinki: Suomalainen Tiedeakatemia, 1977); W. Dietrich, *Prophetie und Geschichte: Eine redaktionsgeschichtliche Untersuchung zum deuteronomistischen Geschichtswerk* [FRLANT 108; Göttingen: Vanderhoeck & Ruprecht, 1972]).

For the sake of consistency, I will follow Römer's use in his dissertation (*Israels Väter*) of the North American terminology of Dtr[1] and Dtr[2]. This is not to say that Römer holds to the view of a double redaction, for his recent treatise on the Deuteronomistic History advocates a three-tiered redaction as a compromise between the North American and European models (*The So-Called Deuteronomistic History: A Sociological, Historical and Literary Introduction* [London: T. & T. Clark, 2007]).

58. Diepold, *Israels Land*, 76–79, 152–54.
59. Römer, *Israels Väter*, 12–14, 195–96, 266–71, and passim.
60. Nocquet's study of Deuteronomic land theology ("Étonnantes variations autour des 'destinataires du pays,'" 341–55) represents the latest example of this tendency. After a perceptive synchronic analysis of the shifting recipients in the Deuteronomic land promise, Nocquet opts for the diachronic explanation that this multiplex land theology derives from univocal building blocks. He argues for three underlying sources that correspond with Deuteronomy's three recipients of the land promise: (1) an early postexilic layer in which the recipients are the children of the first exodus generation (Deuteronomy 1–2); (2) a late postexilic layer in which the recipients are the first exodus generation themselves but are now threatened with dispersion (Deuteronomy 4); and (3) a preexilic layer in which the recipients will certainly possess the land (Deuteronomy 11). Nocquet concludes thus: "Les identifications des destinataires du pays reflètent les différentes périodes de rédaction du Deutéronome" (p. 353).

In response to similar diachronic proposals, however, R. N. Whybray observes that such a conflict between sources and redactions is rather schizophrenic: "Thus the [documentary] hypothesis can only be maintained on the assumption that, while consistency was the hallmark of the various documents, inconsistency was the hallmark of the redactors"

Conclusion

The impasse between redaction-critical proposals such as Diepold's and Römer's suggests that a synchronic reappraisal of the land promise in Deuteronomy is needed. The analysis of texts in chap. 3 operates with the hypothesis that Deuteronomy's variability in describing the land provides evidence of an artful narrative progression within the book. Likewise, the variations in terminology, recipients, verbs of divine and human actions, verbal aspects, grammatical number, and identification of the "fathers" in the Deuteronomic conception of the land can be viewed as literary and rhetorical devices rather than as signs of redactional strata. In its final form, the book of Deuteronomy depicts Israel's impending entry into the land as the intersection between obedience and disobedience, blessing and curse, and ultimately life and death.[61] Israel now stands at a critical point of decision on the plains of Moab,[62] having failed earlier to conquer the promised land of Canaan due to disobedience (1:8–46) but having succeeded in conquering the un-promised land of Transjordan due to obedience (2:1–3:29). The spatial orientation of Israel standing east of the Jordan, on the brink of enjoying the blessings of Canaan while still remembering the barrenness of Egypt and the wilderness leads to a distinctly theological conception of place.

(*The Making of the Pentateuch: A Methodological Study* [JSOTSup 53; Sheffield: JSOT Press, 1994] 49).

61. Brueggemann, *Land*, 43–45.

62. J. G. Millar, *Now Choose Life: Theology and Ethics in Deuteronomy* (Grand Rapids, MI: Eerdmans, 1998) 47–51.

Chapter 3

The "Fathers" and the Land Promise in Deuteronomy: Analysis of Texts

Because references to land in Deuteronomy are too numerous to examine individually,[1] and in keeping with the scope of this book as a whole, I must confine myself to formulaic relative clauses of the land promised to the "fathers." The overarching organizational principle is the land promised to the "fathers" rather than the land itself. Even after narrowing the goal this way, however, we are left with 20 passages, many of which are quite similar in formulaic wording and rhetorical function.[2] Thus I have reduced the number to 5 case studies of the land promise to the "fathers."

First, the three opening references to the "fathers" in Deuteronomy 1 invite us to reexamine Diepold and Römer's redaction-critical distinction between references to an "oath" (נשבע) with and without the terminology of "gift" (נתן), since YHWH's "oath" of the land in 1:35 lacks the "gift" (נתן) terminology found in 1:8 and 1:21. In a reading of the final form of Deuteronomy 1, I will demonstrate the rhetorical progression between these three land-promise formulas.

Second, in an examination of Deut 6:10, 18, and 23, I will interact with von Rad's hypothesis that 6:20–25 represents one of Israel's earliest creeds. The "fathers" formulas in 6:10 and 6:18 are then compared with the similar reference in 6:23, which von Rad classifies as the oldest tradition layer of Deuteronomy 6.

Third, the two references to the "fathers" in Deut 26:3, 15 form an inclusio around the famous reference to the "wandering Aramean" (26:5), von Rad's so-called "little historical credo." I will analyze the literary and genetic relationship between the formulaic references to the plural "fathers" (26:3, 15) and the surprising reference to a singular "father."

Fourth, the two references in Deut 30:5 and 20 juxtapose two seemingly incompatible identities for the Deuteronomic "fathers." On the one hand, 30:5 speaks of the "fathers" as having already possessed the land, whereas 30:20 identifies the "fathers" as the patriarchal trio of Abraham, Isaac, and

---

1. The words ארץ and אדמה occur a combined 235× in Deuteronomy.
2. Deut 1:8, 21, 35; 6:10, 18, 23; 7:13; 8:1; 9:5; 10:11; 11:9, 21; 19:8; 26:3, 15; 28:11; 30:20; 31:7, 23; 34:4.

31

Jacob. This ambiguity in the identity of the "fathers" has contributed to theories of a late Deuteronomistic redaction in the chapter.

Fifth, the reference to the land promised to the patriarchs in Deut 34:4 does not name them as "fathers," unlike 1:8; 6:10; 9:5; and 30:20. As the last chapter of both Deuteronomy and the Pentateuch, Deuteronomy 34 has long been a key chapter in higher criticism. Thus this case study can assist in determining the proper methodological progression from textual analysis to source and redaction criticism.

Of course, Yhwh's land promise to the "fathers" is not confined to formulaic relative clauses or these representative studies. The divine promise of land also arises frequently in Deuteronomy's references to the "God of the fathers" (e.g., Deut 1:11; 4:1; 12:1). Consequently, my treatment of the "God of the fathers" (in part 2) will examine these references in detail.

Land and the "Fathers" in Deuteronomy 1

Formulaic references to the land promised to the "fathers" appear three times in Deuteronomy 1. In Moses' recounting of events at Horeb and Kadesh, the prospect of entering the land promised to the "fathers" is set before Israel twice (1:8, 21) but is then withdrawn when the people disobey Yhwh (1:35). In addition to these formulaic references to the "fathers," Deuteronomy 1 introduces the epithet "God of your fathers" (1:11). The formulaic offer of the land and the title "God of your fathers" converge climactically in the events at Kadesh when the "God of the fathers" offers the ancestral land for possession (1:21). Though the numerous lexical parallels between 1:8 and 1:21 have frequently caused redaction critics to compare these verses without regard for their narrative context, the synchronic approach that I use here will demonstrate that the narrative progression from Horeb to Kadesh is essential for analyzing the "fathers" in Deuteronomy 1.

The initial stages of Israel's journey toward the land are narrated in the events at Horeb (1:6–19) and Kadesh (1:20–46). The account of the events at Horeb (1:6–18) occupies a relatively short portion of the description of Israel's journeys, with the majority of this section dealing with the appointment of leaders for Israel's burgeoning population (1:9–18). Though the emphasis on Israel's judicial matters has led some commentators to view 1:9–18 as an excursus,[3] the selection of Israel's leaders at Horeb forms a critical part of the larger sequence of Horeb events. The events at Horeb provide a fourfold template that will be repeated in similarly stylized fashion

---

3. E.g., M. Weinfeld, *Deuteronomy 1–11*: A New Translation with Introduction and Commentary (AB 5; New York: Doubleday, 1991) 137–40; A. D. H. Mayes, *Deuteronomy* (NCB; Grand Rapids, MI: Eerdmans, 1979) 117–18. In response to this redaction-critical tendency, N. Lohfink ("Darstellungskunst und Theologie in Dtn 1,6–3,29," *Bib* 41 [1960] 124–27) argues convincingly for the judicial nature of the land promises in Deut 1:8. The following section in 1:9–18 could thus be an exposition of the judicial ideas first introduced in 1:8.

at Kadesh. First, Israel is commanded to pack up its present camp and move to a new location (1:6–7). Second, Israel is offered the land promised to the "fathers" (1:8). Third, obedience to the command is postponed by the practical matter of selecting corporate leaders to represent Israel (1:9–18). Fourth, Israel heeds Yhwh's command to advance towards the land promised to the "fathers" (1:19). This fourfold schema occurs twice to describe Israel's movement towards the land, first in a mostly triumphant major key through Israel's obedience at Horeb (1:6–19), then modulated into a poignantly minor key through Israel's disobedience at Kadesh (1:20–46; cf. 2:14–16).[4] The fourth element of obeying Yhwh's command is missing from the Kadesh narrative.

Deuteronomy 1:8

רְאֵה	See!
נָתַתִּי לִפְנֵיכֶם אֶת־הָאָרֶץ	I hereby set before you the land;
בֹּאוּ וּרְשׁוּ אֶת־הָאָרֶץ	enter and possess the land
אֲשֶׁר נִשְׁבַּע יְהוָה לַאֲבֹתֵיכֶם	that Yhwh swore to your fathers,
לְאַבְרָהָם לְיִצְחָק וּלְיַעֲקֹב	to Abraham, to Isaac, and to Jacob,
לָתֵת לָהֶם	to give to them
וּלְזַרְעָם אַחֲרֵיהֶם	and to their seed after them.

As noted, the "fathers" occur for the first time in Deuteronomy in Yhwh's command to Israel to leave Horeb and possess the land promised to the "fathers" (1:8). The identity of these "fathers" is explicitly given in apposition as "Abraham, Isaac, and Jacob." Van Seters and Römer propose that these patriarchal names are late glosses to a narrative that originally referred to the exodus generation as the "fathers."[5] Lohfink disagrees and asserts that the patriarchal names are original to the narrative since they make better sense in the narrative context. At the center of the debate between Römer and Lohfink lie two significant text-critical issues in the אשר relative clause

---

4. The episode at Kadesh represents an ironic reversal of the Exodus/Horeb motifs of deliverance and victory (Lohfink, "Darstellungskunst," 105–35). The same observation for Deut 2:14–16 has been made by W. L. Moran, "The End of the Unholy War and the Anti-Exodus," in *A Song of Power and the Power of Song: Essays on the Book of Deuteronomy* (ed. D. L. Christensen; Sources for Biblical and Theological Study 3; Winona Lake, IN: Eisenbrauns, 1993) 147–55.

5. Römer's redaction-critical proposal for viewing the patriarchal names as a late gloss was anticipated by Van Seters, "Confessional Reformulation," 448–59. Van Seters notes that the Deuteronom(ist)ic prophets typically envision Israel's "fathers" as a generation delivered from Egypt (e.g., Jer 2:4–7; Ezek 20:5–6), with only infrequent or cryptic references to the patriarchs (e.g., Ezek 33:24). Since he views Deuteronomy to be a literary product of the same Deuteronom(ist)ic school, Van Seters concludes that the appositional identification of Deuteronomy's "fathers" with the patriarchs (e.g., Deut 6:10) must be secondary. However, Römer does not share Van Seters's supposition that the individual or school responsible for this redactional insertion also compiled the patriarchal narratives.

of 1:8. The adjudication of these text-critical issues has major implications for the identity of the recipients of Yhwh's ancient oath regarding the land, both in 1:8 and in the similar references to the "fathers" in 1:21 and 1:35.[6]

Text-Critical Issues in Deuteronomy 1:8

The first of several interpretive issues in 1:8 revolves around the numerous variant readings associated with נשבע, the verb denoting the swearing of Yhwh's oath to the "fathers." On the one hand, the third-person reading נשבע יהוה is represented in the MT, DSS, Vulg., Syr., and the targums. On the other hand, the SP and LXX reflect the first-person reading נשבעתי. The discourse context at first glance points to נשבעתי as the *lectio facilior* because 1:8 represents a continuation of Yhwh's speech regarding the command to depart from Horeb (1:6). Since Yhwh is still speaking in 1:8, it seems more natural for Yhwh to refer to himself in the first person than the third person. The awkwardness of the third-person reading for נשבע has led some redaction critics to view the entire אשר clause as the intrusive addition of a third-person oath formula to an earlier first-person speech of Yhwh.[7] According to this view, the references to a patriarchal promise of the land by Yhwh were encapsulated in a formulaic, third-person אשר clause that was often inserted wholesale by later redactors without regard for the grammatical persons of the immediate context. The redaction-critical reconstruction of 1:8 would lack the אשר clause and refer only to a vague promise of the land rather than a specific oath by Yhwh to the three patriarchs. The deletion of the patriarchal names from 1:8 would alter the entire theological outlook of Deuteronomy.

Römer notes three factors that raise doubts about the redaction-critical move to drop the אשר clause from 1:8.[8] First, the abrupt shift from first-person to third-person verbal forms in 1:8 (i.e., the *lectio difficilior* reflected in the MT, DSS, Vulg., and Syr.) is not unparalleled. In 1:36, directly adjacent to another reference to an oath to the fathers (1:35), Yhwh swears that only Caleb from among the exodus generation will see the land because "he has followed Yhwh fully." The very same phenomenon of Yhwh referring to himself in the third person is thus found in proximity to the "fathers" oath in 1:8. Second, Yhwh swears a first-person oath in 10:11 and 31:20. Since these oath formulas with נשבע also occur in אשר clauses, the Deuteronomic internal evidence argues against the view that the Yahwistic oath formulas assumed a standard third-person form that was inserted into earlier texts. Third, the ubiquitous אשר clauses of the land promise that refer to the "fathers" are too tightly woven into the fabric of Deuteronomy to be easily

---

6. Though the detailed analysis of 1:21 and 1:35 must wait until later, the current text-critical treatment of 1:8 still refers to them for internal evidence on the "fathers."

7. E.g., S. Mittmann, *Deuteronomium 1,1–6,3: Literarkritisch und traditionsgeschichtlich untersucht* (BZAW 139; Berlin: de Gruyter, 1975) 20.

8. Römer, *Israels Väter*, 198–99.

discarded. To argue that each instance of an אשר clause that includes נשבע is secondary means that a Priestly redactor would have modified the text in more than 20 places.⁹ Such large-scale redactional intervention is less probable than the supposition that these אשר clauses are original Deuteronomic language.¹⁰

After agreeing that some form of the אשר clause is original, however, Römer argues somewhat surprisingly that the patriarchal names and the associated phrase "to them and their seed after them" in the אשר clause of 1:8 represent expansionistic glosses for the "fathers." Römer begins by arguing for a Priestly redaction in this section of Deuteronomy because the preceding phrase "land of the Canaanite" (1:7) arises from the Priestly strands in Genesis. Next, he notes that the Genesis land-promise texts where this phrase appears also emphasize the eternality of the land promise to the three patriarchs and their descendants. From these two observations, Römer concludes that the same Priestly redactor who inserted the Canaanite reference in 1:7 also inserted two other phrases in 1:8 following the reference to the "fathers": "Abraham, Isaac, and Jacob" and "to them and their seed after them."¹¹ The harmonizing interventions of a Priestly redactor supposedly created an artificial literary link between the patriarchs in Genesis and the Deuteronomic generation.¹² Furthermore, the shorter *Urform* of the land-promise formula is preserved through the abbreviated version in 1:35 that lacks the verb נתן and any reference to the patriarchs, in contrast to the expansive formulation in 1:8.¹³

Römer further challenges the antiquity of the oath to the patriarchs by an unusual assessment of the second text-critical issue in 1:8. In the clause directly following the patriarchal names, the reading להם ולזרעם אחריהם ("to them and their seed after them") is attested by MT, LXX, Vulg., Syr., and *Tg. Onqelos*. The SP alone attests the shorter reading לזרעם ("to their seed"). The possibility that SP's shorter reading arises from homoiarchton with the phrase "to them and" is negated by the occurrence elsewhere of the identical reading "to their seed" in a similar context of an oath to the fathers (11:9).¹⁴ Since a scribal error that could have accidentally created such a

---

9. Some form of נשבע appears in אשר clauses in Deut 1:8, 35; 4:31; 6:10, 18, 23; 7:8, 12, 13; 8:1, 18; 9:5; 10:11; 11:9, 21; 19:8; 26:3, 15; 28:11; 30:20; 31:7, 20; 34:4.

10. So also S. R. Driver, *A Critical and Exegetical Commentary on Deuteronomy* (ICC; Edinburgh: T. & T. Clark, 1901) lxxviii–lxxix n. 4; N. Lohfink, *Das Hauptgebot: Eine Untersuchung literarischer Einleitungsfragen zu Dtn 5–11* (AnBib 20; Rome: Pontifical Biblical Institute, 1963) 86–89, 307–8. This view has been reinforced by the analysis of every Deuteronomic occurrence of אשר and כאשר relative clauses by Skweres, *Rückverweise*.

11. Römer, *Israels Väter*, 212: "Für 1,8 wurde die Erwähnung des Samens zur Redaktion gerechnet, die auch die Patriarchenamen hinzufügte."

12. Römer, *Israels Väter*, 200.

13. Römer, *Israels Väter*, 201.

14. C. McCarthy, *Biblia Hebraica Quinta, Fascicle 5: Deuteronomy* (Stuttgart: Deutsche Bibelgesellschaft, 2007) 50.

lectio brevior is unlikely, the SP's rendering of 1:8 (לזרעם) is probably the original reading. However, Römer argues in the opposite direction and rejects the shorter SP reading in favor of the longer MT reading (עם זרעם להם אחריהם).[15] Römer's reasons for suspending the text-critical principle of *lectio brevis potior* deserve further investigation.[16]

It is telling that the viability of Römer's thesis demands that the longer MT reading provide the basis for the theologized *Textglättung*[17] represented by the shorter SP reading. The probability that a Priestly redactor could simultaneously insert two phrases into 1:8 referring to the patriarchs ("Abraham, Isaac, and Jacob" and "to their seed after them") is significantly increased if there was once a pristine *Urtext* that lacked any reference to the patriarchs and their seed. These two Priestly phrases could then be inserted seamlessly without other redactional modifications to the immediate narrative context, thereby effecting a transformation of a general promise of the land to unspecified "fathers" into a specific oath to the three patriarchs. However, if the SP reading "to their seed" were early, the *Urtext* of Deuteronomy would have already included a reference to an ancient oath to the patriarchs and their seed. The patriarchal promises would then be an ancient and pervasive theme in Deuteronomy, removing the need for a Priestly redactor to intervene on the macroscopic scale proposed by Römer.[18]

Having identified the ideological presuppositions that drive Römer's text-critical analysis, we can now confirm that his text-critical proposal is implausible with these three observations. First, his proposal that the shorter SP reading represents an interpretive truncation of the longer MT reading is out of character with well-established observations about these textual witnesses. SP tends consistently toward expansion and harmonization rather than truncation in the manner advocated by Römer.[19] Even though SP preserves the shorter and likely original reading, the corresponding sense of 1:8 is not substantially modified vis-à-vis the MT reading. The

---

15. Römer, *Israels Väter*, 199, 213.
16. R. W. Klein summarizes the text-critical guideline of *lectio brevior/brevis potior* in this way:

> Unless there is clear evidence for homoeoteleuton or some other form of haplography, a shorter text is probably better. . . . While some scribes may have abbreviated from time to time, we believe that the interpretation of a shorter reading as abbreviation should only be chosen as a last resort. (*Textual Criticism of the Old Testament: The Septuagint after Qumran* [GBS; Philadelphia: Fortress, 1974] 75.)

17. Römer, *Israels Väter*, 213.
18. Lohfink (*Väter*, 28–30) and C. McCarthy (*BHQ*, 50) still argue for Priestly interventions in Deuteronomy 1 but on a much smaller scale.
19. Two characteristics of SP that challenge Römer's thesis are observed by E. Tov, *Textual Criticism of the Hebrew Bible* (Minneapolis: Fortress, 2001) 80–97. First, SP exhibits an expansionist rather than truncating tendency. Second, the Hebrew *Vorlage* for the pre-Samaritan stratum of SP is quite old and often preserves authentic readings.

verse still refers to Yhwh's oath to the patriarchs and to their seed, even after dropping the phrase להם.

Second, the objection just registered against Römer's text-critical work can be supplemented by an argument from the Deuteronomic evidence within SP itself. Römer's suggestion that the short form of 1:8 attested in SP represents an attempt to create chronological distance between the patriarchs and Yhwh's gift of the land is doubtful since SP has the identical short form, לזרעם, in 11:9. Perhaps anticipating this objection, Römer argues that the SP author/scribe truncated the longer "seed" formulas found in the Hebrew *Vorlage* of 1:8 and updated the "fathers" oath in 11:9 to reflect the same short formula.[20] However, this second proposal overlooks the fact that the narrative context of 11:9 contains no references to the three patriarchs, thereby obviating the need for SP to solve a conceptual problem that does not exist there. In contrast, the hypothesis that the shorter SP reading in 1:8 and 11:9 is authentic provides a superior explanation for the origin of the longer readings attested by the MT and other witnesses. Moreover, because the sense of the MT and SP readings is similar, analysis of the oath formulas in 1:8 and 11:9 does not ultimately hinge on adjudicating between textual witnesses.

Third, an objection to Römer's thesis can be raised on purely literary-critical grounds. Since Römer asserts that the patriarchal names in 1:8 were glossed by a Priestly redactor, it is noteworthy that the references to "Abraham, Isaac, and Jacob" appear in a variety of narrative contexts in Deuteronomy that do not necessarily contain specific reference to the "fathers." The patriarchal trio occurs elsewhere as the direct recipients of Yhwh's oath without being mediated through the term "fathers" (34:4), as well as standing in apposition to the term "servants" (9:27) rather than "fathers." Since the references to "Abraham, Isaac, and Jacob" are so varied and distributed throughout Deuteronomy, it is *prima facie* likely that the initial reference to Yhwh's land promise to the "fathers" in 1:8 introduces an integrative motif that permeates Deuteronomy's overall poetics.[21] I will provide additional support for this hypothesis in the detailed analysis of "fathers" texts that follows.

Terminology and Chronology for the "Fathers" in Deuteronomy 1:6–8

The opening reference to the "fathers" in 1:8 introduces all the essential formulaic elements in Deuteronomy's subsequent references to the "fathers." The expansive formulation of the "fathers" in 1:8 need not be

---

20. Römer, *Israels Väter*, 212.
21. A. Berlin notes that the study of narrative poetics "aims to find the building blocks of literature and the rules by which they are assembled" (*Poetics and Interpretation of Biblical Narrative* [Sheffield: Almond, 1983] 15). I argue that the "fathers" constitute this sort of building block for Deuteronomy.

classified as the work of a zealous Priestly redactor, as Römer has proposed. Instead, the expansiveness of the initial reference accords well with the likelihood that 1:8 provides the rhetorical starting point for the repetition, abbreviation, and modification of subsequent "fathers" formulas. The particular formula found in 1:8 contains a superset of the elements found in later references to Yhwh's oath to the fathers: (1) land (ארץ); (2) relative clause marker (אשר); (3) oath (נשבע); (4) God's name (יהוה); (5) "fathers" appellative (אב + suffix); 6) patriarchal names ("Abraham, Isaac, and Jacob"); (7) "giving" (נתן); and (8) "descendants" (לזרעם). Plöger's careful analysis of the "fathers" oath formulas shows that subsequent references to the "fathers" are always missing at least one of the aforementioned eight elements.[22] Since the full formula is found only in 1:8, the superset of oath terminology furnished there introduces the formulaic building blocks that enable the abbreviated references to the "fathers" later in Deuteronomy. Repetition of these building blocks enables both remembrance by the Deuteronomic audience and stylistic variation among occurrences.[23] Thus it is unlikely that similarities and differences between the initial "fathers" formula in 1:8 and its subsequent occurrences furnish any significant criteria for redaction-critical partitioning of Deuteronomy. Indeed, a close reading of the "fathers" references will demonstrate that they cut across the usual redaction-critical seams, thereby undermining the usefulness of the *Numeruswechsel* and other criteria for diachronic reconstructions of Deuteronomy.[24]

The initial portrayal of Deuteronomy's narrative world begins with the delineation of three chronological eras that stand in dialectical tension with one another. In the narrative present, Moses is described by the narrator as speaking התורה הזאת on the plains of Moab (1:1–5). Moses' narration of the past begins not by providing legal exposition but by recounting Israel's departure from Horeb, the place where התורה was first given (1:6–8a).[25] Moses recalls Yhwh's command for Israel to journey toward Canaan, a land to be possessed (1:8b) that was the object of an ancient oath to "your fathers, to Abraham, to Isaac, and to Jacob, and to their seed."[26]

---

22. Plöger, *Literarkritische, formgeschichtliche und stilkritische Untersuchungen*, 65. Since the subsequent references to the "fathers" selectively use some elements of the expansive formula found in 1:8, it is unlikely that the subsequent lack of patriarchal names is of much redaction-critical significance. It is noteworthy that the first instance of the "place formula" (12:5; cf. 12:11, 14, 18, 21, 26; 14:23, 24, 25; 15:20; 16:2, 6, 7, 11, 15, 16; 17:8, 10; 18:6; 26:2; 31:11) is also the most complex.

23. Strawn, "Keep/Observe/Do: Rhetoric," 215–40.

24. Plöger (*Literarkritische, formgeschichtliche und stilkritische Untersuchungen*, 63) shows that the land (גבול, ארץ, אדמה) sworn to the "fathers" appears without noticeable distinctions across singular and plural texts.

25. Lohfink ("Deuteronomy 5," 262–65) notes that the events at Horeb are not fully treated until Deuteronomy 4. Thus Moses recalls the past in reverse order by emphasizing the journey from Horeb to Moab before returning to Horeb.

26. The phrase להם is dropped in this rendering, in keeping with the text-critical decision made earlier.

In these opening verses of Deuteronomy, therefore, the attention of the implied reader is directed to three generations that stand in solidarity and that will be creatively woven together for the sake of Deuteronomy's parenesis.[27] First, the reader stands in continuity with the present generation of Israel on the plains of Moab in the 40th year after the exodus (1:3). Second, the reader is invited to recall the narrative past of 40 years earlier, when Israel experienced the unforgettable events of Horeb. Third, the reader is transported further back to an ancient tradition of Yhwh's swearing an oath to give the land to the three patriarchs. In the span of a few verses, Deuteronomy thus demonstrates its concern for proper continuity among these three generations of Israel.[28] The reader is also led to expect the rhetorical device of shifting frequently between narrative past and present.[29]

Two general observations can be made from the discussion of Deuteronomy 1 thus far. First, Yhwh's initial offer of the land introduces three generational horizons that are bound in corporate solidarity under a single covenant of Yhwh.[30] Thus Deuteronomy constitutes a theological nexus between the distant narrative past of the patriarchs, the recent narrative past at Horeb/Kadesh, and the narrative present at Moab. Second, the temporal and spatial world of Deuteronomy presents a geographical and theological movement toward the land promised to the patriarchs. This is reinforced

---

27. Sonnet argues that Deuteronomy's implied reader is "primarily and ultimately regulated by the narrative text of Deuteronomy" (*Book within the Book*, 6 n. 10). Thus the best mode for understanding the intention of Deuteronomy's author(s) and audience(s) is to enter fully into the narrative world created by the text.

28. J. Taschner ("Die Bedeutung des Generationswechsels für den Geschichtsrückblick im Dtn 1–3," *WD* 26 [2001] 61–72) observes that the transition between the generations in Deuteronomy 1 introduces all the major themes in Deuteronomy: sin, judgment, forgiveness, law, land possession, and political organization.

29. Most notably in Deuteronomy 4, where eyewitness references to past events at Horeb and elsewhere form an essential part of Moses' present exhortations in 4:3–4, 10–15, 20, 33–38.

30. The theological term *corporate solidarity* is preferable to the socioreligious term *corporate personality*. The ambiguity of the latter term in referring to both corporate responsibility and corporate representation has been demonstrated by J. S. Kaminsky, *Corporate Responsibility in the Hebrew Bible* (JSOTSup 196; Sheffield: Sheffield Academic Press, 1995) 16–29; J. W. Rogerson, "The Hebrew Conception of Corporate Personality: A Re-examination," *JTS* 21 (1970) 1–16; and J. R. Porter, "The Legal Aspects of 'Corporate Personality' in the Old Testament," *VT* 15 (1965) 361–68.The term *corporate personality* was originally coined by H. W. Robinson (see *Corporate Personality in Ancient Israel* [rev. ed.; Philadelphia: Fortress, 1980]) on the basis of anthropological models of primitive peoples that have since been discredited. Robinson's notion of "corporate personality" pitted individual and communal identity against one another in a manner that was foreign to the biblical texts.

A thorough case for preferring the term *corporate solidarity* is made by W. C. Kaiser, *Toward Old Testament Ethics* (Grand Rapids, MI: Zondervan, 1983) 67–75. For the purposes of this study, two aspects of Kaiser's definition of corporate solidarity are particularly helpful. First, the whole group is considered to be a single entity. Second, the subject of the discourse frequently oscillates between the individual and the group.

by repetition of *Leitwörter* of motion at strategic points within the first speech of Moses.[31]

Much of the above discussion of Yhwh's initial offer of the land at Horeb (1:8) applies, with minor variations, to Yhwh's reiteration of the land promise at Kadesh (1:21). Before the Kadesh events, however, Deuteronomy introduces another formulaic reference to the ancestors: Yhwh is the "God of the fathers" (1:11) who has fulfilled his past promise to multiply Israel (1:10) and whom Moses beseeches for Israel's continued multiplication in the future (1:11). Subsequently, the completion of Israel's judicial preparations (1:9–18) leads to the journey from Horeb to Kadesh (1:19). Though Kadesh should have been the final stop before entering the land, the dramatic reversal in Israel's itinerary is highlighted by two references to the "fathers" (1:21, 35).

Deuteronomy 1:21

רְאֵה	See!
נָתַן יְהוָה אֱלֹהֶיךָ לְפָנֶיךָ אֶת־הָאָרֶץ	Yhwh your God hereby sets before you the land;
עֲלֵה רֵשׁ	go up, take possession,
כַּאֲשֶׁר דִּבֶּר יְהוָה אֱלֹהֵי אֲבֹתֶיךָ לָךְ	just as Yhwh God of your fathers spoke to you.
אַל־תִּירָא וְאַל־תֵּחָת	Do not fear and do not be afraid.

Upon Israel's arrival in Kadesh, another "fathers" reference appears that combines elements of the command to possess the land sworn to the "fathers" (1:8) with the divine epithet "God of the fathers" (1:11). A comparison of Deut 1:8 and 1:21 reveals the similarities and differences between these two occurrences of the "fathers":

1:8   רְאֵה נָתַתִּי לִפְנֵיכֶם אֶת־הָאָרֶץ בֹּאוּ וּרְשׁוּ אֶת־הָאָרֶץ אֲשֶׁר נִשְׁבַּע יְהוָה לַאֲבֹתֵיכֶם
1:21 רְאֵה נָתַן יְהוָה אֱלֹהֶיךָ לְפָנֶיךָ אֶת־הָאָרֶץ עֲלֵה רֵשׁ כַּאֲשֶׁר דִּבֶּר יְהוָה אֱלֹהֵי אֲבֹתֶיךָ

The verbal correspondences between Deut 1:8 and 1:21 are numerous. As in 1:8, Israel is enjoined to "See!" (ראה) that "Yhwh your God has set the land before you." In both verses, Yhwh has "given" (נתן) with the performative consequence that Israel must "possess" (ירש) the land.[32] The command to possess the land is reinforced in both verses using a relative clause de-

---

31. Plöger (*Literarkritische, formgeschichtliche und stilkritische Untersuchungen*, 13–16) observes that נסע, עבר, עלה, and פנה are *Leitwörter* that narrate Israel's journey in the first speech of Moses (1:19; 2:8, 13; 3:1). Deuteronomy's references to the "way" serve not merely as a geographical marker (1:2; 2:1; 3:1) but also as a spiritual metaphor for Israel's journey with Yhwh (5:33; 9:12; 26:17; 30:16). The physical journey is coterminous with the spiritual journey (see esp. 8:2). See also D. L. Christensen, (*Deuteronomy 1:1–21:9* [WBC 6A; rev. ed.; Nashville: Thomas Nelson, 2001] cvii–cviii) regarding the travel notices in Deuteronomy.

32. The function of ראה in signaling performative language in Deuteronomy 1–4 has been demonstrated by G. Braulik, "Deuteronomium 1–4 als Sprechakt," *Bib* 83 (2002) 249–57. The existence and role of covenantal speech-acts in Deuteronomy is discussed fully in chaps. 6–7.

noting Yhwh's past speech, though with three minor differences. First, the relative-clause marker changes from אשר to כאשר. Second, Yhwh's promise changes from what he has "sworn" (נשבע) to what he "spoke" (דבר). Third, no oath to the patriarchs is found in 1:21, as opposed to their explicit naming in 1:8. Patriarchal times are nonetheless suggested by the appositional reference to Yhwh as "God of the fathers" (1:21; cf. 1:11). Since the similarities between the two verses greatly outweigh the differences, redaction critics have proposed a literary dependence between them.

Even more than from the lexical links between Deut 1:8 and 1:21, redaction-critical proposals for 1:21 receive their impetus from the first occurrence here of the *Numeruswechsel* in Deuteronomy. The preceding and subsequent context is consistently plural, but 1:21 alone shifts to the singular.[33] In addition to the duplicate commands to possess the land in 1:21 and 1:8, this sudden and isolated occurrence of the phenomenon has led redaction critics to view 1:21 as a singular insertion into a plural narrative.[34] However, the observations of *Numeruswechsel* in other Deuteronomic passages cannot be applied so easily here. Unlike other occurrences of the *Numeruswechsel* in Deuteronomy, where entire sections alternate between singular and plural forms,[35] the shift in grammatical number in this section is confined to this one verse. The isolated nature of the *Numeruswechsel* occurrence in Deut 1:21 makes it difficult, if not impossible, to identify an entire strand of singular discourse that might have been incorporated into a plural narrative. Veijola nonetheless argues for the secondary nature of Deut 1:21 by proposing that Deuteronomy 1–3 may contain as many as six singular strata, of which 1:21 occupies one.[36] But approaches that presuppose the viability of the *Numeruswechsel* as a redaction-critical criterion, such as Veijola's, confront mounting improbabilities in order to account for all the textual data. The potentially boundless number of redactors in Veijola's proposal exemplifies how the plausibility of redaction-critical proposals is inversely proportional to their complexity.

---

33. The plural reading in the LXX version of Deut 1:21 is probably an attempt to harmonize with the plural context.

34. E.g., Mayes, *Deuteronomy*, 128; H. Cazelles, "Passages in the Singular within Discourse in the Plural of Dt 1–4," *CBQ* 29 (1967) 208; Mittmann, *Deuteronomium 1,1–6,3*, 35; Perlitt, "Motive und Schichten der Landtheologie im Deuteronomium," 101; Plöger, *Literarkritische, formgeschichtliche und stilkritische Untersuchungen*, 42.

35. Most notably in Deuteronomy 4, which alternates between singular and plural sections. Deut 4:1–8, 12–18 is mostly plural, while 4:9–10 is mostly singular.

36. T. Veijola admits that a large number of redactions is required for the singular sections in Deuteronomy 1–3, since they reflect multiple ideologies that are probably incompatible:

> The number of the redactors has for certain been greater than two or three—perhaps half a dozen, apart from minor glossaic additions. ("Principal Observations on the Basic Story in Deuteronomy 1–3," in *A Song of Power and the Power of Song: Essays on the Book of Deuteronomy* [ed. D. L. Christensen; SBTS 3; Winona Lake, IN: Eisenbrauns, 1993] 141.)

Even granting the common premise of a secondary insertion for Deut 1:21, redaction critics still struggle to explain why this verse might have been added on ideological or literary-critical grounds. Cazelles, who usually advocates the redaction-critical use of *Numeruswechsel*, concedes that this verse fits smoothly into the flow of the narrative.[37] The repetition of such a command in the transition from Horeb to Kadesh encodes a narrative *mise-en-abyme* of Deuteronomy's express claim to be an exposition of Torah (1:5) before Israel's entry into the land.[38] The redundancy between Deut 1:21 and 1:8 is only problematic if one excludes the possibility that repetition can serve the purposes of memory and pedagogy, a doubtful supposition in light of the mnemonic goal of Deuteronomic repetition.[39]

Redactional Approaches to the *Numeruswechsel* in Deuteronomy 1:21

Since redactional explanations for Deut 1:21 have tended to increase in complexity and fragment the text, I hypothesize that reassessment of the final form will potentially offer a better explanation. In this regard, the fact that the commands to possess the land are repeated in direct speech (1:8, 21) rather than in narrative invites two lines of rhetorical-critical questioning. First, what narrative progression or rhetorical function might be served by the repetition and variation of terminology in 1:8 and 1:21? Second, how might this first instance of *Numeruswechsel* be explained as a rhetorical device within the narrative context?

The first question can be addressed by observing the scene shift that takes place in the intervening narrative between 1:8 and 1:21. The earlier instance of Yʜᴡʜ's command to possess the land takes place in the judicial context of Horeb, whereas the repetition of the command takes place in the martial context of Kadesh (1:19). Upon Israel's arrival in Kadesh (1:2), the command to possess the land is repeated with significant lexical shifts that highlight the imminence of Israel's military task. Instead of depicting Israel as outsiders who must בוא ("come, enter"; 1:8), the text now portrays Israel as being in close striking range through the command to עלה ("go up"; 1:21). The shift from בוא to עלה portends more than the topographical shift from the Egyptian wilderness to the Amorite highlands. In contrast to the common verb בוא (e.g., 1:19, 20, 22, 24), the five occurrences of עלה (1:21, 26, 41, 42, 43) introduce a distinctly military and theological dimension to Israel's task of possessing the land. In response to Yʜᴡʜ's original command to עלה (1:21), Israel at first refuses to עלה (1:26) but then undertakes a misguided attempt to עלה (1:41). Yʜᴡʜ warns them of certain defeat in their attempt to עלה (1:42), a prediction that is somberly fulfilled in

---

37. Cazelles, "Passages," 209.
38. On the literary device of *mise-en-abyme* as a "narrative within a narrative," see J.-L. Ska, *'Our Fathers Have Told Us': Introduction to the Analysis of Hebrew Narratives* (SubBi 13; Rome: Pontifical Biblical Institute, 2000) 47–53.
39. Strawn, "Keep/Observe/Do: Rhetoric," 215–40.

Israel's defeat in עלה (1:43).⁴⁰ In 1:21, the previous command to ירש ("possess"; cf. 1:8) is now paired with the verb עלה not only to emphasize the shift from judicial to martial context but also to highlight Israel's disobedience in Yhwh's holy war.⁴¹ Likewise, the conception of land progresses from that of a legal transfer of property (1:8) to a military objective to be won (1:21). The transposition of the previous divine command into a new context pushes the narrative forward and reflects rhetorical artistry.

The issue of *Numeruswechsel* can also be addressed by the preponderance of עלה in the Kadesh narrative. The sudden occurrence of *Numeruswechsel* in Deut 1:21 inflicts an "assault on the listener"⁴² just as Moses introduces the *Leitwort* עלה, the verbal hinge on which Israel's future subsequently turns. Prior to the climactic command to עלה (Deut 1:21), Israel's journey had moved steadily toward the land. But after Israel's disobedience and failure to עלה (Deut 1:26–39), the land recedes from sight as Israel must turn around and return to the wilderness (1:40; cf. 2:1). The *Numeruswechsel* coincides with the zenith of the narrative, at the precise point when Yhwh has commanded Israel most emphatically but before the nation responds disobediently. The *Numeruswechsel* in this instance could then be a rhetorical device to focus the audience's attention on the decision at hand. Though this explanation cannot be judged conclusive, it seems likely that the *Numeruswechsel* in these references to the "fathers" is intentional rather than haphazard.⁴³

Deuteronomy 1:35

אִם־יִרְאֶה אִישׁ בָּאֲנָשִׁים הָאֵלֶּה	Not one of these men shall see,
הַדּוֹר הָרָע הַזֶּה	this evil generation,
אֵת הָאָרֶץ הַטּוֹבָה	the good land
אֲשֶׁר נִשְׁבַּעְתִּי לָתֵת לַאֲבֹתֵיכֶם	that I swore to give to your fathers.

---

40. N. Lohfink notes that this use of the *Leitwort* עלה lies at the center of "die Krise der Erzählung" ("Narrative Analyse von Dtn 1,6–3,29," in *Mincha: Festgabe für Rolf Rendtorff zum 75. Geburtstag* [ed. E. Blum; Neukirchen-Vluyn: Neukirchener Verlag, 2000] 149). Compare with similar observations in P. D. Miller, "The Wilderness Journey in Deuteronomy: Style, Structure, and Theology in Deuteronomy 1–3," in *To Hear and Obey: Essays in Honor of Frederick Carlson Holmgren* (ed. B. J. Bergfalk and P. E. Koptak; Chicago: Covenant, 1997) 52–53.

41. The martial emphasis of Deut 1:21 is also reflected in Moses' injunction for Israel not to fear the enemy (1:21c). Though Moses charged the judges at Horeb not to "fear" (גור; 1:17) human judgment, the present narrative shifts to a different word pair (ירא and חתת) to exhort the people not to fear. Since this hendiadys is typically issued by a military commander to his subordinates before battle (e.g., Deut 31:8; Josh 8:1; 10:25), the new terminology in 1:21 confirms the transition from a judicial to a martial context.

42. Lenchak, *Choose Life*, 13.

43. Millar ("Living at the Place of Decision," 22–23) notes that the shift to singular here may also serve to underline the corporate solidarity of the community in Israel's decision. It is especially striking that the *Numeruswechsel* from plural to singular occurs elsewhere in the context of commands for Israel to take land from the nations (2:24, 25; 3:2).

The next reference to the "fathers" has assumed center stage in the debate over Deuteronomy's audience and the coherence of its narrative world. The Horeb generation to whom Yhwh had sworn to give the land (1:8, 21) is now barred from entering it (1:35), with the exception of Caleb (1:36) and Joshua (1:38). Yhwh's "oath" (נשׁב) to bar the Horeb generation from the land (1:34) stands in stark contrast to two previous references to his "oath" (נשׁבע) to give the land (1:8, 21). More vexingly, the present generation of Moses' listeners is described as having been present at Horeb (1:6–18; cf. 5:2–3) even though the narrative later states that "all the generation of the men of war perished from within the camp, as Yhwh had sworn to them" (2:14; cf. 1:35). Similarly, the pronouns "we" and "you" seemingly denote two mutually exclusive groups: (1) the generation that died at Kadesh (1:20–46; cf. 2:14–16); and (2) the generation that triumphed later over the Amorite kings (2:17–3:29).

Redaction-Critical Proposals for Deuteronomy 1:34–40

The conundrum of *Generationswechsel* has led to countless redaction-critical proposals for Deut 1:35–40. Two representative and influential proposals have been offered by Lohfink and Römer. Though their redaction-critical approaches for dealing with the interpretive difficulties are mutually exclusive, they share the strategy of assigning the various divine oaths in Deuteronomy 1 to separate strata. The proposal presented here concurs with Römer that "[e]ine chronologische Unterscheidung von Generationen in Dtn 1–3 erweist sich nun geradezu als unmöglich"[44] but nonetheless differs from both scholars in its focus on the final form of the text. Deut 1:35–40 introduces a *Leitmotif* of corporate solidarity that prepares the way for the blurring of chronological distinctions in subsequent texts whereby every generation of Israel stands in a filial relationship to the ancestors. Although the "fathers" in Deut 1:35–40 are still the patriarchs, this passage concurrently envisions a transgenerational conception of Israel that undergirds Deuteronomy as a timelessly contemporary document for "today!"[45]

In an essay spun off his 1960 study on Deuteronomy 1–3,[46] Lohfink takes his starting point to be von Rad's contention that "a [newer] stratum that is especially indebted to ideas of community overlays an older one that is more individualistically oriented."[47] The older tradition emphasized Yhwh's grace to Israel in promising the land to the patriarchs, whereas the newer tradition emphasized Yhwh's wrath by threatening the condemna-

---

44. Römer, *Israels Väter*, 203.
45. The transgenerational relevance of Deuteronomy's repeated use of "today" was first noted by von Rad, *OT Theology*, 2:109. Compare with O'Dowd, *Wisdom*, 31–32.
46. Lohfink, "Darstellungskunst," 105–35.
47. N. Lohfink, "The Problem of the Individual and Community in Deuteronomy 1:6–3:29," in *Theology of the Pentateuch* (trans. Linda M. Maloney; Minneapolis: Fortress, 1994) 227.

tion of entire generations even when individuals were innocent. The noncondemnation of Caleb (1:36) reflects the emphasis on the individual in the old source, whereas the condemnation of a blameless Moses (1:37) has been added in exilic times to propagate a new ideology of communal guilt.[48] Lohfink sidesteps the chronological problem of the *Generationswechsel* by opting for a redaction-critical explanation for the apparent discrepancies in covenant ideology. Though his proposal is rather speculative, Lohfink's suggestion of corporate solidarity illustrates the possibilities of a theological rather than chronological approach to the *Generationswechsel*.

In contrast, Römer's redaction-critical approach explicitly addresses the chronological problems in Deuteronomy 1–3 by proposing that Deuteronomy's original temporal horizons referred to two wilderness generations rather than one.[49] Two significant implications follow from Römer's thesis. First, the Deuteronomic "fathers" were once identified with the first wilderness generation rather than the patriarchs. Second, the grammatical and rhetorical function of the "fathers" changes significantly in Yhwh's speech after the faithlessness of the people (1:26–33). Instead of being a formulaic reference to the distant past, the "fathers" in 1:35 actually become part of the narrative in being condemned by Yhwh as "this evil generation," with Caleb and Joshua being the lone exceptions among the "fathers." The patriarchs thus disappear from view, since the chronological horizon of the distant narrative past (i.e., the patriarchs) has been eliminated in favor of the recent narrative past (i.e., the first wilderness generation). The "fathers" now reside on the same temporal plane as "this evil generation," so Yhwh's earlier oath to the "fathers" (1:8, 21) would refer to the first wilderness generation.

The primary evidence that Römer adduces for his hypothesis is that Caleb is numbered among the "fathers" in Num 32:7–15, while the three patriarchs are mentioned there by name (Num 32:11) but are not identified as Israel's "fathers" (Num 32:8, 14).[50] Since Römer classifies Numbers 32 as a pre-Priestly text,[51] he suggests that the pre-Priestly strand of Deuteronomy that once referred to the first wilderness generation as the "fathers" can be recovered by removing the Priestly glosses from Deuteronomy 1. Once Deuteronomy 1 has been harmonized with Numbers 32, there emerges an older stage of Deuteronomistic tradition that views the "fathers" as predominantly negative. This tradition layer also includes the murmuring narratives of the first wilderness generation.[52]

---

48. Lohfink, "Problem," 228.
49. Römer, *Israels Väter*, 148, 202, passim.
50. Römer, *Israels Väter*, 204–5.
51. Römer, *Israels Väter*, 567.
52. Römer, *Israels Väter*, 225, 559.

A Critique of Römer's Redaction-Critical Comparison of Deuteronomy 1 with Numbers 32

Römer's proposal to treat "this evil generation" and the "fathers" in Deut 1:35 as identical groups is problematic on several levels. A brief look at Römer's reading of Numbers suggests that his interpretation disregards the contextual clues in Numbers 32 as well as the chronology and geography of the Numbers narrative itself. The flaws in Römer's analysis of Numbers 32 carry over to his redaction-critical comparison with Deuteronomy 1.

In Numbers 32, Moses rebukes the Reubenites and Gadites for their desire to settle in Gilead before the conquest of the land. The selfishness of these two tribes reminds him of "what your *fathers* did when I sent them from Kadesh to see the land" (Num 32:8). Moses warns that, if Reuben and Gad persist in reenacting the behavior of their "fathers," they will likewise perish (Num 32:14–15). The unhappy prospect of repeating the mistakes of the previous generation induces Moses to use filial language in denouncing the Reubenites and Gadites.

Since Moses equates the second wilderness generation with their "fathers" for rhetorical purposes, such an identification of the "fathers" in Numbers 32 cannot be slavishly applied to other passages when the chronological and rhetorical settings of the narrative are different. The events of Numbers 32 are not set in Kadesh, as they are in the narrative flashback of Deut 1:20–46, but in Gilead nearly four decades later. In Numbers 32, Moses can refer retrospectively to the first wilderness generation as "fathers" precisely because he is now speaking to the children of those who died in the wilderness—namely, the second wilderness generation. Though Joshua and Caleb clearly belong to the same time period as these "fathers" (Num 32:8, 12, 14), Römer's deduction that the "fathers" refers to the first wilderness generation is unwarranted. In this regard, Numbers 14 provides the proper intertextual parallel to Deut 1:20–46.[53]

Similarly, the observation that the patriarchs appear in Num 32:11 but are not identified as the "fathers" misapprehends the rhetorical situation. Since the rhetorical force of Moses' argument hinges on the present disobedience of the children just like their "fathers," a positive reference to "fathers" as patriarchs would have been intrusive at this point in his speech. Once Moses voiced his disgust toward the "fathers" at Kadesh (Num 32:8), the patriarchs were referred to by name in order to avoid conflating them with the sinful "fathers." The difference in terminology in referring to "fa-

---

53. Römer (*Israels Väter*, 204) concedes that a comparison with Numbers 14 suits the context of Deuteronomy 1 better. Even so, he argues that the two generations of Numbers 14 and 32 fuse together because they are both recipients of Yhwh's promise to give the land. However, J. Milgrom (*Numbers* [JPSTC; Philadelphia: Jewish Publication Society, 1990] 268) has demonstrated that the literary and chronological differences between Numbers 14 and 32 militate against the view that these wilderness episodes represent doublets from a single Deuteronom(ist)ic tradition.

thers," on the one hand, and "Abraham, Isaac, and Jacob," on the other, ensures that the positive and negative branches of Israel's genealogical tree are kept separate, as required by Moses' rhetoric.

In fact, Römer's argument for the lack of equation of the "fathers" with the patriarchs could easily be turned on its head. Far from being a redactional seam, the non-equation of the patriarchs with the "fathers" may actually enhance the Mosaic rhetoric in Numbers 32 by providing an element of surprise. If his audience was expecting an equation of the "fathers" with the patriarchs, Moses' unexpected application of the title "fathers" to a generation of condemned, deceased sinners would inflict a particularly devastating blow. The lack of equation of the "fathers" with the patriarchs would provide the linchpin of the argument by forcibly rearranging the branches of Israel's family tree.[54]

The wording of the land promise in Num 32:11 presents a further challenge to Römer's interpretation, especially the clear resemblance between Num 32:7-15 and the various formulas in Deuteronomy: "the land that I swore to Abraham, to Isaac, and to Jacob" (Num 32:11; cf. Deut 1:8; 6:10, etc.). This formulaic expression of the land promise in Numbers 32 occurs in a passage that Römer had previously classified as pre-Priestly because of its negative reference to the "fathers." However, according to Römer's reconstruction of Deut 1:8, a pre-Priestly text should not contain any land promise to the patriarchs because such references to the patriarchs would have been added by a Priestly redactor. Here Römer's proposal is faced with a dilemma. If he continues to regard Numbers 32 as a pre-Priestly text, then it is clear that references to the patriarchs can coexist alongside negative traditions of the "fathers," as in the final form of Deuteronomy, obviating the need for his proposal that the patriarchal names represent a secondary insertion in Deut 1:8. It seems that the only way to salvage his proposal is to argue that the patriarchal names in Numbers 32 were also inserted by a Deuteronomistic or Priestly redactor, but Römer does not pursue this argument.[55] In summary, the text of Numbers 32 strongly resists Römer's dichotomy between patriarchal traditions and exodus/wilderness traditions. Since Römer apparently accepts the final form of this chapter, the chronological horizons and theological distinctions between these traditions need not be collapsed in the manner that he advocates.

A Critique of Römer's Redaction-Critical Proposal for Deuteronomy 1:34–40

A final-form reading of Deut 1:34–40 similarly reinforces the unlikelihood of Römer's redaction-critical proposal. As already noted in the discussion of Deut 1:8, it is unlikely on text-critical grounds that Deut 1:35

---

54. See a similar rhetorical strategy by Ezekiel against the exiles (Ezek 16:3) and Jesus against the Jews (John 8:39-44).
55. In contrast to Blenkinsopp, *Pentateuch*, 117.

preserves a short *Urform* of Yhwh's oath that was subsequently expanded in 1:8 to include the patriarchs.⁵⁶ On the contrary, the expansive formulation in 1:8 prepares the way for the truncated versions of the oath that mix and match the original elements for rhetorical purposes. In the case of Deut 1:35, the reference to the "fathers" oath contains only the elements that epitomize the turnaround in Israel's fortunes. Most notably, the judicial language of the earlier oaths ("See! I *hereby* set the land before you!") is absent from Deut 1:35 because Yhwh's promise to the "fathers" no longer entails an imminent thrust into the land. The only two verbs of motion occurring here are verbs that drive Israel back into the wilderness. First, Yhwh commands Israel to "turn around [פנה] and set out [נסע] for the wilderness" (1:40; cf. 2:1). The use of פנה is both spatially and theologically significant, for Israel is condemned to return to the "great and terrible wilderness" (1:19) from which it came, away from the land of promise. Second, the tragedy of Israel's setback is highlighted by Yhwh's command to נסע, a *Leitwort* with which Yhwh had previously commanded Israel to journey toward the land (1:7, cf. 1:19). In light of these literary features, the withdrawn promise to the "fathers" in 1:35 dashes the hopes for conquest that were inspired by the first reference to Yhwh's oath at Horeb (1:8) and intensified through its repetition at Kadesh (1:21). The ironic tone of the land promise in Deut 1:35 amplifies the tragedy of Israel's disobedience at Kadesh.

Römer's overlooking of the plot reversal at hand is also reflected in his redaction-critical explanation for why the land is characterized here as "good" (1:35). He begins by correctly observing that the patriarchal narratives never refer to the land promised by Yhwh as a "good land," whereas the Exodus–Numbers narratives refer to the land as "good" (Exod 3:8) in conjunction with the frequent phrase "flowing with milk and honey" (Exod 3:8, 17, 13:5; 33:3; Lev 20:24; Num 13:27; 14:8; 16:13–14). Deuteronomy also emphasizes the goodness of the land in a similar manner (Deut 1:25, 35; 3:25; 4:1, 22; 6:18; 8:7, 10; 9:6; 11:17). By this verbal correspondence, Römer concludes that, since Deuteronomy's description of the land mirrors that of Exodus–Numbers rather than Genesis, Deuteronomy originally knew only of Yhwh's promise of land to the first wilderness generation rather than to the patriarchs.⁵⁷ The "goodness" of the land would

---

56. Römer's views on Deut 1:35 seem to oscillate between two mutually exclusive options. In his text-critical proposal for 1:8, he grants the formulaic nature of the land promise in 1:35 in arguing for a redactional expansion in 1:8. The identification of "fathers" in 1:35 would be found within the formulaic אשר clause. In the current discussion on 1:35, however, Römer implicitly denies the presence of a formulaic sense for the אשר clause. He argues that Caleb is numbered among the "fathers," even though syntactically speaking, the name "Caleb" (1:36) lies outside the relative clause (1:35). Here Römer abolishes the distinction between formulaic and nonformulaic language for the sake of his argument on 1:35, thereby suggesting that he tries to have it both ways.

57. Römer, *Israels Väter*, 229.

putatively suggest an Exodus referent for the "fathers" and exclude the patriarchal promises of Genesis from view.

On redaction-critical grounds alone, Römer's redaction-critical hypothesis is certainly admissible, because common terminology may point to the presence of a shared tradition. However, quick recourse to a redactional explanation for the land's being "good" neglects the literary structure of Deut 1:34–40, in which the adjective "good" (טוב; 1:35) in describing the land stands in striking contrast to the "evil" (רע; 1:35; cf. 1:39) of the rebellious generation at Kadesh. The theological consequence of disobedience is unmistakably clear: "this evil generation" will not receive the "good land."[58] Since they refused to enter the land in obedience to YHWH's oath (1:26–33), YHWH promises by swearing another oath that "this evil generation" will never see the land (1:34). Poetic justice is fittingly accomplished when the crime of not entering the "good land" becomes the punishment of never entering the land. Thus there are ample grounds for regarding the identifier "good" as a feature of plot reversal rather than as a redactional marker.

In conclusion, the "fathers" in Deut 1:35 are likely the same patriarchs as in Deut 1:8 and 1:21. The constancy of identifying the "fathers" with the patriarchs provides a theological backdrop of promise and covenant that frames the entire narrative of Deuteronomy 1. The land promise to the patriarchs is first extended to the Horeb/Kadesh generation but then is withdrawn and postponed until the second wilderness generation. Thus the textual unit of Deut 1:34–40 preserves the chronological integrity of three distinct temporal horizons: (1) the distant narrative past of YHWH's land promise to the "fathers"; (2) the recent narrative past of "this evil generation," namely, the first wilderness generation at Horeb/Kadesh; and (3) the narrative present of the second wilderness generation at Moab. Joshua and Caleb provide the bridge between the recent narrative past (horizon 2) and the present (horizon 3) and are not to be numbered among the "fathers" (horizon 1). This chronology resolves the ostensive contradiction between YHWH's promissory oaths (1:8, 21) and maledictory oath (1:35), for the chronological scope of the malediction is explicitly limited to "this evil generation."[59]

I move briefly beyond matters of chronological and narrative coherence: Lohfink's theological conception of דור ("generation"; 1:35) provides a helpful construct with which to understand Deuteronomy 1–3: "[T]he one generation is defined by sin and God's word of punishment that it evokes, the other by obedience and the resulting validation of the promises

---

58. Tigay, *Deuteronomy*, 19.

59. The second wilderness generation obeyed YHWH by resisting the temptations of Baal-Peor (4:4), thereby acquitting Israel of the guilt of the first wilderness generation. YHWH's promise of entering the land is once again available to the obedient (Taschner, "Bedeutung des Generationswechsel," 69).

to the ancestors."[60] Even though Joshua and Caleb would technically belong to the first wilderness generation, their obedience allows them to join the second wilderness generation, which escapes Yhwh's punishment and thereby enters the land. By conceiving of generations in theological terms of disobedience and obedience, Moses confronts his hearers with an urgent choice between which of these two generations they will join.[61] Solidarity with Moses and the evil (first) generation epitomized by him will result in death, whereas solidarity with Joshua, Caleb, and their ilk will result in life.[62] The potential solidarity of Israel with either generation is underscored by Moses' address to both dead and living generations as "you" and "us."[63] Thus the possible destinies of obedience and disobedience are vividly set before the audience of Deuteronomy, who must choose which path to follow.

Land and the "Fathers" in Deuteronomy 6

The three references to the land promised to the "fathers" in Deuteronomy 6 (vv. 10, 18, 23) have been especially significant in the ongoing debate over pentateuchal origins. Two diachronic approaches have dominated the discussion in recent decades. The earlier of these two approaches was taken by von Rad, who argued that Deut 6:20–25 preserves a "little historical credo" (cf. Deut 26:5–9; Josh 24:2–13) of Israel's earliest confessions of faith.[64] The various versions of this credo derived from an ancient Yahwistic festival whereby Israel recalled the patriarchal promises, oppression in Egypt, deliverance from slavery, and Yhwh's bringing Israel into the land of promise. These confessions were subsequently expanded by being combined with originally distinct narrative traditions (e.g., the revelation at Horeb) to form the literary work known as the Hexateuch. Since von Rad considers the Horeb traditions a late addition to the Hexateuch, his approach to Deuteronomy 6 unequivocally identifies Israel's ancestors in the patriarchal era.[65] More recently, Van Seters and Römer have argued for a very different redaction-critical approach that identifies the "fathers" in

---

60. Lohfink, "Problem of the Individual," 229–30.
61. The urgency of this choice is later intensified by Moses' applying the negative language of "generation" to his current audience at Moab (Deut 32:5, 7, 20).
62. K. A. Deurloo, "The One God and All Israel in Its Generations," in *Studies in Deuteronomy in Honour of C. J. Labuschagne on the Occasion of His 65th Birthday* (ed. F. García Martínez et al.; VTSup 53; Leiden: Brill, 1994) 38–39.
63. S. Slater, "Imagining Arrival: Rhetoric, Reader, and Word of God in Deuteronomy 1–3," in *The Labour of Reading: Desire, Alienation, and Biblical Interpretation* (ed. F. C. Black, R. Boer, and E. Runions; SBL Semeia Studies 26; Atlanta: Society of Biblical Literature, 1999) 107–22; Polzin, *Moses*, 31–33.
64. G. von Rad, "The Form-Critical Problem of the Hexateuch," in *From Genesis to Chronicles* (ed. K. C. Hanson; trans. E. W. T. Dicken; Minneapolis: Fortress, 2005) 4–5.
65. Von Rad (*From Genesis to Chronicles*, 43) holds that Israel's oldest ancestor traditions referred to Jacob alone (Deut 26:5; cf. 1 Sam 12:8) rather than to all three patriarchs (6:10). The Yahwist then fleshed out the patriarchal narratives to form the Hexateuch.

Deuteronomy 6 with the exodus generation rather than the patriarchs.[66] Deuteronomy 6 contains three elements that are at the center of the debate over the original identification of the Deuteronomic "fathers": (1) an explicit identification of the "fathers" with the three patriarchs (6:10); (2) a conceptual link between the land promise to the "fathers" and possessing the land (6:18), thereby suggesting the forefathers of the exodus generation; and (3) a secondary version of von Rad's "credo" (6:20–25). These three elements supposedly represent competing traditions of the "fathers" that necessitate a redaction-critical explanation.

In the final-form reading offered here, I will show that variance in the three references to the land promised to the "fathers" (6:10, 18, 23) suggests an intentional progression among them. Specifically, the chronological referent for "fathers" varies according to the speaker's location on the timeline of Israel's history, since Moses can frame life in the land both prospectively (6:10–19) and retrospectively (6:20–25). Life before possession of the land looks back on the "fathers" as the patriarchs (6:10). While the impending fulfillment of the patriarchal promises through the conquest envisions the "fathers" generally as recipients of Yнwн's oath of land but not of its actual possession (6:18), settled life in the land imagines the "fathers" as the entirety of Israel's ancestors, including both patriarchal and exodus generations (6:23). Thus the explicit identification of the "fathers" with the patriarchs in 6:10 serves to provide a starting point for Israel's history rather than fixing this identification for all subsequent occurrences of the "fathers."[67] In addition, the progression from specific "fathers" (v. 10) to general "fathers" (vv. 18; 23) exemplifies Deuteronomy's conception of a single people of God across all generations,[68] thereby rendering unnecessary the choice between patriarchal and exodus referents for the "fathers."

Deuteronomy 6:10

וְהָיָה כִּי יְבִיאֲךָ יְהוָה אֱלֹהֶיךָ אֶל־הָאָרֶץ	When Yнwн your God brings you to the land
אֲשֶׁר נִשְׁבַּע לַאֲבֹתֶיךָ	that he swore to your fathers,
לְאַבְרָהָם לְיִצְחָק וּלְיַעֲקֹב	to Abraham, to Isaac, and to Jacob,
לָתֶת לָךְ	to give to you,
עָרִים גְּדֹלֹת וְטֹבֹת	great and good cities
אֲשֶׁר לֹא־בָנִיתָ	that you did not build . . .

Deuteronomy 6 opens with a summons to covenant loyalty through the *Shemaʿ* (6:4) and the commands to love Yнwн (6:5) and obey "these

---

66. Van Seters, "Confessional Reformulation," 448–59; Römer, *Israels Väter*, 176–81, 231–39.
67. Contra Tigay, *Deuteronomy*, 61; Skweres, *Rückverweise*, 106.
68. J. Scharbert, *Solidarität in Segen und Fluch im Alten Testament und in seiner Umwelt* (Bonn: Hanstein, 1958) 187–91.

words"⁶⁹ in all aspects of life, both internal (6:6–7) and external (6:8–9). Among other features, chap. 6 shares with chap. 5 the insistence that the covenant stipulations at Horeb remain valid for all future generations (6:1-3, 20–25; cf. 5:3, 32–33).⁷⁰ Following his warning about threats to covenant obedience that arise from within the land (6:10–19), Moses institutes the practice of reciting Yhwh's saving deeds as a safeguard against forgetting the purpose of the covenant stipulations (6:20–25).⁷¹

The present reference to the land promised to the "fathers" introduces the first of several threats to covenant obedience.⁷² The threat posed by prosperity will come in the imminent future, "when Yhwh your God brings you into the land that he swore to your fathers" (6:10).⁷³ As a skilled rhetorician, however, Moses begins, not with the expected exhortations to self-vigilance (6:12a),⁷⁴ to avoid forgetfulness (6:12b),⁷⁵ and to worship Yhwh alone (6:13–14),⁷⁶ but with an extended exposition on the goodness of the land (6:10–11). The overflowing abundance of the land is heaped

---

69. Scholars disagree over the exact referent of "these words" (6:6). J. S. DeRouchie (*A Call to Covenant Love: Text Grammar and Literary Structure in Deuteronomy 5–11* [Piscataway, NJ: Gorgias, 2007] 239–40) and N. MacDonald (*Deuteronomy and the Meaning of "Monotheism"* [FAT 2; Tübingen: Mohr Siebeck, 2003] 125–28) argue that "these words" refer to the *Shemaʿ* and the command to love Yhwh. This interpretation is bolstered by the subsequent command to bind these words in small spaces on one's person and house (6:8–9).

70. McConville, *Deuteronomy*, 139.

71. Lohfink (*Hauptgebot*, 116–18) notes the links between Deut 6:10–25, Exod 12:24–27a, and Exod 13:11–16. All three passages use a child's question as an opportunity to expound on earlier material.

72. D. I. Block ("How Many Is God? An Investigation into the Meaning of Deuteronomy 6:4–5," *JETS* 47 [2004] 205–8) notes that Moses' exposition of the *Shemaʿ* (6:4) consists of three sermons on threats to covenant obedience: (1) prosperity in the land (6:10–25); (2) insecurity before conquering the land (7:1–26); and (3) pride after occupying the land.

73. The clause והיה כי יביאך ("so when he [Yhwh] brings you into") is a temporal clause with future referent (i.e., impending life in the land). C. M. Follingstad (*Deictic Viewpoint in Biblical Hebrew Text: A Syntagmatic and Paradigmatic Analysis of the Particle* kî [Dallas: SIL International, 2001] 431) thoroughly discusses the syntax of והיה כי.

Though F. García López ("Analyse littéraire de Deutéronome V–XI," *RB* 84 [1977] 481–522) views והיה כי as a redactional marker, the more likely function of this clause is to join the preceding declaration of the *Shemaʿ* with the following exposition of the Decalogue. Lohfink (*Hauptgebot*, 113–20) rightly argues that the entire unit of 6:10–25 constitutes a *Gebotsrahmung* marked by the כי clause in 6:10.

74. Singular and plural forms of שמר Niphal appear 13× in Deuteronomy. Most notably, an exhortation to "watch yourself!" occurs in a similar context in 8:11, in which the land's prosperity again threatens to overtake Israel's obedience to the covenant.

75. This occurrence of שכח marks the first of five instances where Israel is urged not to forget Yhwh (6:12; 8:11, 14, 19 [2×]). Deuteronomy's use of שכח and זכר is discussed in Blair, "Appeal to Remembrance," 41–47.

76. Lohfink (*Hauptgebot*, 154–57) observes that 6:10–25 exhibits many connections to the Decalogue in Deuteronomy 5, most notably the *Hauptgebot*. Furthermore, the use of השמר in 6:12 links this section to similar passages that prescribe undivided devotion to Yhwh (e.g., Exod 23:13; 34:12; Deut 4:9, 14–23; 8:11; 11:16; 12:30; Josh 23:11).

ever higher by means of five similar clauses that describe blessings for which Israel has done nothing (e.g., "great and wonderful cities you did not build"; 6:10b). The pentadic description of the land not only lulls listeners into smug complacency ("when you eat and are satisfied"; 6:11d) but simultaneously cocks the rhetorical hammer that then falls with the unexpected warning to הִשָּׁמֶר ("watch yourself"; 6:12a).[77] The abrupt yet deft transition from languorous prosperity to imminent peril, from multiple indicative clauses to a solemn asyndetic imperative provides an exemplary case of synergy between literary form and rhetorical function.

The rhetorical reversal from complacency to vigilance in 6:10–15 is buttressed by a contrast in theological geography. The complacency of pleasurable life in Canaan must be countered by remembrance of "Yhwh your God who brought you out of Egypt, out of the house of bondage" (6:12b). Canaan is the place where all the work has already been done (e.g., "hewn cisterns that you did not hew"; 6:11b), whereas Egypt is the "house of bondage" where Israel's labor was as endless as it was inhumane.[78] The antithetical parallels between Canaan and Egypt are further reinforced by Moses' address to his audience as "you" in the entire section of 6:10–15, where Moses warns that those who experienced the exodus (6:12) are the same group that enters the land and faces its manifold temptations (6:10–11). Deliverance, satiety, and apostasy are all within the purview of a single corporate generation represented by "you." The result of apostasy from Yhwh will be destruction off the fecund land (אֲדָמָה; 6:15) that they first entered (אֶרֶץ; 6:10). The good land of Canaan will become the deathtrap that Egypt once represented. Deut 6:10–15 is thus framed by an inclusio of entrance into and destruction off the land of promise.

The rhetorical unity of 6:10–15 is significant for addressing redaction-critical proposals for this section. Most notably, Römer argues for removal of the patriarchal names from the land-promise formula (6:10) since the inventory of the land's features (6:10–11) exhibits lexical parallels to exodus and conquest traditions.[79] For example, Nehemiah 9 highlights the abundance of the land in terms similar to Deuteronomy 6 and 8 (cf. Neh 9:24–25) while also identifying the "fathers" as those who possessed the land (Neh 9:23). Similarly, Van Seters argues that references to the unconditional patriarchal promises could not appear in Deut 6:10–15, since entrance into the land is conditioned upon obedience to Yhwh's covenant.[80] As before, these redaction critics argue that the "fathers" in Deuteronomy 6 originally referred to the exodus generation.

---

77. The abruptness of the transition from prosperity to peril is underscored by the absence of a conjunction between the end of 6:11 (וְשָׂבָעְתָּ) and the imperative at the beginning of 6:12 (הִשָּׁמֶר).
78. García López, "Analyse littéraire de Deutéronome V–XI," 491.
79. Römer, *Israels Väter*, 231–6.
80. Van Seters, "Confessional Reformulation," 451.

In response to redactional proposals of this sort, we should first note that Moses speaks to his audience as individuals who personally experienced the exodus from Egypt (Deut 6:12). Thus Römer is probably incorrect that the "fathers" here originally referred to the exodus generation because the exodus generation cannot simultaneously be "you" and the "fathers." Moreover, this identification of the "fathers" would undermine the aforementioned rhetorical contrast between the leisure of Canaan (6:10–11) and the oppression of Egypt (6:12). The positive description of the "fathers" as recipients of Y<small>HWH</small>'s promise of an abundant land (6:10) would be interrupted by an intrusive allusion to the disobedience of the "fathers," since they would be the wilderness generation that is unequivocally portrayed as disobedient in both Deuteronomy and the Deuteronom(ist)ic prophets.[81] The literary unit resulting from the removal of the patriarchal names in Deut 6:10 would exhibit none of the literary symmetry and rhetorical buildup found in the final form of the text. Furthermore, the discussion on Deut 1:8 already demonstrated the text-critical grounds for keeping the patriarchal names in that reference to the "fathers."[82]

Deuteronomy 6:18

וְעָשִׂיתָ הַיָּשָׁר וְהַטּוֹב	And you shall do right and good
בְּעֵינֵי יְהוָה	in the sight of Y<small>HWH</small>
לְמַעַן יִיטַב לָךְ	so that it may go well for you
וּבָאתָ וְיָרַשְׁתָּ אֶת־הָאָרֶץ הַטֹּבָה	and you may enter and possess the good land
אֲשֶׁר־נִשְׁבַּע יְהוָה לַאֲבֹתֶיךָ	that Y<small>HWH</small> swore to your fathers

Deut 6:18 holds out the prospect of "entering" (בוא) or "possessing" (ירש) the land as motivation (למען) for observing Y<small>HWH</small>'s covenant statutes. Though not every reference to entering or possessing the land refers to the "fathers,"[83] a common feature among these statements is an emphasis on the goodness of the land as motivation for Israel's obedience.[84] Obedience

---

81. E.g., Deut 1:26–40; 6:16; 9:7–21; cf. Jer 2:4–8; Ezek 20:5–6. Van Seters ("Confessional Reformulation," 448–50) is correct that Jeremiah and Ezekiel refer to the wilderness generation as "fathers." But this identification cannot be transferred wholesale to Deuteronomy, since the book speaks prospectively of the impending disobedience of Israel, rather than retrospectively of the actual disobedience of the "fathers" in the wilderness.

82. Skweres (*Rückverweise*, 103–4 n. 418) observes that, if the patriarchal names were really added to Deut 6:10 by a Priestly redactor, then this redactor would likely have made the same addition to the "fathers" references in 6:18 and 6:23. The lack of patriarchal names in the latter two references points to the originality of the patriarchal names in 6:10 and suggests the need for a rhetorical rather than redactional explanation.

83. Deut 4:1; 5:33; 8:1; 11:8, 9; 16:20; 23:21; and 27:3 link Israel's obedience to conquest of the land. However, in these texts, the "fathers" are found in 4:1; 6:18; 8:1; 11:9; and 27:3.

84. R. Sonsino (*Motive Clauses in Hebrew Law: Biblical Forms and Near Eastern Parallels* [SBLDS 45; Chico, CA: Scholars Press, 1980] 101) notes that Deuteronomy exhibits the greatest stylistic variety of all the biblical legal corpora due to its motive clauses. He rightly attributes this to Deuteronomy's expansive hortatory style.

will result in "life" (חיה),⁸⁵ or "prolonging of days" (ארך ימים)⁸⁶ in "the good land" (הארץ הטובה)⁸⁷ or "land flowing with milk and honey" (ארץ זבת חלב ורבש).⁸⁸ Most poignantly, Moses declares that doing "good" (טוב) will issue in Israel's life of "going well" (יטב) and possessing the "good land" that was sworn to the "fathers" (6:18; cf. 6:10, 23). Thus the Israelites would be unthinkably foolish to "test" (נסה) Yнwн in matters of everyday sustenance as they did at Massah (Deut 6:16; cf. Exod 17:1–7).⁸⁹ The pervasive emphasis on the land's goodness confirms the rhetorical unity of the entire section of 6:10–19. Thus the "fathers" in the land formula of 6:18 should be the same patriarchs who were named as recipients of Yнwн's oath of an abundant land (6:10).

The thematic development of Yнwн's goodness and the land's fecundity in Deut 6:10–18 provides an effective rejoinder to the redaction-critical view that the "fathers" in 6:18 originally referred to the exodus generation. However, Römer argues that the militaristic tone of "possessing" (Deut 6:18b) the land and "driving out all your enemies" (Deut 6:19a; cf. Josh 23:4) points to an exodus referent for the "fathers."⁹⁰ But Römer overlooks the entirely circumstantial nature of the reference to "driving out" within the rhetorical unit of Deut 6:16–19. The infinitival clause "driving out" (להדף; 6:19a) is grammatically subordinate to the finitival motive clause denoting possession of the good land (6:18b). This observation can be confirmed by a simple discourse diagram of Deut 6:18–19 (see table 3.1, p. 56). The "driving out" (הדף) of Israel's enemies is hardly the main clause but, rather, the necessary means for Israel's possession of the land ("by driving out"), because this clause constitutes a gerundive or explanatory use of the infinitive construct.⁹¹ Thus the rhetorical center of 6:16–19 remains Israel's possession of the good land sworn to the "fathers" rather than the military campaign required to bring about this result. Thus the "fathers" here are still the patriarchs, though it is noteworthy that the reference to a "good land" comes from the exodus traditions (cf. Exod 3:8; Num 14:7) and reflects the blending of generational horizons in Moses' rhetoric.⁹²

---

85. Deut 4:1; 5:33; 8:1; 16:20.
86. Deut 5:33; 11:9.
87. Deut 6:18.
88. Deut 27:3.
89. Except for Exod 20:20, where Yнwн "tests" Israel, every other instance of נסה in Exodus and Numbers describes how Israel "tests" Yнwн in matters of food and drink (Exod 15:25; 16:4; 17:2, 7; Num 14:22).
90. Römer, *Israels Väter*, 176–81.
91. *IBHS* §36.2.3d–e; Joüon, §124o. In Deuteronomy's only other occurrence of הדף (9:4), it is striking that הדף also reflects circumstances or method of conquest rather than the act of conquest itself (i.e., ירש Hiphil; 9:3, 4, 5; cf. 4:38; 7:17; 11:23; 18:12). In other passages, נשל also refers to the act of driving out the nations (e.g., 7:1, 22).
92. As with 1:35, Römer (*Israels Väter*, 180) asserts that the reference to a "good land" in 6:18 points to an exodus referent for the "fathers," because the terminology of "good" is not found in Genesis. However, this redaction-critical view cannot account for the unmistakable wordplay on "good" (טוב) in 6:18 as well as in the entire section of 6:10–19.

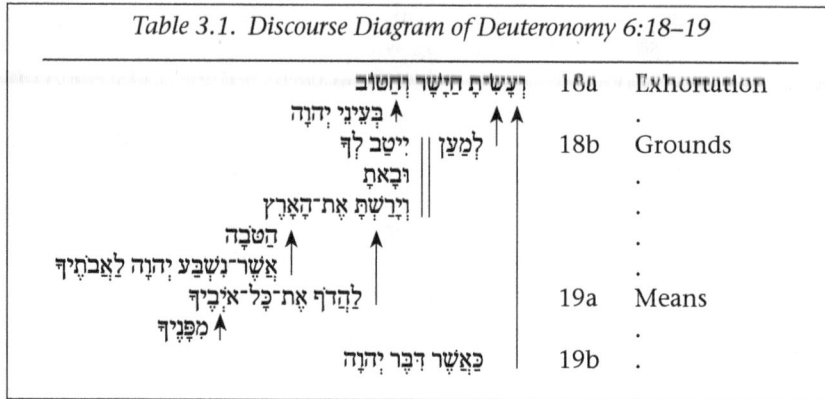

The results of this study of the land promise in Deut 6:10 and 6:18 also apply to the similar references in Deuteronomy 8, 11, and 31. The contrast between Massah and the land anticipates the extended treatment of this theological and geographical contrast in Deuteronomy 8, where the "great and terrible wilderness" (8:15) and the "good land" (8:10) stand in polar opposition. Significantly, Massah and the wilderness were places where water was continually lacking,[93] whereas the land of promise contains "hewn cisterns that you did not hew" (6:11) and "brooks of water, fountains, and springs" (8:7). In Deuteronomy 11, however, the point of comparison for the "land flowing with milk and honey" (11:9) and "good land" (11:21) has shifted from the wilderness to Egypt. The abundance of water in the land also shifts to the issue of farming rather than drinking, for the pervasive need for irrigation in Egypt (11:10) will be solved in the "land . . . that drinks water from the rain of heaven, a land for which YHWH your God cares; the eyes of YHWH your God are always on it, from the beginning even to the end of the year" (11:11–12). As in 6:12–19, the prosperity of this land and the temptations of its fertility deities must not become a snare to Israel (11:16–17).[94] In Deuteronomy 31, Moses also fears that the abundance of the "land flowing with milk and honey" will cause Israel to spurn YHWH in favor of the "other gods" (31:20) of the land. Thus in these chapters, the imminent possession of the abundant land promised to the "fathers" is cause not only for thanksgiving and worship but also for vigilance and self-

---

Deuteronomy blends the Genesis traditions of land promised to the patriarchs with the Exodus traditions of "good land" and "land flowing with milk and honey" in order to demonstrate the continuity of YHWH's oath (11:9; 26:9, 15; 27:3; 31:20).

93. Exod 15:22–27; 17:1–7; Num 20:2–13; 21:4–5.

94. J. M. Hadley, "The De-deification of Deities in Deuteronomy," in *The God of Israel* (ed. R. P. Gordon; Cambridge: Cambridge University Press, 2007) 157–74; M. Fishbane, *Biblical Myth and Rabbinic Mythmaking* (Oxford: Oxford University Press, 2005) 90–91.

reflection.⁹⁵ In light of this overarching theological concern, these passages seem to depict the "fathers" as a symbol for every past generation of Israel that awaited Yʜwʜ's promise of a prosperous land. With the exception of the reference to the patriarchs in 6:3, the referent of the "fathers" is broader than a specific group at a particular time.

Deuteronomy 6:23

וְאוֹתָנוּ הוֹצִיא מִשָּׁם	He brought us out from there
לְמַעַן הָבִיא אֹתָנוּ	in order that he might bring us in,
לָתֶת לָנוּ אֶת־הָאָרֶץ	to give us the land
אֲשֶׁר נִשְׁבַּע לַאֲבֹתֵינוּ	that he swore to our fathers.

This reference to the land promised to the "fathers" falls within Deut 6:20–25, a section indelibly linked to Deut 26:5–9 due to von Rad's tradition-critical thesis. Apart from their creedal tone and similar recitation of Israel's saving history, however, these passages are not as parallel as von Rad maintains. I base this conclusion on four observations. First, the two confessions arise from very different contexts in Israel's life. While 26:5–9 depicts an Israelite's liturgical confession in offering his firstfruits to Yʜwʜ, 6:20–25 records an episode of spontaneous teaching in answer to a child's question. The reciting of Yʜwʜ's saving deeds to the next generation represents the natural outworking of Moses' exhortation to teach Yʜwʜ's commandments to Israel's sons in all spheres of existence (6:7; cf. 4:10; 11:19; 32:7).⁹⁶ Thus it appears that 6:20–25 is more closely connected to its immediate literary context than to 26:5–9.⁹⁷

Second, in contrast to 26:5–9, the Horeb revelation is quite prominent in Deut 6:20–25. Though von Rad had argued that references to Horeb are lacking in both,⁹⁸ the child's question and the father's answer regarding the "stipulations and the statutes and the ordinances" (6:20; cf. 6:24–25) reflect Deuteronomy's standard terminology for the Horeb revelation.⁹⁹ Likewise, Moses' call for Israel to obey "all this commandment before Yʜwʜ our God, *just as he commanded us*" (6:25) represents a standard *Promulgationssatz* for the Horeb revelation.¹⁰⁰ Deuteronomy asserts elsewhere that the exodus

---

95. Brueggemann, *Land*, 45–56.
96. D. J. McCarthy, *Treaty and Covenant*, 161 n. 9.
97. Von Rad (*From Genesis to Chronicles*, 3) implicitly concedes this point when he argues that 6:20-24 has been reworked by a Deuteronomistic redactor.
98. Von Rad, *From Genesis to Chronicles*, 4–5.
99. Skweres, *Rückverweise*, 59–60; G. Braulik, "Die Ausdrücke für 'Gesetz' im Buch Deuteronomium," *Bib* 51 (1970) 39–66. Compare S. J. De Vries ("The Development of the Deuteronomic Promulgation Formula," *Bib* 55 [1974] 301–16), who classifies this as an "authentication formula" rather than a "promulgation formula." Either way, Moses is still clearly referring to antecedent revelation.
100. Braulik, "Ausdrücke," 41–42; Lohfink, *Hauptgebot*, 59–63.

took place in order for YHWH to impart his revelation at Horeb (4:32–40).[101] Thus von Rad's tradition-critical view, which denies the antiquity of the Horeb tradition, is dubious and inconsistent.[102]

Third and on a related note, 6:20–25 accentuates the link between the exodus and the promise of the land much more prominently than 26:5–9.[103] The causal connection between the exodus from Egypt and entrance into the land is captured in a striking juxtaposition of Hiphil verbal forms: "He [YHWH] brought us out [יצא Hiphil] in order to bring us in [בוא Hiphil]" (6:23). The direct rhetorical progression from exodus to conquest means that 6:20–25 lacks the extended meditation on the land's goodness found in 26:9–10, for such an encomium on land was already presented in 6:10–19.

Fourth, while reference to YHWH's oath to the "fathers" occurs in 6:20–24, it is missing from 26:5–9.[104] However, the oath to the "fathers" does appear nearby in 26:3 and 26:15, two verses that frame the inclusio containing the creed (26:5–9). The ability of the "fathers" references to transcend parenesis and narrative (not to mention narrative and direct speech) challenges von Rad's tradition-critical distinction between these genres. Since creedal and parenetic genres often manifest identical concepts and terminology, the immediate literary context in which the creeds are embedded needs to be considered before one proposes a tradition-critical account of how the creeds might have developed. The presence or absence of certain elements from Israel's creeds cannot be said with certainty to possess diachronic significance, for the creeds are often embedded in parenetic or narrative material from which they cannot be readily extricated. Thus the creedal, parenetic, and narrative sections of Deuteronomy 6 should be examined together as a synchronic whole.

Conditional and Unconditional Notions of Land in Deuteronomy 6:20–25

A reassessment of 6:20–25 also reflects Deuteronomy's ability to transcend the usual dichotomy between unconditional and conditional notions of the land promise.[105] In fact, the imagined dialogue between father and son captures in a microcosm the classic dialectic between divine ini-

---

101. Lohfink, *Hauptgebot*, 160. Thus the absence of the words "Horeb" and "Sinai" is of little import (cf. von Rad, *From Genesis to Chronicles*, 4–5).

102. However, von Rad's assertion of a "deuteronomic [*sic*] recension" ("Form-Critical Problem," 4) of Deut 6:20–25 and 26:5–9 may have anticipated this objection by limiting the original credo to the portions of these passages that lacked Deuteronomic language.

103. R. Rendtorff, *The Problem of the Process of Transmission in the Pentateuch* (JSOTSup 89; trans. J. J. Scullion; Sheffield: Sheffield Academic Press, 1990) 197.

104. Rendtorff, *Problem of the Process*, 197 n. 2.

105. E.g., Nocquet, "Étonnantes variations autour des 'destinataires du pays,'" 341–55; Noort, "Land," 136–37; Perlitt, "Motive und Schichten der Landtheologie im Deuteronomium," 104–8.

tiative and human responsibility. While the son's question reflects the misconception that Yhwh's commandments are purely conditional (6:20), the father's answer reflects the theological truth that obedience to Yhwh's commandments is rooted in Yhwh's deeds in the past (6:21–23) while also ensuring life in the future (6:24–25).

The son's question to his father betrays a curious or ignorant nature. When the son initiates the conversation by inquiring about "the stipulations and the statutes and the ordinances,"[106] his emphasis falls squarely on human responsibility to the exclusion of divine initiative. He confesses his shared faith in "Yhwh *our* God"[107] yet states his lack of personal experience in receiving the covenant stipulations "that Yhwh commanded *you*" (6:20).[108] This emphasis on Yhwh's covenant requirements differs notably from Moses' earlier instructions on imbibing the *Shemaʿ* and loving Yhwh (6:4).[109]

The father's delightful non-sequitur reply shifts the rhetorical emphasis to the deliverance that gave rise to Yhwh's covenant requirements. Rather than expositing on the "stipulations and the statues and the ordinances," as the son probably expected, the father launches into a passionate recital of Israel's foundational narrative (6:21–23). This act of remembrance assumes a corporate dimension when the father declares that "*we* were slaves to Egypt. . . . Yhwh brought *us* from Egypt with a mighty hand. . . . before *our* eyes" (6:22–23). To a son inquiring about the "conditional" nature of Yhwh's dealings, the father redirects his son's focus to Yhwh's "unconditional" gifts in the exodus (6:21–22) and possession of the land (6:23).

Furthermore, in his parenetic commentary on the father's reply, Moses transforms the son's distancing statement "just as Yhwh our God commanded *you*" (6:20) back into the inclusive declaration "just as Yhwh our God . . . commanded *us*" (6:25). The commandments now become efficacious for all future generations of "us" in the land who actualize the exodus events through memory and recitation.[110] The obedience demanded by Yhwh always flows from Israel's joyful response to Yhwh's saving deeds. Thus the wise father envisioned by Moses has balanced his son's curiosity about the "conditional" aspects of life with Yhwh by highlighting its "unconditional" aspects.

The taut connection between divine initiative and human responsibility evidenced in 6:20–25 undercuts the historical-critical distinction between unconditionality and conditionality in the land promise. Though

---

106. See Deut 4:1; 6:1.
107. Before its occurrence in Deut 6:20, the phrase "Yhwh our God" last appeared in the *Shemaʿ* itself (6:4), yet the son recites none of the *Shemaʿ* in his question to his father.
108. K. Finsterbusch, *Weisung für Israel: Studien zu religiösem Lehren und Lernen im Deuteronomium und in seinem Umfeld* (FAT 44; Tübingen: Mohr Siebeck, 2005) 250–51.
109. M. Fishbane, *Text and Texture* (New York: Schocken, 1979) 80–81.
110. Finsterbusch, *Weisung für Israel*, 249–53; Childs, *Memory and Tradition*, 50–56.

divine gifts are chronologically and theologically prior to human response (6:22–23), the verdict of human צדקה ("righteousness"; 6:25) before Y<small>HWH</small> still hinges on vigilance in following Y<small>HWH</small>'s commands.[111] On this issue, Brueggemann represents a growing number of scholars who previously argued for the traditional distinction between unconditional and conditional divine promises (including though not limited to land) but who now recognize that "the command of Y<small>HWH</small> is relational and cannot be factored out as conditional or unconditional. Rather, like any thinkable relationship rooted in profound fidelity, this covenant relation is characteristically conditional and unconditional at the same time."[112] Therefore Brueggemann coins the phrase "[e]xodus obedience"[113] to describe the paradigmatic progression from divine initiative to human responsibility as wrought in Israel's exodus from Egypt.[114]

In view of the literary and theological unity of 6:20–25, I may now comment on the historical identification and rhetorical function of the "fathers" in 6:23. Despite the similar wording of 6:23 to the land promises given in 6:10 and 6:18, a significant new feature can be found in 6:23. The time reference in 6:23 has shifted from the narrative present (cf. 6:10–19) to an indeterminate מחר ("tomorrow"; 6:20). When מחר is used elsewhere in the OT to prescribe the cultic recital of past events (e.g., Exod 13:14; Josh 4:6, 21), the historical referents for the terms "fathers" and "children" seem to envision theological rather than strictly chronological generations.[115] The "fathers" in Deut 6:23 may envision all prior generations of Israel coalesced into a single entity (cf. 6:10). From this future perspective, the "fathers" in Deut 6:23 include the patriarchs without being strictly limited to them. However, the "fathers" in Deuteronomy 6 are still the concrete recipients of Y<small>HWH</small>'s oath of the land and probably not the eschatologically charged "fathers" of Deut 30:20 who actually possessed the land.

The rhetorical function of the "fathers" follows closely upon the theological observation that the promise of land encompasses both conditional and unconditional dimensions. On the one hand, the juxtaposition of "bringing out" of Egypt and "bringing in" to the land (6:23) indicates that

---

111. G. Braulik, "Law as Gospel: Justification and Pardon according to the Deuteronomic Torah," *Int* 38 (1984) 5–14.

112. W. Brueggemann, *Theology of the Old Testament: Testimony, Dispute, Advocacy* (Minneapolis: Fortress, 1997) 199.

113. Brueggemann, *Theology*, 200.

114. Deuteronomy's repeated use of the exodus as the quintessential covenant-making event will have significant ramifications for the discussion of the covenant of the "fathers" in chaps. 6–7.

115. In Josh 4:21, for example, the term בנים ("sons") appears twice with מחר. The first instance of "sons" refers to the "sons of Israel" to whom Moses is speaking, whereas the second imagines future "sons" who already live in the land. It seems that the generational distinctions have been deliberately blurred to emphasize Israel's continual need for remembrance after entering the land.

entrance into the land promised to the "fathers" is now cast as the primary purpose for the exodus. Fulfillment of the oath to the "fathers" is mediated through Yhwh's mighty and gracious deeds through the exodus, thereby creating a theological continuity between Yhwh's covenants enacted with the patriarchs and the exodus generation. On the other hand, the prospect of remaining in the land is contingent on Israel's attentiveness to the same covenant stipulations promulgated at Horeb and now reiterated at Moab. Thus the land promised to the "fathers" becomes the theological nexus of covenant blessings and covenant obedience for all generations of Israel in the land. The rhetorical power of the land to encapsulate such a nuanced view of divine and human agency suggests that both the imaginary son (6:20) and redaction critics have asked the wrong questions concerning the conditionality of Yhwh's covenant and the associated role of human obedience.

Land and the "Father(s)" in Deuteronomy 26

The two references in Deuteronomy 26 to a land promised to the "fathers" (26:3, 15) form an inclusio around a liturgical prescription (26:1–15). Once the Israelite worshiper has experienced the fruitfulness of the land promised to the "fathers" (26:3), he should bring his firstfruits to the sanctuary (26:2, 10–11) while declaring his entrance into the land (26:3). Once the priest receives the offering (26:4), the worshiper initiates a second confession of Israel's saving history from patriarchal times until the entrance into the land (26:5–9), which von Rad termed the "little historical credo" (26:5–9). In contrast to the prior reference to plural "fathers" (26:3), the worshiper now expresses his solidarity with a singular ancestor of Israel, "my father" (26:5). After paying his tithe for the Levite and the poor (26:10–14), the worshiper beseeches Yhwh's continual blessing on the "ground" (אדמה) that Yhwh swore to the "fathers" (26:15). The cryptic reference to "my father" (26:5), in contrast to plural "fathers" (26:3, 15), makes this chapter a significant passage for Deuteronomic land theology.

The importance of Deuteronomy 26 is also reflected in its varying terminology, recipients, and conceptions of the land promise. The words אדמה and ארץ appear in Deuteronomy 26 with distinctive as well as nearly synonymous senses.[116] The land is not only promised to the "fathers"; it is also given to "you" (26:1, 2) as a "grant" (26:1). Furthermore, "this land" (26:9) is closely tied to the "place that Yhwh has chosen to establish his name"

---

116. In Deuteronomy 26, the אדמה is the source of פרי ("fruit"; 26:2, 10) whereas the ארץ carries political and territorial connotations (26:1, 2, 3). However, ארץ can also represent fecundity in the Deuteronomic idiom "land [ארץ] flowing with milk and honey" (26:9, 15). Since the phrase "land flowing with milk and honey" stands so close to the use of אדמה in a formulaic relative clause (26:15), Plöger (*Literarkritische, formgeschichtliche und stilkritische Untersuchungen*, 121–30) cites this as a possible example of the synonymy of אדמה and ארץ in formulaic relative clauses referring to the land (cf. 4:40).

(26:2b). As in Deuteronomy 6, land has become the theological intersection for the Deuteronomic motifs of Yhwh's miraculous deliverance from Egypt, Yhwh's generous provision of a homeland, Yhwh's designated place of worship, and Israel's need for continual obedience to the covenant.

As noted, the analysis of the land promise to the plural "fathers" is complicated significantly by the nearby occurrence of a singular "father" in the harvester's confession: "My father was a wandering Aramean" (26:5). Each of the three Hebrew words in this brief confession (ארמי אבד אבי) and their collective syntax are difficult on several counts. First, Deuteronomy never uses the singular אב to denote Israel's ancestors elsewhere, preferring instead to refer to a plurality of אבות (e.g., 1:8; 26:3, 15).[117] The surprising occurrence of the singular has spawned numerous tradition-critical hypotheses that predeuteronomic oral traditions only knew of a single patriarch, whereas later writings such as the patriarchal narratives and Deuteronomy reflect the expanded traditions of a patriarchal trio.[118] Alternatively, אב has been classified as a collective singular denoting Jacob and his entire family (cf. Deut 10:22; Exod 3:6; Num 20:15–16).[119] Second, the usual translation of אֹבֵד as a Qal participle from a Semitic root "to wander"[120] has been challenged on semantic and text-critical grounds. Some scholars have proposed a different Semitic root that means "to perish,"[121] perhaps also with the nuance of "ailing,"[122] "starving,"[123] or "fugitive."[124] Other scholars and several ancient witnesses differ from MT's pointing of אֹבֵד as a

---

117. Deuteronomy's use of singular אב in laws (e.g., 21:19, 22:15), covenant provisions (e.g., 5:16; 27:16), or poetic material (e.g., 32:6) refers to physical fathers in general rather than historical ancestors. The noun ראשנים also refers once to unspecified ancestors (Deut 19:14; cf. Lev 26:45; Ps 79:8).

118. Von Rad, *From Genesis to Chronicles*, 42–47; Wijngaards, *Dramatization of Salvific History*, 68 n. 1, 75.

119. Tigay, *Deuteronomy*, 240; cf. Joüon, §135c.

120. Driver, *Deuteronomy*, 289; P. Buis and J. Leclerq, *Le Deutéronome* (SB; Paris: Lecoffre, 1963) 168; B. Otzen, "אבד," *TDOT* 1:20; E. Lipiński, "'Mon Père était un Araméen errant': l'histoire, carrefour des sciences bibliques et orientales," *OLP* 20 (1989) 23–47.23–47; P. D. Miller, *Deuteronomy* (IBC; Louisville: John Knox, 1990) 181; D. L. Christensen, *Deuteronomy 21:10–34:12* (WBC 6b; Nashville: Thomas Nelson, 2002) 631; McConville, *Deuteronomy*, 376.

121. M. A. Beek, "Das Problem des aramäischen Stammvaters (Deut. XXVI 5)," *OTS* 8 (1951) 193–212; H. F. Fuhs, "Aus der Befreiung leben: Erwägungen zum geschichtlichen Credo in Dtn 26,1–11," in *Schrift und Tradition: Festschrift für Josef Ernst* (ed. K. Backhaus and F. G. Untergassmair; Paderborn: Ferdinand Schöningh, 1996) 3–18. A rendering of "perishing" would link אֹבֵד to Deuteronomy's frequent threat against those who will "perish" as a result of their disobedience to Yhwh's covenant (אבד Qal; e.g., 4:26; 8:19; 30:18) as well as Yhwh's promise to "destroy" (אבד Hiphil; e.g., 8:20; 9:3; 28:51). Thus the internal evidence for classifying אֹבֵד under this root is considerable.

122. P. C. Craigie, *The Book of Deuteronomy* (Grand Rapids, MI: Eerdmans, 1976) 321.

123. J. G. Janzen, "The 'Wandering Aramean' Reconsidered," *VT* 44 (1994) 359–75.

124. So NJPS; Tigay, *Deuteronomy*, 240; W. F. Albright, *From the Stone Age to Christianity* (Garden City, NJ: 1957) 238. A. R. Millard ("A Wandering Aramean," *JNES* 39 [1980] 154–55) argues for a similar connotation of "refugee," though he holds that אֹבֵד still comes from the other root "to wander."

Analysis of Texts 63

Qal participle and treat אבד as a finite verb instead.[125] Whatever is considered to be the etymology of אבד/אֹבֵד, every possible explanation entails an unmistakably negative sense.[126] The third issue concerns whether ארמי is a geographical area or a person. Though some ancient witnesses understand ארמי as "Aram" or "Syria,"[127] most ancient witnesses and rabbinic commentators have taken ארמי as a person, whether Laban, Jacob, or even Abraham during his Mesopotamian sojourn.[128] The identity of ארמי also varies significantly depending on whether אבד/אֹבֵד is taken as a participle or finite verb.

The earlier discussion of Deut 6:20–25 also raised the issue of the literary relationship between the creeds and their broader literary context. Though von Rad isolates the "little historical credo" (26:5–9) as the earliest stratum of oral tradition, the final form of the text embeds the credo within a liturgical framework of offering firstfruits and tithes (26:1–15). The case for reading the credo within the synchronic context of Deuteronomy 26 is bolstered by several features of the text that transcend the generic distinctions between credo and parenesis: (1) the repeated interjection היום (vv. 3, 16, 17, 18); (2) the repeated use of נתן to describe the gifts of Yhwh and worshiper alike (vv. 1, 2, 3, 6, 9, 10, 11, 12, 13, 14, 15, 19);[129] (3) the repetition of בוא (both Qal and Hiphil stems) to denote motion (vv. 1, 2, 3 [2×], 9, 10); (4) the use of מקום (vv. 2, 9b) to denote Israel's final destination;

---

125. See the discussion in C. McCarthy, *BHQ*, 120–21; J. W. Wevers, *Notes on the Greek Text of Deuteronomy* (SBLSCS 39; Atlanta: Scholars Press, 1995) 404–5. The ancient witnesses are split over whether "my father" is the subject or complement of the verb אבד/אֹבֵד. The LXX treats "my father" as subject by rendering "my father [Jacob] cast off Syria." In contrast, the Vulg. treats "my father" as complement of the verb by rendering "the Syrian pursued my father." The Vulg. reading may spring from the targumic traditions that read "Laban, the Aramean sought to destroy my father" (*Tg. Onqelos*) and "our father Jacob descended to Aram-Naharaim at the beginning, where he [Laban] sought to kill him" (*Tg. Jonathan*).

The case for taking אבד as an Aphel perfect from Aramaic has also been argued by R. C. Steiner, "The 'Aramean' of Deuteronomy 26:5: *Peshat* and *Derash*," in *Tehillah le-Moshe: Biblical and Judaic Studies in Honor of Moshe Greenberg* (ed. M. Cogan, B. L. Eichler, and J. H. Tigay; Winona Lake, IN: Eisenbrauns, 1997) 127–38. Steiner's explanation has been criticized by K. H. Zetterholm, *Portrait of a Villain* (Leuven: Peeters, 2002) 47–87. Zetterholm argues that the rabbis understood אבד as a Hebrew transitive verb since Jacob is not named explicitly as an Aramean, whereas Laban clearly is. A full history of interpretation for Deut 26:5 is provided by F. Dreyfus, "'L'Araméen voulait tuer mon père': L'actualisation de Dt 26,5 dans la tradition juive et la tradition chrétienne," in *De la Tôrah au Messie: Mélanges Henri Cazelles* (ed. M. Carrez, J. Doré, and P. Grelot; Paris: Desclée, 1981) 147–61.

126. E. Jenni, "אבד," *TLOT* 1:14.

127. Like the LXX, the Syr. takes ארמי to be geographical in its reading: "my father was taken to Aram."

128. *Laban*: e.g., LXX, Vulg., Syr., Sym., targums. *Jacob*: e.g., Aquila, Abraham Ibn Ezra, David Kimhi, Rashi. *Abraham*: e.g., Rashbam, Joseph Bekhor Shor, Aquila. See discussion of rabbinical sources in Steiner, "'Aramean' of Deuteronomy 26:5," 127–30; C. McCarthy, *BHQ*, 120. Compare with similar arguments for Abraham as the Aramean by N. Krausz, "'Arami oved avi': Deuteronomy 26:5," *JBQ* 25 (1997) 31–34.

129. C. J. H. Wright, *Deuteronomy* (NIBCOT 4; Peabody, MA: Hendrickson, 1996) 270–1.

and (5) the recurrence of the common phrase "land flowing with milk and honey" (vv. 9, 15).[130] The repetition of terms and phrases across creedal and parenetic genres thus reflects the thematic contrasts in the entire section between homelessness and home, hunger and plenty, starvation and multiplication.[131] The credo performs an integral but still minor function in these thematic contrasts because it represents only one of three confessional declarations prescribed for the Israelite in the land (26:3, 5–10, 13–15).

In light of the literary unity of Deuteronomy 26, a rhetorically oriented approach is best equipped to explain the numerous connections between the credo and its broader literary context, as in the previous case study on 6:20–25. A synchronic reading of Deuteronomy 26 also assists in clarifying the aforementioned lexical and syntactical ambiguities of Deut 26:5. The logical flow of 26:1–15 and the dialectic between singular and plural ancestors provide the necessary context for determining the historical referent and rhetorical function of "my father," thereby also furnishing a critique of von Rad's tradition-critical thesis for 26:5–9. [132]

Deuteronomy 26:3b

הִגַּדְתִּי הַיּוֹם לַיהוָה אֱלֹהֶיךָ	I hereby declare today to Yнwн your God
כִּי־בָאתִי אֶל־הָאָרֶץ	that I have entered the land
אֲשֶׁר נִשְׁבַּע יְהוָה לַאֲבֹתֵינוּ	that Yнwн swore to our fathers
לָתֶת לָנוּ	to give us.

---

130. Von Rad (*From Genesis to Chronicles*, 3) and H. Ausloos ("'A Land Flowing with Milk and Honey': Indicative of a Deuteronomistic Redaction?" *ETL* 75 [1999] 305–8) attribute the phrase "land flowing with milk and honey" to a Deuteronom(ist)ic insertion rather than being original to the credo. For an argument that this phrase is original Deuteronomic language, see D. R. Daniels, "The Creed of Deuteronomy XXVI Revisited," in *Studies in the Pentateuch* (ed. J. A. Emerton; VTSup 41; Leiden: Brill, 1990) 231–42.

131. McConville, *Deuteronomy*, 379–80.

132. The declaration of Deut 26:3 poses a text-critical problem that makes it unclear whether the Israelite is praying to God or is speaking to the priest. Though the LXX records the Israelite as speaking to "Yнwн *my* God," the majority of ancient witnesses (MT, SP, Syr., most targums) have the reading "Yнwн *your* God" (i.e., the priest's). The LXX reading probably represents assimilation to the first-person suffix found later in the verse, "our fathers." The probably-original reading of "your God" thus suggests that the Israelite is partaking in a liturgical rite with the officiating priest. The actual confession does not begin until v. 9, when the Israelite shifts to "our God." The declaration of Deut 26:3 poses a text-critical problem that makes it unclear whether the Israelite is praying to God or is speaking to the priest. Though the LXX records the Israelite as speaking to "Yнwн *my* God," the majority of ancient witnesses (MT, SP, Syr., most targums) have the reading "Yнwн *your* God" (i.e., the priest's). The LXX reading probably represents assimilation to the first-person suffix found later in the verse, "our fathers." The probably-original reading of "your God" thus suggests that the Israelite is partaking in a liturgical rite with the officiating priest. The actual confession does not begin until v. 9, when the Israelite shifts to "our God."

This reference to the land promise to the "fathers" appears in the first of the Israelite farmer's three confessions in Deuteronomy 26. Although this occurrence of the oath is similar to others in foreseeing an imminent thrust into the land (e.g., 6:10),[133] the formulation of the land promise in 26:3b marks a significant shift in several respects. First and most generally, the confession marks the first time the people have spoken in the narrative world of Deuteronomy since they beseeched Moses to serve as their mediator (5:24–27).[134] The Mosaic narration and parenesis since then have met with no response by the people other than a series of hypothetical monologues ascribed by Moses to the people's לבב ("heart"; 7:17; 8:17; 9:4; 15:9).[135]

Second and on a related note, Deuteronomy 26 marks the first occasion in the entire book on which the people are portrayed as speaking directly to God. Israel's ability to address God without using a mediator heralds a new era in the divine-human relationship. The confessions of Deuteronomy 26 thus surpass the formality of both the commitment ceremony at Horeb and the covenant renewal at Moab by anticipating the people's direct access to Yhwh in the land. Similarly, the land promise in 26:3b marks the first time that this formula is found on the lips of Israel rather than Yhwh (e.g., 1:8, 35) or Moses (e.g., 1:21; 4:1). The transposition of the land-promise formula from Yhwh/Moses to the lips of the people mirrors the generic shift from sermons by Moses to an offering and confession by the people. The motivation and warning provided by prospective entrance into the land (Deuteronomy 1–25) have now been transformed into a retrospective confession by the people when they experience the land's goodness (Deuteronomy 26). Though entrance into the land is still future in Deuteronomy's narrative world, Moses has heightened its rhetorical immediacy by prescribing a liturgical observance to commemorate life in the land promised to the "fathers" as fait accompli. The strategy of portraying entrance into the land as a completed event is integral to Deuteronomy's rhetoric (e.g., 6:23; 30:5).[136]

---

133. The use of the temporal clause formula (והיה כי) + (imperfect verb) in Deut 26:1 to set a future time context is also found in 6:10; 11:29; 15:16; 30:1 (Follingstad, *Viewpoint*, 431). Each of these temporal clauses sets the chronological stage (e.g., "when Yhwh your God brings you into the land"; 6:10) for a command to govern life in the land (e.g., "watch yourself!"; 6:12).

134. To be more precise, all human and divine speech in Deuteronomy 1–26 has been mediated through the narration of Moses. The direct speech of the people has not been cited by Moses since the events at Horeb in Deuteronomy 5. No one other than Moses and Yhwh speaks in the Deuteronomic narrative until the elders of Israel join Moses in speaking to the people (27:1).

135. García López ("Analyse littéraire de Deutéronome V–XI," 483–86) notes three inner monologues found in 7:17–19, 21; 8:17–18; and 9:4–7. Deut 15:9 should be added to this list. The monologues follow a standard form and can be categorized as monologues of "modesty and timidity" (7:17–19, 21) or "arrogance and pride" (8:17–18; 9:4–7; 15:9).

136. Römer inevitably categorizes such texts as Dtr² (i.e., postexilic). However, it seems equally likely that Moses portrays entrance into the land as a completed event in order to vivify the need for covenant obedience before entering the land.

A brief speech-act analysis confirms these observations on the rhetorical function of Deut 26:3b, especially since the confession of the land promise to the "fathers" is embedded in a liturgical context.[137] Two features of performative speech are readily observable. First, the worshiper's invocation of the first-person perfect verb "I *hereby* declare" (הגד Hiphil; 26:3)[138] reflects more than an affirmation that YHWH's past promise of entering the land has been fulfilled as a present reality. The Israelite's first-person declaration in Deut 26:3b is itself an imaginative speech-act of *believing* and *confessing* rather than a mere statement of fact.[139] While the performative act of believing and confessing is set in the narrative future, the liturgical prescription in the narrative present also issues in a performative force of *guaranteeing* the land promise for Deuteronomy's forward-looking audience.

Second, the prospect of actualizing the land promise היום ("today!"; 26:3; cf. vv. 16, 17, 18) amplifies its rhetorical power to motivate and warn Israel,[140] for the use of היום in the worshiper's confession includes even future life in the land under the theological rubric of היום. The elastic conception of היום in referring to the events and decisions faced at Horeb (1:10), Kadesh (1:39), and Moab (e.g., 4:4; 5:3; 8:1) now climaxes in Canaan (26:3). The dynamic referent of היום not only enforces the theological continuity between the present decisions made at Moab and Israel's future existence in Canaan,[141] it invites every subsequent generation of Israel to return to the

---

137. Speech-act treatments of liturgical and prayer language have been conducted by, e.g., D. Crystal, "Liturgical Language in a Sociolinguistic Perspective," in *Language and the Worship of the Church* (ed. D. Jasper and R. C. D. Jasper; London: Macmillan, 1990) 120–46; J. J. Schaller, "Performative Language Theory: An Exercise in the Analysis of Ritual," *Worship* 62 (1988) 415–32. Deuteronomy 26 has undergone speech-act analyses by N. Lohfink, "Bund als Vertrag im Deuteronomium," *ZAW* 107 (1995) 215–39; and A. Wagner, "Die Bedeutung der Sprechakttheorie für Bibelübsersetzungen, aufgezeigt an Gen 1,29, Ps 2,7 und Dtn 26,17–19," in *Interpretation of the Bible* (ed. J. Krašovec; Ljubljana, Slovenia: Slovenska akadmija znanosti in umetnosti, 1998) 1575–88. However, these studies have confined their attention to Deut 26:17–18.

138. Joüon (§112f) and *IBHS* (§30.5.1d) note the performativity of the Israelite's declaration in Deut 26:3. The best translations of this verse include performative markers such as "hereby" (cf. 26:16–19). Similarly, J. C. Gertz ("Die Stellung des kleinen geschichtlichen Credos in der Redaktionsgeschichte von Deuteronomium und Pentateuch," in *Liebe und Gebot: Studien zum Deuteronomium* [ed. R. G. Kraft and H. Spieckermann; Göttingen: Vandenhoeck & Ruprecht, 2000] 37) renders הגדתי היום dynamically as "ich verkündige *hier* und *jetzt*."

139. In chaps. 6–7, I treat the speech-act significance of imagination in Deuteronomy in detail.

140. Von Rad (*From Genesis to Chronicles*, 22) only ascribed a descriptive sense to Deuteronomy's use of היום. In contrast, Lohfink ("Bund als Vertrag," 222–23), Wagner ("Bedeutung," 1580), and W. Houston ("'Today, in your very hearing': Some Comments on the Christological Use of the Old Testament," in *The Glory of Christ in the New Testament: Studies in Christology in Memory of George Bradford Caird* [ed. L. D. Hurst and N. T. Wright; Oxford: Clarendon, 1987] 37–47) recognize the performative force of "today" in signaling the fulfillment of a promise.

141. Millar, "Living at the Place of Decision," 42–44.

covenant made at Horeb/Moab: "Yhwh our God made a covenant with us at Horeb. *Not with our fathers* did Yhwh make a covenant, but with us, all of us who are alive here *today*" (Deut 5:2–3). This cultic use of היום that is "continually repeated and hence continuously present"[142] suggests that the "fathers" in Deut 26:3b represent every previous generation of Israel that received Yhwh's promise of land without also entering the land, including but not limited to the patriarchs.

The performativity of the Israelite's confession is confirmed by the liturgical events set in motion as a result. The priest responds by accepting the worshiper's offering of firstfruits to present before the altar (26:4). The worshiper then proceeds to the next stage of the liturgy with another reference to the saving history of the nation (26:5–10a). While the second confession of Israel's history expands the scope of Israel's history significantly beyond the first confession's formulaic reference to the plural "our fathers" (26:3b), the scope of Israel's ancestors in the second confession shrinks surprisingly to refer only to a singular figure, "my father" (26:5).

Deuteronomy 26:5b

אֲרַמִּי אֹבֵד אָבִי	My father was a wandering Aramean,
וַיֵּרֶד מִצְרַיְמָה	and he went down to Egypt
וַיָּגָר שָׁם בִּמְתֵי מְעָט	and sojourned there few in number,
וַיְהִי־שָׁם לְגוֹי גָּדוֹל עָצוּם וָרָב	but there became a great and mighty and numerous nation.

As previously noted, the opening clause of the worshiper's confession, ארמי אבד אבי, is fraught with interpretive issues that cannot be resolved on lexical, syntactical, and text-critical grounds alone. Furthermore, tradition critics have long been split on whether an ancient credo provided the historical framework for the Yahwist to assemble the JE narratives,[143] whether preexisting JE narratives were summarized in a credo using Deuteronom(ist)ic language and concepts[144] or the credo was the work of the Pentateuch's

---

142. S. J. De Vries, *Yesterday, Today and Tomorrow: Time and History in the Old Testament* (Grand Rapids, MI: Eerdmans, 1975) 45.

143. E.g., Noth, *History of Pentateuchal Traditions*, 56; von Rad, *From Genesis to Chronicles*, 1–58. Cf. L. Rost, "Das kleine geschichtliche Credo," in *Das kleine Credo*, 11–25. Rost modified von Rad's view in positing that the original credo included only 26:5a and 26:10 while the rest was provided by a Deuteronomistic author.

144. E.g., N. Lohfink, "The 'Small Credo' of Deuteronomy 26:5–9," in *Theology of the Pentateuch* (Minneapolis: Fortress, 1994) 265–89; I. Cairns, *Word and Presence: A Commentary on the Book of Deuteronomy* (ITC; Oxford: Oxford University Press, 1992) 222–23; Daniels, "Deuteronomy XXVI," 231–42; C. Carmichael, "A New View on the Origin of the Deuteronomic Credo," *VT* 19 (1969) 273–89; R. E. Clements, *God's Chosen People: A Theological Interpretation of the Book of Deuteronomy* (London: S.C.M., 1968) 55–56; B. S. Childs, "Deuteronomic Formulae of the Exodus Traditions," in *Hebräische Wortforschung: Festschrift zum 80. Geburtstag von Walter Baumgartner* (ed. B. Hartmann et al.; VTSup 16;

final redactor.[145] Broadly stated, the debate concerns the relative antiquity and priority of creedal genres vis-à-vis the genres within which they are embedded, whether parenetic (6.20–25) or liturgical (26:5–9). Because tradition critics are unable to agree whether creeds came from narrative and oral traditions or vice versa, a reassessment of the final form is necessary to clarify the literary relationship between these genres. As with the land promise to the "fathers" in Deut 6:23, some of the difficulties in finding a satisfactory interpretation for ארמי אבד אבי have stemmed from the tendency to extract Deut 26:5b from both its immediate context within the credo (26:5–9) and its broader liturgical context (26:1–11).

The final-form reading of the "little historical credo" presented here presupposes that the credo represents a selective arrangement of the elements of Israel's saving history that are most pertinent to the liturgical observance of firstfruits (26:1–11).[146] First, I will examine Deut 26:5 in its literary context to determine its rhetorical thrust and prominent themes. This section will also bridge liturgical and creedal genres by exploring possible reasons for the contraction of Israel's ancestry from plural (26:3) to singular (26:5). Second, I will explore a synoptic comparison of the credo with the similar historical recitals in Deut 10:22 and Num 20:14–17. This section will also highlight the importance of differing discourse contexts and narrative audiences as a key to accounting for lexical and conceptual variety. The rhetorical and synoptic approaches to the credo will complement one another in establishing the historical referent and rhetorical function of "my father" in Deut 26:5.

Rhetorical Analysis of Deuteronomy 26:5b

Deut 26:5 can be demarcated as a distinct literary unit with four clauses (see table 3.2, p. 69). An examination of the clause structure of Deut 26:5 reveals a symbiosis of several syntactical and thematic elements in narrating the growth of a single "father" into a populous "nation." First, the verse progresses from a verbless clause (clause 1) to a series of three verbal clauses with *waw*-consecutive imperfect forms (clauses 2–4). The syntacti-

---

Leiden: Brill, 1967) 30–39; J. N. M. Wijngaards, *The Formulas of the Deuteronomic Creed (Dt. 6/20–23; 26/5–9)* (Tilburg: Reinjen, 1963).

145. E.g., Gertz, "Stellung," 30–45; Dreyfus, "L'Araméen voulait tuer mon père," 147–61.

146. A comparison of the credo with Deuteronomy's other recitals of the exodus reveals several distinctive features (see Childs ["Deuteronomic Formulae," 30–39] for a complete listing). In addition to omitting the Horeb revelation, the credo makes no reference to Pharaoh's destruction at the Reed Sea (11:4) and Passover (16:1–8). The terminology of "trials" (4:1) in the "house of bondage" (5:6; 6:12; 7:8; 8:14; 13:6, 11) is also lacking. Rather than possessing tradition-critical significance, these elements are probably missing due to the credo's rhetorical emphasis on the land and its fruitfulness, similar to Deut 6:23. McConville ("Metaphor, Symbol," 329–51) notes that the tradition-critical analysis of so-called "Deuteronomic" phraseology tends to neglect literary contexts in favor of lexical links, as exemplified by M. Weinfeld, *Deuteronomy and the Deuteronomic School* (Oxford: Clarendon, 1972; repr., Winona Lake, IN: Eisenbrauns, 1992).

Table 3.2. Four Clauses of Deuteronomy 26:5

Clause	Hebrew	English
1	אֲרַמִּי אֹבֵד אָבִי	My father was a wandering Aramean
2	וַיֵּרֶד מִצְרַיְמָה	And he went down to Egypt
3	וַיָּגָר שָׁם בִּמְתֵי מְעָט	And he sojourned there few in number
4	וַיְהִי־שָׁם לְגוֹי גָּדוֹל עָצוּם וָרָב	And there he became a great, mighty and numerous nation

cal ambiguity of clause 1 contrasts starkly with the syntactical precision of the subsequent clauses, thereby epitomizing the liminal status of אבי. Second, the languid assonance of the first clause reflects the lamentable state of אבי, whereas the rapid-fire consonance of clauses 2–4 traces the meteoric growth of אבי into a גוי ("nation").[147] Third, the "father" is initially described in three words (clause 1), thereby setting in motion a three-beat rhythm that resonates through the entire credo.[148] Within Deut 26:5 itself, the three-beat rhythm begun by the first clause eventuates in the threefold description of a "great, mighty, and numerous" nation (clause 4). The rhythm of three has thus been transformed from a literary device of desolation to one of abundance. Fourth, table 3.2 (see p. 69) reveals that the four clauses progressively grow in length, as if to mirror the multiplication of "my father" (clause 1) into an entire "nation" (clause 4). The thematic progression from unsettled existence in Aram to settled life in Egypt is encapsulated even in the syntax of 26:5, thereby suggesting that אֹבֵד should be rendered "wandering" rather than "perishing."

The schematized nature of the numerical progression in Deut 26:5 may also shed light on the identity of "my father." Despite the inexorable progression from one person (clauses 1–2) to a few people (clause 3) to a populous nation (clause 4), it is striking that the grammatical number of the verbs in Deut 26:5 remains singular even as the narrative referent of אבי

---

[147]. The accents in ארמי and אבי in clause 1 fall on a final open syllable, thereby reinforcing the poetic effect of languor. However, the *waw*-consecutive verbs that begin clauses 2–4 shift the accent forward, quickly dissipating the languidness of clause 1.

[148]. L. Alonso Schökel, *A Manual of Hebrew Poetics* (trans. A. Graffy; SubBi 11; Rome: Pontifical Biblical Institute, 2000) 22; Fuhs, "Befreiung," 7; Lohfink, "Small Credo," 271–73. The three words of clause 1 each begin with the letter *a*. The immediately following phrases of the credo also exhibit threefold groupings. The Egyptians "treated us harshly [1] and afflicted us [2] and imposed hard labor on us [3]" (26:6). Yʜᴡʜ hears and sees "our affliction [1] and our toil [2] and our oppression [3]" (26:7). Yʜᴡʜ then brought Israel out with "a strong hand [1] and outstretched arm [2] and great terror [3]" (26:8), a trio of phrases that is then supplemented by the stock expression "signs and wonders" (cf. 4:34; 6:22; 34:11).

grows beyond measure.[149] Far from being a solecism, this collective singular representation of Israel's ancestors enables the literary device of hyperbole. By first narrowing the number of Israel's ancestors to one, clause 1 paves the way for the description of Israel's irrepressible growth into a nation. Since Israel is nowhere else described as a גוי before the exodus events (cf. Exod 19:6; 32:10; 33:13),[150] the numerical descriptions of people at both ends of the spectrum in clauses 1 and 4 appear to be symbolic rather than strictly historical.

Synoptic Analysis of Deuteronomy 26:5b

The hypothesis that אבי is a collective singular to represent the nation receives further support through a synoptic comparison of Deut 26:5 with Deut 10:22 and Num 20:14–15, two passages that also recite Israel's history from patriarchal times until the sojourn in Egypt (see table 3.3, p. 71). Among their many similarities, these passages share several elements of particular relevance for this synoptic comparison: (1) the modest status of Israel's ancestor(s); (2) a descent (ירד) of the clan into Egypt; and (3) the growth or longevity of the clan there. Though the lexical similarities among the three passages suggest that they derive from a shared narrative tradition, they also exhibit two striking differences. First, Deut 10:22 and Num 20:14–15 refer to plural "fathers," whereas Deut 26:5 refers to a single "father." While Deut 26:5 specifies an individual as "father" and Deut 10:22 specifies the "fathers" as Jacob's clan of 70 people (cf. Gen 46:27), Num 20:14–15 is more vague regarding their number and identity. Second, the subject of the verb in Deut 26:5 remains the "father" throughout, while the subjects of the other two passages change from the "fathers" to "you" (Deut 10:22) and "we" (Num 20:15). The "father" himself multiplies to become a "great and mighty and numerous nation" (Deut 26:5), whereas "you" multiply to become "like the stars of heaven" (Deut 10:22). Likewise, "our fathers" (Num 20:14) descended to Egypt, whereas "we" denotes the generation that lived there for a long time (Num 20:15). Deut 26:5 thus compresses the pre-exodus generations into a single figure in a way that Deut 10:22 and Num 20:14–15 do not.

In light of these differences, the use of a singular "father" to encompass the entirety of Israel's pre-exodus history supports the view that he is a timeless symbol for the changing fortunes of Israel in patriarchal and pre-exodus times rather than being a strictly historical figure. Deut 26:5 seems to have transformed an existing narrative tradition of Jacob or Abraham (cf. Gen 20:13) into an exemplar of "wandering"[151] for every landless gen-

---

149. After Deut 26:5, however, the grammatical person and number of the credo shift to the first-person plural ("us") in 26:6–9.

150. D. I. Block, "Nations/Nationality," *NIDOTTE* 4:970.

151. If it is correct to render אֹבֵד in Deut 26:5 as "wandering," there remains the question why the compiler of this passage used such a rare homonym of the root אבד. In

Table 3.3. Synoptic Comparison of Deuteronomy 26:5, 10:22; and Numbers 20:14–15

Deut 26:5	Deut 10:22	Num 20:14–15
1. My father [אבי] was a wandering Aramean	1. Your fathers [אבתיך] were seventy in all	1. You know all the trouble we have encountered
2. and he went down [ירד] to Egypt and sojourned there few in number	2. who went down [ירד] to Egypt	2. that our fathers went down [ירד אבתינו] to Egypt
3. and there he became a great and mighty and numerous nation.	3. but now you are like the stars of heaven.	3. and we stayed in Egypt many days

eration of Israel before the exodus. The "seventy people who went down to Egypt" (Deut 10:22) have now fused into a corporate figure. The personal appropriation of such a nomadic phase of Israel's existence occurs through recitation and liturgical observance by the worshipers in Deuteronomy's narrative world.

The rhetorical and synoptic analyses of Deut 26:5b suggest that ארמי אבד אבי should be translated "my father was a wandering Aramean," with אבי referring to Jacob as a corporate figure. The rendering of אבי as a collective singular best captures the rhetorical contrast between a tiny band of Aramean nomads and the mighty settled nation in Egypt. Ironically, this גוי גדול still lacked land,[152] a tension that heightens the rhetorical suspense until its resolution in the rest of the credo and liturgy.

Deuteronomy 26:15

הַשְׁקִיפָה מִמְּעוֹן קָדְשְׁךָ	Look down from your holy habitation,
מִן־הַשָּׁמַיִם	from heaven,
וּבָרֵךְ אֶת־עַמְּךָ אֶת־יִשְׂרָאֵל וְאֵת הָאֲדָמָה	and bless your people Israel and the ground
אֲשֶׁר נָתַתָּה לָּנוּ	that you have given to us,
כַּאֲשֶׁר נִשְׁבַּעְתָּ לַאֲבֹתֵינוּ	just as you swore to our fathers,
אֶרֶץ זָבַת חָלָב וּדְבָשׁ	a land flowing with milk and honey.

The final reference to Israel's ancestor(s) in Deuteronomy 26 appears in the conclusion to the ritual of the triennial tithe (26:12–15). The worshiper

---

Deuteronomy, the root אבד typically means "to perish" (Qal stem; 4:26; 7:20; 8:19; 11:17; 28:20, 22) or "to destroy" (Hiphil stem; 7:10, 24; 8:20; 9:3; 28:51, 63). Thus the diachronic issues remain open.

152. The notion of a גוי גדול ("great nation") necessarily entails a people in possession of its own territory (D. Vetter, "עם/גוי," TLOT 2:910).

professes his obedience to "all your commands that you have commanded me" (26:13b) in terms of faithfully providing the tithe for the marginalized (26:12–13a) and refraining from ritual uncleanness (26:14u). In return for this obedience, the worshiper requests that Yhwh look down from his "holy habitation, from heaven, and bless your people Israel, and the ground [אדמה] that you have given to us, a land [ארץ] flowing with milk and honey, just as you swore to our fathers" (26:15; see text and translation on p. 71). The verbal forms asking Yhwh to "look down" and "bless" are the only imperatives directed by the people toward God in the narrative world of Deuteronomy.[153] The people's ability to speak to God without a mediator represents a reversal from their earlier request at Horeb that Moses should serve as God's spokesman (5:25–27). Faithfulness to Yhwh's covenant not only results in long life in the land, it also restores the direct access to Yhwh that Israel had been missing ever since Moses was appointed as the people's mediator.

The worshiper's prayer is fueled by a description of the lush land that recalls 11:9–12. Canaan is identified in intensely personal terms as אדמה rather than ארץ, which is parallel with the warm request for Yhwh to bless his עם ("people"; 26:15b) rather than merely a גוי ("nation"; 26:5).[154] In 11:9, אדמה rather than ארץ was already used in a formulaic relative clause to emphasize the goodness of the land. This sort of אדמה would far surpass Egypt (11:10), drink from the rain of heaven (11:11), and be the constant object of Yhwh's דרש ("care"; 11:12a). Indeed, the assertion that "the eyes of Yhwh are always on it, from the beginning to the end of the year" (11:12b) locates Yhwh on high, thus mirroring the liturgist's prayer for Yhwh to gaze on the land from "his holy habitation, from heaven" (26:15a).

The similarities between Deuteronomy 11 and 26 provide an important clue for determining the historical referent of the "fathers" in 26:15. In 11:2–7, Moses states that his audience personally witnessed the "discipline [מוסר] of Yhwh your God" by means of the plagues in Egypt, the deliverance at the Reed Sea from Pharaoh and his army, the chastening in the wilderness, and the destruction of Dathan and Abiram. Similarly, the worshiper in Deut 26:9 confesses his participation in the exodus and wilderness events. In both Deuteronomy 11 and 26, the "fathers" of this generation must therefore predate the exodus rather than being the exodus or wilderness generations themselves.[155] On the other hand, the preceding discussion

---

153. In contrast, Moses frequently makes requests of God (e.g., 3:24; 9:27; 33:7, 11).

154. See the discussion of the emotive contrasts between ארץ/אדמה and עם/גוי by Rost, "Die Bezeichnungen für Land und Volk," 89–93; cf. Block, "Nations/Nationality," *NIDOTTE* 4:966.

155. Cf. Römer (*Israels Väter*, 244–45), who asserts that the "fathers" in Deut 26:15 are the exodus generation, based on a comparison with Solomon's confession in 1 Kgs 8:34. Within the same context, Solomon identifies the "fathers" as possessors of the land (1 Kgs 8:21, 40). However, an inordinate amount of redactional revision would be required to undo the fact that Moses speaks from a perspective east of the Jordan, whereas Solomon

of Deut 26:3 has demonstrated that a pre-exodus referent for the "fathers" need not restrict their identity to the three patriarchs, especially since the present references to the "land flowing with milk and honey" (26:9, 15) recall Yhwh's first theophany to Moses and the exodus generation (Exod 3:8). Either way, the tight solidarity between the "fathers and their seed" (11:9) suggests that the "fathers" in Deut 26:15 represent every landless generation in Israel.

In summary, the references to the "father" and "fathers" in Deuteronomy 26 encompass a holistic theology of land. While the land is God's *unconditional* gift to a nomadic people (26:3, 5–9), its concomitantly *conditional* nature is captured in the worshiper's declaration of innocence (26:13–14) before his prayer for divine blessing on the "people" and the "ground" (26:15). Similarly, the phrase "land flowing with milk and honey" (26:9, 15) is used on both sides of the unconditional-conditional dichotomy,[156] thereby challenging the historical-critical tendency to identify univocal layers of tradition. Thus the tapestry of land and "fathers" seems too tightly interwoven with unconditional and conditional threads to be unraveled smoothly into redactional layers. Like Deuteronomy 6, the land promise to the "fathers" provides the essential dialogical links between unconditionality and conditionality in Israel's life under Yhwh's covenant.

Land and the "Fathers" in Deuteronomy 30

Two references to the land promised to the "fathers" (30:5, 20) occur in the third address by Moses (29:1[2]–30:20).[157] In view of the terror of exile (28:64–68) with which the second address concluded, Moses proceeds to secure Israel's commitment through a recital of Yhwh's deeds (29:1–7[2–8]) and a call to keep Yhwh's covenant (29:8[9]). Despite Israel's profession of faith (29:9–12[10–13]) and the applicability of this covenant to all generations (29:13–14[14–15]), the covenant curse of exile will still come upon the people if they persist in idolatry (29:17–27[18–28]). The inevitability of this fate raises the urgent theological question of whether the nation is condemned forever to a cycle of disobedience followed by divine wrath. In Deuteronomy 30, Moses' exposition of the "secret things"

---

speaks of the "fathers" after the land has already been possessed. These discrepancies in geographical and chronological perspective suggest that the "fathers" are different in Deut 26:15 and 1 Kgs 8:34.

156. Ausloos, "Land Flowing with Milk and Honey," 301–3.

157. In addition to land-promise formulas (30:5a, 20), Deuteronomy 30 contains two nonformulaic references to the "fathers" (30:5c, 9). Because these references appear in the context of prosperity and progeny, they resemble several "God of the fathers" texts (e.g., 1:10; 6:3; 27:3) and are treated in chap. 5.

The case for viewing Deut 28:69[29:1] as a colophon for the second Mosaic speech rather than as a superscription for the third speech is presented in chap. 7.

of Yhwh (29:28[29]) reveals that Yhwh will effect a spiritual breakthrough in response to Israel's penitence in a foreign land (30:1–2). Yhwh will not only gather Israel's exiles back to the "land that your fathers possessed" (30:3–5). More importantly, he will also grant Israel a circumcised heart (30:6).[158] A new heart for Israel will result in Yhwh's turning the covenant curses into blessings (30:7), renewed obedience (30:8, 10), and abundant prosperity in the land when Yhwh rejoices over Israel, "just as he rejoiced over your fathers" (30:9; cf. 30:5). The immanence of the divine word (30:11–14) means that obedience to Yhwh's covenant is attainable, thereby providing grounds for Moses' exhortations to love Yhwh and keep his statutes (30:16) in order to avoid destruction (30:17). The result of obeying this injunction to "choose life" (30:19) will be everlasting tenure in the "land that Yhwh swore to your fathers, to Abraham, Isaac, and Jacob, to give them" (30:20).

The seminal nature of Deuteronomy 30 in unifying Israel's past and future history has led redaction critics to isolate exilic and postexilic strands in this chapter's various references to apostasy, exile, and return.[159] A dating within the exilic or postexilic periods is also argued based on thematic correspondence with similarly themed intertexts that emphasize Israel's heartfelt obedience in the aftermath of exile.[160] Likewise, scholars have regarded the numerous links between the covenant formulas of Deuteron-

---

158. The central position occupied by "circumcision of the heart" in Deut 30:1–10 has been demonstrated by P. Barker, *The Triumph of Grace in Deuteronomy: Faithless Israel, Faithful Yahweh in Deuteronomy* (Waynesboro, GA: Paternoster, 2004) 141–67; and G. Vanoni, "Der Geist und der Buchstabe: Überlegungen zum Verhältnis der Testamente und Beobachtungen zu Dtn 30,1–10," *BN* 14 (1981) 65–98. Compare with Christensen (*Deuteronomy 21:10–34:12*, 736–37), who places Deut 30:6–7 at the center of a chiasm in 30:1–10, in addition to arguing that 30:6a is the first element of another chiasm in 30:6–10. K. J. Turner (*The Death of Deaths in the Death of Israel: Deuteronomy's Theology of Exile* [Ph.D. diss., Southern Baptist Theological Seminary, 2005] 206–9) provides the most recent discussion of views on the structure of 30:1–10.

159. Arguments for exilic or postexilic dates for Deuteronomy 30 also apply to similar passages in Deuteronomy 4, 28, and 29. Though differing in specifics, exilic or postexilic strands in Deuteronomy 30 are detected by G. von Rad, N. Lohfink, G. Braulik, L. Perlitt, R. Friedman, H. W. Wolff, R. Smend, R. Albertz, A. Rofé, F. M. Cross, D. N. Freedman, D. Olson, W. Brueggemann, M. Z. Brettler, J. Tigay, P. Miller, and many others. See the recent survey of Deuteronomy research found in E. Otto, "Perspektiven der neueren Deuteronomiumsforschung," *ZAW* 119 (2007) 319–40.

160. The connections between Deuteronomy 30, Jeremiah 31, and Ezekiel 36 have long been noted by, for example, W. E. Lemke, "Circumcision of the Heart: The Journey of a Biblical Metaphor," in *A God So Near: Essays on Old Testament Theology in Honor of Patrick D. Miller* (ed. B. A. Strawn and N. R. Bowen; Winona Lake, IN: Eisenbrauns, 2003) 299–319; M. Z. Brettler, "Predestination in Deuteronomy 30,1–10," in *Those Elusive Deuteronomists: The Phenomenon of Pan-Deuteronomism* (ed. L. S. Schearing and S. L. McKenzie; JSOTSup 268; Sheffield: Sheffield Academic Press, 1999) 171–88; N. Mendecki, "Dtn 30,3–4: Nachexilisch?" *BZ* 29 (1985) 267–71; H. W. Wolff, "The Kerygma of the Deuteronomic Historical Work" (ed. W. Brueggemann; Atlanta: John Knox, 1982) 83–100; Mayes, *Deuteronomy*, 367–68; M. Weinfeld, "Jeremiah and the Spiritual Metamorphosis of Israel," *ZAW* 88 (1976) 17–56.

omy 28–30 and the 7th-century B.C.E. Assyrian treaties as evidence for an exilic or postexilic date.[161] Though space precludes detailed interaction with diachronic proposals, the land-promise formulas in Deut 30:5 and 30:20 may provide a manageable entrée into the discussion. At first sight, the "fathers" in these two verses seem to be identified with two incompatible groups of people. On the one hand, the undefined "fathers" are those who have already "possessed" (ירש) the land (30:5). As Römer and Van Seters observe, the OT references to "fathers" receiving and possessing the land typically occur in texts addressed to exilic or postexilic audiences and refer to the exodus generation rather than the patriarchs (e.g., Jer 7:7; Neh 9:23).[162]

On the other hand, the "fathers" are later identified as the patriarchs "Abraham, Isaac, and Jacob," who received YHWH's "oath" and "gift" of the land (30:20). A referent of the patriarchs seems to accord with texts that portray the "fathers" as landless pilgrims whose descendants will possess the land (e.g., 26:15). The tension between the occurrences of the "fathers" in 30:5, 9, and 20 furnishes a useful opportunity to test the synchronic hypothesis for the generations already offered for Deuteronomy 1, 6, and 26—namely, that the referent for "fathers" shifts according to the rhetorical context rather than being evidence of competing traditions of Israel's ancestors. The previous case studies have indicated that the Deuteronomic "fathers" function flexibly to represent both Israel's chronologically specific generations (e.g., 1:8) as well as rhetorically blended generations (e.g., 6:23).

Deuteronomy 30:5

וֶהֱבִיאֲךָ יְהוָה אֱלֹהֶיךָ אֶל־הָאָרֶץ	Then YHWH your God will bring you back to the land
אֲשֶׁר־יָרְשׁוּ אֲבֹתֶיךָ	that your fathers possessed,
וִירִשְׁתָּהּ	and you will possess it,
וְהֵיטִבְךָ וְהִרְבְּךָ מֵאֲבֹתֶיךָ	and he will prosper and multiply you more than your fathers.

The return to a prosperous land first possessed by the "fathers" stands as a complete reversal of the covenant curse of exile. Much as exile itself represented a reversal from the way that YHWH "rejoiced [שׂושׂ] to prosper [הטיב] and multiply [הרבות] you . . . therefore, he will rejoice [שׂושׂ] to destroy and

---

161. E.g., C. Koch, *Vertrag, Treueid und Bund: Studien zur Rezeption des altorientalischen Vertragsrechts im Deuteronomium und zur Ausbildung der Bundestheologie im Alten Testament* (BZAW 383; Berlin: de Gruyter, 2008); H. U. Steymans, *Deuteronomium 28 und die adê zur Thronfolgeregelung Asarhaddons* (OBO 145; Göttingen: Vandenhoeck & Ruprecht, 1996); R. Frankena, "The Vassal-Treaties of Esarhaddon and the Dating of Deuteronomy," *OTS* 65 (1965) 122–54; Weinfeld, *Deuteronomy and the Deuteronomic School*, 59–146.

162. Van Seters, "Confessional Reformulation," 448–59; Römer, *Israels Väter*, passim. The patriarchal names in 30:20 are a focal point for both Van Seters and Römer, who consider them parallel redactional insertions to 1:8.

annihilate you" (28:63), restoration from exile not only restores a previous blessing but also surpasses it in scope: "Yhwh will prosper [היטיב] and multiply [הרבות] you *more* than your fathers" (30:5b). In addition, Yhwh will "rejoice [שוש] over you for good [טוב]" (30:9). All the verbs that described the curse of exile in Deut 28:63 recur in 30:5 and 30:9 to describe restoration from exile.[163] Thus the tripartite relationship among Yhwh, land, and his people that had come unraveled in the exile has now been restored by Yhwh's bringing the people back to the land.[164]

The lexical links between Deut 28:63 and the "fathers" references in 30:5 and 9 also reflect the forward progression of time in Deuteronomy's narrative world. The terminology of Israel's multiplication with which Moses previously described "you" (1:10; 7:13; 13:18; 28:63) has now been applied to the "fathers" (30:5). The verbal object of ירש in this verse also shifts from the land yet to be possessed by "you" to a past possession of the land by the "fathers." Not only does ירש never appear elsewhere in Deuteronomy with the "fathers" as subject, but 30:5a also contains the only instance in which ירש occurs with perfective aspect (i.e., completed action) outside references to the Transjordan conquest.[165] In short, the verbatim transfer of terminology from "you" in the present to the "fathers" in the past points to an identification of the "fathers" of 30:5a with the populous generation at Moab that would shortly possess the land, rather than the three patriarchs.[166]

At first glance, the rhetorical strategy of referring to possession of the land as a past event seems to mirror the creedal formulations of Deut 6:20–25 and 26:1–11. Unlike the creeds, however, 30:5a envisions the "fathers" as a settled generation in the land rather than individuals who still await the fulfillment of the land promise. Furthermore, it is significant that, although the Deuteronomic "fathers" everywhere represent the ancestors of a landless generation, the landlessness of "you" (i.e., their descendants) in Deuteronomy 30 arises from the covenant curse of exile rather than from any delay in actualizing Yhwh's oath. In fact, Yhwh's faithfulness in fulfilling his covenant promises of "blessing and curse" (30:1) is precisely why Israel now languishes in exile rather than living in the land. In a stunning maneuver, Moses has moved the rhetorical function of the Deuteronomic

---

163. Römer (*Israels Väter*, 39–43) notes that this collocation of שוש, היטב/טוב, and הרבה in Deut 28:63, 30:5, and 30:9 is unique in the entire OT.

164. In Deuteronomy 30, the theme of Israel's return to the land and Yhwh, and Yhwh's return to Israel looms large through repetition of שוב (30:1, 2, 3 [3x], 8, 9, 10). The gracious consequences of return are propounded through various forms of (30:5, 9 [2x], 15). The use of these *Leitwörter* as structuring features of the chapter has been noted by Wolff, "Kerygma of the Deuteronomic Historical Work," 93–97; and W. Brueggemann, "The Kerygma of the Deuteronomistic Historian," *Int* 22 (1968) 387–402.

165. That is, Qal *waw*-consecutive imperfect forms in Deut 2:21, 22; 4:48, and one instance of a perfect form in 3:12. In contrast, ירש with imperfective aspect is pervasive in Deuteronomy.

166. Contra Barker, *Triumph of Grace in Deuteronomy*, 170; Craigie, *Deuteronomy*, 364.

"fathers" along the arc of Israel's redemptive history from the horizon of promise to the horizon of fulfillment. The "fathers" have exchanged their unsettled existence (26:15) for settled life in the land (30:5), placing them diametrically opposite Moses' audience of "you," which faces the danger of exchanging life in the land for exile. Thus the *Leitmotiv* of reversal in 30:5 extends even to the chronological realm, for the "fathers" in the land now occupy the spiritual lot and physical location of their descendants outside the land, and vice versa.

However, the possibility of restoration after exile means that exiled Israel can enjoy solidarity in the land with its "fathers," who once possessed the land. The disparate generations of Israel will no longer stand on opposite sides of the redemptive-historical divide between promise and fulfillment. By ascribing to the "fathers" a different identity from all other instances,[167] Deut 30:1–10 furnishes an outstanding example of the theological continuity between Israel's ancestors and Moses' audience at Moab. Rather than being a static or technical term to denote a particular generation, the referent of the "fathers" modulates frequently in Deuteronomy in order to empower the contemporaneity of the Mosaic speeches. This phenomenon is especially evident in the way that the referent for "fathers" shifts back to the patriarchs in Deut 30:20.

Deuteronomy 30:20

כִּי הוּא חַיֶּיךָ וְאֹרֶךְ יָמֶיךָ	. . . that means life to you and length of days
לָשֶׁבֶת עַל־הָאֲדָמָה	so that you may live on the ground
אֲשֶׁר נִשְׁבַּע יְהוָה לַאֲבֹתֶיךָ	that Yhwh swore to your fathers,
לְאַבְרָהָם לְיִצְחָק וּלְיַעֲקֹב	to Abraham, to Isaac, and to Jacob,
לָתֵת לָהֶם	to give them.

Moses' third address concludes with an impassioned plea for Israel to "choose life!" (30:19). The result of choosing to love Yhwh and obey his commandments will be long life on the "ground [אדמה] that Yhwh swore to . . . Abraham, to Isaac, and to Jacob" (30:20). The names of the patriarchs appear here in a land-promise formula for the first time since 6:10, although they have appeared sporadically in covenant formulas since then.[168] This instance of the land-promise formula belongs to a class of Deuteronomic texts that speak of Yhwh's oath and gift of the land to the "fathers" alone without any reference to their descendants.[169] Deut 30:20 is unique

---

167. Other than Deut 29:24[25], a passage that is analyzed in chaps. 5 and 7.
168. Deut 9:5, 27; 29:12[13]. Strikingly, 9:27 names the three patriarchs as Yhwh's "servants" without calling them "fathers" (cf. 34:4).
169. Deut 1:35; 10:11; 11:21; 30:20; 31:7. Among these texts, 30:20 alone attests a secondary reading whereby the "fathers" receive Yhwh's oath but not his gift of land, since the land gift is offered instead to the Deuteronomic audience: "Yhwh swore to your fathers to give to *you*," where "you" can either be singular (Syr., a few LXX miniscules) or plural

among these passages in placing the patriarchs in apposition to the "fathers," rather than using "fathers" to refer to Israel's ancestors in general.

The uniqueness of Deut 30:20 in identifying the patriarchs as the sole recipients of YHWH's oath and gift of land has been an interpretive crux for pentateuchal criticism. Using somewhat different lines of argument, Van Seters and Römer both propose that the patriarchal names are a secondary insertion into a text that originally referred to the "fathers" as the forefathers of the exodus generation that possessed the land. On the one hand, Van Seters argues that an unconditional oath to the patriarchs cannot be found in a context where tenure in the land is conditioned on obedience to the covenant.[170] The unmistakable emphasis on obedience in 30:15–20 thus obviates a reference to the patriarchs. On the other hand, Römer extends his text-critical argument for deleting the patriarchal names from 1:8 to argue similarly for 30:20. The patriarchal names in both cases were ostensibly added by the same redactor.[171] Van Seters and Römer, though they differ in the specifics of their proposals, share the view that references to the patriarchal promises represent a late accretion to Deuteronomy.

However, the case studies of land-promise formulas thus far have raised doubts about caricaturing Deuteronomic theology as a set of simple dichotomies. The unconditional and conditional elements of the land promise are inextricably connected, thereby challenging the contention of Van Seters and Römer that the patriarchal promises are foreign to Deuteronomic theology. In fact, the patriarchal narratives of promise themselves manifest a theological complexity that defies straightforward redaction-critical partitioning into unconditional and conditional strands. Even granting this presumption, however, the issue of how 30:20 can speak of a land gift to the patriarchs without reference to their descendants still remains. The fact that the patriarchs never conquered the land has been adduced as evidence for deleting the patriarchal names from 30:20.[172]

The surprising reference to the patriarchal names in Deut 30:20 recalls the frequent phenomenon of varying the recipients of YHWH's oath and gift of land. As already noted, Deuteronomy exhibits at least four permutations in this regard: (1) an oath to the "fathers" without any reference to

---

(SP, LXX according to Lucian). These readings probably arose due to the theological difficulty of YHWH's gift to ancestors who never possessed the land, to the exclusion of their descendants who did. Thus the MT reading לתת להם is the *lectio difficilior*, contra Lohfink ("Wann hat Gott," 20–21). Deut 30:20 should still be classified as a land-promise formula with reference to the ancestors alone.

170. Van Seters, "Confessional Reformulation," 451.

171. Römer (*Israels Väter*, 219–22) also argues that the likelihood of a secondary insertion of the patriarchal names in Deut 1:8 and 30:20 is greatly increased by their parallel function in framing the Mosaic speeches.

172. In Gen 15:7–8 (cf. Gen 28:4), YHWH promises Abraham "possession" (ירש) of the land. However, Römer (*Israels Väter*, 42) avers that these promises of Abraham's possession of the land should be deleted as Deuteronom(ist)ic insertions.

a corresponding gift of the land; (2) an oath to the "fathers" with a gift to the same; (3) an oath to the "fathers" but a gift to their "seed," to "us," or to "you"; (4) an oath and gift to both "fathers" and their "seed." The last of these four permutations appears only in the initial land promise: "the land that YHWH swore to your fathers to give to your fathers, to Abraham, to Isaac, and to Jacob, to give to them and to their seed" (1:8). This instance involves a theologically freighted formula that binds all of Israel's generations together as common recipients of YHWH's oath and gift of land. Since the individual elements of every subsequent formula can be traced back to Deut 1:8, the full formula there seems to provide a lexical reservoir from which subsequent occurrences can draw selectively and creatively according to their rhetorical situation.[173] Whether or not subsequent formulas actually cite the transgenerational elements found in Deut 1:8 (e.g., "seed"), the close verbal correspondence between Deut 1:8 and all subsequent formulas suggests that corporate solidarity is explicitly or implicitly conjured up in every instance of the land-promise formula. Thus the differences between the various formulations of the Deuteronomic land promise are probably stylistic variations that do not furnish meaningful redaction-critical seams.[174]

The observation of corporate solidarity in the Deuteronomic land promises provides a potential explanation for why the patriarchs alone are mentioned in Deut 30:20. Here as elsewhere, the formulaic construction "land that YHWH swore" signals a shorthand reference to 1:8, where all of Israel's generations were included as recipients of the land oath and gift.[175] Though Abraham, Isaac, and Jacob here are the recipients of the gift to the exclusion of their descendants, it is unnecessary to posit a contradiction with other Deuteronomic formulas that must be explained away by a redactor's hand in 30:20. Instead, the abbreviated formula found in 30:20 serves as a cipher for the full formula and attendant theological implications contained in 1:8.[176] Corporate solidarity between Israel's generations thus facilitates the literary device of anachronism, since the patriarchs are referred to as recipients of YHWH's gift of land even though it was their descendants who actually took possession of the gift.

In light of the probable originality of the patriarchal names in Deut 30:20, what may be said of their rhetorical function? The mention of the

---

173. Lohfink, *Väter*, 27; Miller, "Gift of God," 454.
174. Plöger, *Literarkritische, formgeschichtliche und stilkritische Untersuchungen*, 81; Scharbert, *Solidarität in Segen und Fluch*, 187.
175. Strawn ("Keep/Observe/Do: Rhetoric," 226–27) notes that repetition in Deuteronomy, as with the land-promise formula, tends to muddle the lexical differences between occurrences while paradoxically sharpening the audience's memory of formulaic language. Brueggemann helpfully labels this phenomenon the "pedagogy of saturation" (*Theology*, 722).
176. Lohfink, *Väter*, 27.

patriarchs enhances the effectiveness of Moses' rhetoric in several ways. First, the conclusion of the third speech of Moses is paired with the opening of the first speech, where the patriarchal names also appeared in a formulaic expression of the land promise (1:8). Thus the patriarchal names in 1:8 and 30:20 form a tidy inclusio around the Mosaic speeches, underscoring the unity of the hortatory material contained within. This observation calls into question the numerous redactional proposals that splice the final form of the Mosaic speeches into earlier components without regard for their rhetorical shape.

Second, the reference to the patriarchs by name indicates that Israel's faithfulness to the covenant at Horeb/Moab results in the ultimate fulfillment of the promises to the patriarchs.[177] Thus the common distinction made between the Abrahamic covenant as unconditional and the Israelite covenant at Horeb/Moab as conditional cannot be sustained.[178] The theological continuity between these covenants indicates that, just as fulfillment of the Abrahamic covenant demands human obedience,[179] fulfillment of the Israelite covenant requires divine grace.[180]

Third, the use of the three patriarchal names here reinforces the triadic cadence of Moses' rhetoric.[181] Immediately prior to the mention of the patriarchs in Deut 30:20, for example, Moses enjoins three tasks upon Israel: love God, obey his voice, and cleave to him. The patriarchal names in 30:20 thus conclude the rhetorical rhythm that has permeated the Mosaic speeches since 1:8.

Fourth, 30:20 pairs the references to Y_HWH's dealings with the patriarchs in the past with the prospect of long life in the future, thereby underscoring Y_HWH's sovereignty and grace over all of Israel's history. By reminding Israel of Y_HWH's incomparability among the gods and the unparalleled blessings of obedience to such a deity,[182] Moses offers a fitting peroration to his exhortation for Israel to love Y_HWH and obey his covenant. In Deut 30:15–20, the promise of the land provides creative inspiration for Moses in this "fugue on the theme of 'life.'"[183]

---

177. Barker, *Triumph of Grace in Deuteronomy*, 213; Clements, *God's Chosen People*, 40.
178. The dichotomy between the Abrahamic covenant as an unconditional land grant and the Israelite covenant as a conditional vassal treaty has been articulated most influentially by M. Weinfeld, "The Covenant of Grant in the Old Testament and the Ancient Near East," *JAOS* 90 (1970) 184–203; and D. N. Freedman, "Divine Commitment and Human Obligation," *Int* 18 (1964) 419–31. This notion is fully analyzed in chaps. 6–7.
179. E.g., Gen 12:2; 17:1; 18:19; 26:5.
180. E.g., Deut 5:6; 6:23; 30:6.
181. Lenchak, *Choose Life*, 216–17.
182. Compare similar emphases in Deut 4:7–8, 32–40; 33:26.
183. McConville, "Deuteronomy: Torah," 39.

Land and the "Fathers" in Deuteronomy 34

The final case involving the Deuteronomic land promise concerns Deuteronomy 34, which stands liminally as the end of Deuteronomy and the Pentateuch while also looking forward to Joshua. The impending death of Moses (1:37–38) has infused a somber and urgent tone into Moses' preaching since the very beginning of Deuteronomy.[184] Though Moses has recounted his successful intercession for sinful Israel in the wilderness (9:25–29), his pleas for himself will not be heeded, for he must die before crossing the Jordan (3:23–28; 31:2, 14). His death is held in abeyance for over 30 chapters, however, until Israel's preparations in covenant ratification and leadership transition are completed. Once Moses has completed these tasks, Yhwh issues the threefold order for him to "ascend" (עלה) the mountain, "look" (ראה) at the land of promise, and "die" (מות). In addition to recording Moses' taciturn compliance with Yhwh's three commands (32:48–52),[185] Deuteronomy 34 describes Yhwh's panoramic presentation of the land to Moses immediately before his death (34:1–3).

Deuteronomy 34:4

וַיֹּאמֶר יְהוָה אֵלָיו	Then Yhwh said to him [Moses]:
זֹאת הָאָרֶץ	"This is the land
אֲשֶׁר נִשְׁבַּעְתִּי לְאַבְרָהָם לְיִצְחָק וּלְיַעֲקֹב	that I swore to Abraham, Isaac, and Jacob,
לֵאמֹר לְזַרְעֲךָ אֶתְּנֶנָּה	saying, 'I will give it to your seed.'"

As the transitional chapter between the Mosaic Torah and the Former Prophets, Deuteronomy 34 has long been the object of historical-critical reconstruction.[186] The older hexateuchal paradigm viewed Deuteronomy

---

184. D. T. Olson (*Deuteronomy and the Death of Moses: A Theological Reading* [OBT; Minneapolis: Fortress, 1994] 47–48) notes that the notice of Moses' imminent departure in Deuteronomy 1 and 3 precipitates a hermeneutical crisis of continuity in Israel's laws and leadership. Thus the rest of Deuteronomy entails the reestablishment of continuity through covenant renewal at Moab and Joshua's accession.

185. R. Lux ("Der Tod des Mose als 'besprochene und erzählte Welt': Überlegungen zu einer literaturwissenschaftlichen und theologischen Interpretation von Deuteronomium 32,48–52 und 34," *ZTK* 84 [1987] 401–2) outlines the numerous lexical parallels in the commands of Deut 32:48–52 and 34:1–6.

186. The interpretive issues in Deuteronomy 34 are at least fourfold. First, from ancient times, *Baba Batra*, Jerome, and many others raised the problem whether Moses could have composed his own death narrative and eulogy. Second, various elements of Deuteronomy 34 have suggested a later date of writing or discontinuity with the preceding narrative. For example, scholars have noted that references to tribal inheritances have not yet been delineated (34:2–3), Moses possesses a unique status as "servant of Yhwh" (34:5) and prophet without equal (34:10), the audience lacks knowledge of Moses' burial place "to this day" (34:6), and the narrative offers an unusual description of Joshua using the language of "wisdom" (34:9). Third, there are apparent contradictions between

34 as a basically Deuteronom(ist)ic composition that summarized JE traditions and incorporated a few Priestly insertions.[187] Following in the footsteps of Noth, the more recent tendency has been to push the dating of Deuteronomy 34 forward into the Persian period as a late compromise between Deuteronomistic and Priestly schools.[188] Between these poles, debate continues over the extent of Priestly influence and reworking in Deuteronomy.[189] Despite this wide spectrum of diachronic views, interpreters who differ on the provenance of Deuteronomy 34 often agree in recognizing Deuteronomic language in the land-promise formula of v. 4.[190]

Lexical Analysis of Deuteronomy 34:4 from a Deuteronomic Perspective

The recognition of Deuteronomic language in Deut 34:4 invites a comparative study of this instance of the land promise in light of the preced-

---

the depictions of the elderly Moses as both frail (31:1) and robust (34:7), and as a figure who knew God "face to face" (34:10) but had earlier denied the possibility of seeing God (4:15). Fourth, the glowing picture of Moses in Deuteronomy 34 vis-à-vis the rest of the Pentateuch is reinforced by the unique transference of exodus terminology from Yhwh to Moses. In Deut 34:12, Moses becomes the one who had exercised a "mighty hand" and performed "terrifying displays of power" against Egypt, in contrast to earlier attributions of these characteristics to Yhwh (e.g., 3:24; 4:34; 5:15; 6:21; 7:8, 19; 9:26; 11:2; 26:8).

187. See the discussion of the older view in F. García López, "Deut 34, DTR History and the Pentateuch," in *Studies in Deuteronomy in Honour of C. J. Labuschagne on the Occasion of His 65th Birthday* (ed. F. García Martínez et al.; VTSup 53; Leiden: Brill, 1994) 47–61; Skweres, *Rückverweise*, 91 n. 363. Deut 34:1*, 2–3, and 5–6 are typically attributed to J; 34:1a, 7a, 8–9 to P; and 34:4, 10–12 to the DH. A striking inversion of the older approach has been attempted by J. Van Seters, "Deuteronomy between Pentateuch and the Deuteronomistic History," *HvTSt* 59 (2003) 947–56. Van Seters largely agrees with the conventional source divisions but argues that the J writer was actually the postexilic compiler of the Pentateuch.

188. E.g., K. Schmid, "The Late Persian Formation of the Torah: Observations on Deuteronomy 34," in *Judah and the Judeans in the Fourth Century B.C.E.* (ed. O. Lipschits, G. Knoppers, and R. Albertz; Winona Lake, IN: Eisenbrauns, 2007) 237–45; H.-C. Schmitt, "Spätdeuteronomistisches Geschichtswerk und Priesterschrift in Deuteronomium 34," in *Textarbeit: Studien zu Texten und ihrer Rezeption aus dem Alten Testament und der Umwelt Israels* (ed. K. Kiesow and T. Meurer; Münster: Ugarit-Verlag, 2003) 407–24; T. C. Römer and M. Z. Brettler, "Deuteronomy 34 and the Case for a Persian Hexateuch," *JBL* 119 (2000) 401–19.

189. See the contrasting views of L. Perlitt ("Priesterschrift im Deuteronomium?" *ZAW* 100 [1988] 65–88), who denies the presence of Priestly strands in Deuteronomy, and P. Stoellger ("Deuteronomium 34 ohne Priesterschrift," *ZAW* 105 [1993] 26–51), who argues for Priestly editing, particularly in Deut 34:7–8a.

190. C. Frevel, "Ein vielsagender Abschied: Exegetische Blicke auf den Tod des Mose in Dtn 34,1–12," *BZ* 45 (2001) 209–34, esp. p. 220 n. 36; Lux, "Tod des Mose," 405; Stoellger, "Deuteronomium 34," 30–31; García López, "Deut 34," 57. Römer and Brettler ("Deuteronomy 34," 405–6) represent exceptions to the view regarding the presence of Deuteronomic language in Deut 34:4. They instead attribute this verse to the "final redaction" of the Pentateuch because the patriarchs are mentioned without referring to them as "fathers." This argument will be examined below.

ing case studies. Without denying the probability of a complex editorial history, I find that a synchronic approach illumines two particular connections between Deuteronomy 34 and the rest of the book. These two connections confirm that the land-promise formula found in Deut 34:4 is thoroughly Deuteronomic, at least in style, if not also in origin.

First, the somber tone of Deut 34:4 is similar to five other passages where Yhwh speaks directly in first person of a land oath to the "fathers."[191] In contrast to Moses' references to Yhwh's oaths in the third person (e.g., 31:7), Yhwh's invocation of a first-person oath formula carries a special urgency. The first-person oaths in 1:35 and 10:11 both appear in contexts of Israel's past apostasy: once at Kadesh (1:35) and once at Horeb (10:11). The first two instances in Deuteronomy 31 appear in the context of future apostasy (31:20, 21), and the final instance appears in Yhwh's charge to Joshua to "be strong and courageous, for you shall bring the sons of Israel into the land that I swore to them" (31:23). From these examples, it is evident that Deuteronomy records Yhwh as speaking directly of his land oath when contrasting his past faithfulness to the "fathers" with the apostasy of the people (e.g., in Kadesh, at Horeb, or in Canaan) or when spiritual challenges are at hand (e.g., Joshua's commissioning). In 34:4, Yhwh's barring of Moses from entering the land through reference to a first-person oath is consistent with these weighty themes.

Second, let us compare Deut 34:4 with the six other contexts that refer to the patriarchs by name.[192] Specifically among these, Deut 9:27 provides the only instance besides 34:4 in which the patriarchal names appear without the appellative "fathers." Though Römer and Brettler view the absence of the title "fathers" as proof that Deut 34:4 is nondeuteronomic,[193] they have overlooked its generic differences from the rest of the patriarchal references that include "fathers." Only Deut 9:27 and 34:4 appear in the context of Moses' private speech with Yhwh rather than in a public setting where Moses is described as addressing "all Israel."[194] In this regard, the generic contrasts between two adjacent occurrences of patriarchal names

---

191. First-person oaths of Yhwh appear 6× (1:35; 10:11; 31:20, 21, 23; 34:4). In contrast, third-person references to Yhwh's oath are much more frequent, occurring 22× (1:8; 2:14; 4:31; 6:10, 18, 23; 7:8, 12, 13; 8:1, 18; 9:5; 11:9, 21; 13:18[17]; 19:8; 26:3; 28:9, 11; 29:12[13]; 30:20; 31:7).

192. Deut 1:8; 6:10; 9:5, 27; 29:12[13]; 30:20; 34:4. Each of these instances provides a rhetorical surprise since Deuteronomic references to the "fathers" without the patriarchal names are much more frequent (> 40×).

193. Römer and Brettler, "Deuteronomy 34," 405–6. J. Van Seters argues similarly that the reference to the three patriarchs indicates that Deut 34:4 is the later work of J rather than being part of the original Deuteronomy (*The Life of Moses: The Yahwist as Historian in Exodus–Numbers* [Louisville: Westminster John Knox, 1994] 452–56).

194. E.g., Deut 1:1; 5:1; 11:6; 13:12; 18:6; 21:21; 27:9; 29:1; 31:1, 7, 11 (2×); 32:45; 34:12. Cf. J. W. Flanagan, "The Deuteronomic Meaning of 'Kol Yisrael,'" *SR* 6 (1977) 159–68.

in Deuteronomy 9 provide an instructive example regarding when Deuteronomy includes or omits the title "fathers."

On the one hand, 9:5 describes Moses as encouraging Israel that dispossessing Canaan's inhabitants will result in confirmation of the "word that Yhwh swore to your *fathers*, to Abraham, Isaac, and Jacob" (9:5c). On the other hand, 9:27 records Moses' intercessory pleas to Yhwh after Israel's sins in the wilderness, where he recalls Yhwh's faithfulness to the patriarchs in order to summon his mercy: "Remember your *servants*, Abraham, Isaac, and Jacob" (Deut 9:27a; cf. Exod 32:13).[195] The difference in titles between Deut 9:27 and 34:4 can thus be attributed to the generic difference between Moses' public speech to Israel and his private speech with Yhwh.[196] While Moses' references to the "fathers" serve as a homiletical device to stress Israel's solidarity with its ancestors, this tactic is unnecessary in his personal conversations with Yhwh. Since Deut 34:4 functions similarly to Deut 9:27 in recording private speech between Yhwh and Moses, the land-promise formula in Deut 34:4 probably arises from a Deuteronomic source.

Deut 34:4 represents the last of 19 instances of Yhwh's formulaic promise of land to the "fathers." In contrast to the first instance in 1:8, however, where Moses had confidently exhorted Israel to approach the land in order to possess it, the last instance of the land-promise formula in 34:4 records a bittersweet viewing of the land by one who will forever stand outside it. Most poignantly, Moses has once again been denied entrance into the land, and the very same formula with which he had repeatedly exhorted Israel is used in the description. He then dies on the mountain "at Yhwh's command" (34:5; cf. 32:48–50), finally fulfilling the various predictions of his demise that have been heard since the beginning of the book.[197] Though Moses embodies the consequences of those who disobey Yhwh and thus cannot enter the land,[198] the reference to the patriarchs in 34:4 indicates that the ancient promises are still on the verge of fulfillment. Thus a comparison of Deut 34:4 with the terminology of the patriarchal narratives of promise becomes necessary.

Lexical Analysis of Deuteronomy 34:4 from a Tetrateuchal Perspective

In Deut 34:4, the reference to Yhwh's oath of land to Abraham, Isaac, and Jacob raises the question of which narrative traditions Deuteronomy

---

195. The vassal terminology of עבד in Deut 9:27 is especially appropriate in light of Moses' pleas for Yhwh to remember his covenant (cf. E. Carpenter, "עבד," *NIDOTTE* 3:304–9).

196. The generic differences between Deut 9:5 and 9:27 are overlooked by Römer, *Israels Väter*, 256–65.

197. Deut 1:37; 3:23–28; 4:21–33; 31:2, 14, 16, 29; 32:48–52.

198. Olson (*Deuteronomy and the Death of Moses*, 165) traces the thematic connections between Moses' death due to disobedience and the similar threat of destruction for Israel in Deut 1:37; 3:26; 4:21.

has in mind. Here as elsewhere, the formulaic brevity of the references to the "fathers," without any narrative elaboration or explanation, suggests that Deuteronomy draws on traditions that its audience knows, both in its intratextual narrative world and in its extratextual setting. The use of לאמר in introducing Yhwh's words reinforces the likelihood that Deut 34:4 cites known texts.[199]

The specific wording of the land-promise formula in Deut 34:4 recalls several tetrateuchal passages. First, Deut 34:4 exhibits lexical parallels to Yhwh's first promise to Abraham (Gen 12:7) and its identical reiteration later (Gen 24:7):

Deut 34:4:   הָאָרֶץ אֲשֶׁר נִשְׁבַּעְתִּי [to the patriarchs] לֵאמֹר לְזַרְעֲךָ אֶתְּנֶנָּה
Gen 12:7:   לְזַרְעֲךָ אֶתֵּן אֶת־הָאָרֶץ הַזֹּאת
Gen 24:7:   לְזַרְעֲךָ אֶתֵּן אֶת־הָאָרֶץ הַזֹּאת

The intentionality of the lexical parallel between Deut 34:4 and the Genesis passages is reinforced by the grammatical awkwardness of referring to descendants with a singular-possessive suffix (לזרעך) despite plural patriarchs (i.e., Abraham, Isaac, and Jacob).[200]

Gen 13:14 provides a second possible intertext for Deut 34:4. In Genesis 13, Yhwh's command for Abraham to scrutinize the boundaries of the land mirrors Yhwh's instructions to Moses before his death in Deuteronomy 34.[201] In the land-promise formula itself, the use of נתן plus 3fs suffix (i.e., אתננה) matches the grammatical form found in Deut 34:4 even more closely than Gen 12:7.[202] In fact, the numerous similarities between Gen 13:14–15 and Deut 34:4 create a striking contrast between Abraham and Moses, for the former "passes through" (עבר; Gen 12:6) the land and walks around in it (Gen 13:17) in a way forbidden to the latter (לא תעבר; Deut 34:4).[203] Abraham experiences a measure of fulfillment of Yhwh's promise that Moses never will, thereby intensifying Moses' tragedy.[204]

---

199. García López, "Deut 34," 55; Römer, *Israels Väter*, 254. Compare with Sonnet (*Book within the Book*, 204–15), who detects numerous echoes of patriarchal death narratives in the entire unit of Deuteronomy 31–34.

200. The LXX, some Syr. manuscripts, and some targums change the MT reading to a plural-possessive suffix—i.e., "to your [pl.] seed/sons." Wevers (*Notes on the Greek Text*, 558) and C. McCarthy (*BHQ*, 168) rightly dismiss these readings as secondary.

201. Frevel, "Ein vielsagender Abschied," 230; García López, "Deut 34," 55; Weinfeld, *Promise of the Land*, 69 n. 41. In contrast to Genesis 13, Genesis 15 describes the land gift using only two landmarks rather than four: "from the river of Egypt as far as the great river, the river Euphrates" (Gen 15:18b). The Genesis 13 passage also links the possession of such a vast land to the promise of innumerable progeny, a cluster of theological ideas in Deuteronomy that I explore in chap. 5.

202. The phrase לזרעך אתננה (Gen 13:14; Deut 34:4) appears elsewhere only in Exod 33:1.

203. D. J. Wiseman ("Abraham in History and Tradition, Part I: Abraham the Hebrew," *BSac* 134 [1977] 126) notes that Abraham's traversal of the land denotes his "acting as one who already held title to it."

204. Sonnet, *Book within the Book*, 218–23; García López, "Deut 34," 55.

Third, the reference in Deut 34:4 to Yhwh's "swearing" (נשבע) an oath recalls the reiteration of Yhwh's promise to Abraham (Gen 24:7), Isaac (Gen 26:3), and Joseph (Gen 50:24). These passages use oath terminology to refer back to the divine promises already given in Genesis 12, 15, and 17. Since the original promises lack the terminology of "oath," it is noteworthy that the language of "oath" typically appears in references to existing promises rather than being the performative language of oath-making itself.[205]

The cumulative force of these lexical parallels indicates that Deut 34:4 is citing or alluding to a multiplicity of promise narratives in Genesis, most prominently Gen 12:7 and 13:14–17. Within both the Tetrateuch and Deuteronomy 34, the extension of a promise's recipients from Abraham (Gen 12:7; 13:14) to all three patriarchs (Gen 17:8; 26:3; 28:4; 35:12; 48:21) as well as Joseph (Gen 50:24) is consistent with our previous observations on corporate solidarity in the gift of land. The land promise to the patriarchs also appears frequently in the exodus and wilderness narratives (Exod 6:8; 13:5, 11; 32:13; 33:1; Lev 26:42; Num 13:12), indicating that the land-promise formula in Deut 34:4 performs the dual function of concluding both Deuteronomy and the Pentateuch at large. Though the ultimate fulfillment of this promise has been pushed into the future once more (34:4), Deuteronomy can also speak of Yhwh's gift of the land as a present reality (e.g., 4:40) and past event (e.g., 30:20; 34:4). The rhetorical blurring of generational and chronological distinctions is thus an integral component of Deuteronomic land theology.

The crucial place of corporate solidarity in Deuteronomic land theology has significant implications for redaction-critical uses of "Deuteronom(ist)ic" concepts in the patriarchal narratives. In this regard, Genesis 15 provides an especially appropriate subject because of the widespread acknowledgment of Deuteronom(ist)ic land terminology in this chapter.[206] Specifically, Gen 15:7 represents a rare instance in which possession of the

---

205. For the verb נשבע, the frequency of the perfect conjugation in the OT (92×) vis-à-vis the imperfect (11×) underscores its predominant function in referring to past promises. In Genesis, most of the references to an "oath" are in the perfect (Gen 21:31; 22:16; 24:7; 26:3; 50:24), the only exception being Abraham's oath to Abimelech (Gen 21:24). This observation challenges the diachronic tendency to separate oath and covenant language into separate strata without regard for the narrative flow of Genesis, as Anbar does: "Genesis 15," 50.

206. E.g., Noort, "Land," 129–43; Blenkinsopp, *Pentateuch*, 122–24; Ha, *Genesis 15*; Anbar, "Genesis 15," 39–55; J. A. Emerton, "The Origin of the Promises to the Patriarchs in the Older Sources of the Book of Genesis," *VT* 32 (1982) 14–32; R. Rendtorff, "Genesis 15 im Rahmen der theologischen Bearbeitung der Vätergeschichten," in *Werken und Wirken des Alten Testaments: Festschrift für Claus Westermann zum 70. Geburtstag* (ed. R. Albertz et al.; Göttingen: Vandenhoeck & Ruprecht, 1980) 74–81; H. H. Schmid, *Der sogenannte Jahwist: Beobachtungen und Fragen zur Pentateuchforschung* (Zurich: Theologischer Verlag, 1976) 121–27; J. Van Seters, *Abraham in History and Tradition* (New Haven, CT: Yale University Press, 1975) 268–69; L. Perlitt, *Bundestheologie im alten Testament* (WMANT 36; Neukirchen-Vluyn: Neukirchener Verlag, 1969) 68–77; Plöger, *Literarkritische, formgeschichtliche*

land is promised to a patriarch himself using the common Deuteronomic verb ירש.[207] Yhwh declares that Abram's exodus (יצא Hiphil) from Ur to Canaan occurred in order "to give you this land to possess [ירש] it" (Gen 15:7). In a similar reiteration of this promise, Isaac blesses Jacob and his descendants, "that you may possess [ירש] the land of your sojournings, which God gave to Abraham" (Gen 28:4). Gen 15:7 and 28:4 thus provide the only instances in Genesis where a patriarch is himself promised "possession" (ירש) of the land. More commonly, Genesis passages use the language of "gift" (נתן) in identifying the recipients of the land as "you" (Gen 13:17), "you and your seed" (Gen 13:15; 17:8; 26:3; 28:4), or only "your seed" (Gen 12:7; 15:18; 24:7; 26:4; 48:4).

As for Deuteronomy, Genesis's varying recipients of the land possession/gift have been viewed as evidence of redactional development, albeit in contrary ways. On the one hand, Rendtorff argues that the gift of land to Abraham alone represents the most abbreviated and therefore earliest conception of the land promise.[208] The land promise was subsequently applied to Abraham's immediate descendants and combined with other covenant promises in becoming a blessing for all humanity.[209] On the other hand, Gosse and Römer follow Van Seters in holding that the Deuteronomistic redaction of the patriarchal narratives originally described the possession of the land as a conditional gift to the exodus generation. The extension of the land promise as an unconditional gift to the patriarchs arose later, either in a Priestly redaction[210] or by the final compiler of the Pentateuch.[211] Though these redaction-critical proposals differ greatly, both schools assert that possession of the land by the patriarchs is an anachronism that must be explained away by redaction criticism.[212] The language of "possession" in Genesis is therefore assigned to a Deuteronom(ist)ic interpolation.

However, the appearances and forms of the land formulas in Deuteronomy have suggested that the gift and possession of land should not be strictly assigned to one group of recipients or another, whether "fathers" or "seed." The principle of corporate solidarity means that the identities and actions of individuals can be attributed to the group, and vice versa, thus raising the possibility of intentional anachronism and historical conflation

---

und stilkritische Untersuchungen, 65; O. Kaiser, "Traditionsgeschichtliche Untersuchung von Genesis 15," *ZAW* 70 (1958) 107–26.

207. The root ירש appears 71× in Deuteronomy in various forms. The ל + Qal infinitive construction in Gen 15:7 is common in Deuteronomy (31×).
208. Rendtorff, *Problem of the Process*, 60–61.
209. Rendtorff, *Problem of the Process*, 74–77.
210. Gosse, "Le don de la terre dans le livre de la Genèse," 290–92.
211. Römer, *Israels Väter*, 41, 254; Van Seters, "Confessional Reformulation," 457–59.
212. See the comparison of Van Seters's and Rendtorff's views on the land oath by Boorer (*Promise of the Land as Oath*, 77–99), who also uses the development of the land-oath formula as a tool for redaction criticism.

with regard to who actually possessed the land promised by Yhwh.[213] As in Deut 1:8 and other places in Deuteronomy, the specification of Abraham (Gen 13:17; 15:7) or Jacob (Gen 28:4) as a recipient of the land may therefore have reflected the Deuteronomic vision of speaking of the "fathers" as possessors of the land, when it was actually their descendants who possessed it. Similarly, the references to their descendants alone are not to be pitted against the references to the patriarchs, because Israel's descendants are vicariously present in receiving the oath that Yhwh swore to the patriarchs.

Conclusion

This study of the final form of Deuteronomy and a few tetrateuchal passages has revealed the remarkable diversity in the relationship between the land and the "fathers" in Deuteronomy. The recipients of the land promise modulate between the "fathers," "their seed," the "fathers" and "their seed," and the patriarchs who may or may not be named as "fathers." The rhetorical conflation of Israel's generations reveals that Deuteronomy conceives of a single people of God across all eras, thereby challenging the viability of exploiting the variable recipients or scope of the promises in the Pentateuch as criteria for detecting redactional seams. The distinctly theological vision of land and people preserved in the final form of Deuteronomy possesses an irreducible sophistication and literary unity that resists diachronic proposals for fragmenting the text. Moreover, the dialectic between Israel's "fathers" and the present generation at Moab empowers Deuteronomy's summons to *"an act of corporate, imaginative remembrance as the insights of the past are brought to bear on the decisions of the present and future."*[214] Though entering the land promised to the "fathers" was forestalled once by disobedience (Deuteronomy 1), the renewal of the covenant at Moab means that Israel now stands on the verge of fulfilling Yhwh's ancient promise (Deuteronomy 34). Thus the omnipresent promise of land to the ancestors as well as present and future generations of Israel bridges the gap between promise and fulfillment in the narrative trajectory of Deuteronomy.

---

213. The possibility of anachronism in the possessors of the land could refine the interpretation offered above for the land-promise formula in Deut 30:5, where the "fathers" are said to possess the land. Though Römer (*Israels Väter*, 36–42) is probably correct in arguing that the "fathers" here refer to the conquest generation, the anachronisms enabled by the Deuteronomic vision of corporate solidarity mean that the "fathers" could also be any generation of Israel's past, not just the generation that actually possessed the land.

214. Millar, "Living at the Place of Decision," 42, italics original.

Part 2

The "God of the Fathers" and the Divine Promises in Deuteronomy

Chapter 4

The "God of the Fathers" and the Divine Promises in Deuteronomy:
History of Research and Method

Deuteronomy's portrayal of the corporate solidarity of Israel across generations is reinforced by strategically located references to the "God of the fathers," one of several epithets that appears in apposition to the divine name Yhwh. Much like references to the recipients of the land promise, which oscillate between "you" and "your fathers," thereby merging Israel's generational horizons, references in Deuteronomy to the appositives of the Tetragrammaton vary between "my/our/your/his God"[1] and "God of the fathers" in order to emphasize Yhwh's sovereignty over past, present, and future eras of Israel's history. The same Yhwh thus superintends the entire trajectory from the making of promises to the patriarchs to their fulfillment for Israel.

However, the timeless unity of God's people and the singularity of Yhwh (cf. 6:4) need not eventuate in the notion of mono-Yahwism whereby Israel must worship at a centralized sanctuary.[2] The analysis of Deuteronomy's eight references to the "God of the fathers"[3] will instead reveal that Deuteronomy portrays Yhwh as both a personal and cosmic god.[4] On the one

---
1. Since English does not differentiate between second-person singular and plural pronouns, I will use "you/your" to indicate both singular and plural forms while distinguishing between them in brackets (e.g., [sg.] or [pl.]) when necessary. Of the 279 total instances of the appositives "your [sg.] God" and "your [pl.] God" in Deuteronomy, the vast majority are singular (234x) rather than plural (45x).
2. The logic of "oneness" across deity, cult, and people is asserted by many. For example, see Philo, *Spec. Laws* 1:67; von Rad, *OT Theology*, 1:227; N. Gottwald, *The Hebrew Bible: A Socio-literary Introduction* (Philadelphia: Fortress, 1985) 390. Similarly, Josephus (*Ant.* 4.201; *Ag. Ap.* 2.193), Driver (*Deuteronomy*, 138–9), S. L. McKenzie (*Covenant* [St. Louis, MO: Chalice, 2000] 127–28), and P. D. Miller (*The Religion of Ancient Israel* [Louisville: Westminster John Knox, 2000] 79) link monotheism with centralization of worship but without inferring that Israel is a single people across generations.
3. Deut 1:11, 21; 4:1; 6:3; 12:1; 26:7; 27:3; 29:24[25].
4. H. Vorländer (*Mein Gott: Die Vorstellungen vom persönlichen Gott im Alten Orient und im Alten Testament* [AOAT 23; Kevelaer: Butzon & Bercker, 1975] 3) provides a useful definition of the ANE notion of the personal god:

> Unter dem Begriff 'persönlicher Gott' ist im folgenden die Funktion einer Gottheit zu verstehen, zu einem Individuum und dessen Familie in einer dauernden, engen

hand, YHWH is portrayed as a personal deity who travels with his people on their journey to the land (e.g., 1:21; 4:1; 6:3).⁵ On the other hand, YHWH is described as a cosmic deity whom Israel is directed to worship in a designated place (e.g., 12:1), though not necessarily a centralized sanctuary (e.g., 27:3).⁶ Deuteronomy's use of the epithet "God of the fathers" can denote both immanent and transcendent aspects of YHWH's locality,⁷ as well as blur the usual ANE distinctions between family and state religion.⁸ This characterization of deity also challenges the common view that Deuteronomy prescribed a radical program of centralization in Israel's worship during the 7th century B.C.E.⁹ The Deuteronomic references to the "God of the fathers" thus provide a broad theological foundation for overcoming some unnecessary dichotomies in the portrayal of Israel's deity.¹⁰

Beziehung als sein spezieller Gott zu stehen. 'Persönlich' wird hier also nicht im Sinne von 'personhaft' verwendet, sondern meint die persönliche Zugehörigkeit eines Menschen zu einer bestimmten Gottheit.

In contrast to a personal deity, a cosmic deity would be one of the creator deities of the Semitic pantheon such as El, Aššur, or Marduk.

5. The "God of the fathers" accompanies Israel through its journeys to Horeb (1:11), Kadesh (1:21), and Moab while anticipating life in the land (4:1; 6:3; 12:1).

6. Deut 12:1 invokes the "God of the fathers" in the context of commanding Israel's worship at the "place that YHWH your God shall choose" (12:5, etc.), while 27:3 commands Israel's cultic observance at Ebal, on the fringes of the land of promise. The theological significance of worshiping the "God of the fathers" at such a liminal place is argued in my examination of Deut 27:3 on pp. 138–143 below.

7. Following a trajectory set by von Rad ("Deuteronomy's 'Name' Theology," 37–44; compare the discussion in McConville, *Deuteronomy*, 442–43), the contrastive pair *transcendent* and *immanent* in Deuteronomy studies has denoted the various modes of God's cultic presence with Israel. This usage in Deuteronomy scholarship contrasts with scholars' usage in Continental philosophy and other disciplines to refer to the possibilities and limitations of human knowledge.

For von Rad, the Priestly document conceives of YHWH's actual presence in the ark and temple as the concrete כבוד ("glory") on earth, whereas Deuteronomy locates YHWH's presence in heaven, with only his abstract שם ("name") remaining on earth. Thus the terms *immanent* and *transcendent* often serve as shorthand for Priestly "glory" theology and Deuteronomic "name" theology, respectively. This dichotomy between modes of divine presence is analyzed in chap 5.

8. See the comparison of family and state religion in J. H. Walton, *Ancient Near Eastern Thought and the Old Testament* (Grand Rapids, MI: Baker, 2006) 135–61; Miller, *Religion of Ancient Israel*, 62–105. While the role of Deuteronomic theology in mediating between family and state religion has been observed by R. Albertz (*A History of Israelite Religion in the Old Testament Period* [trans. J. Bowden; 2 vols.; OTL; Louisville: Westminster John Knox, 1994] 224–31), he argues from his historical-critical framework of Israelite religion rather than from an analysis of the relevant Deuteronomic texts.

9. Following Wellhausen (*Prolegomena*, 32–34), the hypothesis of Israel's centralization of worship has been most influentially advanced by Weinfeld, *Deuteronomy and the Deuteronomic School*. Weinfeld also argues that secularization and demythologization of Israel's worship represent the natural consequences of Deuteronomy's call for centralization. See the survey of research in Vogt, *Deuteronomic Theology*, 1–97.

10. J. G. McConville (*Grace in the End: A Study in Deuteronomic Theology* [Grand Rapids, MI: Zondervan, 1994]) observes that historical-critical views on Deuteronomy are of-

Terminology for Israel's God in Deuteronomy and the Old Testament

Deuteronomy stands at the crucial junction between the Pentateuch and the Deuteronomistic History, not only in narrative and canonical sequence but also theologically and in the history of interpretation. Even as the older consensus regarding the documentary hypothesis has come under criticism, Wilhelm De Wette's dating of Deuteronomy or some significant portion of the book to the time of Josiah's reforms has remained nearly unanimous in OT scholarship.[11] Despite Deuteronomy's central role in reconstructing pentateuchal origins, however, scholarly discussions about Deuteronomy itself have remained largely divorced from two seminal issues in pentateuchal criticism: (1) conflicting accounts of the revelation of the Tetragrammaton Y<small>HWH</small> and (2) the variation in divine names. Julius Wellhausen and Albrecht Alt staked their historical-critical theories on the variation in divine names in the Tetrateuch, mainly in Genesis, while simultaneously relegating Deuteronomy to the fringes of the discussion.[12] Martin Noth subsequently widened the gap between Deuteronomy and the Tetrateuch through his thesis that most of the book originally served as a theological introduction to the Deuteronomistic History (i.e., Joshua–Kings) rather than as the conclusion to the Pentateuch.[13] In the survey of interpretation that follows, I suggest that Deuteronomy's use of divine epithets in general and the "God of the fathers" in particular exhibits closer theological links to the Tetrateuch than to the Deuteronomistic History and Writings. The similarities between Deuteronomy and the Tetrateuch in their use of divine epithets invite an intertextual analysis of the "God of the fathers" within the Pentateuch.

The Divine Name and the "God of the Fathers" in Deuteronomy

In Deuteronomy, the 550 occurrences of the Tetragrammaton are the primary identifier for Israel's God.[14] The divine name Y<small>HWH</small> stands alone

---

ten predicated on the putative inabilities of theological polarities to coexist in the same document (e.g., grace vs. law, unconditionality vs. conditionality, transcendence vs. immanence).

11. The implications of a 7th-century B.C.E. dating of Deuteronomy or some portion thereof for pentateuchal criticism are discussed by G. J. Wenham, "The Date of Deuteronomy: Linch-Pin of Old Testament Criticism, Part One," *Them* 10 (1985) 15–20; idem, "The Date of Deuteronomy: Linch-Pin of Old Testament Criticism, Part Two," *Them* 11 (1985) 15–18. Since Wenham's treatment, however, a minority of scholars have argued for an exilic or postexilic date for Deuteronomy (see p. 1 n. 2 above).

12. Wellhausen, *Prolegomena*, 6–8; A. Alt, "The God of the Fathers," in *Essays on Old Testament History and Religion* (trans. R. A. Wilson; Garden City, NY: Doubleday, 1967) 3–38.

13. Noth, *Deuteronomistic History*.

14. The epithet אל and other אל compounds occur only 13x in Deuteronomy: אל קנא ("a jealous God"; 4:24; 5:9; 6:15), אל רחום ("a compassionate God"; 4:31), האל הנאמן ("the

in 234 of these occurrences (42%), whereas appositive phrases with Yнwн occur 316 times (58%).[15] By decreasing frequency of occurrence, the appositives for Yнwн are "your [sg.] God" (234x), "your [pl.] God" (45x), "our God" (22x), "God of your [sg.] fathers" (4x), "my God" (4x), "his God" (3x), "God of your [pl.] fathers" (2x), "God of our fathers" (1x), and "God of their fathers" (1x). Most notably among these, the second-person appositives occur a total of 279 times, so that the phrases "Yнwн your [sg.] God" and "Yнwн your [pl.] God" account for more than half (51%) of the Deuteronomic references to the Tetragrammaton. Thus Deuteronomy's most frequent identification of Yнwн is as Israel's God in the narrative present on the plains of Moab. Moses' constant appeals in the name of "Yнwн your God" are consistent with the hortatory thrust of the book.

By contrast, Deuteronomy's infrequent references to the "God of the fathers" point to a distant narrative past when Yнwн made promises to Israel's ancestors. The eight instances of this appositive occur primarily in the introductions or conclusions to different sections of Deuteronomy, pre-

---

faithful God"; 7:9), האל הגדל הגבר הנורא ("the great and mighty and awesome God"; 10:17), אל אמונה ("a faithful God"; 32:4), אל ישרון ("the God of Jeshurun"; 33:26), and אל without any descriptors (3:24; 7:21; 32:12, 18, 21). The Tetragrammaton always appears in the literary context of these אל compounds, thereby indicating that expressions such as אל אמונה are adjectival descriptions of Yнwн (i.e., "a faithful God") rather than proper names referring to the head of the Ugaritic pantheon (i.e., "the faithful El"). R. Rendtorff rightly criticizes the tendency to exaggerate the parallels between the OT's use of אל and the Ugaritic evidence ("'El als israelitische Gottesbezeichnung," *ZAW* 106 [1994] 4–21).

The word אלהים in Deuteronomy is much more common than אל, though the former is typically found in apposition (e.g., 4:31) to the Tetragrammaton. When not in apposition, אלהים appears both as an anarthrous proper noun to refer to God (e.g., 4:32; 5:24, 26) and as an articular form to declare Yнwн's uniqueness as האלהים ("the God"; 4:35, 39). Yнwн's incomparability as האלהים (on which see Rendtorff, "'El als israelitische Gottesbezeichnung," 19) contrasts with Deuteronomy's polemical references to אלהים אחרים ("other gods"), an expression that occurs 17× (5:7; 6:14; 7:4; 8:9; 11:16, 28; 13:3[2], 7[6], 14[13]; 17:3; 18:20; 28:14, 36, 64; 29:25[26]; 31:18, 20).

15. There is slight disagreement on the exact number of appositives to the Tetragrammaton in Deuteronomy. Though J. W. Wevers ("Yahweh and Its Appositives in LXX Deuteronomium," in *Studies in Deuteronomy in Honour of C. J. Labuschagne on the Occasion of His 65th Birthday* [ed. F. García Martínez et al.; VTSup 53; Leiden: Brill, 1994] 269) asserts that the Tetragrammaton occurs 561× in Deuteronomy, his calculations are probably incorrect since his figures for nonappositive (233×) and appositive (319×) occurrences of Yнwн do not add up to his total figure (561×).

On a related note, translations and scholars have long differed over whether יהוה אלהינו in the *Shemaʿ* (6:4) should be rendered appositively (i.e., "Yнwн our God" [LXX, NJPS]) or as a verbless clause (i.e., "Yнwн is our God" [NASB, NIV]). The figure of 316 appositives given here reflects the decision to render יהוה אלהינו in the *Shemaʿ* as a verbless clause. For an overview of the possible renderings and a case for translating the first colon in the *Shemaʿ* as a verbless clause, see Block, "Deuteronomy 6:4–5," 193–212. Cf. R. W. L. Moberly ("Yahweh Is One: The Translation of the Shema," in *Studies in Deuteronomy in Honour of C. J. Labuschagne on the Occasion of His 65th Birthday* [ed. F. García Martínez et al.; VTSup 53; Leiden: Brill, 1994] 209–15), who opts for the appositive rendering.

cisely where scholars have often argued for redactional seams.[16] Whether or not diachronic reconstructions of this sort are justified, the relative paucity of references to the "God of the fathers" coupled with their strategic location strongly suggest that they perform a significant function in Deuteronomy. Each invocation of the "God of the fathers" provides a rhetorical climax that highlights the essential continuity in Yhwh's dealings with his people from the patriarchal era to the present time in Moab.

Another rhetorically significant feature of the "God of the fathers" title arises because of its frequent collocation with the phrase "just as he promised you" (1:11, 21; 6:3).[17] Since the promises of land and multiplication are cited without further elaboration, the use of the promise formula likely presumes the audience's awareness of prior promises made to the "fathers."[18] The frequent juxtaposition of the appositives "God of the fathers" and "your God" indicates that a significant stage of redemptive history has now arrived for Israel in Moab, for the promises first given to the patriarchs and reiterated to Israel in Egypt are about to be fulfilled in Deuteronomy's narrative world.

The Divine Name and the "God of the Father(s)" in the Tetrateuch

Though analysis of the Tetragrammaton and its appositives in Deuteronomy will be relatively straightforward, the situation in the Tetrateuch is more complex. The exegetical difficulties in the revelation of the Tetragrammaton and the variation of divine epithets were significant factors in the rise of literary and tradition criticism of the Tetrateuch. However, I argue that literary- and tradition-critical proposals alone cannot yield a satisfactory account for the Tetrateuch's variations in divine epithets. A close reading of the "God of the father(s)" texts of Genesis and Exodus in light of their ANE background suggests that, regardless of when the Tetragrammaton was first known among God's people, the functional significance of the divine name was progressively unfolded over the course of Yhwh's dealings with Israel. Even granting the likelihood of different sources behind the final form of the Pentateuch, all these sources still manifest an indissoluble theological link between the Tetragrammaton and the covenantally

---

16. For example, J. Wellhausen (*Die Composition des Hexateuchs und der historischen Bücher des Alten Testaments* [4th ed.; Berlin: de Gruyter, 1963] 191–93) argued influentially that Deut 12:1, which contains a reference to the "God of the fathers," introduces *Urdeuteronomium*, the original lawbook of Josiah found in Deuteronomy 12–26.

17. J. Milgrom ("Profane Slaughter and a Formulaic Key to the Composition of Deuteronomy," *HUCA* 47 [1976] 3–4) notes that formulaic אשר clauses of promise fulfillment (i.e., "just as he promised [דבר] you"; "just as he swore [נשבע] to you") and Torah promulgation (i.e., "just as he commanded [צוה] you") occur 32× in Deuteronomy.

18. Lohfink, *Väter*, 86–99; cf. Skweres, *Rückverweise*; Milgrom, "Profane Slaughter," 1–17.

motivated deeds associated with it. Thus a theological approach to the divine name is necessary to explain the variation in divine epithets.

These observations about the Tetrateuch will be confirmed through the detailed analysis of Deuteronomic references to the "God of the fathers." Though scholars have tended to bracket out Deuteronomy's use of divine epithets in historical-critical discussions of the Tetrateuch, the book's references to the "God of the fathers" are quite relevant to the tetrateuchal discussion. The book of Deuteronomy stands at the diachronic junction between the purported JE and P sources both in the classical documentary hypothesis[19] and in the newer view that the patriarchal narratives postdate Deuteronomy.[20] Though a previous generation of scholars saw few connections between Deuteronomy and the Tetrateuch, more recent studies have recognized that the presence of Deuteronom(ist)ic elements in the Tetrateuch (e.g., Gen 26:5; Exod 12:24–27) necessitates a reassessment of the extent of Deuteronom(ist)ic reworking in the Tetrateuch.[21]

Divine Names and Literary-Critical Approaches to the Tetrateuch

The revelation of the divine name has played a significant role in literary criticism of the OT.[22] Following an early suggestion of Jean Astruc, Wellhausen and other higher critics used the variations between the divine names Yhwh and Elohim to identify literary strands in the Tetrateuch. On the one hand, Exodus 6 records Yhwh's declaration to Moses that "I appeared to Abraham, Isaac, and Jacob as El-Shaddai, but by my name Yhwh, I did not make myself known to them" (Exod 6:3). On the other hand, the J strand referred to Israel's deity as Yhwh from primeval times, when "men began to

---

19. Wellhausen, *Prolegomena*, 6–10.
20. Van Seters, "Deuteronomy," 947–56; cf. idem, "Confessional Reformulation," 448–59.
21. E.g., J. Blenkinsopp, "Deuteronomic Elements to the Narrative in Genesis–Numbers: A Test Case," in *Those Elusive Deuteronomists: The Phenomenon of Pan-Deuteronomism* (ed. L. S. Schearing and S. L. McKenzie; JSOTSup 268; Sheffield: Sheffield Academic Press, 1999) 84–115; M. Vervenne, "The Question of 'Deuteronomic' Elements in Genesis to Numbers," in *Studies in Deuteronomy in Honour of C. J. Labuschagne on the Occasion of His 65th Birthday* (ed. F. García Martínez et al.; VTSup 53; Leiden: Brill, 1994) 243–68; J. Van Seters, "The So-called Deuteronomistic Redaction of the Pentateuch," in *Congress Volume: Leuven 1989* (ed. J. A. Emerton; VTSup 43; Leiden: Brill, 1991) 58–77; C. Brekelmans, "Die sogenannten deuteronomischen Elemente in Genesis bis Numeri: Ein Beitrag zur Vorgeschichte des Deuteronomiums," in *Volume du Congrès: Genève, 1965* (ed. G. W. Anderson; VTSup 15; Leiden: Brill, 1966) 90–96.
22. See the survey of pentateuchal criticism in A. de Pury and T. C. Römer, "Le Pentateuque en Question: Position du Problème et Brève Histoire de la Recherche," in *Le Pentateuque en Question* (ed. A. de Pury and T. C. Römer; Geneva: Labor et Fides, 2002) 9–80. For reasons of scope, here I must omit the debate over the origin of the Tetragrammaton, for which the most extensive surveys can be found in T. N. D. Mettinger, *In Search of God: The Meaning and Message of the Everlasting Names* (trans. F. H. Cryer; Philadelphia: Fortress, 1988) 14–40; and G. H. Parke-Taylor, *Yahweh: The Divine Name in the Bible* (Waterloo, ON: Wilfrid Laurier University Press, 1975) 1–62.

call upon the name of Yʜᴡʜ" (Gen 4:26). There seemed to be a basic contradiction about when the divine name Yʜᴡʜ was introduced to God's people, because Exod 6:3 indicates that the Tetragrammaton was only revealed to Moses, whereas Gen 4:26 asserts that the same name was known to the ancients. Thus tetrateuchal passages that used the name Yʜᴡʜ were classified as Yahwist (J) traditions, whereas passages that favored Elohim over Yʜᴡʜ were classified as Elohist (E) traditions.

Higher critics subsequently realized that their account of the E traditions still contained narrative doublets, most notably the dual accounts of Moses' call in Exodus 3 and 6. Since narrative doublets were considered evidence of multiple sources, the E traditions were further divided into separate traditions that both used Elohim to refer to Israel's deity. The second call narrative of Exodus 6 was slotted in the exilic period with the Priestly source (P), owing to ostensibly Priestly features such as genealogy (Exod 6:14–27) and the assertion that El-Shaddai was the God of the patriarchs (cf. Gen 17:1, another P passage).[23] In turn, the first call narrative of Exodus 3 was classified as E, which had been joined with J at an early stage of Israel's history to form a combined JE source. The twin criteria of narrative doublets and variation of the divine name were thus central to source-critical logic in positing three literary sources behind the Tetrateuch.[24] Though all three sources agreed that the Tetragrammaton was used nearly exclusively to refer to God after the second call of Moses (Exodus 6), higher critics held that variations in the divine name still furnished a reliable criterion for identifying source-critical strands in Genesis and the early chapters of Exodus.

In light of this literary-critical consensus, the book of Deuteronomy furnished the chronological anchor for Wellhausen's documentary hypothesis. Wellhausen employed De Wette's 7th-century ʙ.ᴄ.ᴇ. dating of Deuteronomy as the fulcrum for dividing the Tetrateuch into predeuteronomic and postdeuteronomic phases of Israel's history. Thus the decentralized worship of the JE sources dated from the 10th and 9th centuries ʙ.ᴄ.ᴇ., before the call for centralized worship in the D source from the 7th century ʙ.ᴄ.ᴇ. The centralized worship described in the P source presupposed that Deuteronomy's summons to a central sanctuary had already happened, thereby necessitating a date in the 6th century ʙ.ᴄ.ᴇ. For the purposes of this study, the most important feature of Wellhausen's JEDP chronology is his sharp dichotomy between the clan-based worship of the patriarchal era (JE) and the cult-based religion of the Mosaic period (DP).[25] In order for

---

23. However, El-Shaddai also appears in non-P passages such as Gen 43:13 and 49:25. The tradition-critical implications of this observation will be explored below.

24. C. Seitz, "The Call of Moses and the 'Revelation' of the Divine Name: Source-Critical Logic and Its Legacy," in *Theological Exegesis: Essays in Honor of Brevard S. Childs* (ed. C. Seitz and K. Greene-McCreight; Grand Rapids, MI: Eerdmans, 1999) 145–46.

25. Wellhausen (*Prolegomena*, 76–82) draws a revealing contrast between the intimate, earthy worship of the patriarchs (JE) and the fixed, legalistic religion of the late monarchy (D) and exile (P). His disdain for institutional religion (i.e., D and P) is evident when he

Wellhausen's schema to work, one must drive a theological wedge between the depictions of Israel's deity in Genesis and Deuteronomy, even though the title "God of the father(s)" is attributed to Y<small>HWH</small> in both books.[26]

Divine Names and Tradition-Critical Approaches to the Tetrateuch

Subsequently on the tradition-critical front, Alt attempted to advance beyond literary-critical approaches to the text by exploring the nature of patriarchal religion during the pre-written, oral stages of Israel's traditions. Though acknowledging that the final form of the Pentateuch asserts that Y<small>HWH</small> was worshiped by both the patriarchs and the Israelites, Alt detected two vestiges of primitive Israelite religion through the references in Genesis to El deities and the "God of the father(s)." First, Alt argued that the various El epithets are appellatives for distinct numina known as *Elim*, who are characterized by "their localization at a holy place in Palestine."[27] According to Alt, Abraham worshiped El-Elyon in Jerusalem (Gen 14:19); Hagar worshiped El-Roi at Beer-Lahai-Roi (Gen 16:13); and Isaac followed Abraham in worshiping El-Olam at Beersheba (Gen 21:33). Jacob worshiped several deities, including El-Bethel at Bethel (Gen 31:13; 35:7) and El-Elohe-Israel at Shechem (Gen 33:20).[28] However, the deity El-Shaddai is somewhat different from the other *Elim* for having appeared to multiple patriarchs in multiple places.[29]

Second, and of greater interest to Alt, the eponymous deities known as the "God of Abraham" (Gen 31:42, 53), the "Fear of Isaac" (Gen 31:42), and the "Mighty One of Jacob" (Gen 49:24)[30] were viewed as personal gods of the patriarchs who accompanied the patriarchs on their journeys and were not to be tied to a specific location. These personal gods represented the oldest religious traditions that were brought by the nomadic patriarchs to

---

describes the P source as "the Judaising tendency to remove God to a distance from man" p. 79).

26. The epithet "God of the father(s)" appears 8× in Genesis (26:24; 28:13; 31:42, 53; 32:10; 46:3; 49:25; 50:17). In these 8 passages, the divine name Y<small>HWH</small> occurs 3× in proximity to the "God of the father(s)" in passages commonly attributed to the J source (Gen 26:24; 28:13; 32:10).

27. Alt, "God of the Fathers," 11.

28. The book of Judges also refers to Israel's ancient worship of El-Berit (Judg 9:46) or Baal-Berit (Judg 9:4) at Shechem.

29. El-Shaddai appears to Abraham (Gen 17:1), Isaac while blessing Jacob (28:3), Jacob in his return to Bethel (35:11), and Jacob in the second commissioning of his sons to buy food in Egypt (43:14). The elderly Jacob in Egypt also recounts to Joseph his encounter with El-Shaddai at Bethel (48:3), as well as invoking El-Shaddai in the final blessing of his sons (49:25).

30. Alt ("God of the Fathers," 32 n. 61) acknowledged that references to the "Mighty One of Jacob" are found in texts such as Isa 49:26; 60:16; Ps 132:2, 5. However, he regarded these texts as a later use of the phrase "Mighty One of Jacob" as a title for Y<small>HWH</small> as the God of Israel.

Canaan, where the family gods were then merged with the fixed local *Elim*. The final tradition-critical stage in the transformation of the itinerant "God of the fathers" into YHWH, Israel's national deity, could be found in Exodus 3 and 6, where YHWH is equated with the "God of Abraham, Isaac, and Jacob" (Exod 3:6, 15), the "God of your father(s)" (Exod 3:6, 13, 15), and El-Shaddai (Exod 6:3).[31] Likewise, Alt averred that the originally disparate genealogies of Abraham, Isaac, and Jacob were artificially joined by the JE redactor through belief in a common deity.[32] The variation between divine epithets thus provided a key criterion for Alt's tradition-critical progression from itinerant to centralized worship, though quite differently from Wellhausen's documentary hypothesis.

Also like Wellhausen, Alt dismissed the relevance of Deuteronomy for any discussion of patriarchal religion. The Deuteronomic references to the "God of the fathers" (i.e., plural) are considered fundamentally different from the Genesis references to the "God of the *father*" (i.e., singular), since only the latter epithet reflects the family-based religion of the patriarchs.[33] Alt's view anticipates the tradition-critical tendency to classify the plural "God of your *fathers*" as a Deuteronom(ist)ic epithet to be compared with the Deuteronomistic History and Chronicles rather than the narratives of Genesis and Exodus.[34] Therefore, it is appropriate to consider briefly the use of this epithet in the Deuteronomistic History and the postexilic literature.

The "God of the Father(s)" in the Deuteronomistic History and the Postexilic Historical Books

Although references to the "God of the father(s)" are rare in the Deuteronomistic History (5×),[35] they are common in the postexilic books of Chronicles (30×) and Ezra (3×).[36] In the Deuteronomistic History, the

---

31. Alt, "God of the Fathers," 15–18.
32. Alt ("God of the Fathers," 38–58) argues for later Yahwism's arrogation of the identities of the Canaanite *Elim* and the Mesopotamian "God of the father" by noting the parallels of patriarchal religion with Nabatean and Palmyrene inscriptions dating from the 1st century B.C.E. to the 4th century C.E. Alt supposed that the transition of the Nabateans from a nomadic to a settled way of life was similar to the Israelites, though dating to a much later time.
33. Alt, "God of the Fathers," 18 n. 32.
34. E.g., Römer, *Israels Väter*, 134–35, 350; cf. G. von Rad, *Das Geschichtsbild des chronistischen Werkes* (BWANT 4; Stuttgart: Kohlhammer, 1930) 7.
35. References to the "God of the fathers" (i.e., plural) occur 4× in the Deuteronomistic History (Josh 18:3; Judg 2:12; 1 Kgs 18:36; 2 Kgs 21:22). Among these, 1 Kgs 18:36 uniquely refers to the "God of Abraham, Isaac, and Israel" without identifying them as "fathers." In contrast to these references to plural "fathers," 2 Kgs 20:5 refers to "YHWH God of David your father" (i.e., singular). This is the only OT occurrence of the phrase "God of David" (אלהי דוד).
36. 1 Chr 5:25; 12:18; 28:9; 29:18, 20; 2 Chr 7:22; 11:16; 13:12, 18; 14:3; 15:12; 17:4; 19:4; 20:6, 33; 21:10; 24:18, 24; 28:6, 9, 25; 29:5; 30:6; 30:7, 19, 22; 33:12; 34:32, 33; 36:15; Ezra 7:27; 8:28; 10:11. In contrast to this list of 33 occurrences, the 29 occurrences given in

ancestral deity is invoked three times in narrative contexts of Israel's idolatry and forsaking of the covenant (Judg 2:12; 1 Kgs 18:36; 2 Kgs 21:11) and once with reference to Yʜᴡʜ's promise of land (Josh 18:3). Since Josh 18:3 also criticizes Israel's reluctance to enter the land promised by the "God of your fathers," every reference in the Deuteronomistic History to the "God of the fathers" possesses a polemical edge. In contrast to the negative tone of the Deuteronomistic History, all but one of the eight invocations of the "God of the fathers" in Deuteronomy are positive, thereby denoting Yʜᴡʜ's imminent fulfillment of his promises of land (1:21; 4:1; 12:1; 27:3) and multiplication (1:11; 6:3). Only Deuteronomy's final reference to the "God of the fathers" assumes a negative tone as Moses warns Israel against forsaking the covenant made with the "God of your fathers" (29:24[25]). Thus the tone and rhetorical function of the references to the "God of the fathers" differ markedly between Deuteronomy and the Deuteronomistic History.[37]

The postexilic corpus also diverges from Deuteronomy in its usage of the "God of the fathers" epithet, albeit in a slightly different way than the Deuteronomistic History. Whereas Deuteronomy invoked the "God of the fathers" in specific contexts where promises first made to the patriarchs and reiterated to the exodus generation are being fulfilled,[38] the books of Chronicles and Ezra refer to "Yʜᴡʜ God of the fathers" more or less synonymously with other epithets such as "Yʜᴡʜ God of Israel" and "Yʜᴡʜ your God."[39] Thus the "fathers" in these passages refer generally to Israel's ancestors rather than any particular generation. In addition, a synoptic comparison of Samuel/Kings and Chronicles reveals that the Chronicler

---

Römer, *Israels Väter*, 345, are missing the single reference to Abraham, Isaac, and Jacob as "our fathers" (1 Chr 29:18) as well as the three references to a singular "God of the father" (1 Chr 28:9; 2 Chr 17:4; 30:6).

37. T. C. Römer ("Deuteronomy in Search of Origins," in *Reconsidering Israel and Judah: Recent Studies on the Deuteronomistic History* [ed. G. N. Knoppers and J. G. McConville; SBTS 8; Winona Lake, IN: Eisenbrauns, 2000] 123–24) downplays this disjunction between Deuteronomy and the Deuteronomistic History by dating Deuteronomy's references to the "God of the fathers" to Dtr², in contrast to his dating of the Deuteronomistic History and Jeremiah mostly to Dtr¹.

38. For example, the "God of the fathers" in Deuteronomy fulfills the promises of multiplication (Deut 1:11) and land (Deut 1:21). Similar connotations of fulfilling covenant promises in the epithet "God of the fathers" can be seen in Exod 3:13, 15–16.

39. S. Japhet, *The Ideology of the Book of Chronicles and Its Place in Biblical Thought* (trans. A. Barber; BFCT 9; Frankfurt am Main: Peter Lang, 1989) 16–17. Japhet notes that, in contrast to Chronicles, Deuteronomy evinces an intentional progression from the simple form "Yʜᴡʜ your God" to the more theological and nuanced epithet "Yʜᴡʜ God of your fathers." This being said, Chronicles may replicate Deuteronomy's strategy of blending past generations of Israel together in the term "fathers." L. C. Allen ("Aspects of Generational Commitment and Challenge in Chronicles," in *The Chronicler as Theologian: Essays in Honor of Ralph W. Klein* [ed. M. P. Graham, S. L. McKenzie, and G. N. Knoppers; JSOTSup 371; New York: T. & T. Clark, 2003] 131–32) observes that the "fathers" in Chronicles can refer to the patriarchs, the exodus generation, or ancestors in general.

occasionally inserts the "God of the fathers" epithet where it was lacking in the parallel passages of Samuel/Kings.[40] The postexilic books also differ from both Deuteronomy and the Deuteronomistic History in their frequent references to the "God of the fathers" as the focus of worship (e.g., Ezra 8:28), the object of spiritual revival (e.g., Ezra 10:11; 2 Chr 14:4; 29:5; 34:33), and the source of help (e.g., 2 Chr 20:6–7; 30:6). Other than the formulaic language used to describe Israel's forsaking of the "God of the fathers,"[41] the Chronicler's use of the "God of the fathers" epithet differs fundamentally from Deuteronomy's, on the one hand, and the Deuteronomistic History's on the other.[42] In conclusion, the suggestion of a direct literary link between the postexilic books and the putatively Dtr² layers of Deuteronomy or the Deuteronomistic History seems unlikely, at least for the "God of the fathers" epithet. Thus the "God of the fathers" texts in Deuteronomy are best treated as a literary continuation of the preceding Tetrateuch rather than using a historical-critical reconstruction of Israel's history.

Method for a Study of the Divine Name and the "God of the Fathers"

While the divine name and its related epithets should be considered in light of the Tetrateuch rather than the Deuteronomistic History and the postexilic literature, the proper method for comparing Deuteronomy's references to the "God of the fathers" with the tetrateuchal narratives requires some discussion in light of the deficiencies of current diachronic approaches. Though detailed assessments of literary and tradition criticism are beyond the purview of this study, two broad lines of critique will be pursued with respect to literary- and tradition-critical accounts of the divine name and the "God of the fathers." First, source critics have frequently reduced the various divine names and epithets to benign lexemes that can be mixed and matched for source-critical purposes without regard for their literary function in the tetrateuchal narrative. Second, the implicit bifurcation posited by tradition critics between family and state religion becomes doubtful when one examines the literary and ANE evidence. Thus a reappraisal of the biblical and ANE data for the "God of the father(s)" will demonstrate how Deuteronomy's references to the Tetragrammaton and the "God of the fathers" bear a closer resemblance to the Tetrateuch than to the Deuteronomistic History and books of Chronicles, as usually held by scholars. As an alternative to literary- and tradition-critical approaches, in the following sections I provide a case for an explicitly theological

---

40. E.g., 1 Chr 5:25 (// 2 Kgs 17:7); 2 Chr 11:16 (// 1 Kgs 12:31).
41. E.g., 2 Chr 7:22; 21:10; 24:18, 24; 28:6, 9, 25; 36:15; cf. Deut 29:24[25]; Judg 2:12.
42. Albertz (*History*, 552) notes that the Chronicler's emphasis on personal piety with regard to the "God of the fathers" recalls the family religion of Genesis rather than the institutional religion of the Deuteronomistic History.

method of treating the Tetragrammaton and the "God of the fathers" in the Pentateuch.

Theological Alternatives to Literary-Critical Proposals for the Tetragrammaton

Though great stock has been placed in the value of the different divine names as a literary-critical criterion,[43] the partitioning of tetrateuchal narratives into J, E, and P sources has been problematic on several counts. First, no convincing explanation has been offered for the fact that the name Yhwh sometimes intrudes into E and P passages,[44] and the name Elohim is likewise found in J passages.[45] Second, the attribution of tetrateuchal passages to a given source has often been unstable. While J has grown by some Anglo-American reckonings,[46] Continental scholars have wrestled with the more fundamental issue of whether it remains meaningful to speak of a distinct J tradition at all, especially if J mirrors P in dating to the exile or later.[47] Third, the criterion of divine names is unusable for much of the Tetrateuch because all the sources consistently use the Tetragrammaton after the second revelation of the divine name to Moses in Exodus 6. The diachronic significance in the shift in divine names, if any, has clearly become a subordinate consideration to the shaping of the narrative in the final form.[48]

---

43. See T. R. Wardlaw, *Conceptualizing Words for God within the Pentateuch: A Cognitive-Semantic Investigation in Literary Context* (LHB/OTS 495; New York: T. & T. Clark, 2008) 169–83; and U. Cassuto, *The Documentary Hypothesis and the Composition of the Pentateuch* (trans. I. Abrahams; Jerusalem: Magnes, 1961) 15–41.

44. Whybray (*Making of the Pentateuch*, 65) lists Gen 5:29; 15:1–6; 17:1; 20:18; 22:1–14; 29:31–30:24; 32:23–32 as passages where the divine epithet used in the narrative contradicts the traditional source analysis.

45. The primary example is the double appellation יהוה אלהים in Gen 2:4b–3:24, a passage traditionally ascribed to J (C. Westermann, *Genesis 1–11: A Commentary* [trans. J. J. Scullion; Minneapolis: Fortress, 1984] 186–90). However, the older attribution of Gen 2:4b–3:24 to J is now challenged by proposals that this passage postdates Gen 1:1–2:4a, which is commonly classified as P (e.g., E. Otto, "Die Paradieserzählung Genesis 2–3: Eine nachpriesterschriftliche Lehrerzählung in ihrem religionshistorischen Kontext," in *"Jedes Ding hat seine Zeit . . .": Studien zur israelitischen und altorientalischen Weisheit. Diethelm Michel zum 65. Geburtstag* [BZAW 241; Berlin: de Gruyter, 1996] 173–89; Blenkinsopp, *Pentateuch*, 60–67).

46. For example, Genesis 20–22 has traditionally been classified as E due to the predominance of the epithet Elohim. However, T. D. Alexander (*Abraham in the Negev: A Source-Critical Investigation of Genesis 20:1–22:19* [Carlisle: Paternoster, 1997]) has demonstrated that Genesis 20–22 not only exhibits several J features, it likely forms the palistrophic conclusion to the Abraham narrative that began in Genesis 12, a text generally acknowledged to be J.

47. T. B. Dozeman and K. Schmid, eds., *A Farewell to the Yahwist? The Composition of the Pentateuch in Recent European Interpretation* (SBLSymS 34; Atlanta: Scholars Press, 2006).

48. C. Seitz, "Call of Moses," 145–61; R. W. L. Moberly, *The Old Testament of the Old Testament* (OBT; Minneapolis: Fortress, 1992) 5–35; G. J. Wenham, "Method in Pentateuchal Source Criticism," *VT* 41 (1991) 85–87; Whybray, *Making of the Pentateuch*, 64.

The third issue of the use of the Tetragrammaton in the putative JE and P narratives after Exodus 6 deserves closer scrutiny, for the shift in divine names from Elohim to YHWH in both these sources potentially presents a theological solution to the puzzle of the divine name. In the larger unit of Exodus 7–14, scholars have observed the recurrence of the so-called "recognition formula" whereby YHWH declares that both Israelites and Egyptians must "know" (עדי) that "I am YHWH."[49] Following Pharaoh's combative pronouncement that "I do not know [עדי] YHWH" (Exod 5:2), the recognition formula occurs eleven times in Exodus 6–14 in order to emphasize that the hardenings of Pharaoh's heart and the escalating plagues against Egypt are divinely designed to bring about humble acknowledgment of YHWH.[50] The audience envisioned by the recognition formula in Exodus 6–14 can be either Egypt or Israel,[51] with Israel continuing as YHWH's sole audience for the recognition formula even after the exodus events.[52] Indeed, the constant repetition of the recognition formula throughout the narrative confirms Eslinger's observation that "liberation is subordinate to the manifestation of the divine name through the miraculous interventions."[53] Irrespective of its underlying sources,[54] the Exodus narrative consistently defines YHWH's name in the *functional* terms of his covenant actions and exercise of power on behalf of Israel.[55] Right knowledge of YHWH thus includes an

---

49. The foundational work is W. Zimmerli, "I Am Yahweh," in *I Am Yahweh* (ed. W. Brueggemann; trans. D. W. Stott; Atlanta: John Knox, 1982) 1–28. Subsequent studies were conducted by L. M. Eslinger, "Knowing Yahweh: Exod 6:3 in the Context of Genesis 1–Exodus 15," in *Literary Structure and Rhetorical Strategies in the Hebrew Bible* (ed. L. J. de Regt, J. de Waard, and J. P. Fokkelman; Assen: Van Gorcum, 1996) 188–98; D. M. Gunn, "The 'Hardening of Pharaoh's Heart': Plot, Character, and Theology in Exodus 1–14," in *Art and Meaning: Rhetoric in Biblical Literature* (ed. D. J. A. Clines, D. M. Gunn, and A. J. Hauser; JSOTSup 19; Sheffield: Sheffield Academic Press, 1982) 72–98; and J. G. Janzen, "What's in a Name? 'Yahweh' in Exodus 3 and the Wider Biblical Context," *Int* 33 (1979) 227–39. J. F. Evans (*An Inner-Biblical Interpretation and Intertextual Reading of Ezekiel's Recognition Formulae with the Book of Exodus* [Th.D. diss.: University of Stellenbosch, 2006]) offers the most recent treatment of the recognition formula.

50. YHWH himself speaks some form of the recognition formula 8x (Exod 6:7; 7:5, 17; 8:22; 9:14; 10:2; 14:4, 18), and Moses speaks it 3x while confronting Pharaoh (Exod 8:10; 9:29; 11:7).

51. Exodus 6–14 identify Pharaoh and Egypt 9x as the audience of the recognition formula (Exod 7:5, 17; 8:10, 22; 9:14, 29; 11:7; 14:4, 18). Israel is named 2x as the target (Exod 6:7; 10:2).

52. Exod 16:6, 12; 29:46 (2x); 31:13.

53. Eslinger, "Knowing Yahweh," 189; cf. idem, "Freedom or Knowledge? Perspective and Purpose in the Exodus Narrative (Exodus 1–15)," *JSOT* 52 (1991) 43–60.

54. The recognition formula in Exodus is assigned alternately to J or P by the commentaries. The source-critical analysis found in the Exodus commentary of B. S. Childs (*The Book of Exodus: A Critical, Theological Commentary* [Philadelphia: Westminster, 1974]) is typical in finding nine P instances (Exod 6:7; 7:5; 14:4, 18; 16:6, 8, 12; 29:46; 31:13) and five J instances (Exod 7:17; 8:10, 22; 9:29; 11:7). See the summary of Exodus commentators in Evans, *Recognition Formulae*, 202–4.

55. Gunn, "Exodus 1–14," 83–84; Fishbane, *Texture*, 73–74; Janzen, "Name," 227; S. Herrmann, *Israel in Egypt* (SBT 27; trans. M. Kohl; Naperville, IL: Allenson, 1973) 53–54;

acknowledgment of his covenantally motivated interventions as the "God of the fathers." The fundamental connection between the Tetragrammaton and the exodus event is exemplified in the prologue to the Decalogue: "I am Yhwh your God who brought you out of Egypt" (Exod 20:2).[56]

The theological connection between the revelation of the Tetragrammaton and Yhwh's covenant actions is extremely pertinent to the current discussion of the Deuteronomic references to the "God of the father(s)." Significantly, three of the purported tetrateuchal sources (i.e., J, E, and P) agree that the Tetragrammaton accumulates theological significance in the course of Yhwh's covenantally motivated dealings with Israel. On the one hand, the account of Exodus 3 generally attributed to E links the introduction of the Tetragrammaton (Exod 3:14) with the impending actualization of the patriarchal promises made by the "God of your fathers, the God of Abraham, the God of Isaac, and the God of Jacob" (Exod 3:15). On the other hand, the instances of the recognition formula in the so-called J and E strands of Exodus 6–14 concur that the full meaning of the Tetragrammaton is displayed through Yhwh's actions in fulfilling his promises to Israel as the "God of the fathers."

If it can be demonstrated that the Deuteronomic collocation of the Tetragrammaton and the "God of the father(s)" fulfills the same function of emphasizing Yhwh's covenant dealings with Israel, then the theological significance of the divine name and the "God of the fathers" would be common to all the putative sources of the Pentateuch. One of the primary disjunctions between the Deuteronomic usage and the three main tetrateuchal sources (i.e., JEP) would thus be bridged, for the divine name and the "God of the fathers" would exhibit a similar theological trajectory of progressive revelation across all pentateuchal sources. Indeed, the use of an overtly theological approach to the Tetragrammaton as an alternative to source criticism is hardly a new development.[57]

M. Greenberg, *Understanding Exodus* (New York: Behrman, 1969) 130–6. Cf. the same phenomenon in ANE theogonies such as *Enuma Elish*, where the functions and names of gods are inextricably intertwined and freely interchanged.

56. C. Seitz, "Call of Moses," 159–60; R. de Vaux, "The Revelation of the Divine Name YHWH," in *Proclamation and Presence: Old Testament Essays in Honour of Gwynne Henton Davies* (ed. J. I. Durham and J. R. Porter; Richmond, VA: John Knox, 1970) 72–73.

57. E.g., C. Seitz, "Call of Moses," 145–61; Moberly, *Old Testament*; C. F. H. Henry, *God, Revelation, and Authority* (6 vols.; Waco, TX: Word, 1976–83) 2:184–209; U. Cassuto, *A Commentary on the Book of Exodus* (trans. I. Abrahams; Jerusalem: Magnes, 1967) 78–79; J. A. Motyer, *The Revelation of the Divine Name* (London: Tyndale, 1959). Similarly, medieval Jewish commentators often argued that, while the patriarchs knew the word Yhwh, the character behind the name was not revealed until the supernatural outworking of Yhwh's covenant through the exodus. See the discussion in N. M. Sarna, *Exodus* (JPSTC; Philadelphia: Jewish Publication Society, 1991) 31; and N. Leibowitz, *Studies in Shemot I* (Jerusalem: World Zionist Organization, 1976) 132–38.

Theological Alternatives to Tradition-Critical Proposals for the "God of the Father(s)"

While theological alternatives to pentateuchal source criticism have frequently been presented, similarly theological approaches to tradition-critical accounts of Israelite religion and the "God of the father(s)" have appeared infrequently.[58] However, the case for a theological approach can be strengthened through an appraisal of the tetrateuchal references to the "God of the father(s)" in the light of recent ANE comparative evidence. A reassessment of the biblical and ANE data used by Alt in light of newer developments will point in a distinctly theological rather than tradition-critical direction, again with major interpretive implications for Deuteronomy's references to the "God of the fathers."

For all its innovation in commencing the study of patriarchal religion, Alt's tradition-critical synthesis has been plagued by three significant problems. First, Alt's contention that the "God of the fathers" was the anonymous deity of the patriarchs is dubious in light of more recently discovered ANE inscriptions and texts. Alt was working with Greco-Roman parallels from the 1st to 4th centuries C.E., but the ANE data from nearer the time of the patriarchs paint a rather different picture for the second and first millennia B.C.E. The epithet "god of the fathers" can refer to well-known gods such as the Sumerian deity Ilabrat, the Assyrian deity Aššur, the Babylonian deities Shamash and Ishtar, the Amorite deity Amurru, and many others.[59] Most notably, the discoveries at Ras Shamra in 1929 revealed that the epithet "god of the father" could be applied to El, the head of the Ugaritic pantheon,[60] a particularly enlightening datum in light of the OT's identification of YHWH using both El-compounds and the name El itself.[61]

---

58. See the studies of patriarchal religion listed in A. Pagolu, *The Religion of the Patriarchs* (JSOTSup 277; Sheffield: JSOT Press, 1998) 15–26; G. J. Wenham, "The Religion of the Patriarchs," in *Essays on the Patriarchal Narratives* (ed. A. R. Millard and D. J. Wiseman; Leicester: Inter-Varsity, 1980) 164–75 (repr., Winona Lake, IN: Eisenbrauns, 1983, pp. 161–95); and W. McKane, *Studies in the Patriarchal Narratives* (Edinburgh: Handsel, 1979) 195–224.

59. The earliest objections to Alt's proposal in light of Old Assyrian texts were registered by J. Lewy, "Les textes paléo-assyriens et l'Ancien Testament," *RHR* 110 (1934) 29–65. More recently discovered ascriptions of the title "God of the father(s)" to named ANE deities are discussed by R. S. Hess, *Israelite Religions: An Archaeological and Biblical Survey* (Grand Rapids, MI: Baker, 2007) 147–49; T. Jacobsen, *The Treasures of Darkness: A History of Mesopotamian Religion* (New Haven, CT: Yale University Press, 1976) 159; and Cross, *Canaanite Myth*, 9–12.

60. Cross, *Canaanite Myth*, 13–43.

61. Debate continues over whether YHWH and El were once identical deities, or whether one or the other came first. J. C. de Moor (*The Rise of Yahwism: The Roots of Israelite Monotheism* [BETL 91; rev. ed.; Leuven: Leuven University Press, 1997] 310–69) and Cross (*Canaanite Myth*, 44–75) offer representative arguments for viewing YHWH as originally synonymous with El. In contrast, J. Day (*Yahweh and the Gods and Goddesses of Canaan* [JSOTSup 265; Sheffield: Sheffield Academic Press, 2000] 13–41) argues that some aspects

Regardless of the taxonomic relationships between these occasionally overlapping or synonymous deities, the ANE data clearly rebut Alt's contention that the title "god(s) of the father(s)" must refer to anonymous gods.

Second, the biblical and ANE data resist Alt's sharp division between the sedentary *Elim* and the nomadic "God of the father(s)." The epithets El-Shaddai and El-Bethel are particularly problematic for Alt's scheme. As I noted above, El-Shaddai frequently appears to the patriarchs in both the land of promise and in Egypt.[62] Though Alt sought to attribute the omnipresence of El-Shaddai to an addition by the Priestly writer in Genesis,[63] the epithet El-Shaddai also occurs with a similar sense in early, non-Priestly texts (Gen 43:14; 49:25).[64] Similarly, El-Bethel's promise to Jacob that "I am with you and will keep you wherever you go" (Gen 28:15; cf. 35:3) is hardly suggestive of a locally confined deity.[65] In fact, El-Bethel's protection of Jacob through his far-flung journeys fits Alt's description of the immanent personal god exactly. Though some tradition critics and history-of-religions scholars have followed Alt in viewing the patriarchs' deities as mainly personal gods,[66] such a polarized view springs from an excessive dichotomy between family and state religion, for the relationship between them in Israel exhibited more of a dynamic continuum than a strict separation.[67] On a similarly interdisciplinary note, the sharp contrast drawn by Alt between nomadic and sedentary models of Israelite society, following

---

of Canaanite El influenced the OT conception of Yhwh, but this conflation was ultimately rejected by the Deuteronom(ist)ic school due to Jeroboam's appropriation of bull imagery from the El cult.

62. See p. 98 n. 26 above.

63. Alt, "God of the Fathers," 17.

64. M. Haran, "The Religion of the Patriarchs: An Attempt at a Synthesis," *ASTI* 4 (1965) 32–33. Regarding Gen 49:25, F. M. Cross and D. N. Freedman (*Studies in Ancient Yahwistic Poetry* [2nd ed.; Grand Rapids, MI: Eerdmans, 1997] 46–63) argue convincingly that the blessing of Jacob in Genesis 49 is an ancient poetic text from the second millennium B.C.E. The reference here to El-Shaddai not only antedates P, but the narrative places it in Egypt, thus challenging Alt's circumscription of the *Elim* to Canaanite sanctuaries. It is surely significant that Jacob presupposes El-Shaddai's sovereignty in Egypt.

65. T. E. McComiskey, "The Religion of the Patriarchs," in *The Law and the Prophets: Old Testament Studies in Honor of Oswald T. Allis* (ed. J. H. Skilton; Nutley, NJ: Presbyterian and Reformed, 1974) 200. For similar reasons, J. Van Seters ("The Religion of the Patriarchs in Genesis," *Bib* 61 [1980] 220–33) argues for an exilic provenance for the Genesis theophanies since their references to El mirror Deutero-Isaiah in holding to a transcendent conception of Israel's God.

66. E.g., E. S. Gerstenberger, *Theologies in the Old Testament* (trans. J. Bowden; Minneapolis: Fortress, 2002) 40, 78–91; J.-M. Heimerdinger, "The God of Abraham," *VE* 22 (1992) 41–55; H. Cazelles, "Le Dieu d'Abraham," in *Autour de l'Exode* (Paris: LeCoffre, 1987) 53–66; R. Albertz, *Persönliche Frömmigkeit und offizielle Religion* (Stuttgart: Calwer, 1978) 88–91; Vorländer, *Mein Gott*, 185–203; J. P. Hyatt, "Yahweh was 'The God of My Father,'" *VT* 55 (1955) 130–36; H. G. May, "The Patriarchal Idea of God," *JBL* 60 (1941) 123–25.

67. K. van der Toorn, *Family Religion in Babylonia, Syria, and Israel: Continuity and Changes in the Forms of Religious Life* (SHANE 7; Leiden: Brill, 1996) 255–65; Jacobsen, *Treasures of Darkness*, 147–64.

Wellhausen, has been exposed as simplistic and inaccurate in light of more recent anthropological research.[68]

Third, the syntactical structure of Exod 6:3 itself points to a theological progression from the patriarchal use of the epithet El-Shaddai to the full understanding of the Tetragrammaton in Mosaic Yahwism. Randall Garr has provided a groundbreaking text-linguistic analysis of the two halves of this verse, demonstrating how El-Shaddai and the divine name YHWH stand in a part-to-whole relationship.[69] On the one hand, in the first half of the verse God asserts that "I appeared to Abraham, Isaac, and Jacob as El-Shaddai [באל שדי]" (Exod 6:3a). Garr demonstrates that, although the ב preposition attached to El-Shaddai has often been miscategorized as a *beth essentiae* construction,[70] text-linguistic comparison with other passages (e.g., Deut 10:22; Ezek 20:41; Ps 39:7) reveals that Exod 6:3a actually contains an instance of the "partitive *beth*."[71] El-Shaddai refers to the same entity as YHWH (i.e., "equireferential") but is subordinate to it, for this "partitive *beth*" expresses a property, function, or state of its nominal referent.[72]

On the other hand, the second half of the verse places the Tetragrammaton in apposition to God's name: "But I, by my name [שמי] YHWH, was not known to them" (Exod 6:3b). Garr shows that the discourse prominence given to "I" (i.e., YHWH) vis-à-vis "my name" in the entire passage demonstrates that "my name" also stands in an equireferential yet subordinate relationship to "I," the first-person voice of YHWH that resounds throughout Exodus 6.[73] Garr's brief survey of the use of El-Shaddai in the Priestly source confirms his text-linguistic conclusion: the epithet El-Shaddai represents a limited aspect of the Israelite deity who made promises to the patriarchs but did not ultimately fulfill them, whereas the god now fully known as YHWH fulfills these ancient promises.[74] Thus the Priestly source, at least, portrays the transition from El-Shaddai to YHWH as a matter of progressive revelation.

In brief, the tetrateuchal references to the "God of the father(s)" can no longer be marshaled in isolation from ANE data in order to use divine

---

68. M. Köckert, *Vätergott und Väterverheissungen: Eine Auseinandersetzung mit Albrecht Alt und seinen Erben* (FRLANT 142; Göttingen: Vanderhoeck & Ruprecht, 1988) 115–61. Compare the reassessment of Abraham as a "short-range semi-nomad" by D. J. Wiseman, "Abraham Reassessed," in *Essays on the Patriarchal Narratives* (ed. A. R. Millard and D. J. Wiseman; Leicester: Inter-Varsity, 1980) 139–44 (repr., Winona Lake, IN: Eisenbrauns, 1983, pp. 141–60).

69. W. R. Garr, "The Grammar and Interpretation of Exodus 6:3," *JBL* 111 (1992) 385–408.

70. E.g., *IBHS* §11.2.5e; Joüon §133c; C. Gordon, "'In' of Predication or Equivalence," *JBL* 100 (1981) 612–13; W. C. Kaiser, *Toward an Old Testament Theology* (Grand Rapids, MI: Zondervan, 1978) 106.

71. GKC §119m; BDB, "ב," 88.

72. Garr, "Grammar and Interpretation of Exodus 6:3," 387–89.

73. Garr, "Grammar and Interpretation of Exodus 6:3," 389–97.

74. Garr, "Grammar and Interpretation of Exodus 6:3," 397–408.

epithets alone as reliable indicators of the nature of Israelite religion. In both the Tetrateuch and ANE, "personal gods" can possess transcendent locality and power, while "state gods" often exercise their authority apart from cultic centers and while performing immanent functions. Already in Genesis–Numbers, the use of the epithet "God of the father(s)" draws together the oft-competing poles of divine immanence and transcendence under a single title.

Conclusion

The history of research of the "God of the fathers" in the Tetrateuch suggests that this epithet describes Y$_{\text{HWH}}$ as a personal god with cosmic authority. Deuteronomy mirrors the Tetrateuch's references to the "God of the fathers" as a deity who both makes and fulfills promises. However, the Pentateuch's references to such a deity who made promises to the patriarchs and fulfilled them to the exodus generation diverges from the Deuteronomistic History and the postexilic literature, in which the "God of the fathers" refers broadly to the deity worshiped by Israel's ancestors. Since the "God of the fathers" epithet in Deuteronomy is closely tied to the patriarchal and exodus generations, in chap. 5 I analyze the pertinent Deuteronomic passages in conjunction with the ancestor traditions in the Tetrateuch. The analysis of these passages in their ANE context reveals that, like the Tetrateuch, Deuteronomy conceives of the "God of the fathers" as both an ANE cosmic god and a personal god, who surpasses the limitations of both. This full-orbed characterization of Y$_{\text{HWH}}$ also bridges the putative theological chasm between patriarchal religion and Mosaic Yahwism.[75]

---

75. While Römer concurs with Van Seters's redactional proposal for the "fathers" in Deuteronomy (see p. 4 n. 16 above), it is important to observe that Römer's views on the extent of Deuteronom(ist)ic editing in the Tetrateuch diverge from those of Van Seters. Van Seters and his school are inclined to see a significant amount of Deuteronom(ist)ic reworking in the Tetrateuch (see n. 21 above), but Römer retains the older dichotomy between patriarchal religion and Mosaic Yahwism. In the vein of Wellhausen and Alt, Römer pits Genesis and Deuteronomy against each other as "[e]ine Opposition zwischen zwei Ursprungskonzeptionen": popular-autochthonous vs. exodic-exilic (*Väter*, 573). In chap. 5, I offer a detailed criticism of dichotomies of this sort.

Chapter 5

The "God of the Fathers" and the Divine Promises in Deuteronomy:
Analysis of Texts

The eight Deuteronomic references to "the God of fathers" can be grouped into three categories. First, two passages identify the "God of the fathers" as the deity who promised to multiply Israel (1:11; 6:3). These passages provide a theological framework with which to understand Deuteronomy's other references to Israel's multiplication (e.g., 7:13; 30:5), especially as they relate to the land promised to the "fathers" (e.g., 28:63). Second, the "God of the fathers" gives the land to Israel in four passages (1:21; 4:1; 12:1; 27:3). Of these passages, the final reference in 27:3 is particularly interesting because it falls in a chapter that is often regarded as secondary. Third, the "God of the fathers" appears twice in explicitly covenantal contexts (26:7; 29:24[25]). While 26:7 looks back positively to Israel's deliverance from Egypt by the "God of the fathers," 29:24 looks forward negatively to Israel's displacement from the land because of disobedience to the covenant made with the "God of the fathers." Deuteronomy's eight references to the "God of the fathers" thus span Israel's entire history from exodus to exile.

My classification of the "God of the fathers" references under the threefold rubric of multiplication, land, and covenant facilitates a synoptic comparison of Deuteronomy with the threefold promises recorded in the tetrateuchal narratives.[1] In particular, Deuteronomy's frequent juxtaposition of the "God of the fathers" with the formulas of covenant promise

---

1. The threefold categorization of the divine promises in the Pentateuch is also advocated by D. J. A. Clines (*The Theme of the Pentateuch*, [JSOTSup 10; Sheffield: JSOT Press, 1978]), although he uses the term *relationship* in place of *covenant*. In contrast to Clines, other scholars have argued for a greater number of divine promises. For example, C. Westermann (*The Promises to the Fathers* [trans. D. E. Green; Philadelphia: Fortress, 1976] 132–63) argues for seven (i.e., a son, new territory, aid, land, increase, blessing, and covenant), whereas W. A. VanGemeren (*The Progress of Redemption: The Story of Salvation from Creation to the New Jerusalem* [Grand Rapids, MI: Baker, 1988] 104–8) argues for four (i.e., seed, land, personal blessing, and blessing to the nations). Regardless of the actual number of promises, all these scholars are agreed that *offspring* represents a prominent category of promise in the Tetrateuch (V. P. Hamilton, "Genesis, Theology of," *NIDOTTE* 4:666–67).

("just as Yhwh promised you") and Torah promulgation ("just as Yhwh commanded you") suggests that Deuteronomy is alluding to specific texts in the Tetrateuch.[2] Thus, in analyzing each Deuteronomic reference to the "God of the fathers," I also identify its most likely intertext in the Tetrateuch.

The "God of the Fathers" and the Promise of Multiplication

Although von Rad once claimed that "Deuteronomy understands the oath to the early patriarchs only as a promise of the land,"[3] the promises to the patriarchs of multiplication are also unmistakably present in Deuteronomy. Among all the references to multiplication that could be adduced,[4] two passages are especially significant because they cite prior promises by the "God of the fathers" to multiply Israel (1:11; 6:3). In Deuteronomy, these promises of multiplication are both fulfilled in the narrative present at Horeb/Moab (e.g., 1:10; 10:22) and yet to be consummated in the land of promise (e.g., 1:11; 6:3). This *already/not-yet* conception of multiplication not only resembles the trajectory of the land promise toward its ultimate fulfillment but becomes intertwined with the multiplication promises so that the two almost blend together. The theological vision for the interpenetration of a fruitful land and a fruitful people will become evident through the analysis of Deut 1:11 and 6:3 in concert with Deuteronomy's other references to multiplication.

Deuteronomy 1:11

יְהוָה אֱלֹהֵי אֲבוֹתֵכֶם	May Yhwh, God of your fathers,
יֹסֵף עֲלֵיכֶם כָּכֶם אֶלֶף פְּעָמִים	multiply you a thousand times
וִיבָרֵךְ אֶתְכֶם	and bless you,
כַּאֲשֶׁר דִּבֶּר לָכֶם	just as he promised you!

This reference to the "God of your fathers" and his fructifying work for Israel appears at the outset of Moses' recollection of events at Horeb (1:6–18). Before the nation can obey Yhwh's command for Israel to advance from Horeb into the land promised to the "fathers" (1:6–8), the practical matter

---

2. Skweres, *Rückverweise*; Milgrom, "Profane Slaughter," 1–17. Though Lohfink (*Hauptgebot*, 59–63) classifies both command and promise formulas under the category of *Promulgationssatz*, I distinguish between promulgation formulas ("just as he commanded [צוה] you"; "just as he taught [למד] you") and promise formulas ("just as he promised [דבר] you"; "just as he swore [נשבע] to you").

3. Von Rad, *From Genesis to Chronicles*, 60; cf. Plöger, *Literarkritische, formgeschichtliche und stilkritische Untersuchungen*, 68.

4. Deut 1:11; 6:3; 7:7, 13–14; 8:1; 9:14; 10:22; 13:17; 28:4, 11, 62–63; 30:5, 9, 16; 33:6, 17. These passages share two features that mark them as multiplication passages: (1) a description of Israel's smallness in the past; (2) a description of Yhwh's multiplying of Israel (e.g., רבה; 1:10) or providing various kinds of fruit (e.g., פרי־בטן; "fruit of the womb"; 7:13).

of the judiciary must be addressed (1:9–18). Quoting himself for the first time, Moses declares that Yʜᴡʜ's abundant multiplication of Israel (1:10) and Israel's own strife (1:12) have resulted in a judicial load that is too burdensome for him (1:9, 12). Thus Moses urges the people to appoint judges to represent smaller units of Israel's population (1:13–15), whom he then enjoins to discharge their duties righteously and without favoritism (1:16–17a). He reserves only the intractable cases for himself (1:17b).

The formulaic reference to Yʜᴡʜ as "God of your fathers" comes in Moses' desire for Yʜᴡʜ to continue multiplying Israel in accordance with his promise (1:11), the fulfillment of which has created the current leadership vacuum. Yʜᴡʜ had previously been described as "our God" (1:6) and "your God" (1:10), but now the transgenerational continuity of Yʜᴡʜ comes to the fore through the epithet "God of your fathers" (1:11). Moses not only invokes the "God of your fathers" at Horeb with reference to Israel's multiplication, but he will also shortly exhort Israel to enter the land, "just as Yʜᴡʜ, God of your fathers, has spoken to you" (1:21). Thus the twofold reference to the "God of your fathers" (1:11, 21) links the promises of multiplication and land in Deuteronomy 1.

Literary-Critical Approaches to Deuteronomy 1:9–18

The reference to Israel's multiplication (1:11) falls within Moses' account of Israel's selection of judges (1:9–18), a section generally acknowledged as a coherent literary unit. However, the origin and placement of 1:9–18 within the larger narrative have posed numerous problems, especially due to the conflation of elements from disparate narratives in Exod 18:13–27 and Num 11:11–17. In terms of chronology, Deuteronomy places the episode at the time of the departure from Horeb (Deut 1:6–8), thus suggesting Num 11:11–17 as a parallel text,[5] even though the majority of Moses' terminology is drawn from the pre-Horeb narrative recorded in Exod 18:13–27.[6] In terms of historiography, the Deuteronomy narrative and the Exodus and Numbers narratives exhibit several discrepancies. In Deuteronomy, the initiative to appoint leaders originates with Moses (Deut 1:13), whereas in Exodus the suggestion arises from Jethro (Exod 18:17–23). The qualifications for these leaders primarily involve moral and spiritual qualities in Exodus (e.g., "men who fear God"; Exod 18:21) and Numbers ("I will put [my Spirit] upon them"; Num 11:17), whereas Deuteronomy emphasizes their intellectual qualities (e.g., "wise and discerning"; Deut 1:13). Another

---

5. Mayes (*Deuteronomy*, 121) argues that the phrase בעת ההוא ("at that time"; Deut 1:9) refers to the time of departure from Horeb rather than the time of arrival. However, Plöger's careful study of all 68 occurrences of בעת ההוא argues that the phrase refers to "eine unbestimmte, chronologisch nicht fixierbare Angabe" (*Literarkritische, formgeschichtliche und stilkritische Untersuchungen*, 224). Thus the temporal references in 1:9–18 may be intentionally vague rather than needing harmonization.

6. The chronological problems are underscored here by the creative solution attempted by the Samaritan Pentateuch, which inserts Deut 1:9–18 after Exod 18:24.

contrast is found in the emphasis in Numbers on their prior leadership experience ("men whom you know . . . to be elders"; Num 11:16–17). One link to Numbers 11 is furnished by the wording of Moses' complaint (משׂא, "burden"; Deut 1:12; cf. Num 11:11). On the other hand, Numbers speaks of the leadership office as זקן ("elder"; Num 11:16) rather than שׂר ("officer"; Deut 1:15) or שׁפט ("judge"; Exod 18:22; Deut 1:16; 16:18–20). Lastly, in contradistinction to Exodus and Numbers, Deuteronomy alone calls for impartiality on the part of the judges (Deut 1:17). These synoptic discrepancies have generated a great deal of discussion.[7]

In addition to synoptic tensions with Exodus and Numbers, two additional reasons are given for classifying Deut 1:9–18 as a secondary insertion within Deuteronomy 1 itself.[8] First, the *Leitwort* of journey (נסע; 1:6) narrating Yhwh's command to leave Horeb is not enacted until 1:19. Because *Leitwort* usage of this sort seems to demand more proximity between repeated occurrences, redaction critics propose that the narrative of Israel's actual departure from Horeb (1:19) originally followed immediately after the command to depart (1:8). Second, some hold that the temporal marker "at that time" (1:9, 6, 18) marks successive stages in the addition of secondary material.[9]

Literary and Rhetorical Structure in Deuteronomy 1:9–18

Though a full response to diachronic reconstructions of Deuteronomy 1 cannot be offered here,[10] two lines of critique are significant for defending the literary coherence and rhetorical unity of 1:9–18. First, the assertion that Deut 1:9–18 represents an intrusive addition to the text, as argued by Weinfeld,[11] overlooks the poetics and narrative placement of 1:9–18 within Deuteronomy 1. Israel's growing population and impending entry into the

---

7. See the history of research on Deut 1:9–18 in Christensen, *Deuteronomy 1:1–21:9*, 17–18.

8. The most influential analysis of Deut 1:9–18 is offered by M. Weinfeld, (*Deuteronomy 1–11*, 137–40), who transforms this section into a *locus classicus* for his view that Deuteronomy portrays a program of theological reform by scribal tradents associated with the reigns of Hezekiah through Josiah. For Deut 1:9–18, in particular, Weinfeld asserts that the D source took over a JE text based on Exodus 18, transformed the spiritual requirements of Exodus 18 into the wisdom-based requirements of Deuteronomy 1, and finally appropriated some elements from Numbers 11 and Deut 16:18–20 to support the scribal agenda of secularizing Israel's institutions.

9. S. E. Loewenstamm ("The Formula *Ba'et Hahi'* in the Introductory Speeches in Deuteronomy," in *From Babylon to Canaan: Studies in the Bible and Its Oriental Background* [Jerusalem: Magnes, 1992] 42–50) argues for three tradition-critical stages. Moses' appointment of judges would be the first stage (1:9–15), to which Moses' charge to the judges was then added (1:16–17). Finally, the command was democratized for all Israel (1:18).

10. For a penetrating critique of Weinfeld, see Vogt, *Deuteronomic Theology*, 98–112. Most significantly, Vogt demonstrates that Weinfeld's dichotomy between spiritual and intellectual qualities of leadership is false, because in Deuteronomy the use of the term צֶדֶק (1:16) and its associated term צְדָקָה entails both sorts of qualities (e.g., 9:4–6).

11. Weinfeld, *Deuteronomy 1–11*, 137, 139.

land (Deut 1:6–8) require a scalable judiciary that can serve the needs of a dispersed people. Miller observes that the placement of this episode here emphasizes "the need for organization and leadership in the fulfillment of the blessing God promised long before to Abraham."[12] Thus it is equally probable that Israel's delay before entering the land is necessitated by the logistical challenges posed by the next stage of the nation's existence. The promises of land and multiplication are closely related, for Israel's transgenerational possession of the land (1:8) demands the transgenerational continuity of Israel's leadership (1:9–18). The divine revelation first given at Horeb must continue to resound through its administration and execution by godly leaders.[13]

Second, the thematic integrity of Deut 1:9–18 within its narrative context can also be defended by observing the elegant literary shaping of the account of the journey between Horeb and Kadesh (1:6–46). The events at Horeb (1:6–18) and Kadesh (1:19–46) exhibit lexical and thematic parallels that would be compromised by removing Deut 1:9–18 as a secondary insertion. Table 5.1 (p. 114) highlights the parallels between the events at Horeb and Kadesh.[14] At both Horeb and Kadesh, the scenes begin with *Leitwörter* of journey (נסע, "to set out") followed by a description of Israel's destination (1:7, 19). Yʜᴡʜ presents the land before the people (1:8a, 21a) for the purpose of imminent possession (1:8b, 21b). The narrative then shifts to the selection of a smaller group of Israelite leaders who will represent and prepare the nation in the new endeavor (1:13–15, 22–25). However, the solidarity of Israel with its leaders that was established at Horeb (1:9–17) and sealed with a call to obedience (1:18) is tragically fractured at Kadesh. Whereas Israel obeyed the command to go up from Horeb to Kadesh (1:19), the nation disobeyed and did not enter from Kadesh into the land (1:26–33).[15] Thus Deut 1:9–18 forms an essential part of the narrative by preparing

---

12. Miller, *Deuteronomy*, 28. It is surprising that Miller grants the literary coherence of Deut 1:9–18, on the one hand, but asserts the need for redactional reconstructions, on the other.

13. The emphasis on judicial continuity in Deut 1:9–18 leads naturally to the observation that leadership succession forms a pervasive *Leitmotif* in the first speech of Moses. The only leader and judge the nation has ever known, Moses himself, will not enter the land (1:37; 3:26; 4:21). The imminence of Moses' death necessitates the commissioning of Joshua (1:38; 3:21–22, 28; 31:1–8). Thus it appears that 1:9–18 intentionally introduces a *Leitmotif* that pervades Deuteronomy rather than being a redactional insertion.

14. Modified slightly from Miller, "Wilderness Journey," 50–56.

15. Deuteronomy 1 highlights the wickedness of the people at Kadesh in a subtle but devastating way. In response to the spies' assertion of the goodness of the land (1:25), the people excuse their unwillingness to possess the land by quoting previously unknown information from the spies: "Our brothers have made our hearts melt, saying, 'The people are bigger and taller than we; the cities are larger and fortified to heaven. And besides, we saw the sons of the Anakim there'" (1:28). Remarkably, the frightening description of the land's occupants is found on the lips of the people in citing the spies rather than the spies themselves (cf. Num 13:28–29). Berlin (*Poetics*, 95–99) notes that the introduction of

Table 5.1. Parallels between Events at Horeb and Kadesh

Literary Feature	Horeb	Kadesh
1. Journey *Leitwörter* + geographical description	"Turn and set your journey, and go to the hill country of the Amorites. . . ." (1:7)	"Then we set out from Horeb, and went through all that great and terrible wilderness. . . ." (1:19)
2. Yhwh's presentation of the land	"See, I have placed the land before you. . . ." (1:8a)	"See, Yhwh your God has placed the land before you. . . ." (1:21a)
3. Yhwh's command to possess the land	"Go in and possess the land. . . ." (1:8b)	"Go up and possess the land. . . ." (1:21b)
4. Corporate selection of leaders	"Set apart . . . men for yourselves. . . ." (1:13)	"Let us send men before us to search out the land for us. . . ." (1:22)
5. Israel's response to these leaders	"I commanded you . . . all the things you should do." (1:18)	"Yet you were not willing to go up but rebelled against the word of Yhwh your God." (1:26)

the ironic contrast between Israel's commitments at Horeb (1:9–18) and its failures to meet these commitments at Kadesh (1:19–46).[16]

In summary, the narrative of Deut 1:9–18 performs two essential literary functions in the larger context of Deuteronomy 1. First, the episode establishes a theological link between Yhwh's promises of land and multiplication. The "God of the fathers" who multiplies Israel (1:11) is the same deity who offers the land for possession (1:21). Second, the obedience of the people at Horeb prepares for the impending contrast with the disobedience that follows at Kadesh. In light of this overarching narrative structure, I now turn to a detailed analysis of the "God of the fathers" reference in Deut 1:11.

Literary and Rhetorical Analysis of the "God of the Fathers" in Deuteronomy 1:11

The initial reference to Yhwh as the "God of the fathers" (1:11) occurs within Deut 1:9–12, a discrete narrative unit framed by references in 1:9

---

new information through direct speech is a powerful characterization device, in this case underscoring Israel's intransigence in disobeying Yhwh's command.

16. E. E. Carpenter ("Literary Structure and Unbelief: A Study of Deuteronomy 1:6–46," *AsTJ* 42 [1987] 78–84) notes the chiastic structure in the entire journey narrative of Horeb and Kadesh. Israel's multiplication and wise leadership (1:9–18) form a contrastive chiastic pair with Israel's defeat and diminution through foolish leadership (1:41–44). Accordingly, the hinge of the chiasm turns on Israel's unwillingness to obey (1:26–28).

and 1:12 to Moses' "bearing" (נשׂא derivatives) of Israel's burdens "alone" (לבדי).[17] The inner two verses express Yhwh's abundant blessing in multiplying Israel (1:10, 11). The verbal and conceptual parallels between the outer and inner frames suggest a chiastic structure for this section (see diagram).

    A "I am not able to bear [נשׂא infinitive construct] you alone [לבדי]" (1:9)
        B "Yhwh your God has multiplied [רבה] you and behold you are today like the stars of heaven in number" (1:10)
        B' "May Yhwh God of your fathers, increase [יסף] you a thousandfold more than you are and bless you, just as he promised you" (1:11)
    A' "How can I alone [לבדי] bear [נשׂא imperfect] the load and burden [משׂא] of you and your strife?" (1:12)

Though the terminological and conceptual parallels in the A/A' chiastic pair are exact, the parallelism of the B/B' pair has provoked debate because of its supposed incongruity. In addition to a change in terminology about growth (רבה versus יסף), the abrupt shift in Moses' tone from negative (1:10) to positive (1:11) has led some scholars to see the positive reference to Israel's multiplication in 1:11 as a secondary insertion into a narrative that was originally negative in tone.[18] The reference to the "God of the fathers" is thus discarded in the redaction-critical reconstruction of 1:9–12.

The move to eliminate 1:11 can be challenged through a form-critical comparison with other Deuteronomic references to the "God of the fathers." Such an analysis reveals that three elements of 1:11 are consistent with other references to the "God of the fathers." First, the epithet "God of the fathers" appears only in apposition to the divine name Yhwh.[19] Second, the identification of Yhwh as "God of the fathers" appears in covenantal contexts where the rhetorical force of Moses' argument is predicated on the present efficaciousness of Yhwh's ancient promises of land and multiplication (e.g., 4:1; 6:3; 12:1) as well as the exodus from Egypt (e.g., 26:7; 29:24[25]). Thus the phrase "just as he [Yhwh] promised you" mirrors other Deuteronomic instances of the promise formula.[20] In light of these common features, the reference to the "God of the fathers" in 1:11 is quite consistent with Deuteronomic usage elsewhere.

---

17. Römer, *Israels Väter*, 107; D. L. Christensen, "Prose and Poetry in the Bible: The Narrative Poetics of Deuteronomy 1,9–18," *ZAW* 97 (1985) 179–89.
18. E.g., Mittmann, *Deuteronomium 1,1–6,3*, 24; Plöger, *Literarkritische, formgeschichtliche und stilkritische Untersuchungen*, 29.
19. See the discussion of "The Divine Name and the 'God of the Fathers' in Deuteronomy" on pp. 93–95 above.
20. The "promise formula" כאשר דבר is also found in 1:21; 2:1; 6:3, 19; 9:3; 10:9; 11:25; 12:20; 15:6; 18:2; 26:18, 19; 27:3; 29:12; 31:3. See the analysis of Deut 6:3 below.

Since Deut 1:11 is probably original, how can the interpreter harmonize the alternation of positive and negative assessments of Yнwн's multiplication of Israel in 1:9–11? When Moses declares that Israel's burgeoning growth (1:10) poses an unbearable burden (1:9), he seems to convey a negative assessment of Yнwн's blessing. Moses apparently seeks to avoid this mistaken impression by declaring his desire that Yнwн's multiplication will continue a thousand times over (1:11).[21] Nonetheless, he complains again of his workload (1:12) and issues an urgent call for new leadership (1:13–18). Trying to follow such mood swings by Moses, the interpreter perceives a rueful, conflicted Moses who is torn between his bitterness over not entering the land (e.g., 1:37; 3:26; 4:21) and his desire for Israel to prosper. Far from being incoherent, this complex portrayal of Moses' character typifies Deuteronomy's powerful depiction of a flawed but still authoritative messenger of Yнwн. The humanness of the narrative's portrayal of Moses evokes sympathy for Moses and reinforces his persuasiveness but ultimately directs attention toward Yнwн rather than Moses as the supreme Torah-giver.[22] Moses will not cross the Jordan with Israel, but the personal deity known as the "God of the fathers" will cross over.[23]

The declaration that Yнwн will be Israel's ultimate leader throughout its history receives further support through the theological dialectic between the appositives for Yнwн whereby "your God" (1:10) stands parallel to the "God of your fathers" (1:11). The appositive "your God" describes Yнwн as the deity of the exodus generation, since Moses is currently recounting the actions and words of Yнwн at Horeb. However, Moses' rhetoric progresses to an invocation of the "God of your fathers" in order to extend Israel's experience of Yнwн's sovereign fidelity back to patriarchal times,[24] for the same "God of your fathers" who journeyed immanently with the patriarchs has now brought Israel to Horeb (1:11) and will continue with his people to Kadesh (1:21). At the same time, Yнwн's transcendence is safeguarded when Moses identifies Israel's deity of the past (i.e., the "God of your fathers") and present (i.e., "your God") as the giver of land be-

---

21. Driver, *Deuteronomy*, 16; Weinfeld, *Deuteronomy 1–11*, 137. However, Moses later blames the people for being barred from the land (1:37; 3:26; 4:21).

22. J. W. Watts, "The Legal Characterization of Moses in the Rhetoric of the Pentateuch," *JBL* 117 (1998) 415–26. Polzin (*Moses*, 35–39) also notes that Deuteronomy simultaneously elevates and undermines Moses.

23. For example, Deut 9:3 speaks of Yнwн himself crossing the Jordan before Israel. The link between Yнwн's anger toward Moses and Moses' inability to cross the Jordan is captured in a wordplay on עבר homonyms in 3:25–26. Moses longs to "cross over" (עבר) to the "other side [בעבר] of the Jordan" (3:25), but Yнwн is "angry" (עבר) with him (3:26).

24. Since Moses is quoting his own speech to the exodus generation, the generation of their "fathers" is likely the patriarchs. In 1:11, this identification of the "fathers" with the patriarchs is consistent with the prior identification of the "fathers" as "Abraham, Isaac, and Jacob" (1:8). The multiplication of Israel in Egypt as a fulfillment of the promises to the patriarchs is similarly attested in Exodus 1–2; this is thus a challenge to Römer's identification of the "fathers" with the exodus generation.

longing to foreign nations (1:7–8)[25] and the multiplier of Israel (1:10). The generation at Horeb has already experienced multiplication by "YHWH your God" (1:10; cf. 10:22),[26] but Moses envisions an even greater fulfillment of this promise by "YHWH God of your fathers" (1:11). The dialectic between appositives thus furnishes an already/not-yet trajectory for the promise of multiplication in Deuteronomy. Ultimate fulfillment of the promise must wait until a numerous people dwell in an abundant land.[27] This promissory nexus of land and multiplication is developed further in Deut 6:3, the next passage to be examined.

Deuteronomy 6:3

וְשָׁמַעְתָּ יִשְׂרָאֵל	You shall listen, O Israel,
וְשָׁמַרְתָּ לַעֲשׂוֹת	and you shall be careful to do,
אֲשֶׁר יִיטַב לְךָ	so that it may go well for you
וַאֲשֶׁר תִּרְבּוּן מְאֹד	and that you may multiply greatly,
כַּאֲשֶׁר דִּבֶּר יְהוָה אֱלֹהֵי אֲבֹתֶיךָ לָךְ	just as YHWH God of your fathers promised you,
אֶרֶץ זָבַת חָלָב וּדְבָשׁ	(in a) land flowing with milk and honey.

The present reference to the "God of the fathers" appears as the conclusion to the first section (5:1–6:3) of Moses' second speech (5:1–28:69[29:1]).[28] After recounting YHWH's declaration of the Decalogue at Horeb (5:1–22), the people's fearful response to YHWH's voice (5:22–27), and YHWH's commissioning of Moses as mediator (5:28–31), Moses offers his own exhortation for Israel to obey YHWH (5:32–6:3). Thus the section of 5:22–6:3 provides a bridge between the covenant document (5:1–21) and covenant exposition (6:4–28:68).[29]

---

25. The sovereignty of ANE national deities over their respective lands is discussed by Block, *Gods of the Nations*, 75–91.

26. Skweres (*Rückverweise*, 173–75) notes that the reference to multiplication as the "stars in the sky" (1:10) recalls a plethora of similar promises to the patriarchs (i.e., Gen 12:2; 13:16; 15:5; 17:2–6; 22:17; 26:3; 26:24; 28:14; 35:11; 46:3). He further notes that Deut 1:11 sets the patriarchs in corporate solidarity with the nation of Israel.

27. Significantly, Moses uses the promise formula "just as he promised you" (1:11) to refer not to Israel's present multiplication at Horeb (cf. 1:10) but to future multiplication in the land.

28. Parallel colophons (5:22; 28:69[29:1]) frame the Decalogue (5:1–21) and the covenant stipulations (6:4–28:68). Deut 28:69[29:1] is often treated as a superscription to a new covenant in Moab (e.g., A. Rofé, "The Covenant in the Land of Moab [Deuteronomy 28:69–30:20]: Historico-literary, Comparative, and Formcritical Considerations," in *A Song of Power and the Power of Song: Essays on the Book of Deuteronomy* [ed. D. L. Christensen; SBTS 3; Winona Lake, IN: Eisenbrauns, 1993] 269–80). However, in the discussion in chap. 7, I argue that 28:69 agrees with 5:22 in summarizing the preceding speeches as "these words."

29. Deut 5:22–6:3 also records the last proleptic references to "the statutes and the ordinances that YHWH your God has commanded me to teach you" (6:1; cf. 4:1, 5, 8, 14, 45; 5:1, 31, 32, 33; 6:2). Millar ("Living at the Place of Decision," 36–41) observes that the

Grammatical and Literary-Critical Issues in Deuteronomy 5:22–6:3

Because of several literary and grammatical tensions, Deut 5:22–6:3 has been the subject of intense redaction-critical scrutiny. First, the shift from a plural (5:22–6:1) to a singular narrative (6:2–3) has prompted the redaction-critical use of the *Numeruswechsel* for identifying literary strata.[30] Second, Moses' account of the people's response to the Horeb theophany (5:22–27) seems to conflate elements of Exodus 19, 20, and 24, even though the narrative chronology in Deuteronomy 5 points to the post-Decalogue events of Exod 20:18–21 as the proper synoptic parallel.[31] Third, Deut 6:1–3 seems to describe the promises of land and multiplication as both unconditional gifts and conditional tasks, prompting redaction critics to subdivide the passage into literary strata that reflect putatively incompatible models of unconditionality and conditionality.[32] Fourth, the syntactical function of the phrase "land flowing with milk and honey" (6:3b) is difficult, since no clear antecedent exists to which it might stand in apposition.[33] The nebulous function of Deut 6:3b has led some scholars to excise Deut 6:2–3a in order to link the phrase "land flowing with milk and honey" appositionally to the "land that you are crossing over to possess" (6:1).[34] Fifth and related to this, the syntax of 6:1–3 is somewhat overcrowded, for the passage intersperses several למען clauses, אשר clauses, and adverbial clauses that begin with the ל preposition.[35]

---

phrase "statutes and ordinances" in Deuteronomy 4 anticipates the covenant stipulations and exposition in Deuteronomy 5–26.

30. Mittmann (*Deuteronomium 1,1–6,3*, 140, 184) argues that the change in grammatical number from singular to plural in the middle of 6:3 indicates that the promise of Israel's multiplication (6:3aβb) is a plural addition to a singular passage. In contrast, García López ("Analyse littéraire de Deutéronome V–XI," 17–18) contends that the singular sections of 6:2–3 are a late insertion into a plural passage.

31. Mayes (*Deuteronomy*, 173–75) and G. von Rad (*Deuteronomy: A Commentary* [OTL; Philadelphia: Westminster, 1966] 59–61) attempt to explain these synoptic discrepancies by arguing for a Deuteronom(ist)ic reworking of the Exodus material.

32. E.g., Köckert, *Vätergott*, 174 n. 48; J. Hoftijzer, *Die Verheissungen an die drei Erzväter* (Leiden: Brill, 1956) 60 n. 18.

33. Contra Ausloos ("Land Flowing with Milk and Honey," 306), Mayes (*Deuteronomy*, 174), and Plöger (*Literarkritische, formgeschichtliche und stilkritische Untersuchungen*, 90), who argue for an appositional construction. Though the LXX attempts to smooth the syntax by inserting δοῦναί σοι before the phrase "land flowing with milk and honey" (cf. Syr.), this reading still leaves an awkward sentence.

34. E.g., R. P. Merendino, "Die Zeugnisse, die Satzungen und die Rechte: Überlieferungsgeschichtliche Erwägungen zu Deut 6," in *Bausteine biblischer Theologie: Festgabe für G. Johannes Botterweck zum 60. Geburtstag dargebracht von seinen Schülern* (BBB 50; Cologne: Hanstein, 1977) 188, 207; Craigie, *Deuteronomy*, 168 n. 3.

35. Römer, *Israels Väter*, 120.

The Rhetoric of Command and Promise in Deuteronomy 5:1–6:3

Despite these literary and grammatical issues, several elements in Deut 5:22–6:3 suggest a rhetorical progression culminating in the promise formula of 6:3. Most significantly, the entire section from 5:1 through 6:3 contains a marked emphasis on speech, both human and divine, through repetition of verbal and nominal forms of דבר and צוה.[36] In 5:1–6:3, five discrete blocks of speech that transcend the typical literary-critical divisions can be demarcated: (1) Moses introduces the prologue to the Decalogue (5:1–5); (2) Yhwh speaks the Decalogue itself (5:6–21); (3) the people respond fearfully in asking Moses to serve as mediator (5:23–27); (4) Yhwh grants the people's request (5:28–31); and (5) Moses concludes with an exhortation based on the Horeb theophany (5:32–6:3).[37] The transition from Yhwh's speech in the narrative past to Moses' speech in the narrative present is reflected in the aspectual modulation of the promulgation formula from "just as Yhwh your God *commanded* [צוה] you" (5:32, 33; 6:1) to "just as I [Moses] am *commanding* you [מצוך]" (6:2).

The central place of Yhwh's speech as mediated through Moses is reinforced through the chiastic structure of 5:27–6:3. Lohfink has demonstrated how key groups of verbs in 5:27–31 are mirrored in reverse order in 6:1–3.[38]

```
A  שמע — עשה (5:27)
   B  ירא — שמר (5:29)
      C  למד — עשה (5:31)
         D  הלך בדרך — סור — עשה — שמר (5:32–33)
      C'  למד — עשה (6:1 )
   B'  ירא — שמר (6:2)
A'  שמע — עשה (6:3)
```

Since the middle of the chiastic pattern (5:32–33) also lies at the center of Yhwh's commissioning of Moses (5:31–6:1), this entire section strongly emphasizes the role of Moses in instructing Israel to obey Yhwh's commands

---

36. Between the twin summons to "Hear!" that frame this section (5:1; 6:4), דבר in its nominal and verbal forms occurs 16× (5:1, 4, 5, 22 [2×], 24, 26, 27 [2×], 28 [5×], 31; 6:3b). Similarly, צוה in its verbal and nominal forms occurs 12× (5:10 [2×], 12, 15, 16, 29, 31, 32, 33; 6:1 [2×], 2 [2×]). These appearances of צו are largely clustered in the six instances of the *Promulgationssatz* (5:12, 16, 32, 33; 6:1, 2).

37. DeRouchie (*Call to Covenant Love*, 235) notes that the shift from Yhwh's embedded speech back to a w^eqatal form (ושמרתם, "and you shall keep"; 5:32) signals the climax of Deut 5:22–6:3.

38. Lohfink, *Hauptgebot*, 66–68.

and avoid idolatry.³⁹ The teaching ministry of Moses thus stands at the junction between divine command and human obedience.

In addition, the constant interplay between forms of דבר and צוה in this section suggests the interweaving of divine command and divine promise. The culmination of this blending of command with promise is found in 5:31–6:3, the syntactically most congested portion of 5:22–6:3, where five instances of the promulgation formula (5:31–6:2) are capped by a single instance of the promise formula (6:3). According to Lohfink, these five instances of the promulgation formula constitute the densest cluster of this sort in all of Deuteronomy:⁴⁰

5:31   אשר תלמדם (Yhwh speaking: "that you shall teach them")
5:32   כאשר צוה יהוה אלהיכם אתכם ("just as Yhwh your God commanded you")
5:33   אשר צוה יהוה אלהיכם אתכם ("that Yhwh your God commanded you")
6:1   אשר צוה יהוה אלהיכם ללמד אתכם ("that Yhwh your God commanded [me] to teach you")
6:2   אשר אנכי מצוך ("that I am commanding you")

It is especially striking that the repetition of promulgation formulas spans both the narrative's recollection of Yhwh's commissioning of Moses (5:31–33) and Moses' preliminary exposition of the "statutes and the ordinances" (6:1–2). Since the promulgation formula is spoken first by Yhwh to Moses and then by Moses to Israel, the same urgency of Yhwh's exhortation to Moses carries over to Moses' own exhortations to Israel. Thus the repetition of the promulgation formula by both Yhwh and Moses is probably a rhetorical device to ensure that Israel recognizes Moses' full authority to speak Yhwh's words.

However, Lohfink's focus on the promulgation formulas of 5:31–6:2 neglects the rhetorical climax of the entire section: the promise formula with the "God of the fathers" (6:3). Lest his audience misinterpret the repetition of the promulgation formula in a legalistic manner, Moses concludes the first part of his second speech by using a promise formula that joins together the fruitfulness of the land with the multiplication of the people. Several rhetorical devices herald the peroration with the "God of the fathers" in 6:3b. First, Moses signals a forthcoming rhetorical apex by addressing the

---

39. This chiastic structure also transcends the variations in singular (6:2–3) and plural (5:27–6:1) address, thereby challenging the redaction-critical usefulness of the *Numeruswechsel*.

40. Lohfink (*Hauptgebot*, 297–98) identifies promulgation formulas in 4:45; 5:1, 12, 16, 31, 32, 33; 6:1, 2, 6, 17, 20, 25; 7:11; 8:1, 11; 9:12, 16; 10:5, 13; 11:8, 13, 22, 27, 28, 32; 12:1, 11, 14, 21, 28; 13:1[12:32], 6[5], 19[18]; 15:5; 17:3; 18:18, 20; 19:9; 20:17; 26:13, 14; 27:1, 4, 10; 28:1, 13, 14, 15, 45. This list shows that the promulgation formula never appears in adjacent verses outside 5:31–6:3, where it is repeated five consecutive times. This suggests that the congested syntax in Deut 5:31–6:3 represents an intentional rhetorical climax achieved through repetition of the promulgation formula.

people using the vocative "O Israel," much like other rhetorical peaks in Deuteronomy (e.g., 5:1b; 6:4). Second, on either side of the vocative "O Israel," Moses shifts suddenly from the language of doing (שמר, עשה) back to the language of hearing (שמע), thus recalling the earlier emphasis on Israel's terrifying privilege of hearing Yhwh's speech at Horeb.[41] Third, a rise in the register of Moses' speech is evident in the aural consonance between ושמעת ("you shall listen") and ושמרת ("you shall keep").[42] These rhetorical features prepare for the shift from Moses' final exhortation to obedience (6:3a) to a climactic infusion of promise theology (6:3b).

The pinnacle of Moses' speech arrives in 6:3b through three אשר clauses denoting the blessed benefits of Israel's obedience: (1) "that [אשר] it may go well for you"; (2) "that [אשר] you may multiply greatly"; and (3) "just as [כאשר] Yhwh God of your fathers promised you, [in] a land flowing with milk and honey." Though the first two אשר clauses have often been classified as rare instances of purpose clauses,[43] closer analysis of Moses' speech in 5:32–6:3 reveals several reasons for identifying them as result clauses pertaining to Yhwh's rewards for covenant obedience. First, Moses had already outlined the purpose of his teaching and Israel's obedience using four למען clauses:[44] (1) "so that you may live" (5:33b); (2) "so that it may go well with you" (5:33c); (3) "so that you may fear Yhwh your God" (6:2a); and (4) "so that your days may be prolonged" (5:33d; 6:2b). In short, Israel's obedience to the covenant was intended to produce life, fear of God, and longevity in the land.

Second, the אשר clauses in 6:3 drive the mostly telic statements of 5:33–6:2 into the concrete realm of benefits for Israel's obedience. Though Moses had previously denoted general well-being (יטב) as one of the goals (למען; 5:33c) of his parenesis, here he transforms the phrase "going well" (6:3b)

---

41. Before the emphasis on obedience through the promulgation formulas (5:31–6:2), the verb שמע appeared 8× in 5:23–28 to denote the directness of communication between Yhwh and Israel.

42. McConville (*Deuteronomy*, 140) notes that the juxtaposition of these similar-sounding words underscores the close connection between hearing and obedience.

43. C. H. J. van der Merwe, J. A. Naudé, and J. H. Kroeze (*A Biblical Hebrew Reference Grammar* [Biblical Languages: Hebrew 3; Sheffield: Sheffield Academic Press, 2002] §40.6) identify the אשר יטב construction in Deut 4:40 as a purpose clause. Though R. D. Holmstedt ("The Story of Ancient Hebrew *'ăšer*," ANES 43 [2006] 7–26) argues for a different syntactical function for אשר, he lists Gen 11:7; 24:3; Exod 20:26; Deut 4:40; 6:3 (2×); 32:46; Josh 3:7; 1 Kgs 22:16; and Neh 8:14 as passages usually cited for the purposive function of אשר (p. 14 n. 19).

44. Joüon (§§168d, 169g) asserts that למען nearly always performs a telic function. Compare H. A. Brongers ("Die Partikel למען in der biblisch-hebräischen Sprache," in *Syntax and Meaning: Studies in Hebrew Syntax and Biblical Exegesis* [ed. C. J. Labuschagne et al.; OtSt 18; Leiden: Brill, 1973] 87–96), who adduces a few passages in Deuteronomy (e.g., 11:8, 25; 14:29; 30:19) where the usual telic function of למען broadens to include aspects of the action's consequence as well as the aim. However, the juxtaposition of למען with אשר in 5:33–6:3 suggests that למען still functions here as a purposive marker.

into a stepping stone to a gushing description of the fecundity of people and land (6:3cd).[45] As a reward for "hearing" and "keeping" Yhwh's commands (6:3a), Israel will "multiply greatly, just as Yhwh, God of your fathers, promised [דבר] you, in a land flowing with milk and honey" (6:3cd). He draws the theological tension between command and promise most tightly by describing the prosperity of people and land as a function of both Israel's covenant compliance ("you shall listen . . . you shall keep") and Yhwh's gracious promise ("just as Yhwh God of your fathers promised you"). However, the balance ultimately tilts toward divine grace because of the rhetorical shift from the promulgation formulas of 5:32–6:2 to the climactic promise formula in 6:3. Divine grace has the last word in the fulfillment of Yhwh's promises, but enjoyment of God's blessings is still predicated on Israel's obedience.[46]

Blended Blessings of Multiplication and Land in Deuteronomy 6:3

Deut 6:3 represents a major shift in Deuteronomy's theology of land in that the phrase "land flowing with milk and honey" appears here for the first time.[47] Though the syntactical function of this clause is problematic, as noted earlier, several scholars have offered the plausible suggestion that the phrase "land flowing with milk and honey" functions as an *accusativus loci*—that is, an accusative of local determination.[48] In the context of 6:3, this sort of adverbial function would denote the physical location where Yhwh's promised blessing of multiplication would take place. If this view is correct, then 6:3 would indicate that Israel's fruitfulness is coterminous with the land's fruitfulness. This hypothesis can be confirmed through an

---

45. Two features of Deut 6:3c accentuate the rhetorical emphasis on multiplication as Yhwh's gracious reward. First, the grammatical number shifts from singular to plural, as if to synchronize Israel's multiplication in population with an increase from a smaller to a larger grammatical number. Second, the adverb מאד emphasizes the boundless nature of Israel's multiplication. Thus the declaration "that you [pl.] will multiply *greatly*" (6:3c) contrasts with the rather pedestrian statement that follows, "that it may go well with you [sg.]" (6:3b). This observation undercuts Mittmann's assertion that the reference to Israel's multiplication is secondary (cf. n. 30 above).

46. Wright, *Deuteronomy*, 93. Compare V. P. Hamilton's caricature of "Deuteronomic theology" as a "system [that is] simple, straightforward, black and white. Those who follow the Lord rightly can instantly expect blessings at every material level; those who repudiate Yahweh's lordship over their lives can expect heartaches, setbacks, sterility, and so forth" (*Handbook to the Pentateuch* [2nd ed.; Grand Rapids, MI: Baker, 2005] 374).

47. The phrase "land flowing with milk and honey" appears 4 more times in Deuteronomy (11:9; 26:9, 15; 27:3) and 14 times outside Deuteronomy (Exod 3:8, 17; 13:5; 33:3; Num 13:27; 14:8; 16:13, 14; Josh 5:6; Jer 11:5; 32:22; Ezek 20:6, 15). See also Deut 31:20, which replaces ארץ with אדמה.

48. E.g., Weinfeld, *Deuteronomy 1–11*, 322–23; Skweres, *Rückverweise*, 165. Compare with similar constructions in Exod 9:19; Judg 20:14; 1 Sam 13:11; 2 Chr 30:13.

examination of the ANE background of both Deut 6:3 and the broader Deuteronomic conception of land.

The view that the final clause in Deut 6:3 functions as an accusative of local determination is supported by a comparison with the Baal cycle from Ugarit. Specifically, the phrase "land flowing with milk and honey" contains striking similarities to El's vision of restored paradisial blessings in the aftermath of Baal's resurrection, as described in lines 10–15 from *KTU* 1.6 iii:[49]

10   In the dream of Beneficent El the Ben[ign,]
11   In the vision of the Creator of Creatures,
12   The heavens rain *oil*,
13   The wadis run with *honey*.
14   Beneficent El the Benign rejoices,
15   His feet on his footstool he stamps.

The correlations between El's vision of a land saturated by "oil" and "honey" and the Deuteronomic idiom have often been noted.[50] Though the parallels between "oil" (line 12) and "milk" (Deut 6:3) are inexact,[51] it should be noted that this passage derives from a broader context in Ugarit that emphasizes Baal's fructifying powers for both people and land,[52] much like the description of YHWH's promises in Deut 6:3. Furthermore, Stern argues that the discrepancy between "oil" and "milk" may be rooted in the conflict between Baal and YHWH. Since this portion of the Baal cycle emphasizes how Baal's return to life allows him to provide a fertile land for his vassals, YHWH's gift of a "land flowing with milk and honey" outdoes Baal by substituting "milk" for "oil," since Israelites probably preferred the former.[53] The pentateuchal references to YHWH as a "living God" (e.g., Num 14:28; Deut 5:23; Josh 3:10) would reinforce YHWH's superiority by underlining his immortality vis-à-vis Baal's cyclical mortality (i.e., *KTU* 1.1–6).

An examination of the overall Deuteronomic theology of land further reinforces the link between the "land flowing with milk and honey" and Israel's own multiplication. In addition to Deut 6:3, Deuteronomy 7 in particular amalgamates the promises of land and multiplication in Moses' polemic against Canaanite fertility religion: "He [YHWH] will love you

---

49. For this translation, see "The Baal Cycle," *KTU* 1.6 iii, lines 10–15 (M. S. Smith, *Ugaritic Narrative Poetry* [ed. S. B. Parker; SBLWAW 9; Atlanta: Scholars Press, 1997] 157–58). Compare with N. Wyatt, *Religious Texts from Ugarit: The Words of Ilimilku and His Colleagues* (Biblical Seminar 53; Sheffield: Sheffield Academic Press, 1998) 137.

50. Wyatt, *Ugarit*, 137 n. 78; W. Herrman, "Baal," *DDD*, 134; Stern, "Origin," 554–57; A. Caquot, "דבש," *TDOT* 3:131.

51. Ausloos, "Land Flowing with Milk and Honey," 300.

52. E.g., in *KTU* 1.4 v, where building Baal's house results in rain, and in *KTU* 1.17 i–ii, where Baal intercedes with El so that Dan'el may receive a son. Moreover, the entire epic of Baal's death and resurrection occurs against the backdrop of the seven-year fertility cult and his restoration to Anat, the goddess of fertility.

53. Stern, "Origin," 555.

and bless you and multiply [רבה] you; he will also bless the fruit [פרי] of your womb and the fruit [פרי] of your ground" (7:13a).[54] Here the organic connection between a fruitful land and fruitful people is obvious through the shared use of "fruit" (פרי) language, for Moses promises that Yhwh will cause fruitfulness to burst forth from the womb (פרי־בטן) and the ground (פרי־אדמה).[55] In addition, Moses subsequently describes Yhwh's blessing of the land using the demythologized names of Mesopotamian and Canaanite fertility deities: "your grain [דגן] and your new wine [תירש] and your oil, the increase [שגר] of your herd and the young [עשתרת] of your flock" (7:13b).[56] Much as in Deut 6:3, the realm where Israel will experience this abundance is the "land that Yhwh swore to your fathers to give you" (7:13c). Thus the polemical use of Canaanite fertility religion in both Deut 6:3 and 7:13 supports the hypothesis that the Deuteronomic references to the "land flowing with milk and honey" represent a partial blending of Yhwh's promises of land and multiplication.[57]

The promises of land and multiplication exhibit a similar interweaving in the rest of Deuteronomy. Much like Deuteronomy 6, Deuteronomy 8 asserts that Israel's attentiveness to Yhwh's commands will result in life and multiplication in an abundant land (8:1; cf. 8:13). In Deuteronomy 11, length of days in the land for the "fathers and their seed" is juxtaposed with fruitful life in the "land flowing with milk and honey" (11:9).[58] In addition, long life itself is described in terms of "increasing" (רבה) days (11:21), an unusual substitution of multiplication terminology for the usual idiom "prolonging [ארך] your days."[59]

---

54. N. MacDonald (*Deuteronomy and the Meaning of "Monotheism"* [FAT 2; Tübingen: Mohr Siebeck, 2003] 159) notes that the purpose of the divine blessings is to demonstrate the character of "Yhwh your God" as the "faithful El" (Deut 7:9).

55. The collocation of פרי and פרי־אדמה also appears in Deut 28:4, 18 (compare 28:53, which refers only to פרי־בטן; and 26:2, 10, which refer only to פרי־אדמה).

56. Hadley ("De-deification," 157–74) argues convincingly that Deuteronomy's use of the terms דגן, תירש, שגר, and עשתרת demythologizes the Mesopotamian and Canaanite deities Dagan, Trt, Shgr, and Ishtar, respectively, in order to refer to the physical entities that they represent rather than the deities themselves. Hadley concludes that "the power of the other deities is virtually eliminated, and Yahweh can reign supreme over the people, keeping the covenant safely intact" (p. 174). Similarly, Weinfeld (*Deuteronomy 1–11*, 373) observes that Deuteronomy's sequence of grain, wine, cattle, and sheep mirrors the sequence of the closing blessings on a Phoenician inscription (see "The Azitawada Inscription," translated by K. L. Younger Jr., *COS* 2:148–49 iii 2–11).

57. O. Eissfeldt ("Der kanaanäische El als Geber der den Israelitischen Erzvätern geltenden Nachkommenschaft- und Landbesitzverheissungen," in *Kleine Schriften* [ed. R. Sellheim and F. Maass; 6 vols.; Tübingen: Mohr, 1962] 4:50–62) also observes the juxtaposition of land and multiplication in the patriarchal narratives. These promises to the patriarchs are vouchsafed by a deity with an El name, as in Deut 7:9.

58. H. C. Brichto ("Kin, Cult, Land and Afterlife: A Biblical Complex," *HUCA* 44 [1973] 30–31) notes that Exod 20:12 (// Deut 5:16) also uses the idiom יארכון ימיך ("you shall prolong your days") in merging the horizons of land and posterity.

59. E.g., Deut 4:40; 5:16, 33; 6:2; 11:9; 17:20; 22:7; 25:15; 30:18, 20; 32:47.

Most significantly, the chronological phases of Israel's experiences of land and multiplication are nearly synchronous in Deuteronomy 28–30. Just as Israel's disobedience will cause possession of the land to be followed by destruction within the land (28:16, 21–24), then exile (28:36, 64–68), and then restoration (30:3–4), disobedience will have the consequences that Israel's multiplication (28:4) will be followed by fruitlessness within the land (28:18, 30, 33, 38–41), population decline through siege-necessitated cannibalism (28:53) and deportation (28:62–63), and finally regrowth upon returning to the land (30:5, 9). In the covenant curses of Deuteronomy 28, followed by the covenant restoration of Deuteronomy 30, land and multiplication follow similar theological trajectories of fulfillment—unfulfillment—refulfillment. However, the horizons of land and multiplication are not completely merged in Deuteronomy, for the multiplication promise is described as partially fulfilled in the narrative present (Deut 1:10; 10:22; cf. Exod 1:7, 12), whereas fulfillment of the land promise is primarily future (1:8; cf. Exod 3:8, 17).

"Yhwh God of the Fathers" as Cosmic and Personal God in Deuteronomy 6:3

Having argued that the polemical portrayal in Deut 7:13–14 represents "a deliberate stab in the jugular of Canaanite religion,"[60] we must balance the Deuteronomic picture of Yhwh's preempting or usurping the roles of Canaanite cosmic deities by noting the features of personal religion that describe Yhwh as the "God of the fathers." Deut 6:3 portrays Yhwh in terms that correspond exactly to the ANE concept of the personal god in three respects. First, the naming of Yhwh as the "God of the fathers" (6:3) mirrors the common ANE use of this title for the personal god.[61] Though scholars once argued that the OT titles "God of the father" and "God of the fathers" referred to personal and cosmic deities, respectively,[62] more-recent ANE comparative studies recognize that the variation between singular "father" and plural "fathers" is simply a matter of how many generations of worshipers are in view.[63] Second, the Deuteronomic portrayal of Yhwh's sovereign but intimate presence with Israel across geographical places differs significantly from the representations of Canaanite cosmic deities, which

---

60. D. I. Block, "Other Religions in Old Testament Theology," in *Biblical Faith and Other Religions: An Evangelical Assessment* (Grand Rapids, MI: Kregel, 2004) 51; cf. Fishbane, *Biblical Myth*, 90–91.

61. For example, the invocation of Aššur as the "god of the fathers" in the witness section of an Old Assyrian letter published in *CCT* 2 6:17–19. A full list of references to Aššur as the "god of the fathers" is found in *CAD* I–J 95; and Vorländer, *Mein Gott*, 12–14.

62. H. G. May, "The God of My Father: A Study of Patriarchal Religion," *JBR* 9 (1941) 155–57; Haran, "Religion," 35–37.

63. Jacobsen (*Treasures of Darkness*, 159) notes that the title of a deity could vary between the "god of the father" and the "god of the fathers," as in the case of Old Assyrian texts that refer to Ilabrat by using both titles.

are mostly attached to places rather than persons.[64] For Israel, the "God of the fathers" who journeyed from Horeb (1:11) to Kadesh (1:21) with his people now promises to accompany them from Moab into the land (6:3; cf. 4:1; 12:1). Third, Yhwh performs the personal god's role of guaranteeing the well-being of his worshipers, especially through providing offspring.[65] While at first glance this function of ANE personal gods might seem identical to the function of Canaanite fertility deities, the ready accessibility of personal gods through prayer distinguishes them from ANE cosmic gods, who typically cannot be bothered with the affairs of ordinary people.[66] For example, Yhwh's gracious intention to fulfill his promises to the "fathers" contrasts strikingly with the Ugaritic depiction of Baal as a cosmic god who constantly battles other deities for supremacy (e.g., Yam, Mot).

In summary, Deut 6:3 describes Yhwh as both Israel's cosmic deity who surpasses the Canaanite fertility deities in promising land and multiplication of his people and the personal deity who serves as the guarantor of these promises.[67] However, Yhwh does not merely possess characteristics of both kinds of deities, for he transcends the categories of cosmic and personal gods by taking promises made to specific individuals (i.e., "fathers") and universalizing them for all Israel. In an extraordinary theological development, Moses declares that every obedient member of the nation can experience the benefits that Yhwh promised to the "fathers."

I conclude briefly with a related redaction-critical issue. The portrayal of Yhwh as both cosmic and personal deity provides a compelling explanation for the question why Moses blends the language of Genesis and Exodus in describing Yhwh's promises in Deut 6:3. On the one hand, Moses speaks of Yhwh's promise of multiplication in terms that recall the patriarchal narra-

---

64. Van der Toorn, *Family Religion*, 81–82; and Mettinger, *In Search of God*, 57. The motif of Yhwh's personal journey with Israel is treated below in the analysis of Deut 12:1 and 27:3.

65. See, for example, the prayer for progeny in *KAI* 216, lines 4–8, cited in Vorländer, *Mein Gott*, 160; see pp. 83, 129–30, and 160–62 for similar prayers from Mesopotamia, Asia Minor, and Syria–Palestine.

66. Walton, *Ancient Near Eastern Thought*, 142–43. Deut 6:3 is unique among ANE texts in that Yhwh is a personal god who speaks (through Moses his mediator), rather than being merely the object of prayers for offspring. Apart from the OT, the characterization of ANE personal gods must be derived circumstantially from laments, vows, incantations, or prayers to the gods rather than from direct speech by the gods themselves (see Jacobsen, *Treasures of Darkness*, 152–55, on the Mesopotamian genres of the "Penitential Psalms" and the "Letters to Gods"). In contrast to the taciturn personal gods who are the object of supplication, the cosmic gods speak frequently in ANE texts (e.g., El in the Baal cycle).

67. D. N. Freedman ("'Who Is like Thee among the Gods?' The Religion of Early Israel," in *Ancient Israelite Religion: Essays in Honor of Frank Moore Cross* [ed. P. D. Miller, P. D. Hanson, and S. D. McBride; Philadelphia: Fortress, 1987] 315–55) notes that, unlike the name Baal, the epithet El could represent both a cosmic and personal god. El was described as both the head of the Canaanite pantheon and an individual's "father," a common term for a personal god.

tives, especially Gen 26:24, 28:13, and 46:3, which involve three episodes where the "God of your father" personally appears to a patriarch in a vision to reiterate the promises. On the other hand, the terminology of a "land flowing with milk and honey" (Deut 6:3) derives from Exodus 3 rather than the patriarchal narratives, since Genesis never characterizes the land of promise in fecund terms of this sort. Therefore, Römer proposes that the references in Deuteronomy to the patriarchal narratives of land promise were added by a postexilic redactor who reworked a text such as Exodus 3 to identify the patriarchs as "fathers."[68] However, the preceding analysis suggests that Deut 6:3 appropriates both Genesis and Exodus language in order to illustrate that Yhwh is both the travel companion of the patriarchs and the almighty deity of the exodus.[69] Much as the terminology of Genesis and Exodus begins to blend in the Deuteronomic portrayal of Israel's past, Moses coalesces the fulfillments of land and multiplication in describing Israel's future. For Israel, the personal and cosmic deity known as the "God of the fathers" and as "your God" is one and the same Yhwh.

The "God of the Fathers" and the Promise of Land

The theological link between the "God of the fathers" appositive and Yhwh's fulfillment of his covenant promises of land is evident in four additional passages (1:21; 4:1; 12:1; 27:3). At first glance, these passages might appear identical to the Deuteronomic land formulas discussed in chaps. 2–3. However, closer examination reveals several differences when the epithet "God of the fathers" appears as the appositive to the Tetragrammaton.

First, these four passages always omit the language of a divine "oath" (נשׁבע) and refer only to a "gift" (נתן) of land. In fact, the four references to a "gift" of land in which Yhwh is identified appositionally as "God of the fathers" are far less common than land-promise formulas in which Yhwh offers the land as both "oath" and "gift" without being identified appositionally as the "God of the fathers" (19×).[70] Second, the identity of the "fathers" in the "God of the fathers" construction is more difficult to determine because this appositive is a relatively fixed idiom that appears throughout the OT. Third, the recipients of the land given by the "God

---

68. Römer, *Israels Väter*, 122.
69. The discourse function of the phrase "land flowing with milk and honey" diverges in Exodus 3 and Deuteronomy 6. The former passage contrasts the "land flowing with milk and honey" to the bondage of Egypt, while Deut 6:3 links a fertile land with the promise of multiplication to the "fathers." Even if Römer were correct that Deut 6:3 cites Exod 3:8 and 17 rather than the patriarchal narratives, he fails to explain why the redactor of Deut 6:3 used the expression "land flowing with milk and honey" differently from Exodus 3. Thus Ausloos ("Land Flowing with Milk and Honey," 304–5) assigns the Exodus 3 references to "land flowing with milk and honey" to the same stratum as other passages that contrast Egypt and Canaan (i.e., Num 13:27; 14:8; 16:13, 14).
70. Deut 1:8, 21, 35; 6:10, 18, 23; 7:13; 8:1; 9:5; 10:11; 11:9, 21; 19:8; 26:3, 15; 28:11; 30:20; 31:7, 23; 34:4. See the detailed analysis in chap. 3.

of the fathers" are always "you," rather than varying among the "fathers" (e.g., 30:20), their "seed" (e.g., 11:9), and "you" (e.g., 6:10), or some combination thereof (e.g., 1:8). The present generation at Moab is thus always the beneficiary of the land gift from the "God of the fathers." Fourth, the "God of the fathers" epithet appears at significant introductory or concluding junctures in Deuteronomy where law and land become rhetorically intertwined (4:1; 12:1). Law is given to govern life in the land, while ongoing life in the land is conditioned on obedience to law.[71] Fifth, the invocation of the "God of the fathers" in fulfilling the land promise is reinforced by the promise formula (i.e., "just as he promised you") in two texts (1:21; 27:3), much like the use of the promise formula in the references to Israel's multiplication (1:11; 6:3). Thus in these four passages, the threefold collocation of land gift, "God of the fathers" appositive, and the promise formula apparently signals a significant milestone in the fulfillment of YHWH's covenant promise with regard to land.

Deuteronomy 12:1 and 27:3 as Putative Historical-Critical Antitheses

Among Deuteronomy's four references to the land promised by the "God of the fathers," Deut 12:1 and 27:3 are particularly intriguing since they are the focus of numerous literary- and tradition-critical debates over Deuteronomy's provenance and theology. Not only do 12:1 and 27:3 form an inclusio around the so-called *Urdeuteronomium* (Deuteronomy 12–26),[72] but these verses seem at first to advocate competing views of Deuteronomy's mandate for the location of Israel's worship. On the one hand, Deut 12:1 forms a superscription to the covenant stipulations found in Deuteronomy 12–26, the first of which calls for the destruction of all places and symbols of Canaanite worship in favor of cultic observance exclusively at "the place that YHWH your God will choose to put his name" (12:5).[73] Scholars thus hold that the demand for a central sanctuary in Deuteronomy 12–26 rep-

---

71. Römer, *Israels Väter*, 114–5; Plöger, *Literarkritische, formgeschichtliche und stilkritische Untersuchungen*, 91–92.

72. Wellhausen regarded Deut 12:1 as the superscription to the *Urdeuteronomium* (see p. 95 n. 16 above). However, W. M. L. De Wette and others who followed him considered 12:2 the beginning of the law code, whereas M. Noth and his followers classified the bulk of 4:44–28:68 as the oldest part of Deuteronomy. For the sake of discussion, I follow Wellhausen's nomenclature in identifying the entire literary unit of Deuteronomy 12–26 as *Urdeuteronomium*.

73. With minor variations, the "place formula" appears 21× in Deuteronomy (12:5, 11, 14, 18, 21, 26; 14:23, 24, 25; 15:20; 16:2, 6, 7, 11, 15, 16; 17:8, 10; 18:6; 26:2; 31:11). See the analysis of the variations of "place" formulas in MT Deuteronomy and other witnesses by L. Laberge, "'Le lieu que YHWH a choisi pour y mettre son Nom' (TM, LXX, Vg, et Targums): Contribution à la critique textuelle d'une formule deutéronomiste," *EstBib* 43 (1985) 209–36; N. Lohfink, "Zur deuteronomischen Zentralisationsformel," *Bib* 65 (1984) 297–328; and B. Halpern, "The Centralization Formula in Deuteronomy," *VT* 31 (1981) 20–38. Halpern's proposal for Deuteronomy 12 is representative. He argues for at least

resents a corrective shift from a multiplicity of cultic sites as allowed by patriarchal religion (e.g., Gen 22:9; 33:20) and prescribed by the Book of the Covenant (Exod 20:24–25).[74] Though the "place" remains anonymous in Deuteronomy, the "place formula" is usually viewed as a cipher for centralization of worship in Jerusalem during the reigns of Hezekiah (2 Kgs 18:3–6, 22) and Josiah (2 Kgs 23:4–20).[75] On the other hand, Deut 27:3 commands Israel to commemorate entry into the land by erecting an altar and a stela at Mount Ebal (27:1–8), instructions that provide the basis for a similar ceremony at Ebal before the conquest (Josh 8:30–35). However, certain elements of the ritual prescribed in Deuteronomy 27 also occur at Gilgal (Joshua 4–5) and Shechem (Joshua 24).[76] Thus Deuteronomy apparently records the "God of the fathers" as commanding Israel to worship at both a central sanctuary (12:1) and a local altar (27:3), a theological paradox in the Deuteronomic conception of "place" that has led to numerous diachronic reconstructions of chaps. 12 and 27.[77]

---

two literary strata on the basis of variation between singular (12:13–31) and plural forms (12:1–12) as well as the variations between שכן and שום in the "place formula."

74. Variations of the centralization thesis are espoused by B. Levinson, A. D. H. Mayes, M. Weinfeld, E. W. Nicholson, R. E. Clements, N. Lohfink, B. Halpern, G. von Rad, S. R. Driver, among many others. While differing on whether centralization represents a new program motivated mainly by religious (Driver, Weinfeld) vis-à-vis nationalistic concerns (Mayes, Nicholson), or rather a tendentious reworking of older cultic regulations (von Rad, Lohfink) or legal traditions (Levinson, Halpern, Clements), these scholars agree that the "place formula" is a polemic against Canaanite religion during the 7th century B.C.E. The variations among centralization hypotheses are thoroughly discussed by Vogt, *Deuteronomic Theology*, 34–58.

75. The identification of the "place" of the "name" as the Jerusalem temple is explicit in 1 Kgs 8:29–30 and 2 Chr 7:15–16. However, the pertinent issue here is whether Jerusalem has always been the sole "place" of worship or whether it was the last "place" in a series. The common use of *altar law* rather than *place formula* tends to foreclose the question whether the "place" must always refer to a central place of worship in Jerusalem. However, the only Deuteronomic collocation of "altar" (מזבח) and "place" (מקום) terminology appears in 26:2–4.

76. The lexical links between Deuteronomy 27 and the Gilgal and Shechem narratives in Joshua are noted by O. Eissfeldt, "Gilgal or Shechem?" in *Proclamation and Presence: Old Testament Essays in Honour of Gwynne Henton Davies* (ed. J. I. Durham and J. R. Porter; Richmond, VA: John Knox, 1970) 90–101. Eissfeldt also proposes that Deuteronomy 27 represents an intentional compromise between Gilgal and Shechem cultic traditions rather than a centralized cult in Jerusalem. Similarly, M. Anbar ("The Story about the Building of an Altar on Mount Ebal," in *Das Deuteronomium: Entstehung, Gestalt und Botschaft* [ed. N. Lohfink; BETL 68; Leuven: Leuven University Press, 1985] 304–9) argues for tradition-critical links between Deut 27:2–8 and Josh 8:30–32 based on shared terminology. In addition to Jerusalem, Gilgal, and Shechem, quite a few other cultic places have been viewed by scholars as the "place formula" instead of its being a reference to a permanent location (e.g., A. C. Welch, T. Oestreicher, W. Stärk, J. N. M. Wijngaards, J. J. Niehaus, J. G. McConville, and G. J. Wenham).

77. Anbar ("Story about the Building of an Altar," 309) concedes that his proposal of a tradition-critical link between the Ebal ceremony (Deuteronomy 27) and the Gilgal tradition (Joshua 8) is incompatible with the Deuteronomic agenda of centralization.

130   Chapter 5: "God of the Fathers" and the Divine Promises

The debate over Deuteronomy's centralization of worship at the "place" is compounded by the tendency to dichotomize Deuteronomic שׁם ("name") theology and Priestly כבוד ("glory") theology as competing conceptions of the divine presence in the cult.[78] In contrast to the Priestly notion of YHWH's presence as an immanent reality in the ark and tabernacle, the Deuteronom(ist)ic school demythologized such corporeal notions by assigning YHWH's presence to heaven (e.g., 26:15), with only YHWH's abstract "name" remaining on earth. Scholarly views on centralization and demythologization in Deuteronomy are thus synergistic by virtue of locating YHWH's hypostatic "name" at a central sanctuary as a substitute for his actual presence.

The differences between Deut 12:1 and 27:3 could also be characterized in theological terms as an antithesis between transcendent and immanent notions of YHWH's presence, respectively. On the one hand, 12:1 putatively headlines the *Urdeuteronomium*, a section that emphasizes YHWH's transcendence in order to support the theological agendas of centralization and demythologization. On the other hand, the reference to a local altar in 27:3–5 (and the theophanic presence usually associated with it)[79] is often attributed to a nondeuteronomic tradition layer in which Israel was allowed to build decentralized, perhaps even multiple altars: "You shall make an altar of earth for me . . . ; in every place where I cause my name to be remembered, I will come to you and bless you" (Exod 20:24; cf. Deut 27:5).[80]

Detailed literary- and tradition-critical operations on Deuteronomy 12 and 27 fall outside the scope of this study. However, a reassessment of 12:1 and 27:3 suggests that the twin references to the "God of the fathers" strike a theological balance between sedentary and mobile notions of YHWH's presence.[81] The close reading of Deuteronomy 12 and 27 presented here attempts to bridge the usual dichotomy between transcendent (i.e., Deu-

---

78. U. Rüterswoorden, "שׁם in Deuteronomium 12," in *Für immer verbündet: Studien zur Bundestheologie der Bible* (ed. C. Dohmen and C. Frevel; SBS 211; Stuttgart: Katholisches Bibelwerk, 2007) 180–86; M. Keller, *Untersuchungen zur deuteronomisch-deuteronomistischen Namenstheologie* (BBB 105; Weinheim: Beltz Athenäum, 1996); T. N. D. Mettinger, *The Dethronement of Sabaoth: Studies in the Shem and Kabod Theologies* (trans. F. H. Cryer; ConBOT 18; Lund: Wallin & Dalholm, 1982); Weinfeld, *Deuteronomy and the Deuteronomic School*, 191–209; R. E. Clements, "Deuteronomy and the Jerusalem Cult Tradition," *VT* 15 (1965) 300–312; von Rad, "Deuteronomy's 'Name' Theology," 37–44.

79. The patriarchs frequently build altars in response to YHWH's personal appearances to them (e.g., Gen 12:7–8; 13:18; 26:24–25; 35:1–7).

80. Von Rad (*Deuteronomy*, 165) assigns the references to (multiple?) altars in Deut 27:5 to a predeuteronomic tradition (cf. Joshua 4), whereas he regards the place formula in Deuteronomy 12 as Deuteronomic (p. 90). Similarly, Levinson (*Deuteronomy and the Hermeneutics*, 28–52) argues that the Deuteronomic place formula borrows and transforms the terminology of Exod 20:24 in order to effect a "double movement of cultic centralization and local secularization" (p. 49).

81. The references to the "God of the fathers" and the land promise in Deut 1:21 and 4:1 are excluded in this chapter, because 1:21 was already treated in chap. 4 in conjunc-

teronomic) and immanent (i.e., Priestly) conceptions of Yhwh. Until now, no exegetical investigation has tested Vorländer's hypothesis that Deuteronomy's references to the "God of the fathers" conceive of Yhwh as the personal god of the entire nation (cf. Deut 4:7).[82] I also propose an alternative explanation for the Deuteronomic "name theology"—namely, that the references to the "God of the fathers" provide rhetorical signals that explicate the divine name and its covenantal character that appear in the narrative of Exodus 3–20, especially the revelation of the Tetragrammaton in Exodus 3 and 6.

Deuteronomy 12:1

אֵלֶּה הַחֻקִּים וְהַמִּשְׁפָּטִים	These are the statutes and the ordinances
אֲשֶׁר תִּשְׁמְרוּן לַעֲשׂוֹת בָּאָרֶץ	that you shall be careful to do in the land
אֲשֶׁר נָתַן יְהוָה אֱלֹהֵי אֲבֹתֶיךָ	that Yhwh God of your fathers has given
לְךָ לְרִשְׁתָּהּ כָּל־הַיָּמִים	for you to possess all the days
אֲשֶׁר־אַתֶּם חַיִּים עַל־הָאֲדָמָה	that you live on the earth.

In Deut 12:1, Moses seems to shift from a general exposition of covenant stipulations (chaps. 5–11) to the specific and detailed consideration of "statutes and ordinances" that will govern Israel's life in the land. Once Israel arrives in the land that the "God of the fathers" has given, its first order of business must be to obliterate "all the places" (כל־המקמות; 12:2), altars, pillars, and idols that the Canaanites use in their pagan worship (12:2–3a). In contrast to this plurality of places and images, 12:3b strikingly goes on to speak of a singular מקום ("place") and שם ("name") for the Canaanite deities that Israel must destroy. This surprising shift to singular nouns in characterizing Canaanite worship sets the stage for a direct contrast to the subsequent description of Yhwh's singular מקום and שם for Israel's worship.[83] The oscillation between plural and singular forms of מקום not only indicates that the term מקום can function distributively in Deuteronomy 12 to refer to multiple places[84] but also that the precise *number* of cultic sites for Israel is less important than Yhwh's *choice* (בחר) of the place in which Israel

---

tion with the exegesis of Deuteronomy 1, and 4:1 is treated in chap. 6's discussion of covenantal forms in Deuteronomy 4.

82. Vorländer, *Mein Gott*, 299.

83. Wright (*Deuteronomy*, 170) helpfully notes that there is a correspondence between singular forms of מקום. Although he is incorrect in contrasting singular and plural forms of "name" (שם never appears in the plural in Deuteronomy), he correctly observes that "[t]o remove the names of Canaan's gods was to remove *their* presence and *their* power, just as the putting of Yahweh's name in a place was to fill it with *his* availability and *his* nearness. But they could not coexist. The names of other gods must be deleted, destroyed, along with all their paraphernalia. The change must be radical" (italics his).

84. Vogt, *Deuteronomic Theology*, 178–79; cf. A. C. Welch, *The Code of Deuteronomy: A New Theory of Its Origin* (London: James Clarke, 1924) 47–49.

worships.⁸⁵ That is to say, Yʜᴡʜ's demand for Israel to worship at a single site springs in part from an intentional break from the Canaanite tendency to worship indiscriminately in every place (e.g., "under every green tree"; 12:2) rather than Yʜᴡʜ's inherent need for a single "place."

In support of this interpretation is the fact that the OT elsewhere records traditions in which Yʜᴡʜ's "name" first dwelled at Shiloh (Jer 7:12; cf. Ps 78:60),⁸⁶ which thus challenges the common notion that mono-Yahwism requires a single sanctuary in Jerusalem. The progression of cultic places in Israel's history, from Shiloh to Jerusalem at the very least, suggests that Deuteronomy 12 was confining worship to a single sanctuary at a given time rather than legislating a permanent cultic center.⁸⁷ However, despite ordaining a single place for Israel's worship, Deuteronomy 12 still asserts that Yʜᴡʜ's holiness extends over the whole land, as in the detailed regulations concerning the slaughter and eating of animals away from the central sanctuary (12:15, 21).⁸⁸ Similarly, Yʜᴡʜ's ability to govern Israel's affairs "in your gates" by forbidding the eating of blood in sacrifice (12:16, 23, 27) and distinguishing between "unclean" and "clean" people (12:23–25) bespeaks his sovereignty away from the "place." Thus "Yʜᴡʜ, God of your fathers" (12:1) is both transcendently powerful in effacing the singular "name" of the Canaanite pantheon that collectively possessed the whole land and immanently present in the way that Israelite worship at a central sanctuary replaced worship of Canaanite gods at a plurality of "places" in the land.⁸⁹

---

85. Y. Suzuki, "'The Place Which Yahweh Your God Will Choose' in Deuteronomy," in *Problems in Biblical Theology: Essays in Honor of Rolf Knierim* (ed. H. T. C. Sun et al.; Grand Rapids, MI: Eerdmans, 1997) 351–52; Miller, *Deuteronomy*, 131–32.

86. The "temple sermon" in Jeremiah 7 exhibits the same collocation of מקום, שם, and שכן Piel found in the Deuteronomic place formula: "But go now to my *place* [מקום] which was in Shiloh, where I made my name [שם] to dwell [שכן] at the first" (Jer 7:12). Such a tradition of cultic worship in the northern city of Shiloh is described by narrative traditions in Joshua 18, Judges 21, and 1 Samuel 1–4.

87. J. G. McConville, "Time, Place and the Deuteronomic Altar-Law," in *Time and Place in Deuteronomy* (JSOTSup 179; Sheffield: Sheffield Academic Press, 1994) 89–139; J. J. Niehaus, "The Central Sanctuary: Where and When?" *TynBul* 43 (1992) 3–30; G. J. Wenham, "Deuteronomy and the Central Sanctuary," *TynBul* 22 (1971) 103–18.

88. Milgrom ("Profane Slaughter," 1–17) observes that the use of זבח in Deut 12:15 and 21 to refer to so-called "profane" slaughter is surprising, since the OT elsewhere uses טבח for slaughter away from the sanctuary. Though Milgrom also suggests that Deuteronomy is conflating זבח and שחט (from P) in order to prescribe that all slaughter should entail slitting the throat, a more likely explanation is that Deuteronomy 12 presumes the holiness of the entire land and not merely the central sanctuary. Vogt (*Deuteronomic Theology*, 183) suggests that the use of זבח to denote "profane" slaughter presumes that all of Israel's life before Yʜᴡʜ is sacred, since all slaughter is sacrifice to Yʜᴡʜ.

89. Maintaining this balance between Yʜᴡʜ's transcendence and immanence in the Deuteronomic place formula provides the best solution for the theological paradox noted by Tigay (*Deuteronomy*, 459): why a transcendent God requires centralization in one place.

The Journey Motif and the Divine Presence in Deuteronomy 12

An examination of the Deuteronomic notion of "place" confirms that the place formulas of Deuteronomy 12 represent one segment of a geographical and theological journey rather than an unequivocal command for centralized worship. First and as already noted,[90] the narrative world of Deuteronomy portrays Israel as continually journeying from Moab ("this place"; 11:5) to the land of promise ("that place"; 12:3). In the chapters preceding Deuteronomy 12, the geographical referent for the term "place" progresses from Kadesh (1:31) to Moab (11:5) to the edge of the land of promise (11:24), thereby identifying way stations in Israel's journey. Upon entering the land, Israel must destroy Canaanite "places" (12:2) on its way to the central "place that YHWH your God will choose from all your tribes" (12:5). McConville rightly observes that the flexible use of מקום to denote both land and sanctuary indicates that "land is a place in a succession of places; the chosen place of worship stands in relationship to the land, and is therefore subordinate to the general tendency of the motif of place in the book."[91] In the vicinity of Deuteronomy 12, the central function of the journey motif is reinforced by Moses' exhortation not to "turn aside [סור] from the way [דרך] that I am commanding you today, to walk after [הלך אחרי] other gods that you have not known" (11:28; cf. 11:22). Israel must therefore stay on the proper physical and spiritual דרך between Horeb and the land of promise rather than being seduced to turn to the "right or left" (e.g., 5:32; 17:11, 20; 28:14). Since these commands to avoid walking to the "right or left" are intended to govern life in the land, it is evident that Israel's metaphorical journey with YHWH continues even after the conquest of Canaan and the long-awaited arrival at the central "place."

Second, the repeated use of the phrase לפני יהוה indicates that Israel's entire journey toward the land takes place in the divine presence. The phrase לפני יהוה not only refers to YHWH's actual presence in the central sanctuary (12:7, 12, 18; 14:23, 26; 15:20; 16:11)[92] but also represents Israel's spatial and theological relationship to YHWH-places outside the land, such as Kadesh (1:45), Horeb (4:10; 9:18, 25), Ebal (27:7), and Moab (29:9[10], 14[15]). The phrase לפני יהוה in Deuteronomy also functions apart from any

---

90. See the discussion of מקום ("place") on pp. 21–22 above.

91. McConville, "Time, Place and the Deuteronomic Altar-Law," 131.

92. Von Rad and Mettinger both assert that D's use of לפני יהוה does not refer to YHWH's actual presence in the sanctuary, as in P (see n. 78). However, I. Wilson (*Out of the Midst of the Fire: Divine Presence in Deuteronomy* [SBLDS 151; Atlanta: Scholars Press, 1995] 131–217) has demonstrated that the spatial and theological coherence of the phrase לפני יהוה in Deuteronomy 12–26 demands YHWH's actual presence in the sanctuary. Far from representing a demythologization of the parallel tetrateuchal narratives, the Deuteronomic descriptions of YHWH's appearances often accentuate his immanence, as in the additional allusions to the divine presence in Deut 9:7b–10:11 vis-à-vis Exodus 32–34 (Wilson, *Out of the Midst of the Fire*, 105–29).

sanctuary or location to denote Israel's timeless posture of living *coram Deo* (6:25; 10:8; 18:7; 19:7; 24:4, 13). This last category of לפני יהוה occurrences is especially significant because it spans both *Urdeuteronomium* and its hortatory framework.

Though Wilson confines his study of לפני יהוה with the place formula to Deuteronomy 12–26,[93] his conclusion that לפני יהוה represents Yhwh's actual presence is supported more broadly by similar uses of the phrase outside *Urdeuteronomium* where a sanctuary may or may not be present. For example, Moses concludes the catechetical conversation between father and son by enjoining Israel's obedience to "all this commandment before Yhwh [לפני יהוה] our God, just as he commanded us" (6:25). Since Moses is referring generally to future life in the land, no reference to cultic centers is presumed in this occurrence of לפני יהוה.[94] Thus it is likely that the existence or nonexistence of a sanctuary is not the paramount issue in living לפני יהוה but, instead, Yhwh's actual presence both in Israel's journeys toward the land and at the central "place." Whether the "name" here denotes a monumental inscription asserting Yhwh's hegemony over the land[95] or functions as a synecdoche for the divine essence and character,[96] the juxtaposition of the "name" with Israel's posture לפני יהוה presupposes a concrete (though not necessarily corporeal)[97] rather than abstract understanding of the presence of Yhwh.[98]

Third, the predominant wording of the place formula using שכן suggests a provisional rather than a permanent dwelling of Yhwh at the "place."[99] The overall use of שכן in the OT indicates resting that is more mobile than ישב but more sedentary than גור.[100] The itinerant sense of שכן is mirrored

---

93. Wilson, *Out of the Midst of the Fire*, 131–97.

94. See also Deut 1:45; 29:9[10]).

95. S. Richter, "The Place of the Name in Deuteronomy," *VT* 57 (2007) 342–66.

96. McConville, *Deuteronomy*, 230; cf. idem, "God's 'Name' and God's 'Glory,'" *TynBul* 30 (1979) 149–63.

97. Deuteronomy 4 repeatedly asserts that Israel hears Yhwh's voice "out of the midst of the fire" while never seeing a physical form to represent Yhwh's presence (4:12, 15, 33, 36; cf. 26:15). Furthermore, Wilson (*Out of the Midst of the Fire*, 68–73) concludes that, since Yhwh's speech comes both from heaven and from the earthly cloud, Yhwh is represented in Deuteronomy as being present in both places (e.g., 4:36).

98. Contra Mettinger, who asserts that לפני יהוה "may well be a sort of linguistic fossil, bearing no semantic cargo of importance," though he grants that "at face value this expression makes it difficult to speak of a Name theology in Deuteronomy" (*Dethronement*, 53).

99. The infinitival verb of the place formula varies between לשכן (12:11; 14:23; 16:2, 6, 11; 26:2) and לשום (12:5, 21, 14:24), or the use of both (12:5). Though arguing from varying diachronic premises, scholars generally agree that the לשכן form is primary and the לשום form secondary, with the latter being an explication or expansion of the former (e.g., Lohfink, "Zur deuteronomischen Zentralisationsformel," 298; Halpern, "Centralization," 30–33). In the discussion below, I suggest that these are synonymous phrases for which no direction of diachronic dependence can conclusively be established.

100. G. H. Wilson, "שכן," *NIDOTTE* 4:109–10. In contrast to Wilson's view, the important monograph by S. Richter (*The Deuteronomistic History and the Name Theology:* lešakkēn

Analysis of Texts   135

by its nominal form מִשְׁכָּן, the Priestly term for the mobile tabernacle that traveled with the Israelites (e.g., Num 10:11; Josh 23:19).[101] While a shared triconsonantal root hardly guarantees an identical semantic range,[102] the use of the same root in שׁכן and מִשְׁכָּן suggests that the Deuteronomic use of שׁכן and the Priestly use of מִשְׁכָּן are somehow linked.[103] It is surprising,

---

šemô šām *in the Bible and the Ancient Near East* [BZAW 318; Berlin: de Gruyter, 2002]) asserts that the Deuteronomic references to לשכן שמו שם are borrowed from the Akkadian idiom *šuma šakānu* ("to place the name"), which typically refers to the erection of a monument or stela by a victorious king to commemorate conquest of a foreign land. Richter's work builds on prior explorations of *šuma šakānu* by Wenham, "Deuteronomy and the Central Sanctuary," 112–14; S. D. McBride, *The Deuteronomic Name Theology* (Ph.D diss., Harvard University, 1969) 86–99; and R. de Vaux, "Le lieu que Yahvé a choisi pour y établir son nom," in *Das ferne und nahe Wort: Festschrift Leonhardt Rost zur Vollendung seines 70. Lebensjahres* (ed. F. Maas; BZAW 105; Berlin: Alfred Töpelmann, 1967) 219–28.

Richter demonstrates conclusively that the Akkadian etymology of שׁכן originates with an East Semitic G-stem ("to put") as opposed to a West Semitic D-stem ("to dwell"). The use of לשכן שמו שם (i.e., Piel infinitive construct) in Deuteronomy would then be borrowed from the transitive sense of the East Semitic G-stem. Richter proposes that, since the borrowed idiom לשכן שמו שם was somewhat opaque to its ancient readers, a redactor inserted the synonymous phrase לשום ("to put") as an explicative calque. By demonstrating that the phrase לשכן שמו שם can refer to sovereignty over the land rather than an abstraction of the divine presence, Richter has provided a viable alternative to the "Deuteronomic name theology" of von Rad and Mettinger, among others.

However, Richter's argument overreaches the textual evidence at times. It seems an etymological fallacy to argue that the Akkadian loan-phrase exhausts the discourse meaning of שׁכן in Deuteronomy 12 (see a similar critique of such approaches by A. R. Hulst, "שׁכן," *TLOT* 3:1327). By arguing that the "name" of Deuteronomy 12 refers primarily to a monumental inscription, she seems to dismiss prematurely the relevance of the juxtaposition of the "name" with "place" formulas elsewhere in 2 Sam 7:23; 1 Kgs 8:16–20; 9:3; 11:36; 14:21; 2 Kgs 21:4, 7. In 1 Kings 8, especially, the lexical sense of the word alternates paronomastically among Yhwh's dwelling, presence, and fame (8:16, 17, 18, 19, 20, 29, 33, 35, 42, 43c, 43e). Richter (*Deuteronomistic History and the Name Theology*, 36–39) thus draws too stark a dichotomy between concrete and abstract notions of "name" when she avers that an abstract sense for "name" necessarily leads to Deuteronomic name theology. Similar criticisms of Richter's lexical distinctions have been registered by T. N. D. Mettinger ("Review of S. L. Richter, *The Deuteronomistic History and the Name Theology*," *JBL* 122 [2003] 754–55) and J. Van Seters ("Review of S. L. Richter, *The Deuteronomistic History and the Name Theology*," *JAOS* 123 [2003] 871–72).

101. In contrast to the putatively Priestly material's use of מקדש to denote the entire cultic complex (Exod 25:8), מִשְׁכָּן refers specifically to the mobile tent within the larger מקדש where Yhwh's presence dwelled. The word מִשְׁכָּן appears 58× in Exodus 25–31 and 35–40, two sections widely acknowledged as Priestly (on which, see Childs, *Exodus*, 529–30).

However, in poetic texts outside the Pentateuch, מִשְׁכָּן can function as a semantic parallel to terms referring to sedentary places such as the temple (Pss 26:8; 74:7; 84:2[1]; 132:5, 7; Jer 9:19) and Jerusalem/Zion (Pss 43:3; 46:5[4]; 87:2; Jer 30:18); or other fixed dwellings (Ps 49:12[11]; Isa 22:16; 32:18; Ezek 37:27).

102. J. Barr, *The Semantics of Biblical Language* (Oxford: Oxford University Press, 1961) 100–106.

103. D. T. Olson ("Deuteronomy as De-centering Center: Reflections on Postmodernism and the Quest for a Theological Center of the Hebrew Scriptures," *Semeia* 71 [1995] 124) suggests that the place formula's use of שׁכן evokes "a mobility and freedom in God's

however, that the various forms of משכן have been claimed by opposing sides in the dialectic between sedentary (i.e., Deuteronomic שם theology) and mobile (i.e., Priestly כבוד theology) conceptions of Yhwh's presence.

This ascription of שכן forms to competing literary strata owes more to tradition-critical views on the centralization of worship than to a careful comparison of the so-called D and P writings in light of ANE evidence.[104] Moreover, if P predates D, as OT scholars increasingly argue,[105] then it may follow that the place formula encapsulates the final destination of Israel's journey with YHWH that begins in the Tetrateuch rather than being a monolithic call to centralized worship.[106] The author of Deuteronomy 12 could easily have used the term ישב rather than שכן to refer to the divine presence if a sedentary sense were required for YHWH's "name."[107]

The Theological Function of the "Name" in Deuteronomy 12

The prominence of the journey motif in Deuteronomy suggests that the "name" of YHWH functions as a synecdoche for YHWH's actual presence in Israel's midst. Having demonstrated the superiority of YHWH's "name" over the "name" of Canaanite gods, YHWH's dwelling at the "place" denotes his claim to sovereignty over the "place" and a corresponding invitation for Israel to worship and perform its cultic duties. Thus Moses commands that the sanctuary where YHWH's "name" dwells be the place where Israel seeks YHWH (12:5) and brings its offerings (12:11, 26, etc.). Once the people have

---

presence and character which may become 'de-centered' from any humanly designated center of worship."

104. Richter (*Deuteronomistic History and the Name Theology*, 106–7) demonstrates that even when the Semitic root *škn* is used in Eastern and Western Semitic languages with the G-stem, transitive sense ("to put"), such dwellings are not necessarily fixed and permanent (e.g., Mari Akkadian *šuma šakānum* referring to setting a tent, and *mšknt* denoting the tent itself). Thus it seems unwise to hold that the Deuteronomic use of שכן and the Priestly use of משכן represent incompatible notions of the divine presence.

105. For example, G. J. Wenham ("The Priority of P," *VT* 49 [1999] 240–58) contends that P forms the backbone for the entire Tetrateuch, including material usually attributed to J. In addition, the idea that D's use of the promulgation and promise formulas presupposes P has been argued convincingly by Milgrom, "Profane Slaughter," 1–17; and Skweres, *Rückverweise*.

106. P. P. Jenson (*Graded Holiness: A Key to the Priestly Conception of the World* [JSOTSup 106; Sheffield: Sheffield Academic Press, 1992] 112–14) similarly concludes that von Rad's dichotomy between theologies of presence (*Präsenztheologie*) and manifestation (*Erscheinungstheologie*) should be recast as a spectrum that includes static and dynamic conceptions of the divine presence. The ANE concept of "sacred space" allows transcendent and immanent dimensions of divine presence to coexist without contradiction.

107. However, both ישב and שכן appear in the narrative of Solomon's dedication of the temple. In response to YHWH's declaration that "he would dwell [שכן] in thick darkness" (1 Kgs 8:12), Solomon responds that "I have surely built . . . a place for you [YHWH] to dwell [ישב] forever" (8:13). This juxtaposition of ישב and שכן suggests that the Deuteronom(ist)ic school that produced this narrative maintained a theological tension between sedentary and mobile notions of the divine presence.

fully obeyed these covenant stipulations, both in destroying the Canaanite religious system (12:2–4) and by instituting proper worship of Yhwh at the "place" (12:5–27), the promise by the "God of the fathers" (12:1) of receiving the land will be completely fulfilled.

The case for a concrete rather than abstract understanding of the "name" is reinforced by the way in which the ancient witnesses interpreted the place formula. Prior to modern theories about the Deuteronomic name theology, these witnesses universally understood the place formula as references to Yhwh's actual presence. A comparison between the MT and the LXX is particularly illuminating in this regard. In the first occurrence of the place formula in Deut 12:5, for example, a comparison of the verbs used by the MT and the LXX reveals that Heb. שׂום ("to place") and שׁכן ("to put, dwell") have been rendered by Gk. ἐπικαλέομαι ("to call by name") and ἐπονομάζω ("to invoke"), respectively. Although the LXX exhibits a tendency to harmonize the MT forms of the place formula,[108] the possibilities of divergent *Vorlagen* and scribal error are mitigated here by the observation that the LXX consistently uses the infinitival form ἐπικληθῆναι ("to be invoked") to render both שׁכן and שׂום.[109] The one-time rendering of Gk. ἐπονομάσαι for Heb. לשׂום in Deut 12:5 arises from this verse's unique juxtaposition of לשׁכן and לשׂום forms.[110] Thus it is probable that the verbs שׁכן and שׂום function in the place formula as virtual synonyms.

It is significant that, of these two Greek verbs in the LXX place formula, ἐπικαλέομαι not only can render Heb. שׁכן elsewhere in the LXX (Exod 29:45—a P text!); it constitutes the most frequent LXX religious term for worship and prayer.[111] Wevers aptly concludes: "What LXX intends is the understanding that God's earthly presence signifies the reality of his invocation, with ἐκεῖ specifying its location."[112] Thus the dynamic rendering of the place formula in the LXX accentuates a concrete understanding of the "name" on the one hand, while deemphasizing the need for a permanent "place" on the other.

In conclusion, the journeying of the "God of the fathers" (12:1) with the nation toward the central "place" supports Vorländer's hypothesis that

---

108. See the LXX's addition of the phrase ἐπικληθῆναι τὸ ὄνομα αὐτοῦ ἐκεῖ in 12:26; 17:8, and 10, even though the infinitival clauses with לשׁכן and לשׂום are lacking.

109. The aorist passive infinitive ἐπικληθῆναι renders both לשׁכן in 12:11; 14:23; 16:2, 6, and 11; and לשׂום in 12:5, 21; and 14:24. Thus C. McCarthy (*BHQ*, 85) notes that the LXX's modifications of the place formula spring from attempts at exegesis rather than the use of a *Vorlage* that differs from the MT.

110. C. McCarthy, *BHQ*, 85.

111. L. Coenen, "Call," *NIDNTT* 1:272; cf. L. Spicq, "ἐπικαλέω," *TLNT* 2:44.

112. Wevers, *Notes on the Greek Text*, 209. Similarly, T. Wittbruck ("The So-Called Antianthropomorphisms in the Greek Text of Deuteronomy," *CBQ* 38 [1976] 29–34) rebuts the tendency by Deuteronomic name theologians to view the LXX's interpretations as part of a demythologizing agenda. Wittbruck shows that the LXX is rendering dynamic equivalents for Yhwh's presence rather than avoiding anthropomorphic terminology.

138   Chapter 5: "God of the Fathers" and the Divine Promises

Deuteronomy portrays Yhwh as Israel's personal god. Though the reference to the "God of the fathers" (12:1) has generally been overlooked, with scarcely any mention in the major commentaries and exegetical studies of Deuteronomy 12,[113] the preceding analysis has demonstrated that "Yhwh, God of the fathers" possesses both immanent and transcendent characteristics in traveling with his people toward the land. The unexpected reappearance in Deut 12:1 of the "God of the fathers" epithet that had been unused since Deut 6:3 signals a "foregrounding"[114] of the *Leitmotif* of the personal God's journey with Israel. The same "God of the fathers" (Exod 3:6, 16) who once promised to bring Israel into the "land flowing with milk and honey" (Exod 3:7–8, 17; cf. Deut 6:3) will soon confirm the faithful character of the divine name through Israel's entrance into "the land that Yhwh, God of your fathers has given you to possess as long as you live on the earth" (Deut 12:1).[115]

Deuteronomy 27:3

לְמַעַן אֲשֶׁר תָּבֹא אֶל־הָאָרֶץ	... so that you might enter the land
אֲשֶׁר־יְהוָה אֱלֹהֶיךָ נֹתֵן לָךְ	that Yhwh your God is giving to you,
אֶרֶץ זָבַת חָלָב וּדְבָשׁ	a land flowing with milk and honey,
כַּאֲשֶׁר דִּבֶּר יְהוָה אֱלֹהֵי־אֲבֹתֶיךָ לָךְ	just as Yhwh God of your fathers promised you.[a]

a. This rendering reflects the MT. The LXX substitutes the appositive "God of your fathers" for "your God" (27:3b), but this additional reference to Yhwh as "God of the fathers" is probably an assimilation to the "God of the fathers" epithet at the end of the verse.

Deuteronomy 27 marks the beginning of a shift in the book from oral to written communication.[116] After Israel crossed the Jordan, Yhwh's revelation to Israel would assume a visual and timeless character through the command for Israel to erect lime-covered stones containing "all the words of this Torah" (27:3a). The recording of these inscriptions will allow Israel to penetrate into the heart of the "land flowing with milk and honey, just

---

113. A survey of the Deuteronomy commentaries by S. R. Driver, G. von Rad, J. A. Thompson, P. Buis and J. Leclerq, P. C. Craigie, H. D. Preuss, E. H. Merrill, J. H. Tigay, C. J. H. Wright, D. L. Christensen, R. D. Nelson, W. Brueggemann, and J. G. McConville reveals voluminous discussion on the role of Deuteronomy 12 in the centralization and demythologization of Israel's worship but no acknowledgment of the significance of the "God of the fathers" epithet in Deut 12:1.

114. As opposed to linguists' use of the term *foregrounding* to denote the discourse function of nonstandard word order, literary critics' use of *foregrounding* can denote the highlighting of an old motif through its reintroduction into the narrative after a hiatus. See the general discussion of foregrounding by W. van Peer and F. Hakemulder, "Foregrounding," in *Encyclopedia of Language and Linguistics* (ed. K. Brown; 14 vols.; Oxford: Elsevier, 2006) 4:546–51.

115. McConville, *Deuteronomy*, 230; Zimmerli, *I Am Yahweh*, 104.

116. Sonnet, *Book within the Book*, 85–92.

as Yhwh, God of your fathers promised you" (27:3c). This use of the "God of the fathers" epithet appears in a promise formula to underscore the imminent actualization of Yhwh's ancient gift of land. At Mount Ebal as well (27:4), Israel must build a stone altar in order to offer burnt offerings and peace offerings (27:5–7). After another exhortation to obedience (27:9–10), Moses divides the people into two groups (27:11–26) for antiphonal recitation of the blessings and the curses on Mts. Gerizim and Ebal, respectively.

Literary-Critical Issues in Deuteronomy 27

As noted earlier, the ritual prescribed at Ebal in Deuteronomy 27 has frequently been treated as the "immanent" and "decentralized" antithesis to the "transcendent" and "centralized" worship of Yhwh prescribed in Deuteronomy 12. The inclination to pit these chapters against one another and, more broadly, to treat the entirety of Deuteronomy 27 as a secondary addition to *Urdeuteronomium* has been buttressed by several literary-critical problems in tracing the flow of argument between Deuteronomy 27 and its neighboring chapters.

First, Deuteronomy 27 seems to interrupt the logical progression between the otherwise adjoining references to Yhwh's setting Israel "high above the nations of the earth" (26:19; 28:1). Second, the sudden narrative reference to Moses in the third person (27:1) breaks the flow of the first-person Mosaic speeches.[117] Third, Deuteronomy 27 lists only curses for disobedience (27:15–26), whereas Deuteronomy 28 lists both blessings (28:3–14) and curses (28:15–68).[118] Fourth, the curses in Deuteronomy 27 focus on the nature of the transgressions, whereas Deuteronomy 28 expounds in detail on the disastrous effects of the curses (28:20–68) with only a brief catalog of the curses themselves (28:16–19). These literary-critical issues have led numerous scholars to regard Deuteronomy 27 or some significant portion thereof as a secondary interpolation between Deut 26:19 and 28:1.[119]

Literary-critical challenges are also found within Deuteronomy 27 itself. First, a solecism occurs when the plurality of persons represented by "Moses and the elders" commands the people using a first-person singular verb (ויצו; "then *he* commanded"; 27:1). Second, the voices speaking in Deuteronomy 27 shift rapidly among Moses and the elders (27:1), Moses

---

[117]. Although narrative references to "Moses" are quite common in Deuteronomy (33×), they are typically confined to the narrative frame of the book in chaps. 1–4 and 31–34. The last explicit reference to Moses before Deut 27:1 occurs at the beginning of the second address when he recapitulates the Decalogue (5:1).

[118]. I. Lewy ("The Puzzle of Dt. XXVII: Blessings Announced, but Curses Noted," *VT* 12 [1962] 207–11) also observes that, despite the listing of the tribes assigned to recite the blessings (27:12), no blessings are actually found in Deuteronomy 27.

[119]. E.g., D. I. Block, "Recovering the Voice of Moses: The Genesis of Deuteronomy," *JETS* 44 (2001) 396–97; Tigay, *Deuteronomy*, 486–89; Cairns, *Word*, 229–33; Mayes, *Deuteronomy*, 340–48; Driver, *Deuteronomy*, 294–95.

and the Levitical priests (27:9), then back to Moses alone (27:11). The shifting of voices stands in stark contrast to Moses' continuous speech in Deut 6:4–26:19. Third, the duplicate instructions on erecting lime-covered stones (27:2, 4) have led scholars to detect a literary doublet. Fourth and similarly, scholars have regarded the dual commands to erect both stelae and an altar as a conflation of two originally distinct traditions. Fifth, there is some chronological ambiguity about whether Israel is to erect the stelae immediately upon crossing the Jordan (27:3) or closer to Ebal (27:4). These and other infelicities lead to the identification of multiple strata within Deuteronomy 27.[120]

The "God of the Fathers" and ANE Covenant Confirmation in Deuteronomy 27

While some of these literary-critical problems can be addressed by synchronic approaches,[121] a more fruitful alternative to the atomizing impulse of diachronic approaches lies in analyzing Deuteronomy 27 within its ANE context. Specifically, the stelae associated with the ritual in Deut 27:1–8 are similar to at least two kinds of Mesopotamian stone monuments: (1) the stelae of Mesopotamian kings; and (2) the *narû* inscriptions denoting a royal land grant, which are usually given the misnomer *kudurru* (i.e., "boundary markers").[122] A comparison with other ANE practices reveals that Deuter-

---

120. E.g., Anbar, "Story about the Building of an Altar," 304–9; E. Bellefontaine, "The Curses of Deuteronomy 27: Their Relationship to the Prohibitives," in *A Song of Power and the Power of Song: Essays on the Book of Deuteronomy* (ed. D. L. Christensen; SBTS 3; Winona Lake, IN: Eisenbrauns, 1993) 256–68; R. P. Merendino, "Dt 27,1–8: Eine literarkritische und überlieferungsgeschichtliche Untersuchung," *BZ* 24 (1980) 194–207; I. Lewy, "Puzzle of Dt. XXVII," 209–11; Eissfeldt, "Gilgal," 90–101; von Rad, *Deuteronomy*, 164–65. Of these authors, Merendino proposes a particularly complex, five-stage textual history: (1) Deut 27:1, 3b, 5a, and 7 derive from Hezekiah's time; (2) 27:5b and 6 were inserted between the reigns of Hezekiah and Josiah; (3) 27:2b–3a and 8 were inserted during Josiah's time; (4) 27:4 was added after Josiah's time but before final Deuteronom(ist)ic editing; and (5) the Deuteronom(ist)ic school added 27:1b and touched up the passage to suit its concerns.

121. Against diachronic approaches, McConville has defended the coherence of Deuteronomy 27 within its present context (*Deuteronomy*, 387–88); see also Christensen, *Deuteronomy 21:10–34:12*, 659; P. Barker, "The Theology of Deuteronomy 27," *TynBul* 49 (1998) 277–303; J. R. Lundbom, "The Inclusio and Other Framing Devices in Deuteronomy I–XXVIII," *VT* 46 (1996) 312–13; Craigie, *Deuteronomy*, 212; and Lohfink, *Hauptgebot*, 233–34. These scholars typically argue that the various elements of Deuteronomy 27 are structured as a chiastic pair with earlier or later sections in the book (e.g., the announcement of the ceremony on Gerizim and Ebal in 11:26–32).

122. K. E. Slanski (*The Babylonian Entitlement* Narûs [Kudurrus]: *A Study in Their Form and Function* [Boston: American Schools of Oriental Research, 2003] 19–64) overturns conventional usage by demonstrating that Akk. *kudurru* refers to boundaries or boundary markers that lack inscriptions, whereas Akk. *narû* refers to inscribed and sculpted stone stelae. The former are found in liminal places, whereas the latter are found in temples. It is noteworthy that the *narû* were also known as Akk. *abnu*, a cognate with Heb. אבן (cf. Deut 27:2, 4, 8).

onomy 27 describes a covenant ratification ceremony to reaffirm Yhwh's sovereignty in consummating his promise to give Israel the land. As in previous passages, the reappearance of the epithet "God of the fathers" (27:3) in apposition to the Tetragrammaton signals an epochal moment in confirming Yhwh's faithfulness to his covenant.

The various stelae of Mesopotamian kings provide a first line of response to redaction-critical objections regarding the juxtaposition of an altar and stelae in Deut 27:1–8. As already noted, some have argued that the altar derives from a Shechem tradition (Joshua 24) whereas the stelae derive from a Gilgal tradition (Joshua 4–5). However, recent archaeological excavations have provided conclusive evidence that the combination of an altar and stelae is a standard feature of Late Bronze cultic sites, as at Shechem and Hazor.[123] The material remains found in the Iron II temple at Arad confirm that altars and stelae were also used together in Israelite worship.[124] Redaction-critical explanations to account for the juxtaposition of altars and stelae in Deuteronomy 27 thus become unnecessary.[125]

Furthermore, to the extent that the monument described in Deuteronomy 27 represents a victory stela where Yhwh's "name" is inscribed (cf. 11:26–12:3),[126] this passage may also portray Yhwh as the cosmic deity who memorializes his victory over the Canaanite pantheon by commanding Israel to erect a stone monument. This interpretation must remain provisional given the multifaceted roles of stelae in the ANE.[127] Nevertheless, in the Ebal ceremony the reader can hear an echo of Exodus 24, a passage that records a juxtaposition of altars and stelae much as in Deuteronomy 27. In this covenant ratification ceremony at Sinai, Israel is also commanded to offer "whole burnt offerings" (עלות) and "peace offerings" (שלמים) on an altar surrounded by "stone pillars" (מצבות; Exod 24:3–4; cf. Deut 27:5–6).[128]

---

123. Richter, "Place of the Name," 358–59.
124. Richter, "Place of the Name," 360.
125. Similarly, Barker ("Deuteronomy 27," 295–97) provides a theological explanation for the juxtaposition of the stelae and altar. He observes that the Torah inscribed on the stones exposes Israel's sin in the land, whereas the altar and the offerings offered on it provide for atonement. Thus the Ebal ceremony reflects the tension between law and grace in Israel's immediate future.
126. As argued by Richter, "Place of the Name," 343–44; cf. idem, *Deuteronomistic History and the Name Theology*, 139–42. However, Richter's argument that Deuteronomy identifies Ebal itself as the "place" overlooks the numerous differences between cultic settings in Deuteronomy 12 and 27. Deuteronomy 12 commands regular cultic observance at the "place," whereas Deuteronomy 27 refers to a one-time event at Ebal, upon crossing the Jordan.
127. Sonnet (*Book within the Book*, 92–94) lists the following functions of inscribed stones in the ANE: treaty commemoration (e.g., Aramean treaties from Sefire), legal material (e.g., Hammurabi's code), commemorative stones for a completed journey (e.g., by Greek settlers in Cyrene and Libya), boundary stones (i.e., *kudurru* inscriptions), and Babylonian entitlement stones (i.e., *narû* inscriptions).
128. Block, *Deuteronomy* (unpublished MS), 767; Sonnet, *Book within the Book*, 92.

Thus the juxtaposition of altars and stelae as prescribed in Deuteronomy 27 is not only quite normal in the ANE but also seems to represent an imaginative reenactment of the covenant ratification ceremony of Exodus 24.[129]

Second, Deut 27:1–8 incorporates two particular functions of the *narû* inscriptions in the royal land grant ceremony that are significant for understanding the invocation of the "God of the fathers" (27:3).[130] The *narû* inscription's first function is to formalize the lines of inheritance for a son to receive the land from his father, since a son could receive the family inheritance only when the father had officially given it to him.[131] In Deuteronomy 27, Israel's entry into the land thus provides a suitable occasion for commemorating the formal adoption of Israel (cf. 26:16–19) as a son by "Yhwh, God of your fathers."

Another function of the *narû* inscription is to express the eternal durability of a land grant by showering imprecations on transgressors of the stipulations of the *narû* and anyone who damaged the *narû* stone itself.[132] The *narû* inscription's role in protecting the rights of the vassal landowner against invaders thus accounts for the absence of blessings in the Ebal ceremony.[133] In short, the *narû*-like inscriptions in Deuteronomy 27 commemorate Israel's entry into the land promised by the "God of the fathers."

Despite these similarities with the Mesopotamian monumental traditions, it should also be noted that Deuteronomy 27 modifies the ANE traditions for the sake of its unique theological agenda. Most significantly, the erection of *narû*-like stones at the liminal location of Ebal represents a striking departure from the usual location of *narû* inscriptions, which were typically set up before the gods in their temples.[134] It is remarkable that, in Deuteronomy 27, the testimonial function of the *narû*-like inscription has been enforced through stelae erected in a *kudurru*-like location. Moses' injunction to erect stelae in Ebal thus presumes both Yhwh's sovereignty over the entire land and his immanent presence with the nation in the outer reaches of Canaan, far away from the "place that Yhwh your God shall choose" (12:5).

In conclusion, a reading of Deuteronomy 27 within its ANE and biblical context indicates that the invocation of the "God of the fathers" is closely associated with Yhwh's confirmation of his covenant. Since Moses had earlier declared that Yhwh and Israel were joined as covenant partners

---

129. However, it is unclear whether the stone pillars in Exodus 24 are inscribed as they are in Deuteronomy 27. Moses writes down the words of Yhwh and then builds an altar with 12 pillars (Exod 24:4), but his writing surface is not specified.

130. The various formal similarities between Deuteronomy 27 and ANE land grants in the *narû* inscriptions are observed by A. E. Hill ("The Ebal Ceremony as Hebrew Land Grant?" *JETS* 31 [1988] 399–406), although he uses the older terminology of *kudurru*.

131. Slanski, *Entitlement* Narûs, 115–16.

132. Slanski, *Entitlement* Narûs, 144.

133. Hill, "Grant," 403.

134. Slanski, *Entitlement* Narûs, 55–57.

(26:16–19),[135] the ceremony prescribed in Deuteronomy 27 now completes the tripartite relationship among deity – land – people by incorporating the newly conquered land into the relationship between deity and people. This tripartite relationship was anticipated at Sinai, but its consummation has been delayed by Israel's disobedience and inability to enter the land.[136] YHWH has remained true to his promises as the "God of the fathers" despite Israel's many failures.

The covenantal import of the "God of the fathers" epithet explains why Moses selects a mountain so near Shechem, the city where the patriarchs often encountered YHWH in the giving of the covenant promises (e.g., Gen 12:6–7; 33:18–20). Israel's return to this place of pilgrimage indicates that the ancient promises are now being fulfilled by the selfsame "God of the fathers" who appeared to the patriarchs and reiterated these promises to the generation enslaved in Egypt (Exod 3:14, 16; cf. 6:3–8).[137] This "God of the fathers" cannot be confined to a single "place," for Moses' injunction to present "whole burnt offerings" (עלות) to YHWH near Shechem reinforces the earlier observation that Israel's immanent god can fulfill promises and receive cultic worship away from the "place."[138] Therefore, the differences between Israel's worship in Deuteronomy 12 and 27 seem to represent a succession of intermediate destinations in Israel's itinerary rather than irreconcilable discrepancies between tradition layers.[139] In both chapters, the "God of the fathers" who accompanied the ancestors also travels with Israel toward the land as both personal and cosmic deity.[140]

---

135. Though the word ברית is not used in Deut 26:16–19, the presence of covenant concepts in the performative speech of the so-called *Bundesformel* (i.e., "YHWH will be your God . . . and you will be his people"; 26:17–18) has been demonstrated by Lohfink, "Bund als Vertrag," 215–39.

136. Block, *Deuteronomy*, 776.

137. Barker ("Deuteronomy 27," 297–300) views the references to Shechem as allusions to the patriarchal narratives, thus suggesting the patriarchs as "fathers." However, Barker neglects to note that the "God of the fathers" epithet occurs in Exodus 3 and 6 to denote YHWH's confirmation of his covenant with the patriarchs and their descendants through the exodus. Thus the "fathers" in the "God of the fathers" epithet could refer generally to Israel's ancestors instead of only to the patriarchs.

138. Compare with Richter ("Place of the Name," 342–66), who regards Mount Ebal itself as the "place" named by Deuteronomy 12. Nonetheless, it is striking that Deuteronomy records injunctions for Israel to present "whole burnt offerings" (עלות) and to "rejoice" (שמח) at both the "place" (12:7, 12, 18) and Ebal (27:6–7).

139. McConville, "Time, Place and the Deuteronomic Altar-Law," 138–39.

140. While in the present analysis I am not explaining all the unusual features of Deuteronomy 27 in its literary context, I am addressing two of the more significant reasons for regarding the chapter as secondary. First, Deuteronomy 27 no longer needs to be regarded as the historical-critical antithesis to Deuteronomy 12 with regard to centralization of worship. Second, the juxtaposition of an altar and stelae in Deuteronomy 27 is native to the ANE.

The "God of the Fathers" and Yhwh's Covenant

The last two Deuteronomic references to the "God of the fathers" demonstrate Yhwh's faithfulness to his word through the actions of exodus (26:7) and exile (29:24[25]). In contrast to the previous five references (1:8; 4:1; 6:3; 12:1; 27:3), where Moses exhorts Israel in the narrative present, these two references to the "God of the fathers" contain proleptic glimpses of Israel's alternative destinies in Deuteronomy's narrative world. In the first occurrence, the Israelite farmer initiates the firstfruits liturgy (26:1–11) by reciting the "little historical creed" (26:5–9).[141] Among other features, this creed asserts every Israelite's solidarity with the oppressed generation that cried out to the "God of the fathers" (26:7), experienced supernatural deliverance from Egypt (26:8), and received the gift of a "land flowing with milk and honey" (26:9). In the second occurrence, an unidentified voice explains to astonished foreign observers that Israel's uprooting from the land is divine punishment for violating "the covenant of Yhwh, God of their fathers, which he made with them when he brought them out of the land of Egypt" (29:24[25]). The first occurrence of the "God of the fathers" anticipates Israel's immediate future in the land, whereas the second occurrence foretells a more distant future when Israel disobeys Yhwh.

Technically speaking, both these references to the "God of the fathers" are found on the lips of Moses. However, a closer examination of each context indicates that Moses introduces a hypothetical interlocutor as a rhetorical device. Rather than speaking for himself or addressing Israel directly, Moses portrays a future Israelite in the land (26:7; see text and translation, p. 144) and an imaginary foreigner gazing from afar (29:24[25]) as witnesses to the covenantally motivated interventions of the "God of the fathers." As Deuteronomy accelerates toward its rhetorical climax in chap. 30, with its urgent choice between "life and prosperity, death and destruction" (30:15), Israel must remember that it stands at the critical juncture between the exodus of the narrative past and the prospect of exile in the narrative future. The "God of the fathers" thus superintends the bookends of Israel's history.

Deuteronomy 26:7

וַנִּצְעַק אֶל־יְהוָה אֱלֹהֵי אֲבֹתֵינוּ	Then we cried out to Yhwh, God of our fathers,
וַיִּשְׁמַע יְהוָה אֶת־קֹלֵנוּ	and Yhwh heard our voice
וַיַּרְא אֶת־עָנְיֵנוּ	and saw our affliction
וְאֶת־עֲמָלֵנוּ וְאֶת־לַחֲצֵנוּ	and our toil and our oppression.

---

141. Von Rad, *From Genesis to Chronicles*, 3.

The history of interpretation for the "little historical creed" within its broader Deuteronomic context has already been discussed.[142] Within the boundaries of the creed itself (26:5–9), two features highlight the eminent status of "YHWH, God of our fathers" as Israel's personal and cosmic deity who journeys with the people toward the land. First, the people's desperation in the face of Egyptian cruelty and YHWH's faithful response as the "God of our fathers" represent the central element in a chiasmus (see diagram).[143]

> A (Homelessness): "my father was a wandering Aramean" (26:5a)
>   B (Oppression): "Egypt treated us harshly" (26:6a)
>   C (Response): "We cried out to YHWH, God of our fathers and YHWH heard our voice" (26:7a)
>   B′ (Deliverance): "YHWH brought us out of Egypt" (26:8a)
> A′ (Home): "he has brought us to this place . . . a land flowing with milk and honey" (26:9)

The key moment in the reversal of Israel's lot from homelessness (A) to home (A′) and from oppression (B) to deliverance (B′) is reflected by the introduction of "YHWH, God of our fathers" into the narrative. Thus the chiasmus turns on the way that YHWH overthrows Egypt's oppression (26:8) and brings Israel into an abundant land (26:9). For ease of presentation, the skeletal diagram shown above omits some elements of the creed, most notably its rhetorical flourishes.[144] Nonetheless, it is clear that the creed's structure centers on Israel's salvation by the "God of our fathers." Though this epithet only appears once, reiteration of the appositive "God of our fathers" is unnecessary since the twofold repetition of the Tetragrammaton (26:7a, 8a) alludes back to YHWH's first appearance in the creed as the "God of our fathers."

Second, the "God of the fathers" epithet in the creed heralds YHWH's unique ability to encompass both immanent and transcendent notions of the divine presence. On the one hand, YHWH is portrayed as the personal deity who "heard" (שמע) and "saw" (ראה) Israel's deplorable condition in Egypt (26:7b). The emphasis here on the immediacy of "YHWH, God of the fathers" (26:7a) in responding to Israel's "voice" (קול) stands in contrast to the Exodus accounts, where Israel's cries must "ascend to" (עלה אל) a more remote "God" (אלהים) in order to be "heard" (שמע; Exod 2:23–24). Similarly, the book of Exodus identifies YHWH (without any appositive) as the deity who "saw" (ראה) Israel's affliction (Exod 3:7). The apposition of the epithet "God of the fathers" with the Tetragrammaton only appears later in

---

142. See the discussion of "Land and the 'Fathers' in Deuteronomy 26" on pp. 61–64 above.
143. Modified slightly from Christensen, *Deuteronomy 21:10–34:12*, 634.
144. For example, see the threefold repetition of elements in 26:7b: (1) "our affliction"; (2) "our toil"; and (3) "our oppression."

the Exodus narrative, when YHWH commissions Moses to lead the people: "YHWH, God of your fathers, the God of Abraham, the God of Isaac, and the God of Jacob, has sent me to you" (Exod 3:15; cf. 3:6, 13, 16). Whatever the precise diachronic relationship between the Deuteronomic creed and its Exodus intertexts, it is striking that Deuteronomy has characterized the "God of the fathers" as the personal deity who first sees and hears of Israel's pain. The heightened importance and transformation of the "God of the fathers" appositive in the Deuteronomic creed vis-à-vis the Exodus narratives have gone unnoticed by redaction critics, who are primarily focused on the lexical correspondence between texts.[145]

On the other hand, the unrivaled power of the "God of the fathers" is reinforced through a string of prepositional phrases describing the exodus: (1) "by a mighty hand"; (2) "by an outstretched arm"; (3) "by great terror"; and (4) "by signs and by wonders" (26:8).[146] This fourfold paean for YHWH's supremacy not only interrupts the three-beat rhythm of the creed with an unexpected addition;[147] it echoes Deut 4:34 in preserving the second-largest collection of exodus descriptors anywhere in the OT.[148] Though redaction critics simplify the complex syntax of Deut 26:7 by excising the repeated exodus descriptors as secondary,[149] it seems more likely that this repetition serves the rhetorical function of heaping up praises for the dominion of "YHWH, God of our fathers." Following this sequence of breathless superlatives, the creed again accentuates YHWH's intimacy with the people through his personal escorting (יצא Hiphil) of Israel into the fecund "land flowing with milk and honey" (26:9).

---

145. Redaction critics observe the lexical correspondence between the credo's reference to the "God of the fathers" and Exodus 3 without noticing that the epithet functions differently in Deut 26:7 (e.g., Daniels, "Creed," 235–36; Fuhs, "Befreifung," 11).

146. Except for Exod 7:3 ("my signs and my wonders"), the Exodus narrative always refers separately to "signs" (Exod 4:9; 17, 28, 30, 7:3; 10:1, 2) and "wonders" (Exod 4:21; 7:3; 11:9, 10, 11). In contrast, Deuteronomy nearly always joins them in the stock phrase "by signs and by wonders" (Deut 4:34; 6:22; 7:19; 13:2, 3; 26:8; 28:46; 29:2[3]; 34:11). Thus the phrase "by signs and by wonders" is treated as a single element in Deut 26:7.

147. Fuhs, "Befreiung," 7–8; Lohfink, "Small Credo," 271–73.

148. The six exodus descriptors of Deut 4:34 represent a superset of the elements found in Deut 26:7: (1) "by trials"; (2) "by signs and by wonders" (see n. 146 above); (3) "by war"; (4) "by a mighty hand"; (5) "by an outstretched arm"; and (6) "by great terrors." Jer 32:21 contains the same four exodus descriptors as Deut 26:7. A complete comparison of exodus terminology in Deuteronomy with the rest of the OT is provided by Childs, "Formulae," 30–39.

149. In assessing the conflicting views of Lohfink and Rost on the extent of diachronic editing in the credo, I consider it to be telling that Daniels observes the common tendency to regard the confluence of Deuteronomic language as secondary: "The evidence thus indicates that all the prepositional phrases of v. 8aβb are Deuteronomic additions. There is general agreement on this point" (Daniels, "Deuteronomy XXVI," 236).

The Identity and Rhetorical Function of the "Fathers" in Deuteronomy 26:7

As was the case with the above analysis of the "wandering Aramean" (26:5),[150] here a synoptic comparison with Num 20:15–16 (see comparison diagram) can elucidate the significance of the Deuteronomic creed's invocation of the "God of the fathers" (Deut 26:7):

Deuteronomy 26:6–8	Numbers 20:15–16
[6] And Egypt treated us harshly and afflicted us and imposed hard labor on us.	[15c] And Egypt afflicted us and our fathers
[7] And we cried out to Yʜᴡʜ, God of our fathers, and Yʜᴡʜ heard our voice and saw our affliction and our toil and our oppression.	[16a] And we cried out to Yʜᴡʜ, and he heard our voice.

In addition to the aforementioned tendency for Deuteronomy to heap up exodus terminology, the summaries of Israel's history preserved in Deut 26:6–8 and Num 20:15–16 differ in two important respects. First, the victims of Egypt's brutality are identified as "us" in the Deuteronomic creed, while Numbers enumerates "us" and "our fathers" as discrete groups who suffered in Egypt. Since Num 20:15–16 distinguishes between the second generation ("us") and the first generation ("our fathers") that departed from Egypt, it seems likely that Deut 26:6–8 has conflated the generations in order to personalize these seminal events for every Israelite who dwells in the land. Once it is observed that the creed uses "we" and "us" to transport every Israelite back to Egypt in imaginative remembrance,[151] it becomes unnecessary to hypothesize that the creed's first-person-plural sections are secondary additions to an older, third-person narrative.[152] Much like the preceding reference to the "wandering Aramean," the creed appears to subordinate chronological precision to the theological agenda of declaring the essential unity of Israel's generations.

A second difference between Num 20:15–16 and Deut 26:6–8 arises in the former passage's reference to Israel's "fathers" as part of the "God of the fathers" appositive (Deut 26:7) rather than as a distinguishable generation in Egypt (Num 20:15c). In so doing, Deut 26:7 introduces some ambiguity into the historical referent for the "fathers." On the one hand, a comparison with Exodus reveals that the "God of the fathers" is concurrently identified as the "God of Abraham, the God of Isaac, and the God of Jacob" (Exod

---

150. See the synoptic analysis of Deut 26:5b on pp. 70–71 above.
151. See the discussion of imagination in Israel's life, and especially in Deuteronomy, by Brueggemann, "Imagination," 13–36.
152. As argued, for example, by Lohfink, "Small Credo," 269–71.

Table 5.2. Lexical Parallels between
Deuteronomy 26 and Exodus 3, 6

Term or Phrase in Deuteronomic Creed	Lexical Parallels in Exodus[a]
Deut 26:7a "We cried out" (צעקה/צעק)	Exod 3:13, 15, 16 (J)
Deut 26:7a "God of our father[s]" (אלהי אב / אלהי אבות)	Exod 2:24 (P); 3:7 (J); 6:5 (P)
Deut 26:7b "he heard" (שמע)	Exod 3:7 (J), 9 (E)
Deut 26:7b "he saw" (ראה)	Exod 2:24 (P), 3:7 (J), 9 (E)
Deut 26:7b "our affliction" (עני)	Exod 3:7 (J)
Deut 26:7b "our oppression" (לחץ)	Exod 3:9 (E)
Deut 26:8a "Yhwh brought us out" (יצא Hiphil)	Exod 3:10, 11, 12 (all E texts) Exod 6:6, 7, 13, 26, 27 (P)
Deut 26:8a "by a mighty hand" (ביד חזקה)	Exod 3:19 (J) Exod 6:1 (P)
Deut 26:8b "by an outstretched arm" (בזרע נטויה)	Exod 6:6 (P)
Deut 26:9b "land flowing with milk and honey"	Exod 3:8 (J), 17 (J)

a. The Exodus texts usually classified as J and E are listed in Noth, *History of Pentateuchal Traditions*, 30–36. Additionally, J. I. Durham (*Exodus* [WBC 3; Waco, TX: Word, 1987] 73) notes that Exodus 6 is typically attributed to P.

3:15, 16; 4:5), thereby suggesting that the patriarchs are the "fathers."[153] On the other hand, the creed's earlier reference to a singular "father" (26:5; cf. 10:22) who descended to Egypt could indicate that the plural "fathers" represent a settled generation in Egypt before the exodus.[154]

In distinction from these conflicting options, the preceding analysis suggests that the conflation of distinct generations of Israel in the first-person plural (i.e., "we" and "us") encapsulates the corporate solidarity of all Israel. Parallel to the catechism of 6:20–25, the creed's linking of exodus ("he brought us out"; יצא Hiphil; 26:8) and conquest ("he brought us in"; בוא Hiphil; 26:9) in an imagined future suggests that the "fathers" here portray every unlanded generation in Israel that has received Yhwh's promise of land (cf. 26:3, 15). Just as the "fathers" represent every homeless generation of Israel, the "God of the fathers" is the ancestral deity who now brings his people home by fulfilling his promise of land.

This nexus of exodus and land suggests that the ability of the future Israelite in the land to recite the creed (26:5–9) represents the fulfillment of the covenant promises made by the "God of the fathers" in Exodus 3 and

---

153. Tigay, *Deuteronomy*, 241; Skweres, *Rückverweise*, 106.
154. Römer, *Israels Väter*, 66.

reiterated in Exodus 6. Table 5.2 (p. 148) demonstrates that nearly every phrase in Deut 26:7–9 has lexical parallels in the commissioning narratives of Moses. Deut 26:7–9 displays a plethora of lexical links with Exodus 3 and 6,[155] in contrast to the skeletal account of Israel's history preserved in Num 20:15–16.[156] The diachronic relationship between these texts is difficult if not impossible to determine, but it is striking that the creed evinces identical terminology with texts usually attributed to J, E, and P. Whatever the diachronic relationship between the credo and these JEP texts,[157] Deut 26:7–9 clearly portrays the fulfillment of the promises first made by the "God of the fathers" in Exodus 3 and reiterated in Exodus 6. By using the same terminology but transforming the Exodus promises into actuated realities, the Israelite's confession in the creed completes the promissory trajectory begun by Yhwh's self-revelation as "God of the fathers." Therefore, the use of the epithet "God of the fathers" thrusts a cluster of related theological ideas into the foreground: (1) Yhwh's faithful character in fulfilling his promises to Israel; (2) Yhwh's sovereignty over his opponents; and (3) Yhwh's transcendent and immanent journey with Israel toward the land.

Deuteronomy 29:24[25]

וְאָמְרוּ	Then they will say,
עַל אֲשֶׁר עָזְבוּ	"[It is] because they abandoned
אֶת־בְּרִית יְהוָה אֱלֹהֵי אֲבֹתָם	the covenant of Yhwh, God of their fathers,
אֲשֶׁר כָּרַת עִמָּם	that he cut with them
בְּהוֹצִיאוֹ אֹתָם מֵאֶרֶץ מִצְרָיִם	when he brought them out of the land of Egypt."

This reference to the "fathers" presents an unambiguous link between the epithet "God of the fathers" and Yhwh's status as a deity who cuts and keeps his "covenant" (ברית) with Israel. Though detailed commentary must wait until the analysis of ברית terminology in chap. 6 below,[158] two

---

155. Only two phrases in Deut 26:7–9 have no parallels in Exodus: (1) "our toil" (26:7b; used nowhere else in the OT to describe the exodus); and (2) "this place," a Deuteronomic phrase for the land of promise (cf. 11:5; 29:6).

156. Even if Römer (*Israels Väter*, 66–67, 124–25) were correct that Num 20:15–16 is the sole intertext for Deut 26:7–9, it should be noted that Num 20:15–16 is typically classified as an Elohist text (P. J. Budd, *Numbers* [WBC 5; Nashville: Thomas Nelson, 1984] 222). Thus the Deuteronomic credo still contains many parallels to the ostensive Elohist traditions in Exodus 3 that fall outside 3:13–16, a section viewed by Römer (*Israels Väter*, 552–54) as an addition by the final editor of the Pentateuch.

157. The presence of JEP language in the creed leads numerous scholars to suggest that Deut 26:5–9 is the work of the Pentateuch's final redactor (e.g., Gertz, "Stellung," 30–45; Dreyfus, "L'Araméen," 147–61).

158. The ambiguous syntax of Deut 29:24[25] creates an exegetical difficulty with respect to the "fathers." The repeated use of 3mp forms could mean that the "fathers" are co-referential with the generation of "them" (3mp object marker) that exited Egypt.

features of this reference to the "God of the fathers" (29:24[25]; see text and translation, p. 149) are significant for the present discussion. First, the horrific prospect of covenant curses is described in the context primarily as "plagues and diseases" (29:21[22]) on the *land* rather than the *people*: "All the nations will say, 'Why has Yhwh done thus to this land? Why this great outburst of anger?'" (29:23[24]; cf. 28:20–21). In fact, the section following the reference to the "God of the fathers" (29:24–27[25–28]) emphasizes unmistakably the reversal of the exodus and gift of land by means of exile: (1) Yhwh rescues Israel from the "land of Egypt" (29:24b[25b]); (2) his wrath burns against "that land" (29:26[27]); (3) he uproots them from "their land" (29:27a[28a]); and (4) he banishes them to "another land" (29:27b[28b]). This repetition of ארץ constitutes a *Leitwort* that traces the dynamic contours of Israel's relationship with various lands (i.e., Egypt – Canaan – exile).

The "God of the fathers" epithet in 29:24[25] not only signals the foregrounding of the promise motif of land; it also conveys the notion of withdrawing this gift when Israel disobeys the covenant made with the "God of the fathers." The tight connections between the "God of the fathers" and the various phases of the land promise thus challenge redaction-critical attempts to correlate Deuteronomy with the postexilic writings of the OT (i.e., Dtr[2], Ezra/Nehemiah, Chronicles). As noted above, the postexilic writings use the "God of the fathers" appositive as a synonym for "your God," rather than communicating the uniquely Deuteronomic nuance of Yhwh's transcendence and immanence in fulfilling his promises.[159]

Second, Deut 29:24–25[25–26] exhibits ironic connections with the "recognition formula" of the Exodus narratives by collocating the "God of the fathers" epithet with the need to "know" (ידע) Israel's ancestral deity. In Exodus, Yhwh desires for both Israel and Egypt to "know [ידע] that I am Yhwh" (e.g., Exod 6:7; cf. 6:3).[160] As discussed above, the recognition formula refers back to Yhwh's self-revelation as the "God of the fathers" by using the *functional* terms of his covenantal interventions for Israel.[161] In a reversal of the recognition formula, the writer attributes Israel's removal from the land by the "God of the fathers" (29:24[25]) to Israel's rejection of the known "God of the fathers" in favor of unknown deities: "[the Is-

---

Accordingly, the "covenant" (ברית) that was made "with them" (3mp prepositional suffix) would refer to the Horeb revelation. Alternatively, the epithet "God of their fathers" could constitute a fixed idiom whereby the "fathers" always signifies the ancestors of the first exodus generation—that is, the patriarchs (1:8, 11). In the analysis in chap. 7, I will argue in favor of the former.

159. See the discussion of "The 'God of the Father(s)' in the Deuteronomistic History and the Post-exilic Historical Books" on pp. 99–101 above.

160. With slight variations, the "recognition formula" is found in Exod 6:7; 7:5, 17; 8:10, 22; 9:14, 29; 10:2; 11:7; 14:4, 18; 16:6, 8, 12; 29:46; 31:13.

161. Eslinger, "Knowing Yahweh," 188–98; Garr, "Grammar and Interpretation of Exodus 6:3," 385–408; cf. pp. 105–108 above.

raelites] served other gods and worshiped them, gods whom they have not known [ידע]" (29:25[26]). This informed remembrance of the "God of the fathers," the deity who rescued Israel from Egypt, thus contrasts with the irrational forgetfulness of serving "other gods" who are incapable of doing anything for Israel.[162] Deut 29:21-27[22-28] evinces a theological trajectory similar to Exodus's through the sovereign power and covenantal fidelity implied by use of the epithet "God of the fathers" but adds the ironic twist of this personal and cosmic deity's steadfastness in punishing an idolatrous nation (cf. 5:9; 7:10). Accordingly, the "God of the fathers" enacts both covenant blessings and covenant curses.

Conclusion

Chapter 5's analysis of the "God of the fathers" in the Pentateuch suggests that this epithet strikes a delicate theological balance between transcendence and immanence in the depiction of Israel's deity. In particular, Deuteronomy's invocations of the "God of the fathers" reveal that the author uses this term to present YHWH as a personal deity who makes covenant promises to Israel as well as a cosmic deity who possesses supreme power to fulfill them. By transcending the typical ANE distinctions between family and state religion, Deuteronomy echoes the tetrateuchal depiction of the "God of the fathers," who journeys with his people while acting supernaturally on their behalf yet does not require a permanent sanctuary where they must worship.

I suggest that Deuteronomy represents a fitting conclusion to the promise narratives of Genesis and Exodus, rather than being fundamentally discontinuous from the narratives attributed to the Tetrateuch's JE and P sources, as usually argued. Many difficult questions regarding the relationship between Deuteronomy and the Tetrateuch remain, especially in accounting for the manifold differences between patriarchal religion and Mosaic Yahwism.[163] But these disjunctions have often been staked on sharp theological dichotomies that should be reexamined in light of Deuteronomy's multifaceted depiction of the "God of the fathers."

Having analyzed the promises of land and multiplication of population on a detailed level, I will broaden the discussion in part 3 by identifying

---

162. Similarly, Deut 28:63 asserts that exiled Israel will worship "other gods, wood and stone, which neither you nor your fathers have known." Moses has already mocked the impotence of such idols as: "the work of man's hands, wood and stone, which neither see nor hear nor eat nor smell" (Deut 4:28).

163. Moberly (*Old Testament*, 87–104) provides a convenient summary: (1) patriarchal religion is monotheistic but not threatened by other gods; (2) patriarchal religion is not threatened by the Canaanites; (3) patriarchal religion allows multiple cultic centers; (4) patriarchal religion lacks priests and prophets; (5) patriarchal religion lacks possessiveness with regard to Canaan; and (6) patriarchal religion lacks an explicit moral framework and the terminology of holiness.

Deuteronomy's referent when it speaks of the covenant (ברית) between Yhwh and the "fathers" (4:31; 5:3; 7:12; 8:18; 29:24[25]). From the narrative perspective in Moab, which covenant is in view—the Abrahamic covenant of Genesis or the Israelite covenant of Exodus, or some combination of the two? In the following section, I examine the exegetical and biblical-theological function of ANE treaty and covenant forms in Deuteronomy as well as in the Pentateuch as a whole.

Part 3

The "Fathers" and the Divine-Human Covenant in Deuteronomy

Chapter 6

The "Fathers" and the Divine-Human Covenant in Deuteronomy: History of Research and Method

That the canonical form of Deuteronomy represents the pinnacle of covenant theology in Israel is something of a truism in OT scholarship.[1] Beyond this basic consensus, little agreement exists on the proper method for identifying and elucidating these covenantal features in Deuteronomy, especially insofar as they relate diachronically to covenantal concepts in the rest of the OT, on the one hand, and ANE treaty forms, on the other. Though scholars have spilled much ink on these issues,[2] they have often overlooked the fact that *historical-critical* judgments on the provenance of Deuteronomic covenant theology are inextricably linked to *theological* judgments regarding the message of Deuteronomy and its relationship to

---

1. As witnessed by the affirmations of those who otherwise disagree on the provenance and message of Deuteronomy—e.g., C. J. H. Wright, *The Mission of God: Unlocking the Bible's Grand Narrative* (Downers Grove, IL: InterVarsity, 2006) 375–76; Miller, *Religion of Ancient Israel*, 5; J. D. Levenson, *Sinai and Zion: An Entry into the Jewish Bible* (Minneapolis: Winston, 1985) 81; Craigie, *Deuteronomy*, 33; M. Fishbane, "Varia Deuteronomica," *ZAW* 84 (1972) 349; K. Baltzer, *The Covenant Formulary in Old Testament, Jewish, and Early Christian Writings* (trans. D. E. Green; Philadelphia: Fortress, 1971) 31; D. R. Hillers, *Covenant: The History of a Biblical Idea* (Baltimore: Johns Hopkins University Press, 1969) 151; W. L. Moran, "The Ancient Near Eastern Background of the Love of God in Deuteronomy," *CBQ* 25 (1963) 82; J. Muilenburg, "The Form and Structure of the Covenantal Formulations," *VT* 9 (1959) 350.

2. Complete histories of research on covenant in OT studies are provided by S. Hahn, "Covenant in the Old and New Testaments: Some Current Research (1994–2004)," *CBR* 3 (2005) 263–92; D. C. Lane, *The Meaning and Use of Berith in the Old Testament* (Ph.D. diss., Trinity Evangelical Divinity School, 2000) 29–162; E. Zenger, "Die Bundestheologie: Ein derzeit vernachlässigtes Thema der Bibelwissenschaft und ein wichtiges Thema für das Verhältnis Israel-Kirche," in *Der neue Bund im alten: Studien zur Bundestheologie der beiden Testamente* (ed. E. Zenger; QD 146; Freiburg: Herder, 1993) 13–49; R. A. Oden Jr., "The Place of Covenant in the Religion of Israel," in *Ancient Israelite Religion: Essays in Honor of Frank Moore Cross* (ed. P. D. Miller, P. D. Hanson, and S. D. McBride; Philadelphia: Fortress, 1987) 429–47; R. Davidson, "Covenant Ideology in Ancient Israel," in *The World of Ancient Israel: Sociological, Anthropological, and Political Perspectives* (ed. R. E. Clements; Cambridge: Cambridge University Press, 1989) 323–47; E. W. Nicholson, *God and His People: Covenant and Theology in the Old Testament* (Oxford: Clarendon, 1986) 3–118; and H. Tadmor, "Treaty and Oath in the Ancient Near East: A Historian's Approach," in *Humanizing America's Iconic Book: Society of Biblical Literature Centennial Addresses* (ed. G. M. Tucker and D. A. Knight; Chico, CA: Scholars Press, 1982) 127–52.

the narrative traditions that undergird its rhetoric of covenant renewal—that is, the Abrahamic and Israelite covenants.³ Based on the LXX title of the book (δευτερονόμιον, "second law"), Deuteronomy has generally been considered a recapitulation of "conditional" (i.e., Israelite) rather than "unconditional" (i.e., Abrahamic) notions of covenant.

In contrast to this theological reductionism, I argue for an irreducible relationship between divine initiative and human responsibility in Deuteronomy's references to YHWH's covenant with the "fathers."⁴ The rhetorical blending of the oath with the patriarchs and the covenant-making events at Sinai in the renewal ceremony at Moab challenges the sharp distinctions usually drawn between the Abrahamic and Israelite covenants as unconditional and conditional, respectively, for elements of promise and obligation are found in both covenants. The book of Deuteronomy thus envisages the renewal of a single, simultaneously unconditional and conditional, covenantal relationship between YHWH and his people throughout all generations (5:3; 29:9–14[10–15]).⁵ In the narrative world of Deuteronomy, the corporate solidarity of Israel in the land (part 1) under the sovereignty of a singular "God of the fathers" across the people's history (part 2) reflects a timeless covenant between YHWH and his people (part 3). With the assistance of speech-act theory, my reassessment of Deuteronomic covenant theology seeks to overcome the dichotomy between unconditionality and conditionality that has been both influential and problematic in OT studies and, in so doing, clarifies the role of the "fathers" in Deuteronomy.

Past Approaches to Covenant in the Old Testament and the Ancient Near East

In the history of covenant studies, OT scholars have typically operated on the continuum bracketed by the minimalist followers of Julius Wellhausen, on the one hand, and the maximalist followers of Walther Eichrodt, on the other.⁶ Wellhausen held that covenant ideas originated in the tumultuous centuries of the Deuteronom(ist)ic movement and were absent from Israel's earliest history.⁷ By contrast, Eichrodt viewed the covenant,

---

3. Space considerations necessitate excluding the historical-critical debate over how many Abrahamic and Israelite covenants are preserved in the Pentateuch. For my purposes, it is sufficient to note that the Abrahamic and Israelite covenant(s) are often treated as monolithic entities that exemplify unconditionality and conditionality, respectively.

4. Deut 4:31; 7:12; 8:18; 29:11–12[12–13], 24[25].

5. So also R. Rendtorff, *The Covenant Formula: An Exegetical and Theological Investigation* (trans. M. Kohl; Edinburgh: T. & T. Clark, 1998) 78–92.

6. Cf. J. Barton, "Covenant in Old Testament Theology," in *Covenant as Context: Essays in Honour of E. W. Nicholson* (ed. A. D. H. Mayes and R. B. Salters; Oxford: Oxford University Press, 2003) 23–32, for a similar comparison of Wellhausen and Eichrodt.

7. According to Baltzer (*Covenant Formulary*, 1 n. 3), those who followed Wellhausen's views on covenant included Gesenius, H. Schultz, A. Dillman, R. Kraetzschmar, and E. König, among many other German scholars.

not only as an ancient and timeless metaphor for God's gracious relationship with his people, but also as the organizational principle for all of OT theology.⁸

Before undertaking analysis of the pertinent Deuteronomic references to covenant, we must survey the research—a necessity that is underscored by the vastly different understandings of ברית advocated by Wellhausen and Eichrodt. In Wellhausen's view, the introduction of ברית terminology by the 8th-century prophets (e.g., Amos) heralded a theological revolution in which "the [previously unconditional] relation of Jehovah to Israel was conditioned by the demands of His righteousness, as set forth in His word and instruction."⁹ The carefree, immanent religion of the patriarchal age was now superseded by the postexilic demand "to familiarise the Jewish mind with the idea that the covenant depended on conditions, and might possibly be dissolved."¹⁰

In contrast to Wellhausen, who regarded covenant as a late, negative development in Israel's history, Eichrodt viewed the ברית as an expression of mutual commitment in which "the relationship with God has the character of a relationship of grace; that is to say, it is founded on a primal act in history, maintained on definite conditions and protected by a powerful divine Guardian."¹¹ Though Eichrodt thus acknowledged the presence of "definite conditions" in the covenant, he decried legalistic distortions of the Sinai ברית as mechanistic *do ut des* religion, since the biblical conception of covenant always emphasizes prior divine acts of grace more than the attendant human obligations.¹² Responding to Wellhausen in particular, Eichrodt asserted that the term ברית was avoided by the 8th-century prophets because its meaning had already taken on legalistic connotations.¹³ Since the fundamentally incompatible ideas of Wellhausen and Eichrodt are still propagated today, it is essential to begin with a reassessment of covenant terminology and its related concepts in the OT. In the overview of interpreters that follows, I use Deuteronomy as a case study to examine competing scholarly views on covenant.

Semantic and Literary-Critical Approaches

The frequency (283×) and semantic breadth of the word ברית have invited very different approaches to lexical analysis, each of which reflects

---

8. Though not as far-reaching as Eichrodt, B. S. Childs (*Biblical Theology of the Old and New Testaments: Theological Reflection on the Christian Bible* [Philadelphia: Fortress, 1993] 413–28) argues similarly for the ubiquity of covenant concepts in Israel even if the terminology is absent before the Deuteronom(ist)ic movement.
9. Wellhausen, *Prolegomena*, 418.
10. Wellhausen, *Prolegomena*, 419.
11. Eichrodt, *Theology*, 1:36.
12. Eichrodt, *Theology*, 1:44–45.
13. Eichrodt, *Theology*, 1:51–52.

the individual scholar's theological presuppositions.[14] A prominent example of theological biases influencing etymological studies can be found in the work of Ernst Kutsch, who argued, following Wellhausen, that ברית refers solely to "obligation" (*Verpflichtung*).[15] Kutsch's survey of ברית in the OT led him to categorize every instance of the term as one of four sorts of obligation: (1) an obligation of oneself (*Selbstverpflichtung und Zusage*); (2) an obligation by another party (*Verpflichtung eines anderen*); (3) a mutual obligation by two parties (*wechselseitige Verpflichtung*); and (4) a mutual obligation brokered by a third party (*Verpflichtung durch einen Dritten*).[16] Since the notion of obligation underlies each of these meanings, Kutsch averred that any relational connotations in ברית were secondary.

In a convincing critique of Kutsch, James Barr not only exposed the lexical fallacies inherent in any attempt to discover a shared etymology for all senses of ברית;[17] he observed that Kutsch's analysis in particular "seems dominated by a strong sense of the opposition between grace and law, promise and law, which makes the reader uncomfortable."[18] Similarly, Dennis McCarthy concluded regarding Kutsch's analysis that "there is more than merely scientific interest at work. There are theological positions, probably subconscious but still very real, in the background. There is the fear of seeming to tie God to a contract and creating a *quid pro quo* pharisaism."[19] Kutsch's emphasis on ברית as unilateral obligation evidently sought to redeem OT scholarship from antiquated notions of Israelite covenant as totemism or a bond of blood, as argued by William Robertson Smith and Wellhausen.[20] Ironically, Kutsch's attempt to progress beyond

---

14. For example, the BDB entry for ברית renders the term variously as "pact," "compact," "covenant," "treaty," "alliance," "league," "constitution," "ordinance," "agreement," and "pledge." The corresponding *HALOT* entry adds the notion of "contract."

15. E. Kutsch (*Verheissung und Gesetz: Untersuchungen zum sogenannten 'Bund' im Alten Testament* [BZAW 131; Berlin: de Gruyter, 1973] 38–39) defines ברית as *Verpflichtung* using an uncertain etymology deriving from ברה II ("to look"; cf. Akkadian *barû*), which undergoes an etymological development through several phases: *sehen → ersehen → auswählen → bestimmen → Bestimmung → Verpflichtung*.

16. Kutsch, *Verheissung*, 6–16.

17. J. Barr ("Some Semantic Notes on the Covenant," in *Beiträge zur alttestamentlichen Theologie: Festschrift für Walther Zimmerli zum 70. Geburtstag* [ed. H. Donner, R. Hanhart, and R. Smend; Göttingen: Vandenhoeck & Ruprecht, 1977] 23–38) criticizes Kutsch on two fronts. First, any etymology of ברית cannot be determinative for discourse meaning since "the effective semantic function of ברית was far removed from any sense that can be detected by etymology" (p. 24). Second, Kutsch's analysis of ברית in narrative texts conflates the descriptions of ברית-making with the implications of the ברית itself (p. 37). Cf. K. A. Kitchen ("Egypt, Qatna, and Covenant," *UF* 11 [1979] 453–64), who undercuts Kutsch's etymological study from a different angle by demonstrating that ברית cognates are attested in ANE texts much earlier than the Deuteronom(ist)ic period.

18. Barr, "Some Semantic Notes," 37.

19. D. J. McCarthy, *Treaty and Covenant*, 17.

20. E.g., W. Robertson Smith, *Lectures on the Religion of the Semites. First Series: The Fundamental Institutions* (London: Black, 1956) 316–18; Wellhausen, *Prolegomena*, 71. Compare the discussion by M. Weinfeld, "*Berît*: Covenant vs. Obligation," *Bib* 56 (1975) 123–24.

19th-century views on covenant was still indebted to the theological dichotomy found in Wellhausen's account of Israel's history as a devolution from grace to law.

Similar strictures apply to the work of Lothar Perlitt, who asserted that the introduction of ברית terminology in the 7th century B.C.E. coincided with the Deuteronom(ist)ic impulse to place Israel under divine sanction for idolatry.[21] Using Kutsch's definition of ברית as a starting point, Perlitt argued that the concept of a bilateral relationship between YHWH and his people was originally absent from the 8th-century prophets, patriarchal narratives, Sinai theophany, and Davidic traditions. Through a redaction-critical analysis, Perlitt concluded that any references to ברית in older texts were secondary additions of the Deuteronom(ist)ic school.

A detailed critique of Perlitt's redaction-critical conclusions appears in chap. 7 below. However, it is noteworthy here that Perlitt operated with a hidden premise regarding the theological incompatibility of promise and obligation, much as Kutsch did. The final form of Deuteronomy posed a particular dilemma for Perlitt because ברית is able to encompass both promissory and obligatory dimensions of the divine-human relationship, as found in Deut 7:12 and 5:2. Deut 7:12 uses ברית to denote YHWH's promissory oath to the "fathers," but Deut 5:2 uses ברית to identify the promulgation of "statutes and ordinances" (5:1) at Horeb. Perlitt resolved the theological tension between promise and obligation by assigning these texts to different tradition layers. Thus the promissory sense of ברית (7:12b) is an earlier use from a time when Israel experienced little threat of destruction, whereas the obligatory sense of ברית (5:2) arose later as a reflection of either the preexilic agenda to place Israel on notice or the postexilic need to account for the exile.[22]

Though the details of Perlitt's literary-critical methods were quite different from the etymological methods of Kutsch, a significant presupposition at work in both authors was the putative incompatibility of conditional and unconditional notions of covenant. Their work also showed that semantic (e.g., Kutsch) and literary-critical (e.g., Perlitt) approaches to covenant tended to focus inordinately on the term ברית to the exclusion of related terminology; they also deemphasized the literary contexts in which ברית occurs. Thus the stage was set for form-critical studies of covenant, which focused on the significance of larger literary units rather than individual words or isolated phrases.

Initial Form-Critical Approaches

Source-critical and redaction-critical approaches to covenant dominated the scholarly scene in the decades following Wellhausen and again in the 1970s through the works of Kutsch and Perlitt. Between these two waves

---

21. Perlitt, *Bundestheologie*.
22. Perlitt, *Bundestheologie*, 80–81.

of literary criticism, a new course in OT covenant studies was charted in the 1950s through the advent of form-critical approaches incorporating the latest discoveries from the ANE.[23] Drawing on the publication of ANE treaty documents,[24] George Mendenhall observed that the Israelite covenant (i.e., Exodus 19–24) exhibited numerous links with the Hittite suzerainty treaties from the second millennium B.C.E.[25] Such treaty texts reflected an identifiable literary genre with six parts: (1) preamble; (2) historical prologue; (3) stipulations; (4) document clause; (5) list of divine witnesses, and (6) curses and blessings.[26] The Decalogue apparently contained a preamble ("I am YHWH your God . . ."), a historical prologue (". . . who brought you out of Egypt, out of the house of bondage"), and stipulations (i.e., the apodictic pronouncements of the Decalogue). Though the Decalogue lacked the elements of the document clause, divine witnesses, and listing of curses and blessings, Mendenhall suggested that the missing ANE treaty elements could be found elsewhere in the Pentateuch, notably in the concluding chapters of Deuteronomy.[27]

Meredith Kline also applied the Hittite treaty form to Deuteronomy but with strikingly different results from Mendenhall. Rather than identifying ANE treaty features in an ad hoc fashion, Kline asserted that the entire book was structured as a five-part suzerainty treaty: (1) preamble (1:1–5); (2) historical prologue (1:6–4:49); (3) stipulations (chaps. 5–26); (4) curses and blessings (chaps. 27–30); and (5) succession arrangements (chaps. 31–34).[28] Despite viewing the entire book as a treaty document, Kline acknowledged that smaller units within Deuteronomy contain miniature instances of the treaty form, most notably Deuteronomy 4.[29] The methodological

---

23. The tension between literary- and form-critical approaches to OT covenant studies is reflected by Perlitt (*Bundestheologie*, 4) when he cavalierly dismisses the pertinence of ANE treaty forms for his study.

24. Most notably V. Korošec, *Hethitische Staatsverträge: Ein Beitrag zu ihrer juristischen Wertung* (Leipziger rechtswissenschaftliche Studien 60; Leipzig: Weicher, 1931).

25. G. E. Mendenhall, *Law and Covenant in Israel and the Ancient Near East* (Pittsburgh: Biblical Colloquium, 1955) 35–38. Other parallels between the Sinai narratives and the newly published ANE treaties were observed by Baltzer, *Covenant Formulary*, 27–31; and Muilenburg, "Form and Structure of the Covenantal Formulations," 351–57.

26. Mendenhall, *Law*, 32–34. Baltzer (*Covenant Formulary*, 11–17, 27–31) independently proposed a six-part treaty structure that was slightly different from Mendenhall's in distinguishing between general stipulations (element 3) and specific stipulations (element 4) while lacking a document clause (Mendenhall's element 4). However, Mendenhall and Baltzer were basically in agreement on the presence of the preamble, historical prologue, and listing of curses and blessings in Exodus 19–24.

27. Mendenhall, *Law*, 39–42, 48–49. However, Mendenhall also held that Deuteronomy dated largely from the post-Mosaic period (pp. 47–50), after the monarchy, when "the older form of covenant was no longer widely known" (pp. 30–31).

28. M. G. Kline, *The Treaty of the Great King* (Grand Rapids, MI: Eerdmans, 1963) 27–44.

29. Kline (*Treaty*, 31, 58–61) observes that the ANE treaty pattern recurs in the rhetorical subsections of Deuteronomy 4: (1) identification of the speaker (4:1, 2, 5, 10); (2) historical prologue (4:3–4, 10–12, 20, 32–34, 36–38); (3) stipulation of undivided alliance

tension between Mendenhall's "bottom–up" (i.e., inductive) approach and Kline's "top–down" (i.e., deductive) approach highlights an enigmatic feature of Deuteronomy—namely, the relationship between the parts and the whole with respect to ANE treaty forms. Thus, any analysis of the Deuteronomic references to covenant should provide a satisfactory account of the way the book functions both as a collection of smaller rhetorical units of treaty forms and in its entirety as a literary record of a covenant renewal ceremony.

Subsequent Refinements in Form-Critical Criteria

The form-critical criteria applied in these initial studies underwent substantial refinement through the identification of additional genres among ANE diplomatic documents. First, McCarthy noted the distinctions between Hittite vassal treaties that governed relationships between a great king and his subjects, on the one hand, and Hittite parity treaties between equals, on the other.[30] Since vassal treaties could only be distinguished from parity treaties on the basis of content rather than form-critical markers, McCarthy made the important observation that treaties could not be classified a priori as unilateral or bilateral documents based on their literary form alone.[31] The questionable decision to designate treaties as either unilateral or bilateral, or unconditional as opposed to conditional, on the basis of strictly formal considerations became commonplace soon after the publication of the first-millennium ANE treaties, the next form-critical development to be considered.

Second, the available corpus of ANE treaties grew significantly through the publication of Neo-Assyrian treaties from the first millennium.[32] These treaties differed from their Hittite counterparts in lacking a historical prologue and blessings,[33] while also displaying a long and creative list of curses.[34] The provenance of many Neo-Assyrian treaties could be firmly established in the 8th–6th centuries B.C.E., an era in which the Assyrian

---

(4:5, 9, 15–18, 23); (4) blessing-curse sanctions (4:27–31); and (5) invocation of witnesses (4:26); and (6) succession arrangements (4:9, 10, 21, 22).

30. D. J. McCarthy, *Treaty and Covenant*, 37–85.

31. D. J. McCarthy, *Treaty and Covenant*, 50; cf. Mendenhall, *Law*, 30.

32. S. Parpola and K. Watanabe, *Neo-Assyrian Treaties and Loyalty Oaths* (SAA 2; Helsinki: Helsinki University Press, 1988); D. J. Wiseman, "The Vassal-Treaties of Esarhaddon," *Iraq* 20 (1958) 1–99.

33. K. A. Kitchen, *On the Reliability of the Old Testament* (Grand Rapids, MI: Eerdmans, 2003) 283–94; idem, "The Fall and Rise of Covenant, Law and Treaty," *TynBul* 40 (1989) 123–32. However, the absence of historical prologues in Neo-Assyrian treaties has been contested by Weinfeld, *Deuteronomy and the Deuteronomic School*, 68; and A. F. Campbell, "An Historical Prologue in a Seventh-Century Treaty," *Bib* 50 (1969) 534–35.

34. M. Weinfeld ("The Loyalty Oath in the Ancient Near East," *UF* 8 [1976] 379–414) coined the phrase "loyalty oaths" for the Neo-Assyrian treaties because they apparently differed from the Hittite treaties in forcibly extracting rather than graciously motivating the vassal's promise to obey.

Empire exercised major political and military clout in Israel's affairs (see 2 Kgs 15–19). Thus it was natural that scholars would argue for literary-critical connections with Deuteronomy, the core of which was typically dated to Josiah's reforms in the 7th century. The lexical similarities between the elaborate Neo-Assyrian curse formulas and Deuteronomy 28 only reinforced this view.[35]

Third, in distinction to both Hittite and Neo-Assyrian treaties, another ANE literary form known as the royal grant was isolated by scholars. In a widely cited 1970 article, Moshe Weinfeld argued that, whereas the suzerainty treaties codified a vassal's obligations to the suzerain, the royal grant confirmed the suzerain's commitment to the vassal, usually the promise of land or kingship.[36] While the distinction between treaties and grants may be admissible on form-critical grounds,[37] Weinfeld's interpretation of the ANE data also revealed a decidedly theological bias. Regarding the OT covenants, he asserted that the "promissory type" (i.e., Abrahamic, Davidic) reflects the *unconditionality* of the royal grant, while the "obligatory type" (i.e., Israelite) reflects the *conditionality* of the suzerainty treaty.[38] Though Weinfeld's views on the strict contrast between grants and treaties have become nearly axiomatic in the academy,[39] newer research indicates that

---

35. Koch, *Vertrag*; E. Otto, "Treueid und Gesetz: Die Ursprünge des Deuteronomiums im Horizont neuassyrischen Vertragsrechts," *ZABR* 2 (1996) 1–52; Steymans, *Deuteronomium 28*; Frankena, "Vassal-Treaties," 122–54.

36. M. Weinfeld, "The Covenant of Grant in the Old Testament and the Ancient Near East," *JAOS* 90 (1970) 184–203; cf. idem, *Deuteronomy and the Deuteronomic School*, 74–81.

37. The distinctive formal features of royal grants vis-à-vis treaties have been confirmed by the meticulous analysis of Slanski, *Entitlement* Narûs. Weinfeld ("Covenant of Grant," 185) had noted that the Mesopotamian *narû* inscriptions (formerly known as *kudurru* stones) represented the prototypical royal grant.

38. Weinfeld, "Covenant of Grant," 184–85, 189, 195–96.

39. The conditional-unconditional taxonomy for ANE treaty documents has been adopted by a wide spectrum of biblical scholars and theologians. Among ANE/OT specialists, see E. H. Merrill, *Everlasting Dominion: A Theology of the Old Testament* (Nashville: Broadman & Holman, 2006) 238–45, 432–42; G. Davies, "Covenant, Oath, and the Composition of the Pentateuch," in *Covenant as Context: Essays in Honour of E. W. Nicholson* (ed. A. D. H. Mayes and R. B. Salters; Oxford: Oxford University Press, 2003) 71–83; B. W. Anderson, *Contours of Old Testament Theology* (Minneapolis: Fortress, 1999) 101–3, 142–44; J. Krašovec, "Two Types of Unconditional Covenant," *HBT* 18 (1996) 61–63; A. Rofé, "Promise and Covenant: The Promise to the Patriarchs in Late Biblical Literature," in *Divine Promises to the Fathers in the Three Monotheistic Religions* (ed. A. Niccacci; Jerusalem: Franciscan Printing Press, 1995) 52–59. G. E. Mendenhall, "Covenant," *ABD* 1:1188–92; N. Lohfink, "Die Abänderung der Theologie des priesterlichen Geschichtswerks im Segen des Heiligkeitsgesetzes: Zu Lev. 26,9.11–13," in *Studien zum Pentateuch* (SBAB 4; Stuttgart: Katholisches Bibelwerk, 1988) 157–68; B. K. Waltke, "The Phenomenon of Conditionality within Unconditional Covenants," in *Israel's Apostasy and Restoration: Essays in Honor of Roland K. Harrison* (ed. A. Gileadi; Grand Rapids, MI: Baker, 1988) 129–39; T. E. McComiskey, *The Covenants of Promise: A Theology of Old Testament Covenants* (Grand Rapids, MI: Baker, 1985) 62–63; S. M. Paul, "Adoption Formulae: A Study of the Cuneiform and Biblical Legal Clauses," *Maarav* 2 (1979–80) 176–78; J. D. Levenson, "The Davidic

these ANE documents cannot be categorized so easily in unconditional and conditional terms. Not only are all covenants and treaties conditional to some degree,[40] but continued use of the legal designations "unconditional" and "conditional" to describe royal grant and the suzerainty treaties, respectively, tends to be misleading since these terms obscure the relational aspects that inhere in all covenants and treaties.[41]

Fourth, the discovery of additional Hittite texts has demonstrated that royal grants and suzerainty treaties could be linked in a chronological progression rather than pitted against one another. Though an initial grant might appear unconditional, subsequent treaties drew out the implicitly conditional aspects of the relationship between the Great King and his vassals. The various treaties between the Hittite king Mursili II of Ḫatti and several vassal kings in Arzawa provide a clear case of treaties that describe the suzerain-vassal relationship over multiple generations.[42] The historical prologue of the latest pact between Mursili II and Kupanta-Kurunta details the generosity previously shown by Mursili II to Mashuiluwa, Kupanta-Kurunta's adoptive father, through a royal grant of land and kingship

---

Covenant and Its Modern Interpreters," *CBQ* 41 (1979) 205–19; S. E. Loewenstamm, "The Divine Grants of Land to the Patriarchs," *JAOS* 91 (1971) 509–10; Freedman, "Commitment," 419–31; W. Zimmerli, "Sinaibund und Abrahambund: Ein Beitrag zum Verständnis der Priesterschrift," in *Gottes Offenbarung: Gesammelte Aufsätze zum Alten Testament* (Munich: Chr. Kaiser, 1963) 205–16.

Systematic theologians who have adopted the theological dichotomy between treaties and grants include M. S. Horton, *Covenant and Salvation: Union with Christ* (Louisville: Westminster John Knox, 2007) 12–27; and R. L. Saucy, *The Case for Progressive Dispensationalism: The Interface between Dispensational and Non-dispensational Theology* (Grand Rapids, MI: Zondervan, 1993) 65–66.

40. G. N. Knoppers ("David's Relation to Moses: The Contexts, Content and Conditions of the Davidic Promises," in *King and Messiah in Israel and the Ancient Near East: Proceedings of the Oxford Old Testament Seminar* [JSOTSup 170; Sheffield: Sheffield Academic Press, 1998] 91–118; idem, "Ancient Near Eastern Royal Grants and the Davidic Covenant: A Parallel?" *JAOS* 116 [1996] 670–97) demonstrates that even royal grants are generally conditional rather than unconditional in nature. Though grants do not specify the suzerain's obligations to the vassal, they reflect both a reward for the vassal's past loyalty and an incentive for future loyalty. Thus the relationship between suzerain and vassal is irreducibly reciprocal. Compare G. H. Johnston ("'Unconditional' and 'Conditional' Features of the Davidic Covenant in the Light of Ancient Near Eastern Grants and Grant Treaties" [paper presented at the National Meeting of the Evangelical Theological Society, Providence, RI, 19 November 2008] 1–26) and R. S. Hess ("The Book of Joshua as a Land Grant," *Bib* 83 [2002] 493–506), who register similar objections to Weinfeld's unconditional-conditional schema.

41. In chap. 7, I develop this argument at length. For now it suffices to observe that biblical scholars and theologians have often used the *legal* metaphors of unconditionality and conditionality to describe *relational* concepts such as mutuality and temporality.

42. See G. Beckman, *Hittite Diplomatic Texts* (SBLWAW 7; 2nd ed.; Atlanta: Scholars Press, 1999) 69–93, for the various treaties between Mursili II and the vassal kings of Arzawa (i.e., treaties 10–13). The treaty between Mursili II and Kupanta-Kurunta (74–82) represents the most completely preserved of this type.

(§3). Mursili II affirms the efficaciousness of the original royal grant to Mashuiluwa's son Kupanta-Kurunta (§8) despite the rebellion of his father (§§4–7), but warns that the perpetuity of kingship and land is contingent on Kupanta-Kurunta's ongoing fealty.[43] This blend of unconditional and conditional features through the generations led Amnon Altman to classify the treaty between Mursili II and Kupanta-Kurunta as a hybrid, the "grant reaffirmation treaty," since the present and apparently conditional treaty is constructed on the prior and apparently unconditional grant to Mashuiluwa, Kupanta-Kurunta's father.[44] Altman noted further that the grant reaffirmation treaty belongs to the broader class of the "follow-up treaty," a genre in which the suzerain's magnanimity in the past toward either the vassal or the vassal's ancestor provides relational grounds for the new stipulations to be levied on the vassal in the present.[45]

Though Altman confined his study to the Hittite historical prologues, it is noteworthy that his category of "follow-up treaty" resembles several features of Deuteronomy as a literary account of covenant renewal.[46] Most importantly among these, the mutuality of the suzerain-vassal relationship in Deuteronomy is evidenced by the rhetorical links between Yhwh's past provision for Israel in its journeys (e.g., Deuteronomy 2–3) and the present injunctions to obey Yhwh (e.g., Deuteronomy 4).[47] Thus the form-critical taxonomy of unconditionality and conditionality proves inadequate to account for the vagaries of suzerain-vassal relations through the generations. Weinfeld's schema erroneously leads to analyzing grants, covenants, and treaties as autonomous literary entities when they are actually multigenerational documents linked by and reflective of an unfolding relationship.[48]

---

43. As exemplified by Mursili II's repeated warnings about the consequences of disobedience for Kupanta-Kurunta: "The oath gods shall pursue you unrelentingly" (§§10, 14, 16, 17, 18, 19, 21, 26).

44. A. Altman, *The Historical Prologue of the Hittite Vassal Treaties: An Inquiry into the Concepts of Hittite Interstate Law* (Ramat-Gan: Bar-Ilan University Press, 2002) 60–61.

45. Altman, *Historical Prologue*, 54–55.

46. However, Deuteronomy in its final form is not an ANE treaty. The canonical book does exhibit numerous points of contact with second-millennium ANE treaties, but it is more accurate to follow Deuteronomy's self-description of its genre in the opening verses: a series of Mosaic speeches to the people (i.e., "the words that Moses spoke to all Israel"; 1:1a) that is embedded in a historical narrative (i.e., "across the Jordan in the wilderness . . . in the fortieth year"; 1:1a, 3a).

47. In the treaty between Mursili II and Miqmepa of Ugarit (Beckman, *Hittite Diplomatic Texts*, 64–69), from the same collection of Hittite grant reaffirmation treaties, the grammatical person of suzerain and vassal shifts frequently in a manner reminiscent of the *Numeruswechsel* in Deuteronomy. Although the Hittite treaty does not shift the grammatical number as Deuteronomy does, it seems likely that grammatical shifts are a normal feature of grant reaffirmation treaties and also suggests that the suzerains and vassals express personal knowledge of one another from a variety of grammatical vantage points.

48. Even if Neo-Assyrian documents furnish closer parallels to Deuteronomy, Parpola and Watanabe (*Neo-Assyrian Treaties*, xv–xvi) have shown that even the relatively one-sided stipulations of the Neo-Assyrian loyalty oaths required the assent of the conquered

The form-critical and theological reductionism of Weinfeld's conclusions is especially problematic in interpreting the book of Deuteronomy, since the book contains features of both royal grants and Hittite treaties (e.g., historical prologue), on the one hand, and Neo-Assyrian treaties (e.g., extended curses section), on the other.[49]

Fifth, form-critical theories on the origins of OT covenant theology have returned full circle to the relational setting first proposed by Eichrodt. The trend since the discovery of the ANE treaties and grants had been to emphasize their legal and political aspects after it became evident that Deuteronomy in particular draws from a common pool of ANE diplomatic vocabulary for describing the suzerain-vassal relationship. The early decision to deemphasize ANE parity treaties in favor of the suzerainty treaties, as exemplified by Weinfeld's work,[50] led to the conclusion that familial language in Deuteronomy (e.g., אהב, "to love") served primarily as a cipher for political, legal, and cultic-religious realities rather than denoting relationship and emotions.[51]

In response to the tendency to downplay the affective dimensions of covenant, the study of parity treaties in the OT narratives, also known as "secular covenants," has provided a helpful corrective by recovering the clan and tribal settings of covenant-making.[52] Building on some early explorations in this area,[53] Paul Kalluveettil undertook a systematic study of covenant-making narratives in the OT and exposed several problems in previous lexical studies on ברית.[54] First, his analysis revealed that ברית and its various synonyms (e.g., ערות) could refer to alliances in general, with God serving implicitly as witness rather than as party to the accord (e.g.,

---

vassal. Thus, Weinfeld is still incorrect to view Neo-Assyrian documents as unilateral rather than bilateral in nature (see n. 34 above).

49. Deuteronomy's eclectic features thus undercut any definitive attempts to correlate its literary *Gattung* with its provenance, whether we are referring to Kitchen's arguments for the second millennium or Weinfeld's arguments for the first millennium.

50. As noted by Knoppers, "Ancient Near Eastern Royal Grants," 672 n. 9; cf. Weinfeld, "Covenant of Grant," 185.

51. Moran, "Ancient Near Eastern Background of the Love of God," 77–87. Compare the similar argument of D. J. McCarthy, "Notes on the Love of God in Deuteronomy and the Father-Son Relationship between Yahweh and Israel," *CBQ* 27 (1965) 144–47.

52. Contrast a recent attempt to regard covenant as primarily a legal and political institution to the exclusion of its relational aspects by G. W. Buchanan, "The Covenant in Legal Context," in *The Concept of the Covenant in the Second Temple Period* (ed. S. E. Porter and J. C. de Roo; Leiden: Brill, 2003) 27–52.

53. E.g., F. C. Fensham, "Father and Son as Terminology for Treaty and Covenant," in *Near Eastern Studies in Honor of William Foxwell Albright* (ed. H. Goedicke; Baltimore: Johns Hopkins University Press, 1971) 122–35; D. J. McCarthy, "Three Covenants in Genesis," *CBQ* 26 (1964) 179–89.

54. P. Kalluveettil, *Declaration and Covenant: A Comprehensive Review of Covenant Formulae from the Old Testament and the Ancient Near East* (AnBib 68; Rome: Pontifical Biblical Institute, 1982).

Gen 31:25–32:3).[55] Even when no synonyms for ברית were used, pacts of kingship, vassalage, marriage, and trade could still be established.[56] Second and more significantly, covenants between parties could still be ratified in the absence of ברית terminology through various *declaration formulas*.[57] The utterance of these formulas in either unilateral (e.g., "I will be X to you") or bilateral ("I will be X to you, and you will be Y to me") terms effected a mutual commitment between vassal and lord, father and son, brother and brother, friend and ally; alternatively, the covenanting parties could utter a unity declaration (e.g., "we are all one") to bind themselves to one another.[58]

Kalluveettil not only cast a wider semantic net than the usual fixation on ברית (e.g., Nicholson, Perlitt); his analysis of *declaration formulas* in both secular and nonsecular OT covenant narratives also demonstrated that relationships between parties are always reciprocal in nature rather than denoting a one-sided obligation (e.g., Kutsch).[59] More recently, Frank Moore Cross has arrived at similar conclusions in a socioanthropological study of West Semitic kinship and tribal groups.[60] Though kinship language is usually characterized as *covenant terminology*, Cross rightly concludes that "[t]his is to turn things upside down. The language of covenant, kinship-in-law, is taken from the language of kinship, kinship-in-flesh."[61] Because the declaration formula is grounded in familial realities (e.g., marriage, adoption),[62] it follows logically that ברית is frequently explicated with a

---

55. Kalluveettil, *Declaration*, 17–57.
56. Kalluveettil, *Declaration*, 57–90.
57. Usually known in English as the *covenant formula/formulary* and in German as the *Bundesformel* or *Bundesformular*, following R. Smend, *Die Bundesformel* (ThSt 68; Zurich: EVZ, 1963); and the German title of Baltzer's work, *Das Bundesformular*. However, German scholars who argue for a one-to-one correspondence between ברית occurrences and covenant concepts avoid referring to the word *Bund* in favor of a term such as *Zugehörigskeitsformel* (e.g., Kutsch, *Verheissung*, 146–49).
58. Kalluveettil, *Declaration*, 92–210.
59. Against scholars who ascribe redaction-critical significance to the variations among unilateral and bilateral formulas (e.g., Rendtorff, *Covenant Formula*), Kalluveettil's analysis conclusively demonstrates that all varieties of the declaration formula presume the ratification of a mutual relationship. Similarly, A. Schenker ("L'origine de l'idée d'une alliance entre Dieu et Israël dans l'Ancien Testament," *RB* 92 [1988] 184–94) shows that, even if one accepts Kutsch's definition of ברית as "obligation," the accompanying oath that verbally ratifies the ברית is always mutual in nature: "Dans le serment, nous sommes en présence de l'idée *d'obligation mutuelle d'un dieu et d'un homme* par rapport à un même objet" (p. 186, emphasis original).
60. F. M. Cross, "Kinship and Covenant in Ancient Israel," in *From Epic to Canon: History and Literature in Ancient Israel* (Baltimore: Johns Hopkins University Press, 1998) 3–21. Building on Cross's work is S. Hahn, *Kinship by Covenant: A Canonical Approach to the Fulfillment of God's Saving Promises* (ABRL; New Haven, CT: Yale University Press).
61. Cross, "Kinship," 11; cf. Kalluveettil, *Declaration*, 213.
62. S.-T. Sohn, "'I Will Be Your God and You Will Be My People': The Origin and Background of the Covenant Formula," in *Ki Baruch Hu: Ancient Near Eastern, Biblical, and Judaic Studies in Honor of Baruch A. Levine* (ed. R. Chazan, W. W. Hallo, and L. H. Schiffman; Winona Lake, IN: Eisenbrauns, 1999) 355–72.

relational sense through collocation with the declaration formula (e.g., Gen 17:7–8).[63] The arguments in favor of the irreducible mutuality of covenant relationships thus rest on a broad linguistic and socioanthropological foundation.

Sixth, Kalluveettil's conclusions about the establishment of reciprocal relationships by means of a "declarative act of fellowship"[64] suggests that covenant ratification can be analyzed as an *oral performative* act that effects changes in the extratextual world, rather than a merely *textual* phenomenon that is confined to the narrative world of the text. Particularly in Deuteronomy, the verbally enacted renewal of the covenant between YHWH and Israel is not limited to the immediate audience on the plains of Moab but expands to include every future generation of God's people (29:9–14[10–15]; cf. 26:17–19; 27:9). As noted in the earlier discussion of the land promised to the "fathers," Deuteronomy's resounding appeals to היום ("today!") imaginatively transport every generation of Israel back to Moab, the archetypal "place of decision."[65] In addition, Moses' command for the Levitical priests to recite periodically the covenantal revelation (31:9–13; cf. 1:6–30:20) coupled with Moses' recording of the "words of this Torah" (31:24–26; cf. 32:44–47) ensure that Israel will always possess a written record of Moses' addresses.[66] Thus the book of Deuteronomy is self-consciously canonical and designed to speak perpetually to God's people.

However, purely historical-critical or textual approaches to exegesis such as form criticism are unable to do justice to these features of "emphatic contemporaneity"[67] in Deuteronomy, much less traverse the millennia so that the "words of Moses" (1:1) can speak effectually to the modern reader of the book. Unless literary approaches are supplemented by exegetical methods that elucidate the timeless performativity in Deuteronomy's references to covenant, they risk pigeonholing the book as a solely literary document that makes no claim on future audiences.[68]

---

63. S. van den Eynde, "Covenant Formula and *Bᵉrît*: The Links between a Hebrew Lexeme and a Biblical Concept," *OTE* 12 (1999) 135–6.
64. Kalluveettil, *Declaration*, 1.
65. Millar, "Living at the Place of Decision," 15–88.
66. The dialogical relationship between speaking and writing in Deuteronomy's narrative world has been ably explored by Sonnet, *Book within the Book*.
67. Von Rad, *From Genesis to Chronicles*, 23; cf. idem, "Ancient Word and Living Word," in ibid., 89–98.
68. Similarly, M. Haran ("The *Bĕrît* 'Covenant': Its Nature and Ceremonial Background," in *Tehillah le-Moshe: Biblical and Judaic Studies in Honor of Moshe Greenberg* [ed. M. Cogan, B. L. Eichler, and J. H. Tigay; Winona Lake, IN: Eisenbrauns, 1997] 203–19) has demonstrated that covenant-making comprises at least three ritual elements, none of which can be circumscribed by a literary text: (1) the suzerain's oral pronouncement of the covenant's stipulations; (2) the vassal's oath of consent; and (3) the ratification of the agreement by placing the covenant document at the feet of the deity. Treaty documents only contain the literary record of covenant-making and do not exhaustively describe the covenantal relationship.

Strengths and Weaknesses of Past Approaches

Before I outline a method to supplement current approaches, it is appropriate to summarize the strengths and weaknesses of past approaches to *covenant* in OT studies. First, the concept of *covenant* includes not only the word ברית but the related concepts of *oath, declaration formula,* and *kinship.* Because covenant is basically a familial metaphor that has been extended into the legal and political realms, the meaning of ברית cannot be relegated to the antiseptic notion of *Verpflichtung.* Though any precise definition of ברית is potentially reductionistic,[69] a reasonable working definition for ברית is "a chosen relationship of mutual obligation guaranteed by oath sanctions."[70]

Second, the formal differences between grants and treaties should be considered as points along a spectrum rather than strictly separate entities.[71] Form-critical distinctions remain legitimate on their own terms but cannot be extended to support a theological dichotomy between unconditionality and conditionality. Moreover, the unconditional-conditional taxonomy is itself problematic because covenants are, by definition, a relational mixture of "unconditional" and "conditional" elements. Because Deuteronomy cannot be easily classified as either a grant or a treaty or as unconditional or conditional, proper analysis of the book should proceed from smaller rhetorical units rather than a priori conceptions of the book as a whole.

Third and finally, proper analysis of covenant as both a textual and an oral phenomenon cannot be undertaken by historical-critical and literary methods working alone. The book of Deuteronomy enacts its own oral and textual propagation to future generations. Thus the interpretation of Deuteronomic covenant theology always entails, in Dietrich Bonhoeffer's inimitable terms, the hermeneutical "turn from the phraseological to the real."[72] The limitations of current methods require an approach that also operates in front of the text in order to grasp the full import of Deuteronomy's references to a covenant with the "fathers."

---

69. P. Buis (*La Notion d'Alliance dans l'Ancien Testament* [Paris: Cerf, 1976] 45) asserts that "il n'existe dans le monde actuel aucune realité juridique que recouvre le champ sémantique de *berît* en son entier."

70. S. J. Foster, "A Prototypical Definition of *Běrît,* 'Covenant' in Biblical Hebrew," *OTE* 19 (2006) 35–46; cf. G. P. Hugenberger's definition of ברית as "an elected, as opposed to natural, relationship of obligation established under divine sanction" (*Marriage as a Covenant: A Study of Biblical Law and Ethics Governing Marriage Developed from the Perspective of Malachi* [VTSup 52; Leiden: Brill, 1994] 171). Foster's definition represents a slight improvement over Hugenberger's because it emphasizes the mutuality of the relationship. In both definitions, the chosen (i.e., non-kinship) rather than natural (i.e., kinship) character of the relationship is the crucial element.

71. Hahn, *Kinship by Covenant,* 31.

72. D. Bonhoeffer, *Letters and Papers from Prison* (enl. ed.; New York: Macmillan, 1972) 275.

Speech-Act Theory and Deuteronomic Covenant Theology

Speech-act theory offers a useful tool for illuminating Deuteronomy's assertions of covenantal relationships and changes that are effected in the "real world." Because speech-act theory is concerned with illustrating, in John Austin's terms, *How to Do Things with Words*,[73] it holds great promise for illustrating how covenant renewal narratives effect changes in the narrative world, on the one hand, and link textual propositions to extratextual institutions and readers of the text, on the other. Gordon McConville has similarly observed the synergy between speech-act theory and the exegesis of Deuteronomy: "The application of speech-act theory to Deuteronomy is evocative because it resonates with themes and features of the book itself."[74] However, scholars have used speech-act theory sparingly for Deuteronomy,[75] no doubt because of the perceived philosophical impenetrability of its terminology and ideas. Thus what follows is an overview of speech-act principles and their potential for exploring the intrinsic "hermeneutics of self-involvement"[76] in Deuteronomic covenant theology.

Speech-Act Theory in Biblical and Theological Studies

The application of speech-act theory in biblical and theological studies has been controversial.[77] Since speech-act theory was originally conceived by Austin and his student John Searle as a subdiscipline within the philosophy of language[78] rather than as an exegetical method in itself, biblical scholars have frequently disagreed over whether speech-act theory operates

---

73. J. L. Austin, *How to Do Things with Words* (2nd ed.; Cambridge: Harvard University Press, 1975).

74. McConville, "Metaphor, Symbol," 343.

75. Besides McConville's methodological sketch, three exegetical studies using speech-act theory have been conducted to date on portions of Deuteronomy: Braulik, "Deuteronomium 1–4 als Sprechakt," 249–57; Wagner, "Bedeutung," 1575–88; and Lohfink, "Bund als Vertrag," 215–39.

76. A phrase coined by A. C. Thiselton (*New Horizons in Hermeneutics: The Theory and Practice of Transforming Biblical Reading* [Grand Rapids, MI: Zondervan, 1992] 272–312) to capture the existentialist bent of speech-act theory, following D. D. Evans, *The Logic of Self-Involvement: A Philosophical Study of Everyday Language with Special Reference to the Christian Use of Language about God as Creator* (New York: Herder & Herder, 1969).

77. See the surveys of speech-act theory in biblical studies in J. W. Adams, *The Performative Nature and Function of Isaiah 40–55* (LHB/OTS 448; New York: T. & T. Clark, 2006) 1–86; A. Wagner, "Die Stellung der Sprechakttheorie in Hebraistik und Exegese," in *Congress Volume: Basel 2001* (ed. A. Lemaire; VTSup 92; Leiden: Brill, 2002) 55–83; and R. S. Briggs, "The Uses of Speech-Act Theory in Biblical Interpretation," *CBR* 9 (2001) 229–76.

78. In addition to Austin's pioneering work (*How to Do Things with Words*), see J. R. Searle, *Speech Acts: An Essay in the Philosophy of Language* (Cambridge: Cambridge University Press, 1969); idem, *Expression and Meaning: Studies in the Theory of Speech Acts* (Cambridge: Cambridge University Press, 1979).

as a supplement to existing exegetical methods[79] or whether it recasts the entire enterprise of exegesis in speech-act categories.[80] On a related note, text-oriented uses of speech-act theory tend to confine themselves to examining performative utterances in Hebrew and Greek,[81] whereas reader-oriented uses move toward reader-response theory through integration with rhetorical or performance criticism.[82] In light of this penchant for turning speech-act theory into a wax nose, it is less than surprising that biblical scholars have often voiced "the suspicion that speech-act theory is all so much jargon for finding complicated ways of saying what we all knew already."[83]

Speech-Act Theory and Old Testament Covenant Theology

Despite these methodological disputes over speech-act theory, a selective reexamination of its basic tenets will demonstrate that speech-act theory illuminates heretofore neglected elements in Deuteronomy's account of covenant-making and renewal. Among the numerous ways in which Searle refined Austin's views,[84] three items are especially suggestive for Deuteronomic covenant theology: (1) the "direction of fit" between words and the world; (2) "institutional facts" within both intratextual and extratextual social worlds; and (3) the unreliability of mapping vocabulary markers to speech-acts, especially in the case of divine-human covenants. As a result of using these elements combined, I suggest that covenant in Deuteronomy is a relational institution that is initiated by Y<small>HWH</small>'s grace, ratified by the performative speech of Y<small>HWH</small> and his people rather than explicit references to a ברית, and sustained by the faithfulness of both parties, even as Y<small>HWH</small>'s fidelity remains primary in the divine-human relationship. The Abrahamic and Israelite covenants that covenant renewal in Deuteronomy presupposes must therefore exist both in the narrative world and in the real world.

Searle's first contribution derives from his attempt to move beyond Platonic views of language as merely referential. Working with Austin's insight

---

79. E.g., Adams, *Performative Nature*, 87–119; Thiselton, *New Horizons*, 31–35.

80. E.g., D. Neufeld, *Reconceiving Texts as Speech Acts: An Analysis of 1 John* (Leiden: Brill, 1994) 37–60.

81. E.g., D. R. Hillers, "Some Performative Utterances in the Bible," in *Pomegranates and Golden Bells: Studies in Biblical, Jewish, and Near Eastern Ritual, Law, and Literature in Honor of Jacob Milgrom* (ed. D. P. Wright, D. N. Freedman, and A. Hurvitz; Winona Lake, IN: Eisenbrauns, 1995) 757–66.

82. E.g., D. Patrick, *The Rhetoric of Revelation in the Hebrew Bible* (OBT; Minneapolis: Fortress, 1999).

83. Briggs, "Uses of Speech-Act Theory," 231.

84. See the detailed account of Searle's refinement of Austin's views by R. S. Briggs, *Words in Action: Speech Act Theory and Biblical Interpretation* (Edinburgh: T. & T. Clark, 2001) 43–63.

that words (i.e., locutions) perform actions (i.e., illocutions), Searle shows that "[s]ome illocutions have as part of their illocutionary point to get the words (more strictly, their propositional content) to match the world, others to get the world to match the words."[85] Searle thus coins the term *direction of fit* to depict the descriptive and prescriptive capacities of language. He proceeds to identify four possibilities for direction of fit between words and the world: (1) words-to-world (↓); (2) world-to-words (↑); (3) double direction of fit (↕); and (4) null or empty direction of fit (Ø).[86]

Using these four directions of fit, Searle constructs a taxonomy of five illocutionary acts that he proposes can encompass all speech-acts: (1) assertives (↓), which describe true or false states of affairs (e.g., weather forecasts); (2) commissives (↑), which commit oneself to do something (e.g., promises); (3) directives (↑), which obligate someone else to do something (e.g., commands); (4) declaratives (↕), which both accurately describe and efficaciously enact a new state of affairs (e.g., a judge's pronouncement of guilt); and (5) expressives (Ø), in which feelings and attitudes are communicated (e.g., apologies).[87] Of these five speech-acts, Searle considers the declarative speech-act the purest form of "performative utterance," since it is the only type in which "the successful performance of this [declarative] class brings about the correspondence between the propositional content and reality, [and] successful performance guarantees that the propositional content corresponds to the world."[88] By its ability both to *portray* and to *project* changes in the world, the dual direction of fit encapsulated in the declarative speech-act represents a unique contribution of speech-act theory that has no parallel in literary, rhetorical, and performance criticism.[89]

Searle's notion of "directions of fit" provides a compelling linguistic explanation for Kalluveettil's observations about the efficaciousness of declaration formulas in biblical narratives. In 2 Kgs 16:7, for example, Kalluveettil demonstrates that Ahaz's appeal to Tiglath-pileser using the declaration formula confirms a relationship of vassalage with the Assyrian king. First, Ahaz declares, "I am your servant and your son" (2 Kgs 16:7b), a statement

---

85. Searle, *Expression*, 3.
86. Borrowing from Elizabeth Anscombe's illustration, Searle (*Expression*, 3–4) asserts that the distinction between words-to-world (↓) and world-to-words (↑) directions of fit is exemplified by a list of grocery items for a shopper at the market vis-à-vis a detective who is investigating the shopper for suspicious behavior. Whereas the shopper attempts to match the contents of the shopping cart to the grocery list (i.e., world-to-words fit), the detective follows the shopper and records the shopper's purchases (i.e., words-to-world fit). The identical lists obviously serve different purposes.
87. Searle, *Expression*, 12–27.
88. Searle, *Expression*, 16–17.
89. See the discussion of such "strong illocutions" by Adams, *Performative Nature*, 35–37; and Briggs, *Words*, 64–65, 95–97. Both Adams and Briggs note that "perlocutions" in speech-act theory are more or less identical to "audience effects" in rhetorical and performance criticism.

by which "Ahaz implicitly takes on all the obligations, as well as claims all the rights that ensue from the covenant."[90] Second, Ahaz's vassalage is a reciprocal relationship that emboldens his request for Tiglath-pileser's help. "Come up and deliver me from the hand of the king of Aram and the hand of the king of Israel, who are rising up against me" (2 Kgs 16:7c). Aided by a vassal's tribute (2 Kgs 16:8), the performativity of Ahaz's appeal is confirmed by Tiglath-pileser's prompt response and defeat of Judah's opponents (2 Kgs 16:9–10). Although the narrative of Ahaz's interactions with Tiglath-pileser lacks any references to an official ברית, his utterance of the declaration formula is sufficient to set in motion the covenantal interventions leading to his deliverance. This phenomenon fits Searle's category of the declarative speech-act exactly—the declaration both describes and enacts a new reality, in this case Ahaz's obligations and privileges as Tiglath-pileser's "servant" and "son."[91] The correlation between Kalluveettil's declaration formula and Searle's declarative speech-act is especially pertinent to the study of Deuteronomy. Three instances of the declaration formula occur in proximity toward the end of the book (26:17–18; 27:9; 29:12[13]), precisely at the climax of the covenant renewal ceremony.

A second and related theme in Searle's exposition of speech-act theory is his concept of *institutional facts*. If the aforementioned "directions of fit" enable the identification of performative utterances in the narrative world of the text, the concept of *institutional facts* facilitates the mapping of the narrative world to social realities that stand outside the text. Building on Austin's notion of "felicity conditions,"[92] Searle observes that the intelligibility and performativity of speech-acts depend on extralinguistic factors that he dubs "institutional facts."[93] In contrast to "brute facts," which are empirical observations from the natural world, "institutional facts" presuppose the existence of human institutions in the real world, such as a relationship between two persons. In this vein, the speech-act of an individual making a promise to another not only becomes one among many institutional facts that govern a relationship; promises themselves possess power to generate other institutional facts, such as the speaker's obligation to keep the promise and the listener's expectation that the promise will be

---

90. Kalluveettil, *Declaration*, 134.
91. Even among speech-act pioneers, the concept of *covenant* has been miscategorized as a commissive speech-act in which speakers unilaterally commit themselves to a course of action (e.g., Searle, *Expression*, 8; Thiselton, *New Horizons*, 305–6). This reproduces the erroneous literary-critical view that covenant is a one-sided affair. In response, the case for classifying covenant as a declarative speech-act is presented by G. Alster-Elata and R. Salmon, "Biblical Covenants as Performative Language," in *Summoning: Ideas of the Covenant and Interpretive Theory* (ed. E. Spolsky; Albany, NY: State University of New York, 1993) 27–29.
92. Austin, *How to Do Things with Words*, 12–24.
93. Searle, *Speech Acts*, 50–53; idem, *Expression*, 178.

kept.⁹⁴ Since the promise binds the speaker and the listener together until it is either kept or broken, the promise and its related institutional facts now exist as extralinguistic entities that cannot be confined to an intralinguistic world—for example, a literary text.

Two promissory speech-acts of this sort are woven into the narrative fabric of institutional facts in the opening verses of Deuteronomy. First, Moses cites Yhwh's promise of the land at Horeb: "I have *hereby* placed the land before you" (1:8a). Second, Israel's invitation to possess the land is built on an ancient pledge of the same land to the patriarchs: "the land that Yhwh swore to give to your fathers, to Abraham, to Isaac, and to Jacob, and to their seed" (1:8c).⁹⁵ These promises of the land to the ancestors not only set the narrative trajectory of Deuteronomy, as previously argued, but these promissory speech-acts and the respective covenants that they embody are depicted within Deuteronomy as institutional facts requiring neither description nor proof. Briggs thus summarizes the unique ability of divine speech-acts to reach beyond the narrative world into the real world, thus transcending the boundaries between them: "[T]he language of the narrative-world draws its currency from the world behind the text, and cannot be entirely cashed out without reference to it."⁹⁶

Third, in distinguishing between brute facts and institutional facts, Searle observes that ignorance of institutional facts distorts the referential relationship between words and concepts. Overlooking institutional facts is especially problematic for lexical studies, which are now forced to work "with only a conceptual structure of brute facts and ignoring the semantic rules that underlie the brute regularities."⁹⁷ As a result, words and concepts are wrongly viewed as existing in a one-to-one correspondence, an error that linguists dub the "word-concept fallacy."⁹⁸ When institutional facts are incorporated in lexical analysis, however, it becomes apparent that concepts (e.g., human institutions) typically exist in an extralinguistic world, apart from the words used to describe them. The existence of institutional facts (e.g., covenants) should be decoupled from the presence or absence of specific vocabulary markers (e.g., covenant terminology).

Searle's observations on lexical analysis underscore the implications of the axiomatic status of the Abrahamic and Israelite covenants in Deuteronomy. Since the opening verses of Deuteronomy introduce both covenants as institutional facts, the covenantal narratives of Genesis–Numbers provide an indelible background to the narrative world of Deuteronomy, although ברית is not always used in Deuteronomy to characterize this background. This conclusion vitiates the literary-critical tendency to treat

---

94. Searle, *Speech Acts*, 57–62.
95. See the analysis of Deut 1:8 on pp. 33–40 above.
96. Briggs, "Uses of Speech-Act Theory," 245.
97. Searle, *Speech Acts*, 53.
98. See Cotterell and Turner, *Linguistics*, 115–25.

occurrences of ברית as the sole object of analysis. Speech-act theory also provides a timely reminder that ברית terminology is unnecessary either for making or for renewing covenants, since the uttering of declaration formulas is sufficient for ratifying a covenantal relationship. Just as the speech-act of promise can be enacted in myriad ways without uttering the exact phrase "I promise," the presence or absence of ברית or its associated idioms (e.g., כרת ברית) in a given biblical passage cannot be considered a definitive indicator of covenantal speech-acts. [99]

Covenantal Speech-Acts in Deuteronomy

This final section outlines a method for applying speech-act principles to Deuteronomy's references to a covenant between YHWH and the "fathers." Working in conjunction with synchronic methods such as "new literary criticism" and rhetorical criticism, a speech-act approach to interpretation presents a solution to the historical-critical problem mentioned earlier—that is, the relationship between the parts and the whole with respect to ANE treaty forms in Deuteronomy. Both the macrostructure and microstructure of the book evince a repeated threefold progression of historical glances backward or forward, commands, and covenant ratification. Rather than analyzing this progression from only a form-critical perspective, which tends to fragment the text, we can describe this ubiquitous sequence in Moses' preaching as three speech-acts: (1) imaginative; (2) directive; and (3) declarative. The repetition of this rhetorical progression on the level of individual pericopes (e.g., 4:1–8) mirrors the broader logic in the three addresses of Moses: (1) historical prologue (1:6–4:43); (2) stipulations (5:1–28:68); and (3) ratification (29:1[2]–30:20). The "words of Moses" (1:1) thus comprise a single speech-act of covenant renewal that aggregates the cumulative rhetoric of smaller speech-acts.

The most important step in this rhetorical progression is the *imaginative* speech-act, a concept that modifies Searle's definition of the *assertive* speech-act. Searle had described the assertive speech-act as the communication of information that is basically true or false.[100] If one were to correlate speech-act categories with the historiographical categories usually used by biblical scholars, the scientifically oriented epistemology underlying Searle's assertive speech-act would correspond to the historicists' tendency to excavate literary texts for history *wie es eigentlich gewesen* (*ist*)—that is, in true or false terms.[101] However, this mapping of categories is problematic

---

99. Cf. J. Goldingay's similar observation regarding the book of Exodus that "paucity of use of [ברית] language points us to the fact that a covenant between YHWH and this people already exists" (*Old Testament Theology: Israel's Gospel* [Downers Grove, IL: InterVarsity Press Academic, 2003] 370).

100. Searle, *Expression*, 12.

101. See the treatment of Leopold von Ranke's historicism and its influence on OT scholarship in I. W. Provan, V. P. Long, and T. Longman III, *A Biblical History of Israel* (Louisville: Westminster John Knox, 2003) 18–24.

since the analysis of prologue sections in treaty documents has already been marred by historicists' studies of them as annalistic chronicles, on the one hand, and skepticism toward them as unreliable ideology, on the other.[102] For the historical prologue of Deuteronomy, in particular, Martin Noth's view that the itineraries in Deuteronomy 1–3 represent an unreliable, late reworking of the Exodus–Numbers narratives is perhaps the most notable example of the latter tendency.[103]

An imaginative speech-act refines Searle's assertive speech-act by recognizing that historical flashbacks in treaty documents embody more than history (and certainly not less). Rather than being disinterested accounts of the suzerain-vassal relationship, historical prologues in both vassal and parity treaties use "careful and selective argumentation to establish the rights to be claimed in the document," as McCarthy's meticulous analysis reveals.[104] This parenetic thrust in the historical flashbacks of Deuteronomy is all the more evidence that Deuteronomy is a book of preaching rather than a law code or treaty.[105] Since the bulk of Deuteronomy's תורה (1:6–30:20) is actually a series of second-person sermons that must be recited verbatim to future generations (31:9–13),[106] the precise referent of "you" becomes ambiguous in subsequent performances of the book. The voice of Moses speaking to "you" draws future audiences into the narrative world of Deuteronomy by whisking them to the plains of Moab and pointing to an even more remote past with the "fathers," thereby collapsing the historical distance between original and future audiences.[107] The coalescing of present and future generations of "you" into a singular entity thus reinforces Deuteronomy's conception of the corporate solidarity of Israel.[108]

The rhetorical power of anachronism in Deuteronomy leads Walter Brueggemann to adopt the concept of *imagination*.[109] Brueggemann argues that Deuteronomy's narrative flashbacks invite "the imaginative recovery of the root of memory," thus binding together all generations of God's people in "a regular and periodic *liturgic processing of the normative memory.*"[110]

---

102. Altman, *Historical Prologue*, 23–34.
103. Noth, *Deuteronomistic History*, 12–17.
104. D. J. McCarthy, *Treaty and Covenant*, 37; cf. 53–57.
105. Von Rad, *From Genesis to Chronicles*, 89–90.
106. See B. Lindars ("Torah in Deuteronomy," in *Words and Meanings: Essays Presented to David Winton Thomas* [ed. P. R. Ackroyd and B. Lindars; Cambridge: Cambridge University Press, 1968] 117–36), who views תורה as an all-encompassing word for law.
107. Polzin, *Moses*, 69–72. Similarly, T. Polk (*The Prophetic Persona* [JSOTSup 32; Sheffield: JSOT Press, 1984] 58–126) uses a speech-act approach to demonstrate the audience-involving effects of the ambiguous "I" in the book of Jeremiah.
108. J. G. McConville, "Singular Address in the Deuteronomic Law and the Politics of Legal Administration," *JSOT* 97 (2002) 25–29.
109. See the discussion of imagination as a mode of theological reflection by L. G. Perdue, *The Collapse of History: Reconstructing Old Testament Theology* (OBT; Minneapolis: Fortress, 1994) 263–98.
110. Brueggemann, "Imagination," 23, emphasis original.

Deut 5:3 binds past generations to the present generation by asserting that YHWH's covenant was *"not with our fathers, but with all of us who are alive here today* [היום]*."* Similarly, Deut 29:13–14[14–15] links future generations to the present generation by declaring that *"[n]ot with you alone am I making this covenant and oath but with both those who are standing here with us today* [היום] *before* YHWH *our God and those who are not here with us today* [היום]*."*[111] By subordinating chronological precision in Israel's generations to "the elastic quality of genealogical time,"[112] Deuteronomy invites all of God's people to imagine themselves at Moab reenacting the cultic היום of covenant commitment. The *imaginative* speech-act in Moses' preaching thus transports his audience backward or forward through time in order to actualize Israel's past and future for the sake of the present.[113]

In contrast to discussion of the imaginative speech-act, discussion of the directive and declarative speech-acts can be brief since they largely reproduce Searle's categories. The case for mapping declarative speech-acts to the ANE declaration formulas of covenant ratification has already been presented above. Thus it is sufficient to conclude with some minor modifications of Searle's directive speech-act. Although Searle mostly classifies commands as directive speech-acts, he also notes that the promulgation of law has "both a declarational status (the propositional content becomes law) and a directive status (the law is directive in intent)."[114] In Deuteronomy, however, the performative nature of the covenant stipulations goes beyond even this synergy between the propositional content of the laws and their normative status. The homiletical, second-person character of Deuteronomy's covenant stipulations places its audience under an obligation to exemplify a community that is dedicated to upholding the rights of the "other," whether fellow Israelites or YHWH himself. The directive speech-acts found in Deuteronomy's covenant stipulations not only describe and govern the relationships between YHWH and his people; they can even create these relationships by speaking performatively into existence a community that is relationally constituted by covenant rather than impersonally bound to law.[115]

---

111. Braulik ("Deuteronomium 1–4 als Sprechakt," 249–53) and Lohfink ("Bund als Vertrag," 222–23) note that the interjection היום often functions in Deuteronomy as a marker of performative speech.

112. R. S. Hendel ("The Exodus in Biblical Memory," *JBL* 120 [2001] 601) coins this phrase to describe the function of collective memory in the OT's use and reuse of the exodus traditions, especially in the Passover Haggadah.

113. Pannell, *Those Alive Here Today*, 41–48; Millar, "Living at the Place of Decision," 41–49; von Rad, *From Genesis to Chronicles*, 20–26.

114. Searle, *Expression*, 28.

115. The "transactional" nature of God's commands is ably explored by D. Patrick, "God's Commandment," in *God in the Fray: A Tribute to Walter Brueggemann* (ed. T. Linafelt and T. K. Beal; Minneapolis: Fortress, 1998) 93–103; idem, *Rhetoric*, 202.

Conclusion

The book of Deuteronomy preserves a striking balance between *textuality* and *orality* in its account of covenant renewal at Moab. In this regard, neither the literary-critical view of Deuteronomy as "essentially an independent law-book"[116] nor the form-critical impulse to classify Deuteronomy as an ANE treaty document reckons adequately with the book's self-description as "the *words* of Moses that he *spoke* to all Israel across the Jordan in the wilderness" (1:1). In contrast to literary approaches working alone, speech-act theory provides helpful tools to explore the book of Deuteronomy as both an oral pronouncement of the divine-human covenant (i.e., prescriptive) and a kaleidoscopic window into (i.e., descriptive) the dynamic relationship between Yhwh and his people through the ages. Thus, in chap. 7, I apply the heuristic categories of imaginative, directive, and declarative speech-acts to the Deuteronomic appearances of Yhwh's oath and covenant with the "fathers."

---

116. Wellhausen, *Prolegomena*, 6.

Chapter 7
The "Fathers" and the Divine-Human Covenant in Deuteronomy:
Analysis of Texts

Moses' enigmatic declaration that Yhwh's covenant at Horeb was made "not with our fathers, but with all of us who are alive here today" (Deut 5:3) has proven to be a difficult crux for Deuteronomic covenant theology. While Jewish tradition has generally viewed this verse as an expression of the eternal ברית at Horeb between Yhwh and his people,[1] redaction critics have taken divergent approaches to reconciling this verse's theological and chronological problems with other passages in Deuteronomy. As already observed, Lothar Perlitt advances the theological argument that the identification of ברית with the Decalogue stipulations (5:1–21) belongs to a different stratum from Yhwh's promise (e.g., 7:12b).[2] In contrast, Thomas Römer classifies Deut 5:3 as one side of the chronological incoherence of the *Generationswechsel*, since Moses' present assertion regarding his audience's presence at Horeb is difficult to reconcile with other passages in which the first exodus generation is said to have perished (1:35–39; 2:14–16).[3] Though Römer allows that Deuteronomy's conflated generations may represent an intentional theological construct,[4] he ultimately regards the phenomenon of *Generationswechsel* as either a vestige of redaction-critical editing or the literary fiction of the Deuteronom(ist)ic school[5] rather than as an essential feature of the book's rhetoric of covenant actualization.

---

1. Jewish approaches to Deut 5:3 vary. Abravanel asserted that, because God knew that the first exodus generation would not enter the land, he gave it to the following generations who are "with us here today." Ibn Ezra understood the phrase "not with our fathers" as a relative negation: "not *only* with our fathers but *also* with us." Weinfeld (*Deuteronomy 1–11*, 239) provides a survey of Jewish interpretations.
2. Perlitt (*Bundestheologie*, 80–81) also argues for multiple layers and glosses within Deut 5:1–5 itself. Compare with a similar approach by C. Brekelmans, "Deuteronomy 5: Its Place and Function," in *Das Deuteronomium: Entstehung, Gestalt und Botschaft* (ed. N. Lohfink; BETL 68; Leuven: Leuven University Press, 1985) 165.
3. Römer, *Israels Väter*, 47–53.
4. Römer (*Israels Väter*, 52 n. 229) avows agreement with the "covenant actualization" view of Deut 5:3 held by Jewish scholars and von Rad, *From Genesis to Chronicles*, 20–26. Von Rad synthesized the Jewish and diachronic views by proposing that Deut 5:3 was the microcosm of the covenant renewal ceremony at Shechem that was reflected in the final form of Deuteronomy.
5. Römer, *Israels Väter*, 20–21, passim.

The previous sections make a preliminary case for subordinating chronological precision in Deuteronomy to the cultic identification of the generations, especially through the *imaginative* speech-act of transporting future generations of Israel back to the plains of Moab. While the broad contours of this interpretation are not new,[6] past explorations of this use of anachronism have been largely restricted to Deut 5:3.[7] Thus, in this chapter I analyze Deuteronomy's seven references to an oath or covenant with the "fathers" (4:31; 7:8, 12; 8:18; 29:11[12], 13[14], 24[25]) in order to demonstrate that all of Deuteronomy's narrative flashbacks with respect to Yhwh's covenant are imaginatively rather than dispassionately historical in nature. The dynamic conception of *covenant* in Deuteronomy can be explained as a rhetorical device that unifies Israel's generations under a single covenant rather than as evidence of different redactional layers.

The six verses in which ברית is collocated with אבות (4:31; 7:12; 8:18; 29:11[12], 13[14], 24[25]) sketch only the broad outlines of Yhwh's relationship with Israel's ancestors. In the surrounding context of these passages, the broad lexical sense of ברית assumes greater specificity through its juxtaposition with familial (e.g., חסד) and diplomatic (e.g., ידע) language.[8] Thus every Deuteronomic occurrence of ברית connotes relational ideas.[9] However, the precise nuance of ברית in a given pericope hinges, not only on identifying the proper referent for the "fathers" with whom the ברית was made, but also on taking into account the juxtaposed terms and concepts for covenant relationship (e.g., שבעה, אלה).

An Overview of Deuteronomic Covenant Theology

Though Deuteronomic covenant theology has been labeled the "piety-prosperity equation,"[10] a survey of the book's terminology and concepts of covenant quickly exposes the inaccuracy of this caricature. Deuteronomy

---

6. The view that Deut 5:3 encapsulates the actualization of Yhwh's covenant has been adopted with minor modifications by many scholars, although they do not always trace their view to Ibn Ezra. For example, see McConville, *Deuteronomy*, 124; W. Brueggemann, *Deuteronomy* (AbOTC; Nashville: Abingdon, 2001) 64–65; Miller, *Deuteronomy*, 67; Mayes, *Deuteronomy*, 165.

7. E.g., Pannell, *Those Alive Here Today*, 42–48.

8. On חסד as familial language (e.g., 2 Sam 7:15), see K. D. Sakenfeld, *The Meaning of Hesed in the Hebrew Bible: A New Inquiry* (HSM 17; Missoula, MT: Scholars Press, 1978); N. Glueck, *Hesed in the Bible* (trans. A. Gottschalk; Cincinnati: Hebrew Union College Press, 1967). On ידע as diplomatic language, see H. B. Huffmon, "The Treaty Background of Hebrew YĀDA‘," *BASOR* 181 (1966) 31–37; idem, and S. B. Parker, "A Further Note on the Treaty Background of Hebrew YĀDA‘," *BASOR* 184 (1966) 36–38.

9. See the discussion of form-critical approaches to OT covenant theology on pp. 159–168 above. In addition to denoting divine-human covenants (e.g., 5:3), the term ברית denotes a parity treaty between human parties (7:2) one time in Deuteronomy.

10. C. H. H. Scobie, *The Ways of Our God: An Approach to Biblical Theology* (Grand Rapids, MI: Eerdmans, 2003) 196, 205–6.

unquestionably contains many formulaic commands to obey,[11] but this obedience is always couched in the imaginative recitation of Yʜᴡʜ's prior dealings with Israel.

History and Kinship in Deuteronomy's Covenant with the "Fathers"

Five of Yʜᴡʜ's gracious actions in Israel's history receive special attention in Deuteronomy 1–4. First, Yʜᴡʜ provides the gift of a lush land (1:35; 4:21), thereby fulfilling his promise to the "fathers" (1:8, 21). Second, Yʜᴡʜ has delivered his people through the mighty deeds of the exodus (1:30; 4:20, 34; 6:21–22; 26:6–8). Third, the theophany at Horeb represents Yʜᴡʜ's unparalleled gift of covenant stipulations (4:6, 8) to a people that is privileged to hear the divine voice (4:7, 12, 33, 36). Fourth, Israel's survival through the wilderness and victory in the Transjordan after the apostasy at Kadesh is the result of Yʜᴡʜ's faithful provision (2:1–3:29; cf. 8:2–4; 29:4–8[5–9]). Fifth, Israel's arrival at Moab as an innumerable people fulfills Yʜᴡʜ's ancient promise of multiplication (1:10; 10:22). In light of this wondrous history, it is appropriate for Moses to conclude his summary of Yʜᴡʜ's dealings with Israel with two emphatic pronouncements of Yʜᴡʜ's incomparability (4:35, 39; cf. 3:24). Thus it is the theological paradox of holiness and mercy in Israel's experience of Yʜᴡʜ as "a god so near" (4:7) more than the impersonal calculus of seeking prosperity that furnishes Israel with the proper motivation to obey Yʜᴡʜ (4:40). The imaginative speech-acts of Israel's history designed to inspire the people's obedience are not confined to the opening chapters of Deuteronomy but occur throughout the book (e.g., 6:20–25; 26:5–9).

In addition to his gracious actions, the affective component of the relationship between Yʜᴡʜ and multiple generations of his people is evident through Deuteronomy's use of kinship language. The current generation at Moab is identified not only as the "seed" (1:8; 4:37; 10:15; 11:9; 34:4) of the "fathers" but also as "son(s)" of Yʜᴡʜ himself (1:31; 8:5; 14:1; cf. 32:6).[12] The "fathers" are the object of Yʜᴡʜ's אהב ("to love"; 4:37a) and חשק ("to desire, show affection"; 10:15a),[13] which eventuates for their descendants

---

11. Even granting this, many fail to see that Deuteronomy does not speak monolithically but has a rich vocabulary of obedience: עשה ("to do"), שמר (Qal: "to keep"; Niphal: "to be careful"), למד (Qal: "to learn"; Piel: "to teach"), זכר ("to remember"), שמע ("to listen/obey").

12. Fensham ("Father and Son as Terminology," 122–35) notes that "father" and "son" are standard terms in ANE treaties for suzerain and vassal, respectively. However, Deuteronomy depicts human "fathers" as recipients of Yʜᴡʜ's promises (e.g., 1:8) and teachers of Yʜᴡʜ's truth (e.g., 6:20–25) but not as suzerains.

13. J. E. Lapsley ("Feeling Our Way: Love for God in Deuteronomy," CBQ 65 [2003] 350–69) nuances the consensus view, first argued by W. L. Moran, that the use of אהב in Deuteronomy is diplomatic language that signifies a vassal's duty to obey the suzerain. Lapsley shows that אהב in Deuteronomy also entails an emotive component.

in divine election (בחר, "to choose"; 4:37b; 10:15b), deliverance from Egypt (4:37c), and the gift of land (4:38). This conceptual cluster of Yhwh's love, affection, election, exodus, and land gift is applied both to the generation of the "fathers" (4:37; 10:15) and to the present generation of "you" at Moab (7:7–8). Since Yhwh's "love" precedes the demand for obedience, the present duty of Israel to "love" Yhwh (5:10; 6:5: 10:12; 11:1) is clearly a reciprocation of divine favor rather than a unilateral means of earning it.[14]

Yhwh's fidelity to his people is communicated both in other constructions with ברית and in the absence of the term. Similar to the way that verbs (e.g., בחר, אהב) are used to denote Yhwh's affection for both past and present generations, the hendiadys ברית וחסד describes Yhwh's relationship with both the "fathers" (7:12) and the present generation at Moab (7:9).[15] The word ברית appears later in a different hendiadys with אלה ("oath") in the context of a transgenerational covenant with both the present generation (29:9–10[10–11]) and the "fathers" (29:12[13]). Deuteronomy 29 also contains a bilateral declaration formula, "that you might be his people . . . and he might be your God" (29:12[13]), which makes explicit the mutuality of the ברית (29:11[12]). This reciprocal relationship between Yhwh and Israel, with the deity himself as its primary guarantor, is buttressed through Deuteronomy's frequent use of the verb נשבע (e.g., 1:8) and its rarer, nominal form, שבעה (7:8).[16] Like other covenantal expressions, נשבע can take both the "fathers" (e.g., 1:8, 34) and the current generation at Moab as verbal objects (e.g., 26:5; 28:9). In sum, Deuteronomy uses a smorgasbord of terms to describe covenant-making and covenant-keeping with multiple generations of God's people, thus blurring the chronological and theological distinctions between them.

Historical-Critical and Canonical Perspectives in OT Covenant Theology

Since the broader contexts of these passages contain every major term and concept for covenant, the seven references to Yhwh's oath and

---

14. B. E. Willoughby, "A Heartfelt Love: An Exegesis of Deuteronomy 6:4–19," *ResQ* 22 (1970) 63–79. Despite the reciprocity in Deuteronomy's use of אהב, S. Ackerman ("The Personal Is Political: Covenantal and Affectionate Love (*'ĀHĒB, 'AHĂBÂ*) in the Hebrew Bible," *VT* 52 [2002] 437–58) notes that the OT's use of the אהב lexical family is typically reserved for the love of a superior party (e.g., a parent) for an inferior (e.g., a child). Though Israel is commanded in Deuteronomy to "love" God (e.g., 6:5), Ackerman is correct that "Deuteronomy never describes the people or their ancestors as actually offering Yahweh this love" (p. 445). Deuteronomy continually portrays divine love as prior and primary (compare with Solomon's אהב for Yhwh in 1 Kgs 3:3, a passage that is traditionally classified as Deuteronom[ist]ic).

15. Sakenfeld (*Meaning of Hesed*, 134) notes that here the hendiadys of ברית and חסד emphasizes "the keeping of the covenant by the powerful party," thus prioritizing divine grace over human commitment without negating the latter.

16. Schenker ("L'origine," 184–94) demonstrates the mutual character of oaths (e.g., שבעה, אלה) in covenant-making, even when the term ברית is not present.

covenant with the "fathers" (4:31; 7:8, 12; 8:18; 29:11, 13, 24) constitute a representative cross-section of Deuteronomic covenant theology. Deut 4:31 falls within 4:9–31, a section in which the ratification of a ברית is described using three different verbs: (1) הגיד ("to declare"; 4:13); (2) כרת ("to cut/make"; 4:23); and (3) נשבע ("to swear"; 4:31). Deut 7:8 and 7:12 belong to the broader pericope of 7:1–13, a passage that contains various nouns (e.g., חסד, אלה) and verbs (e.g., נשבע, שמר) denoting covenant relationship. Deut 8:18 marks a rare instance in which the verb הקים ("to establish") denotes the consummation of Yhwh's ברית with the "fathers."

Most importantly, Deut 29:11–13[12–14] contains a superset of all the covenant parties, terminology, and concepts found elsewhere in the entire Pentateuch. Moses invites Israel to ratify its relationship with Yhwh:

> to enter [עבר] into the covenant [ברית] with Yhwh your God and into his oath [אלה] that he is making [כרת] with you today, in order to establish [הקים] you as his people and that he may be your God, just as he swore [נשבע] to your *fathers*, to Abraham, to Isaac, and to Jacob. (29:11–13[12–14])

This reference to Yhwh's timeless relationship with both the patriarchs and the present generation is intriguing because it combines the idioms of every putative pentateuchal stratum. The use of כרת to ratify covenants with the generation at Moab is generally attributed to the Deuteronom(ist)ic school;[17] the use of נשבע for an oath to the patriarchs is assigned to J or E;[18] and the use of הקים for covenant-making is universally classified as P.[19] In addition to 29:11–13, the final reference to Yhwh's covenant in 29:24[25] is also unusual since it preserves the only occurrence of כרת to denote the ratification of a ברית with the "fathers" rather than "you." In light of this chapter's unparalleled convergence of covenant terminology, particularly in vv. 9–14, Rolf Rendtorff rightly affirms that Deuteronomy 29 is a key text for bridging the usual redaction-critical divisions in the Pentateuch and thereby unlocking the puzzle of OT covenant theology.[20]

Because Deuteronomy's references to a covenant with the "fathers" contain a useful microcosm of OT covenant concepts, the analysis of these seven passages can provide a methodological foundation for answering the biblical-theological question posed in chap. 6—what are the taxonomic relationships among covenant renewals in Deuteronomy, the Abrahamic covenant with the patriarchs in Genesis, and the Israelite covenant with the entire nation in Exodus–Numbers? In this analysis (chap. 7), I

---

17. Römer, *Israels Väter*, 50–51, 132, passim.
18. Van Seters ("Confessional Reformulation," 448–59) acknowledges the attribution of an oath with the patriarchs to JE but argues that JE postdates rather than predates D.
19. J. Day, "Why Does God 'Establish' Rather Than 'Cut' Covenants in the Priestly Source?" in *Covenant as Context: Essays in Honour of E. W. Nicholson* (ed. A. D. H. Mayes and R. B. Salters; Oxford: Oxford University Press, 2003) 91–109.
20. Rendtorff, *Covenant Formula*, 68–69.

also address the much-debated issue of whether the "covenant at Moab" (28:69[29:1]–30:20) constitutes a new and distinct covenant or whether it recapitulates earlier material in the book.[21]

I will undertake this examination of Deuteronomy's seven references to Y<small>HWH</small>'s oath and covenant with the "fathers" (4:31; 7:8, 12; 8:18; 29:11[12], 13[14], 24[25]) by introducing three case studies. First, the various references to ברית in Deuteronomy 4 form a single study. Second, the three references in Deuteronomy 7–8 (7:8, 12; 8:18) are treated together since these chapters form a coherent unit detailing the privileges and responsibilities of divine election. Third, the three references to covenant and oath in 29:11–13 and 29:24 form a single study on Deuteronomy 29. Rather than restricting the present analysis to the occurrences of covenant and oath terminology, I trace Moses' rhetorical strategy in each case study through the imaginative, directive, and declarative speech-acts that constitute the larger speech-act of covenant renewal.

Divine-Human Covenant and the "Fathers" in Deuteronomy 4

The hortatory thrust of Deuteronomy 4 provides a fitting conclusion to the first Mosaic speech (1:6–4:40). Although Perlitt argues that Deuteronomy 4 is primarily an exposition of covenant stipulations,[22] closer examination reveals that this chapter contains far more imaginative speech-acts about Y<small>HWH</small>'s gracious relationship with the "fathers" and the present generation than actual commands. Here Y<small>HWH</small> is characterized, not only as the deity whose love for the "fathers" resulted in the exodus (4:37) and the "God of the fathers" who now gives the land (4:1), but also as the one who rescues Israel from exile by remembering the "covenant of your fathers that he swore to them" (4:31). Deuteronomy 4 ties Y<small>HWH</small>'s dealings with the "fathers" closely to three seminal events in Israel's history: (1) exodus; (2) conquest; and (3) restoration. The imaginative speech-acts outlining these events in Israel's past and future provide the rhetorical basis for the directive (i.e., parenetic) and declarative (i.e., covenant-ratifying) speech-acts for the present generation at Moab, thereby making Deuteronomy 4 a summary statement of Y<small>HWH</small>'s timeless covenant with Israel. However, the microcosmic character of this chapter also places it at the heart of numerous historical-critical and theological debates in OT studies. Thus it is

---

21. See the history of research in D. T. Olson, "How Does Deuteronomy Do Theology? Literary Juxtaposition and Paradox in the New Moab Covenant in Deuteronomy 29–32," in *A God So Near: Essays on Old Testament Theology in Honor of Patrick D. Miller* (ed. B. A. Strawn and N. R. Bowen; Winona Lake, IN: Eisenbrauns, 2003) 202–5.

22. Perlitt argues that the legal character of Deuteronomy 4 undermines the earlier notion in Deut 1:8 of land as a free gift: "Zwischen Dtn 1,8 und Dtn 4 . . . liegt ein Zeitraum der Relativierung von Landverheißung und Verheißungsland durch Gesetz und 'Bund'" (*Bundestheologie*, 34).

necessary to argue briefly for a final-form reading of Deuteronomy 4 as the conclusion to the first Mosaic speech before I return to examining its imaginative, directive, and declarative speech acts.

Diachronic and Synchronic Approaches to Deuteronomy 1–4

The hands of source and redaction critics have performed a significant amount of surgery on the first speech of Moses. Three general trends may be summarized from the numerous diachronic proposals that have been adduced. First, at the macroscopic level of Deuteronomy as a whole, Martin Noth proposed that "Deut. 1–3(4) is not the introduction to the Deuteronomic law [i.e., Deuteronomy 12–26] but the beginning of the Deuteronomistic historical narrative"[23] from Joshua to 2 Kings. Noth held that the narrative of Israel's failures in the wilderness in Deuteronomy 1–3 provided the theological background for the Deuteronomistic History's account of the fall of the Judean monarchy. The hortatory and legal material of Deut 4:44–30:20, which existed earlier as a separate collection, was then joined together with Deuteronomy 1–3(4) by the exilic Deuteronom(ist)ic Historian.[24] Noth's proposal to divide these initial chapters from the rest of the book as a later insertion has been widely adopted.[25]

Second, redaction critics have often separated Deuteronomy 1–3 from Deuteronomy 4 on literary and theological grounds.[26] On literary grounds, scholars note that the first Mosaic speech shifts abruptly from the historical narratives of chaps. 1–3 to the hortatory genre of chap. 4.[27] Moreover, historical and temporal references tend to diverge in chaps. 1–3 and chap. 4. On the one hand, chaps. 1–3 lack the eyewitness appeals to the Horeb revelation (4:10–15, 23, 33) and exodus (4:20, 34–38) that dominate chap. 4. In contrast, chap. 4 lacks references to judicial details (1:9–18), the events

---

23. Noth, *Deuteronomistic History*, 14.
24. Noth was ambivalent regarding the place of Deuteronomy 4 in his scheme (on which, see A. D. H. Mayes, "Deuteronomy 4 and the Literary Criticism of Deuteronomy," *JBL* 100 [1981] 23–51).
25. H. D. Preuss (*Das Deuteronomium* [EdF 164; Darmstadt: Wissenschaftliche Buchgesellschaft, 1982] 77) affirms the hegemony of Noth's theory: "Wer heute etwas zu Dtn 1 sagt, muß zu dieser These [Noths] Stellung nehmen bzw. (schlicht ausgedrückt) einleuchtend machen, was Dtn 1–3 sonst noch sein könnten, wenn sie nicht die Einleitungsreden zum DtrG sind." Scholarly developments since 1982 are well-documented by J. C. Gertz, "Kompositorische Funktion und literarhistorischer Ort von Deuteronomium 1–3," in *Die deuteronomischen Geschichtswerke in den Büchern Genesis bis 2 Könige* (ed. M. Witte, K. Schmid, and D. Prechel; BZAW 365; Berlin: de Gruyter, 2006) 103–23.
26. See the surveys of interpretation by N. MacDonald, "The Literary Criticism and Rhetorical Logic of Deuteronomy I–IV," *VT* 56 (2006) 203–24; and D. Knapp, *Deuteronomium 4: Literarische Analysen und theologische Interpretation* (GTA 35; Göttingen: Vandenhoeck & Ruprecht, 1987) 27–29.
27. Von Rad (*Deuteronomy*, 48) and Mayes ("Deuteronomy 4," 31–32) consider the transitional interjection ועתה ("and now"; 4:1) to be secondary.

at Kadesh (1:19–46), and chronology and geography (2:1–25) as found in chaps. 1–3. On theological grounds, Deuteronomy 4 putatively exhibits a theological sophistication that necessitates a dating during the Divided Monarchy or even later, most notably due to the radical monotheism associated with the so-called *Bilderverbot*.[28] In contrast, the wilderness narratives of chaps. 1–3 are identified as the recasting of J or E material during the United Monarchy.[29]

The *Numeruswechsel* presents a third line of redaction-critical approaches to Deuteronomy 1–4.[30] Although Samuel Driver long ago suggested that variations in person and number were literary indicators of corporate solidarity,[31] Deuteronomy research has instead been dominated by the tendency to view such variations as evidence of multiple sources.[32] In similar publications on Deuteronomy 1–3, for example, Henri Cazelles and Josef Plöger propose that an originally plural narrative was supplemented by a singular narrative.[33] In response, Siegfried Mittmann proposes that the pre-deuteronomic plural narrative extends to Deuteronomy 6 rather than ending in Deuteronomy 3.[34] Providing further contrast, Norbert Lohfink takes a tradition-critical approach by proposing that 1:6–3:29 resulted from the joining of a newer narrative emphasizing collective identity and an older narrative emphasizing individual guilt.[35] With such plurality and even incommensurability among redaction-critical proposals, the inclination to view the *Numeruswechsel* as evidence for redactional seams has diminished in recent decades.

The impasse among diachronic approaches has given rise to an increasing number of synchronic studies on Deuteronomy 1–4. The morphological and syntactical phenomena of *Numeruswechsel* and generic shift that first inspired diachronic studies have now been examined convincingly as rhetorical and stylistic features.[36] Though some redaction-critical holdouts

---

28. Braulik, "Birth," 99–130, 237–47.
29. M. Z. Brettler, *The Creation of History in Ancient Israel* (New York: Routledge, 1995) 62–78; G. W. Coats, *Rebellion in the Wilderness: The Murmuring Motif in the Wilderness Traditions of the Old Testament* (Nashville: Abingdon, 1968) 192–96.
30. Though the term *Numeruswechsel* traditionally refers to oscillation in grammatical number, Millar ("Living at the Place of Decision," 18) notes that the discourses of Deuteronomy also vary in grammatical person.
31. Regarding the *Numeruswechsel* in 1:21 and 6:2, Driver (*Deuteronomy*, 89) opines that "the Writer's thought passes from the nation to the individual Israelite."
32. Minnette de Tillesse, "Sections," 29–87. Cf. C. T. Begg, "The Literary Criticism of Deuteronomy 4,1–40: Contributions to a Continuing Discussion," *ETL* 56 (1980) 10–55.
33. Cazelles, "Passages," 207–19; Plöger, *Literarkritische, formgeschichtliche und stilkritische Untersuchungen*, 5–24.
34. Mittmann, *Deuteronomium 1,1–6,3*, 170–72.
35. Lohfink, "Problem," 227–33.
36. E.g., N. Lohfink, "Verkündigung des Hauptgebots in der jüngsten Schicht des Deuteronomiums (Dt 4,1–40)," in *Höre Israel: Auslegung von Texten aus dem Buch Deuteronomium* (Die Welt der Bibel 18; Düsseldorf: Patmos, 1965) 247–56; Braulik, *Mittel*; cf.

remain,³⁷ a growing number of Deuteronomy scholars recognize that a final-form reading of the text provides fresh grist for the diachronic mill that had heretofore stalled on diachronic readings alone. The urgent need for synchronic reappraisal of diachronic work has been echoed notably by Norbert Lohfink and Georg Braulik, who have both offered insightful final-form studies of the very same texts on which they previously used a redaction-critical approach.

Several decades ago, Lohfink conducted a diachronic study on 1:6–3:29 that took Noth's theory for granted.³⁸ However, in a more recent article, he concedes the shortcomings of his earlier article and offers a brilliant synchronic analysis on 1:6–3:29.³⁹ In a similar way, Braulik currently uses speech-act theory to argue for the coherence of Deuteronomy 1–4,⁴⁰ despite asserting in the past that Deuteronomy 4 was a postexilic insertion between the Deuteronomic Torah and the Deuteronomistic History.⁴¹ Since these preeminent Deuteronomy scholars now admit that final-form approaches are viable for texts that they previously analyzed as redacted collections, it is clearly acceptable to examine the first speech of Moses as a unified argument.

A final-form reading of Deuteronomy 1–4 also takes into account in a better way the ANE context of Deuteronomy, since the progression from historical recital to covenant stipulations is a common feature of second-millennium treaties.⁴² Both the hypothesis of a Deuteronomistic History and other attempts to separate Deuteronomy 1–3 from Deuteronomy 4 neglect the similarities between the book and the second-millennium treaties that allow for a seamless transition from history to parenesis.⁴³ The various attempts to partition Deuteronomy 1–4 using generic divisions (e.g., historiography vs. parenesis) or historical antecedents (e.g., preexilic vs.

Lenchak, *Choose Life*. Mayes ("Deuteronomy 4," 24–30) also considers Deuteronomy 4 to be a unified, though postexilic, composition.

37. See Perlitt's severe criticism of Braulik's work on Deuteronomy 4: "Es ist mir unbegreiflich, daß G. Braulik seiner rhetorischen Analyse von Dtn 4 . . . die literarkritische im Druck nicht vorangestellt hat" ("Deuteronomium 1–3 im Streit der exegetischen Methoden," in *Deuteronomium-Studien*, 118 n. 43).

38. Lohfink, "Darstellungskunst," 105–35.

39. Lohfink, "Narrative Analyse," 121–76.

40. Braulik, "Deuteronomium 1–4 als Sprechakt," 249–57.

41. G. Braulik, "Wisdom, Divine Presence and Law," in *The Theology of Deuteronomy* (trans. U. Lindbad; N. Richland Hills, TX: BIBAL, 1993) 2–3.

42. See, for example, the shift from historical recital to parenetic future in the treaty between Suppiluliuma I of Ḫatti and and Niqmaddu II of Ugarit in Beckman, *Texts*, 34–36. Cf. Kline, *Treaty*, 31.

43. This is not to say that Deuteronomy in its final form is an ANE treaty (see discussion on p. 164 n. 46 above) but only that the generic similarities between Deuteronomy 1–4 and the first three sections of the Hittite treaties (i.e., preamble, historical prologue, covenant stipulations) offer a *prima facie* case for presuming the literary integrity of Deuteronomy 1–4.

postexilic Sitz im Leben) rest more on extratextual theories of Deuteronomy's provenance than on a close reading of the text itself. Thus our study of Yhwh's oath and covenant with the "fathers" in Deuteronomy 4 can proceed with the assumption that this chapter represents the conclusion of the first Mosaic speech.

Covenantal Speech-Acts in Deuteronomy 4

Braulik's speech-act analysis of Deuteronomy 4 provides a useful starting point for the present study of Yhwh's oath and covenant with the "fathers." He progresses beyond literary-critical approaches by recognizing that deictic particles (e.g., ראה, ועתה) and chronological markers (e.g., היום, בעת ההיא) often signal the presence of declarative speech-acts of covenant ratification (e.g., "I *hereby* call heaven and earth to witness against you *today*"; 4:26; cf. 4:5).[44] Braulik's guidelines for identifying speech-acts in Deuteronomy 4 will be useful for the exegetical case studies that follow.

However, it is necessary first to modify Braulik's characterization of Deut 4:9–31 as parenesis,[45] since this sort of all-encompassing category tends to overlook the fact that Moses' exhortation to covenant fidelity is driven more by imaginative speech-acts of reciting episodes in Israel's history than by directive speech-acts of commanding Israel's obedience. For example, each directive speech-act in which Moses briefly exhorts the people to "keep watch" (שמר Niphal; e.g., 4:9, 15, 23) is immediately followed by an extended imaginative speech-act in which he details the seminal events of Israel's history. Moses not only looks back to the theophany at Horeb (4:10–14; cf. 15b) and his own disqualification at Kadesh from entering the land (4:21–22); he also looks ahead to a terrifying future in which Israel faces exile in a foreign land (4:26b–28).

Even when Moses forbids Israel to worship images or rival gods of Yhwh, the rhetorical priority of the imaginative speech-act over the directive speech-act is confirmed by the narrative framework within which each command is embedded. Moses' recollections of Horeb in Deuteronomy 4 emphasize the visual and aural phenomena experienced there (e.g., darkness, cloud, fire, Yhwh's voice; cf. 4:11–13) far more than Yhwh's actual commands in the Decalogue (4:13; cf. 5:8–10).[46] The *Bilderverbot* is also narrated rather than commanded through Israel's hearing of God's

---

44. Braulik, "Deuteronomium 1–4 als Sprechakt," 249–53.
45. Braulik, "Deuteronomium 1–4 als Sprechakt," 254.
46. The word אש ("fire") appears 14× in Deuteronomy 4–5 (4:11, 12, 15, 24, 33, 36 [2×]; 5:4, 5, 22, 24, 25) as a visual representation of Yhwh's presence both in heaven (e.g., 4:11) and on earth (e.g., 4:36). In conjunction with אש, the noun קול appears 9× in Deuteronomy 4–5 as an acoustic *Leitwort* to denote Yhwh's terrifying voice (4:12, 20, 33, 36; 5:22, 23, 24, 25, 26). The polysemy of קול as both "sound" and "voice" in these chapters is particularly apt for capturing the transcendent and immanent qualities of Yhwh's speech.

transcendent voice without seeing any immanent form (4:12, 15a).[47] Thus it is essential to parse Braulik's category of *parenesis* into the subcategories of *imaginative* and *directive* speech-acts, especially since the imaginative speech-act predominates in the larger unit of Deut 4:9–31.

Deuteronomy 4:1

וְעַתָּה יִשְׂרָאֵל	And now, O Israel,
שְׁמַע אֶל־הַחֻקִּים וְאֶל־הַמִּשְׁפָּטִים	listen to the statutes and the ordinances
אֲשֶׁר אָנֹכִי מְלַמֵּד אֶתְכֶם לַעֲשׂוֹת	that I am teaching you today to do,
לְמַעַן תִּחְיוּ וּבָאתֶם	in order that you may live and enter
וִירִשְׁתֶּם אֶת־הָאָרֶץ	and possess the land
אֲשֶׁר יְהוָה אֱלֹהֵי אֲבֹתֵיכֶם נֹתֵן לָכֶם	that YHWH God of your fathers is giving to you.

Deuteronomy 4 opens with the deictic particle ועתה ("and now"), an interjection that ascribes a performative force to Moses' reminiscence of Israel's travels in Deuteronomy 1–3.[48] Despite the usual function of ועתה to denote a shift from historical lessons to parenesis,[49] here it is conspicuous that ועתה actually introduces a chapter that reaches further back in Israel's history than the first three chapters of the book. By waiting until Deuteronomy 4 to provide an extended account of the Horeb events (4:9–31; cf. 1:6–18), Moses has chosen to recite Israel's history in reverse order since the previous three chapters had focused on Israel's journeys from Kadesh, the wilderness, and Transjordan (1:19–3:29).[50] Thus ועתה does not simply mark the arrival of the narrative present at Moab but heralds a timeless conception of Israel's history in which the distant past is brought to bear on the present audience. More than merely linking law and land,[51] the introductory section of 4:1–4 asserts the theological continuity in YHWH's dealings with all generations, for Israel now stands at Moab on the verge of possessing "the land that YHWH God of your *fathers* is giving *you*" (4:1b).

Three lexical shifts in the land-gift formula of Deut 4:1 are significant vis-à-vis the three land-promise formulas of Deuteronomy 1. Each of these shifts reflects the forward progression of covenant actualization in the first Mosaic speech. First, the earlier language of Yahweh's "oath" (נשבע; 1:8, 21,

---

47. Lohfink ("Bund als Vertrag," 218–20) makes a similar case for the priority of *Darstellung* (i.e., "narrative") over *Bericht* (i.e., "report") in Deuteronomy's accounts of covenant-making.

48. Braulik, "Deuteronomium 1–4 als Sprechakt," 249: "Mit 4,1 erreicht die erste Moserede also ihre eigentliche Aussage. Was die Erzählung in den ersten drei Kapiteln in Errinerung gerufen hatte, war den Zuhörern Moses bereits weitgehend bekannt. Moses Geschichtsrésumee sollte vor allem begründend und legitimierend das vorbereiten, was Mose im Anschluss daran sagen würde."

49. Weinfeld, *Deuteronomy 1–11*, 199; cf. H. A. Brongers, "Bemerkungen zum Gebrauch des adverbialen wᵉʿattah im Alten Testament (ein lexikologischer Beitrag)," *VT* 15 (1965) 289–99.

50. Cf. Lohfink, "Deuteronomy 5," 262–65.
51. Römer, *Israels Väter*, 128.

35) has now narrowed to the terminology of "gift" (נתן) that is so characteristic of Deuteronomy 4 (vv. 1, 21, 38, 40). The verb נתן previously appeared in Deuteronomy 1 only in infinitive construct form as a complementary infinitive to נשבע (i.e., "Yhwh swore to give"). Second, the verbal aspect of נתן has shifted from the past to the narrative present through the use of the Qal participle נֹתֵן. The *past* sense of נתן as a complementary infinitive to the perfect verb נשבע is exchanged for a durative participle that underlines Yhwh's *present* gift of the land, perhaps even suggesting that its conquest has already begun.[52] Third, as already noted, the recipient of Yhwh's "gift" (נתן) of land has been updated from "your fathers" to "you." The cumulative effect of these shifts is that Yhwh can be identified appositionally both as the "God of the fathers" (4:1) and "your God" (3× in 4:2–4, both plural and singular "your"). The ancient promise of the land has been actualized and reiterated at Moab with stunning vividness, since Yhwh has been the same deity for all generations of Israel.

Additionally, the same "God of the fathers" who once invited Israel to possess (ירש) the land at Kadesh (1:21) now repeats this offer at Moab (4:1b), thereby giving Israel the opportunity to overlay the unsavory history at Kadesh with a new chapter of obedience. In fact, the terminology of "possessing" (ירש) the land is accompanied by that of "entering" (בוא; cf. 1:8) rather than "going up" (עלה; cf. 1:21), thereby avoiding the frequent *Leitwort* עלה from the Kadesh narrative (e.g., 1:41–43) in favor of the Horeb term בוא (4:1b). Unlike Israel's laxity at Kadesh, possession of the land can occur imminently by the people's vigilance in obeying Yhwh's word "now" (4:1) and "today" (4:4) in a manner reminiscent of the earlier covenant ratification at Horeb.

In summary, the invocation of the "God of your fathers" in Deuteronomy 4 binds the generations together by bringing the present audience into a filial relationship with both the patriarchs and the Horeb/Kadesh generation. The current generation at Moab can count both these generations as its "fathers" since it represents only the latest group to have received the same promise of the land. Much as the "God of the fathers" is now contemporized as "your God" (4:1–4), the future-oriented hermeneutic of this chapter anticipates Moses' proclamation that the book's audience includes every coming generation that faces the theological nexus of life and land (29:9–14[10–15]). Thus the initial section of 4:1–4 broadens the chronological horizons of the entire chapter by heaping every past tradition of the "fathers" onto Israel's present. The rhetorical power of the imaginative speech-act becomes especially evident in the subsequent references to Yhwh's ברית with his people (4:13, 23, 31), in which Moses asserts that

---

52. See Deut 4:38; 6:19; 9:5. Joüon (§121c) notes that participles take their time and aspect features from the context. Since a present-time context is demanded by the use of the imperative ("listen!" 4:1a) followed by *waw*-consecutive perfect forms ("that you may live, enter, and possess the land"; 4:1b), the Qal active participle נֹתֵן also carries a continuing or durative sense in the present.

the present generation of "you" will experience the nation's entire history from exodus to restoration from exile.

Deuteronomy 4:31

כִּי אֵל רַחוּם יְהוָה אֱלֹהֶיךָ	For Yhwh your God is a compassionate El.
לֹא יַרְפְּךָ וְלֹא יַשְׁחִיתֶךָ	He will neither fail you nor destroy you;
וְלֹא יִשְׁכַּח אֶת־בְּרִית אֲבֹתֶיךָ	he will not forget the covenant with your fathers
אֲשֶׁר נִשְׁבַּע לָהֶם	that he swore to them.

The ברית with the "fathers" in Deut 4:31 involves the third and final reference to a ברית in this chapter. Because the first two references to ברית (4:13, 23) unquestionably denote the Israelite covenant at Horeb with "you," while the final reference speaks of Yhwh's covenant with the "fathers" (4:31),[53] redaction critics have often assigned the references to competing tradition layers. On the one hand, Yhwh "declared [הגיד] to you his covenant" (4:13a) at Horeb, which is immediately linked to the writing of the Decalogue (4:13b), though the ambiguous syntax here raises the question whether ברית also includes other stipulations. In 4:23, Moses warns Israel not to worship other gods and thereby forget "the covenant of Yhwh that he made [כרת] with you." Moses' homily on the Horeb events in 4:9–31, which may exhibit the structure of a suzerainty treaty,[54] often leads redaction critics to assign this passage to a stratum in which ברית denotes human obligation.[55] The demand for obedience to the ברית is ostensibly rooted in Yhwh's character as "a consuming fire, an impassioned El" (4:24).[56]

On the other hand, Deut 4:31 foresees a time when Yhwh will save his repentant people (4:29–30) after the punishment of exile for worshiping other gods (4:25–28). Because Yhwh is the "compassionate El" (4:31a; cf. 4:24), Moses promises that "he will neither fail you nor destroy you; [he will] not forget the covenant [ברית] with your fathers that he swore to them" (4:31b). This emphasis on Yhwh's restoration of Israel after captivity generally leads scholars to view 4:25–31 as an *ex eventu* prophecy from a postexilic writer.[57]

---

53. The covenant with the "fathers" is identified as the Abrahamic covenant by the vast majority of scholars: e.g., McConville, *Deuteronomy*, 111; R. D. Nelson, *Deuteronomy: A Commentary* (OTL; Philadelphia: Westminster John Knox, 2002) 68–69; E. H. Merrill, *Deuteronomy* (NAC 4; Nashville: Broadman & Holman, 1994) 129; G. Braulik, *Deuteronomium 1–16,17* (NEchtB; Würzburg: Echter Verlag, 1986) 45; Mayes, *Deuteronomy*, 157; Kutsch, *Verheissung*, 150.

54. So Mayes, "Deuteronomy 4," 25–26; D. J. McCarthy, *Treaty and Covenant*, 190–94; and Braulik, *Mittel*, 101–4.

55. E.g., Kutsch, *Verheissung*, 81, 136.

56. This emphasis contrasts with Exod 19:5, which links obedience to Yhwh's voice.

57. See Weinfeld, *Deuteronomy 1–11*, 223–26. Compare with Nelson (*Redaction*, 93–94) and Wolff ("Kerygma of the Deuteronomic Historical Work," 96–98), who propose that the references to Israel's restoration in 4:29–31 and 30:1–10 come from an even later hand

Despite the historical-critical consensus that Deut 4:25–31 is late, this passage's atypical mixture of oath and covenant terminology has generated considerable debate over the identity of the "fathers" in 4:31. In contrast to the present phrase in Deuteronomy, "covenant [ברית] of your fathers that he swore [נשבע] to them" (4:31), the verb נשבע ("to swear") never takes the noun ברית ("covenant") as an object in the Tetrateuch.[58] Deuteronomy usually makes a similar distinction between oath and covenant terminology, as when Yhwh "swore" an oath to the "fathers" (e.g., 1:8) or that he "made" (כרת) a covenant with the present audience at Horeb or Moab (e.g., 4:13; 29:11[12]).[59] Because the idiomatic distinctions between oath and covenant appear consistently enough elsewhere to be used as source-critical criteria,[60] the conflation of terminology from Genesis's patriarchal traditions and Exodus's Israel traditions in Deut 4:31 presents a unique problem: does the "covenant of the fathers" refer to the oath (Gen 26:3) or covenant(s) with the patriarchs (Gen 15:18; 17:2),[61] or does it refer to the covenant(s) at Sinai/Horeb (Exod 19:5; 24:7–8; 34:10)?[62]

The key to answering this question lies in analyzing the logical progression of the earlier references to ברית (4:13, 23) in Moses' exposition of the Horeb events (4:9–31). Though the first two references to the ברית at Horeb are usually attributed to a different stratum from 4:31, as already noted, a reexamination of Deut 4:9–31 reveals that its three references to ברית portray different but complementary aspects of a single divine-human covenant. The definition of ברית in chap. 6 above as "a chosen relationship of mutual obligation guaranteed by oath sanctions"[63] is thus broad enough to encompass the spectrum of Yhwh's holy and gracious actions in Israel's unfolding history.

---

than the references to exile in 4:25–28. To contrast further, see n. 36 above for a list of those who regard the entirety of Deuteronomy 4 as a unified postexilic work.

58. In Genesis, Yhwh either "swears an oath" (נשבע; Gen 26:3; cf. 24:7; 50:24), or "makes" (כרת; 15:18) and "establishes" (הקים; 17:2) a "covenant" (ברית). A similar dichotomy between oath and covenant is found in Exodus, where Yhwh "swore" (נשבע) to give the land to the patriarchs (Exod 6:8; 13:5, 11; 33:1) but has "remembered" (זכר; 2:24; 6:5), "established" (הקים; 6:4), or "made" (כרת; 34:10, 12, 15) a "covenant" (ברית). Exodus 6 represents the only passage where oath and covenant terms occur in proximity—where Yhwh declares both that "I established my covenant with them [i.e., the patriarchs in 6:3]" (6:4) and that "I swore to give [the land] to Abraham, Isaac, and Jacob" (6:8).

59. An identical collocation of נשבע and ברית appears only in Deut 7:12 and 8:18, two passages that also speak of Yhwh's covenant with the "fathers." The diachronic and theological significance of this datum will be discussed below.

60. See the discussion of Deut 29:11–13 on p. 182 above.

61. See p. 190 n. 53 above.

62. So Römer, *Israels Väter*, 139–41; cf. Köckert, *Vätergott*, 313.

63. Foster, "Prototypical Definition," 35–46; see the discussion of "Strengths and Weaknesses of Past Approaches" to form criticism on p. 168 above.

The Phenomenological and Relational ברית at Horeb (Deuteronomy 4:9–24)

The two references to Yhwh's ברית at Horeb (Deut 4:13, 23) in the exposition of proper worship of Yhwh (4:9–31) are not as closely tied to covenant stipulations as is often supposed. Past analysis of 4:13 and 4:23 has tended to neglect Deuteronomy 4's emphasis on the phenomenological and relational character of the Horeb revelation. Not only is legal material completely absent from Deuteronomy 4[64] but, even when the Decalogue is mentioned briefly in the context of a ברית (4:13b), Moses withholds the *content* of the "Ten Words" (cf. 5:6–21) in favor of repeatedly emphasizing the *fact* that Yhwh spoke "out of the midst of the fire" (4:12; cf. vv. 15, 33, 36). Since Yhwh's purpose for the Horeb revelation was "so that I may have them hear [שמע Hiphil] my words" (Deut 4:10), Moses proceeds to portray Horeb as a place where Israel experienced Yhwh's presence and speech, rather than where the people received the law. In fact, Moses' account of the Horeb events in Deut 4:9–20 differs markedly from Exodus 19, since Deuteronomy 4 deemphasizes Moses' mediatory role (cf. Deut 5:1–5) in favor of highlighting Yhwh's presence at Horeb.[65] Because Moses focuses in 4:9–20 on Yhwh's theophany and the people's response, it is necessary to consider the imaginative speech-acts of the Horeb revelation that form the background for the ברית references in 4:13 and 4:23.

The ברית and the Decalogue in Deuteronomy 4:13

Immediately before the reference to ברית in Deut 4:13, Moses directs his audience to remember the otherworldly sights of Horeb: "Watch yourself ... lest you forget the things that *your eyes have seen*" (4:9a), thereby creating the expectation that his own recollections will assume an existentialist posture. Accordingly, his exhortation to "make known to your sons and your grandsons" (4:9c) refers to the "day that you stood before Yhwh your God at Horeb" (4:10),[66] a time when "the mountain burned with fire to

---

64. Millar ("Living at the Place of Decision," 36–41) notes that this chapter's references to "statutes and ordinances" (vv. 1, 5, 8, 14, 45) are proleptic glances at Deuteronomy 5–26. The exposition of the legal material does not begin until later: "Now *this* is the commandment, the statutes and the ordinances that Yhwh your God commanded me to teach you" (6:1a).

65. Wilson, *Out of the Midst of the Fire*, 51–52; D. C. Sherrifs, "The Phrases *ina IGI DN* and *liphney Yhwh* in Treaty and Covenant Contexts," *JNSL* 7 (1971) 61–65. The lone reference to Moses in Deut 4:9–20 is Yhwh's command to him to teach Israel "statutes and ordinances" (4:14), while the narrative of Exodus 19 refers constantly to the words and actions of Moses (vv. 3, 7, 8, 9, 10, 14, 17, 19, 20, 21, 23, 35).

66. The usual rendering of the initial clause of Deut 4:10 as "remember the day when you stood" (e.g., NIV, NASB) obscures the awkwardness of the Hebrew construction, which contains no verb and begins abruptly with a relative clause: יום אשר עמדת לפני יהוה. The foregrounding of יום reflects the centrality of the "day" of Horeb.

the heart of heaven—darkness, clouds, and gloom" (4:11b). This summary of the Horeb events constitutes an imaginative speech-act on three levels. First, Moses avers that the theophanic events possess timeless significance through his command to *"make them known* [ידע Hiphil] to your sons and grandsons," providing another instance in Deuteronomy where future generations of "you" and "your son(s)" are explicitly incorporated into Israel's past and future history.[67] Second, his assertion that *"you stood* before YHWH your God" transports every generation of Israel back to Horeb, thus fueling the Jewish conception of מעמד הר סיני ("standing at Mount Sinai").[68] Third, the description of "fire ... darkness, clouds, and gloom" paints an arresting picture of the *mysterium tremendum et fascinans* that simultaneously attracts and repels God's people.[69] Moses' multifaceted description of the sights at Horeb is designed to stir the imagination of future generations of "sons and grandsons" (4:9) who had never experienced the theophany themselves.

More important than the visual phenomena, however, is that Horeb was the place of divine revelation, where "YHWH spoke to you from the midst of the fire" (4:12a).[70] Having described the "fire" as a visible symbol of divine presence both in heaven (4:11b) and on earth (4:12a; cf. 4:36),[71] Moses now reminds the people of what they heard but did not see: "You heard the sound of words, but you saw no form—only a voice" (4:12b). The shift from YHWH's transcendent presence to his immanent speech provides the phenomenological context for understanding the next verse's reference to ברית primarily as a verbal declaration (4:13a) and only secondarily as a written document (4:13c).

Deut 4:13 preserves the book's first references to both a ברית and the Decalogue, although the conceptual link between them is less than clear. Moses asserts that YHWH "declared [הגיד] to you his covenant [בריתו]" (4:13a), an unusual construction on two counts. First, the noun ברית appears only here in the OT as the object of the verb הגיד. In contrast to the ritual connotations of כרת (the usual verb for covenant-making in Deuteronomy), the denotation of הגיד is a "personal word event" of verbal communication

---

67. Compare with other imaginative speech-acts of generational inclusion in Deut 4:25–31; 6:20–25; 26:3–15.

68. Weinfeld argues (*Deuteronomy 1–11*, 203) that the theophany at Horeb "was understood as a collective experience of Israel bequeathed to all coming generations."

69. MacDonald, *Deuteronomy and the Meaning of "Monotheism,"* 192–201; cf. R. Otto, *The Idea of the Holy: An Inquiry into the Non-rational Factor in the Idea of the Divine and Its Relation to the Rational* (2nd ed.; trans. J. W. Harvey; New York: Oxford University Press, 1958) 12–41.

70. Wilson (*Out of the Midst of the Fire*, 55–62) notes that the Deuteronomic idiom "the midst of the fire" (4:15–16, 33, 36; 5:24, 26; 9:10; 10:4) serves to highlight the reality of YHWH's presence at Horeb in a manner distinct from the Exodus parallels.

71. Wilson (*Out of the Midst of the Fire*, 66–73) observes that the assertion of YHWH's presence both in heaven and on earth, as exemplified in Deut 4:36, challenges the common notion that Deuteronomy presents YHWH's name on earth as a hypostasis for the divine presence. Cf. von Rad, "Deuteronomy's 'Name' Theology," 37–44.

between parties.[72] This occurrence of נגד Hiphil to reflect Yhwh's accessible speech to Israel is the reciprocal dimension of Moses' earlier assertion regarding Israel's access in speaking to God. "What great nation has a god so near as Yhwh our God whenever we call on him?" (4:7).[73] The relational dimension of covenant-making is reinforced by the second unusual feature in this verse, the identification of the agreement as בריתו ("his covenant"). The references to "his covenant" elsewhere in the OT always emphasize Yhwh's initiative in enacting or remembering his relationship with his people.[74] Thus the unique phrase "Yhwh declared his covenant" (4:13a) reflects Yhwh's unequivocal commitment to his people.

These observations regarding Yhwh's relational motivations in his speech at Horeb assist in adjudicating the ambiguous syntax of the אשר clause in v. 13aβ that immediately follows בריתו, a decision that has significant implications for the relationship between Yhwh's ברית and the Decalogue. The Masoretic accentuation of Deut 4:13 places a *zaqep parvum* above the infinitival construction לַעֲשׂוֹת ("to do"), thereby moving the subsequent phrase עֲשֶׂרֶת הַדְּבָרִים ("Ten Words") into apposition with אֶת־בְּרִיתוֹ ("his covenant"):

4:13aα	וַיַּגֵּד לָכֶם אֶת־בְּרִיתוֹ	Then he declared to you his covenant
4:13aβ	אֲשֶׁר צִוָּה אֶתְכֶם לַעֲשׂוֹת	that he commanded you to do:
4:13b	עֲשֶׂרֶת הַדְּבָרִים	*that is*, the Ten Words.

Nearly all scholars have accepted the Masoretic interpretation that "his covenant" (4:13aα) is equivalent to the Decalogue (4:13b), thereby limit-

---

72. On the ritual dimensions of the idiom כרת ברית, see G. F. Hasel, "The Meaning of the Animal Rite in Genesis 15," *JSOT* 19 (1981) 61–78; and G. J. Wenham, "The Symbolism of the Animal Rite in Genesis 15: A Response to G. F. Hasel, *JSOT* 19 [1981] 61–78," *JSOT* 22 (1982) 134–37. Although disagreeing on the exact ritual underpinnings of Gen 15:7–21 and Jer 34:18–19, Hasel and Wenham concur that the act of cutting the animal in covenant confirmation parallels the idiomatic use of כרת with ברית.

C. Westermann ("נגד," *TLOT* 2:715) notes three other interesting features of נגד Hiphil: (1) it denotes "essentially and properly an interpersonal occurrence" (p. 716); (2) it "is usually not used in the context of the announcement of judgment" (p. 717); and (3) its most frequent theological usage occurs in liturgical contexts of praising God (p. 717).

73. Moses' rhetorical question about Yhwh's proximity to his people (4:7) is strikingly juxtaposed with another rhetorical question about the righteousness of Yhwh's revelation (4:8). Miller (*Deuteronomy*, 56) rightly notes that "the nearness of God and the righteous laws are closely related" in the parallel rhetorical questions of 4:7–8. The same observation applies to the juxtaposition of Yhwh's personal speech and his righteous revelation in 4:13.

74. Exod 2:24; Deut 4:13; 8:18; 17:2; 2 Kgs 13:23; 17:15; 18:12. Whether for Israel's good or ill, the aforementioned references to "his covenant" always describe God as the initiating party. The same observation holds for biblical references to the divine-human covenant as "my covenant" (Gen 6:18; 9:9, 11, 15; 17:2, 4, 7, 9, 10, 13, 14, 19, 21; Exod 6:4, 5; Lev 26:9, 15, 42, 44; Deut 31:16, 20; Josh 7:11; Judg 2:11, 20; 1 Kgs 11:11; Pss 50:16; 89:28, 34; 132:12; Isa 59:21; Jer 11:10; 31:32; 33:20, 21, 25; Ezek 16:60, 62; 44:7; Hos 8:1; Zech 11:10; Mal 2:4, 5) and "your covenant" (Deut 33:9; 2 Sam 3:12; 1 Kgs 19:10, 14; Ps 44:17; Isa 28:18; Jer 14:21; Ezek 16:61).

ing the scope of Yhwh's ברית to what Yhwh immediately wrote on tablets of stone (4:13c).⁷⁵

While acknowledging the close connection between Yhwh's covenant and the Decalogue, Braulik and Lohfink provide three compelling reasons for viewing the "Ten Words" as the object of the infinitival clause "to do" rather than standing in apposition to "his covenant."⁷⁶ First, Lohfink argues that ברית never occurs in Deuteronomy as a technical term for the Decalogue as a written text.⁷⁷ Second, Braulik notes that the Deuteronomic use of the verb צוה never takes ברית as the direct object. Third, Braulik points out that making the עשרת הדברים the verbal object of the infinitival clause לעשות creates a natural parallelism between vv. 13a and 14a, with an identical structure of the verb צוה (with Yhwh as subject) + addressee (people/Moses) + object clause:⁷⁸

4:13a   אשר צוה אתכם לעשות עשרת הדברים
4:14a   ואתי צוה יהוה בעת ההוא ללמד אתכם חקים ומשפטים

Lohfink and Braulik conclude that "his covenant" refers to the narrative action of covenant-making at Horeb by means of Yhwh's speech, as opposed to being limited to the "Ten Words" themselves. The אשר clause in 4:13 functions not as a conventional relative clause but as an appositional clause to "his covenant":⁷⁹

וַיַּגֵּד לָכֶם אֶת־בְּרִיתוֹ	Then he declared to you his covenant:
אֲשֶׁר צִוָּה אֶתְכֶם לַעֲשׂוֹת עֲשֶׂרֶת הַדְּבָרִים	*that is,* he commanded you to do the Ten Words.

---

75. E.g., Nelson, *Deuteronomy*, 57; Tigay, *Deuteronomy*, 48; Merrill, *Deuteronomy*, 120; Weinfeld, *Deuteronomy 1–11*, 193; Craigie, *Deuteronomy*, 132; Buis and Leclerq, *Deutéronome*, 56.

76. N. Lohfink, "Prolegomena zu einer Rechtshermeneutik des Pentateuchs," in *Studien zum Deuteronomium und zur deuteronomistischen Literatur V* (SBAB 38; Stuttgart: Katholisches Bibelwerk, 2005) 193 n. 45; G. Braulik, "Deuteronomium 4,13 und der Horebbund," in *Für immer verbündet: Studien zur Bundestheologie der Bibel* (ed. C. Dohmen and C. Frevel; SBS 211; Stuttgart: Katholisches Bibelwerk, 2007) 30–33.

77. However, the book of Exodus attests the term "tablets of the stipulations" (Exod 31:18; 32:15; 34:29). The similar phrase "tablets of the covenant" appears in Deut 9:9, 11, 15 (cf. Heb 9:4).

78. A statistical analysis supports Braulik's assertion ("Deuteronomium 4,13," 32) that the infinitival form לעשות rarely concludes clauses in Deuteronomy. Besides the contested case in 4:13a, לעשות only stands alone 4× in the book (1:14; 4:1; 6:3; 8:1), as opposed to being followed 31× by an object or adverbial clause (4:5; 5:15, 32; 6:1, 24, 25; 8:8; 9:18; 11:32; 12:1; 13:1[12:32], 12[11], 19[18]; 15:5; 17:10; 18:9; 19:19, 20; 20:18; 24:8, 18, 22; 26:16; 27:26; 28:1, 15, 58; 29:28[29]; 31:12; 32:46; 34:11).

79. Earlier treatments of אשר argued that it served primarily as a relative and complement clause marker. But the recent work of Holmstedt ("Story," 7–26) demonstrates that אשר performs the more basic function of nominalizing clauses. The syntactical function of אשר nominal clauses thus derives from their discourse context rather than being locked into inflexible grammatical categories. Deut 4:13 presents an appositional use of אשר (cf. Braulik, "Deuteronomium 4,13," 31; GKC §138a).

Lohfink and Braulik have rightly shifted the referent of "his covenant" from a fixed, unilaterally given text to a verbally enacted, mutual commitment between Yhwh and Israel. Yhwh's covenant includes the Decalogue but cannot be confined to it. The essence of covenant is the relationship between Yhwh and his people, for Yhwh has joined himself to Israel through his declarative speech-act and Israel must reciprocate this relationship by obeying the Decalogue. The textualization of the Decalogue (4:13c) now enshrines the divine-human relationship for future generations. Therefore, it would be inaccurate to characterize the ברית in Deut 4:9 as primarily a matter of legal obligation, for Moses concludes his remarks on the Horeb theophany by reminding Israel that "Yhwh took you and brought you out of the iron furnace, from Egypt, to be a people for his own possession, as it is this day" (4:20).

The ברית *and the* Bilderverbot *in* Deuteronomy 4:23

The relational component that is inherent in the concept ברית also explains why the sense of the term can shift quickly from Yhwh's oral declaration (4:13) to Moses' warning about the *Bilderverbot* (4:23). While 4:13 focuses more on the existential aspects of Yhwh's ברית in the theophany at Horeb, 4:23 further develops its affective dimensions by linking Israel's forgetfulness of the covenant with Yhwh's jealousy for Israel: "So watch yourselves lest you forget the covenant [ברית] of Yhwh your God that he made with you by making an idol in the likeness [תבנית] of anything against which Yhwh your God commanded you." Previously, in 4:16–18, Moses had enumerated the various kinds of iconic "likeness" (תבנית 5×) that were forbidden for Israel's worship of Yhwh. The solemnity of Moses' warning is heightened by his adducing himself as a poignant example of one who will die in "this land" before Israel crosses the Jordan to enter the "good land" (4:21–22). This imaginative speech-act leads to the current exhortation for Israel to guard against forgetting Yhwh's ברית (4:23b) by violating the *Bilderverbot* (4:23c).

The nature of the parallelism between Yhwh's ברית and the *Bilderverbot* requires detailed examination. As with Deut 4:13, regarding 4:23 scholars have commonly asserted that these concepts are synonymously parallel, thereby imparting a legal sense to Yhwh's ברית through its equation with the *Bilderverbot*.[80] Although some link between them is undeniable, the usual view that ברית is coextensive with the *Bilderverbot* overlooks four features of the passage indicating that ברית here retains its basic sense of mutual relationship. First, the object of the common Deuteronomic verbs שכח ("to forget") and זכר ("to remember") is nearly always either Yhwh himself (e.g., 6:12; 8:11, 14) or an episode from Israel's saving history as directed

---

80. E.g., Braulik, *Deuteronomium 1–16,17*, 43–44; Skweres, *Rückverweise*, 185; Kutsch, *Verheissung*, 138, 151.

by Yhwh (e.g., 5:15; 8:18; 24:9).[81] Thus it is doubtful that forgetfulness of the ברית in 4:23 refers to Israel's religious duties apart from Yhwh's gracious relationship with his people. Since Moses has already warned Israel not to "forget [שכח] the things that your eyes have seen" (4:9), Moses' present exhortation not to "forget" (שכח; 4:23) Yhwh's ברית constitutes a warning against forgetting Yhwh himself as revealed in the theophany and divine words at Horeb.

Second, the description of the *Bilderverbot* itself indicates that the act of idol-making is more a willful act of forgetting Yhwh than the benign transgression of a legal stipulation. Several polemical features of Moses' warning suggest that the crafting of an idol entails an ominous existential turn from Yhwh to the self. In Deut 4:23, Moses' insertion of the prepositional phrase לכם ("for yourselves") as an adverbial modifier of עשׂה ("to make") highlights the sinister motivations of artisans who make idols or false representations of Yhwh. When the grammatical person of the verb (i.e., עשׂיתם 2mp perfect) corresponds to that of the suffixed ending attached to the ל preposition (i.e., לכם; 2mp suffix on ל), as in 4:23, Driver incisively observes that

> the reflexive ל, throwing back the action denoted by the verb upon the subject, and referring it, as it were, to the pleasure or option of the agent, gives more or less pathetic expression to the *personal* feelings—the satisfaction, or the interest, or the promptitude—with which the action in question is (or is to be) accomplished.[82]

Thus the use of the reflexive ל in 4:23 unmasks the selfish hearts of idolaters who act "for yourselves," thereby forgetting the divine Deliverer (4:20) in favor of worthless idols. Moses further reveals the rebellious motives of idolaters by describing their lust to make an "idol in the form of anything [כל]" (4:23b; cf. 5:8).[83]

---

81. Blair, "Appeal," 44–45. In Deut 26:13, the sole instance in which a legal regulation might be the verbal object of שכחה, the collocation of שכח and מצוה ("commandment") appears within the Israelite farmer's confession of the "little historical credo" (26:5–9) and affirmation that he has brought his firstfruits to share joyfully ("you shall rejoice" [שׂמח]; 26:11) with the Levite, foreigner, orphan, and widow (26:10–14). The impersonal notion of *Verpflichtung* is completely lacking in this reference to מצוה, because the broader context asserts that Israel enthusiastically offers back to Yhwh the manifold gifts of the "land flowing with milk and honey" (26:9, 15).

82. Driver, *Deuteronomy*, 10–11 (emphasis original). Compare T. Muraoka's similar observation that the so-called "centripetal dative . . . serves to convey the impression on the part of the speaker or author that the subject establishes his own identity, recovering or finding his own place by determinedly dissociating himself from his familiar surrounding" ("On the So-Called *Dativus Ethicus* in Hebrew," *JTS* 29 [1978] 497). Muraoka also finds instances of the reflexive/centripetal dative in Gen 12:1; 27:43; Deut 1:6; 2 Kgs 18:21; Isa 2:22; Jer 7:4; and Ps 120:6, among other passages.

83. Compare a similarly sarcastic use of כל in Moses' polemic against the indiscriminate nature of Canaanite worship: תחת כל עץ רענן ("under every green tree"; 12:2).

Third and more broadly, Deut 4:23–24 reinforces the link between right relationship with Yhwh and righteous living that Moses had asserted earlier. Besides the already-discussed passage of 4:9–14, Moses declares in 4:16 and 4:25 that idolatry is the natural outcome when "you corrupt yourself" (והשחתם), a surprising intransitive occurrence of שחת Hiphil that focuses attention on the idolater's malicious intent to destroy his/her relationship with Yhwh.[84] Likewise, in 4:39–40, Moses first exhorts Israel to "take it to your *heart* that Yhwh, he is God in heaven above and on earth below" (4:39) before he enjoins the people to "keep his statutes and his commandments" (4:40). The theological progression in 4:23 from *attitude* ("do not forget the covenant of Yhwh your God") to *action* ("and make an idol in the form of anything") reflects a broader biblical nexus between the disposition of the heart and the behavior that results, rather than a solely legislative prohibition on sinful actions.

Fourth, the relational dimension of ברית is stressed through Moses' contrast between Israel's animate deity and the inanimate idols. The reason (כי) given by Moses for forbidding iconic worship is because Yhwh is the "impassioned El" (4:24), an epithet that denotes "an emotion springing from the very depths of personality: as the zealous [קנא] one Jahweh is a person to the highest possible degree."[85] In contrast to Yhwh, who treasures his relationship with his people and whose jealous passions are quickly aroused, the idols are incapable of basic sensory perception (4:28), to say nothing of defending their own honor or acting miraculously on Israel's behalf (cf. 4:20, 34). In addition, since every assertion in Deuteronomy of Yhwh's status as the "impassioned El" is tied either to the *Bilderverbot* (4:24; 5:9) or to the need for faithful remembrance of Yhwh (6:15), the prohibition on images is clearly a matter of safeguarding the divine-human relationship rather than of a legal obligation devoid of affective dimensions. The distinctiveness of Yhwh's relational rather than contractual covenant with Israel paves the way for the third and final reference to ברית in Deut 4:31.

ברית *and the Divine-Human Covenant in Deuteronomy 4:23–31*

The third and final reference to Yhwh's ברית in Deuteronomy 4 appears in a context that envisions Israel's future in a land where prosperity has engendered complacency ("you have grown stale"; ישן Niphal; 4:25)[86] and thus led to violating the *Bilderverbot*. For such disobedience to Yhwh, Moses places Israel under threat of divine sanction by uttering a declarative

---

84. J. Conrad, "שחת," *TDOT* 14:584, 589; cf. Deut 31:29.

85. Von Rad, *OT Theology*, 1:207. The application of the human emotions of jealousy (Gen 26:14) and zeal (e.g., Prov 6:34) to Yhwh with regard to his worshipers is a completely unique description of deity in the ANE (so G. Sauer, קנאה, *TLOT* 3:1146).

86. Compare the references to rotten grain in Lev 13:11 and 26:10, the only other two appearances of ישן Niphal in the entire OT.

speech-act: "I *hereby* call heaven and earth to witness against you today that you will surely perish quickly from the land that you are crossing the Jordan to possess" (4:26).[87] Though Israel has grown numerous in the land (4:25a), Moses now warns that Yhwh will scatter them among the nations as a people "few in number" (4:27; cf. 1:10). Poetic justice will be amply served when exiled Israel worships the impotent "work[s] of human hands that neither see nor hear nor eat nor smell" (4:28; cf. 4:16–19). However, the violation of the "covenant of Yhwh your God that he made with you" (4:23) by tolerating competitors to Yhwh (4:25) will not result in Israel's permanent demise, for distress in a foreign land (4:29) will impel the people to seek Yhwh anew (4:30). The people will now experience the kindness of the "compassionate El," who vows never to forget the "covenant of the fathers that he swore to them" (4:31).

As noted above, the contrasting references to covenant in Deut 4:23 and 4:31 are typically assigned to incompatible strata in which ברית denotes obligation and promise, respectively. But redactional approaches of this sort are doubtful in light of the rhetorical unity of 4:23–31. Though Israel's proclivity to "corrupt yourself" (שחת Hiphil intransitive; 4:25) will incite Yhwh's wrath as "an impassioned El" (4:24), the same deity who is the "compassionate El" (4:31) promises never to "destroy you" (שחת Hiphil transitive; 4:31). Israel is commanded never to "forget" (שכח) Yhwh's covenant with "you" (4:23), though the consequences of the people's disobedience ultimately cannot overcome Yhwh's commitment never to "forget" (שכח) his "covenant of the fathers" (4:31). The contrast between Israel's faithlessness and Yahweh's faithfulness forms a striking inclusio that frames the unit of 4:23–31, challenging the redaction-critical tendency to excise this passage as postexilic. The references to ברית in 4:23 and 4:31 obviously stand in some sort of parallel relationship, but what sort of conceptual or chronological parallelism is envisioned in this section? Even scholars who argue for the final form of Deut 4:23–31 tend to conclude that the two references to ברית represent antithetical covenants.[88]

Corporate Solidarity in Deuteronomy 4:23–31

Though most scholars identify the "covenant that Yhwh made with *you*" (4:23) and the "covenant of the *fathers*" (4:31) as the Israelite and Abrahamic covenants, respectively, a rhetorical analysis suggests that chronological precision is subordinate in Deut 4:23–31 to the theological conception of corporate solidarity in Israel's generations. Rather than contrasting conditional and unconditional covenants, Moses is depicting different aspects of a single covenant by drawing a contrast between Yhwh's faithfulness and

---

87. Braulik, "Deuteronomium 1–4 als Sprechakt," 251–53.
88. E.g., McConville, *Deuteronomy*, 111: "[T]he covenant [in 4:31] is characterized as that which goes back to the patriarchal promise, a commitment to his people that predates and takes priority over that of Horeb and the Mosaic preaching."

his people's unfaithfulness in Israel's unfolding history. The "covenant of the fathers" represents both the Abrahamic and Israelite covenants as seen from the future vantage point of the exile. Moses has transported his audience to the endpoint of Israel's history so that the "fathers" include both the patriarchal and the exodus generations.

The first indication that corporate solidarity is in view appears in Moses' address to disparate generations of Israel using second-person singular pronouns.[89] Not only does Moses announce a transgenerational vision by anticipating a time when "you" have borne "sons and grandsons" (4:25); he asserts that this same generation of "you" will experience every successive stage of judgment and restoration: (1) quick destruction from the land (4:26); (2) exile among the nations (4:27); (3) pointless worship of powerless deities (4:28); and (4) pricked consciences to repent and seek YHWH (4:29–30). While it is theoretically possible for a single generation to cycle through this prolonged sequence of events, this possibility is obviated by several clues that Moses envisions a broader referent for "you" than only his present audience. Moses emphatically warns that "you will surely perish quickly" (4:26; אבד infinitive absolute + 2ms imperfect + מהר) and be left "few in number" (4:27). Interpreted literalistically, Moses would then be asserting that the vast majority of "you" would expire (4:26–27) before YHWH's promised restoration experienced by "you" (4:29–30). Since literalism of this sort would render Moses' statement self-defeating, it is more likely that the second-person singular pronouns refer to Israel as a singular entity throughout history.

This view of the corporate solidarity of "you" is reinforced by the chronological problems in Moses' statement that Israel's repentance will not occur until the period באחרית הימים ("in the latter days"; 4:30). The phrase באחרית הימים would connote an era beyond the lifespan of his current audience (cf. 31:29),[90] even though Moses concretely identifies "you" as a

---

89. Compare similar observations on the collective use of 2ms forms in the Deuteronomic legal stipulations by McConville, "Singular Address," 19–36; and D. Patrick, "The Rhetoric of Collective Responsibility in Deuteronomic Law," in *Pomegranates and Golden Bells: Studies in Biblical, Jewish, and Near Eastern Ritual, Law, and Literature in Honor of Jacob Milgrom* (ed. D. P. Wright, D. N. Freedman, and A. Hurvitz; Winona Lake, IN: Eisenbrauns, 1995) 421–36.

90. The phrase באחרית הימים appears 13× in the OT (Gen 49:1; Num 24:14; Deut 4:30; 31:29; Isa 2:2; Jer 23:20; 30:24; 48:47; 49:39; Ezek 38:16; Dan 10:14; Hos 3:5; Mic 14:1). *Pace* J. H. Sailhamer (*The Pentateuch as Narrative: A Biblical-Theological Commentary* [Grand Rapids, MI: Zondervan, 1992] 34–37), the phrase באחרית הימים is not necessarily eschatological in its referent. G. A. Klingbeil ("Looking at the End from the Beginning: Studying Eschatological Concepts in the Pentateuch," *JATS* 11 [2000] 182–83) rightly observes that באחרית הימים in Deut 31:29 points to Israel's apostasy immediately following Moses' death rather than the eschatological future. However, it is noteworthy that the use of באחרית הימים in 4:30 refers not only to Israel's apostasy (cf. 31:29) but also to its exile and restoration, thereby suggesting that here Moses no longer has only his current audience in mind. Compare the discussion of באחרית הימים in D. I. Block, "Gog and Magog in Ezekiel's

remnant that has survived exile. It is thus more plausible that Moses uses "you" in an anachronistic manner to reinforce the unity of present and future generations.

A Singular and Timeless Covenant in Deuteronomy 4:23–31

The blending of terminology from the Abrahamic and Israelite covenant narratives provides another reason for viewing the "covenant of the fathers" (4:31) as a summary declaration of the divine-human relationship throughout Israel's history rather than merely the Abrahamic covenant. Despite the aforementioned tendency by scholars to classify the Abrahamic covenant as an unconditional royal grant, several features of the "unconditional" covenant in Deut 4:29–31 actually suggest that the passage is referring to the events surrounding the "conditional" Israelite covenant at Horeb. First, Moses' prediction that Israel will return and "obey" (שמע; 4:30) YHWH's voice represents the ultimate fulfillment of the *Leitmotif* of hearing/obedience that was commanded in the Israelite covenant by constant repetition of the verb שמע (4:1, 10, 12, 33, 36). Second, the divine epithet אל רחום (4:31) appears in the Tetrateuch only in Exod 34:6 (cf. Deut 5:9). YHWH's motivation for remembering the "covenant of the fathers" (Deut 4:31) echoes a narrative in which the Israelite covenant is renewed after the apostasy with the golden calf. These links lead some scholars to propose that the word ברית used in 4:23 and 4:31 refers to the same entity—namely, the Israelite covenant at Horeb.[91]

On the other hand, some aspects of the ברית with the "fathers" (4:31) cannot be correlated readily with the ברית at Horeb with "you" (4:23). As noted above, the collocation of the noun ברית and the verb נשבע is never attested in the Tetrateuch. The rare Deuteronomic instances of this pairing (cf. 7:12; 8:18) bridge the lexical divide that usually separates the patriarchs to whom YHWH "swore an oath" (נשבע; e.g., 1:8) from Moses' current audience of the (first? second?) exodus generation, with whom a ברית has been "made" (כרת; 5:3, etc.). This combination of ברית and נשבע terminology foreshadows the covenant ratification ceremony in Deut 29:9–14, a passage in which the Abrahamic and Israelite covenants converge through YHWH's ratification of both oath and covenant with all generations of Israel. Similarly, the prediction that Israel will "return" (שוב) to YHWH not only anticipates the "fugue on the theme of שוב"[92] found in Deut 30:1–10[93] but

---

Eschatological Vision," in *Eschatology in Bible and Theology: Evangelical Essays at the Dawn of a New Millennium* (ed. K. Brower and M. Elliott; Downers Grove, IL: InterVarsity, 1997) 85–116.

91. Römer, *Israels Väter*, 137–8; cf. Braulik, *Mittel*, 119.
92. Rofé, "Covenant in the Land of Moab," 370.
93. However, Deut 4:29–31 differs from 30:1–10 in speaking only of Israel's "return" (שוב) to YHWH (4:30; cf. 30:2, 10) and not to the land (30:3).

also amplifies Moses' assertion that Israel will "seek" (בקשׁ) and "find" (מצא) Yhwh when the people "search" (דרשׁ) for Yhwh "with all your heart and with all your soul" (4.29; cf. 6:5, 11:1). This note resonates beyond Deuteronomy to the "new covenant" oracles of Jeremiah 29–31.[94]

In summary, Moses' declarative speech-act of setting "the blessing and the curse" (Deut 11:26; cf. 4:26; 30:1, 19) before the people performatively creates the entire spectrum of possibilities for Israel's future: fruitful life in the land (4:5, 40), exile for disobedience (4:27–29; 30:1), and restoration to Yhwh and the land (4:30–31; 30:1–10). Since neither the Abrahamic nor the Israelite covenant narrative deals much with Israel's restoration from exile,[95] while Deut 30:2–10 spells out this promise in vivid detail, it seems likely that Moses' invocation of the "covenant of the fathers" is an intentional canonical moment in which the book of Deuteronomy refers to its own promises of exile and restoration in chaps. 28–30.[96] In other words, the clear links among Deut 4:23–31, the panhistorical covenant in Deut 29:9–14[10–15], and the "new covenant" in Jeremiah 29–31 raise the intriguing possibility that Moses' citation of the "covenant of the fathers" in Deut 4:31 extends outside the narrative world of Deuteronomy to encompass all of Yhwh's past and future dealings with Israel—from the patriarchal promises to the return from exile, under a singular and all-encompassing covenant that is simultaneously "unconditional" and "conditional."[97] Thus the relationship of the Abrahamic and Israelite covenants to the "covenant of the fathers" (4:31) would constitute that of a part to the whole: the "covenant of the fathers" includes both covenants but is not limited to them since it glances retrospectively at Israel's entire history. As a corollary, the "fathers" here would telescopically include all of Israel's ancestors

---

94. Such lexical links are viewed as evidence that the book of Jeremiah was produced or influenced by the Deuteronom(ist)ic school. See, for example, T. C. Römer, "How Did Jeremiah Become a Convert to Deuteronomic Ideology?" in *Those Elusive Deuteronomists: The Phenomenon of Pan-Deuteronomism* (ed. L. S. Schearing and S. L. McKenzie; JSOTSup 268; Sheffield: Sheffield Academic Press, 1999) 189–99.

95. The covenant blessings and curses in Lev 26:1–45 may briefly mention a return to the land: "I [Yhwh] will remember the land" (v. 42). See P. Buis, "Comment au septième siècle envisageait-on l'avenir de l'alliance? Étude de Lv. 26,3–45," in *Questions disputées d'Ancien Testament: Méthode et Théologie* (ed. C. Brekelmans; BETL 33; Leuven: Leuven University Press, 1989) 131–40.

96. McConville ("Metaphor, Symbol," 329) argues similarly for Deuteronomy's "sharp hermeneutical self-awareness."

97. This hypothesis accounts for the repetition of various forms of the *Bundesformel* at so many critical junctures in Israel's history and across ostensibly different covenants (e.g., Gen 17:7; Exod 6:7; 19:4–6; Lev 26:12; Deut 29:9–14[10–15]; 1 Sam 12:20; 2 Sam 7:23–24; Jer 31:31–34; Ezek 11:19–20; Zech 8:8). See Rendtorff, *Covenant Formula*, 11–37. R. T. Beckwith ("The Unity and Diversity of God's Covenants," *TynBul* 38 [1987] 93–118) presents the similar thesis that the OT envisions a single people of God, though it lives under multiple divine-human covenants.

whose faithlessness caused them to experience Yhwh's covenant faithfulness as both an "impassioned El" (4:24) and a "compassionate El" (4:31).

Deuteronomy 4:37

וְתַחַת כִּי אָהַב אֶת־אֲבֹתֶיךָ	Because he [Yhwh] loved your fathers,
וַיִּבְחַר בְּזַרְעוֹ אַחֲרָיו	he choose his seed after him,
וַיּוֹצִאֲךָ בְּפָנָיו בְּכֹחוֹ הַגָּדֹל מִמִּצְרָיִם	and he personally brought you out by his great power from Egypt.

Moses' assertion that Yhwh's "love" (אהב; 4:37a)[98] for the "fathers" motivated Yhwh to "choose" (בחר; 4:37b) their descendants by means of the exodus needs to be treated briefly even though this passage contains no explicit references to covenant and oath (see text and translation, p. 203).[99] If the "fathers" in 4:31 refer to all of Israel's ancestors from a postexilic perspective, as suggested above, the identification of the "fathers" in 4:37 as a generation who experienced the exodus would seem problematic since other references to their "seed" (זרע) identify the "fathers" as the patriarchs (e.g., Gen 13:15–16; Deut 1:8). However, I will show that the "fathers" in Deut 4:37 represent more of a timeless symbol of divine faithfulness than a concrete generation in Israel's history. Any exegetical attempt to fix a particular generation as the "fathers," as in the conflicting redactional proposals of Römer and Lohfink,[100] tends to underestimate the rhetorical force of the imaginative speech-acts in Deut 4:32–40. Here Moses transports his audience from the imaginative future (4:29–31) back to the imaginative past ("Ask now concerning the *former days*"; 4:32; cf. 4:9–20) in order to actualize Yhwh's marvelous actions and speech in the exodus and Horeb revelation (4:33–34, 36–38). Without explicitly using oath and covenant

---

98. The English rendering of Deut 4:37 in the citation reflects two text-critical decisions. First (and following *BHQ*), I reject the suggestion of *BHS* to emend ותחת to ותחי ("and live"; cf. v. 33 LXX, Vulg.). The OT elsewhere attests the use of ותחת as the conjunction "because" (e.g., Prov 1:9) as well as the more common phrase תחת אשר ("because of that"; e.g., Deut 21:14; 22:29; 28:47, 62; Jer 29:19). Second, the MT's singular suffixes on בזרעו אחריו ("his seed after him") are the *lectio difficilior* because plural suffixes ["their," "them"] would have been more likely for denoting a multitude of descendants (cf. MT at Deut 10:15; and LXX, Syr., SP, and Vulg. at 4:37). Contra Wijngaards (*Dramatization of Salvific History*, 68 n. 1), the MT's singular reading need not denote either a singular ancestor or descendant, because Moses often conceives of Israel as a corporate entity.
99. A fuller analysis of בחר and related terms of divine election (e.g., אהב) are provided in the case study on Deuteronomy 7 that follows.
100. Römer (*Israels Väter*, 23–29) exhibits a tension between using his Nothian presuppositions to identify the "fathers" as a settled generation in Egypt and viewing them as symbolic of "[die] Kontinuität von Yhwhs Solidarität mit seinem Volk" (p. 28). Compare Lohfink (*Väter*, 71–72), who argues here for the patriarchs. Though Römer and Lohfink argue consistently according to their respective diachronic presuppositions, their debate over the identity of the "fathers" largely ignores the imaginative character of Moses' rhetoric in Deut 4:32–40.

terminology, the peroration in 4:32–40 points again to the unworkability of the unconditional-conditional dichotomy in OT scholarship by virtue of the seamless integration between imaginative speech-acts of divine grace (4:32–34, 36–38) and directive speech-acts of divine commands (4:35, 39–40).

Deut 4:32–40 is structured as two panels (columns 3–4) in table 7.1 (p. 205), in which the imaginative speech-acts of Yhwh's actions in the past and future greatly outnumber the directive speech-acts of the actions demanded of Israel in the present. I have highlighted the sensory language (in italics) and temporal markers (in bold) that enable Moses' audience to experience afresh the seminal moments of Israel's history.[101]

Though space prevents extensive discussion, I offer two observations on the dialectic between imaginative and directive speech-acts in Deut 4:32–40. First, Moses' imaginative speech-acts not only actualize past events for the second exodus generation (i.e., past history, Horeb, Egypt); they also treat the future event of "driving out nations greater and mightier than you" as inaugurated "this day" (4:38). This contemporizing of both past and future events as present realities imparts a timeless quality to "this Torah" (1:5; cf. 4:43; 17:18; 27:3; 31:11).[102] Thus "this Torah" is actuated, not only for future generations of Israel through regular recitation at the Feast of Tabernacles (31:9–13), but even for Moses' present audience of "you," the second exodus generation at Horeb, which never actually witnessed these events (cf. 1:35; 2:14–16).

Second, among the three imperative sentences that are classified as directive speech-acts (vv. 35, 39, 40), only Moses' final command to "keep his statutes and commandments" (v. 40) might qualify as a "conditional" matter. On the one hand, the earlier directive speech-acts acknowledging that Yhwh alone is God (vv. 35, 39) constitute the only reasonable con-

---

101. Adapted from MacDonald, *Deuteronomy and the Meaning of "Monotheism*," 171; and Römer, *Israels Väter*, 25; cf. G. Braulik, "Monotheismus im Deuteronomium: Zu Syntax, Redeform und Gotteserkenntnis in 4,32–40," *ZABR* 10 (2004) 180–83.

102. Schaper ("Publication," 225–36) convincingly argues that the unusual use of באר Piel in Deut 1:5 (cf. 27:8; Hab 2:2) entails the "publication" of the Mosaic speeches as authoritative revelation through written recording and oral recitation. The need for oral recitation lends credence to the speech-act approach taken here. A similar thesis of "publication" is argued by G. Braulik and N. Lohfink, "Deuteronomium 1,5 באר את־התורה הזאת: 'Er verlieh dieser Tora Rechtskraft,'" in *Textarbeit—Studien zu Texten und ihrer Rezeption aus dem Alten Testament und der Umwelt Israels: Festschrift für Peter Weimar zur Vollendung seines 60. Lebensjahres mit Beiträgen von Freunden, Schülern and Kollegen* (ed. K. Kiesow and T. Meurer; AOAT 294; Münster: Ugarit-Verlag, 2003) 34–51. Compare E. Otto's view that באר Piel in Deut 1:5 introduces Moses' exposition of the Torah previously given at Sinai rather than the impending propagation of his speeches in Deuteronomy (Otto, "Mose, der erste Schriftgelehrte: Deuteronomium 1,5 in der Fabel des Pentateuch," in *L'Écrit et l'Esprit. Études d'histoire du texte et de théologie biblique: Festschrift für Adrian Schenker* [ed. D. Böhler, I. Himbaza, and P. Hugo; OBO 214; Fribourg: Academic Press / Göttingen: Vandenhoeck & Ruprecht, 2005] 273–84).

Table 7.1. Sensory Language and Temporal Markers in Deuteronomy 4:32–40

Speech-Act	Category	Panel 1	Panel 2
Imaginative Speech-Acts	Past History	Ask now about **the former days**, when God created humans on the earth, and from one end of heaven to the other! Has anything been done like this great thing? Or has anything been *heard* like it? (v. 32)	∅
	Horeb	Has any people heard the voice of God speaking from the midst of the fire, as you yourselves heard, and survived? (v. 33)	*Out of the heavens, he let you hear his voice to discipline you, and on earth he let you see his great fire, and you heard his words from the midst of the fire.* (v. 36)
	Egypt	Or has a god tried to take for himself a nation from within another, by trials, by signs, and by wonders, by battle, and by a strong hand, by an outstretched arm, and by great terrors, *as* Y{\sc hwh} *did for you in Egypt before your eyes?* (v. 34)	Because he loved your fathers, he chose their seed after them. And he brought you *personally* [פָּנָיו] by his great power from Egypt.... (v. 37)
	Canaan	∅	... by driving out *before you* nations greater and mightier than you in order to give you their land as an inheritance, **as on this day.** (v. 38)
Directive Speech-Acts	Acknowledgment	*To you it was shown* [רָאָה Hophal] that you might know that Y{\sc hwh}, he is God; there is no other! (v. 35)	Know **today** and bring back to your heart that Y{\sc hwh}, he is God in heaven above and on earth below; there is no other! (v. 39)
	Command	∅[a]	Thus you shall keep his statutes and commandments that I am commanding you **today**.... (v. 40)

a. Though no formal "Command" concludes the first panel, the directive speech-act in Deut 4:40 serves as a fitting conclusion for both panels. The ellipsis at the end of the first panel heightens the rhetorical anticipation provided in Moses' final injunction to "keep his statutes and commandments that I am commanding you today" (4:40).

clusion to the imaginative speech-acts portraying Y{\sc hwh}'s marvels in the exodus and Horeb theophany (4:33–34, 36–38). On the other hand, the final "Command" (v. 40) is predicated upon the theological reality of the "Acknowledgment" (vv. 35, 39), because Moses' recital of Israel's history has conclusively answered his rhetorical questions with an emphatic "No!" (4:32–33), thereby rebutting every conceivable objection to Yhwh's call to "obey my voice" (4:10).[103] Thus Moses' final directive speech-act for Israel to obey Yhwh (4:40) is not only the lone command in the entire passage, but this exhortation also finds its grounds in the persuasive power of divine speech and presence.

Since Yhwh's undeserved affection for the "fathers" (4:37) initiates the historical chain of events resulting in the present command to obey (4:40),[104] it is appropriate to conclude with some reflections on the fathers' identity. Römer argues that the "fathers" are the ancestors of the exodus generation because the verb אהב never occurs in the patriarchal narratives but is applied first to the exodus generation (Hos 11:1) and is extended to the patriarchs only in late texts (e.g., 2 Chr 20:7; Isa 41:8). In conjunction with Deut 4:37 and 10:15, he regards the references to זרע in Genesis as originating from a similarly late, postdeuteronomic hand.[105] Lohfink answers that the Priestly writer's use of זרע language is close enough in dating to Deut 4:37, which he considers a late Deuteronomistic text, to allow for the possibility that אבות still refers to the patriarchs.[106]

In response to redactional proposals, I note that it is significant that all the putative strata of the Genesis and Exodus narratives agree that Yhwh cared for the ancestors of the exodus generation (e.g., Gen 12:2; 15:13; 17:7; 50:24; Exod 1:7, 20; 2:23–25). Römer and Lohfink appear to be caught up in arguing over a false dichotomy, since the expression "fathers" in Deut 4:37 is ambiguous enough to include both groups. More importantly, the strategy of Deuteronomy in embedding the means of its own oral and written propagation ensures that subsequent performances of the book transform the "fathers" into the beloved ancestors of every generation that experiences Yhwh's miraculous deliverance.[107] Braulik is right to observe

---

103. Similarly, Moses' assertion that the purpose of Yhwh's speech was to "discipline" (יסר Piel; 4:36) Israel is an outstanding use of kinship language (cf. Deut 8:5; 21:18; 22:18; 1 Kgs 12:11; Job 4:3; Prov 19:18) to bridge the putative dichotomy between grace and law. See J. W. McKay, "Man's Love for God in Deuteronomy and the Father/Teacher–Son/Pupil Relationship," *VT* 22 (1972) 426–35.

104. The later Jewish tendency to view Deut 4:37 as an expression of the זכות אבות ("merit of the fathers"; cf. Sir 44:19–21; J. H. Shmidman, "Zekhut Avot," *EncJud* 21:497–98; Tigay, *Deuteronomy*, 56–57) by which the patriarchs earned Yhwh's favor through obedience thus misses the emphasis on divine grace in Deut 4:32–40.

105. Römer, *Israels Väter*, 27–28.

106. Lohfink, *Väter*, 72.

107. Sonnet (*Book within the Book*) provides a detailed treatment of Deuteronomy's references to its own writing and recitation in 6:6–9; 11:18–21; 17:18–20; 27:1–8; 31:9–13. Cf. S. Amsler, "Loi orale et loi écrite dans le Deutéronome," in *Das Deuteronomium: Entstehung, Gestalt und Botschaft* (ed. N. Lohfink; BETL 68; Leuven: Leuven University Press, 1985) 51–54.

that the references to the "fathers" in Deuteronomy 4 provide "eine Art *Motivcrescendo*"[108] of Yhwh's enduring faithfulness that climaxes in Deut 4:37. Thus Deuteronomy 4 consistently envisages Yhwh's ברית as an essentially relational institution that is governed by covenant stipulations rather than being a strictly legal matter. This ברית transcends Israel's generations and thereby conceives of Israel's ancestors and descendants as a corporate whole.

Divine-Human Covenant and the "Fathers" in Deuteronomy 7–8

Yhwh's oath and covenant with the "fathers" also maintain a theological balance between grace and law in Deuteronomy 7–8, a passage that fleshes out the ethical implications of divine election (4:37). This section represents the middle section of Moses' exposition of the *Hauptgebot* (5:1–11:32).[109] Following Moses' restatement of Israel's unique election (7:6–8) and an exhortation for Israel to remember Yhwh's unique status as האלהים (7:9–11; cf. 4:35, 39; 5:9–10), the covenant segments in 7:12–26 and 8:1–20 form a complementary unit that "both asserts the truth of Yahweh's election of Israel and problematizes it; that is, it shows that a wrong concept of election will have disastrous results."[110] In 7:12–26, Moses asserts that the privilege of divine election as Yhwh's "holy people" (7:6) entails the responsibilities of conquering the land (7:17–24; cf. 7:1) and eradicating its pagan elements (7:25–26; cf. 7:2–6). In 8:1–20, Moses warns that the privileges of divine election, as exemplified by the gift of an abundant land (8:7–13), must not eventuate in a failure to "remember" (זכר; 8:2) Yhwh's provision during the painful journeys through the wilderness or his continued provision in the land. Here the goodness of Yhwh's gifts creates a paradox in which Israel may "forget" (שכח; 8:11; cf. 8:18) the Giver himself. Since divine election can be a dangerous doctrine in its extreme forms,[111] Moses asserts that confident obedience in conquering the land (7:12–26)

---

108. Braulik, *Mittel*, 119.
109. Regarding Deuteronomy 4(5)–11, J. R. Lundbom ("Inclusio," 304–6), D. L. Christensen (*Deuteronomy 1–11* [WBC 6A; Nashville: Thomas Nelson, 1991] 69), and R. H. O'Connell ("Deuteronomy VIII 1–20: Asymmetrical Concentricity and the Rhetoric of Providence," *VT* 40 [1990] 451–52) differ slightly in the chiasms proposed, but they concur in placing the covenant sermons of 7:12–26 and 8:1–20 at the center. Whereas Christensen and O'Connell view the deictic particle ועתה ("and now"; 4:1; 10:12) as delimiting the outermost frame of 4:1–11:25, Lundbom holds that the chiasm is framed by the paired references to "statutes and ordinances" (5:1; 11:32).
110. McConville, *Deuteronomy*, 159.
111. R. Rendtorff ("Die Erwählung Israels als Thema der deuteronomischen Theologie," in *Die Botschaft und die Boten: Festschrift für Hans Walter Wolff zum 70. Geburtstag* [ed. J. Jeremias and L. Perlitt; Neukirchen-Vluyn: Neukirchener Verlag, 1981] 83–86) observes that various theological tensions in divine election (e.g., universalism vs. exclusivism) are well balanced in Deuteronomy's final form.

must remain inseparable from sober remembrance while living in the land (8:1–20).[112]

Moses illustrates the theological balance between grace and law in divine election by uttering two kinds of imaginative speech-acts, the first of which is not found in Deuteronomy 4. First, Deuteronomy 7 and 8 each contain an inner monologue ("If you say in your heart . . .") with which Moses illustrates the people's contrasting attitudes toward the land. The people must not succumb either to timidity before the conquest ("These nations are greater than I; how can I dispossess them?"; 7:17) nor to arrogance after the conquest ("My power and the strength of my hand made me this wealth!"; 8:17).[113] This imaginative speech-act is not a matter of historical anachronism as in other cases (e.g., 5:3) but is the preempting of Israel's disobedience through the use of a hypothetical thought process.

Second, Moses undercuts Israel's potential timidity and arrogance in the future by conjuring up the great episodes of Israel's history as if his present audience had experienced them. In order to embolden the people against the Canaanites, whom he had acknowledged are "greater and mightier than you" (7:1), Moses emphatically reminds (זכר תזכר; "you shall *surely* remember"; 7:18) his audience that they witnessed Yhwh's mighty deliverance from Egypt ("which *your eyes saw*"; 7:19) and that he is present "in your midst" to dispossess the Canaanites (7:21). The manifestation of Yhwh's power against Egypt furnishes a theological template for the conquest of Canaan. Similarly, Moses warns against hedonistic enjoyment of the land's blessings by transporting his audience back to the privation of the "great and terrible wilderness, with its fiery serpents and scorpions, and thirsty ground where there was no water" (8:15). The remembrance of Yhwh's sustenance in the wilderness must therefore guard Israel against forgetting that the land is always a divine gift and never a human entitlement. The imaginative speech-acts of inner monologue and vivification of the past channel the prior experience of Yhwh's grace into Israel's present decision at Moab and its future obligations in the land. These glimpses into Israel's saving history provide the rhetorical foundation for the directive (e.g., 7:9–11) and declarative (e.g., 8:19) speech-acts of Yhwh's ברית that will be treated shortly.

---

112. R. H. O'Connell, "Deuteronomy VII 1–26: Asymmetrical Concentricity and the Rhetoric of Conquest," *VT* 42 (1992) 263–65; J. H. Gammie, "The Theology of Retribution in the Book of Deuteronomy," *VT* 32 (1970) 9–12.

113. García López ("Analyse littéraire de Deutéronome V–XI," 483–86) notes that the monologues of timidity (7:17-19, 21) and arrogance (8:17–18; 9:4–7; cf. 15:9) follow a standard form: (1) introduction; (2) the monologue proper; (3) and Moses' rebuttal of the monologue's concerns, whether timidity or arrogance. Block ("Investigation," 207–8) also notes that each of the covenant segments in Deuteronomy 6–8 possesses a threefold structure: (1) rhetorical presentation of a test of love for Yhwh (6:10–19; 7:1–16; 8:1–16); (2) audience response (6:20; 7:17; 8:17); and (3) rhetorical answer (6:21–25; 7:18–26; 8:18–20).

The case for reading Deuteronomy 7 and 8 as a unified exposition of divine election and covenant recommitment is strengthened further by several structural features. First, the parallel phrases עקב תשמעון ("if you obey"; 7:12) and עקב לא תשמעון ("because you would not obey"; 8:20) form an inclusio around the adjacent sermons in 7:12–26 and 8:1–20.[114] These lexical markers indicate that these sections belong together in outlining the blessings for obedience and curses for disobedience to the *Hauptgebot*, respectively. Second, and more significantly, Robert O'Connell has demonstrated in two articles that these chapters exhibit similar structures of "assymetrical concentricity" that encapsulate the complementarity of the "rhetoric of conquest" (7:1–26) and the "rhetoric of providence" (8:1–20).[115] O'Connell refines Lohfink's literary analysis of these chapters by showing that chiastic pairs may be indicated by conceptual correspondence in addition to lexical parallels, and by recognizing that Deuteronomy 7 and 8 conclude with miniature chiasms (7:26; 8:19–20) of their own. Moses amplifies the original warnings at the beginning of each chapter (cf. 7:1; 8:1) by restating them in antithetical terms.[116]

Though the asymmetrical structures of O'Connell diverge in some details from the symmetrical structures of Lohfink, it is noteworthy for the present discussion that the two authors correspond exactly on the chiastic pairing of the various references to Y<small>HWH</small>'s oath and covenant with Israel (7:8–9 // 7:12–13), the need for Israel to "remember" (זכר) Y<small>HWH</small> and his ברית (8:2 // 8:18),[117] and Y<small>HWH</small>'s past dealings with the "fathers" (8:3 // 8:16). This rhetorical artistry does not preclude the possibility of editorial activity in Deuteronomy 7–8,[118] for it should be noted that diachronic proposals for these chapters have often exposed genuine textual difficulties with which synchronic approaches still need to grapple.[119] Though the *Numeruswechsel*

---

114. Christensen (*Deuteronomy 1:1–21:9*, 164) notes that עקב תשמעון appears only here in the entire OT.
115. O'Connell, "Deuteronomy VII," 248–65; idem, "Deuteronomy VIII," 437–52.
116. Lohfink, *Hauptgebot*, 181–83, 194–95.
117. R. C. Van Leeuwen ("What Comes out of God's Mouth: Theological Wordplay in Deuteronomy 8," *CBQ* 47 [1985] 55–57) simplifies Lohfink's proposal by structuring the entirety of Deuteronomy 8 as a contrast between Moses' admonitions to "remember" (8:2–5) and not "forget" (8:11–16). Because Van Leeuwen essentially agrees with Lohfink and O'Connell on the overarching contrast between remembrance and forgetfulness in Deuteronomy 8, I will use a modified version of his structure here for the sake of simplicity.
118. Cf. O'Connell ("Deuteronomy VII," 264), who poses the provocative question of whether diachronic reconstructions for these chapters remain necessary: "[T]here is evidence of redactional processes in the development of the present form of Deuteronomy, but are such processes likely to have given rise to chapters so architecturally analogous and, at the same time, so mutually integrated with their context?" His answer is clearly "no."
119. T. Veijola ("'Der Mensch lebt nicht vom Brot allein': Zur literarischen Schichtung und theologischen Aussage von Deuteronomium 8," in *Bundesdokument und Gesetz: Studien zum Deuteronomium* [HBS 4; Freiburg: Herder, 1995] 143) acknowledges the presence

remains problematic as a redaction-critical criterion,[120] the marked tension between "unconditional" and "conditional" notions of YHWH's covenant has provided an understandable impetus for redaction critical proposals.[121] Thus my analysis below of the references to YHWH's oath and covenant acknowledges these tensions in the final form but attempts to explain them as a necessary theological dialectic between grace and law rather than as literary-critical contradictions.[122] Moses' interweaving of imaginative, directive, and declarative speech-acts in Deuteronomy 7–8 captures the symbiosis between grace and law in the four references to YHWH's שבעה and ברית (7:8, 9, 12; 8:18; see text and translation, p. 211).

The theological dialectic between grace and law comes to the fore in the three references to YHWH's oath and covenant in Deut 7:7–12, a tension often viewed as an irresolvable contradiction between "unconditional" and "conditional" ideas. On the one hand, the "unconditional" aspect of covenant arises in Israel's deliverance through the exodus because "he [YHWH] loved you and kept the oath [שבעה] that he swore to your fathers" (7:8). This description of YHWH's שבעה emphasizes its antecedent and undeserved character, since the divine election of Israel occurred despite Israel's status as "the smallest of the peoples" (7:7). Moses concludes that, because YHWH is "the faithful El, keeping his covenant [ברית] and lovingkindness [חסד]" (7:9), Israel ought therefore to "keep the commandment and the statutes and the ordinances" (7:11). On the other hand, the "conditional" aspect of the covenant appears immediately in the next verse. Moses asserts that, if Israel obeys YHWH's commands (7:12a), YHWH will keep his "covenant [ברית] and his lovingkindness [חסד]" (7:12b). Though here the phrase ברית וחסד is identical to 7:9, YHWH's covenant faithfulness has apparently shifted from being the prior motivation for Israel's obedience (ושמרת את המצוה; "*therefore* you shall keep the commandment"; 7:11) to being its contingent result

---

of "eine kunstvolle literarische Struktur mit chiastischem Aufbau" in Deuteronomy 8 but asserts that "[dies] vermag nicht über die literargeschichtlich bedingte Mehrschichtigkeit des Kapitels hinwegzutäuschen." Veijola cites the uniquely long sentence in 8:7–18 ("die monströse grammatikalische Struktur") as a probable example of redactional layering.

120. See the discussion of "A Singular and Timeless Covenant in Deut 4:23–31" on pp. 201–203 above.

121. Veijola ("Deuteronomium 8," 143–58), F. García López ("'Un Peuple Consacré': Analyse Critique de Deutéronome VII," *VT* 32 [1982] 438–63; idem, "Yahvé, fuente última de vida: Análisis de Dt 8," *Bib* 62 [1981] 21–54), and Perlitt (*Bundestheologie*, 55–77) posit reconstructions of varying complexity, sometimes using the *Numeruswechsel*, but placing greater weight on the putative shifts in the (un)conditionality of land and covenant.

122. Hoftijzer (*Verheissungen*, 61 n. 25) summarizes thus the presuppositions behind stratifying Deuteronomic covenant theology into "conditional" and "unconditional" layers that ostensibly reflect Israel's historical circumstances: "Da die Erwählungstat ein immer wiederkehrendes Heute ist, ist sie nicht von der Gesetzestreue abhängig und ist von einer möglichen Krise nicht die Rede. Erst in den jüngeren Teilen Deuteronomiums, ist unter Einfluss der historischen Ereignisse der Akzent auf die menschliche Leistung verlegt worden."

Deuteronomy 7:7–12

לֹא מֵרֻבְּכֶם מִכָּל־הָעַמִּים	⁷Not because you were the largest of the peoples
חָשַׁק יְהוָה בָּכֶם וַיִּבְחַר בָּכֶם	did Yhwh desire you and choose you,
כִּי־אַתֶּם הַמְעַט מִכָּל־הָעַמִּים	for you were the smallest of the peoples.
כִּי מֵאַהֲבַת יְהוָה אֶתְכֶם	⁸But because Yhwh loved you
וּמִשָּׁמְרוֹ אֶת־הַשְּׁבֻעָה	and kept the oath
אֲשֶׁר נִשְׁבַּע לַאֲבֹתֵיכֶם	that he swore to your fathers,
הוֹצִיא יְהוָה אֶתְכֶם בְּיָד חֲזָקָה	Yhwh brought you out by a strong hand
וַיִּפְדְּךָ מִבֵּית עֲבָדִים	and redeemed you from the house of slavery,
מִיַּד פַּרְעֹה מֶלֶךְ־מִצְרָיִם	from the hand of Pharaoh king of Egypt.
וְיָדַעְתָּ כִּי־יְהוָה אֱלֹהֶיךָ	⁹Thus you shall know that Yhwh your God,
הוּא הָאֱלֹהִים הָאֵל הַנֶּאֱמָן	he is God, the faithful El,
שֹׁמֵר הַבְּרִית וְהַחֶסֶד	keeping his covenant and lovingkindness
לְאֹהֲבָיו וּלְשֹׁמְרֵי מִצְוֹתָו	for those who love him and keep his commands,
לְאֶלֶף דּוֹר	for a thousand generations,
וּמְשַׁלֵּם לְשֹׂנְאָיו אֶל־פָּנָיו	¹⁰but repaying those who hate him to his face
לְהַאֲבִידוֹ	to destroy him.
לֹא יְאַחֵר לְשֹׂנְאוֹ	He will not delay with the one who hates him, [but]
אֶל־פָּנָיו יְשַׁלֶּם־לוֹ	will repay him to his face.
וְשָׁמַרְתָּ אֶת־הַמִּצְוָה	¹¹Thus you shall keep the commandment
וְאֶת־הַחֻקִּים וְאֶת־הַמִּשְׁפָּטִים	and the statutes and the ordinances
אֲשֶׁר אָנֹכִי מְצַוְּךָ הַיּוֹם לַעֲשׂוֹתָם	that I am commanding you today, to do them.
וְהָיָה עֵקֶב	¹²Then it will come about,
תִּשְׁמְעוּן אֵת הַמִּשְׁפָּטִים הָאֵלֶּה	if you obey these ordinances
וּשְׁמַרְתֶּם וַעֲשִׂיתֶם אֹתָם	and keep and do them,
וְשָׁמַר יְהוָה אֱלֹהֶיךָ לְךָ	that Yhwh will keep with you
אֶת־הַבְּרִית וְאֶת־הַחֶסֶד	the covenant and lovingkindness
אֲשֶׁר נִשְׁבַּע לַאֲבֹתֶיךָ	that he swore to your fathers.

(והיה עקב תשמעון המשפטים האלה; "*if* you obey these ordinances"; 7:12a). The contrasting instances of ברית וחסד lead Perlitt to excise 7:12a as a plural Deuteronomistic insertion into an older singular layer in which ברית still referred to the pre- or protodeuteronomic promise to the patriarchs (cf. Gen 12:7).[123] If the grounds clause (והיה עקב) in 7:12a were removed, the phrase ברית וחסד would signify a uniformly "unconditional" notion of covenant.

Though Römer strongly criticizes the theological reductionism of Perlitt's study,[124] his own proposal falls into a similar though less severe dichotomy between promise and obligation. Römer offers two counter-arguments in favor of a "conditional" interpretation of ברית וחסד as the

---

123. Perlitt, *Bundestheologie*, 59–60, 64–68. Cf. von Rad, *From Genesis to Chronicles*, 25–26.
124. Römer, *Israels Väter*, 144–45.

covenant at Horeb in response to Perlitt's view that the hendiadys refers to YHWH's "unconditional" promise to the patriarchs. First, the predominant use of ברית in Deuteronomy and the Deuteronom(ist)ic literature refers to the stipulations given at Horeb (Deut 4:13, 31; cf. 1 Kgs 8:21, 23).[125] Second, the present reference to חסד (7:9, 12) echoes the blessing and curse sections of the various Decalogues (Deut 5:9–10; Exod 20:5–6; cf. 34:7), thereby suggesting that this use of חסד primarily denotes Israel's impersonal obedience instead of personal commitment.[126] Römer concludes that the "fathers" to whom YHWH swore ברית וחסד (7:9, 12) must either be the Horeb generation or their immediate forebears, since the "unconditional" oath received by the patriarchs differs markedly from the "conditional" covenant described in 7:7–12 as well as Deuteronomy's other descriptions of Horeb (e.g., chaps. 4–5, 9–10).[127]

In brief, Perlitt regards Deut 7:7–12 as an originally "unconditional" passage into which "conditional" phraseology was added by the Deuteronom(ist)ic school, whereas Römer reverses Perlitt's historical-critical timeline by arguing that a "conditional" passage only became "unconditional" in the postexilic period through the recasting of the "fathers" as the patriarchs instead of the Horeb generation(s). Despite all the differences between Perlitt and Römer, however, their proposals do share three presuppositions: (1) "unconditionality" and "conditionality" are irreconcilable paradigms; (2) the patriarchal covenant is "unconditional"; and (3) the Horeb covenant, and Deuteronomic covenant theology by extension, is "conditional." This sort of theological dichotomy inevitably leads to the conclusion that the function of "conditional" obedience for Moses' audience (7:12a) in fulfilling the "unconditional" promise to the "fathers" (7:12b) is an illogical and secondary development.

שמר as Leitwort of Theological Dialectic in Deuteronomy 7:7–12

A synchronic reexamination of Deut 7:7–12 reinforces the earlier conclusion that divine promise and human obligation operate as contrasting points along a relational spectrum that unfolds in Israel's history, rather than an ahistorical dichotomy between unconditionality and conditionality. The smooth interweaving of grace and law in the divine-human relationship is exemplified by this passage's sixfold repetition of the verb שמר

---

125. Römer, *Israels Väter*, 144.
126. Against the consensus that חסד is essentially a relational term (see n. 8 above), Römer (*Israels Väter*, 146) argues that Deuteronomy's collocation of ברית and חסד makes the latter term a matter of human duty ("eine menschliche Handlung"), thus defining the entire hendiadys in terms of his understanding of ברית.
127. This point represents the corollary to the earlier assertion of Römer (*Israels Väter*, 49–50) that the term ברית was only associated with the patriarchal traditions in late, Priestly texts (Exod 2:24; 6:3; Lev 26:42).

using various subjects, objects, verbal aspects, and time markers.[128] First, Yhwh's "irrational, free decision of love"[129] (חשק in 7:7; אהב in 7:8) in electing Israel indicates that Yhwh "kept" (שמר infinitive construct) his oath with the "fathers" (7:8a) by delivering his people from Egypt (7:8b). Second and third, Moses declares that Yhwh is the "faithful El, keeping [שמר participle] his covenant and lovingkindness for those who keep [שמר participle] his commandments" (7:9). Fourth and fifth, Israel must respond to this divine grace with obedience: "you shall keep [שמר imperfect] the commandment" (7:11), and "if you obey these ordinances and keep [שמר imperfect] and do them" (7:12a). Sixth and finally, Moses promises that "he [Yhwh] will keep [שמר imperfect] with you the covenant and lovingkindness that he swore to your fathers" (7:12b). This sixfold repetition marks the verb שמר as a *Leitwort* in 7:7–12 that draws intentional parallels between Yhwh's "keeping" and Israel's "keeping" of the covenant, especially in the liturgical oration of 7:9. The ברית וחסד that was once sworn to the "fathers" obligates both Yhwh and Israel to exercise their mutual commitment to one another in the past (7:7–8), present (7:9–11), and future (7:12).

Against the dominant characterization of Deuteronomic covenant theology, however, it should be noted that the symbiosis between divine and human agency in Deut 7:7–12 is hardly a quid pro quo matter. Yhwh's faithfulness to his ברית and חסד frames the passage at both the beginning (7:8) and the end (7:12), thus enclosing all of Israel's history in divine grace with human obedience sandwiched in between. Even in the middle section, in which Moses emphasizes Israel's duties (7:9–11), the asymmetry between divine commitment and human obligation is clear in the contrast between Yhwh's vast faithfulness "for those who love him ... for a thousand generations" (7:9) and the limited scope of divine punishment returned upon "those who hate him" (7:10). The exponential disproportion between Yhwh's "vertical" faithfulness and "horizontal" retribution highlights the primacy of divine grace in Israel's history.[130]

The rhetorical intentionality of this confluence of שמר verbal forms in Deut 7:7–12 comes into even sharper relief in a synoptic comparison. Though the subunit of 7:9–10 is usually grouped with other OT references to so-called "collective retribution,"[131] a closer examination shows that 7:9–10 is unique on three counts.

---

128. Cf. Buchanan, "Covenant," 40 n. 46.
129. W. Zimmerli, *Old Testament Theology in Outline* (trans. D. E. Green; Edinburgh: T. & T. Clark, 1978) 45.
130. The pervasiveness of this motif in Deuteronomy is demonstrated at length by Barker in *Triumph of Grace in Deuteronomy*, though not with direct reference to Deuteronomy 7.
131. J. Krašovec ("Is There a Doctrine of 'Collective Retribution' in the Hebrew Bible?" *HUCA* 65 [1994] 35–89) contends that Exod 20:5–6 (// Deut 5:9–10), Num 14:18, Deut 7:9–

First, Deut 7:9–10 alone uses the verb שמר to denote Yhwh's "keeping" his חסד, as opposed to "doing" (עשה; Exod 20:6 // Deut 5:10, Jer 32:18) or "guarding" (נצר, Exod 34:7); or using no participial form ("abundant in lovingkindness [חסד]"; Num 14:18). Whatever the diachronic relationship between the parallel orations in Deut 5:9–10 and 7:9–10,[132] the latter passage represents more than a simple recapitulation of the Decalogic formula. Second, Deut 7:7–12 repeatedly uses the same verb (i.e., שמר) to denote both the divine and human actions of "keeping" the covenant, while the other passages do not reuse the verbs associated with Yhwh's חסד (i.e., נצר, עשה) as *Leitwörter*. Third, Deut 7:9–10 does not contain the characteristic phrase עון אבות ("iniquities of the fathers"; e.g., 5:9) that is always found in other texts of "collective retribution." Whether or not one regards these texts as asserting vertical judgment (i.e., "upon the third and fourth generations"; Exod 20:5 // Deut 5:9), Deut 7:9–10 does not belong in this contested category.[133] From this reassessment of Deut 7:7–12 in literary and synoptic context, it is apparent that the repetition of the *Leitwort* שמר emphasizes the bilateral nature of the relationship between Yhwh and Israel while concurrently prioritizing the role of divine grace in sustaining the covenant.

The Referent of the "Fathers" and the ברית וחסד in Deuteronomy 7:7–12

Having demonstrated that Yhwh's promise is both prior and posterior to Israel's obedience, I must reexamine the historical referent for the "fathers" who received Yhwh's ברית וחסד (7:9, 12). As I already indicated, Perlitt and Römer disagree on the identity of the "fathers," though paradoxically, they have similar presuppositions about the obligatory nature of the covenant at Horeb. The preceding analysis of Deut 7:7–12 has determined that the phrase ברית וחסד encapsulates a mutual commitment between Yhwh and his people that necessarily contains both "unconditional" and "conditional" features. Since Moses explicitly links fulfillment of the ברית וחסד that were once sworn to the "fathers" (7:8, 9, 12) to the covenant stipulations "that I am commanding you *today*" (7:11), it appears that he conceives of Israel's

---

10, and Jer 32:18 share two features marking them as formulas of "collective retribution": (1) an antithesis between Yhwh's mercy and judgment; and (2) participial verb forms. Krašovec reluctantly concludes that "ancestral guilt is inheritable" (p. 35). See Gammie ("Theology of Retribution," 9–10) for a more nuanced view of Deuteronomy 7.

132. Perlitt (*Bundestheologie*, 61–62) argues that the use of ברית to refer to the Decalogue (7:9–11) arises in the late Deuteronomic or early Deuteronomistic period between the purely "unconditional" (i.e., pre- or protodeuteronomic) and "conditional" (i.e., Deuteronomistic) phases of the term. Deut 7:9–12 would thus belong to the same early Deuteronomistic layer as the Decalogue.

133. Contra Krašovec, "Retribution," 52–53. Thus the debate over whether "collective retribution" is asserted in the OT is impertinent for the present discussion.

history as governed either by a single covenant[134] or by an original and overarching promise whose implicit demand for the vassal's loyalty is only fleshed out according to the vicissitudes of history.[135] Both views find support in Moses' liturgically charged characterization of Yhwh as "keeping" (שמר participle) his singular ברית for a thousand generations (7:9). On the one hand, the active participle of שמר "indicates a person or thing conceived as being in the continual uninterrupted *exercise* of an activity."[136] On the other hand, Yhwh's timeless devotion to a singular rather than plural ברית suggests that the various OT covenants represent the continuation of the divine-human relationship that was first established in patriarchal times.[137] For 7:7-12, an understanding of ברית as relationship accounts more plausibly for the essential continuity in Yhwh's dealings than a rather schizophrenic shift between "unconditional" and "conditional" covenants, as required by the contractual notion of obligation.[138]

The relational character of this covenant is reinforced by the already/not-yet trajectory of Yhwh's ברית וחסד with the "fathers." The ancestral ברית is both partially fulfilled in the exodus deliverance (7:8) and yet to be fulfilled through Israel's obedience in the land (7:12).[139] These instances of the phrase ברית וחסד form imaginative speech-acts that transport his present audience into both the past (7:8) and the future (7:12) in order to motivate Moses' present audience to obey his directive speech-acts (7:9-11). The imaginative blending of past, present, and future horizons of ברית וחסד for parenetic purposes suggests that, while the "fathers" in 7:7-12 primarily signify the patriarchs who first received Yhwh's oath, they also become the ancestors of every generation that reenacts the exodus, hears the call of Yhwh/Moses for decision at Moab, and thus stands at the boundary between promise and fulfillment (cf. 5:3).[140]

---

134. See 201-203 above; and Rendtorff, *Covenant Formula*, 82-83.

135. Altman, *Historical Prologue*, 54-55, 60-61. Cf. McComiskey (*Covenants*, 59-76), whose otherwise helpful approach is marred by an appeal to Weinfeld's sharp distinctions between royal grants and suzerainty treaties (pp. 62-63).

136. GKC §116a, emphasis original; cf. Krašovec, "Retribution," 41-42.

137. Barr ("Some Semantic Notes," 29-31) observes that, in contrast to other "covenantal" words such as אלה, חק, and עדה/עדות, the word ברית is never attested in the plural in the OT. While Barr downplays the theological ramifications of this, Rendtorff uses Barr's observation to argue that the inability of ברית to form plurals points to the presence of the "one, continually 'new' covenant" (*Covenant Formula*, 78-79).

138. Contra Kutsch, *Verheissung*, 121-23.

139. The already/not-yet tension of ברית וחסד reflects the multiplex character of divine חסד itself. Glueck (*Ḥesed*, 102) notes that the OT use of חסד denotes both the grounds and the result of God's promise.

140. Römer (*Israels Väter*, 151-52) also sees a temporal progression from promise to fulfillment in Deut 7:7-12. Though my analysis diverges from his view that the "fathers" are the ancestors of the first exodus generation, Römer has rightly identified the textual tensions in his suggestion that the "fathers" here represent more than just the patriarchs.

Deuteronomy 8:18

וְזָכַרְתָּ אֶת־יְהוָה אֱלֹהֶיךָ	But you shall remember YHWH your God,
כִּי הוּא הַנֹּתֵן לְךָ	for he is the one who is giving you
כֹּחַ לַעֲשׂוֹת חָיִל	power to make wealth,
לְמַעַן הָקִים אֶת־בְּרִיתוֹ	in order to establish his covenant
אֲשֶׁר־נִשְׁבַּע לַאֲבֹתֶיךָ	that he swore to your fathers,
כַּיּוֹם הַזֶּה	as it is this day.

The need for a theological conception of the generations is reinforced in Deuteronomy 8, a chapter that contains four dissimilar references to the "fathers" (8:1, 3, 16, 18). At first glance, the formulaic references to the land (8:1) and the covenant (8:18; see text and translation, p. 216) sworn to the "fathers" apparently denote the patriarchs (cf. 1:8; 6:10). However, the parallelism between generations in YHWH's provision of manna "which *you* did not know, nor did *your fathers* know" (8:3, 16) suggests that Moses is speaking to the children of the first generation that ate manna in the wilderness with their parents (cf. Exod 16:15). While some translations distinguish two generations by rendering אבות variously as "forefathers" (8:1, 18) and "fathers" (8:3, 16),[141] other translations view the repetition and shared context of the four אבות instances as pointing to the same entity, whether to the patriarchs[142] or to the Horeb generation.[143]

Even more troublesome than these chronological ambiguities, however, is the reemerging, difficult problem of the *Generationswechsel* in the ostensive contradiction between Moses' statement that his present audience experienced YHWH's leading in the wilderness during "these forty years" (8:2, 4) and his earlier assertion that the first wilderness generation perished in the wilderness (1:34–36; 2:14–16). The final form of Deuteronomy 8 thus evinces a chronological tension between collapsing the generations into "these forty years" and distinguishing between "you" and "your fathers." This chronological difficulty is accompanied by the tension between "unconditionality" and "conditionality" in Moses' arresting depiction of the land's abundance as both a gift to be enjoyed (8:7–10) and a temptation to be guarded against (8:12–13).[144]

---

141. So the NASB and NIV. The chronological ambiguity for אבות is retained by rendering all instances of אבות as either "fathers" (NJPS, RSV) or "ancestors" (NLT). In 8:1, some LXX manuscripts and the SP explicitly add the names of the patriarchal trio.

142. E.g., McConville, *Deuteronomy*, 164–65; Diepold, *Israels Land*, 78.

143. E.g., B. Gosse, "Le souvenir de l'alliance avec Abraham, Isaac et Jacob et le serment du don de la terre dans le Pentateuque," *EstBib* 51 (1993) 469; Römer, *Israels Väter*, 153.

144. Brueggemann, *Land*, 45–56.

The Rhetorical Progression of the "Fathers" in Deuteronomy 8

These chronological and theological difficulties must be kept in mind when one is identifying the proper referent for the ברית with the "fathers." While exegetes tend to regard the ברית with the "fathers" (8:18) as more or less synonymous with the land promise to the patriarchs (8:1; cf. 1:8; 34:4),[145] a reassessment of Deuteronomy 8 reveals several signs of a progression in the "fathers" from the patriarchs to the exodus generation and, finally, to including all of Israel's ancestors from a landed perspective.

First, Deut 8:18 represents only one of three instances in Deuteronomy (cf. 7:12; 29:11–12[12–13]) in which Moses applies the language of ברית to an oath (נשבע) with the "fathers." Not only do most of the Deuteronomic occurrences of ברית refer to the covenant at Horeb (e.g., 4:23; 5:2–3), but (as already argued above) the preceding reference to a ברית with the "fathers" (7:7–12) refers to an ongoing relationship between YHWH and his people rather than any particular "unconditional" or "conditional" covenant. Even if the ברית in 8:18 envisions the patriarchs, a view to be reexamined shortly, YHWH's current intention to "establish" (הקים)[146] the covenant on "this day" (e.g., 4:20, 38; 6:24; 29:28) scrolls forward the recital of Israel's history to the present time, with the exodus directly in the background.[147] Moses' assertion that YHWH is currently "giving" (נתן participle) Israel the means to prosper in the land (8:18a) also heightens the immediacy of the moment.[148] From the narrative perspective of Moab, it is chronologically coherent for the "fathers" to include both the patriarchal and exodus generations as the contemporized ancestors of the present audience.

---

145. E.g., Millar, *Now Choose Life*, 55, 62–65; O'Connell, "Deuteronomy VIII," 439–42; Lohfink, *Hauptgebot*, 86–89, 195.

146. In contrast to the putatively D and JE idiom כרת ברית, the expression הקים ברית has usually been viewed as P language (cf. n. 19). The surprising use of הקים ברית in Deut 8:18 recalls YHWH's second theophany to Moses, an ostensibly P text: "I established [הקים] my covenant [ברית] with them [Abraham, Isaac, and Jacob], to give them the land of Canaan" (Exod 6:4). Since Exodus records YHWH as declaring that he has already "established" his covenant with the patriarchs, yet Deuteronomy records this action as taking place "this day" (8:18), it is likely that the use of הקים ברית does not refer to a once-for-all event but maintains an already/not-yet tension for a previously ratified covenant. The use of קום Hiphil to denote ratification of an existing covenant is defended by J. Milgrom, *Leviticus 23–27* (AB 3B; New York: Doubleday, 2001) 2343–46; G. J. Wenham, *Genesis 1–15* (WBC 1; Waco, TX: Word, 1987) 175; and W. J. Dumbrell, *Covenant and Creation: A Theology of the Old Testament Covenants* (Grand Rapids, MI: Baker, 1984) 26. Though rightly criticizing the extremes of Dumbrell's view, Day ("Why Does God 'Establish' Rather Than 'Cut' Covenants," 99) agrees with Dumbrell that Deut 8:18 entails the renewal of an existing covenant.

147. Block (*Deuteronomy*, 359) and McConville (*Grace in the End*, 125–6) note that the expression "this day" typically refers to the day at Horeb or the exodus events.

148. Compare the frequency of Deuteronomy's durative use of the נתן active participle to denote YHWH's present gift of land (e.g., 1:20; 2:29; 4:1, 40; 5:16; 7:16; 9:6; 12:9; 15:7; 19:2; 24:4; 26:1; 27:3; 28:8; 32:52).

Second, the usual characterization of the ברית in 8:18 as an "unconditional" gift of land, thereby recalling the Abrahamic covenant, is untenable given the numerous references to Horeb in the literary context.[149] In Deuteronomy 8, Moses issues directive speech-acts for Israel to "keep" (שׁמר) YHWH's commands (8:1, 2, 6, 11) and thereby "remember" (זכר; 8:2, 18) and not "forget" (שׁכח; 8:11, 14, 19) YHWH. The urgent need for obedience is also punctuated by two references to the Decalogue (8:14, 19). Immediately after the reference to ברית in 8:18, Moses concludes this section of the sermon with a declarative speech-act that warns of dire consequences for forgetfulness: "If you ever forget YHWH your God and walk after other gods and serve them and worship them, I *hereby* testify against you *today* that you will surely perish" (8:19). Since forgetfulness through violating the *Hauptgebot* (8:19; cf. 4:23) is the antithesis of remembering YHWH (8:18), Israel's tenure in the land is inextricably linked with continual loyalty to the deity who swore a ברית with the "fathers." All this is not to say that the ברית at Horeb is "conditional" but that reference to the "fathers" in Deuteronomy 8 hardly signals an "unconditional" gift of land to the patriarchs.

Third and most important, Moses' exhortations for Israel to "remember" and not "forget" are imaginative speech-acts that initiate a rhetorical progression in the referent of the "fathers" from the patriarchs to all of Israel's ancestors. In Deuteronomy 8, Moses uses imaginative speech-acts to address his hearers as a single generation that experiences everything from the "house of slavery" (8:14) to the "good land" (8:7, 10), as well as "these forty years" (8:2, 4; cf. 2:14) in between. Moses transports his audience backward in time to "remember" (8:2) the wilderness, which he then describes using language that has no parallel in the OT except in Deuteronomy itself (i.e., chap. 29). The wilderness was the place not only of punishment (1:34–35; cf. Num 14:22–25) but also of humbling (8:2–3, 16) and discipline (8:5) that ultimately resulted in Israel's "good" (8:16). Likewise, Moses recalls the hunger (8:3) and physical threats (8:15) of the wilderness suffered by his audience only for the purpose of contrast with YHWH's provision of food (8:3; 29:5[6]), clothing (8:4; 29:4[5]), and water (8:15b; 29:5[6]) there. Thus the real objects of remembrance are YHWH and his faithfulness rather than the privations of the wilderness.[150]

Moses' description of the manna as that which "your fathers did not know" (8:3, 16) not only emphasizes its unexpected character but also recalls the narrative account of manna-giving in Exodus 16. In response to the grumbling hunger of the Israelites (Exod 16:2–3), YHWH promised to

---

149. Cf. Perlitt ("Motive und Schichten der Landtheologie im Deuteronomium," 105–6), who recognizes a mixture of "conditional" and "unconditional" elements in Deuteronomy 8 but regards them as evidence of redactional layers.

150. C. T. Begg ("Bread, Wine, and Strong Drink in Deut 29:5a," *Bijdr* 41 [1980] 260–75) discusses the pedagogical link between the wilderness wanderings (29:2–5a[3–6a]) and the "recognition formula" ("so that you might know that I am YHWH your God"; 29:5b[6b]).

provide food (Exod 16:4–12). The gift of manna was initially befuddling to the people: "When the sons of Israel saw [the manna], they said to one another, 'What is it?' For they did *not know* [לֹא יָדְעוּ] what it was" (Exod 16:15).[151] In the same context, Israel's "not-knowing" of manna (Exod 16:15) prominently contrasts with two preceding instances of ידע in the "recognition formula":[152] YHWH earnestly desires his people to "know" (ידע) him as (1) the God of the exodus (16:6); and (2) the God who alone can provide food in the wilderness (16:12). The repeated use of ידע in proximity constitutes a *Leitwort* usage in which Israel's "not-knowing" of manna (Exod 16:15) highlights its supernatural quality and signals its greater purpose in helping Israel to "know" YHWH (Exod 16:12).

The same pedagogical link between food and knowledge of YHWH is found in Deut 8:3, for the "not-knowing" (ידע Qal) of manna was designed to "make known" (ידע Hiphil) to Israel that "man does not live by bread alone but by everything that comes out of the mouth of YHWH."[153] Because Exodus 16 furnishes Deuteronomy 8's narrative and paronomastic background, Deuteronomy 8 seems to envision "you" and "your fathers" as the first and second wilderness generations, respectively, who at first did not "know" (i.e., recognize) YHWH's gift of manna but eventually consumed it during "these forty years" (8:2, 4). This emphasis on generational continuity mirrors the theological transformation of the wilderness from a death-giving (chaps. 1–3) to a life-giving place (chap. 8).[154] The parallelism between "your fathers" and "you" thus enables Moses to highlight the two generations' common experience of YHWH's provision in the wilderness.

Moses' rhetorical strategy of identifying "you" as the generation at Moab also empowers the imaginative speech-act of catapulting his audience forward into a "good land" (8:7, 10). Much like Deut 6:10, Moses vivifies the land's prosperity by characterizing Israel's future settlement as an accomplished reality: "When you have eaten and are satisfied, and have built good houses and lived in them, and when your herds and your flocks

---

151. Though Römer (*Israels Väter*, 78) excludes Exod 16:15 from his consideration of Deut 8:18 because Exod 16:15 is ostensibly a Priestly and therefore postdeuteronomic text, the formulaic and scanty description of the manna in Deuteronomy 8 presumes awareness of manna's etiology. In Deut 8:3, the shared terminology of לחם ("bread"; Exod 16:3, 4, 8, 12, 15, 22, 29, 32) and פה ("mouth"; Exod 16:18, 21) provide further evidence that Exodus 16 stands in the background. Regardless of which text came first, the two are likely intended to be read together.

152. See discussion of the "recognition formula" on pp. 103–104 above.

153. J. T. Willis ("Man Does Not Live by Bread Alone," *ResQ* 16 [1973] 141–49) demonstrates that Deut 8:3 is asserting Israel's need to trust YHWH in everything rather than drawing a dichotomy between physical and spiritual realities.

154. See Gomes de Araújo (*Theologie der Wüste*, 325–32), who uses the differing conceptions of the wilderness as a negative place of punishment (i.e., Deuteronomy 1–3) and a positive place of discipline (i.e., Deuteronomy 8) as redaction-critical criteria. However, Miller (*Deuteronomy*, 115) notes that the same father-son imagery is used in 1:31 and 8:5 to denote God's protection and discipline.

multiply, and your silver and gold multiply, and all that you have multiplies . . ." (8:12–13). The dangers of corporate amnesia amidst such abundance (8:11, 14) lead Moses to interrupt his forward looking imaginative speech-act of the land with another backward-looking imaginative speech-act of the wilderness: "He [Yhwh] led you through the great and terrible wilderness, with fiery serpents and scorpions and thirsty ground where there was no water; he brought water for you out of the rock of flint. In the wilderness he fed you manna that your fathers did not know" (8:15–16a; cf. 8:2–4). Though Moses' idyllic description of water (8:7), food (8:8–9a), and natural resources (8:9b) in the land contrasts starkly with the lack of basic sustenance in the wilderness (8:15–16), it is quite astonishing that Moses' imaginative speech-acts of these vastly divergent places share the pedagogical aim of stimulating Israel to corporate remembrance of Yhwh's faithfulness, whether in poverty or prosperity.[155]

The Dynamic Referent of the ברית with the "Fathers" in Deuteronomy 8:18

Moses further supplements his directive speech-acts for "this day" (8:11, 18, 19) with another imaginative speech-act that undermines the errant imagination of the people. Just as the challenges of conquest may lead Israel to further grumbling (7:17–18), the future day of satiety may lead to a narcissistic monologue: "*My* power and the strength of *my* hand have made *for myself* this wealth" (8:17). Moses counters that "Yhwh your God . . . is the one who is giving you power to make wealth, so that he may confirm his covenant that he swore to your fathers" (8:18). The reversal of the people's monologue rebuts an act of "disobedient imagination" with Moses' own act of "radical obedient imagination."[156] However, Moses' assertion that the fulfillment of Yhwh's covenant with the "fathers" entails the ability for Israel to "make wealth" (עשׂה חיל) never appears in Genesis and is only hinted at in Exodus–Numbers in the numerous references to a "good land" (e.g., Exod 3:8; Num 14:7) and a "land flowing with milk and honey" (e.g., Exod 3:17; 33:3; Num 14:8). Ultimately the language of the land's potential for creating prosperity finds its closest parallels in the covenant blessings and curses of Deuteronomy itself. In terms of blessings, Moses' stress on the land as the place where Israel and its possessions will "multiply" (4× in Deut 8:1, 13) mirrors the various predictions of Israel's multiplication in Deut 1:11; 6:3; 7:13–14; 26:1–2, 15; 28:3–12. These Deuteronomic passages emphasize the interpenetration of a fruitful people

---

155. Van Leeuwen ("What Comes out of God's Mouth," 55–57), F. I. Andersen (*The Sentence in Biblical Hebrew* [The Hague: Mouton, 1974] 138–39), and J. Cogswell ("Lest We Forget: A Sermon," *Int* 15 [1961] 32–34) demonstrate that the contrast between remembrance and forgetfulness is programmatic for Deut 8:11–18.

156. Brueggemann, "Imagination," 22.

with a fruitful land in a manner not found in the Tetrateuch.[157] In terms of curses, Moses' declarative speech-act in 8:19 asserting that "you will *surely perish*" (אבד תאבדון) for "walking after other gods" (הלך אחרי אלהים אחרים) mirrors the covenant curses of Israel's de-multiplication found in Deut 4:26; 11:26–28; 28:15–68; 30:18.

The numerous lexical links between Deut 8:18–19 and these declarative speech-acts suggest that Yhwh's ברית with the "fathers" in 8:18 may refer to none other than the moment of covenant renewal reflected in the book of Deuteronomy itself. As in Deut 4:31 and 7:12, 8:18 captures Moses speaking to Israel as a singular entity of "you"[158] that now views Israel's entire history retrospectively from within the land.[159] In another canonical moment, the generation that renews the covenant at Moab has become the ancestors of all landed generations of Israel so that this reference to Yhwh's ברית with the "fathers" (8:18) constitutes a *mise-en-abyme* for the entire book of Deuteronomy. But even if the ברית with the "fathers" (8:18) does not refer to Deuteronomy itself, the "fathers" in this passage clearly represent more than the patriarchs in light of the forward progression of the "fathers" in 8:3 and 8:16. At the very least, Moses has refracted an ancient promise to the patriarchs through the imaginative lenses of the wilderness wanderings and conquest (8:2–17) so that the "fathers" in 8:18 now recall both the patriarchs and the exodus generation as Israel's ancestors.

The oath of land to the ancestors (Deut 8:1) is no longer primarily a matter of territory (cf. Gen 13:14–17) or of a destination after deliverance from Egypt (cf. Exod 6:6–8) but has now been actuated in chaps. 7–8 as a full-orbed symbol of the inherent dialectic in divine election (7:6–8). Land captures the theological tensions between promise and peril, divine grace and human obligation, and victorious confidence and sober humility. The rhetorical progression in the "fathers" in Deuteronomy 8 from the distant past to the immediate ancestors of Moses' audience imaginatively channels the lessons from Israel's past and future into the directive (8:1, 6, 11) and declarative (8:19–20) speech-acts of covenant renewal in the narrative present, perhaps even including his immediate hearers as "fathers." In the covenant renewal ceremony at Moab, the Abrahamic and Israelite covenants seem to blend into a unified covenant that defies simple description by virtue of including both "unconditional" and "conditional" elements.

---

157. See the discussion of "The 'God of the Fathers' and the Promise of Multiplication" on pp. 110–127.

158. Compare with the discussion of Deuteronomy's theologically fraught use of the second-person singular by McConville, "Singular Address," 19–36.

159. It is striking that Moses' directive speech-act *"You shall remember* [Qal imperfect, future sense] that it is Yhwh your God who *is giving* [Qal participle, present sense] you power to make wealth . . . *as on this day"* (Deut 8:18) prescribes a future act of remembrance within the land, not a present act of remembrance at Moab. The object of future remembrance is the covenant renewal at Moab.

Divine-Human Covenant and the "Fathers" in Deuteronomy 29

The thesis that Deuteronomy envisions a single divine-human covenant for all of Israel's history finds its most explicit support in the two references to a ברית with the "fathers" in Deuteronomy 29. In Deut 29:9–14[10–15], Moses asserts that the present moment of decision at Moab stands in essential continuity with Yhwh's covenantal dealings with present, past, and future generations of Israel. In addition, the referent of "fathers" shifts forward in time to denote both the patriarchs (29:12[13]; cf. 30:20) and a later generation with whom Yhwh made a covenant after the exodus (29:24[25]; cf. 30:5, 9).

Although these shifting chronological horizons have been the object of frequent redaction-critical reconstruction,[160] space considerations dictate that this final case study will take a mostly synchronic approach to Deuteronomy 29. Similar diachronic issues have been discussed extensively in the analyses of Deuteronomy 4, 30, and 34 in part 1 above. In the present analysis, I proceed from a brief speech-act analysis of Deuteronomy 29 to explore the wider theological implications of a single divine-human covenant in Deuteronomic covenant theology. If the covenant renewal ceremony at Moab not only looks backward to the patriarchal and Israelite covenants but also looks forward to anticipate and perhaps even include the "new covenant" found in Jeremiah and Ezekiel, how would this theologoumenon refine the appropriation of Deuteronomic covenant theology in OT scholarship? The reappraisal of Deuteronomic covenant theology as the imaginative and indefinite continuation of a gracious oath that began with Israel's ancestors can offer a corrective to caricatures of Deuteronomy as "second law," "obligation," and "conditional."

The first reference to a divine-human covenant in Deuteronomy 29 is the contested chapter heading found in Deut 28:69[29:1] rather than Moses' actual utterance of the declarative speech-acts that renew the divine-human covenant (29:9–14[10–15]). The verse in question reads as follows: "These are the words of the covenant that Yhwh commanded Moses to make with the Israelites in the land of Moab, *in addition to* [מלבד] the covenant that he had made with them at Horeb" (28:69[29:1]). The difference in versification between the MT, on the one hand (i.e., 28:69[29:1]), and the LXX, Vulgate, and English versions, on the other (i.e., 29:1), represents a longstanding debate over whether Deut 28:69[29:1] functions as a colophon for the preceding chapters or as a superscription to the third

---

160. While the history of interpretation for Deuteronomy 29 is contentious, historical critics generally regard this chapter as a late, composite text based on its extensive references to exile. The latest survey of Deuteronomy research by E. Otto ("Perspektiven," 319–40) affirms the consensus of exilic or postexilic dates for Deuteronomy 4, 29, and 30.

speech of Moses (29:1[2]–30:20). As a colophon, 28:69[29:1] would indicate that the "words of the covenant" at Moab supplement Moses' exposition of the Horeb covenant (4:44–28:68) and thereby emphasize the continuity between the words spoken at Horeb and Moab.[161] As a superscription, 28:69[29:1] would indicate that the phrase "words of the covenant" at Moab is anticipatory in nature and therefore distinct from the covenant at Horeb.[162]

The debate over the function of Deut 28:69[29:1] is significant, because the central issue at stake is the theological relationship between the covenant(s) at Horeb and Moab. Adherents of the superscription view typically argue that Deuteronomy 29 was added by postexilic writers in order to draw a distinction between Horeb and Moab.[163] Whether or not Deuteronomy 29 is a secondary insertion,[164] however, the rhetorical strategy of the final form of this chapter is similar to the Deuteronomic passages already treated in the above case studies. First, Moses opens his third address by repeating the imaginative speech-acts that transport his audience back to the exodus ("your eyes have seen"; 29:1–2[2–3]; cf. 4:34; 7:19), the wilderness wanderings ("I have led you forty years in the wilderness"; 29:4–5[5–6]; cf. 8:2–4), and the defeat of the Amorite kings and the partitioning of their land (29:6–7[7–8]; cf. 2:26–3:17). The same appeals to Yhwh's past benevolence are central to Moses' parenetic strategy.

Second, Moses issues a directive speech-act for Israel to "keep [שמר] the words of this covenant" (29:8[9]). Even if 28:69[29:1] is a superscription, it is striking that this command is only intelligible with reference to the

---

161. H. F. van Rooy ("Deuteronomy 28:69: Superscript or Subscript?" *JNSL* 14 [1988] 215–22) argues for the minority view that the phrase "words of the covenant" usually denotes both the covenant statutes and the curses befalling the disobedient (e.g., Jer 11:8). Since Deuteronomy 29–30 is devoid of such obligations (cf. 29:27[28]), van Rooy regards 28:69[29:1] as a concluding colophon to Deut 1:1 ("these are the words that Moses spoke . . ."). The colophon view is shared by Lundbom ("Inclusio," 312–13), Craigie (*Deuteronomy*, 353), and Driver (*Deuteronomy*, 319), among others.

162. N. Lohfink ("Dtn 28,69: Überschrift oder Kolophon?" *BN* 64 [1992] 40–52) argues for the majority view that Deut 28:69[29:1] is one of four superscriptions with demonstrative pronouns that introduce new sections in Deuteronomy (e.g., 1:1; 4:44; 28:69[29:1]; 33:1). Lohfink also argues that the use of ברית in 28:69[29:1] anticipates the seven uses in 29:1–24[2–25], since the term is mostly absent from the preceding chapters.

163. Olson, *Deuteronomy and the Death of Moses*, 155, 175–76; Lenchak, *Choose Life*, 167; A. Cholewinski, "Zur theologischen Deutung des Moabbundes," *Bib* 66 (1985) 96–111; Preuss, *Deuteronomium*, 157–59; Braulik, "Ausdrücke," 43–45, 61–62; N. Lohfink, "Der Bundesschluß im Land Moab: Redaktionsgeschichtliches zu Dt 28,69–32,47," *BZ* 6 (1962) 32–36.

164. Cholewinski asserts that the use of מלבד in 28:69[29:1] indicates that the covenant at Moab is "ein neuer selbständiger Bund" ("Zur theologischen Deutung des Moabbundes," 96). However, Barker (*Triumph of Grace in Deuteronomy*, 113) notes that מלבד usually means "in addition to" (e.g., Gen 26:1; Lev 9:17; Num 29:16; 1 Kgs 10:13) rather than "in place of" (Dan 11:4).

stipulations in Deuteronomy 5–26 since Deuteronomy 29–30 contains no covenant stipulations for Israel to "keep" (cf. 4:44; 5:1).[165]

Third, Moses ratifies the covenant through his performative declaration of the *Bundesformel*: "that he [Y<small>HWH</small>] may establish you *today* as his people and that he may be your God" (cf. 26:16–19; 27:9).[166] The continuity between Horeb and Moab is reflected especially in the parallels between Deuteronomy 29 and the theological progression of imaginative, directive, and declarative speech-acts in Deuteronomy 4, Moses' most detailed exposition of the Horeb theophany and revelation.[167] The imaginative use of anachronism coalesces the generations so that the "you" who stood at Horeb becomes the same "you" who now stand at Moab on the verge of entering the land.[168] Since the theological continuity between Horeb and Moab is generally recognized even by scholars who regard Deut 28:69[29:1] as a superscription,[169] this verse probably performs a transitional function in linking Horeb to Moab (see Deut 29:11–13[12–14]).[170]

Deuteronomy 29:11–13[12–14]

¹¹לְעָבְרְךָ בִּבְרִית יְהוָה אֱלֹהֶיךָ וּבְאָלָתוֹ	¹²... to [enter] into the covenant of Y<small>HWH</small> your God and into his oath
אֲשֶׁר יְהוָה אֱלֹהֶיךָ כֹּרֵת עִמְּךָ הַיּוֹם	that Y<small>HWH</small> your God is making with you today,
¹²לְמַעַן הָקִים־אֹתְךָ הַיּוֹם לוֹ לְעָם	¹³in order that he might establish you today as his people,
וְהוּא יִהְיֶה־לְּךָ לֵאלֹהִים	and that he might be your God,
כַּאֲשֶׁר דִּבֶּר־לָךְ	just as he promised you
וְכַאֲשֶׁר נִשְׁבַּע לַאֲבֹתֶיךָ	and just as he swore to your fathers,
לְאַבְרָהָם לְיִצְחָק וּלְיַעֲקֹב	to Abraham, Isaac, and Jacob.
¹³וְלֹא אִתְּכֶם לְבַדְּכֶם	¹⁴Now, not with you only
אָנֹכִי כֹּרֵת אֶת־הַבְּרִית הַזֹּאת	am I making this covenant
וְאֶת־הָאָלָה הַזֹּאת	and this oath ...

Moses' speech-acts expand beyond the blending of the Horeb and Moab generations to establish Y<small>HWH</small>'s covenant with all generations of Israel in

---

165. Rofé ("Covenant in the Land of Moab," 276–78) sees a Hittite treaty structure in Deut 28:69[29:1]–30:20. Though Rofé identifies 29:14–20[15–21] as covenant stipulations, he concedes that the final form of these verses is more like curses than stipulations.

166. Lohfink ("Bund als Vertrag," 226–28) notes that the performative marker היום appears 5× in Deut 29:9–14[10–15]. Cf. also Braulik, "Deuteronomium 1–4 als Sprechakt," 249–53.

167. See the discussion of "Covenantal Speech-Acts in Deuteronomy 4" on pp. 187–188.

168. Millar, "Living at the Place of Decision," 41–49.

169. E.g., Barker, *Triumph of Grace in Deuteronomy*, 112–6; N. Lohfink, "Zur Fabel des Deuteronomiums," in *Bundesdokument und Gesetz: Studien zum Deuteronomium* (HBS 4; Freiburg: Herder, 1995) 65–78.

170. Christensen, *Deuteronomy 21:10–34:12*, 664–66; cf. E. Otto (*Das Deuteronomium im Pentateuch und Hexateuch: Studien zur Literaturgeschichte von Pentateuch und Hexateuch im Lichte des Deuteronomiumrahmens* [FAT 30; Tübingen: Mohr Siebeck, 2000] 138–41), who arrives at the same conclusion using a redaction-critical method.

Deut 29:9–14[10–15] (see table 7.2, p. 226). The chiastic structure of this section indicates that past, present, and future generations are all included in the invocation of the bilateral *Bundesformel* at the center.[171]

Several features of this section bespeak the corporate solidarity of Israel's generations under a singular covenant. First, Moses' audience in this ratification ceremony includes both the present generation who is "arraying yourselves here today . . . before YHWH your God" (29:9[10]; cf. 14a[15a]) as well as future generations who are "not with us here today" (14b[15b]).[172] Much as Moses links the present generation to the covenant at Horeb ("YHWH made a covenant with *us* at Horeb. Not with our fathers did YHWH make this covenant, but with all of us who are alive here today!"; 5:2–3), he now scrolls Israel's history forward to include future generations in the covenant renewal at Moab. Since Moab is itself an imaginative recapitulation of Horeb, as already demonstrated, the broad chronological horizons covered by Deut 5:3 and 29:9–14[10–15] ensure that the covenant at Horeb/Moab will remain valid for an unspecified number of future generations. Indeed, the lexical and conceptual links between Deuteronomy 4 and 29–30 and the "new covenant" oracles of the prophets have often been noted,[173] thereby raising the tantalizing possibility that the forward-looking ceremony at Moab anticipates every future divine-human covenant.[174]

---

171. Lenchak, *Choose Life*, 175; Lohfink, "Bundesschluß," 39.

172. Christensen, *Deuteronomy 21:10–34:12*, 718; Brueggemann, *Deuteronomy*, 261; Tigay, *Deuteronomy*, 278; Miller, *Deuteronomy*, 209; Mayes, *Deuteronomy*, 363–64; von Rad, *Deuteronomy*, 180. Compare the unlikely suggestion of Rofé ("Covenant in the Land of Moab," 272) that the phrase "those who are not here with us today" (29:13[14]) refers to absentees from the ratification ceremony, rather than all future generations. Since Moses has taken special pains to include "all of you" and "every man of Israel" (29:9[10]) among his present audience of "those who are *here with us today*" (29:14b[15b]), it seems that future generations are Moses' most likely referent for "those who are *not here with us* today." McConville rightly notes that "Deuteronomy 29, in fact, strains for inclusiveness" ("Singular Address," 28).

173. P. Buis ("La Nouvelle Alliance," *VT* 18 [1968] 1–7) identifies five formal features of "new covenant" oracles such as Jer 32:37–41: (1) restoration to the land; (2) definition of the covenant—that is, the *Bundesformel*; (3) interior renovation of God's people; (4) YHWH's promise to ratify a covenant; and (5) covenant blessings. Buis notes that Deut 30:1–10 contains element 1 ("YHWH your God will restore your captivity"; 30:3), element 3 ("YHWH your God will circumcise your heart"; 30:6), and element 5 ("YHWH your God will give you excess"; 30:9). Cholewinski ("Zur theologischen Deutung des Moabbundes," 10–19) comments further that elements 2 and 4 are found in Deut 29:12[13], leading him to assert that the covenant at Moab prefigures the "new covenant" of the prophets. In contrast, Lohfink, ("Der neue Bund im Buch Deuteronomium?," *ZABR* 4 [1998] 113–18) is more inclined to view Deuteronomy 4 and 29–30 as reflecting a general postexilic expectation of hope (e.g., the "unconditional" Abrahamic covenant of the Priestly school) rather than being literarily dependent on the prophets.

174. Rendtorff (*Covenant Formula*, 78–87) argues that the constancy of the *Bundesformel* in the Abrahamic (e.g., Gen 17:7), Israelite (e.g., Exod 19:5; 29:45; Deut 29:12[13]), and "new" covenants (Jer 31:33) suggests the existence of "the one, continually 'new' covenant" between YHWH and his people.

Table 7.2. Yhwh's Covenant with All Generations of Israel
(Deut 29:9–14[10–15])

Marker	Hebrew	English
A. vv. 9–10 [10–11] (Audience)	אַתֶּם נִצָּבִים הַיּוֹם כֻּלְּכֶם לִפְנֵי יְהוָה אֱלֹהֵיכֶם טַפְּכֶם נְשֵׁיכֶם . . . וְגֵרְךָ אֲשֶׁר בְּקֶרֶב מַחֲנֶיךָ מֵחֹטֵב עֵצֶיךָ עַד שֹׁאֵב מֵימֶיךָ	You are arraying yourselves *today*,[a] all of you before Yhwh your God, . . . your children, your wives, and the alien who is in your camps, from the one who chops your wood to the one who draws your water,
B. v. 11[12] (Purpose)	לְעָבְרְךָ בִּבְרִית יְהוָה אֱלֹהֶיךָ וּבְאָלָתוֹ אֲשֶׁר יְהוָה אֱלֹהֶיךָ כֹּרֵת עִמְּךָ הַיּוֹם	to [enter] into the covenant of Yhwh your God and into his oath that Yhwh your God is making with you *today*,
C. v. 12[13] (Declaration)	לְמַעַן הָקִים־ אֹתְךָ הַיּוֹם לְעָם וְהוּא יִהְיֶה־לְּךָ לֵאלֹהִים כַּאֲשֶׁר דִּבֶּר־לָךְ וְכַאֲשֶׁר נִשְׁבַּע לַאֲבֹתֶיךָ לְאַבְרָהָם לְיִצְחָק וּלְיַעֲקֹב	in order that he might establish you *today* as his people and that he might be your God, just as he promised *you* and just as he swore to your *fathers*, to Abraham, Isaac, and Jacob.
B′. v. 13[14] (Purpose)	וְלֹא אִתְּכֶם לְבַדְּכֶם אָנֹכִי כֹּרֵת אֶת־הַבְּרִית הַזֹּאת וְאֶת־הָאָלָה הַזֹּאת	Now, not with you only am I making this covenant and this oath
A′. v. 14[15] (Audience)	כִּי אֶת־אֲשֶׁר יֶשְׁנוֹ פֹּה עִמָּנוּ עֹמֵד הַיּוֹם לִפְנֵי יְהוָה אֱלֹהֵינוּ וְאֵת אֲשֶׁר אֵינֶנּוּ פֹּה עִמָּנוּ הַיּוֹם	but with those who are here with us standing *today* before Yhwh our God and those who are not here with us *today*.

a. The chiastic diagram shown here omits the comprehensive list of Israel's persons in vv. 9b–10, which Lenchak (*Choose Life*, 96–101) identifies as the most comprehensive "participant list" in the entire OT. Cf. McConville, "Singular Address," 27–29.

Second, the oneness of Israel in Deut 29:9–14[10–15] is reinforced by Moses' rapid shifts between singular and plural, and first- and second-person forms. He addresses all the diverse sorts of individuals in his audience ("all of you," "every man of Israel"; 29:9[10]) in the second-person plural (A, B′), shifts to the collective singular in the performative language of covenant ratification (B, C), and concludes with an inclusive description of his present audience in the first-person plural (A′). Lenchak's remarks concerning the theological significance of the *Numeruswechsel* are equally applicable to the rhetorical shift from second- to first-person forms:

> Such sudden shifts from singular to plural or vice versa were probably noticeable to listeners of the discourse. Members of the audience were addressed both as individuals and as a whole, reinforcing both of these

identities. The audience is not merely a mass of individuals, nor is it merely a cohesive whole. It is somehow both, and the speaker appeals to both. His appeal to the solidarity of the group reinforces his appeal to each individual.[175]

Moses not only asserts the *vertical* solidarity of Israel across generations; he also emphasizes the *horizontal* solidarity of the present generation at Moab/Horeb standing together "before Yhwh" (29:9[10], 14[15]).[176] The covenant renewal at Moab thus includes individual members of the people as well as the entire people as a timeless unity.[177]

Third and most important for this study, several aspects of the ברית and *Bundesformel* language introduce a transgenerational trajectory that leads to the creative conflation of the patriarchs and exodus generation(s) later in Deuteronomy 29–30. The covenantal formulations in Deut 29:11–12[12–13] are a mixture of those found especially in Genesis 17 and Exodus 6, two key Priestly texts. On the one hand, Deut 29:11–12[12–13] represents one of only two OT instances (cf. Gen 17:7) in which the *Bundesformel* specifies the content of a divine-human ברית,[178] demonstrating conclusively that this ברית is a relational matter that includes stipulations, rather than a solely legal matter that lacks relational components.[179] The lexical links between Deut 29:12[13] and Gen 17:7 are strengthened by their common use of the verb הקים ("to establish, confirm") to denote covenant-making.[180] As already noted, this terminology in Deut 29:12[13] is a surprising use of Priestly language that differs from the Deuteronomic idiom (i.e., כרת ברית).

On the other hand, several features of Deut 29:11–12[12–13] are not found in Gen 17:7 and evoke Exodus 6, another passage attributed to the Priestly school that draws upon Genesis 17 but expands the divine promises found there from a familial to a national scope.[181] While the *Bundesformel* in Gen 17:7 contains only the unilateral formula that Yhwh will be God to Abraham and his descendants, the *Bundesformel* in Exod 6:7 also contains the reciprocal statement that Israel will be a people to Yhwh, thereby anticipating the bilateral *Bundesformel* found in Deut 29:12[13].[182]

These connections between Deuteronomy 29 and Exodus 6 are reinforced by two other features. First, the motivation for establishing the *Bundesformel* in both passages is Yhwh's remembrance of an ancient promise to

---

175. Lenchak, *Choose Life*, 106.
176. The collocation of the verb עמד and the prepositional phrase לפני יהוה recalls Moses' imaginative speech-act of Horeb in Deut 4:10–11. See the discussion of לפני יהוה and the Deuteronomic journey motif on pp. 133–134 above.
177. Polzin, *Moses*, 69–71.
178. Rendtorff, *Covenant Formula*, 42, 69; Skweres, *Rückverweise*, 131.
179. Contra Kutsch, *Verheissung*, 146–8.
180. However, Deut 29:12[13] differs slightly from Gen 17:7 in that Yhwh "establishes" (הקים) his "people" (עם; Deut 29:12[13]) rather than his "covenant" (ברית; Gen 17:7). The Deuteronomic language of "making" a ברית is retained in 29:11[12].
181. Rendtorff, *Covenant Formula*, 49–51; Childs, *Exodus*, 114.
182. Skweres, *Rückverweise*, 179.

Abraham, Isaac, and Jacob (Exod 6:4, 8; cf. 2:24; Deut 29:12[13]). Second, the means of consummating the *Bundesformel* in Exodus 6 and Deuteronomy 29 is the miraculous deliverance from Egypt (Exod 6:6; Deut 29:1[2]; cf. 4:20; 7:8).

A Single, Timeless Covenant in Deuteronomy 29:9–14[10–15]

The same collocation of bilateral *Bundesformel* and the exodus from Egypt is found in Exodus 19 and Leviticus 26, two seminal texts that begin and end Moses' promulgation of the covenant at Sinai. In light of the rhetorical prominence of the *Bundesformel* in the canonical form of the Pentateuch, Rolf Rendtorff incisively concludes that the ratification ceremony in Deuteronomy 29 is the endpoint of the narrative journey that began with YHWH's desire to "establish" a covenant with Abraham in Genesis 17.[183] Exodus 6, 19, and Leviticus 26 serve as theological bridges between the promises to Abraham's family and their fulfillment for the Israelite people.[184] In light of Rendtorff's observations, it seems that the ברית עולם ("eternal covenant") that YHWH inaugurates with Abraham in Gen 17:7 corresponds to the timeless covenant and oath that Moses ratifies "both with those who stand here with us today ... and with those who are not with us here today" (Deut 29:14[15]; cf. 5:3).[185]

The transgenerational significance of this *Bundesformel* is confirmed by the double "promise formulas" in Deut 29:12b[13b]. The bilateral establishment of YHWH as Israel's God and Israel as YHWH's people (29:12a[13a])

---

183. Rendtorff, *Covenant Formula*, 25–28.

184. The links between Deuteronomy 29 and Genesis 17, Exodus 19, Leviticus 26 are strengthened not only by the recurrence of the *Bundesformel* but also by recent studies indicating that the covenant theology of each of these passages is simultaneously "unconditional" and "conditional." Scholars once commonly argued that the Holiness Code's conception of covenant is a late compromise between the conditionality of Deuteronomy and the unconditionality of the Priestly writer. See the discussion by Lohfink, "Abänderung," 157–68; and Zimmerli, "Sinaibund," 205–16.

However, the unworkability of the older view about the unconditional covenant theology of the Priestly source, especially Genesis 17, has been demonstrated by S. D. Mason (*'Eternal Covenant' in the Pentateuch: The Contours of an Elusive Phrase* [LHB/OTS 494; New York: T. & T. Clark, 2008] 89–122). Similarly, J. Milgrom ("Covenants: The Sinaitic and Patriarchal Covenants in the Holiness Code [Leviticus 17–27]," in *Sefer Moshe: The Moshe Weinfeld Jubilee Volume: Studies in the Bible and the Ancient Near East, Qumran, and Postbiblical Judaism* [ed. C. Cohen, A. Hurvitz, and S. M. Paul; Winona Lake, IN: Eisenbrauns, 2004] 91–101) shows that Leviticus 26 not only regards both the Abrahamic and the Israelite covenants as conditional; it even blends them into a single entity, much like Deuteronomy's reference to a covenant with the "fathers." Cf. J. Joosten, "Covenant Theology in the Holiness Code," *ZABR* 4 (1998) 146–64.

185. Despite this pregnant possibility, Mason's study (*Eternal Covenant*) reflects the unfortunate tendency to analyze the Priestly phrase ברית עולם without reference to Deut 29:9–14[10–15] even though Priestly language (i.e., הקים ברית) and a timeless covenant are also found there.

represents a long-awaited fulfillment for two different generations of God's people (29:12b[13b]): (1) "just as he promised *you*";[186] and (2) "just as he swore to *your fathers*, to Abraham, Isaac, and Jacob." While the "fathers" are still identified here as the patriarchs, the parallelism between "you" and "your fathers" in these promise formulas indicates that they are common participants in a *Bundesformel* that radiates outward from the ceremony at Moab into the past and the future. The "emphatic contemporaneity"[187] of the current moment in unifying Israel is punctuated further by five occurrences of the performative interjection היום, which binds past and future generations in a cultic היום that is "continually repeated and hence continuously present."[188] In summary, the performative force of the present *Bundesformel* in coalescing Israel's ancestors into a unified entity prepares for the rhetorical shift in the following reference to the "fathers" as the Horeb/Moab generation (29:24[25]).

Deuteronomy 29:24[25]

וְאָמְרוּ	Then they will say,
עַל אֲשֶׁר עָזְבוּ	"[It is] because they abandoned
אֶת־בְּרִית יְהוָה אֱלֹהֵי אֲבֹתָם	the covenant of Yhwh, God of their fathers,
אֲשֶׁר כָּרַת עִמָּם	that he made with them
בְּהוֹצִיאוֹ אֹתָם מֵאֶרֶץ מִצְרָיִם	when he brought them out of the land of Egypt."

The final Deuteronomic reference to Yhwh's ברית with the "fathers" falls within a section in which the audience's perspective shifts forward to "the generation to come, your sons who arise after you" (29:21[22]). The contingent blessings and curses of Deuteronomy 29 now become concretized as serial events in Israel's future.[189] In preempting the wayward Israelite who "blesses himself [ברך Hithpael] in his heart, saying, 'I have peace though I walk in the stubbornness of my heart'" (29:18[19]),[190] Moses warns that this sort of hubris will result in the fiery destruction of the land in a manner akin to Sodom and Gomorrah (29:21–23[22–24]). In addition, Moses counters

---

186. Contra Skweres (*Rückverweise*, 179–80), the narrative referent for this promise to "you" (29:12[13]) is probably the bilateral *Bundesformel* found in 26:17–18 rather than the unilateral formula from Exod 19:5 (on which, see N. Lohfink, "Dt 26,17–19 und die 'Bundesformel,'" in *Studien zum Deuteronomium und zur deuteronomistischen Literatur* [SBAB 8; Stuttgart: Katholisches Bibelwerk, 1995] 211–61). In addition to these lexical links, Deut 26:17–18 is more closely related to 29:9–14[10–15] in the narrative world of the book. As in 26:1–19, the rhetoric of Moses in 29:1–20[2–21] treats the first and second exodus generations as the singular entity "you."
187. Von Rad, *From Genesis to Chronicles*, 22–23.
188. De Vries, *Yesterday*, 45.
189. McConville, *Grace in the End*, 134–39.
190. Compare similar monologues of arrogance in 8:17; 9:4–7; 15:9. The self-absorption connoted in the use of ברך Hithpael ("to bless oneself; 29:18[19]) contrasts starkly with the use of ברך passive participles to denote Yhwh's covenant blessings in 28:1–14.

the disobedient imagination in Israel's לבב ("heart"; 2× in 29:18[19])[191] by placing an imaginative speech-act on the lips of horrified pagan observers: "All the nations [גוים] will say, 'Why has YHWH done thus to this land? Why this great outburst of anger?'" (29:23[24]). An unspecified voice responds: "[It is] because they abandoned the covenant of YHWH, God of their fathers, that he made with them when he brought them out of the land of Egypt'" (29:24[25]).[192] The anonymous speaker's comments on Israel's violation of the *Hauptgebot* (29:25[26]) and its punishment in the form of "every curse that is written in this book" (29:26[27]) betray a familiarity with YHWH's ways that Israel sadly lacks. Moses imagines the ironic day when pagans will comprehend the *Bundesformel* (29:12[13]) more fully than God's own people, who foolishly turn aside to worship "gods whom they have not known and whom he [YHWH] had not allotted to them" (29:25[26]).[193]

Speaking imaginatively from a vantage point after the exile, Moses' referent for the ברית with the "fathers" in Deut 29:24[25] is unclear due to the ambiguous referent of "them" in the two clauses in the latter part of the verse. First, the relative clause describing YHWH's covenant "that he made with *them*" could identify "them" as either "their fathers" or those who abandoned YHWH's covenant. Second, the temporal clause describing the occasion of covenant-making as "when he brought *them* out of Egypt" suffers from the same ambiguity. Are the "fathers" in Deut 29:24[25] the Horeb/Moab generation or a pre-exodus generation, perhaps even the patriarchs? In slightly different ways, the LXX and Vulgate disambiguate the Hebrew syntax by identifying the "fathers" as the Horeb/Moab generation.[194] Römer draws the same conclusion using a somewhat convoluted redactional comparison with 2 Chr 7:22, 1 Kgs 9:9, and Jer 22:9.[195]

In contrast to text- and redaction-critical proposals working alone, the view that Moses recasts the "fathers" as the blended generation at Horeb/

---

191. Barker (*Triumph of Grace in Deuteronomy*, 157–68) observes that לבב functions as a *Leitwort* in Deuteronomy 29–30 (e.g., 29:3[4], 17[18], 18[19]; 30:1, 2, 6, 10). Israel's lack of a "heart to know" (29:3; cf. vv. 17, 18) will find its ultimate remedy in YHWH's promise to "circumcise your heart and that of your seed, to love YHWH your God with all your heart [לבב] and with all your soul so that you may live" (30:6; cf. 10:15).

192. The reference to deliverance from Egypt (29:24) is especially poignant since Moses had just imagined Israel in Egypt, with its empty idolatry of "their abominations and their idols of wood, stone, silver, and gold" (29:15–16[16–17]). Yet Israel later succumbs to these very same vices (29:25[26]).

193. This use of ידע is an ironic reversal of the "recognition formula" found elsewhere in Deuteronomy (e.g., 4:35, 49; 29:5[6]; cf. 5:6).

194. The LXX inserts the phrase ἃ διέθετο τοῖς πατράσιν αὐτῶν after the divine name and epithet κυρίου θεοῦ τῶν πατέρων αὐτῶν, thus identifying the "fathers" with the generation that received the covenant at Horeb. Similarly, the Vulg. does not translate the appositive אלהי אבתם and renders the subordinate clauses "quod pepigit cum patribus eorum quando eduxit eos de terra Aegypti."

195. Römer, *Israels Väter*, 130–33.

Moab receives broader support by observing the broader movement from the present to the future in Deut 29:21[22]–30:20. Earlier Moses had portrayed the "fathers" as a generation that received but had not experienced the divine promises, whether it was the generation of the patriarchs (e.g., 1:8) or of a landless people (e.g., 26:15). But the "fathers" now become the very audience to whom Moses is speaking in order to highlight the gravity of Israel's present decision between "life and prosperity, and death and destruction" (30:15). While the Horeb/Moab generation can potentially be the cursed generation of "fathers" that forsakes Yhwh's covenant (29:24[25]), Moses does not hesitate to transform the "fathers" into the blessed generation that possesses the land and experiences multiplication (30:5, 9; cf. 28:63). Thus Moses' imaginative speech-acts project the "fathers" into different lights and time periods (cf. 30:20) in order to illustrate the whole range of Israel's destinies, both potential and actual. The possibility of Moses' audience's becoming both cursed and blessed generations of "fathers" in Deuteronomy 29–30 mirrors the theological use of "you" in the *Generationswechsel* of Deuteronomy 1–3.[196]

These imaginative speech-acts of corporate solidarity furnish the rhetorical backing for the climactic speech-acts in 30:19-20. Moses actualizes the covenant through a declarative speech-act: "I *hereby* call heaven and earth to witness against you *today*, that I have *hereby* set before you life and death, the blessing and the curse" (30:19a).[197] Now that the covenant is in effect, Moses adds a directive speech-act for Israel to act wisely for the sake of present and future generations: "So *choose life* in order that you may live, both *you and your seed*" (30:19b). Finally, Moses ascribes to the Horeb/Moab generation the ability to obey Yhwh (30:20a) and thereby remain in the land for "length of days" (30:20b), creatively positioning his present audience as the ancestors of all who dwell continually in the land. This constitutes a final imaginative speech-act that binds the Horeb/Moab generation with Israel's original ancestors in a shared promise of the "land that Yhwh swore to give to your *fathers*, to Abraham, Isaac, and Jacob" (30:20b).[198]

---

196. See the analysis of Deuteronomy 30 on pp. 73–80 above.

197. Braulik ("Deuteronomium 1–4 als Sprechakt," 252 n. 5) identifies the entire unit of Deut 30:15-20 as performative speech. However, the declarative speech-act in 30:19 is a discrete utterance that is distinguished by its first-person perfect forms of עוד Hiphil (cf. 4:26) and נתן לפני (cf. 1:8) as well as the interjection היום (see p. 167 above). The efficaciousness of the covenant curses and blessings is proven by Yhwh's private warning to Moses that Israel's disobedience (31:16) will surely result in divine punishment (31:17–18).

198. Deut 30:20 is unique in the book in that it identifies the patriarchs as the sole recipients of the land gift. However, the corporate solidarity of Israel's generations found explicitly in the first land-promise formula (i.e., 1:8) is implicitly continued in 30:20 by identifying the Horeb/Moab generation as "fathers" (i.e., 29:24[25]; 30:5, 9) who, like the patriarchs, receive Yhwh's gift of land.

Conclusion

The examination of Deuteronomic covenant theology has revealed the ubiquity of rhetorical progressions among imaginative, directive, and declarative speech-acts of Yhwh's oath and covenant with the "fathers." The artful rhetorical linkage between the imaginative speech-acts of Yhwh's past and future grace and the directive speech-acts of Yhwh's present commands indicates that divine initiative always entails human responsibility, while human obedience is never demanded without a prior act of divine grace. The theological interplay between grace and law suggests that Deuteronomy cannot be separated as readily into unconditional and conditional strands of covenant theology as has been claimed by redaction critics. Kutsch's view that covenant is essentially an issue of *Verpflichtung* must be discarded as theologically reductionistic, since Deuteronomy's account of covenant portrays Israel as experiencing different aspects of Yhwh's personal character in an unfolding history of obedience and disobedience.

Moreover, a speech-act approach to the book demonstrates that the *Generationswechsel* functions as an intentional rhetorical device that empowers the actualization of Yhwh's covenant with the "fathers" for the present generation at Moab and for future generations in the land and in exile. The referent of the "fathers" expands from the patriarchs in Deuteronomy 1 to encompass even Moses' present audience in Deuteronomy 30—if only for a brief rhetorical moment—in a climactic statement regarding the present generation's solidarity with all of Israel's ancestors who had received but still awaited fulfillment of Yhwh's promises. Deuteronomic covenant theology conceives of Israel in all its generations as a corporate entity that is bound to a single covenant that Yhwh made with the "fathers," which is a symbolic group that minimally includes the patriarchs but also expands to include other groups, depending on the chronological horizon occupied by the audience of the book. The rhetorical flexibility of the "fathers" enables Moses to proclaim to both his original and his later audiences the urgent need to actualize Yhwh's covenant for a new generation: "Not with our fathers did Yhwh make this covenant, *but with us, all of us who are alive here today*" (5:3).

Chapter 8
The "Fathers" in Deuteronomy: Conclusions and Avenues for Future Research

The shadow of Israel's "fathers" looms large in Deuteronomy. Throughout the book, the references to Israel's ancestors provide the dialogical connections between various generations of Israel's ancestors and Moses' current audience at Moab. I have indicated in this book that, rather than being strictly limited to a single generation of patriarchs or the Israelite adults and children who exited Egypt, the "fathers" function in Deuteronomy as a timeless symbol of every generation of God's people that receives Yhwh's promises but still awaits their fulfillment. The rhetorical flexibility of the "fathers" is evident in the way that they are first identified as the patriarchs in Deuteronomy 1–3, modulate between the patriarchs and the exodus generations in Deuteronomy 4–29, and finally encompass even Moses' current audience of "you" at Moab for a brief rhetorical moment in Deuteronomy 30.

The blending of the "fathers" with multiple generations of "you" into a corporate entity underscores the theological continuity in Yhwh's dealings across all of Israel's history. This transgenerational conception also envisions the divine-human relationship as a singular covenant that is simultaneously grounded in divine initiative and contingent on human obedience. A foundational promise to the patriarchs of Israel is fleshed out according to the shifting needs of salvation history in such a way that, not only does Yhwh's grace remain primary,[1] even the giving and recapitulation of the law are a gift rather than a burden for Israel.[2]

This theological and mostly synchronic analysis of the "fathers" has several significant implications for diachronic treatments of the "fathers" in Deuteronomy and the Tetrateuch. First, the rhetorical progression of the "fathers" within Deuteronomy suggests that the dynamic referent of "you" in the so-called *Generationswechsel* is probably not a redactional seam[3] but

---
1. Beckwith, "Unity and Diversity," 93–118 ; McComiskey, *Covenants*, 59–76.
2. D. I. Block, "The Grace of Torah: The Mosaic Prescription for Life (Deut. 4:1–8; 6:20–25)," *JETS* 162 (2005) 3–22; Barker, *Triumph of Grace in Deuteronomy*, 175–78; Braulik, "Law as Gospel," 5–14; G. J. Wenham, "Grace and Law in the Old Testament," in *Law, Morality, and the Bible* (ed. B. Kaye and G. J. Wenham; Downers Grove, IL: InterVarsity, 1978) 3–23.
3. Cf. Römer, *Israels Väter*, 18–21.

an integral part of the book's rhetorical strategy to coalesce all of Israel's generations into a singular people of God. Second, the seamless weaving of divine initiative and human responsibility in Deuteronomy's references to the "fathers" indicates that the book cannot be characterized reductionistically as an exemplar of covenant conditionality[4] or separated easily into unconditional (i.e., Abrahamic) and conditional strands (i.e., Israelite) of covenant theology.[5] Third, Deuteronomy's portrayal of "Yhwh, God of the fathers" as a cosmic and personal deity who travels with the nation offers a challenge to the prevailing view that the book is a programmatic statement for centralizing the cult in Jerusalem.[6]

Due to the fact that these conclusions bear on many topics currently debated in pentateuchal criticism, future research will need to extend this mostly synchronic analysis of the Deuteronomic "fathers" by interacting in greater detail with diachronic studies that use "Deuteronom(ist)ic" ideas as redactional criteria in the Tetrateuch.[7] In contrast to my emphasis on Deuteronomy, these diachronic studies have generally used the ancestral narratives of Genesis–Numbers as their center of gravity. Thus the time is ripe for another iteration of the hermeneutical circle to proceed from this study of the Deuteronomic "fathers" back toward diachronic examinations of Deuteronomy's links to the ancestor narratives of the Tetrateuch.[8] Polzin rightly observes regarding interpretive methods that "[t]he priority of synchrony . . . over diachrony is not in rank but only in operation. Thus we are still allowed to call both approaches truly complementary: each must eventually take the other's conclusions into account."[9] Although Polzin was referring to older literary methods such as "new literary criticism" and structuralism, my research on the "fathers" in Deuteronomy indicates that newer synchronic methods such as speech-act theory, collective memory, and rhetorical criticism can also provide useful critiques of diachronic proposals.

---

4. Cf. Van Seters, "Confessional Reformulation," 451: "Deuteronomy makes possession of the land conditional upon obedience to the covenant, but this would be contradictory to an unconditional promise made previously to the patriarchs."

5. Cf. Perlitt, "Motive und Schichten der Landtheologie im Deuteronomium," 97–108.

6. Cf. Wellhausen, *Prolegomena*, 28–38.

7. E.g., Westermann, *Promises*; Van Seters, *Moses*; idem, *Abraham*; E. Blum, *Studien zur Komposition des Pentateuch* (BZAW 189; New York: de Gruyter, 1990); Rendtorff, *Problem of the Process*; K. Schmid, *Genesis and the Moses Story*.

8. Indeed, the diachronic iteration of the hermeneutical circle has already begun in the critical reaction to the synchronic study of Deuteronomy's relationship to the tetrateuchal narratives recently offered by Johannes Taschner (*Mosereden im Deuteronomium*), which bears some similarities to mine. Taschner's attempt to offer a synchronic corrective to diachronic approaches has met with criticism from E. Otto, "Ist das Deuteronomium 'nicht mehr und nicht weniger als eine Lehrstunde der Geschichtsdidaktik'? Zu einem Buch von Johannes Taschner," *ZABR* 14 (2008) 463–74.

9. Polzin, *Moses*, 6.

More broadly, Deuteronomy's notion of a single divine-human covenant with the "fathers" opens several theological avenues for future research. Within OT theology, the reassessment of Deuteronomic covenant theology as simultaneously unconditional and conditional needs to be integrated with recent studies arriving at similar conclusions regarding the covenant theologies of the Priestly source and the Holiness Code.[10] On the NT front, the irreducible dialectic between grace and law in the Deuteronomic references to the "fathers" has obvious parallels to the single covenant envisioned by proponents of covenant nomism.[11] Similarly, some Catholic and Reformed theologians have argued for subsuming grace and law under a single covenant.[12]

The ability of Deuteronomy to touch on so many areas in biblical and theological studies confirms its central place in the canon of Scripture. Though this book on the "fathers" has diverged from consensus views on Deuteronomy in many important respects, Wellhausen's observations regarding the pivotal function of Deuteronomy in OT criticism are equally reflective of the unifying function of the "fathers" in the final form of the book: "The connecting link between old and new, between Israel and Judaism, is everywhere Deuteronomy."[13]

---

10. E.g., Mason, *Eternal Covenant*; Milgrom, "Covenants," 91–101.

11. E.g., E. P. Sanders, *Paul and Palestinian Judaism* (Philadelphia: Fortress, 1977). Cf. K. J. Turner, "Moses on the New Perspective: Does Deuteronomy Teach Covenant Nomism?" (paper presented at the national meeting of the Evangelical Theological Society, Providence, RI, 19 November 2008) 1–28.

12. E.g., Pope Benedict XVI, *Many Religions—One Covenant: Israel, the Church and the World* (trans. G. Harrison; San Francisco: Ignatius, 1999); J. Murray, *The Covenant of Grace: A Biblico-theological Study* (London: Tyndale, 1954). Cf. Horton, *Covenant and Salvation*.

13. Wellhausen, *Prolegomena*, 362.

Bibliography

Abba, R. "The Divine Name Yahweh." *Journal of Biblical Literature* 80 (1961): 320–28.
Abel, E. L. "The Nature of the Patriarchal God 'El Sadday.'" *Numen: International Review for the History of Religions* 20 (1973): 48–59.
Achenbach, R. *Israel zwischen Verheißung und Gebot: Literarkritische Untersuchungen zu Deuteronomium 5–11.* Europäische Hochschulschriften 422. Frankfurt am Main: Peter Lang, 1991.
Ackerman, S. "The Personal Is Political: Covenantal and Affectionate Love (ʾĀHĒB, ʾAHĂBÂ) in the Hebrew Bible." *Vetus Testamentum* 52 (2002): 437–58.
Adams, J. W. *The Performative Nature and Function of Isaiah 40–55.* Library of Hebrew Bible / Old Testament Studies 448. New York: T. & T. Clark, 2006.
Albertz, R. *A History of Israelite Religion in the Old Testament Period.* Translated by J. Bowden. 2 vols. Old Testament Library. Louisville: Westminster John Knox, 1994.
———. *Persönliche Frömmigkeit und offizielle Religion.* Stuttgart: Calwer, 1978.
Albright, W. F. *From the Stone Age to Christianity.* 2nd ed. Garden City, NY: Doubleday, 1957.
Alexander, T. D. *Abraham in the Negev: A Source-Critical Investigation of Genesis 20:1–22:19.* Carslisle: Paternoster, 1997.
———. "Genesis 22 and the Covenant of Circumcision." *Journal for the Study of the Old Testament* 25 (1983): 17–22.
Allen, L. C. "Aspects of Generational Commitment and Challenge in Chronicles." Pp. 123–32 in *The Chronicler as Theologian: Essays in Honor of Ralph W. Klein.* Edited by M. P. Graham, S. L. McKenzie, and G. N. Knoppers. Journal for the Study of the Old Testament Supplement 371. New York: T. & T. Clark, 2003.
Alonso Schökel, L. *A Manual of Hebrew Poetics.* Translated by A. Graffy. Subsidia Biblica 11. Rome: Pontifical Biblical Institute, 1988.
Alster-Elata, G., and R. Salmon. "Biblical Covenants as Performative Language." Pp. 27–45 in *Summoning: Ideas of the Covenant and Interpretive Theory.* Edited by E. Spolsky. Albany, NY: State University of New York, 1993.
Alt, A. "The God of the Fathers." Pp. 3–86 in *Essays on Old Testament History and Religion.* Translated by R. A. Wilson. Garden City, NY: Doubleday, 1967.
Alter, R. *The Art of Biblical Narrative.* New York: Basic Books, 1981.
———. *The Five Books of Moses: A Translation with Commentary.* New York: Norton, 2004.
Altman, A. *The Historical Prologue of the Hittite Vassal Treaties: An Inquiry into the Concepts of Hittite Interstate Law.* Ramat-Gan: Bar-Ilan University Press, 2004.
Amsler, S. "Loi orale et loi écrite dans le Deutéronome." Pp. 51–54 in *Das Deuteronomium: Entstehung, Gestalt und Botschaft.* Edited by N. Lohfink.

Bibliotheca Ephemeridum Theologicarum Lovaniensium 68. Leuven: Leuven University Press, 1985.

Anbar, M. "Genesis 15: A Conflation of Two Deuteronomic Narratives." *Journal of Biblical Literature* 101 (1982): 39–55.

———. "The Story about the Building of an Altar on Mount Ebal." Pp. 304–9 in *Das Deuteronomium: Entstehung, Gestalt und Botschaft*. Edited by N. Lohfink. Bibliotheca Ephemeridum Theologicarum Lovaniensium 68. Leuven: Leuven University Press, 1985.

Andersen, F. I. *The Sentence in Biblical Hebrew*. The Hague: Mouton, 1974.

Anderson, B. W. *Contours of Old Testament Theology*. Minneapolis: Fortress, 1999.

Aristotle. *Rhetoric*. New York: Random, 1954.

Ausloos, H. "'A Land Flowing with Milk and Honey': Indicative of a Deuteronomistic Redaction?" *Ephemerides theologicae lovanienses* 75 (1999): 297–314.

Austin, J. L. *How to Do Things with Words*. 2nd ed. Cambridge: Harvard University Press, 1975.

Bächli, O. *Israel und die Völker: Eine Studie von Deuteronomium*. Abhandlungen zur Theologie des Alten und Neuen Testaments 41. Zurich: Zwingli, 1962.

Baker, D. L. "Covenant: An Old Testament Study." Pp. 21–53 in *The God of Covenant: Biblical, Theological, and Contemporary Perspectives*. Edited by J. A. Grant and A. I. Wilson. Leicester: Apollos, 2005.

Baltzer, K. *The Covenant Formulary in Old Testament, Jewish, and Early Christian Writings*. Translated by D. E. Green. Philadelphia: Fortress, 1971.

Bar-Efrat, S. *Narrative Art in the Bible*. Journal for the Study of the Old Testament Supplement 70. Sheffield: Almond, 1989.

Barker, P. "The Theology of Deuteronomy 27." *Tyndale Bulletin* 49 (1998): 277–303.

———. *The Triumph of Grace in Deuteronomy: Faithless Israel, Faithful Yahweh in Deuteronomy*. Paternoster Biblical Monographs. Waynesboro, GA: Paternoster, 2004.

Barr, J. *The Semantics of Biblical Language*. Oxford: Oxford University Press, 1961.

———. "Some Semantic Notes on the Covenant." Pp. 23–38 in *Beiträge zur alttestamentlichen Theologie: Festschrift für Walther Zimmerli zum 70. Geburtstag*. Edited by H. Donner, R. Hanhart, and R. Smend. Göttingen: Vandenhoeck & Ruprecht, 1977.

———. "The Symbolism of Names in the Old Testament." *Bulletin of the John Rylands University Library of Manchester* 52 (1969): 11–29.

Barrick, W. D. "The Authorship of Deuteronomy 34: Moses or a Redactor?" Paper presented at the National Meeting of the Evangelical Theological Society. Colorado Springs, 14–16 November 2001.

Barton, J. "Covenant in Old Testament Theology." Pp. 23–38 in *Covenant as Context: Essays in Honour of E. W. Nicholson*. Edited by A. D. H. Mayes and R. B. Salters. Oxford: Oxford University Press, 2003.

———. *Reading the Old Testament: Method in Biblical Study*. London: Darton, Longman & Todd, 1984.

Beckman, G. *Hittite Diplomatic Texts*. 2nd ed. Society of Biblical Literature Writings from the Ancient World 7. Atlanta: Scholars Press, 1999.

Beckwith, R. T. "The Unity and Diversity of God's Covenants." *Tyndale Bulletin* 38 (1987): 93–118.

Beek, M. A. "Das Problem des aramäischen Stammvaters (Deut. XXVI 5)." *Old Testament Studies* 8 (1951): 193–212.

Begg, C. T. "Bread, Wine, and Strong Drink in Deut 29:5a." *Bijdragen: Tijdschrift voor filosofie en theologie* 41 (1980): 266–75.

———. "The Literary Criticism of Deuteronomy 4,1–40: Contributions to a Continuing Discussion." *Ephemerides theologicae lovanienses* 56 (1980): 10–55.

Bellefontaine, E. "The Curses of Deuteronomy 27: Their Relationship to the Prohibitives." Pp. 256–68 in *A Song of Power and the Power of Song: Essays on the Book of Deuteronomy*. Edited by D. L. Christensen. Sources for Biblical and Theological Study 3. Winona Lake, IN: Eisenbrauns, 1993.

Benedict XVI, Pope. *Many Religions—One Covenant: Israel, the Church and the World*. Translated by G. Harrison. San Francisco: Ignatius, 1999.

Berlin, A. *Poetics and Interpretation of Biblical Narrative*. Bible and Literature Series 9. Sheffield: Almond, 1983.

Blair, E. P. "An Appeal to Remembrance: The Memory Motif in Deuteronomy." *Interpretation* 15 (1961): 41–47.

Blenkinsopp, J. "Deuteronomic Elements to the Narrative in Genesis–Numbers: A Test Case." Pp. 84–115 in *Those Elusive Deuteronomists: The Phenomenon of Pan-Deuteronomism*. Edited by L. S. Schearing and S. L. McKenzie. Journal for the Study of the Old Testament Supplement 268. Sheffield: Sheffield Academic Press, 1999.

———. "Memory, Tradition, and the Construction of the Past in Ancient Israel." Pp. 1–17 in *Treasures Old and New: Essays in the Theology of the Pentateuch*. Grand Rapids, MI: Eerdmans, 2004.

———. *The Pentateuch: An Introduction to the First Five Books of the Bible*. Anchor Bible Reference Library. New York: Doubleday, 1992.

———. "The Structure of P." *Catholic Biblical Quarterly* 38 (1976): 275–92.

Block, D. I. *Deuteronomy*. Unpublished manuscript. [private communication, 2008]

———. "Deuteronomy, Book of." Pp. 165–73 of *Dictionary for Theological Interpretation of the Bible*. Edited by K. J. Vanhoozer. Grand Rapids, MI: Baker, 2005.

———. *The Foundations of National Identity: A Study in Ancient Northwest Semitic Perceptions*. D.Phil. dissertation. University of Liverpool, 1981.

———. *The Gods of the Nations: Studies in Ancient Near Eastern National Theology*. 2nd ed. Evangelical Theological Society Studies. Grand Rapids, MI: Baker, 2000.

———. "Gog and Magog in Ezekiel's Eschatological Vision." Pp. 85–116 in *Eschatology in Bible and Theology: Evangelical Essays at the Dawn of a New Millennium*. Edited by K. Brower and M. Elliott. Downers Grove, IL: InterVarsity, 1997.

———. "The Grace of Torah: The Mosaic Prescription for Life (Deut. 4:1–8; 6:20–25)." *Journal of the Evangelical Theological Society* 162 (2005): 3–22.

———. "How Many Is God? An Investigation into the Meaning of Deuteronomy 6:4–5." *Journal of the Evangelical Theological Society* 47 (2004): 193–212.

———. "Other Religions in Old Testament Theology." Pp. 43–78 in *Biblical Faith and Other Religions: An Evangelical Assessment*. Grand Rapids, MI: Kregel, 2004.

———. "Recovering the Voice of Moses: The Genesis of Deuteronomy." *Journal of the Evangelical Theological Society* 44 (2001): 385–408.

Blum, E. *Die Komposition der Vätergeschichte*. Wissenschaftliche Monographien zum Alten und Neuen Testament 57. Neukirchen-Vluyn: Neukirchener Verlag, 1984.

———. *Studien zur Komposition des Pentateuch*. Beihefte zur Zeitschrift für die alttestamentliche Wissenchaft 189. New York: de Gruyter, 1990.

Bonhoeffer, D. *Letters and Papers from Prison*. Enl. ed. New York: Macmillan, 1972.

Boorer, S. *The Promise of the Land as Oath: A Key to the Formation of the Pentateuch*. Beihefte zur Zeitschrift für die alttestamentliche Wissenschaft 205. Berlin: de Gruyter, 1993.

Bottéro, J. *Religion in Ancient Mesopotamia*. Chicago: University of Chicago Press, 2001.

Braulik, G. "Die Ausdrücke für 'Gesetz' im Buch Deuteronomium." *Biblica* 51 (1970): 39–66.

———. "Deuteronomium 1–4 als Sprechakt." *Biblica* 83 (2002): 249–57.

———. *Deuteronomium 1–16,17*. Neue Echter Bibel. Würzburg: Echter Verlag, 1986.

———. "Deuteronomium 4,13 und der Horebbund." Pp. 27–36 in *Für immer verbündet: Studien zur Bundestheologie der Bible*. Edited by C. Dohmen and C. Frevel. Stuttgarter Bibelstudien 211. Stuttgart: Katholisches Bibelwerk, 2007.

———. "Deuteronomy and the Birth of Monotheism." Pp. 99–130, 237–47 in *The Theology of Deuteronomy*. Translated by U. Lindbad. N. Richland Hills, TX: BIBAL, 1985.

———. "Deuteronomy and the Commemorative Culture of Israel: Redactio-historical Observations on the Use of *lmd*." Pp. 183–98, 263–70 in *The Theology of Deuteronomy*. Translated by U. Lindbad. N. Richland Hills, TX: BIBAL, 1993.

———. "Law as Gospel: Justification and Pardon according to the Deuteronomic Torah." *Interpretation* 38 (1984): 5–14.

———. "Literarkritik und die Einrahmung von Gemälden: Zur literarkritischen und redaktions-geschichtlichen Analyse von Dtn 4,1–6,3 and 29,1–30,10 durch D. Knapp." *Revue biblique* 96 (1989): 266–88.

———. *Die Mittel deuteronomischer Rhetorik, erhoben aus Deuteronomium 4,1–40*. Analecta Biblica 68. Rome: Pontifical Biblical Institute, 1978.

———. "Monotheismus im Deuteronomium: Zu Syntax, Redeform und Gotteserkenntnis in 4,32–40." *Zeitschrift für altorientalische und biblische Rechtsgeschichte* 10 (2004): 169–94.

———. "Wisdom, Divine Presence and Law." Pp. 1–25, 199–209 in *The Theology of Deuteronomy*. Translated by U. Lindbad. N. Richland Hills, TX: BIBAL, 1993.

———, ed. *Bundesdokument und Gesetz: Studien zum Deuteronomium*. Herders biblische Studien 4. Freiburg: Herder, 1995.

_____, and N. Lohfink. "Deuteronomium 1,5 באר את־התורה הזאת: 'Er verlieh dieser Tora Rechtskraft.'" Pp. 34–51 in *Textarbeit—Studien zu Texten und ihrer Rezeption aus dem Alten Testament und der Umwelt Israels: Festschrift für Peter Weimar zur Vollendung seines 60. Lebensjahres mit Beiträgen von Freunden, Schülern and Kollegen*. Edited by K. Kiesow and T. Meurer. Alter Orient und Altes Testament. Münster: Ugarit-Verlag, 2003.

Brekelmans, C. "Deuteronomy 5: Its Place and Function." Pp. 164–73 in *Das Deuteronomium: Entstehung, Gestalt und Botschaft*. Edited by N. Lohfink. Bibliotheca Ephemeridum Theologicarum Lovaniensium 68. Leuven: Leuven University Press, 1985.

_____. "Die sogenannten deuteronomischen Elemente in Genesis bis Numeri: Ein Beitrag zur Vorgeschichte des Deuteronomiums." Pp. 90–96 in *Volume du Congrès: Genève, 1965*. Edited by G. W. Anderson. Supplements to Vetus Testamentum 15. Leiden: Brill, 1966.

Brettler, M. Z. *The Creation of History in Ancient Israel*. New York: Routledge, 1995.

_____. "Predestination in Deuteronomy 30.1–10." Pp. 171–88 in *Those Elusive Deuteronomists: The Phenomenon of Pan-Deuteronomism*. Edited by L. S. Schearing and S. L. McKenzie. Journal for the Study of the Old Testament Supplement 268. Sheffield: Sheffield Academic Press, 1999.

_____. "The Promise of the Land of Israel to the Patriarchs in the Pentateuch." *Shnaton* 5–6 (1982): vii–xxiv.

Brichto, H. C. "Kin, Cult, Land and Afterlife: A Biblical Complex." *Hebrew Union College Annual* 44 (1973): 1–54.

_____. *The Names of God: Poetic Readings in Biblical Beginnings*. New York: Oxford University Press, 1998.

Briggs, R. S. "The Uses of Speech-Act Theory in Biblical Interpretation." *Currents in Biblical Research* 9 (2001): 229–76.

_____. *Words in Action: Speech Act Theory and Biblical Interpretation*. Edinburgh: T. & T. Clark, 2001.

Bright, J. *Covenant and Promise: The Prophetic Understanding of the Future in Preexilic Israel*. Philadelphia: Westminster, 1976.

_____. *A History of Israel*. 4th ed. London: SCM, 2000.

Brongers, H. A. "Bemerkungen zum Gebrauch des adverbialen $w^{e\zeta}\bar{a}ttah$ im Alten Testament (Ein lexikologischer Beitrag)." *Vetus Testamentum* 15 (1965): 289–99.

_____. "Die Partikel למען in der biblisch-hebräischen Sprache." Pp. 87–96 in *Syntax and Meaning: Studies in Hebrew Syntax and Biblical Exegesis*. Edited by C. J. Labuschagne et al. Oudtestamentische Studiën 18. Leiden: Brill, 1973.

Brueggemann, W. *Deuteronomy*. Abingdon Old Testament Commentary. Nashville: Abingdon, 2001.

_____. *Genesis*. Interpretation. Atlanta: John Knox, 1982.

_____. "Imagination as a Mode of Fidelity." Pp. 13–36 in *Understanding the Word: Essays in Honor of Bernhard W. Anderson*. Edited by J. T. Butler, E. W. Conrad, and B. C. Ollenburger. Journal for the Study of the Old Testament Supplement 37. Sheffield: JSOT Press, 1985.

_____. "The Kerygma of the Deuteronomistic Historian." *Interpretation* 22 (1968): 387–402.

_____. *The Land*. 2nd ed. Overtures in Biblical Theology. Philadelphia: Fortress, 2002.

_____. "Pharaoh as Vassal: A Study of a Political Metaphor." *Catholic Biblical Quarterly* 57 (1995): 27–51.

_____. *Theology of the Old Testament: Testimony, Dispute, Advocacy*. Minneapolis: Fortress, 1997.

Buchanan, G. W. "The Covenant in Legal Context." Pp. 27–52 in *The Concept of the Covenant in the Second Temple Period*. Edited by S. E. Porter and J. C. de Roo. Leiden: Brill, 2003.

Budd, P. J. *Numbers*. Word Biblical Commentary 5. Nashville: Thomas Nelson, 1984.

Buis, P. "Comment au septième siècle envisageait-on l'avenir de l'alliance? Étude de Lv. 26,3–45." Pp. 131–40 in *Questions disputées d'Ancien Testament: Méthode et Théologie*. Edited by C. Brekelmans. Bibliotheca Ephemeridum Theologicarum Lovaniensium 33. Leuven: Leuven University Press, 1989.

_____. *La Notion d'Alliance dans l'Ancien Testament*. Paris: Cerf, 1976.

_____. "La Nouvelle Alliance." *Vetus Testamentum* 18 (1968): 1–15.

_____, and J. Leclercq. *Le Deutéronome*. Sources Bibliques. Paris: Lecoffre, 1963.

Buss, M. J. "Potential and Actual Interactions between Speech Act Theory and Biblical Studies." *Semeia* 41 (1988): 125–34.

Cairns, I. *Word and Presence: A Commentary on the Book of Deuteronomy*. International Theological Commentary. Oxford: Oxford University Press, 1992.

Campbell, A. F. "An Historical Prologue in a Seventh-Century Treaty." *Biblica* 50 (1969): 534–35.

Carmichael, C. "A New View on the Origin of the Deuteronomic Credo." *Vetus Testamentum* 19 (1969): 273–89.

Carpenter, E. E. "Literary Structure and Unbelief: A Study of Deuteronomy 1:6–46." *Asbury Theological Journal* 42 (1987): 78–84.

Cassuto, U. *A Commentary on the Book of Exodus*. Translated by I. Abrahams. Jerusalem: Magnes, 1967.

_____. *The Documentary Hypothesis and the Composition of the Pentateuch*. Translated by I. Abrahams. Jerusalem: Magnes, 1961.

Cazelles, H. *Autour de l'Exode (Études)*. Sources Bibliques. Paris: Lecoffre, 1987.

_____. "Passages in the Singular within Discourse in the Plural of Dt 1–4." *Catholic Biblical Quarterly* 29 (1967): 207–19.

Childs, B. S. *Biblical Theology of the Old and New Testaments: Theological Reflection on the Christian Bible*. Philadelphia: Fortress, 1993.

_____. *The Book of Exodus: A Critical, Theological Commentary*. Old Testament Library. Philadelphia: Westminster, 1974.

_____. "Deuteronomic Formulae of the Exodus Traditions." Pp. 30–39 in *Hebräische Wortforschung: Festschrift zum 80. Geburtstag von Walter Baumgartner*. Edited by B. Hartmann et al. Supplements to Vetus Testamentum 16. Leiden: Brill, 1967.

_____. *Introduction to the Old Testament as Scripture*. Philadelphia: Fortress, 1979.

_____. *Memory and Tradition in Israel*. Naperville, IL: Allenson, 1962.

———. "Speech-Act Theory and Biblical Interpretation." *Scottish Journal of Theology* 58 (2005): 375–92.
Cholewinski, A. "Zur theologischen Deutung des Moabbundes." *Biblica* 66 (1985): 96–111.
Christensen, D. L. *Deuteronomy 1–11*. Word Biblical Commentary 6A. Nashville: Thomas Nelson, 1991.
———. *Deuteronomy 1:1–21:9*. Rev. ed. Word Biblical Commentary 6A. Nashville: Thomas Nelson, 2001.
———. *Deuteronomy 21:10–34:12*. Word Biblical Commentary 6b. Nashville: Thomas Nelson, 2002.
———. "New Evidence for the Priestly Redaction of Deuteronomy." *Zeitschrift für die alttestamentliche Wissenschaft* 104 (1992): 197–201.
———. "Prose and Poetry in the Bible: The Narrative Poetics of Deuteronomy 1,9–18." *Zeitschrift für die alttestamentliche Wissenchaft* 97 (1985): 179–89.
———, ed. *A Song of Power and the Power of Song: Essays on the Book of Deuteronomy*. Sources for Biblical and Theological Study 3. Winona Lake, IN: Eisenbrauns, 1993.
Clements, R. E. *Abraham and David: Genesis XV and Its Meaning for Israelite Tradition*. Naperville, IL: Allenson, 1967.
———. "Covenant and Canon in the Old Testament." Pp. 1–12 in *Creation, Christ, and Culture: Studies in Honor of T. F. Torrance*. Edited by B. W. A. McKinney. Edinburgh: T. & T. Clark, 1976.
———. "Deuteronomy and the Jerusalem Cult Tradition." *Vetus Testamentum* 15 (1965): 300–312.
———. *God's Chosen People: A Theological Interpretation of the Book of Deuteronomy*. London: S.C.M., 1968.
———, R. W. L. Moberly, and J. G. McConville. "A Dialogue with Gordon McConville on Deuteronomy." *Scottish Journal of Theology* 56 (2003): 508–31.
Clines, D. J. A. *The Theme of the Pentateuch*. Journal for the Study of the Old Testament Supplement 10. Sheffield: JSOT Press, 1978.
Coats, G. W. *Rebellion in the Wilderness: The Murmuring Motif in the Wilderness Traditions of the Old Testament*. Nashville: Abingdon, 1968.
———. "A Structural Transition in Exodus." *Vetus Testamentum* 22 (1972): 129–42.
Coggins, R. "What Does 'Deuteronomistic' Mean?" Pp. 22–35 in *Those Elusive Deuteronomists: The Phenomenon of Pan-Deuteronomism*. Edited by L. S. Schearing and S. L. McKenzie. Journal for the Study of the Old Testament Supplement 268. Sheffield: Sheffield Academic Press, 1999.
Cogswell, J. "Lest We Forget: A Sermon." *Interpretation* 15 (1961): 32–40.
Cohen, Jeremy. *'Be Fertile and Increase, Fill the Earth and Master It': The Ancient and Medieval Career of a Biblical Text*. Ithaca, NY: Cornell University Press, 1989.
Cotterell, P., and M. Turner. *Linguistics and Biblical Interpretation*. Downers Grove, IL: InterVarsity, 1989.
Craigie, P. C. *The Book of Deuteronomy*. New International Commentary on the Old Testament. Grand Rapids, MI: Eerdmans, 1976.
Cross, F. M. *Canaanite Myth and Hebrew Epic: Essays in the History of Religion of Israel*. Cambridge: Harvard University Press, 1973.

———. "Kinship and Covenant in Ancient Israel." Pp. 3–21 in *From Epic to Canon: History and Literature in Ancient Israel*. Baltimore: Johns Hopkins University Press, 1998.

———. "Yahweh and the God of the Patriarchs." *Harvard Theological Review* 55 (1962): 225–59.

———, and D. N. Freedman. *Studies in Ancient Yahwistic Poetry*. 2nd ed. Grand Rapids, MI: Eerdmans, 1997.

Crüsemann, F. *The Torah: Theology and Social History of the Old Testament*. Translated by A. W. Mahnke. Minneapolis: Fortress, 1996.

Crystal, D. "Liturgical Language in a Sociolinguistic Perspective." Pp. 120–46 in *Language and the Worship of the Church*. Edited by D. Jasper and R. C. D. Jasper. London: Macmillan, 1990.

Daniels, D. R. "The Creed of Deuteronomy XXVI Revisited." Pp. 231–42 in *Studies in the Pentateuch*. Edited by J. A. Emerton. Supplements to Vetus Testamentum 41. Leiden: Brill, 1990.

Davidson, R. "Covenant Ideology in Ancient Israel." Pp. 323–47 in *The World of Ancient Israel: Sociological, Anthropological, and Political Perspectives*. Edited by R. E. Clements. Cambridge: Cambridge University Press, 1989.

Davies, G. "Covenant, Oath, and the Composition of the Pentateuch." Pp. 71–89 in *Covenant as Context: Essays in Honour of E. W. Nicholson*. Edited by A. D. H. Mayes and R. B. Salters. Oxford: Oxford University Press, 2003.

Davies, P. R. *Scribes and Schools: The Canonization of the Hebrew Scriptures*. Louisville: Westminster John Knox, 1998.

Day, J. "Why Does God 'Establish' Rather Than 'Cut' Covenants in the Priestly Source?" Pp. 91–109 in *Covenant as Context: Essays in Honour of E. W. Nicholson*. Edited by A. D. H. Mayes and R. B. Salters. Oxford: Oxford University Press, 2003.

———. *Yahweh and the Gods and Goddesses of Canaan*. Journal for the Study of the Old Testament Supplement 265. Sheffield: Sheffield Academic Press, 2000.

DeRouchie, J. S. *A Call to Covenant Love: Text Grammar and Literary Structure in Deuteronomy 5–11*. Gorgias Dissertations 30. Piscataway, NJ: Gorgias, 2007.

Deurloo, K. A. "The One God and All Israel in Its Generations." Pp. 31–46 in *Studies in Deuteronomy in Honour of C. J. Labuschagne on the Occasion of His 65th Birthday*. Edited by F. García Martínez et al. Supplements to Vetus Testamentum 53. Leiden: Brill, 1994.

De Vries, S. J. "The Development of the Deuteronomic Promulgation Formula." *Biblica* 55 (1974): 301–16.

———. *Yesterday, Today and Tomorrow: Time and History in the Old Testament*. Grand Rapids, MI: Eerdmans, 1975.

Diepold, P. *Israels Land*. Beiträge zur Wissenschaft vom Alten und Neuen Testament 15. Stuttgart: Kohlhammer, 1972.

Dietrich, W. *Prophetie und Geschichte: Eine redaktionsgeschichtliche Untersuchung zum deuteronomistischen Geschichtswerk*. Forschungen zur Religion und Literatur des Alten und Neuen Testaments 108. Göttingen: Vanderhoeck & Ruprecht, 1972.

Doan, W., and T. Giles. *Prophets, Performance, and Power: Performance Criticism of the Hebrew Bible*. New York: T. & T. Clark, 2005.

Dozeman, T. B., and K. Schmid, eds. *A Farewell to the Yahwist? The Composition of the Pentateuch in Recent European Interpretation.* Society of Biblical Literature Symposium Series 34. Atlanta: Scholars Press, 2006.

Dreyfus, F. "'L'Araméen voulait tuer mon père': L'actualisation de Dt 26,5 dans la tradition juive et la tradition chrétienne." Pp. 147–61 in *De la Tôrah au Messie: Mélanges Henri Cazelles.* Edited by M. Carrez, J. Doré, and P. Grelot. Paris: Desclée, 1981.

Driver, S. R. *A Critical and Exegetical Commentary on Deuteronomy.* 3rd ed. International Critical Commentary. Edinburgh: T. & T. Clark, 1901.

Duke, R. K. *The Persuasive Appeal of the Chronicler: A Rhetorical Analysis.* Journal for the Study of the Old Testament Supplement 88. Sheffield: Sheffield Academic Press, 1990.

Dumbrell, W. J. *Covenant and Creation: A Theology of the Old Testament Covenants.* Grand Rapids, MI: Baker, 1984.

―――――. "The Prospect of Unconditionality in the Sinaitic Covenant." Pp. 141–55 in *Israel's Apostasy and Restoration: Essays in Honor of Roland K. Harrison.* Edited by A. Gileadi. Grand Rapids, MI: Baker, 1988.

Durham, J. I. *Exodus.* Word Biblical Commentary 3. Waco, TX: Word, 1987.

Eichrodt, W. *Theology of the Old Testament.* Translated by J. A. Baker. 2 vols. Old Testament Library. Philadelphia: Westminster, 1967.

Eissfeldt, O. "Gilgal or Shechem?" Pp. 90–101 in *Proclamation and Presence: Old Testament Essays in Honour of Gwynne Henton Davies.* Edited by J. I. Durham and J. R. Porter. Richmond, VA: John Knox, 1970.

―――――. "Der kanaanäische El als Geber der den Israelitischen Erzvätern geltenden Nachkommenschaft- und Landbesitzverheissungen." Pp. 50–62 in vol. 4 of *Kleine Schriften.* 6 vols. Edited by R. Sellheim and F. Maass. Tübingen: Mohr, 1962.

Emerton, J. A. "The Origin of the Promises to the Patriarchs in the Older Sources of the Book of Genesis." *Vetus Testamentum* 32 (1982): 14–32.

―――――. "The Priestly Writer in Genesis." *Journal of Theological Studies* 39 (1988): 382–400.

Eslinger, L. M. "Freedom or Knowledge? Perspective and Purpose in the Exodus Narrative." *Journal for the Study of the Old Testament* 52 (1991): 43–60.

―――――. "Knowing Yahweh: Exod 6:3 in the Context of Genesis 1–Exodus 15." Pp. 188–98 in *Literary Structure and Rhetorical Strategies in the Hebrew Bible.* Edited by L. J. de Regt, J. de Waard, and J. P. Fokkelman. Assen: Van Gorcum, 1996.

Evans, D. D. *The Logic of Self-Involvement: A Philosophical Study of Everyday Language with Special Reference to the Christian Use of Language about God as Creator.* New York: Herder & Herder, 1969.

Evans, J. F. *An Inner-Biblical Interpretation and Intertextual Reading of Ezekiel's Recognition Formulae with the Book of Exodus.* Th.D. dissertation. University of Stellenbosch, 2006.

Eynde, S. van den. "Covenant Formula and $B^e r\hat{\imath}t$: The Links between a Hebrew Lexeme and a Biblical Concept." *Old Testament Essays* 12 (1999): 122–48.

Fensham, F. C. "Father and Son as Terminology for Treaty and Covenant." Pp. 122–35 in *Near Eastern Studies in Honor of William Foxwell Albright.* Edited by H. Goedicke. Baltimore: Johns Hopkins University Press, 1971.

Finsterbusch, K. *Weisung für Israel: Studien zu religiösem Lehren und Lernen im Deuteronomium und in seinem Umfeld.* Forschungen zum Alten Testament 44. Tübingen: Mohr Siebeck, 2005.

Firth, D. G. "Speech Acts and Covenant in 2 Samuel 7:1–17." Pp. 79–99 in *The God of Covenant: Biblical, Theological, and Contemporary Perspectives.* Edited by J. A. Grant and A. I. Wilson. Leicester: Apollos, 2005.

Fishbane, M. *Biblical Interpretation in Ancient Israel.* Oxford: Clarendon, 1985.

———. *Biblical Myth and Rabbinic Mythmaking.* Oxford: Oxford University Press, 2005.

———. *Text and Texture.* New York: Schocken, 1979.

———. "Varia Deuteronomica." *Zeitschrift für die alttestamentliche Wissenschaft* 84 (1972): 49–50.

Flanagan, J. W. "The Deuteronomic Meaning of 'Kol Yisrael.'" *Studies in Religion* 6 (1977): 159–68.

Fokkelman, J. P. *Reading Biblical Narrative: An Introductory Guide.* Translated by I. Smit. Louisville: Westminster John Knox, 1999.

Follingstad, C. M. *Deictic Viewpoint in Biblical Hebrew Text: A Syntagmatic and Paradigmatic Analysis of the Particle kî.* Dallas: SIL International, 2001.

Forshey, H. O. "The Construct Chain *naḥᵃlat* Y$_{HWH}$/*ʾĕlōhîm*." *Bulletin of the American Schools of Oriental Research* 220 (1975): 51–53.

———. "The Hebrew Root NḤL and Its Semitic Cognates." *Harvard Theological Review* 66 (1973): 505–6.

Foster, S. J. "A Prototypical Definition of *Bĕrît*, 'Covenant' in Biblical Hebrew." *Old Testament Essays* 19 (2006): 35–46.

Fowler, M. D. "The Meaning of *liphne* Y$_{HWH}$ in the Old Testament." *Zeitschrift für die alttestamentliche Wissenschaft* 99 (1987): 384–90.

Frankena, R. "The Vassal-Treaties of Esarhaddon and the Dating of Deuteronomy." *Old Testament Studies* 65 (1965): 122–54.

Freedman, D. N. "Divine Commitment and Human Obligation." *Interpretation* 18 (1964): 419–31.

———. "'Who Is Like Thee among the Gods?' The Religion of Early Israel." Pp. 315–55 in *Ancient Israelite Religion: Essays in Honor of Frank Moore Cross.* Edited by P. D. Miller, P. D. Hanson, and S. D. McBride. Philadelphia: Fortress, 1987.

———, and D. Miano. "People of the New Covenant." Pp. 7–26 in *The Concept of the Covenant in the Second Temple Period.* Edited by J. E. Porter and J. C. R. de Roo. Leiden: Brill, 2003.

Fretheim, T, E. *Deuteronomic History.* Nashville: Abingdon, 1983.

Frevel, C. "Ein vielsagender Abschied: Exegetische Blicke auf den Tod des Mose in Dtn 34,1–12." *Biblische Zeitschrift* 45 (2001): 209–34.

Friedman, R. E. "From Egypt to Egypt: Dtr[1] and Dtr[2]." Pp. 167–92 in *Traditions in Transformation: Turning Points in Biblical Faith.* Edited by B. Halpern and J. D. Levenson. Winona Lake, IN: Eisenbrauns, 1981.

Fuhs, H. F. "Aus der Befreiung leben: Erwägungen zum geschichtlichen Credo in Dtn 26,1–11." Pp. 3–18 in *Schrift und Tradition: Festschrift für Josef Ernst.* Edited by K. Backhaus and F. G. Untergassmair. Paderborn: Ferdinand Schöningh, 1996.

Gammie, J. H. "The Theology of Retribution in the Book of Deuteronomy." *Vetus Testamentum* 32 (1970): 1–12.
García López, F. "Analyse littéraire de Deutéronome V–XI: Part 1." *Revue biblique* 84 (1977): 481–522.
_____. "Analyse littéraire de Deutéronome V–XI: Part 2." *Revue biblique* 85 (1978): 5–49.
_____. "Deut. VI et la Tradition-Rédaction du Deutéronome." *Revue biblique* 85 (1977): 161–200.
_____. "Deut 34, DTR History and the Pentateuch." Pp. 47–61 in *Studies in Deuteronomy in Honour of C. J. Labuschagne on the Occasion of His 65th Birthday*. Edited by F. García Martínez et al. Supplements to Vetus Testamentum 53. Leiden: Brill, 1994.
_____. "'Un Peuple Consacré': Analyse Critique de Deutéronome VII." *Vetus Testamentum* 32 (1982): 438–63.
_____. "Yahvé, fuente última de vida: Análisis de Dt 8." *Biblica* 62 (1981): 21–54.
García Martínez, F., et al., eds. *Studies in Deuteronomy in Honour of C. J. Labuschagne on the Occasion of His 65th Birthday*. Supplements to Vetus Testamentum 53. Leiden: Brill, 1994.
Garr, W. R. "The Grammar and Interpretation of Exodus 6:3." *Journal of Biblical Literature* 111 (1992): 385–408.
Gemser, B. "God in Genesis." Pp. 1–21 in *Studies on the Book of Genesis*. Oudtestamentische Studien 52. Leiden: Brill, 1958.
Gerstenberger, E. S. "Covenant and Commandment." *Journal of Biblical Literature* 84 (1965): 38–51.
_____. *Theologies in the Old Testament*. Translated by J. Bowden. Minneapolis: Fortress, 2002.
Gertz, J. C. "Kompositorische Funktion und literarhistorischer Ort von Deuteronomium 1–3." Pp. 103–23 in *Die deuteronomischen Geschichtswerke in den Büchern Genesis bis 2 Könige*. Edited by M. Witte, K. Schmid, and D. Prechel. Beihefte zur Zeitschrift für die alttestamentliche Wissenschaft 365. Berlin: de Gruyter, 2006.
_____. "Die Stellung des kleinen geschichtlichen Credos in der Redaktionsgeschichte von Deuteronomium und Pentateuch." Pp. 30–45 in *Liebe und Gebot: Studien zum Deuteronomium*. Edited by R. G. Kraft and H. Spieckermann. Göttingen: Vandenhoeck & Ruprecht, 2000.
Giesen, G. *Die Wurzel* שבע *'schworen': Eine semasiologische Studie zum Eid im Alten Testament*. Bonner Biblische Beiträge 56. Bonn: Hanstein, 1981.
Glueck, N. *Ḥesed in the Bible*. Translated by A. Gottschalk. Cincinnati: Hebrew Union College Press, 1967.
Goldingay, J. *Old Testament Theology: Israel's Faith*. Downers Grove, IL: InterVarsity Press Academic, 2006.
_____. *Old Testament Theology: Israel's Gospel*. Downers Grove, IL: InterVarsity Press Academic, 2003.
_____. *Theological Diversity and the Authority of the Old Testament*. Grand Rapids, MI: Eerdmans, 1987.
Gomes de Araújo, R. *Theologie der Wüste im Deuteronomium*. Österreichische Biblische Studien 17. Frankfurt: Peter Lang, 1999.

Gordon, C. "'In' of Predication or Equivalence." *Journal of Biblical Literature* 100 (1981): 612–3.
Gosse, B. "Le don de la terre dans le livre de la Genèse: En rapport aux rédactions deutéronomiste et sacerdotale du Pentateuque." *Estudios Bíblicos* 52 (1994): 289–301.
_____. "Moïse entre l'alliance des patriarches et celle du Sinaï." *Scandinavian Journal of the Old Testament* 11 (1997): 3–15.
_____. "Le souvenir de l'alliance avec Abraham, Isaac et Jacob et le serment du don de la terre dans le Pentateuque." *Estudios Bíblicos* 51 (1993): 459–72.
Gottwald, N. *The Hebrew Bible: A Socio-literary Introduction*. Philadelphia: Fortress, 1985.
Greenberg, M. *Understanding Exodus*. New York: Behrman, 1969.
Guillén Torralba, J. "La fórmula *kol ʾîš yiśᵉraʾel*." *Estudios Bíblicos* 34 (1975): 5–21.
Gunn, D. M. "The 'Hardening of Pharaoh's Heart': Plot, Character, and Theology in Exodus 1–14." Pp. 72–98 in *Art and Meaning: Rhetoric in Biblical Literature*. Edited by D. J. A. Clines, D. M. Gunn, and A. J. Hauser. Journal for the Study of the Old Testament Supplement 19. Sheffield: Sheffield Academic Press, 1982.
Ha, J. *Genesis 15: A Theological Compendium of Pentateuchal History*. Berlin: de Gruyter, 1989.
Habel, N. C. *The Land Is Mine: Six Biblical Land Ideologies*. Overtures to Biblical Theology. Minneapolis: Fortress, 1995.
Habets, G. "Bund im Alten Testament: Gabe und Aufgabe." *Teresianum* 35 (1982): 3–35.
Hadley, J. M. "The De-deification of Deities in Deuteronomy." Pp. 157–74 in *The God of Israel*. Edited by R. P. Gordon. Cambridge: Cambridge University Press, 2007.
Hahn, S. "Covenant in the Old and New Testaments: Some Current Research (1994–2004)." *Currents in Biblical Research* 3 (2005): 263–92.
_____. *Kinship by Covenant: A Canonical Approach to the Fulfillment of God's Saving Promises*. Anchor Bible Reference Library. New Haven, CT: Yale University Press, 2009.
Halpern, B. "The Centralization Formula in Deuteronomy." *Vetus Testamentum* 31 (1981): 20–38.
Hamilton, V. P. *Handbook to the Pentateuch*. 2nd ed. Grand Rapids, MI: Baker, 2005.
Haraguchi, T. "A Rhetorical Analysis of Deuteronomy 29–30." *Asia Journal of Theology* 15 (2001): 24–37.
Haran, M. "The *Bĕrît* 'Covenant': Its Nature and Ceremonial Background." Pp. 203–19 in *Tehillah le-Moshe: Biblical and Judaic Studies in Honor of Moshe Greenberg*. Edited by M. Cogan, B. L. Eichler, and J. H. Tigay. Winona Lake, IN: Eisenbrauns, 1997.
_____. "The Divine Presence in the Israelite Cult and the Cultic Institutions." *Biblica* 50 (1969): 222–41.
_____. "The Religion of the Patriarchs: An Attempt at a Synthesis." *Annual of the Swedish Theological Institute* 4 (1965): 30–55.
Hasel, G. F. "The Meaning of the Animal Rite in Genesis 15." *Journal for the Study of the Old Testament* 19 (1981): 61–78.

Heimerdinger, J.-M. "The God of Abraham." *Vox evangelica* 22 (1992): 41–55.
Hendel, R. S. "The Exodus in Biblical Memory." *Journal of Biblical Literature* 120 (2001): 601–22.
_____. *Remembering Abraham: Culture, Memory, and History in the Hebrew Bible*. Oxford: Oxford University Press, 2005.
Henry, C. F. H. *God, Revelation, and Authority*. 6 vols. Waco, TX: Word, 1976–83.
Herrmann, S. *Israel in Egypt*. Translated by M. Kohl. Studies in Biblical Theology 27. Naperville, IL: Allenson, 1973.
Hertog, C. den. "The Prophetic Dimension of the Divine Name: On Exodus 3:14a and Its Context." *Catholic Biblical Quarterly* 64 (2002): 213–28.
Hess, R. S. "The Book of Joshua as a Land Grant." *Biblica* 83 (2002): 493–506.
_____. *Israelite Religions: An Archaeological and Biblical Survey*. Grand Rapids, MI: Baker, 2007.
Hill, A. E. "The Ebal Ceremony as Hebrew Land Grant?" *Journal of the Evangelical Theological Society* 31 (1988): 399–406.
Hillers, D. R. *Covenant: The History of a Biblical Idea*. Baltimore: Johns Hopkins University Press, 1969.
_____. "Some Performative Utterances in the Bible." Pp. 757–66 in *Pomegranates and Golden Bells: Studies in Biblical, Jewish, and Near Eastern Ritual, Law, and Literature in Honor of Jacob Milgrom*. Edited by D. P. Wright, D. N. Freedman, and A. Hurvitz. Winona Lake, IN: Eisenbrauns, 1995.
Hoftijzer, J. *Die Verheissungen an die drei Erzväter*. Leiden: Brill, 1956.
Holmstedt, R. D. *The Relative Clause in Biblical Hebrew: A Linguistic Analysis*. Ph.D. dissertation. University of Wisconsin–Madison, 2002.
_____. "The Story of Ancient Hebrew 'ăšer." *Ancient Near Eastern Studies* 43 (2006): 7–26.
Horton, M. S. *Covenant and Salvation: Union with Christ*. Louisville: Westminster John Knox, 2007.
Houston, W. "'Today, in your very hearing': Some Comments on the Christological Use of the Old Testament." Pp. 37–47 in *The Glory of Christ in the New Testament: Studies in Christology in Memory of George Bradford Caird*. Edited by L. D. Hurst and N. T. Wright. Oxford: Clarendon, 1987.
Howard, D. M. "Rhetorical Criticism in Old Testament Studies." *Bulletin for Biblical Research* 4 (1994): 87–104.
Huffmon, H. B. "The Exodus, Sinai, and the Credo." *Catholic Biblical Quarterly* 27 (1965): 101–13.
_____. "The Treaty Background of Hebrew YĀDAʿ." *Bulletin of the American Schools of Oriental Research* 181 (1966): 31–37.
_____, and S. B. Parker. "A Further Note on the Treaty Background of Hebrew YĀDAʿ." *Bulletin of the American Schools of Oriental Research* 184 (1966): 36–38.
Hugenberger, G. P. *Marriage as a Covenant: A Study of Biblical Law and Ethics Governing Marriage Developed from the Perspective of Malachi*. Supplements to Vetus Testamentum 52. Leiden: Brill, 1994.
Hurowitz, A. (V.). *I Have Built You An Exalted House: Temple Building in the Bible in Light of Mesopotamian and Northwest Semitic Writings*. Journal for the Study of the Old Testament Supplement 115. Sheffield: Sheffield Academic Press, 1992.

Hyatt, J. P. "Yahweh as 'The God of My Father.'" *Vetus Testamentum* 55 (1955): 130–36.
Isbell, C. "Exodus 1–2 in the Context of Exodus 1–14: Story Lines and Key Words." Pp. 37–59 in *Art and Meaning: Rhetoric in Biblical Literature*. Edited by D. J. A. Clines, D. M. Gunn, and A. J. Hauser. Journal for the Study of the Old Testament Supplement 19. Sheffield: Sheffield Academic Press, 1982.
Jackson, J. J., and M. Kessler, eds. *Rhetorical Criticism: Essays in Honor of James Muilenburg*. Pittsburgh Theological Monograph Series 1. Pittsburgh: Pickwick, 1974.
Jacobsen, T. *The Treasures of Darkness: A History of Mesopotamian Religion*. New Haven, CT: Yale University Press, 1976.
Janzen, J. G. "The 'Wandering Aramean' Reconsidered." *Vetus Testamentum* 44 (1994): 359–75.
―――. "What's in a Name? 'Yahweh' in Exodus 3 and the Wider Biblical Context." *Interpretation* 33 (1979): 227–39.
Japhet, S. *The Ideology of the Book of Chronicles and Its Place in Biblical Thought*. Translated by A. Barber. Beiträge zur Erforschung des Alten Testaments und des antiken Judentum 9. Frankfurt am Main: Peter Lang, 1989.
Jenson, P. P. *Graded Holiness: A Key to the Priestly Conception of the World*. Journal for the Study of the Old Testament Supplement 106. Sheffield: Sheffield Academic Press, 1992.
Johnston, G. H. "'Unconditional' and 'Conditional' Features of the Davidic Covenant in the Light of Ancient Near Eastern Grants and Grant Treaties." Paper presented at the National Meeting of the Evangelical Theological Society. Providence, RI, 19 November 2008.
Johnstone, W. "From the Mountain to Kadesh." Pp. 449–67 in *Deuteronomy and Deuteronomistic Literature: Festschrift C. H. W. Brekelmans*. Edited by J. Lust and M. Vervenne. Bibliotheca Ephemeridum Theologicarum Lovaniensium 83. Leuven: Leuven University Press, 1997.
Joosten, J. "Covenant Theology in the Holiness Code." *Zeitschrift für altorientalische und biblische Rechtsgeschichte* 4 (1998): 146–64.
Kaiser, O. "Traditionsgeschichtliche Untersuchung von Genesis 15." *Zeitschrift für die alttestamentliche Wissenchaft* 70 (1958): 107–26.
Kaiser, W. C. *Toward an Old Testament Theology*. Grand Rapids, MI: Zondervan, 1978.
―――. *Toward Old Testament Ethics*. Grand Rapids, MI: Zondervan, 1983.
Kalluveettil, P. *Declaration and Covenant: A Comprehensive Review of Covenant Formulae from the Old Testament and the Ancient Near East*. Analecta Biblica 68. Rome: Pontifical Biblical Institute, 1982.
Kaminsky, J. S. *Corporate Responsibility in the Hebrew Bible*. Journal for the Study of the Old Testament Supplement 196. Sheffield: Sheffield Academic Press, 1995.
Keller, M. *Untersuchungen zur deuteronomisch-deuteronomistischen Namenstheologie*. Bonner Biblische Beiträge 105. Weinheim: Athenäum, 1996.
Kennedy, G. A. *A New History of Classical Rhetoric*. Princeton: Princeton University Press, 1994.
Kitchen, K. A. "Egypt, Qatna, and Covenant." *Ugarit-Forschungen* 11 (1979): 453–64.

———. "The Fall and Rise of Covenant, Law and Treaty." *Tyndale Bulletin* 40 (1989): 118–35.

———. *On the Reliability of the Old Testament.* Grand Rapids, MI: Eerdmans, 2003.

Klein, R. W. "The Message of P." Pp. 57–66 in *Die Botschaft und die Boten: Festschrift für Hans Walter Wolff zum 70. Geburtstag.* Edited by J. Jeremias and L. Perlitt. Neukirchen-Vluyn: Neukirchener Verlag, 1981.

———. *Textual Criticism of the Old Testament: The Septuagint after Qumran.* Guides to Biblical Scholarship. Philadelphia: Fortress, 1974.

Kline, M. G. "Dynastic Covenant." *Westminster Theological Journal* 23 (1960): 1–15.

———. *The Treaty of the Great King.* Grand Rapids, MI: Eerdmans, 1963.

Klingbeil, G. A. "Looking at the End from the Beginning: Studying Eschatological Concepts in the Pentateuch." *Journal of the Adventist Theological Society* 11 (2000): 174–87.

Kloppenborg, J. S. "Joshua 22: The Priestly Editing of an Ancient Tradition." *Biblica* 62 (1981): 347–71.

Knapp, D. *Deuteronomium 4: Literarische Analysen und theologische Interpretation.* Göttinger theologischen Arbeiten 35. Göttingen: Vanderhoeck & Ruprecht, 1987.

Knoppers, G. N. "Ancient Near Eastern Royal Grants and the Davidic Covenant: A Parallel?" *Journal of the American Oriental Society* 116 (1996): 670–97.

———. "David's Relation to Moses: The Contexts, Content and Conditions of the Davidic Promises." Pp. 91–118 in *King and Messiah in Israel and the Ancient Near East: Proceedings of the Oxford Old Testament Seminar.* Journal for the Study of the Old Testament Supplement 170. Sheffield: Sheffield Academic Press, 1998.

Koch, C. *Vertrag, Treueid und Bund: Studien zur Rezeption des altorientalischen Vertragsrechts im Deuteronomium und zur Ausbildung der Bundestheologie im Alten Testament.* Beihefte zur Zeitschrift für die alttestamentliche Wissenschaft 383. Berlin: de Gruyter, 2008.

Köckert, M. "Das nahe Wort: Zum entscheidenden Wandel des Gesetzesverständnisses im Alten Testament." *Theologie und Philosophie* 60 (1985): 496–519.

———. *Vätergott und Väterverheissungen: Eine Auseinandersetzung mit Albrecht Alt und seinen Erben.* Forschungen zur Religion und Literatur des Alten und Neuen Testaments 142. Göttingen: Vanderhoeck & Ruprecht, 1988.

Korošec, V. *Hethitische Staatsverträge: Ein Beitrag zu ihrer juristischen Wertung.* Leipziger rechtswissenschaftliche Studien 60. Leipzig: Weicher, 1931.

Krašovec, J. "Is There a Doctrine of 'Collective Retribution' in the Hebrew Bible?" *Hebrew Union College Annual* 65 (1994): 35–89.

———. "Two Types of Unconditional Covenant." *Horizons in Biblical Theology* 18 (1996): 55–77.

Kratz, R. G. *The Composition of the Narrative Books of the Old Testament.* Translated by J. Bowden. London: T. & T. Clark, 2005.

———, and H. Spieckermann, eds. *Liebe und Gebot: Studien zum Deuteronomium.* Forschungen zur Religion und Literatur des Alten und Neuen Testaments 190. Göttingen: Vanderhoeck & Ruprecht, 2000.

Krausz, N. "'*Arami oved avi*': Deuteronomy 26:5." *Jewish Bible Quarterly* 25 (1997): 31–34.
Kugler, R. A. "The Deuteronomists and the Latter Prophets." Pp. 127–44 in *Those Elusive Deuteronomists: The Phenomenon of Pan-Deuteronomism*. Edited by L. S. Schearing and S. L. McKenzie. Journal for the Study of the Old Testament Supplement 268. Sheffield: Sheffield Academic Press, 1999.
Kutsch, E. *Verheissung und Gesetz: Untersuchungen zum sogenannten 'Bund' im Alten Testament*. Beihefte zur Zeitschrift für die alttestamentliche Wissenschaft 131. Berlin: de Gruyter, 1973.
Laberge, L. "'Le lieu que Yhwh a choisi pour y mettre son Nom' (TM, LXX, Vg, et Targums): Contribution à la critique textuelle d'une formule deutéronomiste." *Estudios Bíblicos* 43 (1985): 209–36.
Labuschagne, C. J. "Divine Speech in Deuteronomy." Pp. 111–26 in *Das Deuteronomium: Entstehung, Gestalt und Botschaft*. Edited by N. Lohfink. Bibliotheca Ephemeridum Theologicarum Lovaniensium 68. Leuven: Leuven University Press, 1985.

———. "Some Significant Composition Techniques in Deuteronomy." Pp. 121–31 in *Scripta signa vocis*. Groningen, Netherlands: Forsten, 1986.
Lane, D. C. *The Meaning and Use of Berith in the Old Testament*. Ph.D. dissertation. Trinity Evangelical Divinity School, 2000.
Lang, B. "The Number Ten and the Iniquity of the Fathers: A New Interpretation of the Decalogue." *Zeitschrift für die alttestamentliche Wissenchaft* 118 (2006): 218–38.
Lapsley, J. E. "Feeling Our Way: Love for God in Deuteronomy." *Catholic Biblical Quarterly* 65 (2003): 350–69.
Leibowitz, N. *Studies in Shemot I*. Jerusalem: World Zionist Organization, 1976.
Lemke, W. E. "Circumcision of the Heart: The Journey of a Biblical Metaphor." Pp. 299–319 in *A God So Near: Essays on Old Testament Theology in Honor of Patrick D. Miller*. Edited by B. A. Strawn and N. R. Bowen. Winona Lake, IN: Eisenbrauns, 2003.
Lenchak, T. A. *Choose Life! A Rhetorical-Critical Investigation of Deuteronomy 28,69–30,20*. Analecta Biblica 129. Rome: Pontifical Biblical Institute, 1993.
Levenson, J. D. "The Davidic Covenant and Its Modern Interpreters." *Catholic Biblical Quarterly* 41 (1979): 205–19.

———. *Sinai and Zion: An Entry into the Jewish Bible*. Minneapolis: Winston, 1985.

———. "Who Inserted the Book of the Torah?" *Harvard Theological Review* 68 (1975): 203–33.
Levine, E. "The Land of Milk and Honey." *Journal for the Study of the Old Testament* 87 (2000): 43–57.
Levinson, B. M. *Deuteronomy and the Hermeneutics of Legal Innovation*. New York: Oxford University Press, 1998.

———. "The Hermeneutics of Tradition in Deuteronomy: A Reply to J. G. McConville." *Journal of Biblical Literature* 119 (2000): 268–86.
Lewy, I. "The Puzzle of Dt. XXVII: Blessings Announced, but Curses Noted." *Vetus Testamentum* 12 (1962): 207–11.
Lewy, J. "Les textes paléo-assyriens et l'Ancien Testament." *Revue de l'histoire des religions* 110 (1934): 29–65.

Lindars, B. "Torah in Deuteronomy." Pp. 117–36 in *Words and Meanings: Essays Presented to David Winton Thomas*. Edited by P. R. Ackroyd and B. Lindars. Cambridge: Cambridge University Press, 1968.

Linington, S. "The Term *berith* in the Old Testament—Part I: An Enquiry into the Meaning and Use of the Word in the Contexts of the Covenants between God and Humans in the Pentateuch." *Old Testament Essays* 15 (2002): 687–714.

Lipiński, E. "'Mon Père était un Araméen errant': L'histoire, carrefour des sciences bibliques et orientales." *Orientalia lovaniensia periodica* 20 (1989): 23–47.

Loewenstamm, S. E. "The Divine Grants of Land to the Patriarchs." *Journal of the American Oriental Society* 91 (1971): 509–10.

⸻. "The Formula *Baʿet Hahiʾ* in the Introductory Speeches in Deuteronomy." Pp. 42–50 in *From Babylon to Canaan: Studies in the Bible and Its Oriental Background*. Jerusalem: Magnes, 1992.

Lohfink, N. "Die Abänderung der Theologie des priesterlichen Geschichtswerks im Segen des Heiligkeitsgesetzes: Zu Lev. 26,9.11–13." Pp. 157–68 in *Studien zum Pentateuch*. Stuttgarter Biblische Aufsatzbände 4. Stuttgart: Katholisches Bibelwerk, 1988.

⸻. "Der Begriff 'Bund' in der biblischen Theologie." Pp. 19–36 in *Der Gott Israels und die Volker: Untersuchungen zum Jesajabuch und zu den Psalmen*. Edited by N. Lohfink and E. Zenger. Stuttgarter Bibelstudien 154. Stuttgart: Katholisches Bibelwerk, 1994.

⸻. "Bund als Vertrag im Deuteronomium." *Zeitschrift für die alttestamentliche Wissenschaft* 107 (1995): 215–39.

⸻. "Der Bundesschluß im Land Moab: Redaktionsgeschichtliches zu Dt 28,69–32,47." *Biblische Zeitschrift* 6 (1962): 32–56.

⸻. "Darstellungskunst und Theologie in Dtn 1,6–3,29." *Biblica* 41 (1960): 105–35.

⸻. "Dtn 12,1 und Gen 15,18: Das dem Samen Abrahams geschenkte Land als der Geltungsbereich der deuteronomischen Gesetze." Pp. 183–210 in *Die Väter Israels: Beiträge zur Theologie der Patriarchenüberlieferungen im Alten Testament*. Edited by M. Görg. Stuttgart: Katholisches Bibelwerk, 1989.

⸻. "Dt 26,17–19 und die 'Bundesformel.'" Pp. 211–61 in *Studien zum Deuteronomium und zur deuteronomistischen Literatur I*. Stuttgarter biblische Aufsatzbände 8. Stuttgart: Katholisches Bibelwerk, 1995.

⸻. "Dtn 28,69: Überschrift oder Kolophon?" *Biblische Notizen* 64 (1992): 40–52.

⸻. *Das Hauptgebot: Eine Untersuchung literarischer Einleitungsfragen zu Dtn 5–11*. Analecta Biblica 20. Rome: Pontifical Biblical Institute, 1963.

⸻. *Die Landverheissung als Eid: Eine Studie zu Gn 15*. Stuttgart: Katholisches Bibelwerk, 1967.

⸻. "Moab oder Sichem: Wo wurde Dtn 28 nach der Fabel des Deuteronomiums proklamiert?" Pp. 139–53 in *Studies in Deuteronomy in Honour of C. J. Labuschagne on the Occasion of His 65th Birthday*. Edited by F. García Martínez et al. Supplements to Vetus Testamentum 53. Leiden: Brill, 1994.

_____. "Narrative Analyse von Dtn 1,6-3,29." Pp. 121-76 in *Mincha: Festgabe für Rolf Rendtorff zum 75. Geburtstag*. Edited by F. Blum, Neukirchen Vluyn: Neukirchener Verlag, 2000.

_____. "Der neue Bund im Buch Deuteronomium?" *Zeitschrift für altorientalische und biblische Rechtsgeschichte* 4 (1998): 100-25.

_____. "The Problem of the Individual and Community in Deuteronomy 1:6-3:29." Pp. 227-33 in *Theology of the Pentateuch: Themes of the Priestly Narrative and Deuteronomy*. Translated by Linda M. Maloney. Minneapolis: Fortress, 1994.

_____. "Prolegomena zu einer Rechtshermeneutik des Pentateuchs." Pp. 181-231 in *Studien zum Deuteronomium und zur deuteronomistischen Literatur V*. Stuttgarter Biblische Aufsatzbände 38. Stuttgart: Katholisches Bibelwerk, 2005.

_____. "Reading Deuteronomy 5 as Narrative." Pp. 261-81 in *A God So Near: Essays on Old Testament Theology in Honor of Patrick D. Miller*. Edited by B. A. Strawn and N. R. Bowen. Winona Lake, IN: Eisenbrauns, 2003.

_____. "The 'Small Credo' of Deuteronomy 26:5-9." Pp. 265-89 in *Theology of the Pentateuch: Themes of the Priestly Narrative and Deuteronomy*. Translated by Linda M. Maloney. Minneapolis: Fortress, 1994.

_____. *Die Väter Israels im Deuteronomium: Mit einer Stellungnahme von Thomas Römer*. Orbis Biblicus et Orientalis 111. Göttingen: Vandenhoeck & Ruprecht, 1991.

_____. "Verkündigung des Hauptgebots in der jüngsten Schicht des Deuteronomiums (Deut. 4,1-40)." Pp. 82-120 in *Höre Israel! Auslegung von Texten aus dem Buch Deuteronomium*. Die Welt der Bibel 18. Dusseldorf: Patmos, 1965.

_____. "Wann hat Gott dem Volk Israel das den Vätern verheissene Land gegeben? Zu einem rätselhaften Befund im Buch Numeri." Pp. 9-30 in *Väter der Kirche—ekklesiales Denken von den Anfängen bis in die Neuzeit: Festgabe für Hermann Josef Sieben SJ zum 70. Geburtstag*. Edited by J. Arnold, R. Berndt, and R. M. W. Stammberger. Paderborn: Schöningh, 2004.

_____. "Zur deuteronomischen Zentralisationsformel." *Biblica* 65 (1984): 297-328.

_____. "Zur Fabel des Deuteronomiums." Pp. 65-78 in *Bundesdokument und Gesetz: Studien zum Deuteronomium*. Herders Biblische Studien 4. Freiburg: Herder, 1995.

_____, ed. *Das Deuteronomium: Entstehung, Gestalt and Botschaft*. Bibliotheca Ephemeridum Theologicarum Lovaniensium 68. Leuven: Leuven University Press, 1985.

Lundbom, J. R. "The Inclusio and Other Framing Devices in Deuteronomy I-XXVIII." *Vetus Testamentum* 46 (1996): 296-315.

_____. *Jeremiah: A Study in Ancient Hebrew Rhetoric*. Society of Biblical Literature Dissertation Series 18. Missoula, MT: Scholars Press, 1975.

_____. "The Lawbook of the Josianic Reform." *Catholic Biblical Quarterly* 38 (1976): 293-302.

Lust, J., and M. Vervenne, eds. *Deuteronomy and Deuteronomistic Literature: Festschrift C. H. W. Brekelmans*. Bibliotheca Ephemeridum Theologicarum Lovaniensium 83. Leuven: Leuven University Press, 1997.

Lux, R. "Der Tod des Mose als 'besprochene und erzählte Welt': Überlegungen zu einer literaturwissenschaftlichen und theologischen Interpretation von Deuteronomium 32,48-52 und 34." *Zeitschrift für Theologie und Kirche* 84 (1987): 395-425.
MacDonald, N. *Deuteronomy and the Meaning of "Monotheism."* Forschungen zum Alten Testament 2. Tübingen: Mohr Siebeck, 2003.
———. "The Literary Criticism and Rhetorical Logic of Deuteronomy I-IV." *Vetus Testamentum* 56 (2006): 203-24.
Magonet, J. "The Rhetoric of God: Exodus 6.2-8." *Journal for the Study of the Old Testament* 27 (1983): 56-67.
Manley, G. T. "The God of Abraham." *Tyndale Bulletin* 14 (1964): 3-7.
Mann, T. W. "Theological Reflections on the Denial of Moses." *Journal of Biblical Literature* 98 (1979): 481-94.
Mason, S. D. *'Eternal Covenant' in the Pentateuch: The Contours of an Elusive Phrase*. Library of Hebrew Bible/Old Testament Studies 494. New York: T. & T. Clark, 2008.
May, H. G. "The God of My Father: A Study of Patriarchal Religion." *Journal of Bible and Religion* 9 (1941): 155-200.
———. "The Patriarchal Idea of God." *Journal of Biblical Literature* 60 (1941): 113-28.
Mayes, A. D. H. "Deuteronomistic Ideology and the Theology of the Old Testament." *Journal for the Study of the Old Testament* 82 (1999): 424-55.
———. *Deuteronomy*. New Century Bible Commentary. Grand Rapids, MI: Eerdmans, 1979.
———. "Deuteronomy 4 and the Literary Criticism on Deuteronomy." *Journal of Biblical Literature* 100 (1981): 23-51.
———, and R. B. Salters. *Covenant as Context: Essays in Honour of E. W. Nicholson*. Oxford: Oxford University Press, 2003.
McBride, S. D. *The Deuteronomic Name Theology*. Ph.D dissertation. Harvard University, 1969.
McCarthy, C. *Biblia Hebraica Quinta, Fascicle 5: Deuteronomy*. Stuttgart: Deutsche Bibelgesellschaft, 2007.
McCarthy, D. J. "*Bᵉrît* and Covenant in the Deuteronomistic History." Pp. 65-85 in *Studies in the Religion of Ancient Israel*. Edited by P. A. H. Boer. Supplements to Vetus Testamentum 23. Leiden: Brill, 1972.
———. "*Bᵉrît* in Old Testament History and Theology." *Biblica* 53 (1972): 110-21.
———. "Exod 3:14: History, Philology, and Theology." *Catholic Biblical Quarterly* 40 (1978): 311-22.
———. "Moses' Dealings with Pharaoh: Ex 7,8-10,27." *Catholic Biblical Quarterly* 27 (1965): 336-47.
———. "Notes on the Love of God in Deuteronomy and the Father-Son Relationship between Yahweh and Israel." *Catholic Biblical Quarterly* 27 (1965): 144-47.
———. "Three Covenants in Genesis." *Catholic Biblical Quarterly* 26 (1964): 179-89.
———. *Treaty and Covenant*. Analecta Biblica 21a. Rome: Pontifical Biblical Institute, 1981.

McComiskey, T. E. *The Covenants of Promise: A Theology of Old Testament Covenants*. Grand Rapids, MI: Baker, 1985.

———. "The Religion of the Patriarchs." Pp. 195–206 in *The Law and the Prophets: Old Testament Studies in Honor of Oswald T. Allis*. Edited by J. H. Skilton. Nutley, NJ: Presbyterian and Reformed, 1974.

McConville, J. G. *Deuteronomy*. Apollos Old Testament Commentary 5. Downers Grove, IL: InterVarsity, 2002.

———. "Deuteronomy: Torah for the Church of Christ." *European Journal of Theology* 9 (2000): 33–47.

———. "God's 'Name' and God's 'Glory.'" *Tyndale Bulletin* 30 (1979): 149–63.

———. *Grace in the End: A Study in Deuteronomic Theology*. Studies in Old Testament Biblical Theology. Grand Rapids, MI: Zondervan, 1993.

———. *Law and Theology in Deuteronomy*. Eugene, OR: Wipf & Stock, 1984.

———. "Metaphor, Symbol, and the Interpretation of Deuteronomy." Pp. 329–51 in *After Pentecost: Language and Biblical Interpretation*. Edited by C. Bartholomew, C. Green, and K. Möller. Grand Rapids, MI: Zondervan, 2001.

———. "Singular Address in the Deuteronomic Law and the Politics of Legal Administration." *Journal for the Study of the Old Testament* 97 (2002): 19–36.

McKane, W. *Studies in the Patriarchal Narratives*. Edinburgh: Handsel, 1979.

McKay, J. W. "Man's Love for God in Deuteronomy and the Father/Teacher-Son/Pupil Relationship." *Vetus Testamentum* 22 (1972): 426–35.

McKenzie, S. L. *Covenant*. St. Louis, MO: Chalice, 2000.

———, and M. P. Graham, eds. *The History of Israel's Traditions: The Heritage of Martin Noth*. Journal for the Study of the Old Testament Supplement 182. Sheffield: Sheffield Academic Press, 1994.

McNulty, T. M. "Pauline Preaching: A Speech-Act Analysis." *Worship* 53 (1979): 207–14.

Mendecki, N. "Dtn 30,3–4: Nachexilisch?" *Biblische Zeitschrift* 29 (1985): 267–71.

Mendenhall, G. E. *Law and Covenant in Israel and the Ancient Near East*. Pittsburgh: Biblical Colloquium, 1955.

———. "The Suzerainty Treaty Structure: Thirty Years Later." Pp. 85–100 in *Religion and Law: Biblical-Judaic and Islamic Perspectives*. Edited by E. B. Firmage, B. G. Weiss, and J. W. Welch. Winona Lake, IN: Eisenbrauns, 1990.

Merendino, R. P. *Das Deuteronomische Gesetz*. Bonner biblische Beiträge. Bonn: Hanstein, 1969.

———. "Dt 27,1–8: Eine literarkritische und überlieferungsgeschichtliche Untersuchung." *Biblische Zeitschrift* 24 (1980): 194–207.

———. "Die Zeugnisse, die Satzungen und die Rechte: Überlieferungsgeschichtliche Erwägungen zu Deut 6." Pp. 185–208 in *Bausteine biblischer Theologie: Festgabe für G. Johannes Botterweck zum 60. Geburtstag dargebracht von seinen Schülern*. Bonner Biblische Beiträge 50. Cologne: Hanstein, 1977.

Merrill, E. H. *Deuteronomy*. New American Commentary 4. Nashville: Broadman & Holman, 1994.

———. *Everlasting Dominion: A Theology of the Old Testament*. Nashville: Broadman & Holman, 2006.

Merwe, C. H. J. van der, J. A. Naudé, and J. H. Kroeze. *A Biblical Hebrew Reference Grammar*. Biblical Languages: Hebrew. Sheffield: Sheffield Academic Press, 2002.
Mettinger, T. N. D. *The Dethronement of Sabaoth: Studies in the Shem and Kabod Theologies*. Translated by F. H. Cryer. Coniectanea biblica: Old Testament Series 18. Lund: Wallin & Dalholm, 1982.
———. *In Search of God: The Meaning and Message of the Everlasting Names*. Translated by F. H. Cryer. Philadelphia: Fortress, 1988.
———. Review of S. L. Richter, *The Deuteronomistic History and the Name Theology*: lešakkēn šemô šām *in the Bible and the Ancient Near East*. *Journal of Biblical Literature* 122 (2003): 753–55.
Michel, A. "Deuteronomium 26,16–19: Ein 'ewiger' Bund." Pp. 141–49 in *Für immer verbündet: Studien zur Bundestheologie der Bible*. Edited by C. Dohmen and C. Frevel. Stuttgarter Bibelstudien 211. Stuttgart: Katholisches Bibelwerk, 2007.
Milgrom, J. "Covenants: The Sinaitic and Patriarchal Covenants in the Holiness Code (Leviticus 17–27)." Pp. 91–101 in *Sefer Moshe: The Moshe Weinfeld Jubilee Volume: Studies in the Bible and the Ancient Near East, Qumran, and Postbiblical Judaism*. Edited by C. Cohen, A. Hurvitz, and S. M. Paul. Winona Lake, IN: Eisenbrauns, 2004.
———. *Leviticus 23–27*. Anchor Bible 3B. New York: Doubleday, 2001.
———. *Numbers*. The Jewish Publication Society Torah Commentary. Philadelphia: Jewish Publication Society, 1990.
———. "Profane Slaughter and a Formulaic Key to the Composition of Deuteronomy." *Hebrew Union College Annual* 47 (1976): 1–17.
Millar, J. G. "Living at the Place of Decision: Time and Place in the Framework of Deuteronomy." Pp. 15–88 in *Time and Place in Deuteronomy*. Journal for the Study of the Old Testament Supplement 179. Sheffield: Sheffield Academic Press, 1994.
———. *Now Choose Life: Theology and Ethics in Deuteronomy*. Grand Rapids, MI: Eerdmans, 1998.
Millard, A. R. "A Wandering Aramean." *Journal of the Near Eastern Studies* 39 (1980): 153–5.
———, and D. J. Wiseman, eds. *Essays on the Patriarchal Narratives*. Leicester: Inter-Varsity, 1980. Reprinted, Winona Lake, IN: Eisenbrauns, 1983.
Miller, P. D. *Deuteronomy*. Interpretation. Louisville: John Knox, 1990.
———. "The Gift of God: The Deuteronomic Theology of the Land." *Interpretation* 23 (1969): 450–65.
———. *Israelite Religion and Biblical Theology: Collected Essays*. Journal for the Study of the Old Testament Supplement 267. Sheffield: Sheffield Academic Press, 2000.
———. "Moses My Servant: The Deuteronomic Portrait of Moses." *Interpretation* 41 (1987): 245–55.
———. *The Religion of Ancient Israel*. Louisville: Westminster John Knox, 2000.
———. "The Wilderness Journey in Deuteronomy: Style, Structure, and Theology in Deuteronomy 1–3." Pp. 50–68 in *To Hear and Obey: Essays in Honor of Frederick Carlson Holmgren*. Edited by B. J. Bergfalk and P. E. Koptak. Chicago: Covenant, 1997.

Minnette de Tillesse, G. "Sections 'Tu' et Sections 'Vous' dans le Deutéronome." *Vetus Testamentum* 12 (1982): 29–87.

Mittmann, S. *Deuteronomium 1,1–6,3: Literarkritisch und traditionsgeschichtlich untersucht*. Beihefte zur Zeitschrift für die alttestamentliche Wissenschaft 139. Berlin: de Gruyter, 1975.

Moberly, R. W. L. *At the Mountain of God: Story and Theology in Exodus 32–34*. Journal for the Study of the Old Testament Supplement 22. Sheffield: JSOT Press, 1983.

———. "How May We Speak of God? A Reconsideration of the Nature of Biblical Theology." *Tyndale Bulletin* 53 (2002): 177–202.

———. *The Old Testament of the Old Testament*. Overtures to Biblical Theology. Minneapolis: Fortress, 1992.

———. "Toward an Interpretation of the Shema." Pp. 124–44 in *Theological Exegesis: Essays in Honor of Brevard S. Childs*. Edited by C. Seitz and K. Greene-McCreight. Grand Rapids, MI: Eerdmans, 1999.

———. "Yahweh Is One: The Translation of the Shema." Pp. 209–15 in *Studies in Deuteronomy in Honour of C. J. Labuschagne on the Occasion of His 65th Birthday*. Edited by F. García Martínez et al. Supplements to Vetus Testamentum 53. Leiden: Brill, 1994.

Mölle, H. *Genesis 15: Eine Erzählung von den Anfängen Israels*. Forschung zur Bibel 62. Würzburg: Echter Verlag, 1988.

Moor, J. C. de. *The Rise of Yahwism: The Roots of Israelite Monotheism*. Rev. ed. Bibliotheca Ephemeridum Theologicarum Lovaniensium 91. Leuven: Leuven University Press, 1997.

———, ed. *Synchronic or Diachronic? A Debate on Method in Old Testament Exegesis*. Old Testament Studies 34. Leiden: Brill, 1995.

Moran, W. L. "The Ancient Near Eastern Background of the Love of God in Deuteronomy." *Catholic Biblical Quarterly* 25 (1963): 77–87.

———. "The End of the Unholy War and the Anti-Exodus." Pp. 147–55 in *A Song of Power and the Power of Song: Essays on the Book of Deuteronomy*. Edited by D. L. Christensen. Sources for Biblical and Theological Study 3. Winona Lake, IN: Eisenbrauns, 1993.

Motyer, J. A. *The Revelation of the Divine Name*. London: Tyndale, 1959.

Mowinckel, S. "The Name of the God of Moses." *Hebrew Union College Annual* 32 (1961): 121–33.

Muilenburg, J. "The Form and Structure of the Covenantal Formulations." *Vetus Testamentum* 9 (1959): 347–65.

———. "Form Criticism and Beyond." *Journal of Biblical Literature* 88 (1969): 1–18.

Muraoka, T. "On the So-Called *Dativus Ethicus* in Hebrew." *Journal of Theological Studies* 29 (1978): 495–98.

Murray, J. *The Covenant of Grace: A Biblico-theological Study*. London: Tyndale, 1954.

Nelson, R. D. *Deuteronomy: A Commentary*. Old Testament Library. Philadelphia: Westminster John Knox, 2002.

———. *The Double Redaction of the Deuteronomistic History*. Journal for the Study of the Old Testament Supplement 18. Sheffield: JSOT Press, 1981.

_____. "The Double Redaction of the Deuteronomistic History: The Case Is Still Compelling." *Journal for the Study of the Old Testament* 29 (2005): 319–37.

Neufeld, D. *Reconceiving Texts as Speech Acts: An Analysis of 1 John*. Leiden: Brill, 1994.

Nicholson, E. W. "The Centralisation of the Cult in Deuteronomy." *Vetus Testamentum* 13 (1963): 380–89.

_____. "The Covenant Ritual in Exodus XXIV 3–8." *Vetus Testamentum* 32 (1982): 74–86.

_____. *Deuteronomy and Tradition*. Philadelphia: Fortress, 1967.

_____. *Exodus and Sinai in History and Tradition*. Oxford: Blackwell, 1973.

_____. *God and His People: Covenant and Theology in the Old Testament*. Oxford: Clarendon, 1986.

_____. *The Pentateuch in the Twentieth Century: The Legacy of Julius Wellhausen*. Oxford: Clarendon, 1998.

Niehaus, J. J. "An Argument against Theologically Constructed Covenants." *Journal of the Evangelical Theological Society* 50 (2008): 259–73.

_____. "The Central Sanctuary: Where and When?" *Tyndale Bulletin* 43 (1992): 3–30.

_____. "Covenant: An Idea in the Mind of God." *Journal of the Evangelical Theological Society* 52 (2009): 225–46.

_____. *The Deuteronomic Style: An Examination of the Deuteronomic Style in the Light of Ancient Near Eastern Literature*. Unpublished manuscript, 1985.

_____. *God at Sinai: Covenant and Theophany in the Bible and the Ancient Near East*. Grand Rapids, MI: Zondervan, 1995.

Nocquet, D. "Étonnantes variations autour des 'destinataires du pays' dans le Deutéronome: Significations synchroniques et historiques." *Zeitschrift für die alttestamentliche Wissenschaft* 119 (2007): 341–54.

Noort, E. "'Land' in the Deuteronomistic Tradition." Pp. 128–44 in *Synchronic or Diachronic? A Debate on Method in Old Testament Exegesis*. Edited by J. C. de Moor. Leiden: Brill, 1995.

Noth, M. *The Deuteronomistic History*. Translated by J. Doull. Journal for the Study of the Old Testament Supplement 15. Sheffield: JSOT Press, 1981.

_____. *A History of Pentateuchal Traditions*. Translated by B. W. Anderson. Chico, CA: Scholars Press, 1981.

O'Brien, M. "The Book of Deuteronomy." *Currents in Research: Biblical Studies* 3 (1995): 95–128.

O'Connell, R. H. "Deuteronomy VII 1–26: Asymmetrical Concentricity and the Rhetoric of Conquest." *Vetus Testamentum* 42 (1992): 248–65.

_____. "Deuteronomy VIII 1–20: Asymmetrical Concentricity and the Rhetoric of Providence." *Vetus Testamentum* 40 (1990): 437–52.

_____. "Deuteronomy IX 7–X 7, 10–11: Panelled Structure, Double Rehearsal and the Rhetoric of Covenant Rebuke." *Vetus Testamentum* 42 (1992): 492–509.

Oden, R. A., Jr. "The Place of Covenant in the Religion of Israel." Pp. 429–47 in *Ancient Israelite Religion: Essays in Honor of Frank Moore Cross*. Edited by P. D. Miller, P. D. Hanson, and S. D. McBride. Philadelphia: Fortress, 1987.

O'Dowd, R. *The Wisdom of Torah: Epistemology in Deuteronomy and the Wisdom Literature*. Forschungen zur Religion und Literatur des Alten und Neuen Testaments 225. Göttingen: Vandenhoeck & Ruprecht, 2009.

Olbricht, T. H. "Rhetorical Criticism in Biblical Commentaries." *Currents in Biblical Research* 7 (2008): 11–36.

Olson, D. T. *Deuteronomy and the Death of Moses: A Theological Reading*. Overtures to Biblical Theology. Minneapolis: Fortress, 1994.

―――――. "Deuteronomy as De-centering Center: Reflections on Postmodernism and the Quest for a Theological Center of the Hebrew Scriptures." *Semeia* 71 (1995): 119–32.

―――――. "How Does Deuteronomy Do Theology? Literary Juxtaposition and Paradox in the New Moab Covenant in Deuteronomy 29–32." Pp. 201–13 in *A God So Near: Essays on Old Testament Theology in Honor of Patrick D. Miller*. Edited by B. A. Strawn and N. R. Bowen. Winona Lake, IN: Eisenbrauns, 2003.

Olyan, S. M. "Honor, Shame, and Covenant Relations in Ancient Israel and Its Environment." *Journal of Biblical Literature* 115 (1996): 201–18.

Orlinsky, H. M. "The Biblical Concept of the Land of Israel: Cornerstone of the Covenant between God and Israel." Pp. 27–64 in *The Land of Israel: Jewish Perspectives*. Edited by L. A. Hoffman. Notre Dame, IN: University of Notre Dame Press, 1986.

Otto, E. "Das Deuteronomium als Archimedischer Punkt der Pentateuchkritik auf dem Wege zu einer Neubegründung der De Wette'schen Hypothese." Pp. 321–39 in *Deuteronomy and Deuteronomistic Literature: Festschrift C. H. W. Brekelmans*. Edited by J. Lust and M. Vervenne. Bibliotheca Ephemeridum Theologicarum Lovaniensium 83. Leuven: Leuven University Press, 1997.

―――――. *Das Deuteronomium im Pentateuch und Hexateuch: Studien zur Literaturgeschichte von Pentateuch und Hexateuch im Lichte des Deuteronomiumrahmens*. Forschungen zum Alten Testament 30. Tübingen: Mohr Siebeck, 2000.

―――――. "Mose, der erste Schriftgelehrte: Deuteronomium 1,5 in der Fabel des Pentateuch." Pp. 273–84 in *L'Écrit et l'Esprit. Études d'histoire du texte et de théologie biblique: Festschrift für Adrian Schenker*. Edited by D. Böhler, I. Himbaza, and P. Hugo. Orbis Biblicus et Orientalis 214. Fribourg: Academic Press / Göttingen: Vandenhoeck & Ruprecht, 2005.

―――――. "Die Paradieserzählung Genesis 2–3: Eine nachpriesterschriftliche Lehrerzählung in ihrem religionshistorischen Kontext." Pp. 167–92 in *"Jedes Ding hat seine Zeit . . .": Studien zur israelitischen und altorientalischen Weisheit. Diethelm Michel zum 65. Geburtstag*. Beihefte zur Zeitschrift für die alttestamentliche Wissenschaft 241. Berlin: de Gruyter, 1996.

―――――. "Perspektiven der neueren Deuteronomiumsforschung." *Zeitschrift für die alttestamentliche Wissenschaft* 119 (2007): 319–40.

―――――. "Treueid und Gesetz: Die Ursprünge des Deuteronomiums im Horizont neuassyrischen Vertagsrechts." *Zeitschrift für altorientalische und biblische Rechtsgeschichte* 2 (1996): 1–52.

Otto, R. *The Idea of the Holy: An Inquiry into the Non-rational Factor in the Idea of the Divine and Its Relation to the Rational*. Translated by J. W. Harvey. 2nd ed. New York: Oxford University Press, 1958.

Pagolu, A. *The Religion of the Patriarchs*. Journal for the Study of the Old Testament Supplement 277. Sheffield: JSOT Press, 1998.
Pakkala, J. "The Date of the Oldest Edition of Deuteronomy." *Zeitschrift für die alttestamentliche Wissenschaft* 121 (2009): 388–401.
Pannell, R. J. "El Deuteronomio y su hermenéutica de la tradición." *Diálogo Teológico* 21 (1983): 47–56.
———. *Those Alive Here Today: The "Day of Horeb" and Deuteronomy's Hermeneutical Locus of Revelation*. Longwood, FL: Xulon, 2004.
Pardee, D. "The 'Epistolary Perfect' in Hebrew Letters." *Biblische Notizen* 22 (1983): 34–40.
Parker, S. B., ed. *Ugaritic Narrative Poetry*. Society of Biblical Literature Writings from the Ancient World 9. Atlanta: Scholars Press, 1997.
Parke-Taylor, G. H. *Yahweh: The Divine Name in the Bible*. Waterloo, ON: Wilfrid Laurier University Press, 1975.
Parpola, S., and K. Watanabe. *Neo-Assyrian Treaties and Loyalty Oaths*. State Archives of Assyria 2. Helsinki: Helsinki University Press, 1988.
Patrick, D. "God's Commandment." Pp. 93–111 in *God in the Fray: A Tribute to Walter Brueggemann*. Edited by T. Linafelt and T. K. Beal. Minneapolis: Fortress, 1998.
———. "The Rhetoric of Collective Responsibility in Deuteronomic Law." Pp. 421–36 in *Pomegranates and Golden Bells: Studies in Biblical, Jewish, and Near Eastern Ritual, Law, and Literature in Honor of Jacob Milgrom*. Edited by D. P. Wright, D. N. Freedman, and A. Hurvitz. Winona Lake, IN: Eisenbrauns, 1995.
———. *The Rhetoric of Revelation in the Hebrew Bible*. Overtures to Biblical Theology. Minneapolis: Fortress, 1999.
———, and A. Scult. *Rhetoric and Biblical Interpretation*. Journal for the Study of the Old Testament Supplement 82. Sheffield: Sheffield Academic Press, 1990.
Patte, D. "Speech Act Theory and Biblical Exegesis." *Semeia* 41 (1988): 85–102.
Paul, S. M. "Adoption Formulae: A Study of the Cuneiform and Biblical Legal Clauses." *Maarav* 2 (1979–80): 176–78.
Peer, W. van, and F. Hakemulder. "Foregrounding." Pp. 546–51 in vol. 4 of the *Encyclopedia of Language and Linguistics*. Edited by K. Brown. 14 vols. Oxford: Elsevier, 2006.
Perdue, L. G. *The Collapse of History: Reconstructing Old Testament Theology*. Overtures to Biblical Theology. Minneapolis: Fortress, 1994.
———. *Reconstructing Old Testament Theology After the Collapse of History*. Overtures to Biblical Theology. Minneapolis: Fortress, 2005.
Perelman, C., and L. Olbrechts-Tyteca. *The New Rhetoric: A Treatise on Argumentation*. Notre Dame, IN: University of Notre Dame Press, 1969.
Perlitt, L. *Bundestheologie im alten Testament*. Wissenschaftliche Monographien zum Alten und Neuen Testament 36. Neukirchen-Vluyn: Neukirchener Verlag, 1969.
———. *Deuteronomium-Studien*. Forschungen zum Alten Testament 8. Tübingen: Mohr, 1994.
———. "Priesterschrift im Deuteronomium?" *Zeitschrift für die alttestamentliche Wissenschaft* 100 (1988): 65–88.

_____. "Wovon der Mensch lebt (Dtn 8,3b)." Pp. 404–26 in *Die Botschaft und die Boten: Festschrift für Hans Walter Wolff zum 70. Geburtstag*. Edited by J. Jeremias and L. Perlitt. Neukirchen-Vluyn: Neukirchener Verlag, 1981.

Plöger, J. G. *Literarkritische, formgeschichtliche und stilkritische Untersuchungen zum Deuteronimum*. Bonner Biblische Beiträge 26. Bonn: Hanstein, 1967.

Polk, T. *The Prophetic Persona*. Journal for the Study of the Old Testament Supplement 32. Sheffield: JSOT Press, 1984.

Polzin, R. *Moses and the Deuteronomist*. New York: Seabury, 1980.

_____. "Reporting Speech in the Book of Deuteronomy: Toward a Compositional Analysis of the Deuteronomic History." Pp. 193–211 in *Traditions in Transformation: Turning Points in Biblical Faith*. Edited by B. Halpern and J. D. Levenson. Winona Lake, IN: Eisenbrauns, 1981.

Porter, J. R. "The Legal Aspects of 'Corporate Personality' in the Old Testament." *Vetus Testamentum* 15 (1965): 361–68.

Porter, S. E., and D. L. Stamps, eds. *Rhetorical Criticism and the Bible*. Journal for the Study of the New Testament Supplement 195. London: Sheffield Academic Press, 2002.

Preuss, H. D. *Das Deuteronomium*. Erträge der Forschung 164. Darmstadt: Wissenschaftliche Buchgesellschaft, 1982.

_____. *Old Testament Theology*. 2 vols. Old Testament Library. Louisville: Westminster John Knox, 1995.

Provan, I. W., V. P. Long, and T. Longman III. *A Biblical History of Israel*. Louisville: Westminster John Knox, 2003.

Pury, A. de, and T. C. Römer. "Le Pentateuque en question: Position du problème et brève histoire de la recherche." Pp. 9–80 in *Le Pentateuque en Question*. Edited by A. de Pury and T. C. Römer. Geneva: Labor et Fides, 2002.

Rad, G. von. *Deuteronomy: A Commentary*. Old Testament Library. Philadelphia: Westminster, 1966.

_____. "Deuteronomy's 'Name' Theology and the Priestly Document's 'Kabod' Theology." Pp. 37–44 in *Studies in Deuteronomy*. Translated by D. Stalker. Studies in Biblical Theology 9. London: SCM, 1953.

_____. *From Genesis to Chronicles*. Edited by K. C. Hanson. Translated by E. W. T. Dicken. Minneapolis: Fortress, 2005.

_____. *Das Geschichtsbild des chronistischen Werkes*. Beiträge zur Wissenschaft vom Alten und Neuen Testament 4. Stuttgart: Kohlhammer, 1930.

_____. *Old Testament Theology*. Translated by D. M. G. Stalker. 2 vols. Louisville: Westminster John Knox, 2001.

Rendtorff, R. "'El als israelitische Gottesbezeichnung." *Zeitschrift für die alttestamentliche Wissenschaft* 106 (1994): 4–21.

_____. "'Covenant' as a Structuring Concept in Genesis and Exodus." *Journal of Biblical Literature* 108 (1989): 385–93.

_____. *The Covenant Formula: An Exegetical and Theological Investigation*. Translated by M. Kohl. Edinburgh: T. & T. Clark, 1998.

_____. "El, Ba'al und Jahwe: Erwägungen zum Verhältnis von kanaanäischer und israelitischer Religion." *Zeitschrift für die alttestamentliche Wissenchaft* 78 (1966): 277–92.

_____. "Die Erwählung Israels als Thema der deuteronomischen Theologie." Pp. 75–86 in *Die Botschaft und die Boten: Festschrift für Hans Walter Wolff zum 70. Geburtstag*. Edited by J. Jeremias and L. Perlitt. Neukirchen-Vluyn: Neukirchener Verlag, 1981.

———. "Genesis 15 im Rahmen der theologischen Bearbeitung der Vätergeschichten." Pp. 74–81 in *Werken und Wirken des Alten Testaments: Festschrift für Claus Westermann zum 70. Geburtstag*. Edited by R. Albertz et al. Göttingen: Vandenhoeck & Ruprecht, 1980.

———. *The Problem of the Process of Transmission in the Pentateuch*. Translated by J. J. Scullion. Journal for the Study of the Old Testament Supplement 89. Sheffield: Sheffield Academic Press, 1990.

Renz, T. *The Rhetorical Function of the Book of Ezekiel*. Supplements to Vetus Testamentum 76. Leiden: Brill, 1999.

Richter, S. *The Deuteronomistic History and the Name Theology*: lešakkēn šemô šām *in the Bible and the Ancient Near East*. Beihefte zur Zeitschrift für die alttestamentliche Wissenschaft 318. Berlin: de Gruyter, 2002.

———. "The Place of the Name in Deuteronomy." *Vetus Testamentum* 57 (2007): 342–66.

Robinson, H. W. *Corporate Personality in Ancient Israel*. Rev. ed. Philadelphia: Fortress, 1980.

Rofé, A. "The Covenant in the Land of Moab (Deuteronomy 28:69–30:20): Historico-literary, Comparative, and Formcritical Considerations." Pp. 269–80 in *A Song of Power and the Power of Song: Essays on the Book of Deuteronomy*. Edited by D. L. Christensen. Sources for Biblical and Theological Study 3. Winona Lake, IN: Eisenbrauns, 1993.

———. "The Monotheistic Argumentation in Deuteronomy iv 32–40: Contents, Composition and Text." *Vetus Testamentum* 35 (1985): 434–45.

———. "Promise and Covenant: The Promise to the Patriarchs in Late Biblical Literature." Pp. 52–59 in *Divine Promises to the Fathers in the Three Monotheistic Religions*. Edited by A. Niccacci. Jerusalem: Franciscan Printing Press, 1995.

Rogerson, J. W. "The Hebrew Conception of Corporate Personality: A Re-examination." *Journal of Theological Studies* 21 (1970): 1–16.

Römer, T. C. "The Book of Deuteronomy." Pp. 178–212 in *The History of Israel's Traditions: The Heritage of Martin Noth*. Journal for the Study of the Old Testament Supplement 182. Sheffield: Sheffield Academic Press, 1994.

———. "Deuteronomy in Search of Origins." Pp. 112–38 in *Reconsidering Israel and Judah: Recent Studies on the Deuteronomistic History*. Edited by G. N. Knoppers and J. G. McConville. Sources for Biblical and Theological Study 8. Winona Lake, IN: Eisenbrauns, 2000.

———. "How Did Jeremiah Become a Convert to Deuteronomic Ideology?" Pp. 189–99 in *Those Elusive Deuteronomists: The Phenomenon of Pan-Deuteronomism*. Edited by L. S. Schearing and S. L. McKenzie. Journal for the Study of the Old Testament Supplement 268. Sheffield: Sheffield Academic Press, 1999.

———. Israels Väter: Untersuchungen zur Väterthematik im Deuteronomium und in der deuteronomistischen Tradition. Orbis Biblicus et Orientalis 99. Freiburg: Universitätsverlag / Göttingen: Vandenhoeck & Ruprecht, 1990.

———. *The So-Called Deuteronomistic History: A Sociological, Historical and Literary Introduction*. London: T. & T. Clark, 2007.

_____, and M. Z. Brettler. "Deuteronomy 34 and the Case for a Persian Hexateuch." *Journal of Biblical Literature* 119 (2000): 401–19.

Rooy, H. F. van. "Deuteronomy 28:69: Superscript or Subscript?" *Journal of Northwest Semitic Languages* 14 (1988): 215–22.

Rost, L. *Das kleine Credo und andere Studien zum Alten Testament.* Heidelberg: Quelle & Meyer, 1965.

Rütersworden, U. "Bundestheologie ohne ברית." *Zeitschrift für altorientalische und biblische Rechtsgeschichte* 4 (1998): 85–99.

_____. "שם in Deuteronomium 12." Pp. 180–86 in *Für immer verbündet: Studien zur Bundestheologie der Bible.* Edited by C. Dohmen and C. Frevel. Stuttgarter Bibelstudien 211. Stuttgart: Katholisches Bibelwerk, 2007.

Sailhamer, J. H. *The Pentateuch as Narrative: A Biblical-Theological Commentary.* Grand Rapids, MI: Zondervan, 1992.

Sakenfeld, K. D. *The Meaning of Hesed in the Hebrew Bible: A New Inquiry.* Harvard Semitic Monograph 17. Missoula, MT: Scholars Press, 1978.

Sanders, E. P. *Paul and Palestinian Judaism.* Philadelphia: Fortress, 1977.

Sanders, P. *The Provenance of Deuteronomy 32.* Leiden: Brill, 1996.

Sarna, N. M. *Exodus.* The Jewish Publication Society Torah Commentary. Philadelphia: Jewish Publication Society, 1991.

_____. *Genesis.* The Jewish Publication Society Torah Commentary. Philadelphia: Jewish Publication Society, 1991.

Saucy, R. L. *The Case for Progressive Dispensationalism: The Interface between Dispensational and Non-dispensational Theology.* Grand Rapids, MI: Zondervan, 1993.

Schaller, J. J. "Performative Language Theory: An Exercise in the Analysis of Ritual." *Worship* 62 (1988): 415–32.

Schaper, J. "The 'Publication' of Legal Texts in Ancient Judah." Pp. 225–36 in *The Pentateuch as Torah: New Models for Understanding Its Promulgation and Acceptance.* Edited by G. N. Knoppers and B. M. Levinson. Winona Lake, IN: Eisenbrauns, 2007.

Scharbert, J. "'B^{e}rît' im Pentateuch." Pp. 163–70 in *De la Tôrah au Messie: Mélanges Henri Cazelles.* Edited by M. Carrez, J. Doré, and P. Grelot. Paris: Desclée, 1981.

_____. *Solidarität in Segen und Fluch im Alten Testament und in seiner Umwelt.* Bonner Biblische Beiträge. Bonn: Hanstein, 1958.

Schearing, L. S., and S. L. McKenzie, eds. *Those Elusive Deuteronomists: The Phenomenon of Pan-Deuteronomism.* Journal for the Study of the Old Testament Supplement 268. Sheffield: Sheffield Academic Press, 1999.

Schenker, A. "L'origine de l'idée d'une alliance entre Dieu et Israël dans l'Ancien Testament." *Revue biblique* 92 (1988): 184–94.

_____. "Unwiderrufliche Umkehr und neuer Bund: Vergleich zwischen der Wiederherstellung Israels in Dt 4,25–31; 30,1–14 und dem neuen Bund in Jer 31,31–34." *Freiburger Zeitschrift für die Philosophie und Theologie* 27 (1980): 93–106.

Schmid, H. H. *Der sogenannte Jahwist: Beobachtungen und Fragen zur Pentateuchforschung.* Zurich: Theologischer Verlag, 1976.

Schmid, K. *Genesis and the Moses Story: Israel's Dual Origins in the Hebrew Bible*. Translated by J. D. Nogalski. Siphrut: Literature and Theology of the Hebrew Scriptures 3. Winona Lake, IN: Eisenbrauns, 2010.
⸻. "The Late Persian Formation of the Torah: Observations on Deuteronomy 34." Pp. 237–45 in *Judah and the Judeans in the Fourth Century* B.C.E. Edited by O. Lipschits, G. N. Knoppers, and R. Albertz. Winona Lake, IN: Eisenbrauns, 2007.
Schmitt, H.-C. "Spätdeuteronomistisches Geschichtswerk und Priesterschift in Deuteronomium 34." Pp. 407–24 in *Textarbeit: Studien zu Texten und ihrer Rezeption aus dem Alten Testament und der Umwelt Israels*. Edited by K. Kiesow and T. Meurer. Münster: Ugarit-Verlag, 2003.
Scobie, C. H. H. *The Ways of Our God: An Approach to Biblical Theology*. Grand Rapids, MI: Eerdmans, 2003.
Searle, J. R. *The Construction of Social Reality*. London: Lane, 1995.
⸻. *Expression and Meaning: Studies in the Theory of Speech Acts*. Cambridge: Cambridge University Press, 1979.
⸻. *Speech Acts: An Essay in the Philosophy of Language*. Cambridge: Cambridge University Press, 1969.
Seebass, H. "Garizim und Ebal als Symbole von Segen und Fluch." *Biblica* 63 (1982): 22–31.
Segal, M. H. *The Pentateuch: Its Composition and Its Authorship and Other Biblical Studies*. Jerusalem: Magnes, 1967.
Seitz, C. "The Call of Moses and the 'Revelation' of the Divine Name: Source-Critical Logic and Its Legacy." Pp. 145–61 in *Theological Exegesis: Essays in Honor of Brevard S. Childs*. Edited by C. Seitz and K. Greene-McCreight. Grand Rapids, MI: Eerdmans, 1999.
Seitz, G. *Redaktionsgeschichtliche Studien zum Deuteronomium*. Beiträge zur Wissenschaft vom Alten und Neuen Testament 13. Stuttgart: Kohlhammer, 1971.
Sénéchal, V. *Rétribution et intercession dans le Deutéronome*. Beihefte zur Zeitschrift für die alttestamentliche Wissenschaft 408. Berlin: de Gruyter, 2009.
Shafer, B. E. "The Root *bḥr* and Pre-exilic Concepts of Chosenness in the Hebrew Bible." *Zeitschrift für die alttestamentliche Wissenschaft* 89 (1977): 20–42.
Sherrifs, D. C. "The Phrases *ina IGI DN* and *liphney Yhwh* in Treaty and Covenant Contexts." *Journal of Northwest Semitic Languages* 7 (1971): 55–65.
Silva, M. *Biblical Words and Their Meaning: An Introduction to Lexical Semantics*. Rev. ed. Grand Rapids, MI: Zondervan, 1994.
Ska, J.-L. *'Our Fathers Have Told Us': Introduction to the Analysis of Hebrew Narratives*. Subsidia Biblica 13. Rome: Pontifical Biblical Institute, 2000.
⸻. "La structure du Pentateuque dans sa forme canonique." *Zeitschrift für die alttestamentliche Wissenchaft* 113 (2001): 331–52.
Skweres, D. E. *Die Rückverweise im Buch Deuteronomium*. Analecta Biblica 79. Rome: Pontifical Biblical Institute, 1979.
Slanski, K. E. *The Babylonian Entitlement* Narûs (Kudurrus): *A Study in Their Form and Function*. Boston: American Schools of Oriental Research, 2003.
Slater, S. "Imagining Arrival: Rhetoric, Reader, and Word of God in Deuteronomy 1–3." Pp. 107–22 in *The Labour of Reading: Desire, Alienation, and Biblical Interpretation*. Edited by F. C. Black, R. Boer, and E. Runions. Society of

Biblical Literature Semeia Studies 26. Atlanta: Society of Biblical Literature, 1999.

Smend, R. *Die Bundesformel.* Theologische Studien 68. Zürich: EVZ, 1963.

———. "The Law and the Nations: A Contribution to Deuteronomistic Tradition History." Translated by P. T. Daniels. Pp. 95–110 in *Reconsidering Israel and Judah: Recent Studies on the Deuteronomistic History*. Sources for Biblical and Theological Study 8. Winona Lake, IN: Eisenbrauns, 2000.

Smith, M. S. "Remembering God: Collective Memory in Israelite Religion." *Catholic Biblical Quarterly* 64 (2002): 631–51.

———. *Ugaritic Narrative Poetry*. Society of Biblical Literature Writings from the Ancient World 9. Atlanta: Scholars Press, 1997.

Smith, W. Robertson. *Lectures on the Religion of the Semites—First Series: The Fundamental Institutions*. London: Black, 1956.

Sohn, S.-T. *The Divine Election of Israel*. Grand Rapids, MI: Eerdmans, 1991.

———. "'I Will Be Your God and You Will Be My People': The Origin and Background of the Covenant Formula." Pp. 355–72 in *Ki Baruch Hu: Ancient Near Eastern, Biblical, and Judaic Studies in Honor of Baruch A. Levine*. Edited by R. Chazan, W. W. Hallo, and L. H. Schiffman. Winona Lake, IN: Eisenbrauns, 1999.

Sonnet, J.-P. *The Book within the Book: Writing in Deuteronomy*. Leiden: Brill, 1997.

———. "Review of T. C. Lenchak, *Choose Life! A Rhetorical-Critical Investigation of Deuteronomy 28,69–30,20*." *Biblica* 76 (1995): 93–98.

Sonsino, R. *Motive Clauses in Hebrew Law: Biblical Forms and Near Eastern Parallels*. Society of Biblical Literature Dissertation Series 45. Chico, CA: Scholars Press, 1980.

Steiner, R. C. "The 'Aramean' of Deuteronomy 26:5: *Peshat* and *Derash*." Pp. 127–38 in *Tehillah le-Moshe: Biblical and Judaic Studies in Honor of Moshe Greenberg*. Edited by M. Cogan, B. L. Eichler, and J. H. Tigay. Winona Lake, IN: Eisenbrauns, 1997.

Stern, P. D. "The Origin and Significance of 'The Land Flowing with Milk and Honey.'" *Vetus Testamentum* 42 (1992): 554–57.

Sternberg, M. *The Poetics of Biblical Narrative: Ideological Literature and the Drama of Reading*. Bloomington: Indiana University Press, 1985.

Steymans, H. U. *Deuteronomium 28 und die adê zur Thronfolgeregelung Asarhaddons*. Orbis Biblicus et Orientalis 145. Göttingen: Vandenhoeck & Ruprecht, 1996.

Stoellger, P. "Deuteronomium 34 ohne Priesterschrift." *Zeitschrift für die alttestamentliche Wissenschaft* 105 (1993): 26–51.

Strawn, B. A. "Keep/Observe/Do — Carefully — Today! The Rhetoric of Repetition in Deuteronomy." Pp. 215–40 in *A God So Near: Essays on Old Testament Theology in Honor of Patrick D. Miller*. Edited by B. A. Strawn and N. R. Bowen. Winona Lake, IN: Eisenbrauns, 2003.

Suzuki, Y. "'The Place Which Yahweh Your God Will Choose' in Deuteronomy." Pp. 338–52 in *Problems in Biblical Theology: Essays in Honor of Rolf Knierim*. Edited by H. T. C. Sun et al. Grand Rapids, MI: Eerdmans, 1997.

Tadmor, H. "Treaty and Oath in the Ancient Near East: A Historian's Approach." Pp. 127–52 in *Humanizing America's Iconic Book: Society of Biblical Litera-*

ture Centennial Addresses. Edited by G. M. Tucker and D. A. Knight. Biblical Scholarship in North America 6. Chico, CA: Scholars Press, 1982.

Talstra, E. "Deuteronomy 9 and 10: Synchronic and Diachronic Observation." in *Old Testament Studies*. Edited by J. C. de Moor. Old Testament Studies 34. Leiden: Brill, 1995.

Taschner, J. "Die Bedeutung des Generationswechsels für den Geschichtsrückblick im Dtn 1–3." *Wort und Dienst* 26 (2001): 61–72.

———. *Die Mosereden im Deuteronomium: Eine kanonorientierte Untersuchung*. Forschungen zum Alten Testament 59. Tübingen: Mohr Siebeck, 2008.

Thiselton, A. C. "Communicative Action and Promise in Interdisciplinary, Biblical, and Theological Hermeneutics." Pp. 133–231 in *The Promise of Hermeneutics*. Grand Rapids, MI: Eerdmans, 1999.

———. *Language, Liturgy, and Meaning*. Grove Liturgical Study 2. Bramcote, Nottingham: Grove Books, 1975.

———. *New Horizons in Hermeneutics: The Theory and Practice of Transforming Biblical Reading*. Grand Rapids, MI: Zondervan, 1992.

———. "The Supposed Power of Words in the Biblical Writings." *Journal of Theological Studies* 25 (1974): 283–99.

———. *The Two Horizons: New Testament Hermeneutics and Philosophical Description*. Grand Rapids, MI: Eerdmans, 1980.

Thompson, T. L. *The Historicity of the Patriarchal Narratives*. Beihefte zur Zeitschrift für die alttestamentliche Wissenschaft 133. Berlin: de Gruyter, 1974.

———. "How Yahweh Became God: Exodus 3 and 6 and the Heart of the Pentateuch." *Journal for the Study of the Old Testament* 68 (1995): 57–74.

Tigay, J. H. *Deuteronomy*. The Jewish Publication Society Torah Commentary. Philadelphia: Jewish Publication Society, 1996.

Toorn, K., van der. *Family Religion in Babylonia, Syria, and Israel: Continuity and Changes in the Forms of Religious Life*. Studies in the History of the Ancient Near East 7. Leiden: Brill, 1996.

———. *Scribal Culture and the Making of the Hebrew Bible*. Cambridge: Harvard University Press, 2007.

Tov, E. *Textual Criticism of the Hebrew Bible*. 2nd rev. ed. Minneapolis: Fortress, 2001.

Trible, P. *Rhetorical Criticism: Context, Method, and the Book of Jonah*. Guides to Biblical Scholarship. Minneapolis: Fortress, 1994.

Turner, K. J. *The Death of Deaths in the Death of Israel: Deuteronomy's Theology of Exile*. Ph.D. dissertation. Southern Baptist Theological Seminary, 2005.

———. "Moses on the New Perspective: Does Deuteronomy Teach Covenant Nomism?" Paper presented at the National Meeting of the Evangelical Theological Society. Providence, RI, 19 November 2008.

VanGemeren, W. A. *The Progress of Redemption: The Story of Salvation from Creation to the New Jerusalem*. Grand Rapids, MI: Baker, 1988.

Van Leeuwen, R. C. "What Comes out of God's Mouth: Theological Wordplay in Deuteronomy 8." *Catholic Biblical Quarterly* 47 (1985): 55–57.

Vanoni, G. "Der Geist und der Buchstabe: Überlegungen zum Verhältnis der Testamente und Beobachtungen zu Dtn 30,1–10." *Biblische Notizen* 14 (1981): 65–98.

Van Seters, J. *Abraham in History and Tradition*. New Haven, CT: Yale University Press, 1975.
———. "Confessional Reformulation in the Exilic Period." *Vetus Testamentum* 22 (1972): 448–59.
———. "Deuteronomy between Pentateuch and the Deuteronomistic History." *Hervormde theologiese studies* 59 (2003): 947–56.
———. *The Life of Moses: The Yahwist as Historian in Exodus–Numbers*. Louisville: Westminster John Knox, 1994.
———. *Prologue to History: The Yahwist as Historian in Genesis*. Philadelphia: Westminster John Knox, 1992.
———. "The Religion of the Patriarchs in Genesis." *Biblica* 61 (1980): 220–33.
———. Review of S. L. Richter, *The Deuteronomistic History and the Name Theology*: lešakkēn šemô šām *in the Bible and the Ancient Near East*. *Journal of the American Oriental Society* 123 (2003): 871–2.
———. "The So-called Deuteronomistic Redaction of the Pentateuch." Pp. 58–77 in *Congress Volume: Leuven 1989*. Edited by J. A. Emerton. Supplements to Vetus Testamentum 43. Leiden: Brill, 1991.
Vaux, R. de. "Le lieu que Yahvé a choisi pour y établir son nom." Pp. 219–28 in *Das ferne und nahe Wort: Festschrift Leonhardt Rost zur Vollendung seines 70. Lebensjahres*. Edited by F. Maas. Beihefte zur Zeitschrift für die alttestamentliche Wissenschaft 105. Berlin: Alfred Töpelmann, 1967.
———. "The Revelation of the Divine Name Y<small>HWH</small>." Pp. 48–75 in *Proclamation and Presence: Old Testament Essays in Honour of Gwynne Henton Davies*. Edited by J. I. Durham and J. R. Porter. Richmond, VA: John Knox, 1970.
Veijola, T. *Das Königtum in der Beurteilung der deuteronomistischen Historiographie: Eine redaktionsgeschichtliche Untersuchung*. Helsinki: Suomalainen Tiedeakatemia, 1977.
———. "'Der Mensch lebt nicht vom Brot allein': Zur literarischen Schichtung und theologischen Aussage von Deuteronomium 8." Pp. 143–58 in *Bundesdokument und Gesetz: Studien zum Deuteronomium*. Herders Biblische Studien 4. Freiburg: Herder, 1995.
———. "Principal Observations on the Basic Story in Deuteronomy 1–3." Pp. 137–46 in *A Song of Power and the Power of Song: Essays on the Book of Deuteronomy*. Edited by D. L. Christensen. Sources for Biblical and Theological Study 3. Winona Lake, IN: Eisenbrauns, 1993.
Vervenne, M. "The Question of 'Deuteronomic' Elements in Genesis to Numbers." Pp. 243–68 in *Studies in Deuteronomy in Honour of C. J. Labuschagne on the Occasion of His 65th Birthday*. Edited by F. García Martínez et al. Supplements to Vetus Testamentum 53. Leiden: Brill, 1994.
Vogt, P. T. *Deuteronomic Theology and the Significance of Torah: A Reappraisal*. Winona Lake, IN: Eisenbrauns, 2006.
Vorländer, H. *Mein Gott: Die Vorstellungen vom persönlichen Gott im Alten Orient und im Alten Testament*. Alter Orient und Altes Testament 23. Kevelaer: Butzon & Bercker, 1975.
Wagner, A. "Die Bedeutung der Sprechakttheorie für Bibelübsersetzungen, aufgezeigt an Gen 1,29, Ps 2,7 und Dtn 26,17–19." Pp. 1575–88 in *Interpretation of the Bible*. Edited by J. Krašovec. Ljubljana, Slovenia: Slovenska akadmija znanosti in umetnosti, 1998.

———. *Sprechakte und Sprechaktanalyse im Alten Testament: Untersuchungen im biblischen Hebräisch an der Nahtstelle zwischen Handlungsebene und Grammatik*. Beihefte zur Zeitschrift für die alttestamentliche Wissenschaft 253. Berlin: de Gruyter, 1997.

———. "Die Stellung der Sprechakttheorie in Hebraistik und Exegese." Pp. 55–83 in *Congress Volume: Basel 2001*. Edited by A. Lemaire. Supplements to Vetus Testamentum 92. Leiden: Brill, 2002.

Waltke, B. K. "The Phenomenon of Conditionality within Unconditional Covenants." Pp. 123–39 in *Israel's Apostasy and Restoration: Essays in Honor of Roland K. Harrison*. Edited by A. Gileadi. Grand Rapids, MI: Baker, 1988.

Walton, J. H. *Ancient Near Eastern Thought and the Old Testament*. Grand Rapids, MI: Baker, 2006.

———. *Covenant: God's Purpose, God's Plan*. Grand Rapids, MI: Zondervan, 1994.

Wardlaw, T. R. *Conceptualizing Words for God within the Pentateuch: A Cognitive-Semantic Investigation in Literary Context*. Library of Hebrew Bible / Old Testament Studies 495. New York: T. & T. Clark, 2008.

Warning, W. "Terminological Patterns and the Divine Epithet *El Shaddai*." *Tyndale Bulletin* 52 (2001): 149–52.

Waterhouse, S. D. "A Land Flowing with Milk and Honey." *Andrews University Seminary Studies* 1 (1963): 152–66.

Watson, D. F., and A. J. Hauser. *Rhetorical Criticism of the Bible: A Comprehensive Bibliography with Notes on History and Method*. Leiden: Brill, 1994.

Watson, W. G. E. *Classical Hebrew Poetry: A Guide to Its Techniques*. Journal for the Study of the Old Testament Supplement 26. Sheffield: JSOT Press, 1984.

Watts, J. W. "The Legal Characterization of Moses in the Rhetoric of the Pentateuch." *Journal of Biblical Literature* 117 (1998): 415–26.

———. *Reading Law: The Rhetorical Shaping of the Pentateuch*. Sheffield: Sheffield Academic Press, 1999.

Weidmann, H. *Die Patriarchen und ihre Religion im Licht der Forschung seit Julius Wellhausen*. Forschungen zur Religion und Literatur des Alten und Neuen Testaments 94. Göttingen: Vandenhoeck & Ruprecht, 1968.

Weinfeld, M. "$B^e r\hat{\imath}t$: Covenant vs. Obligation." *Biblica* 56 (1975): 120–28.

———. "The Covenant of Grant in the Old Testament and the Ancient Near East." *Journal of the American Oriental Society* 90 (1970): 184–203.

———. "Covenant Terminology in the Ancient Near East and Its Influence on the West." *Journal of the American Oriental Society* 93 (1973): 190–99.

———. *Deuteronomy 1–11: A New Translation with Introduction and Commentary*. Anchor Bible 5. New York: Doubleday, 1991.

———. *Deuteronomy and the Deuteronomic School*. Oxford: Clarendon, 1972. Reprinted, Winona Lake, IN: Eisenbrauns, 1992.

———. "Jeremiah and the Spiritual Metamorphosis of Israel." *Zeitschrift für die alttestamentliche Wissenchaft* 88 (1976): 17–56.

———. "The Loyalty Oath in the Ancient Near East." *Ugarit-Forschungen* 8 (1976): 379–414.

———. *The Promise of the Land: The Inheritance of the Land of Canaan by the Israelites*. Berkeley: University of California Press, 1993.

Welch, A. C. *The Code of Deuteronomy: A New Theory of Its Origin.* London: James Clarke, 1924.
Wellhausen, J. *Die Composition des Hexateuchs und der historischen Bücher des Alten Testaments.* 4th ed. Berlin: de Gruyter, 1963.
———. *Prolegomena to the History of Israel.* Cleveland: World Publishing, 1957.
Wenham, G. J. "The Date of Deuteronomy: Linch-Pin of Old Testament Criticism, Part One." *Themelios* 10 (1985): 15–20.
———. "The Date of Deuteronomy: Linch-Pin of Old Testament Criticism, Part Two." *Themelios* 11 (1985): 15–18.
———. "The Deuteronomic Theology of the Book of Joshua." *Journal of Biblical Literature* 90 (1971): 140–48.
———. "Deuteronomy and the Central Sanctuary." *Tyndale Bulletin* 22 (1971): 103–18.
———. *Genesis 1–15.* Word Biblical Commentary 1. Waco, TX: Word, 1987.
———. *Genesis 16–50.* Word Biblical Commentary 2. Waco, TX: Word, 1994.
———. "Grace and Law in the Old Testament." Pp. 3–23 in *Law, Morality, and the Bible.* Edited by B. Kaye and G. J. Wenham. Downers Grove, IL: InterVarsity, 1978.
———. "Method in Pentateuchal Source Criticism." *Vetus Testamentum* 41 (1991): 84–109.
———. "Pondering the Pentateuch: The Search for a New Paradigm." Pp. 116–44 in *The Face of Old Testament Studies.* Edited by D. W. Baker and B. T. Arnold. Grand Rapids, MI: Baker, 1999.
———. "The Priority of P." *Vetus Testamentum* 49 (1999): 240–58.
———. "The Religion of the Patriarchs." Pp. 157–88 in *Essays on the Patriarchal Narratives.* Edited by A. R. Millard and D. J. Wiseman. Leicester: InterVarsity, 1980. [Reprinted, Winona Lake, IN: Eisenbrauns, 1983, pp. 161–95.]
———. "The Symbolism of the Animal Rite in Genesis 15: A Response to G. F. Hasel, JSOT 19 [1981] 61–78." *Journal for the Study of the Old Testament* 22 (1982): 134–7.
Westermann, C. *Genesis 1–11: A Commentary.* Translated by J. J. Scullion. Minneapolis: Fortress, 1984.
———. *Genesis 12–36: A Commentary.* Translated by J. J. Scullion. Minneapolis: Fortress, 1985.
———. *The Promises to the Fathers.* Translated by D. E. Green. Philadelphia: Fortress, 1976.
Wevers, J. W. *Notes on the Greek Text of Deuteronomy.* Society of Biblical Literature Septuagiant and Cognate Studies 39. Atlanta: Scholars Press, 1995.
———. "Yahweh and Its Appositives in LXX Deuteronomium." Pp. 269–80 in *Studies in Deuteronomy in Honour of C. J. Labuschagne on the Occasion of His 65th Birthday.* Edited by F. García Martínez et al. Supplements to Vetus Testamentum 53. Leiden: Brill, 1994.
White, H. C. "The Divine Oath in Genesis." *Journal of Biblical Literature* 92 (1973): 165–79.
———. "The Value of Speech Act Theory for Old Testament Hermeneutics." *Semeia* 41 (1988): 41–63.
Whitley, C. F. "Covenant and Commandment in Israel." *Journal for Near Eastern Studies* 22 (1963): 37–48.

Whybray, R. N. *The Making of the Pentateuch: A Methodological Study*. Journal for the Study of the Old Testament Supplement 53. Sheffield: JSOT Press, 1994.

Wijngaards, J. N. M. *The Dramatization of Salvific History in the Deuteronomic Schools*. Oudtestamentische Studiën 16. Leiden: Brill, 1969.

―――. *The Formulas of the Deuteronomic Creed (Dt. 6/20–23: 26/5–9)*. Tilburg: Reinjen, 1963.

Wildberger, H. *Jahwes Eigentumswolk: Eine Studie zur Traditionsgeschichte und Theologie des Erwählungsgedankens*. Abhandlungen zur Theologie des Alten und Neuen Testaments 37. Zurich: Zwingli, 1960.

Williamson, P. R. *Abraham, Israel, and the Nations*. Journal for the Study of the Old Testament Supplement 315. Sheffield: Sheffield Academic Press, 2000.

Willis, J. T. "'Man Does Not Live by Bread Alone.'" *Restoration Quarterly* 16 (1973): 141–49.

Willoughby, B. E. "A Heartfelt Love: An Exegesis of Deuteronomy 6:4–19." *Restoration Quarterly* 22 (1970): 73–87.

Wilson, I. *Out of the Midst of the Fire: Divine Presence in Deuteronomy*. Society of Biblical Literature Dissertation Series 151. Atlanta: Scholars Press, 1995.

Wiseman, D. J. "Abraham in History and Tradition." *Bibliotheca Sacra* 134 (1977): 123–30.

―――. "Abraham Reassessed." Pp. 139–56 in *Essays on the Patriarchal Narratives*. Edited by A. R. Millard and D. J. Wiseman. Leicester: Inter-Varsity, 1980. [Reprinted, Winona Lake, IN: Eisenbrauns, 1983, pp. 141–60.]

―――. "The Vassal-Treaties of Esarhaddon." *Iraq* 20 (1958): 1–99.

Wittbruck, T. "The So-Called Anti-anthropomorphisms in the Greek Text of Deuteronomy." *Catholic Biblical Quarterly* 38 (1976): 29–34.

Witte, M., et al., eds. *Die deuteronomistischen Geschichtswerke: Redaktions- und religionsgeschichtliche Perspektiven zur "Deuteronomismus"—Diskussion in Tora und Vorderen Propheten*. Beihefte zur Zeitschrift für die alttestamentliche Wissenschaft 365. Berlin: de Gruyter, 2006.

Wolff, H. W. "The Kerygma of the Deuteronomic Historical Work." Pp. 83–100 in *The Vitality of Old Testament Traditions*. Edited by W. Brueggemann. Translated by F. C. Prussner. Atlanta: John Knox, 1982.

Wright, C. J. H. *Deuteronomy*. New International Bible Commentary on the Old Testament 4. Peabody, MA: Hendrickson, 1996.

―――. *God's People in God's Land: Family, Land, and Property in the Old Testament*. Grand Rapids, MI: Eerdmans, 1990.

―――. *The Mission of God: Unlocking the Bible's Grand Narrative*. Downers Grove, IL: InterVarsity, 2006.

Wuellner, W. "Where Is Rhetorical Criticism Taking Us?" *Catholic Biblical Quarterly* 49 (1987): 448–63.

Wyatt, N. "The Problem of the 'God of the Fathers.'" *Zeitschrift für die alttestamentliche Wissenschaft* 90 (1978): 101–4.

―――. *Religious Texts from Ugarit: The Words of Ilimilku and His Colleagues*. Biblical Seminar 53. Sheffield: Sheffield Academic Press, 1998.

Young, E. J. "The God of the Fathers." *Westminster Theological Journal* 3 (1940): 25–40.

Zakovitch, Y. *'And You Shall Tell Your Son . . .': The Concept of the Exodus in the Bible*. Jerusalem: Magnes, 1991.

Zenger, E. "Die Bundestheologie: Ein derzeit vernachlässigtes Thema der Bibelwissenschaft und ein wichtiges Thema für das Verhältnis Israel-Kirche." Pp. 13–49 in *Der neue Bund im alten. Studien zur Bundestheologie der beiden Testamente.* Edited by E. Zenger. Quaestiones disputatae 146. Freiburg: Herder, 1993.

Zetterholm, K. H. *Portrait of a Villain.* Leuven: Peeters, 2002.

Zimmerli, W. "I Am Yahweh." Pp. 1–28 in *I Am Yahweh.* Edited by W. Brueggemann. Translated by D. W. Stott. Atlanta: John Knox, 1982.

———. *Old Testament Theology in Outline.* Translated by D. E. Green. Edinburgh: T. & T. Clark, 1978.

———. "Sinaibund und Abrahambund: Ein Beitrag zum Verständnis der Priesterschrift." Pp. 205–16 in *Gottes Offenbarung: Gesammelte Aufsätze zum Alten Testament.* Munich: Chr. Kaiser, 1963.

Index of Authors

Abravanel 178
Ackerman, S. 181
Adams, J. W. 169, 170, 171
Albertz, R. 74, 92, 101, 106
Albright, W. F. 62
Alexander, T. D. 102
Allen, L. C. 100
Alonso Schökel, L. 69
Alster-Elata, G. 172
Alt, A. 11, 93, 98, 99, 105, 106, 108
Alter, R. 18, 62
Altman, A. 164, 175, 215
Amsler, S. 206
Anbar, M. 16, 86, 129, 140
Andersen, F. I. 220
Anderson, B. W. 162
Aquila 63
Araújo, R. G. de 20, 219
Astruc, J. 96
Ausloos, H. 64, 73, 118, 123, 127
Austin, J. L. 169, 170, 171, 172

Baltzer, K. 155, 156, 160, 166
Barker, P. 74, 76, 80, 140, 141, 143, 213, 223, 224, 230, 233
Barr, J. 135, 158, 215
Barton, J. 156
Beckman, G. 163, 164, 186
Beckwith, R. T. 202, 233
Beek, M. A. 62
Begg, C. T. 185, 218
Bekhor Shor, J. 63
Bellefontaine, E. 140
Benedict XVI, Pope 235
Berlin, A. 37, 113
Blair, E. P. 7, 52, 197
Blenkinsopp, J. 2, 8, 16, 47, 86, 96, 102
Block, D. I. 3, 21, 23, 52, 70, 72, 94, 117, 125, 139, 141, 143, 200, 208, 217, 233
Bonhoeffer, D. 168
Boorer, S. 15, 87
Braulik, G. 1, 7, 9, 40, 57, 60, 74, 169, 176, 185, 186, 187, 188, 190, 195, 196, 199, 201, 204, 206, 207, 223, 224, 231
Brekelmans, C. 96, 178
Brettler, M. Z. 25, 74, 82, 83, 185
Brichto, H. C. 124
Briggs, R. S. 169, 170, 171, 173
Bright, J. 3
Brongers, H. A. 121, 188
Brueggemann, W. 8, 20, 24, 25, 30, 57, 60, 74, 76, 79, 138, 147, 175, 179, 216, 220, 225
Buchanan, G. W. 165, 213
Budd, P. J. 149
Buis, P. 62, 138, 168, 195, 202, 225

Cairns, I. 67, 139
Campbell, A. F. 161
Caquot, A. 123
Carmichael, C. 67
Carpenter, E. E. 84, 114
Cassuto, U. 102, 104
Cazelles, H. 41, 42, 106, 185
Childs, B. S. 7, 8, 59, 67, 68, 103, 135, 146, 157, 227
Cholewinski, A. 223, 225
Christensen, D. L. 40, 62, 74, 112, 115, 138, 140, 145, 207, 209, 224, 225
Clements, R. E. 1, 67, 80, 129, 130
Clines, D. J. A. 109
Coats, G. W. 185
Coenen, L. 137
Coggins, R. 1
Cogswell, J. 220
Conrad, J. 198
Cotterell, P. 17, 173
Craigie, P. C. 62, 76, 118, 138, 140, 155, 195, 223
Cross, F. M. 28, 74, 105, 106, 166
Crüsemann, F. 2
Crystal, D. 66

Daniels, D. R. 64, 67, 146

Davidson, R. 155
Davies, G. 162
Davies, P. R. 1
Day, J. 105, 182, 217
DeRouchie, J. S. 52, 119
Deurloo, K. A. 50
De Vries, S. J. 57, 67, 229
De Wette, W. M. L. 1, 93, 97, 128
Diamond, A. R. P. 17
Diepold, P. 5, 25, 29, 30, 31, 216
Dietrich, W. 29, 168
Dillman, A. 156
Dozeman, T. B. 102
Dreyfus, F. 63, 68, 149
Driver, S. R. 1, 35, 62, 91, 116, 129, 138, 139, 185, 197, 223
Duke, R. K. 10
Dumbrell, W. J. 217
Durham, J. I. 148

Eichrodt, W. 3, 156, 157, 165
Eissfeldt, O. 124, 129, 140
Emerton, J. A. 86
Eslinger, L. M. 103, 150
Evans, D. D. 169
Evans, J. F. 103
Eynde, S. van den 167

Fensham, F. C. 165, 180
Finsterbusch, K. 59
Fishbane, M. 2, 56, 59, 103, 125, 155
Flanagan, J. W. 83
Follingstad, C. M. 52, 65
Forshey, H. O. 21
Foster, S. J. 168, 191
Frankena, R. 75, 162
Freedman, D. N. 74, 80, 106, 126, 163
Fretheim, T. E. 1
Frevel, C. 82, 85
Friedman, R. E. 28, 74
Fuhs, H. F. 62, 69, 146

Gammie, J. H. 208, 214
García López, F. 52, 53, 65, 82, 85, 118, 208, 210
García Martínez, F. 50, 82, 94, 96
Garr, W. R. 107, 150
Gerstenberger, E. S. 106
Gertz, J. C. 66, 68, 149, 184
Gesenius, W. 156

Giesen, G. 16
Glueck, N. 179, 215
Goldingay, J. 174
Gordon, C. 107
Gosse, B. 15, 87, 216
Gottwald, N. 91
Greenberg, M. 104
Gunn, D. M. 103

Ha, J. 15, 86
Habel, N. C. 16, 21
Hadley, J. M. 56, 124
Hahn, S. 155, 166, 168
Hakemulder, F. 138
Halpern, B. 1, 128, 129, 134
Hamilton, V. P. 109, 122
Haran, M. 106, 125, 167
Hasel, G. F. 194
Heimerdinger, J.-M. 106
Hendel, R. S. 8, 176
Henry, C. F. H. 104
Herrman, W. 123
Herrmann, S. 103
Hess, R. S. 105, 163
Hill, A. E. 142
Hillers, D. R. 155, 170
Hoftijzer, J. 118, 210
Holmstedt, R. D. 121, 195
Horton, M. S. 163, 235
Houston, W. 66
Howard, D. M. 9, 10
Huffmon, H. B. 179
Hugenberger, G. P. 168
Hulst, A. R. 135
Hyatt, J. P. 106

Ibn Ezra, Abraham 63, 178, 179

Jacobsen, T. 105, 106, 125, 126
Janzen, J. G. 62, 103
Japhet, S. 100
Jenni, E. 63
Jenson, P. P. 136
Jerome 81
Johnston, G. H. 163
Joosten, J. 228
Josephus 91
Joüon, P. 26, 55, 62, 66, 107, 121, 189

Kaiser, O. 87

Kaiser, W. C. 39, 107
Kalluveettil, P. 165, 166, 167, 171, 172
Kaminsky, J. S. 39
Keller, M. 130
Kennedy, G. A. 10
Kimhi, David 63
Kitchen, K. A. 158, 161, 165
Klein, R. W. 36
Kline, M. G. 160, 161, 186
Klingbeil, G. A. 200
Kloppenborg, J. S. 17
Knapp, D. 184
Knoppers, G. N. 163, 165
Koch, C. 75, 162
Köckert, M. 28, 107, 118, 191
König, E. 156
Korošec, V. 160
Kraetzschmar, R. 156
Krašovec, J. 162, 213, 214, 215
Kratz, R. G. 1
Krausz, N. 63
Kroeze, J. H. 121
Kutsch, E. 158, 159, 166, 190, 196, 215, 227, 232

Lane, D. C. 155
Lang, B. 2
Lapsley, J. E. 180
Leclerq, J. 62, 138, 195
Leibowitz, N. 104
Lemke, W. E. 74
Lenchak, T. A. 7, 8, 10, 43, 80, 186, 223, 225, 226, 227, 228
Levenson, J. D. 155, 162
Levine, E. 24
Levinson, B. M. 1, 2, 129, 130
Lewy, I. 139, 140
Lewy, J. 105
Lindars, B. 175
Lipiński, E. 62
Loewenstamm, S. E. 112, 163
Lohfink, N. 1, 4, 5, 7, 15, 25, 27, 32, 33, 35, 36, 38, 43, 44, 45, 49, 50, 52, 53, 57, 58, 66, 67, 68, 74, 78, 79, 80, 95, 110, 119, 120, 128, 129, 134, 140, 143, 146, 147, 162, 169, 176, 185, 186, 188, 195, 196, 203, 204, 206, 209, 217, 223, 224, 225, 228, 229
Long, V. P. 174

Longman, T., III 174
Lundbom, J. R. 1, 9, 140, 207, 223
Lux, R. 81, 82

MacDonald, N. 52, 124, 184, 193, 204
Mason, S. D. 228, 235
May, H. G. 106, 125
Mayes, A. D. H. 1, 32, 41, 74, 111, 118, 129, 139, 179, 184, 186, 190, 225
McBride, S. D. 135
McCarthy, C. 35, 36, 63, 85, 137
McCarthy, D. J. 8, 57, 158, 161, 165, 175, 190
McComiskey, T. E. 106, 162, 215, 233
McConville, J. G. 3, 7, 9, 24, 29, 52, 62, 64, 68, 80, 92, 121, 129, 132, 133, 134, 138, 140, 143, 169, 175, 179, 190, 199, 200, 202, 207, 216, 217, 221, 225, 228, 229
McKane, W. 105
McKay, J. W. 206
McKenzie, S. L. 91
Mendecki, N. 74
Mendenhall, G. E. 160, 161, 162
Merendino, R. P. 118, 140
Merrill, E. H. 22, 138, 162, 190, 195
Merwe, C. H. J. van der 121
Mettinger, T. N. D. 96, 126, 130, 133, 134, 135
Milgrom, J. 46, 95, 110, 132, 136, 217, 228, 235
Millar, J. G. 7, 8, 30, 43, 66, 88, 117, 167, 176, 185, 192, 217, 224
Millard, A. R. 62
Miller, P. D. 16, 24, 43, 62, 74, 79, 91, 92, 113, 132, 155, 179, 194, 219, 225
Mittmann, S. 34, 41, 115, 118, 122, 185
Moberly, R. W. L. 94, 102, 104, 151
Mölle, H. 15
Moor, J. C. de 105
Moran, W. L. 33, 155, 165, 180
Motyer, J. A. 104
Muilenburg, J. 9, 10, 155, 160
Muraoka, T. 197
Murray, J. 235

Naudé, J. A. 121

Nelson, R. D.   28, 138, 190, 195
Neufeld, E.   170
Nicholson, E. W.   1, 129, 155, 166
Niehaus, J. J.   129, 132
Nocquet, D.   29, 30, , 58
Noort, E.   15, 58, 86
Noth, M.   1, 2, 5, 29, 67, 82, 93, 128, 148, 175, 184, 186

O'Connell, R. H.   207, 208, 209, 217
Oden, R. A., Jr.   155
O'Dowd, R.   7, 44
Oestreicher, T.   129
Olson, D. T.   74, 81, 84, 135, 183, 223
Orlinsky, H. M.   21
Otto, E.   74, 102, 162, 204, 222, 224, 234
Otto, R.   193
Otzen, B.   62

Pagolu, A.   105
Pakkala, J.   1
Pannell, R. J.   8, 176, 179
Parker, S. B.   179
Parke-Taylor, G. H.   96
Parpola, S.   161, 164
Patrick, D.   8, 9, 170, 176, 200
Paul, S. M.   162
Peer, W. van   138
Perdue, L. G.   175
Perlitt, L.   15, 41, 58, 74, 82, 86, 159, 160, 166, 178, 183, 186, 210, 211, 212, 214, 218, 234
Philo   91
Plöger, J. G.   16, 23, 24, 25, 38, 40, 41, 61, 79, 86, 110, 111, 115, 118, 128, 185
Polk, T.   175
Polzin, R.   10, 50, 116, 175, 227, 234
Porter, J. R.   39
Preuss, H. D.   138, 184, 223
Provan, I. W.   174
Pury, A. de   96

Rad, G. von   1, 5, 6, 7, 15, 21, 22, 31, 44, 50, 51, 57, 58, 61, 62, 63, 64, 66, 67, 74, 91, 92, 99, 110, 118, 129, 130, 133, 135, 136, 138, 140, 144, 167, 175, 176, 178, 184, 193, 198, 211, 225, 229

Ranke, L. von   174
Rashbam (Rabbi Shmuel ben Meir)   63
Rashi (Rabbi Shelomo Yitzhaki)   63
Rendtorff, R.   58, 86, 87, 94, 156, 166, 182, 202, 207, 215, 225, 227, 228, 234
Renz, T.   10
Richter, S.   134, 135, 136, 141, 143
Robinson, H. W.   39
Rofé, A.   74, 117, 162, 201, 224, 225
Rogerson, J. W.   39
Römer, T. C.   4, 5, 6, 7, 10, 23, 25, 27, 28, 29, 30, 31, 33, 34, 35, 36, 37, 38, 44, 45, 46, 47, 48, 49, 50, 51, 53, 54, 55, 56, 65, 72, 75, 76, 78, 82, 83, 84, 85, 87, 88, 96, 99, 100, 108, 115, 116, 118, 127, 128, 148, 149, 178, 182, 188, 191, 201, 202, 203, 204, 206, 211, 212, 214, 215, 216, 219, 230, 230
Rooy, H. F. van   223
Rost, L.   20, 67, 72, 146
Rütersworden, U.   130

Sailhamer, J. H.   200
Sakenfeld, K. D.   179, 181
Salmon, R.   172
Sanders, E. P.   235
Sanders, P.   17
Sarna, N. M.   104
Saucy, R. L.   163
Sauer, G.   198
Schaller, J. J.   66
Schaper, J.   8, 204
Scharbert, J.   51, 79
Schenker, A.   166, 181
Schmid, H. H.   86
Schmid, K.   5, 82, 102, 234
Schmitt, H.-C.   82
Schultz, H.   156
Scobie, C. H. H.   179
Scult, A.   8, 9
Searle, J. R.   169, 170, 171, 172, 173, 174, 175, 176, 177
Seitz, C.   97, 102, 104
Sherrifs, D. C.   192
Shmidman, J. H.   206
Ska, J.-L.   42

Index of Authors

Skweres, D. E.   2, 7, 35, 51, 54, 57, 82, 95, 110, 117, 122, 136, 148, 196, 227, 229
Slanski, K. E.   140, 142, 162
Slater, S.   50
Smend, R.   29, 74, 166
Smith, M. S.   8, 123
Smith, W. Robertson   158
Sohn, S.-T.   166
Sonnet, J.-P.   8, 10, 39, 85, 138, 141, 167, 206
Sonsino, R.   54
Stärk, W.   129
Steiner, R. C.   63
Stern, P. D.   23, 123
Sternberg, M.   17
Steymans, H. U.   75, 162
Stoellger, P.   82
Strawn, B. A.   7, 38, 42, 79
Suzuki, Y.   132

Tadmor, H.   155
Taschner, J.   6, 7, 39, 49, 234
Thiselton, A. C.   169, 170, 172
Thompson, J. A.   138
Tigay, J. H.   5, 49, 51, 62, 63, 74, 132, 138, 139, 148, 195, 206, 225, 228
Tillesse, G. M. de   25, 185
Toorn, K. van der   106, 126
Tov, E.   36
Trible, P.   9, 11
Turner, K. J.   74, 235
Turner, M.   17, 173

VanGemeren, W. A.   109
Van Leeuwen, R. C.   209, 220
Vanoni, G.   74
Van Seters, J.   2, 4, 33, 50, 51, 53, 54, 75, 78, 82, 83, 86, 87, 96, 106, 108, 135, 182, 234
Vaux, R. de   104, 135
Veijola, T.   29, 41, 209, 210
Vervenne, M.   96

Vetter, D.   71
Vogt, P. T.   7, 92, 112, 129, 131, 132
Vorländer, H.   91, 106, 125, 126, 131, 137

Wagner, A.   66, 169
Waltke, B. K.   162
Walton, J. H.   92, 126
Wardlaw, T. R.   102
Watanabe, K.   161, 164
Waterhouse, S. D.   24
Watts, J. W.   9, 116
Weinfeld, M.   1, 3, 15, 18, 32, 68, 74, 75, 80, 85, 92, 112, 116, 122, 124, 129, 130, 158, 161, 162, 163, 164, 165, 178, 188, 190, 193, 195, 215
Welch, A. C.   129, 131
Wellhausen, J.   1, 3, 11, 29, 92, 93, 95, 96, 97, 98, 99, 107, 108, 128, 156, 157, 158, 159, 177, 234, 235
Wenham, G. J.   1, 93, 102, 105, 129, 132, 135, 136, 194, 217, 233
Westermann, C.   102, 109, 194, 234
Wevers, J. W.   63, 85, 94, 137
Whybray, R. N.   30, 102
Wijngaards, J. N. M.   21, 62, 68, 129, 203
Willis, J. T.   219
Willoughby, B. E.   181
Wilson, G. H.   134
Wilson, I.   133, 134, 192, 193
Wiseman, D. J.   85, 107, 161
Wittbruck, T.   137
Wolff, H. W.   74, 76, 190
Wright, C. J. H.   16, 21, 63, 122, 131, 138, 155
Wuellner, W.   9
Wyatt, N.   123

Zenger, E.   155
Zetterholm, K. H.   63
Zimmerli, W.   103, 138, 163, 213, 228

Index of Scripture

Hebrew Bible

Note to reader: Citations in this section of the index follow the order of the traditional Hebrew canon and its versification.

Genesis
1–11   102
1–15   217
1:1–2:4   102
2–3   102
2:4–3:24   102
2:7   23
2:19   19, 23
3:18   19
4:26   97
5:29   102
6:18   194
9:9   194
9:11   194
9:15   194
11:7   121
12   86, 102
12–50   3
12:1   197
12:2   80, 117, 206
12:6   85
12:6–7   143
12:7   85, 86, 87, 211
12:7–8   130
13   85
13:14   85, 86
13:14–15   85
13:14–17   86, 221
13:15   87
13:15–16   203
13:16   117
13:17   85, 87, 88
13:18   130
14:19   98
15   15, 85, 86, 87, 194
15:1–6   102
15:5   117

Genesis (cont.)
15:7   86, 87, 88
15:7–8   78
15:7–21   194
15:13   206
15:18   85, 87, 191
16:13   98
17   86, 227, 228
17:1   80, 97, 98, 102
17:2   191, 194
17:2–6   117
17:4   194
17:7   194, 202, 206, 225, 227, 228
17:7–8   167
17:8   17, 86, 87
17:9–10   194
17:13–14   194
17:19   194
17:21   194
18:19   80
20–22   102
20:1–22:19   102
20:13   70
20:18   102
21:24   86
21:31   86
21:33   98
22:1–14   102
22:9   129
22:16   86
22:17   117
24:3   121
24:7   85, 86, 87, 191
26:1   223
26:3   86, 87, 117, 191
26:4   87

Genesis (cont.)
26:5   80, 96
26:14   198
26:24   98, 117, 127
26:24–25   130
27:43   197
28:3   98
28:4   78, 86, 87, 88
28:13   98, 127
28:14   117
28:15   106
29:31–30:24   102
31:13   98
31:14   21
31:25–32:3   166
31:42   98
31:53   98
32:10   98
32:23–32   102
33:18–20   143
33:19   20
33:20   98, 129
34:7   19
35:1–7   130
35:3   106
35:7   98
35:11   98, 117
35:12   86
36:35   19
43:13   97
43:14   98, 106
46:3   98, 117, 127
46:27   70
48:3   98
48:4   87
48:21   86
49   106

Genesis (cont.)
49:1   200
49:24   98
49:25   97, 98, 106
49:27   20
50:17   98
50:24   86, 191, 206

Exodus
1–2   116
1–14   103
1–15   103
1:7   125, 206
1:12   125
1:20   206
2:23–24   145
2:23–25   206
2:24   191, 194, 212, 228
3   97, 99, 103, 104, 127, 131, 143, 146, 148, 149
3–20   131
3:6   62, 99, 138, 146
3:7   145
3:7–8   138
3:8   48, 55, 73, 122, 125, 127, 220
3:13   99, 100, 146
3:13–16   149
3:14   104, 143
3:15   99, 104, 146
3:15–16   100, 148
3:16   138, 143
3:17   48, 122, 125, 127, 138, 220
4:5   148
4:9   146
4:17   146
4:21   146
4:28   146
4:30   146
5:2   103
6   96, 97, 99, 102, 103, 107, 131, 143, 148, 149, 191, 227, 228
6–14   103, 104
6:3   96, 97, 99, 103, 107, 150, 191, 212

Exodus (cont.)
6:4   191, 217, 228
6:4–5   194
6:5   191
6:6   228
6:6–8   221
6:7   103, 150, 202, 227
6:8   86, 191, 228
6:14–27   97
7–14   103
7:3   146
7:5   103, 150
7:6–8   221
7:17   103, 150
8:10   103, 150
8:22   103, 150
9:14   103, 150
9:19   122
9:25   19
9:29   103, 150
10:1–2   146
10:2   103, 150
11:7   103, 150
11:9–11   146
12:24–27   52, 96
13:5   15, 48, 86, 122, 191
13:11   15, 86, 191
13:11–16   52
13:14   60
14:4   103, 150
14:18   103, 150
15:17   21
15:22–27   56
15:25   55
16   218, 219
16:2–3   218
16:3–4   219
16:4   55
16:4–12   219
16:6   103, 150, 219
16:8   103, 150, 219
16:12   103, 150, 219
16:15   216, 219
16:18   219
16:21   219
17:1–7   55, 56
17:2   55
17:7   55
18   112

Exodus (cont.)
18:13–27   111
18:17–23   111
18:21   111
18:22   112
18:24   111
19   192, 228
19–20   118
19–24   160
19:4–6   202
19:5   190, 191, 225, 229
19:6   70
20   2
20:2   104
20:5   214
20:5–6   212, 213
20:6   214
20:12   124
20:18–21   118
20:20   55
20:24   130
20:24–25   129
20:26   121
21–23   2
23:13   52
23:16   19
24   118, 141, 142
24:3–4   141
24:4   142
25–31   135
25:8   135
29:45   137, 225
29:46   103, 150
31:13   103, 150
31:18   195
32–34   133
32:10   70
32:13   15, 84, 86
32:15   195
33:1   15, 85, 86, 191
33:3   48, 122, 220
33:13   70
34:6   201
34:7   212, 214
34:10   191
34:12   52, 191
34:15   191
34:29   195
35–40   135

Leviticus
9:17 223
13:11 198
14:34 17
17–26 2
17–27 228
19:9 19
20:24 48, 122
23–27 217
26 228
26:1–45 202
26:9 194
26:10 198
26:12 202
26:15 194
26:22 19
26:42 86, 194, 212
26:44 194
26:45 62

Numbers
10:11 135
11 112
11:11 112
11:11–17 111
11:16 112
11:16–17 112
11:17 111
13:12 86
13:27 48, 122, 127
13:28–29 113
14 46
14:7 55, 220
14:8 48, 122, 127, 220
14:18 213, 214
14:22 55
14:22–25 218
14:23 15
14:28 123
16:13–14 48, 122, 127
20:2–13 56
20:14 70
20:14–15 70, 71
20:14–17 68
20:15 70, 147
20:15–16 62, 147, 149
21:4–5 56
21:20 19
24:14 200
24:18 18

Numbers (cont.)
29:16 223
32 45, 46, 47
32:7–15 45, 47
32:8 45, 46
32:11 15, 45, 46, 47
32:12 46
32:14 45, 46
32:14–15 46
34:1–12 18
35:2 21

Deuteronomy
1 31, 32, 36, 39, 44, 45, 46, 49, 75, 81, 88, 111, 112, 113, 114, 131, 188, 189, 232
1–2 29
1–3 20, 41, 43, 44, 45, 49, 50, 175, 184, 185, 186, 188, 219, 231
1–4 40, 180, 184, 185, 186
1–11 3, 32, 112, 116, 122, 124, 178, 188, 190, 193, 195, 207
1–25 65
1–26 65
1:1 8, 20, 83, 164, 167, 174, 177, 223
1:1–5 38, 160
1:1–21:9 112, 209
1:2 22, 40, 42
1:3 39, 164
1:5 42, 204
1:6 34, 111, 112, 197
1:6–7 33
1:6–8 18, 37, 38, 110, 111, 113
1:6–18 32, 44, 110, 113, 188
1:6–19 32, 33
1:6–46 113, 114
1:6–3:29 44, 185, 186
1:6–4:40 183
1:6–4:43 174
1:6–4:49 160

Deuteronomy (cont.)
1:6–30:20 167, 175
1:7 35, 48, 113
1:7–8 117
1:8 3, 4, 5, 16, 18, 23, 24, 25, 27, 31, 32, 33, 34, 35, 36, 37, 38, 40, 41, 42, 43, 44, 45, 47, 48, 49, 54, 62, 65, 75, 78, 79, 80, 83, 84, 88, 112, 113, 116, 125, 127, 128, 144, 150, 173, 180, 181, 183, 188, 189, 191, 201, 203, 216, 217, 231
1:8–46 30
1:9 111, 112, 114, 116
1:9–11 116
1:9–12 114, 115
1:9–15 112
1:9–17 113
1:9–18 32, 33, 40, 111, 112, 113, 114, 184
1:10 40, 66, 73, 76, 110, 111, 115, 116, 117, 125, 180, 199
1:10–11 115
1:11 4, 32, 40, 41, 91, 92, 95, 100, 109, 110, 111, 114, 115, 116, 117, 126, 128, 150, 220
1:12 111, 112, 115, 116
1:13 111
1:13–15 111, 113
1:13–18 116
1:14 195
1:15 112
1:16 112
1:16–17 111, 112
1:17 43, 111, 112
1:18 112, 113

Index of Scripture

Deuteronomy (cont.)
1:19   20, 22, 33, 40, 42, 48, 112, 113
1:19–20   42
1:19–46   113, 114, 185
1:19–3:29   188
1:20   217
1:20–46   32, 33, 44, 46
1:21   4, 16, 18, 31, 32, 34, 40, 41, 42, 43, 44, 45, 48, 49, 65, 91, 92, 95, 100, 109, 111, 113, 114, 115, 116, 126, 127, 128, 130, 180, 185, 188, 189
1:22   22, 42
1:22–25   113
1:24   42
1:25   23, 48, 113
1:26   42
1:26–28   114
1:26–33   45, 49, 113
1:26–39   43
1:26–40   54
1:26–46   18
1:27   23
1:28   113
1:30   180
1:31   20, 21, 22, 133, 180, 219
1:33   21, 22
1:34   44, 49, 181
1:34–35   218
1:34–36   216
1:34–40   44, 47, 49
1:35   4, 6, 16, 23, 25, 31, 32, 34, 35, 40, 43, 44, 45, 46, 47, 48, 49, 55, 65, 77, 83, 127, 180, 189, 204
1:35–38   178
1:35–40   44
1:36   22, 34, 44, 45, 48
1:37   45, 84, 113, 116
1:37–38   81
1:38   21, 44, 113
1:39   49, 66

Deuteronomy (cont.)
1:40   20, 22, 43, 48
1:41   42
1:41–43   42, 189
1:41–44   114
1:42   42
1:43   43
1:45   133, 134
2–3   164
2:1   20, 22, 40, 43, 48, 115
2:1–25   185
2:1–3:29   30, 180
2:4   19
2:5   18
2:7   20
2:8   22, 40
2:9   18
2:12   18
2:13   40
2:14   44, 83, 218
2:14–16   6, 33, 44, 178, 204, 216
2:17–3:29   44
2:18   19
2:19   18
2:21–22   76
2:24   18
2:24–25   43
2:26   20
2:26–3:17   223
2:27   22
2:29   217
2:31   18
3   81, 185
3:1   22, 40
3:2   43
3:4   17, 18
3:12   18, 76
3:13–14   17, 18
3:14   19
3:16   146
3:16–17   19
3:18   18, 21, 24
3:20   18, 24
3:21–22   113
3:23–28   81, 84
3:24   23, 72, 82, 94, 180
3:25   23, 48

Deuteronomy (cont.)
3:25–26   116
3:26   84, 113, 116
3:28   21, 113
4   30, 38, 39, 41, 74, 118, 131, 134, 160, 164, 183, 184, 185, 186, 187, 188, 189, 190, 191, 192, 198, 207, 208, 222, 223, 224, 225
4–5   187
4–29   233
4:1   4, 18, 32, 48, 54, 55, 59, 65, 68, 91, 92, 100, 109, 115, 117, 126, 127, 128, 130, 131, 144, 183, 184, 188, 189, 195, 201, 207, 217, 218
4:1–2   160
4:1–4   188, 189
4:1–8   41, 174, 233
4:1–11:25   207
4:2–4   189
4:3   203
4:3–4   39, 160
4:4   49, 66, 189
4:5   26, 117, 160, 161, 187, 195, 202
4:6   180
4:7   131, 180, 194
4:7–8   80, 194
4:8   117, 180, 194
4:9   52, 161, 187, 192, 193, 196, 197
4:9–10   41, 161
4:9–14   198
4:9–20   192, 203
4:9–24   192
4:9–31   182, 187, 188, 190, 191, 192
4:10   23, 57, 133, 160, 192, 201, 206
4:10–11   227
4:10–12   160
4:10–14   187

Deuteronomy (cont.)
4:10–15 39, 184
4:11 187, 193
4:11–12 187
4:11–13 187
4:12 134, 180, 187, 188, 192, 193, 201
4:12–18 41
4:13 182, 187, 189, 190, 191, 192, 193, 194, 195, 196, 212
4:14 26, 117, 192, 195
4:14–23 52
4:15 82, 134, 187, 188, 192
4:15–16 193
4:15–18 161
4:16 198
4:16–18 196
4:16–19 199
4:17 23
4:18 23
4:20 21, 39, 160, 180, 184, 187, 196, 197, 198, 217, 228
4:20–21 20
4:21 26, 84, 113, 116, 180
4:21–22 23, 161, 187, 196
4:21–33 84
4:22 48
4:23 161, 182, 184, 187, 189, 190, 191, 192, 196, 197, 198, 199, 201, 217, 218
4:23–24 198
4:23–31 198, 199, 201, 202, 210
4:24 93, 187, 190, 198, 199, 203
4:25 198, 199, 200
4:25–28 190, 191
4:25–31 190, 191, 193
4:26 23, 62, 71, 161, 187, 199, 200, 202, 221, 231

Deuteronomy (cont.)
4:26–27 200
4:26–28 187
4:27 199, 200
4:27–13 161
4:27–20 202
4:28 151, 198, 199, 200
4:29 199, 202
4:29–30 190, 200
4:29–31 191, 201, 203
4:30 199, 200, 201
4:30–31 202
4:31 4, 35, 83, 93, 94, 152, 156, 179, 182, 183, 189, 190, 191, 198, 199, 201, 202, 203, 221, 222
4:32 23, 94, 203
4:32–33 206
4:32–34 160, 204
4:32–40 58, 80, 203, 204, 205, 206
4:33 134, 180, 184, 187, 192, 193, 201
4:33–34 203, 205
4:33–38 39
4:34 69, 82, 146, 180, 198, 223
4:34–38 184
4:35 94, 180, 204, 207, 230
4:36 23, 134, 180, 187, 193, 201, 206
4:36–38 160, 203, 204, 205
4:37 27, 180, 181, 183, 203, 206, 207
4:38 20, 21, 55, 181, 189, 204, 217
4:39 23, 94, 180, 198, 207
4:39–40 198
4:40 23, 24, 61, 86, 121, 124, 180, 198, 202, 205, 206, 217
4:43 20, 204

Deuteronomy (cont.)
4:44 223, 224
4:44–28:68 128, 223
4:44–30:20 184
4:45 117, 120
4:48 76
4:49 230
5 2, 7, 38, 52, 65, 118, 188
5–11 52
5–26 118, 192, 224
5:1 83, 117, 119, 120, 121, 139, 159, 207, 224
5:1–5 119, 178, 192
5:1–21 117, 178
5:1–22 117
5:1–6:3 117, 119
5:1–11:32 207
5:1–28:68 174
5:1–28:69 117
5:2 159
5:2–3 44, 67, 217, 225
5:3 4, 6, 52, 66, 152, 156, 176, 178, 179, 201, 208, 215, 225, 228, 232
5:4–5 119, 187
5:6 23, 68, 80, 230
5:6–21 119, 192
5:7 94
5:8 23, 197
5:8–10 187
5:9 93, 151, 198, 201, 214
5:9–10 207, 212, 213, 214
5:10 119, 181, 214
5:12 119, 120
5:15 23, 82, 195, 197
5:15–16 119
5:16 4, 23, 62, 119, 120, 124, 217
5:21 19
5:22 117, 119
5:22–25 187
5:22–27 117, 118
5:22–6:1 118

Index of Scripture

Deuteronomy (cont.)
5:22–6:3   117, 118, 119, 120
5:23   123
5:23–27   119
5:23–28   121
5:24   94, 119, 193
5:24–27   65
5:25–27   72
5:26   94, 193
5:26–28   119
5:27–31   119
5:27–6:1   120
5:27–6:3   119
5:28–31   117, 119
5:29   119
5:31   24, 119, 120
5:31–33   117, 119, 120
5:31–6:1   119
5:31–6:2   120, 121
5:31–6:3   120
5:32   119, 120, 133, 195
5:32–33   52, 119
5:32–6:2   122
5:32–6:3   117, 119, 121
5:33   22, 23, 40, 54, 55, 120, 121, 124
5:33–6:2   121
5:33–6:3   121
6   31, 50, 51, 53, 58, 60, 62, 73, 75, 118, 124, 127, 185
6–8   208
6:1   59, 117, 118, 119, 120, 192, 195
6:1–2   119, 120
6:1–3   52, 118, 119
6:2   23, 117, 119, 120, 121, 124, 185
6:2–3   118, 120
6:3   4, 23, 57, 73, 91, 92, 95, 100, 109, 110, 115, 117, 118, 119, 120, 121, 122, 123, 124, 125, 126, 127, 128, 138, 144, 195, 220
6:3–8   143

Deuteronomy (cont.)
6:4   51, 52, 59, 91, 94, 119, 121
6:4–5   52, 94
6:4–19   181
6:4–26:19   140
6:4–28:68   117
6:5   51, 181, 202
6:6   52, 120
6:6–7   52
6:6–9   206
6:7   22, 57
6:8–9   52
6:10   3, 4, 16, 23, 24, 25, 27, 28, 31, 32, 33, 35, 47, 50, 51, 52, 53, 54, 55, 56, 60, 65, 77, 83, 127, 128, 216, 219
6:10–11   52, 53, 54
6:10–15   53
6:10–18   55
6:10–19   51, 52, 55, 58, 60, 208
6:10–25   52
6:11   53, 56
6:12   23, 52, 53, 54, 65, 68, 196
6:12–19   56
6:13–14   52
6:14   94
6:15   53, 93, 198
6:16   54, 55
6:16–19   55
6:17   120
6:18   4, 16, 23, 24, 25, 31, 35, 48, 51, 54, 55, 56, 60, 83, 127
6:18–19   55, 56
6:19   55, 115, 189
6:20   57, 59, 60, 61, 120, 208
6:20–24   57, 58
6:20–25   31, 50, 51, 52, 57, 58, 59, 60, 63, 64, 68, 76, 148, 180, 193, 233
6:21   82

Deuteronomy (cont.)
6:21–22   59, 180
6:21–23   59
6:21–25   208
6:22   69, 146
6:22–23   59, 60
6:23   4, 16, 24, 25, 26, 27, 31, 35, 51, 54, 55, 57, 58, 59, 60, 65, 68, 75, 80, 83, 127
6:24   217
6:24–25   57, 59, 195
6:25   57, 59, 60, 120, 134
7   123, 203, 208, 209, 213, 214
7–8   183, 207, 209, 210
7–11   20
7:1   24, 55, 207, 208, 209
7:1–13   182
7:1–16   208
7:1–26   52, 209
7:2   179
7:2–6   207
7:4   94
7:6   207
7:6–8   207
7:7   110, 210, 213
7:7–8   181, 213
7:7–12   4, 210, 211, 212, 213, 214, 215, 217
7:8   35, 68, 82, 83, 179, 181, 182, 183, 210, 213, 215, 228
7:8–9   209, 210, 214
7:9   94, 124, 181, 210, 212, 213, 214, 215
7:9–10   213, 214
7:9–11   207, 208, 213, 214, 215
7:9–12   214
7:10   71, 151, 213
7:11   120, 210, 213, 214

Deuteronomy (cont.)
7:12   152, 156, 159,
       178, 179, 181,
       182, 183, 191,
       201, 209, 210,
       211, 212, 213,
       214, 215, 217, 221
7:12–13   35, 83, 209
7:12–26   207, 209
7:13   4, 16, 23, 25, 27,
       31, 76, 109, 110,
       124, 127
7:13–14   110, 125, 220
7:16   217
7:17   55, 65, 208
7:17–18   220
7:17–19   65, 208
7:17–24   207
7:18   208
7:18–26   208
7:19   82, 146, 208, 223
7:20   71
7:21   65, 94, 208
7:22   19, 55
7:24   71
7:25–26   207
7:26   209
8   53, 54, 56, 124, 208,
    209, 210, 216,
    217, 218, 219, 221
8:1   3, 4, 16, 24, 25,
      31, 35, 54, 55, 66,
      83, 110, 120, 124,
      127, 195, 207,
      209, 216, 217,
      220, 221
8:1–2   218
8:1–16   208
8:1–20   207, 208, 209
8:2   20, 22, 40, 207,
      209, 216, 218,
      219
8:2–3   218
8:2–4   180, 220, 223
8:2–5   209
8:2–17   221
8:3   3, 20, 209, 216,
      218, 219, 221
8:4   216, 218, 219
8:5   180, 206, 218, 219
8:6   22, 218, 221

Deuteronomy (cont.)
8:7   23, 48, 56, 218,
      219, 220
8:7–10   216
8:7–13   207
8:7–18   210
8:8   195
8:8–9   220
8:9   94, 220
8:10   23, 48, 56, 218,
       219
8:11   52, 120, 196,
       218, 220, 221
8:11–16   209
8:11–18   220
8:12–13   216, 220
8:13   124, 220
8:14   23, 52, 68, 196,
       218, 220
8:15   20, 56, 208, 218
8:15–16   20, 220
8:16   20, 209, 216,
       218, 221
8:17   65, 208, 220, 229
8:17–18   65, 208
8:18   4, 35, 83, 152,
       156, 179, 182,
       183, 191, 194,
       197, 201, 207,
       209, 210, 216,
       217, 218, 219,
       220, 221
8:18–19   221
8:18–20   208
8:19   52, 62, 71, 208,
       218, 220, 221
8:19–20   209, 221
8:20   62, 71, 209
9   84
9:2   22
9:3   62, 71, 115, 116
9:3–5   55
9:4   55, 65
9:4–6   112
9:4–7   65, 208, 229
9:5   3, 4, 16, 25, 31,
      32, 35, 77, 83, 84,
      127, 189
9:6   23, 48, 217
9:7   20, 21, 23
9:7–21   54

Deuteronomy (cont.)
9:7–10:11   133
9:9   195
9:10   193
9:11   195
9:12   40, 120
9:14   110
9:15   195
9:16   22, 120
9:18   133, 195
9:23   24
9:25   133
9:25–29   81
9:26   20, 21, 82
9:27   37, 72, 77, 83, 84
9:28   20
9:29   20, 21
10:4   193
10:5   120
10:7   23
10:8   134
10:9   20, 21, 115
10:11   4, 16, 24, 25,
        27, 31, 34, 35, 77,
        83, 127
10:12   22, 181, 207
10:13   120
10:14   23
10:15   27, 180, 181,
        203, 206, 230
10:17   94
10:19   23
10:22   4, 62, 68, 70,
        71, 107, 110, 117,
        125, 148, 180
11   30, 56, 72, 73, 124
11:1   181, 202
11:2   82
11:2–7   72
11:4   68
11:5   20, 21, 133, 149
11:6   83
11:8   24, 120, 121
11:8–9   23, 54
11:9   4, 16, 23, 25, 27,
       31, 35, 37, 54, 55,
       56, 72, 73, 83,
       122, 124, 127,
       128, 180
11:9–12   72
11:10   23, 56, 72

Deuteronomy (cont.)
11:11 72
11:11–12 56
11:12 72
11:13 120
11:15 19
11:16 52, 94
11:16–17 56
11:17 23, 48, 71
11:18–21 206
11:19 22, 57
11:21 4, 16, 23, 25,
    26, 27, 31, 35, 56,
    77, 83, 124, 127
11:22 18, 22, 120, 133
11:23 55
11:24 19, 20, 21, 133
11:24–25 19, 22
11:25 115, 121
11:26 202
11:26–28 221
11:26–32 140
11:26–12:3 141
11:27–28 120
11:28 22, 94, 133
11:29 65
11:30 22
11:32 120, 195, 207
12 26, 128, 130, 131,
    132, 133, 135,
    136, 138, 139,
    141, 143
12–26 2, 20, 95, 128,
    133, 134, 184
12:1 4, 23, 24, 25, 26,
    32, 91, 92, 95,
    100, 109, 115,
    120, 126, 127,
    128, 129, 130,
    131, 132, 137,
    138, 144, 195
12:1–12 129
12:2 22, 128, 131,
    132, 133, 197
12:2–3 21, 131
12:2–4 137
12:3 22, 131, 133
12:5 21, 22, 38, 92,
    128, 133, 134,
    136, 137, 142
12:5–27 137

Deuteronomy (cont.)
12:7 133, 143
12:9 20, 21, 26, 217
12:11 21, 22, 38, 120,
    128, 134, 136,
    137
12:12 20, 21, 133, 143
12:13–14 21
12:13–31 129
12:14 22, 38, 120, 128
12:15 132
12:16 23, 132
12:18 21, 22, 38, 128,
    133, 143
12:19 23
12:20 19, 115
12:21 21, 22, 38, 120,
    128, 132, 134,
    137
12:23 132
12:23–25 132
12:24 23
12:26 21, 22, 38, 128,
    136, 137
12:27 132
12:28 120
12:30 52
13:1 120, 195
13:2–3 146
13:3 94
13:6 22, 23, 68, 120
13:7 94
13:11 23, 68
13:12 83, 195
13:14 94
13:17 110
13:18 76, 83
13:19 120, 195
14:1 180
14:22 19
14:23 133, 134, 137
14:23–25 21, 22, 38,
    128
14:24 22, 134, 137
14:26 133
14:27 20, 21
14:29 20, 21, 121
15:1–2 16
15:4 20
15:5 120, 195
15:6 115

Deuteronomy (cont.)
15:7 217
15:9 65, 208, 229
15:15 23
15:16 65
15:20 21, 22, 38, 128,
    133
15:23 23
16:1–8 68
16:2 21, 22, 38, 128,
    134, 137
16:3 23
16:4 19
16:6 134, 137
16:6–7 21, 22, 38, 128
16:11 21, 22, 38, 128,
    133, 134, 137
16:12 219
16:15 219
16:15–16 21, 22, 38,
    128
16:18–20 112
16:20 54, 55
16:22 219
16:29 219
16:32 219
17:2 194
17:3 94, 120
17:8 21, 22, 38, 128,
    137
17:10 21, 22, 38, 128,
    137, 195
17:11 133
17:14 24
17:16 22
17:18 3, 204
17:18–20 206
17:20 23, 124, 133
18:1 20
18:1–2 20, 21
18:2 115
18:6 21, 22, 38, 83,
    128
18:7 134
18:8 20
18:9 195
18:12 55
18:18 120
18:20 94, 120
19 19
19:1 26

Deuteronomy (cont.)
19:2 217
19:2–3 24
19:3 19, 22
19:6 22
19:7 134
19:8 4, 16, 19, 25, 31, 35, 83, 127
19:9 22, 120
19:10 20
19:14 19, 20, 24, 62
19:19–20 195
20:1 23
20:16 20
20:17 120
20:18 195
20:19 19
21:1 19, 24
21:7–8 20
21:10–34:12 74, 145, 224, 225
21:14 203
21:18 206
21:19 21, 62
21:21 83
21:23 20
22:4 22
22:7 23, 124
22:15 62
22:18 206
22:25 19
22:27 19
22:29 203
23:3 27
23:5 22
23:17 21, 22
23:21 54
24:4 20, 134, 217
24:7–8 191
24:8 195
24:9 22, 197
24:13 134
24:18 195
24:19 19
24:22 23, 195
25:15 23, 124
25:17–18 22
25:19 20, 23, 24
26 61, 63, 64, 65, 66, 71, 72, 73, 75, 148

Deuteronomy (cont.)
26:1 20, 24, 61, 65, 217
26:1–2 61, 220
26:1–3 61
26:1–11 68, 76, 144
26:1–15 22, 23, 61, 63, 64
26:1–19 229
26:2 21, 22, 23, 38, 61, 62, 124, 128, 134
26:2–4 129
26:3 4, 16, 25, 27, 31, 35, 58, 61, 62, 64, 65, 66, 67, 68, 73, 83, 127, 148
26:3–15 193
26:4 61, 67
26:5 4, 31, 50, 57, 61, 62, 63, 64, 67, 68, 69, 70, 71, 72, 145, 147, 148, 181
26:5–9 50, 57, 58, 61, 63, 64, 67, 68, 73, 144, 145, 148, 149, 180, 197
26:5–10 64, 67
26:6 69, 145
26:6–8 147, 180
26:6–9 70
26:7 69, 91, 109, 115, 144, 145, 146, 147, 149
26:7–9 149
26:8 69, 82, 144, 145, 146, 148
26:9 21, 22, 23, 56, 61, 72, 73, 122, 144, 145, 146, 148, 197
26:9–10 58
26:10 23, 61, 67, 124
26:10–11 61
26:10–14 61, 197
26:11 197
26:12–13 72
26:12–15 71
26:13 72, 197
26:13–14 73, 120
26:13–15 64

Deuteronomy (cont.)
26:14 72
26:15 4, 16, 23, 25, 31, 35, 56, 58, 61, 62, 71, 72, 73, 75, 77, 122, 127, 130, 134, 148, 197, 220, 231
26:16 22, 195
26:16–19 66, 142, 143, 224
26:17 40
26:17–18 22, 66, 143, 172, 229
26:17–19 167
26:18–19 115
26:19 139
27 129, 130, 138, 139, 140, 141, 142, 143
27:1 65, 120, 139, 140
27:1–8 129, 140, 141, 142, 206
27:2 140
27:2–3 140
27:2–8 129
27:3 4, 23, 54, 55, 56, 73, 91, 92, 100, 109, 115, 122, 126, 127, 128, 129, 130, 138, 139, 140, 141, 142, 144, 204, 217
27:3–5 130
27:4 120, 139, 140
27:5 130, 140
27:5–6 141
27:5–7 139
27:6 140
27:6–7 143
27:7 133, 140
27:8 140, 204
27:9 83, 140, 167, 172, 224
27:9–10 139
27:11 140
27:11–26 139
27:12 139
27:15–26 139
27:16 62

Index of Scripture

Deuteronomy (cont.)
27:17   19
27:22   4
27:26   195
27:28   120
28   74, 125, 139, 162
28:1   120, 139, 195
28:1–14   229
28:3   19
28:3–12   220
28:3–14   139
28:4   23, 110, 124, 125
28:7   22
28:8   217
28:9   22, 83, 181
28:11   4, 16, 23, 25, 27, 31, 35, 83, 110, 127
28:13–15   120
28:14   94, 133
28:15   195
28:15–68   19, 139, 221
28:16   19, 125
28:16–19   139
28:18   23, 124, 125
28:20   71
28:20–21   150
28:20–68   139
28:21   23
28:21–24   125
28:22   71
28:24   23
28:25   22
28:26   23
28:29   22
28–30   75, 125
28:30   125
28:33   23, 125
28:36   94, 125
28:38   19
28:38–41   125
28:40   19
28:42   23
28:45   120
28:46   146
28:47   203
28:51   23, 62, 71
28:53   124, 125

Deuteronomy (cont.)
28:58   195
28:62   203
28:62–63   110, 125
28:63   23, 71, 76, 109, 151, 231
28:64   94
28:64–68   73, 125
28:68   19, 22
28:69   73, 117, 222, 223, 224
28:69–30:20   8, 117, 183, 224
29   74, 181, 182, 183, 222, 223, 224, 225, 227, 228, 229
29–30   222, 223, 224, 225, 227, 228, 230, 231
29–32   183
29:1   23, 73, 83, 222, 223, 228
29:1–20   229
29:1–24   223
29:1–30:20   73, 174, 223
29:2   146
29:2–5   218
29:3   230
29:4   20, 218
29:4–5   223
29:4–8   180
29:5   218, 230
29:6   21, 149
29:6–7   223
29:7   20, 21
29:8   73, 223
29:9   133, 134, 225, 226, 227
29:9–10   181
29:9–12   73
29:9–14   4, 7, 156, 167, 189, 201, 202, 222, 224, 225, 226, 228, 229
29:11   179, 181, 182, 183, 191, 227
29:11–12   156, 217, 227
29:11–13   182, 183, 191, 224

Deuteronomy (cont.)
29:12   3, 77, 83, 115, 172, 181, 222, 225, 227, 228, 229, 230
29:13   179, 182, 183, 225
29:13–14   73, 176
29:14   133, 225, 227, 228
29:14–20   224
29:15   23
29:15–16   230
29:17–18   230
29:17–27   73
29:18   229, 230
29:21   150, 229
29:21–23   229
29:21–27   151
29:21–30:20   231
29:23   150, 230
29:24   4, 23, 77, 91, 100, 101, 109, 115, 144, 149, 150, 152, 156, 179, 182, 183, 222, 229, 230, 231
29:24–25   150
29:24–27   150
29:25   94, 151, 230
29:26   150, 230
29:27   150, 223
29:28   74, 195, 217
30   73, 74, 76, 125, 222, 231, 232
30:1   65, 76, 202
30:1–2   74, 230
30:1–3   76
30:1–10   74, 77, 191, 201, 202, 225
30:2   201
30:2–10   202
30:3   201, 225
30:3–4   125
30:3–5   74
30:5   28, 31, 65, 73, 74, 75, 76, 77, 88, 109, 110, 125, 222, 231
30:6   74, 80, 225, 230

Deuteronomy (cont.)
30:6–7   74
30:6–10   74
30:7   74
30:8   74
30:8–10   76
30:9   23, 73, 74, 75, 76, 110, 125, 222, 225, 231
30:10   74, 201, 230
30:11–14   74
30:15   76, 144, 231
30:15–20   6, 20, 78, 80, 231
30:16   22, 24, 40, 74, 110
30:17   74
30:18   23, 62, 124, 221
30:19   23, 74, 77, 121, 202, 231
30:19–20   231
30:20   3, 4, 16, 23, 24, 25, 26, 27, 31, 32, 35, 60, 73, 74, 75, 77, 78, 79, 80, 83, 86, 124, 127, 128, 222, 231
31   56, 57
31–34   85
31:1   21, 82, 83
31:1–8   113
31:2   81, 84
31:3   115
31:7   4, 16, 25, 27, 28, 31, 35, 77, 83, 127
31:8   43
31:9–13   8, 167, 175, 204, 206
31:11   22, 38, 83, 128, 204
31:12   195
31:13   23
31:14   81, 84
31:16   84, 194, 231
31:17–18   231
31:18   94
31:20   23, 25, 34, 35, 56, 94, 122, 194

Deuteronomy (cont.)
31:20–21   83
31:21   25, 27
31:23   4, 16, 25, 31, 83, 127
31:24–26   167
31:28   23
31:29   22, 84, 198, 200
32   17
32:1   23
32:1–43   17
32:4   22, 94
32:5   50
32:6   62, 180
32:7   50, 57
32:9   17, 18, 20, 21
32:10   20
32:10–14   19
32:12   94
32:13   19
32:18   94
32:20   50
32:21   94
32:41   17
32:44–47   167
32:45   83
32:46   121, 195
32:47   124
32:48–50   84
32:48–52   81, 84
32:49   17
32:51   20
32:52   217
33:1   223
33:6   110
33:7   72
33:9   194
33:11   72
33:13   23
33:17   110
33:26   80, 94
33:28   23
33:29   22
34   32, 81, 82, 83, 85, 88, 222
34:1   82
34:1–3   81, 82
34:1–6   81
34:2–3   81

Deuteronomy (cont.)
34:4   4, 16, 25, 28, 31, 32, 35, 37, 77, 81, 82, 83, 84, 85, 86, 127, 180, 217
34:5   81, 84
34:5–6   82
34:6   81
34:7   82
34:7–8   82
34:7–9   82
34:9   81
34:10   81, 82
34:10–12   82
34:11   23, 69, 146, 195
34:12   82, 83

Joshua
1:3–4   18
1:15   18
3:7   121
3:10   123
4   130
4–5   129, 141
4:6   60
4:21   60
5:6   122
7:11   194
8   129
8:1   43
8:30–32   129
8:30–35   129
10:25   43
13:7   20
14:1   21
14:3   21
14:4   20
15:3   20
17:5   17
18   132
18:3   99, 100
19:9   17
22:19   17
23:4   55
23:11   52
23:19   135
24   129, 141
24:2–13   50

Index of Scripture

Judges
2:11 194
2:12 99, 100, 101
2:20 194
9:4 98
9:46 98
20:14 122
21 132

1 Samuel
1–4 132
12:8 50
12:20 202
13:11 122

2 Samuel
3:12 194
7:15 179
7:23 135
7:23–24 202
17:13 17

1 Kings
3:3 181
8 135
8:12 136
8:13 136
8:16–20 135
8:21 72, 212
8:23 212
8:29 135
8:29–30 129
8:33 135
8:34 72, 73
8:35 135
8:40 72
8:42–43 135
9:3 135
9:9 230
10:13 223
11:11 194
11:36 135
12:11 206
12:31 101
14:21 135
18:36 99, 100
19:10 194
19:14 194
20:31 17
22:16 121

2 Kings
13:23 194
15–19 162
16:7 171, 172
16:8 172
16:9–10 172
17:7 101
17:15 194
18:3–6 129
18:12 194
18:21 197
18:22 129
20:5 99
21:4 135
21:7 135
21:11 100
21:22 99
23:4–20 129

Isaiah
2:2 200
2:22 197
22:16 135
28:18 194
32:18 135
40–55 169
41:8 206
49:26 98
59:21 194
60:16 98

Jeremiah
2:4–7 33
2:4–8 54
2:7 21
7 132
7:4 197
7:7 75
7:12 132
9:19 135
11:5 122
11:8 223
11:10 194
14:21 194
22:9 230
23:20 200
29–31 202
29:19 203
30:18 135
30:24 200

Jeremiah (cont.)
31 74
31:31–34 202
31:32 194
31:33 225
32:18 214
32:21 146
32:22 122
32:37–41 225
33:20–21 194
33:25 194
34:18–19 194
48:47 200
49:39 200

Ezekiel
11:19–20 202
16:3 47
16:60 194
16:61 194
16:62 194
20:5–6 33, 54
20:6 122
20:15 122
20:41 107
33:24 33
36 74
37:27 135
38:16 200
44:7 194

Hosea
3:5 200
8:1 194
11:1 206

Amos
7:17 17

Micah
2:5 17
14:1 200

Habakkuk
2:2 204

Zechariah
8:8 202
11:10 194

Malachi
 2:4–5   194

Psalms
 22:19   20
 26:8   135
 39:7   107
 43:3   135
 44:17   194
 46:5   135
 49:12   135
 50:16   194
 74:7   135
 78:60   132
 79:1   21
 79:8   62
 84:2   135
 87:2   135
 89:28   194
 89:34   194
 120:6   197
 132:2   98
 132:5   98, 135
 132:7   135
 132:12   194

Job
 4:3   206

Proverbs
 1:9   203
 6:34   198
 19:18   206

Daniel
 10:14   200
 11:4   223

Ezra
 7:27   99
 8:28   99, 101
 10:11   99, 101

Nehemiah
 8:14   121
 9   53
 9:23   53, 75
 9:24–25   53

1 Chronicles
 5:25   99, 101
 12:18   99
 28:9   99, 100
 29:18   99, 100
 29:20   99

2 Chronicles
 7:15–16   129
 7:22   99, 101, 230

2 Chronicles (cont.)
 11:16   99, 101
 13:12   99
 13:18   99
 14:3   99
 14:4   101
 15:12   99
 17:4   99, 100
 19:4   99
 20:6   99
 20:6–7   101
 20:7   206
 20:11   18
 20:33   99
 21:10   99, 101
 24:18   99, 101
 24:24   99, 101
 28:6   99, 101
 28:9   99, 101
 28:25   99, 101
 29:5   99, 101
 30:6   99, 100, 101
 30:7   99
 30:13   122
 30:19   99
 30:22   99
 33:12   99
 34:32–33   99
 34:33   101
 36:15   99, 101

New Testament

John
 8:39–44   47

Hebrews
 9:4   195

Deuterocanonical Literature

Sirach
 44:19–21   206

www.ingramcontent.com/pod-product-compliance
Lightning Source LLC
Chambersburg PA
CBHW021958090426
42811CB00001B/74